2.2.68 Russell + Russell 1167 (Sweringen)

MODERN FRANCE

MODERN FRANCE

A COMPANION TO FRENCH STUDIES

EDITED BY

ARTHUR TILLEY, M.A.

FELLOW AND LECTURER OF KING'S COLLEGE, CAMBRIDGE

NEW YORK / RUSSELL & RUSSELL

FIRST PUBLISHED IN 1922
REPRINTED BY PERMISSION OF THE CAMBRIDGE UNIVERSITY PRESS
REISSUED, 1967, BY RUSSELL & RUSSELL
A DIVISION OF ATHENEUM HOUSE, INC.
L. C. CATALOG CARD NO: 66–27168

PRINTED IN THE UNITED STATES OF AMERICA

PREFACE

THE task of comprising within the limits of a single volume a survey of Modern France has been far more difficult than in the companion volume on Medieval France. Firstly, the advance of knowledge and the development of government and society have necessitated several chapters which have nothing corresponding to them in the Medieval volume—chapters on Finance, Law, Music, the Stage, Mathematics, Science. Secondly, though this volume covers a shorter period than the other, every topic, except architecture, demands more space for its treatment. We can see this from the analogy of the History of France in the two works edited by M. Lavisse, in which five volumes are allotted to medieval history from Hugh Capet and seventeen to modern history, or from that of the *History of French Literature* edited by Petit de Julleville, in which the share of modern literature is between five and six times as large as the share of medieval literature.

Thus, though this volume is nearly twice as long as its companion, the need for compression has been far greater. This is especially the case with the chapter on History, which has only been kept within the limits assigned to it by the skill and self-renunciation of the writers. They have aimed at putting before the reader, not a summary of events, but a clear picture of the period with which they are dealing—a picture, in which details of no special significance are omitted, while the salient features are brought into prominence. And, as in order to make a picture the artist must stand at a certain distance from his subject, the principle, not only in this chapter but throughout the volume, has been to touch very lightly on events which are too near to us to admit of their being seen in the right perspective.

The long chapter on History is followed by five chapters which are more or less subsidiary to it—on the Army, on the Navy, on Economic and Social Life, on the Finance of the *Ancien Régime*, and on Law. In the chapters by M. Caron and M. de la Roncière in this and the companion volume, we have for the

first time complete historical sketches of the French Army and
the French Navy. M. Sagnac's chapter on Economic and Social
Life is equally novel as a comprehensive survey of a vast subject,
the materials for which have had to be gathered from innumerable documents, monographs, and articles in reviews. The two
chapters which follow constitute a formidable indictment against
the Finance and Law of the *Ancien Régime*, and they leave us
with the impression that the spirit of inequality with which
they were both administered was the main cause of the overthrow of the whole fabric.

Down to the middle of the seventeenth century Education
and Learning go hand in hand, and can be conveniently treated
together; but later, as they become more and more organised,
they follow separate paths. Education is national and state-
controlled; Learning, having abandoned the medium of Latin,
allies itself with Literature and sometimes is Literature. In
the chapter on Literature only writers whose work is of the
first importance, either in itself or for the influence it has
exercised, have been taken into account, thus making it easier
to follow the general development and to characterise the various
movements. But after 1870 it becomes increasingly difficult to
estimate the relative importance of writers, and the ground has
to be surveyed more in detail. This delicate task, requiring
wide knowledge and calm judgment, has naturally been entrusted to a Frenchman.

The other arts follow—Architecture, Painting, Sculpture,
Decorative Art, Music, the Stage. It is rash to generalise about
national characteristics, but French art has certain qualities
which, though they are sometimes in abeyance, are never far
absent—constructive power, which shows itself in careful
planning and a sense of proportion, fine and skilled workmanship, and, in portraiture, the same psychological insight that
distinguishes French literature. Lastly, however revolutionary
may be the experiments of new schools of art, reason is always
at hand to resume control.

It was natural that a Frenchman, Descartes, should be the
founder of modern philosophy, for Frenchmen have, as Professor Robinson says, a philosophic, or at least a thinking mind.
Few thinkers have more deeply influenced European thought

in the past than Descartes, Rousseau, or Comte, and in the thought of to-day the philosophy of Henri Bergson is a powerful factor. After Philosophy comes Science, with which in France, notes Bergson, it has always been in close union. In Mathematics the French have been distinguished for lucidity of expression and a love of fine and delicate workmanship. In the seventeenth century they had mathematicians of the first rank in Descartes, Fermat, and Pascal, and these had worthy successors in Clairaut and D'Alembert, in Lagrange, Laplace and Legendre, in Fourier and Cauchy, and in our own day Poincaré. Descartes and Pascal were also accomplished physicists, but, though the natural sciences were increasingly studied throughout the eighteenth century, and though Buffon was remarkable as a pioneer in more than one direction, the great era of science did not open in France till the days of Lamarck and Lavoisier. When the latter, after helping to found modern chemistry, perished by the guillotine in 1794, three men of the next generation, who were to play a brilliant part in French science, had just begun their life-work. These were Cuvier, Geoffroy Saint-Hilaire, and Bichat, one of the heroes of science, who died at thirty-one. Only a year or two younger, but later in finding his career, was the Newton of electricity, André-Marie Ampère. It is not for a layman to single out the most illustrious of their numerous successors, but the name of Louis Pasteur is revered throughout the civilised world, and Claude Bernard deserves mention, not only as a great physiologist, but as one whose influence on French thought and literature has been wide and lasting.

To all the contributors who have taken part in this venture the warmest thanks are due, particularly to our French friends, without whose co-operation it could not have been realised. That their work has suffered somewhat from the process of translation is inevitable. You can reproduce in a foreign idiom the substance of a writer's thought, but not the style, nor always the writer's mode of thought—the position, so to speak, from which he views a particular event. For help in revising the translations the editor is indebted not only to the original writers, but also, for some of the chapters, to English specialists—to Professor Hazeltine for the chapter on Law, to Mr Vulliamy for that on Painting, Sculpture, and Decorative Art, to Mr Barcroft, Mr McCombie, and Mr Dampier-Whetham for that on Science. The editor is also specially indebted for much kind assistance in writing the summary account of modern French learning which he has attempted in chapter VII, and particularly to the distinguished Orientalists, Professor E. G. Browne, Professor H. A. Giles, and Sir Edward Ross. As in the companion volume he has again to thank Mr H. S. Bennett for the index. Lastly, Mr A. R. Waller, the Secretary of the Syndics of the University Press, has continued to follow with active sympathy this story of the life of a great nation, which has touched our own at so many points and so often in the past, and which with greater knowledge will, we hope, come into closer contact with us in the future.

A. T.

July 1, 1922.

CONTENTS

CHAPTER I

HISTORY

§ I. SIXTEENTH CENTURY

By HENRI HAUSER, Professor in the University of Paris

§ II. Seventeenth Century

By Émile Bourgeois, Professor in the University of Paris and
Director of the National Manufactory of Porcelain at Sèvres

Henry IV and Sully

Louis XIII and Richelieu

The Reign of Louis XIV

§ III. Eighteenth Century
By É. Bourgeois
The Reign of Louis XV

The Reign of Louis XVI

§ IV. The Church in the Seventeenth and Eighteenth Centuries
By É. Bourgeois
Seventeenth Century

Eighteenth Century

§ V. THE FRENCH REVOLUTION AND NAPOLEON

By A. AULARD, Professor in the University of Paris

§ VI. NINETEENTH CENTURY

By GEORGES WEILL, Professor in the University of Caen

The Restoration, 1814–1830

CHAPTER II

THE ARMY

By PIERRE CARON of the *Archives Nationales*

CHAPTER III

THE NAVY

By CH. DE LA RONCIÈRE of the *Bibliothèque Nationale*

CHAPTER IV

ECONOMIC AND SOCIAL LIFE

By PH. SAGNAC, Professor in the University of Lille

§ I. PROVINCIAL ECONOMY (16TH CENTURY)

§ II. National Economy from 1600 to 1750

§ III. Attempts at Reform (1750–1789)

§ IV. The Revolution and the achievement
of National Economy

CONTENTS

CHAPTER V

THE FINANCE OF THE *ANCIEN RÉGIME*

By G. B. PERRETT, M.A., Fellow of Selwyn College

CHAPTER VI

LAW

By A. DE LAPRADELLE, Professor in the University of Paris

§ I. THE *ANCIEN RÉGIME*

Public Law

Private Law

CHAPTER VII

EDUCATION AND LEARNING

§ I. 1494–1660

By ARTHUR TILLEY, M.A., Fellow of King's College, Cambridge

§ II. Education from 1660

By J. W. Adamson, M.A., Professor at King's College, London

§ III. Learning from 1660

By A. Tilley, M.A.

CHAPTER VIII

LITERATURE

§ I. Sixteenth Century

By A. Tilley, M.A.

§ II. SEVENTEENTH CENTURY

By A. TILLEY, M.A.

§ III. EIGHTEENTH CENTURY

By H. F. STEWART, D.D., Reader in French in the University of Cambridge and Fellow of Trinity College

§ IV. Nineteenth Century

By A. Tilley, M.A.

Romanticism

§ V. After 1870

By Gonzague Truc

The Novel

The Drama

Poetry

The literature of ideas

CONTENTS

CHAPTER IX

ARCHITECTURE

By W. H. WARD, F.R.I.B.A., M.A., of Clare College

§ I. TRANSITION AND EARLY RENAISSANCE (1494–1589)

Styles of Louis XII and Francis I.—French Masons and Italian Decorators

Style of Henry II.—The first architects

§ II. MATURE CLASSIC (1589–1793)

Style of Henry IV and Louis XIII.—Utilitarianism and Baroque

Style of Louis XIV.—Baroque-Classic Compromise

Style of the Regency and Louis XV.—Rococo

Style of Louis XVI.—Classical Reaction

CHAPTER X

PAINTING, SCULPTURE, AND DECORATIVE ART

By LOUIS HOURTICQ, Professor at the *École Nationale
des Beaux Arts*

§ II. Sculpture

§ III. DECORATIVE ART

CHAPTER XI

MUSIC

By E. J. DENT, M.A., formerly Fellow of King's College, Cambridge

CHAPTER XII
THE STAGE

By Alphonse Séché, *Lecteur-Examinateur*
at the *Comédie-Française*

§ IV. NINETEENTH CENTURY

Lighting and Auditorium

CHAPTER XIII

PHILOSOPHY

By A. ROBINSON, D.C.L., Professor in the University
of Durham and Vice-Chancellor

§ I. SEVENTEENTH CENTURY

§ II. EIGHTEENTH CENTURY

§ III. NINETEENTH CENTURY

(*a*) 1800–1850

(*b*) 1850–1870

(*c*) 1870–1900

CHAPTER XIV
MATHEMATICS

By F. S. Carey, M.A., Professor in the University of Liverpool, formerly Fellow of Trinity College, Cambridge

§ I. Seventeenth Century

§ II. Eighteenth Century

§ III. Nineteenth Century

CHAPTER XV
SCIENCE

§ I. The Biological Sciences

By Étienne Rabaud, Professor in the University of Paris

§ II. Chemistry

By Audré Job, Professor at the *Conservatoire des Arts et Métiers*

§ III. Physics

By H. Cotton, Professor in the University of Paris

Heat

CONTENTS

In the Bibliographies the place of publication is omitted for English books published in London and for French books published at Paris.

§ II. Chemistry

By Audré Job, Professor at the *Conservatoire des Arts et Métiers*

The Elements

The Compounds

Atoms and Structure

Chemical Energy

§ III. Physics

By H. Cotton, Professor in the University of Paris

Heat

CONTENTS

In the Bibliographies the place of publication is omitted for English books published in London and for French books published at Paris.

LIST OF PLATES

CHAPTER I

HISTORY

§ I. SIXTEENTH CENTURY

THE 16th century in France begins with the year 1494 and closes in 1598. The former date marks the moment when the French State, emerging from feudal struggles, entered the sphere of European politics by way of the Italian wars. The latter (Peace of Vervins and Edict of Nantes) marks the end both of the wars arising out of the Italian wars and of the Wars of Religion.

The year 1559 (Treaty of Cateau-Cambrésis and death of Henry II, prelude to the Wars of Religion) divides the century into two parts.

The intense interest of this period lies in the fact that France, which, next to Italy, produced the most brilliant achievements of the Renaissance, was to become the battle-field of the struggle between the old Church and the new; and that this same France, though threatened to the point of extinction by the monstrous growth of the Habsburg-Burgundian power, actually created and defended a new political formula, the balance of European power.

This twofold evolution took place in the midst of violent convulsions which lend to this period a highly dramatic character, revealing a medley of heroic exploits, plots and revolts, sumptuous follies, touching or scandalous romances, ardent faith, impiety, superb courage, nameless vices, virtue, mire and blood. But beneath these adventures in which individualism, released from all restraint, ran riot, the historic process followed its course—a process which led the French government towards a centralised and absolute monarchy, and transformed a people of landed gentry, *vilains*, small *bourgeois*, and artisans, into a nation composed of court nobles, peasants who became landowners, a *bourgeoisie* growing rich and eager for public office, and an industrial and commercial class dominating an already important urban proletariat.

France at the Time of the Italian Wars

The reign of Louis XI definitely transformed France into a modern state.

Geographical Aspect. In spite of the feudal reaction which marked the early years of Charles VIII's reign, the wisdom of Anne of Beaujeu and her husband saved the essential parts of the web woven by the "universal spider." In spite of the retrocessions which, in order to facilitate his Italian plans, Charles VIII made to Maximilian (the County of Burgundy and Artois), and to Ferdinand (Roussillon), France presented in 1494 a compact geographical figure, within the limits of which not more than four large feudal enclaves continued to exist: the Bourbon domains, spreading over the whole of central France, which through the Constable's treason were to fall into the hands of Francis I; in the mid-Loire region, those of the Valois-Orléans family, which by the accession of Louis XII were to become embodied in the royal domain; in the south-west and along the Pyrenees, those of the Albrets, a family dependent on the King and posted by him as sentinels on the Spanish frontier, which was destined in the person of Henry IV to unite the crown of Navarre to that of France; in the extreme west, the Duchy of Brittany, which, through the two successive marriages of Anne with Charles VIII and Louis XII and that of Claude of France, Anne's heiress, with Francis I, was to be linked up with the kingdom, first by a personal, and later, in 1532, by an administrative union.

The eastern boundary of France ran, roughly, from Cape Gris-Nez to the sources of the Meuse and the Saône; it then followed the latter river more or less closely and after skirting Savoy embraced the Alps of Dauphiné and Provence. This boundary was, of course, not drawn with precision, but it should be remembered that in the 16th century the term frontier did not possess the rigid meaning which it has acquired since the French Revolution. A strong state, in full growth, would send out feelers beyond its fluctuating borders; an inheritance, a lawsuit, the encroachments of administrative or judicial bodies, were all used as pretexts for expansion. Owing to a common language and culture, the countries of the Meuse, the Scheldt,

the Saône, and even of the Alps, did not consider themselves
wholly foreign to France. The Holy Roman Empire, at that time
hardly more than a name, exercised on such of these lands as it
legally possessed an ever-decreasing power of attraction. The aim
of France, on the other hand, was to fill up the geographical outline
of ancient Gaul and to establish herself on her natural frontiers.

The " Marches " of France. Some of these French countries,
such as Franche-Comté and Artois, though not yet definitely
incorporated in the kingdom, belonged for brief periods to the
King. Savoy was French from 1536 to 1559, and this annexation, which was fairly well received by the inhabitants, paved
the way for future developments. Piedmont too met with the
same fate. In 1552 Henry II permanently acquired the three
Bishoprics of Metz, Toul, and Verdun, and from that moment
commanded the routes across the Duchy of Lorraine. Thus, by
fulfilling Ronsard's saying and "watering his horses at the
Rhine," he established the first political contact between France
and Alsace.

The French Monarchy. "One faith, one law, one king "—thus
runs the golden legend which, in paintings of David's coronation, hangs from the beak of the mystic dove above a king,
clothed in azure robes embroidered with fleur-de-lis, whose
features recall those of Louis XII. These words exactly express
the feeling of worship for their monarch which possessed the
French after the English wars and the war between the two
parties of the nobility—the Armagnacs and the Burgundians.
Bourgeois, peasants, and scholars were all alike grateful to the
King for having re-established order and security throughout
the kingdom. Anointed with the holy oil from the sacred
chrism in Reims cathedral, his person became the centre of
manifold traditions: (1) the biblical tradition, which saw in the
successors of Clovis the royal line of the House of Israel, the
most Christian kings, kings by the grace of God, whose mere
touch by its holiness worked miracles on the sores of the
scrofulous, members of the ecclesiastical hierarchy, lay bishops,
or rather, bishops over bishops; (2) the feudal tradition, which
saw in the King the universal suzerain, the lord paramount,
whose legal decisions over-ruled all other legal decisions; (3) the
Roman tradition, carefully preserved by the lawyers of the

schools of the south, especially of that of Toulouse, and which, endowed with new life by the classical revival, saw in the King of Paris the heir of the Caesars and of Charlemagne, the embodiment, like Justinian, of the will of the people, that is of supreme law; (4) a literary tradition, originating in humanism, which claimed to see in the Francs the descendants of Francus, the son of Hector; and finally (5) the purely historic tradition, symbolised by the name of St Louis, which revered in the Valois heir of the Capets, the good and upright judge, the protector of the weak, the eldest son and right arm of the Church, the leader of the crusade against the infidel. Thanks to the false interpretation put upon the salic law this monarchy could rest assured of a perpetual continuity and of the maintenance in male hands of the sceptre of the fleurs-de-lis.

As early as the reign of Charles V, Christine de Pisan used the terms pontifical and imperial when referring to the power of the kings of France. These terms assumed their full value in the 16th century. Charles VII, in consultation with an assembly of bishops, was able to give the Gallican Church a real "civic constitution." The Pragmatic Sanction, which, according to the fluctuations of his Italian policy, Louis XI used at times as a basis for bargaining with Rome, remained nevertheless a law of the State. It enabled Charles VIII to enter Italy in spite of the Pope, and Louis XII to make war on Julius II and to set up the schismatic Council of Pisa in opposition to the Lateran Council. It was in vain that Julius II hurled the thunderbolts of the Church at the son of St Louis; in France the most Christian King was by law exempt from excommunication. In this contest Louis XII had on his side the clergy, the *Parlement*, and public opinion as represented both by lawyers and men of learning, such as Jean Bouchet, Jean Lemaire de Belges, and Pierre Gringore.

Scholars vied with one another in efforts to search out and extol the *insignia peculiaria Christianissimi Francorum regni*. They demonstrated that the Empire had passed from the Romans to the Greeks (Byzantines), and from the Greeks to the Franks, that is to say the French; it was by virtue of this *translatio imperii* that Francis I, whom Louise of Savoy proudly called "my son, my Caesar, my King," became a candidate for

the imperial crown. Both the populace and the lawyers looked
upon the King of France as standing alone among kings,
"emperor in his kingdom," for he holds his crown from no one
"save God and himself." In a political play of 1512 a poet
represented Henry VIII as being rebuked by his father's shade
in these terms:

> Car obéi tu n'es de ton arroy,
> Ainsi comme est le noble roy de France,
> Qui n'a de gens, d'or ni d'argent, souffrance,
> *Empereur est*, non seulement régent,
> Car il règne sur la terre et la gent.

He lacked neither gold nor silver. The feudal principle, by
virtue of which taxes had to be sanctioned, had indeed fallen
into disuse. The States General, which had played a great part
in the English wars, had come into bad odour. Louis XI
managed without them. The assemblies of the year 1484 were
bold in their utterances, but the Regent, her father's true
daughter, succeeded in ridding herself of them, and the people
continued to pay *tailles* and *aides*. Thanks to an economical
administration and to the skill with which he made the countries
he had conquered pay the expenses of his wars, Louis XII was
able at first to maintain and later to reduce slightly the sums
levied by his predecessor. *Bourgeois* and peasants contributed
with little remonstrance to taxes which were not on the increase and which seemed relatively light by reason of the real
prosperity that the kingdom was enjoying. Thus even the
very merits of the "Father of his People" served the cause of
absolutism by making it popular.

Francis I therefore attributed to himself the right of fixing
as he pleased the amount of the taxes. "If he wishes to
increase the *tailles* on his people," wrote the Venetian Marino
Giustiniani, as early as the year 1536, "whatever tax he
may levy it will be paid without objection." And it was
Francis I himself who in 1542 reminded Matteo Dandolo of
Maximilian's famous saying, "The Emperor is king of kings,
the Catholic King is king of men, the King of France is
king of beasts, because, whatever he commands, he is instantly
obeyed, like man by beasts." This was not altogether true of
provinces such as Brittany, Burgundy, Languedoc, etc. where

Provincial Estates which sanctioned and assessed taxes continued to exist.

As a matter of fact, after the abortive rebellion of the Constable of Bourbon, the King had no longer need to fear a rival in his kingdom. "For such is our pleasure," the formula which preceded the royal signature in letters-patent, was not merely an empty phrase. Later, his grandsons went so far as to adopt the title of "Majesty," reserved till then for the Emperor alone.

Even the personality of Francis I contributed, as did that of Louis XII, though from opposite reasons, towards strengthening the tendency towards absolutism. The young Duc d'Angoulême had not been a "Dauphin," and Louis XII's marriage with Mary of England came near to losing him the rank of heir-presumptive. Nevertheless on January 1, 1515, the dream of his ambitious mother, Louise of Savoy, henceforward known as *Madame*, was fulfilled, and the brilliant cavalier entered on his reign as a triumphant conqueror. Skilled in all physical exercises, endowed with personal charm, graced, at least superficially, by intellectual gifts, he was surrounded by a polished and cultured court. This court, while serving as an instrument for the social power of royalty, rivalled in brilliance those of the Italian princes. The King's sister, Margaret of Angoulême, Duchesse d'Alençon, and later, through her second marriage with Henri d'Albret, Queen of Navarre, known as *la Marguerite des Princesses*, was the living incarnation of the subtle feminine grace of this shifting capital, which migrated from palace to palace across the forests stocked with game and the gardens bright with flowers of the valley of the Loire. Other feminine figures, less chaste, passed across the stage. But the amours of the *roi chevalier*, which were by no means platonic and sometimes very brief, even his commonplace adventures, were far from prejudicing him in public opinion; they did but add the final touch to his popularity.

Francis I and, later on, his son Henry II governed almost as autocrats, with the assistance of a council, to which they summoned whomsoever they pleased; the Chancellor, who had charge of the State seals, the Constable—Anne de Montmorency—marshals, ecclesiastical dignitaries, great nobles, representatives of the *Parlement*, all of whom the King honoured or disgraced according to his pleasure. Moreover the council only gave advice. The King, God's elect, could always have recourse by meditation and prayer to the inspiration of the Almighty. While the council awaited his decision, the "secretaries of State," standing in a corner of the chamber, scribbled at their desks—an unassuming group, whose destiny it was to become in time the true ministers of the monarch.

The Elements of Opposition. Beneath the pompous show sung by the poets, disturbing realities were taking shape. Taxes were heavy, and though the people paid them, unaccustomed to legal resistance, this was not always done without expostulation. It became doubtful whether the edifice would not be shaken, should the royal splendour suffer an eclipse like that of the king's captivity in 1525–1526. Songs insulting him were current, such as the celebrated one on M. de la Palice:

> Ils le prirent et le menèrent
> Droit au chasteau de Madrid...
> Un courrier par là passait:
> " Courrier qui portes lettre,
> Que dit-on du roy à Paris ?"
> "—Par ma foy, mon gentilhomme,
> On ne sait s'est mort ou vif."

Even school-children were in the habit of singing irreverent songs about the captive king. The famine of 1529 let loose revolutionary troubles at Lyons and in other towns. Dandolo wrote that in 1542 in Normandy, the richest but at the same time the most heavily burdened province, "the peasants were fleeing with their children on their backs, not knowing where to go, hopeless refugees, rendered destitute by the *tailles*." In the same year the people of La Rochelle rebelled in defence of their franchises, and all the south-west of France was engaged in a struggle to prevent the extension of the *gabelle* (salt-tax) to the regions of the salt marshes. The condition of the kingdom was at that time sufficiently grave for Mary of Hungary to submit to Charles V a plan to dethrone Francis I with the help of his disaffected nobles. In 1548, in Henry II's reign, this same question of the *gabelle* caused a real revolution amongst the peasants in the same part of the country, a revolution led by the landed gentry, in which the priests often took part with their parishioners. Documents were proudly signed in this wise:

"the Colonel, by the grace of God, commanding the whole
commonwealth of Guyenne." Stern measures, directed by
Montmorency, became necessary to put down this revolt, of
which England, still inconsolable for the loss of her "ancient
patrimony," and Spain might have taken advantage.

But serious as these incidents were, they did not, at any rate
till 1559, prevent the royal power from making itself more and
more felt by all classes of the nation.

The Clergy.—The Concordat of 1516. In spite of its good points,
the constitution given to the Gallican Church by the Pragmatic
Sanction of 1438 was beginning to fall into disuse. Pope Leo X
threatened to have it condemned by the Lateran Council, a
course which would have placed France definitely in a state of
schism. Moreover on the morrow of the battle of Marignano
Francis I's Italian policy demanded a reconciliation with the
Court of Rome. The King therefore, acting chiefly on the advice
of the Chancellor Antoine du Prat, sacrificed the Pragmatic
Sanction by signing at Bologna the Concordat of 1516.

The abolition of the Pragmatic Sanction raised great opposition in France; it was in vain the King stated that the Concordat
confirmed the Pragmatic Sanction; no one was deceived. The
Parlement of Paris, which considered itself the born defender of
the rights of the Gallican Church, refused to record the act till
the year 1518 and even continued until 1527 to try cases according to the Pragmatic law. The University uttered protests.
On several occasions the bishops and abbots, nominated
according to the new law, were treated as intruders by the
Chapters and Communities. The abolition of the Concordat was
demanded in the States General of 1560 and in the national
councils until 1583. It remained neverth₃less a law of the State
until 1790.

By this agreement the King nominated the bishops, while the
Pope afterwards conferred the canonical authority. The few
abbeys which were exempt from this rule became subject to
it after 1531. The King thus held the nominations to ten
archbishoprics, eighty-two bishoprics, five hundred and twenty-
seven abbeys and many priories and canonries, that is to say
he was able to dispose autocratically of the immense fortune of
the Gallican Church and to make use of it at his pleasure to

reward those who had served him. Thus was formed a clergy of high rank to which the King appointed foreigners, particularly Italians when he wished to please Rome, and younger sons of the great families of the nobility. He drew his ambassadors and statesmen from this rich, learned, and submissive clergy. After du Prat, who was successively archbishop, abbot, and cardinal, came Jean du Bellay, Guillaume Pellicier, Tournon, Noailles, etc.

What completed the transformation of the Church's revenues into the King's civil list was the fact that these ecclesiastical benefices could be held in *commendam*, that is to say they could be conferred on laymen who found graduates to act for them for a small salary. Artists and authors shared with soldiers and aged officials these benefices of commendatory abbots. The King then rewarded and pensioned them without having to unloose his purse-strings.

While in Germany one of the principal motives which drove the Princes towards the Reformation was the desire to acquire the property of the Church, and while the same motive partly explained the schism in England, the secularisation of this property had ceased to have any object in France after 1516. On the other hand, by the Concordat the King had actually saved the financial provisions of the Pragmatic Sanction, those which prevented the Court of Rome enriching itself from the revenues of the Gallican Church. By sacrificing the independence of the Church, the University, and the *Parlement* in France, he had strengthened the country politically and financially. At times of tension with the Curia it was possible to stop all payments to Rome. Henry II went so far as to threaten to create a patriarch of the Gallican Church. When in need of money the King applied to his clergy, sometimes under the form of tenths authorised by the Pope, sometimes, when he had not obtained or did not wish to ask for the authority of the Pope, under the form of "free gift," a term which gives a false impression since he had power to seize part of the temporal possessions of the recalcitrant clergy.

Below the court clergy, which alone counted, there lived in poverty the crowd of graduates employed by the commendatories, of monks, parish priests, and curates. Men of university education, often faithful to the old traditions, in close touch with the poor and humble, they were excluded from the government of the Church and ceased to play a part in public affairs till the day when the religious disturbances turned them into a revolutionary force.

The Nobles. Feudal lords had really ceased to exist. The royal jurisdiction, represented by the *Parlement, bailliages,* and *sénéchaussées,* were encroaching on the feudal jurisdiction. In their place were the "nobility," that is men who by virtue of their birth had the double privilege of being exempt from direct taxation and of bearing arms. They formed a hierarchy, some being direct vassals of the King, others vassals of other nobles, and all having tenants paying them rents.

They tended more and more however to fall into two classes. First there was an aristocracy composed of the princes of the blood, the dukes and peers, and the owners of rich estates; they often lived at the court, following it in its migrations, grouped round a king who called himself the first of the nobles, sharing amongst themselves the high places, the great military commands, the *commendams.* Their wives were ladies-in-waiting to queens and princesses. They formed factions amongst themselves; Henry II's reign was destined to be the story of a struggle for power between the younger sons of the House of Lorraine—the Guises—who had acquired immense wealth through offices of State and Church, and the Constable Montmorency, "first Christian baron," with his following of the Chastillon family.

The mass of the nobles lived in the country in their châteaux, in the midst of the peasants over whom they exercised a local authority. Their position, fairly prosperous at the beginning of the century, deteriorated gradually with the progress of the economic revolution, that is to say with the continuous decrease of the value of money. Their incomes were diminishing because they consisted chiefly of rents and dues, formerly fixed in *livres, sols,* and *deniers.* The country noble became a poor creature when he did not succeed, by means of a pleasing address, in insinuating himself among the court nobles or becoming the "domestic" of some great man. He saw increasing in importance round him the rich class of newly made nobles who owed their titles to royal favour or had acquired them in public office of a judicial or administrative nature.

The Country-folk. France was still chiefly an agricultural country, producing corn, wine, hemp, and woad, and rearing cattle, especially sheep for their wool. These products and raw materials even gave rise to an export trade, when France was at peace with her neighbours, and thus it happened that periods of peace coincided with periods of rising prices.

Serfdom had, as a matter of fact, almost disappeared and personal dues were tending more and more to be transformed into dues paid in kind or money. Though the peasants were still subject to many feudal duties—dues in kind, forced labour, succession duties, judicial rights, feudal services attached to the lord of the manor, tolls and hunting rights—and though they paid church tithes, and though they bore almost the whole burden of direct taxation (the *taille*), and in part that of the *gabelle* and the *aides*, yet their position was improving, because the decrease in the value of money served them in two ways: it reduced the dues estimated in money and it raised the value of agricultural products. The peasant, the farmer, the *metayer*, and the tenant, all were more and more becoming landowners. In contradistinction to the property belonging to the nobility, the property of the country-folk consisted of very small holdings, which remained subject to dues. But it was growing in area by the acquisition of new holdings, and thus by degrees was formed the very complicated map of the peasant holdings of France. Small country landowners moreover often combined some industrial occupation with their agricultural labours; they were wheelwrights, farriers, masons, and especially weavers.

Town life. In this agricultural country, towns began to acquire a very real importance as markets for agricultural produce, junctions of roads, centres of administration, industry, and intellectual development.

Though royalty led a very migratory existence, Paris already formed a centre of immense importance compared to the other towns of the kingdom. The population was estimated at from 400,000 to 500,000 souls, doubtless an exaggerated figure, but one which bears witness to the impression produced on visitors by "this town, which was superior," wrote Marino Cavalli in 1546, "not only to all other towns of this kingdom but to those of the rest of Europe." It was noted for its University, the students of which were sometimes reckoned at more than 20,000, including the grammar schools, its *Parlement*, the first in the kingdom, its public buildings. In the provinces there were: Rouen, enriched by the cloth industry and the commerce of the Seine and the sea, and improved under Francis I by a port on the coast, *Le Havre de Grâce*; Orleans, the gateway to the lands beyond the Loire; Tours, at the very centre of the châteaux in which the Valois court mostly resided, where an attempt was made to establish a silk industry; Dijon, a frontier town, a royal outpost facing the Burgundian lands which remained in the hands of Spain; Lyons, magnificently situated at the junction of the routes from the Mediterranean, northern Italy, and upper Germany, which since Charles VII's reign had replaced Geneva as the town of fairs, and had also become a town of banking and financial houses, a cosmopolitan centre for all money business, a town of printers and booksellers, and was definitely taking the place of Tours as the centre of the silk industry; Marseilles, a fortunate acquisition of Louis XI, which by its activity monopolised the trade of the Levant and northern Africa; Toulouse, proud of its architecture, its *Parlement*, and its schools, where the theory of the royal power was elaborated; Bordeaux, the former capital of British Guyenne, grown wealthy by the export of wines; learned Poitiers, situated like Orleans on one of the great strategic routes linking the north to the south-west; on the coast, La Rochelle, Saint-Malo, and further east Dieppe, nests of daring sailors, ship-owners, explorers and captains of privateers, who visited the west coast of Africa, sailed to Canada to search for the route to China through the estuary of the St Lawrence, and guarded the Azores to intercept, on their passage, the Spanish galleons laden with the precious metals of the New World, or the Portuguese caravels with their cargoes of spices.

Town life was developing. In such towns as possessed a *Parlement*, the magistrates built themselves splendid residences, decorated by works of art. From the time of Louis XI they always bought their official posts. More and more frequently they bequeathed them to their sons, thus forming magisterial dynasties, a legal nobility. Around them swarmed a crowd of barristers, attorneys, notaries, proctors, clerks—known collectively as the *basoche*. In towns of lesser importance the *bailliage*, the *sénéchaussée*, and, dating from Henry II, the *présidial* represented the *Parlement* on a small scale.

Theoretically towns were always divided into royal towns and communes. The latter, also theoretically, retained extensive rights, possessing their own police, law-courts, economic control and financial independence, which made of them feudal corporations, especially in the south and south-east, where the office of consul had survived. But the royal officers encroached more and more on the communes and endeavoured to reduce the towns to the pattern of Paris, where the Provost and the sheriffs were little more than mere officials. But this evolution was not completed till the 17th century.

The *bourgeois* proper, owners of houses in the towns and generally also of market gardens in the suburbs, had been enriched by the rise in the value of land, and they, like the nobles, escaped from part of the direct taxation. Besides these the town population was composed of industrial classes—masters, journeymen, and apprentices. It was then on the increase, though one must beware of contemporary statistics which speak of 40,000 people in the same town earning their living by a single trade. Besides it is necessary to distinguish (1) traditional trades, sometimes organised into guilds, which, with the unique exception of the cloth-trade, belonged to the type of the small manufactory, the isolated handicraft complete in itself and subject to invariable rules; (2) the new trades, printing, silk, and paper-making, which demanded a large staff and a stock of intricate and costly manufacturing tools—in short, capital. These trades underwent the changes already accomplished in the cloth-trade, the separation of the capitalist, the owner of tools, raw materials, and manufactured goods, from the mass of artisans who possessed only their strength and skill. Violent conflicts burst forth, such as the printers' strike at Lyons which, breaking out in 1539, did not subside till 1571 and even spread to the printers in Paris.

Even in the traditional trades and in the guilds the owners were inclined to form an oligarchy which became almost hereditary. The manual worker was looked upon more and more as doing servile work. The efforts made by royalty (especially

in 1581 and 1597) to regularise the system of the guilds and to
correct its abuses had in the main a fiscal object. They did not
remedy the general condition. They did not prevent the workmen, who were being more and more ousted from the government of their trades, from forming amongst themselves defensive
associations, which seemed mysterious because they were forbidden and which were known as *compagnonnages*.

Besides these associations for trade purposes, the industrial
world formed religious associations or brotherhoods, which were
an integral part of town life and which were to play a rôle of
the first importance in the times of the League.

The Italian Wars

In spite of all attempts to vindicate it, one can hardly deny
that Charles VIII's expedition was a deviation from national
policy, a "war of display." The young king found as part of
his heritage the claims of the House of Anjou to the two Sicilies,
and even its claims to the kingdoms of Jerusalem and Cyprus;
he dreamed of restoring the empire of the Palaeologi. Louis XI's
Italian intrigues had prepared the way for the expedition of
1494; they had not made it a necessity.

The Expedition of 1494. This expedition brought about a
revolution. First in the art of war: war, as carried on by the
condottieri in the service of the Italian republics or princes, was
a very scientific art, but one which caused comparatively little
bloodshed. The great army of Charles VIII numbered national
elements of great variety and was a violent and brutal army.
It was provided with a large force of artillery, superior in
quality to any known up till then. Therefore in its first stages
the expedition was nothing but a promenade. Armies fled and
walls crumbled before the most Christian King, and with the
walls princedoms crumbled too. Pisa flung the Lion of Florence
into the Arno; Florence expelled the Medici. The Borgia Pope
shut himself up in the castle of St Angelo and, not being safe
there from the French cannon, induced his conqueror to
celebrate mass on his behalf. Charles VIII entered Naples in
triumph.

There was also a revolution in diplomacy. French simplicity
moved very clumsily over the unstable and difficult ground of

Italian politics. The King and his councillors, with the exception perhaps of Commines, would not believe that Sforza, who had invited the French into Italy, was the soul of the League which was being formed at Venice to drive them in the Italian *cul-de-sac*. As the kingdom of Naples had been taken by Charles VIII from a branch of the House of Aragon, Ferdinand the Catholic, sovereign lord of Valencia, Catalonia, and the Balearic Isles, candidate for the lordship of the western Mediterranean, entered the anti-French league. Italian history was expanding into European history.

The Milanese Question. This expansion became still more noticeable when, on Charles VIII dying without children, the Duke of Orleans became king. Not only did he take over the "rights" of his predecessor to Naples, but he claimed those of his grandmother Valentine Visconti to Milan which he declared to have been usurped by Ludovico Sforza. But Milan was a fief of the Empire and Ludovico had managed to give his niece in marriage to Maximilian. This therefore is what happened: whereas Charles VIII had sacrificed to his "Italian dreams" the policy of Louis XI, who wished to absorb the Burgundian inheritance, Louis XII, by alarming the head of the House of Austria, mixed up the Burgundian with the Italian question; thus France, engaged beyond the Alps, was dangerously threatened on her left flank. In addition to this the valleys of Lombardy were at that time a land of promise for the Alpine communities of Switzerland; by closing to them as Duke of Milan the southern passes of the Alps, the King of France threatened them with ruin. These mountaineers, in whom Louis XI had divined the best foot-soldiers of the age and whom he had made his allies, became the allies of France's enemies, and above all the allies of the Pope, when Julius II tried to push the French out of Italy and to establish in a peninsula which hated foreigners the primacy of St Peter's see. By laying siege to Dijon in 1513, the Swiss nearly succeeded in completely re-establishing for Maximilian's benefit the Flemish-Burgundian state. They were prevented from doing so by the skill of La Trémoille.

But it was no longer only the Catholic King, the Emperor, and the cantons who were interfering in the quarrel of which Naples and Milan were the pawns. In 1513 England intervened and it was a moot point whether the English (Anglo-Burgundian) wars would not begin again. Louis XII's marriage with Mary of England warded off this danger.

The Flemish-Burgundian inheritance and the struggle for the balance of power. Francis I inherited all the Italian claims of his predecessor Louis XII. He immediately crossed the Alps and thanks to his artillery and to the powerful onslaught of his cavalry he crushed the formidable Swiss infantry at Marignano. To defeat the Swiss at that time was above all to defeat the Pope. But Francis I needed the Pope's support for his Neapolitan policy; he became reconciled with Leo X at Bologna and, renouncing his schismatic tendencies, signed with him as we have seen the Concordat. He made peace with the Swiss and formed with them a permanent alliance which, during nearly three hundred years, placed contingents recruited from the cantons at the service of the King of France and made the King's ambassador at Soleure a kind of mediator between the confederated cantons.

All his life Francis I continued to dream of Milan and Naples, kept up armies in the peninsula, intrigued, protected princes and republics, and wore out in this useless enterprise the resources of the kingdom. But other cares were to claim his attention.

When Francis became King of France, Charles, through his father, Philip the Fair, was heir to the Flemish-Burgundian State. Through his mother, Juana of Castile, he was Charles I, King of Spain, and consequently master of the West Indies. His grandfather Maximilian dreamed of making him King of the Romans, a future Emperor. Francis I, whose head had been turned by the French doctrines of the imperial dignity of the kings of France, committed the folly of becoming a candidate for the Empire. The contest began before the Electors; the most Christian King threw into the balance the money-bags of his submissive people; the Catholic King countered this by the bonds issued through the German banks. The election of Charles V was the first great triumph of the credit system, the work of the Fuggers of Augsburg.

The situation of France became dangerous from that moment; on the Pyrenees, the Saône, and the Somme she was face to

face with the powerful House of Burgundy, which was eager to
recover the native lands of Charles the Bold; she came into conflict
with it at Milan, a fief of the Empire, and at Naples, a Spanish
possession, and this power of the Habsburgs rested not only on
the hereditary lands of Austria but on that vague entity, the Holy
Roman Empire. If the Emperor succeeded in creating a universal
monarchy, the first victim to be crushed would be France.

The drama seemed to be definitively ended in Lombardy, in
1525, by the capture of Francis I at Pavia. Here was the most
Christian King imprisoned in the melancholy castle of Madrid;
the victor insisted on the restoration of the old Duchy, where
slept his ancestors, the Dukes of Burgundy; Francis surrendered
even his suzerainty over the other parts of the Burgundian
heritage; he re-established for the Constable of Bourbon a great
feudal power in central France, renounced his Italian claims
and forsook his allies in Italy. The history of France seemed to
be at an end.

France was saved by *two men*: the Chancellor Du Prat and
the regent Louise of Savoy. They obtained from the Estates of
Burgundy a protest against the surrender of the province to
Charles V—an early and wonderful expression of the rights
of a people to self-determination. By drawing attention to
the immense power of the Emperor they roused the concern
of the Pope, the Venetians, the Italian princes, and the King of
England. Immediately upon his release the prisoner of Madrid
became at Cognac the head of a league to re-establish the
balance of power. He completed his task by forming an *entente*,
strange in the eyes of his contemporaries, with the Turk Soliman,
who was to detain the imperial armies in Hungary and the
imperial fleets in the Mediterranean. He went further; thanks
to the skilful policy of the Du Bellays, he made allies in Germany
itself of the Protestant princes, and even of all the princes who
were unwilling to see the Holy Roman Empire transformed
into a monarchy.

The conflict continued through innumerable vicissitudes, interrupted by periods of peace. It recommenced under Francis I's
son, Henry II, who was launched once more into the Italian
adventures by the ambition of the Guises, and who intervened in
Germany as defender of German liberties, a new Brutus opposing

a new Caesar. He acquired the three Bishoprics and had the joy of recovering Calais from the English (1558). But the disaster of Saint-Quentin, where the Constable Montmorency allowed himself to be defeated and captured by Duke Emmanuel-Philibert of Savoy, brought about the peace of Cateau-Cambrésis (1559), which closed the brilliant period of the history of France in the 16th century.

The King ceded Piedmont and Savoy, countries which had both belonged to France since 1536, and of which one at least was in process of becoming French. He renounced his Italian possessions or claims, and even Corsica, which also had for a time been French. He sacrificed all his allies and subordinated his policy to that of Philip II, who was to become the leader of the Catholic reaction in Europe.

The beginnings of the French Reformation. France, the country where the doctrines of the great councils of the 15th century had been worked out and preserved, had early been roused by an intense need of religious and moral revival. The movement began in the circle of the learned, devout humanists who often belonged to the regular or secular clergy and who applied to the sacred text the same critical methods as were applied by scholars to classical texts. In these sacred texts, restored to their early purity, they found the doctrine of justification by faith alone and they condemned the abuse of the doctrine of works. The foremost representative of this first reformation was Jacques Lefèvre d'Étaples, who published his *Psalter* in 1508, and his *Commentary on St Paul's Epistles* in 1512. The new doctrine was developed in the circle of Guillaume Briçonnet, Bishop of Meaux, and also in that of Marguerite d'Angoulême in the little court of Nérac. It was soon to be influenced by the doctrine of Luther, some of whose tracts had been translated into French by Louis de Berquin. The preaching of the learned had a special influence on the poor and humble, particularly the artisans, whose unhappy social position predisposed them to listen to this appeal to individual reason and to the equality of all Christians, as had been the case earlier in England in Wiclif's time. These "Bible Christians" of Meaux were weavers and carders, like the artisans of Saintonge with whom Bernard Palissy used to sing Marot's psalms.

This first French reformation, which was gentle and timid, far removed from any idea of violent rupture with Rome and slightly nationalist, humanist, and democratic, was denounced and fought against by the theologians, notably by the Sorbonne. The *Parlements* were somewhat divided, for a certain number of their members had been won over to the new ideas; on the whole they saw in the religious dissent a revolt against established order and acted all the more severely because, with rare exceptions such as. Berquin, their victims were people of no consequence. During periods of violent persecution the Protestant population emigrated to Geneva, Lausanne, Strasburg and, after the accession of Elizabeth, to England; this migration was facilitated by the fact that the Protestants were chiefly recruited from the working class.

Owing to his ties with the humanists, his rôle of creator of the Royal College of the three languages, and his sister's influence, Francis I was somewhat inclined to sympathise with the new ideas. But the Concordat having settled in his favour the question of ecclesiastical property, there no longer existed for him one of the reasons which was driving the German princes to Lutheranism. His Italian policy obliged him to deal cautiously with the Pope. The violent manifestations of reformed zeal amongst the people—which from 1528 took the form of demolishing statues and in 1533 of posting up placards attacking the mass—made him listen to those who denounced the French Reformers as anarchists, rivals of the Swabian peasants, and anabaptists. Although the requirements of his German policy drove him, even after a period of pitiless reaction, to negotiate with the German Lutherans, and even to outline with Melanchthon a somewhat insincere attempt at reconciliation between the two professions of faith, he remained faithful to his rôle of "eldest son of the Church," and he stained the close of his reign with the blood of the Vaudois.

Nevertheless the "father of letters" remained the hope of the Protestants. Jean Calvin of Noyon, the jurist who had studied at the universities of Orleans, Bourges, and Paris, and who in 1533 had been obliged to flee from the latter town, wrote the famous preface to the *Institution Chrétienne* at Bâle in 1535; addressing Francis I, he protested against the calumnies

of which the Reformers were victims and showed them to be
loyal subjects who rendered unto Caesar the things which were
Caesar's. His book, written with a severe and pitiless logic,
gave the French-speaking Reformers a terribly rigid doctrine.
He first settled in Geneva in 1536, was banished thence in 1538,
took refuge in Strasburg, and was recalled in 1541, from which
date till his death in 1564 he exercised a commanding influence
on the little republic. Towards Geneva flocked Frenchmen who
wished to revive their faith and prepare for the ministry at this
living source; from Geneva pastors and martyrs set out towards the provinces of France. In the eyes of France, England,
and the Low Countries, Geneva was indeed, according to
Michelet's saying, the "school of martyrs."

Thanks to the great power of organisation possessed by Calvin
and his lieutenants, amongst whom stood out the Burgundian
Theodore Beza, the French Reformation changed its character.
Spontaneous and isolated gatherings were gradually replaced
by "organised Churches" provided with constitutions of a
hierarchical character, in which the lay element had its place
beside the pastors, and which were able to group themselves
in "conferences" and "synods." Theirs was an ordered force
which the fierce persecution of Henry II's time was to render
still more powerful. To use a figure of speech familiar to
the Reformers, the hammer by dint of striking wore itself
out on the anvil and hardened it. By the end of Henry II's
reign a large number of provinces, Guyenne, Languedoc, Poitou,
Normandy, Lyonnais, and Dauphiné were "infested" by heresy;
Brittany, Burgundy, Auvergne, and Provence were affected;
even the country folk, overwhelmed by the burden of the taxes,
rebelled against the tithes. Paris itself was not immune in spite
of the power of the clergy and the marshalling of the lower
middle-class into religious confraternities. In 1559 councillors
of the *Parlement* were not afraid of protesting against the
persecution and of sacrificing their lives for Calvin's doctrine.
A new feature was to be seen in the fact that great nobles (the
Chastillons) did not hesitate to proclaim their faith, and without
flinching allowed themselves to be thrown into the Bastille. The
Reformers were in sufficient numbers for a new name to be
coined for them in common speech, that of "Huguenots,"

borrowed no doubt from the Swiss *Eidgenossen*. Henry II's accidental death was considered by the Huguenots as a chastisement of God, and the fear of the heretics had been largely accountable for the facility with which he had reconciled himself with Philip II. It is noticeable that Calvin's departure from Paris took place no long time before the day (August 15, 1534) on which, in a chapel of Montmartre, Ignatius Loyola and his companions enrolled their first recruits. France therefore appeared to be the arena in which was to be fought out the struggle between the Reformation and the counter-Reformation.

The Civil Wars

Henry II's death was the beginning of a crisis in the history of France. The consolidation of the royal power, the transition of royalty from a feudal to an almost absolute type, national unity, an active and able foreign policy holding in cheque the Burgundian-Habsburg power, all these results of a century-old evolution seemed to be called in question by Montgomery's spear-thrust. In reality it lanced an abscess just ready to burst.

The first Wars of Religion. Bourbon and Guise. We have seen that from 1559 the Reformation issued from the monasteries and the cobblers' stalls to enter the châteaux. The Protestant nobles, whose fathers and grandfathers had known the days of the Armagnacs and Burgundians and who had themselves taken part in the Italian wars, were not of a nature to meet persecution with the scriptural resignation of the poor preaching monk or the journeyman cobbler. The struggle between the two religions was to become a "War of Religion," and because, partly from religious motives and partly under the pretext of religion, it brought opposing factions into conflict, it was also to become a civil war.

The two factions had existed under Henry II. It was during his reign that had been built up, largely under cover of the Italian wars, the fortune of the Guises, foreign princes and great French lords, men of the sword and princes of the Church; it was their policy that had triumphed both in the persecution of 1559 and in the Treaty of Cateau-Cambrésis. Since then there had arisen against them, as the leader of another party, the

Constable de Montmorency, the aged minister of Francis and Henry. He, like the Lorraine princes, was a Catholic, but his nephews, the three Chastillons—Odet, a bishop, Gaspard de Coligny, Admiral of France, François d'Andelot, Colonel-General of the Infantry—were openly Protestant. They had more or less with them princes of the blood, the Bourbons, a branch which had remained faithful at the time of the Constable's treason: Antoine, by his marriage King of Navarre and Vicomte de Béarn, a shifty and unstable individual, whose wife, Jeanne d'Albret, was an ardent Huguenot; and Louis, Prince de Condé, who, under the influence of Coligny, was to figure as leader of the party.

In short Henry II's death precipitated the crisis. He left behind him a family of sickly children, doomed to tuberculosis and neurasthenia. In eighteen months France experienced two changes of reign, the second of which began with a minority. The regency, which should have been claimed by Antoine de Bourbon, was administered by the Queen-mother, a Medici. Destitute of all real authority, this clever Florentine was obliged to manœuvre between the parties and to attach herself to one or other alternately so as to prevent any from ever becoming the strongest. Thanks to this complex and shifty rôle, Catherine won a not unmerited reputation for cunning and duplicity which caused her to be detested by all parties. It cannot however be denied that, placed as she was in a most difficult position, she gave proof of real ability.

The entry of an important part of the nobility into the ranks of the reformed party had not only the effect of exciting war-like passions and of transforming into civil war the conflict over religious doctrines, it opened up a question of authority. Francis II and Charles IX were such weak kings that it was sufficient, in order to become master of the political machinery, to have possession of the royal person, to hold the hand that signed the decrees. It was therefore the endeavour of each faction in turn to get possession of the King and to isolate him, each party professing to act in His Majesty's name and interests. Whichever party found itself temporarily in a state of rebellion, owing to the King being in the hands of the opposing party, pretended to be fighting for His Majesty's deliverance. It was

thus that the "religious Huguenots" became "political Huguenots" (*Huguenots d'État*).

At the head of the "political Huguenots" were the Bourbons.
In the event of the failure of male issue it was they who according to the salic law would be called to the throne. But in
opposition to their rights arose the claims of the House of
Lorraine—the Guises, who called themselves the descendants of
the Carolingians and victims of the Capet usurpation. They
established their power through the marriage of their niece
Mary Stuart with Francis II, and they stamped out with blood
the conspiracy of Amboise, which had for its express object their
overthrow. After this, Charles IX's accession and Catherine's
policy seemed to give power to the Huguenots. It was possible momentarily to believe, at the time of the meeting of
the Conference of Poissy (1561), that a *modus vivendi* between
the two parties might be found. The Cardinal of Lorraine
wrecked a plan which would have deprived the Guises of their
raison d'être, and dissension recommenced. In those times
moreover the periods of "peace" were destined to be of short
duration, mere truces between two wars, truces during which
neither local disturbances, nor massacres by either side, nor
petty provincial wars were suspended. The massacre at Vassy
(March 1, 1562) caused a renewal of fighting and plundering of
churches; there were revolts at Lyons and Rouen. The Huguenots, masters of Normandy, implored the help of adjacent
England against the triumvirate formed by the Guises, the aged
Montmorency, now become their tool, and the Maréchal de Saint-
André. The Treaty of Hampton Court, in which their delegate,
the Vidame de Chartres, no doubt exceeded the instructions of
Condé and Coligny, unfortunately gave them the appearance of
being allies of a foreign nation. The conflict, marked by the
murder of François de Guise, conqueror of Calais, called by the
Huguenots the "Tiger of France" (1563), began to assume an
intensely cruel character. If the Huguenots had turned to
England, they accused the House of Lorraine of being in the
pay of Spain and of having led the young King to Bayonne to
plan with the Duke of Alba a general massacre of the Protestant
leaders.

The war spread over the whole kingdom. Its principal

theatre was in Poitou, in the border land between the Parisian districts and those parts of Guyenne in which the Reformers had at their disposal large forces amongst the nobility, in the principality of Béarn, and in the little maritime republic of La Rochelle. The Catholics tried to ascribe to the Duke of Anjou, Henry II's third son, the prestige of the victories of Jarnac and Moncontour.

St Bartholomew. For the second time, after the Treaty of Saint-Germain (1570), it was possible to believe that religious peace was about to reappear and France to resume her traditional policy. King Charles IX made a display of his veneration for Coligny. The latter had always taken seriously his rôle of Admiral and had patronised French enterprise in Brazil (expedition of Villegagnon), Florida, and Barbary. In the revolt of the Low Countries against Philip II he saw a way both of extending the naval power of France and of uniting against Spain the whole French nobility without distinction of religion. This policy was guaranteed by the marriage of Margaret, Henry II's daughter, with Henry of Navarre, heir of the Bourbons and Albrets.

This bold policy tended to eliminate the Guises and withdraw the King from his mother's influence. Hence arose an alliance between the House of Lorraine and Catherine and her son the Duke of Anjou against Coligny. Jeanne d'Albret's death, which had wrongly aroused suspicion, had already thrown a tragic light upon the wedding of Henry and Margaret. An attempt planned by the Guises on the life of Coligny only succeeded in severely wounding him. It was represented to the King that the Huguenot leaders assembled in Paris for the wedding were about to revolt to avenge Coligny, and thus was wrung from him his consent to the general massacre of August 24, 1572. From Paris the movement spread to many towns.

The consequences of this event were far-reaching. The Huguenots had had faith in the royal word; they had been betrayed. Their anger turned against the kingship itself, against the Queen-mother, called Jezebel by the ministers of religion, against the perjured King and his eventual successor. They declared the original contract between subject and king to have been broken. Abandoning the position adopted by Calvin, they claimed the right of subjects to overthrow tyrants. In the provinces the direction of the movement passed into the hands of violent spirits, bigoted pastors and the fanatical masses. The latter found leaders amongst the small landed gentry, whose feudal pretensions were reviving, and allies amongst certain Catholic parties, upright and patriotic spirits who were horrified by the intolerance of the slaughterers, and amongst the disaffected great nobles who wished to use the Huguenot force to fight the Guises. The Huguenots, who were organising themselves more and more into a small federated republic in the very heart of the kingdom, had as protector in the first instance a prince of the blood who had been ill-provided for, the Duc d'Alençon, youngest son of Henry II, on whose behalf an attempt was even made to resume Coligny's Flemish plan. He was succeeded later by a Montmorency. Certain great Protestant communes, such as La Rochelle and Montpellier, were real capitals, at war with Catholic and royalist Paris.

The massacre, hailed as a victory at Rome and Madrid, produced an impression of horror on the Protestant allies of France and even on many foreign Catholics. It almost prevented the Poles from adopting as king, Henry of Anjou, the victor of Moncontour. His reign was of the shortest duration, for hardly had the newly made king arrived at Cracow when he heard of Charles IX's death. In all haste he left his kingdom and, not without stopping on his way for rejoicings, returned to his kingdom of France (1574).

The League. Henry III's reign (1574–89) is assuredly one of the saddest periods in the history of France. The King was a commonplace creature, without will-power, of effeminate habits, who divided his time between the most degrading vices and the most puerile devotions, and whose sole ability lay in betraying his own officers and in playing them off against each other. The States General of 1576 were powerless to re-establish order in the country and to restore civil peace.

The King and the Catholics inspired the Protestants with so little confidence that the latter, during the short periods of peace which occurred between two wars, exacted Edicts of pacification guaranteeing them places of safety. These places of safety were fortified towns, generally chosen from among those in which the Huguenots were numerous, and of which the governor and garrison were of necessity Protestant. They also obtained *chambres mi-parties* (courts composed of both Catholics and Protestants) in the *Parlements* and places of worship in every *bailliage*.

These concessions to the minority filled the Catholics with indignation. In opposition to the groups of nobles and reformed Communes they organised themselves into associations, ranging from the "holy unions" of nobles and church adherents, which were directed by Duke Henry of Guise and the Cardinal of Lorraine, down to the pious brotherhoods of the *bourgeoisie* and the artisans led by monks and parish priests whose semi-military processions periodically rekindled enthusiasm. In order to avoid receiving a Condé as governor of Picardy, there was formed in 1576 at Amiens the particular association which gave birth to the League. Similar associations were established in Burgundy, Provence, etc. In opposition to the reformed federal Republic arose a kind of Catholic Republic, a State within the State, a suspicious and imperious patron rather than a vassal of royalty. This Republic, supported by Rome, upheld and subsidised by Spain, assisted by the great army of the Regular Orders and by the Society of the Jesuits, held sway in large towns such as Paris, Marseilles, Toulouse and, at various times, Lyons; *Parlements* and provincial Estates were on its side.

The question of the dynasty was openly discussed, for Henry III and his brother d'Alençon, now Duc d'Anjou, after having missed the opportunity of becoming Count of Flanders, were childless. The Carolingian claims, either of the Guises themselves or of the head of the family, Duke Charles III of Lorraine, were beginning to take shape.

The event which led to the dynastic crisis was the death, in 1584, of "Monsieur," the Duc d'Anjou. The accession of Henry of Navarre, leader of the Huguenots, appeared no longer merely a possibility but an imminent danger. This prince of Béarn was poor, always short of money, always in danger of being defeated and captured by his enemies and deserted by his followers. But he was a brave soldier, who fought with the zeal and wit of a cadet of Gascony and who fascinated his followers by his apparent good-nature, his free and easy manners and absence of arrogance. He inspired enthusiasm and devotion, and obtained in Switzerland, Germany, and England valuable financial and military assistance.

A formidable question was then raised. Was the so-called "salic law," by virtue of which St Louis's descendant should succeed the last of the Valois, the "fundamental law" of the French State? or was it that other law which through the coronation at Reims made the most Christian King the Lord's anointed, and thereby implicitly excluded all heretics? It was against the heretic King that the Holy League strove and obtained from Pope Sixtus V the excommunication of the "Béarnais" and his Catholic followers. As the King was suspected of favouring the heretic, the revolt of the brotherhoods and the Parisian army was organised against him and in favour of Henry of Guise, the conqueror of the German mercenaries (day of the Barricades, May 7, 1588). Henry III, forced to flee from his capital to Chartres, never forgave the man who had caused his humiliation.

From that time the civil war was a war between Guise, the real King of Paris, and the King of Chartres, the ally of the heretic. In nearly all the towns with *Parlements*, there arose, besides the *Parlement* of the League, a royalist *Parlement*, which held its sittings outside the provincial capital. France was really divided against itself, or rather, divided into hostile regions, and her neighbours were taking advantage of this state of dissension to enlarge their own boundaries. The House of Savoy, both in the person of the Duke himself and in that of his relative the Duc de Nemours, was trying to extend its territory to Lyons. Philip II had hopes of dominating a worn-out France. The unity of France was in process of being completely broken up.

As in 1576, recourse was had to a meeting of the States General, which opened at Blois in December 1588. With his vindictive temperament Henry III took advantage of it to bring about the assassination of his enemy Henry of Guise and the Cardinal of Lorraine. This murder let loose among the Catholic masses a tempest of indignation and wrath against the man whom the preachers in their raging sermons never alluded to

otherwise than as "wicked Herod," and who was looked upon
as still more odious than the heretic himself. Excommunicated
in his turn, deprived of his rights, marked down for the dagger,
he was assassinated at Saint-Cloud by the monk Jacques
Clément, and the memory of his murderer was lauded as that
of a hero, the saviour of France, the avenger of Christ, the
instrument of divine justice (1589). The Catholics then, in their
turn, took up in their own interests the republican doctrines of
the Reformers, while the latter, by way of reply, defended the
rights of kings.

The Accession of Henry IV. "Better to die a thousand
deaths than have a Huguenot king" was the cry of many
Catholic nobles, while others, in unison with the Reformers,
hailed the King of Navarre as Henry IV, King of France. But
this king had yet to conquer his kingdom. In opposition to
him and to facilitate the transition, the Leaguers tried to raise
a phantom king; they discovered another Prince of the Blood,
an authentic Bourbon, an old man and a cardinal, therefore
doubly incapable of carrying on the line, whom they called
"Charles X," a strange king, prisoner of his nephew, the Béarnais.

A mere captain of mercenaries, or, if you prefer it, a knight
errant, the Béarnais had nothing in his favour but his white
plume. He had, like an adventurer, to scour the highways of
his kingdom to recruit his adherents. He rushed to Normandy
to receive the support sent over by Elizabeth; he opened war
on the Duc de Mayenne, the one prince of the House of Lorraine
who had remained in Paris, and defeated his troops at Arques,
near Dieppe. After a fresh victory at Ivry he had the daring
to besiege Paris, the great city of the League, but the blockade
was raised by the Duke of Parma, one of the ablest strategists
of the time, who had come from Flanders at the head of the
renowned Spanish *tercios*. Paris was actually in the hands of
a revolutionary government organized by heads of districts—
the *Seize*—who kept the whole population in a state of feverish
excitement. In nearly all the towns of the League, members of
the *Parlements* and the municipal authorities played a similar
part. In spite of everything Henry was gaining ground; between
the Protestants and the Catholics of the League a third party
was formed which placed the interests of the State before those

of religion; as a term of abuse its members were called *politiques*, or in the south *bigarrats* (parti-coloured). In the League itself shades of opinion were becoming apparent, ranging from the absolute leaguers, who were entirely under the influence of Spain, to the French leaguers, who wished to save the Roman religion without ruining France.

This was the state of public opinion at the beginning of the second siege of Paris and the opening of the constitutional crisis of 1593. The States General, assembled in Paris under the direction of Philip II's envoys and the Pope's legate, had to solve the difficult question of choosing a most Christian King in succession to "Charles X." Should it be Philip II, or his daughter Isabella Clara Eugenia, or the Duke of Savoy, or Mayenne, or Charles III of Lorraine? But royalist propaganda was at work among the people of Paris, and famine, a wise counsellor, was influencing them towards peace. The *Seize* were losing power, and dissension reigned in their midst. In spite of the *Parlement's* adhesion to the League, its members bore in mind that its power was based on the fleurs-de-lis and that a King of France should be of the royal lineage. Henry IV's hour was about to strike. But he seemed to be involved in an *impasse*; it was impossible for a foreigner, not of the blood of St Louis, to be made king (or queen), but it was equally impossible for a heretic. Henry IV, who on matters of religion held much the same views as the *politiques*, extricated himself from the *impasse* by abjuring Protestantism (1593), a course which allowed the royalist bishops to crown him king (1594).

It must not be taken for granted that this abjuration, which angered and alarmed the Reformers, settled everything. Rome took time to pronounce herself satisfied with the penitence of the heretic who had already once fallen from grace. Those who benefited by the League were slow to let themselves be ousted from their posts, or else they insisted on being paid for their compliance. "They have not given me back my kingdom, but they have sold it me," said the King. Nevertheless he entered Paris amid the cheers of the crowd, which had suffered more than enough, and gained the submission of Lyons and Orleans. Marseilles did not give in till 1596 and Brittany not till two years later.

In order to enter Dijon, he had first to defeat the Spanish
forces and Mayenne at Fontaine-Française (June 5, 1595).

Close of the Wars of Religion and the Italian Wars. Henry
IV proceeded with the task of reconquering his kingdom
under the almost constant menace of criminal attempts instigated by the ultra-Catholics, who did not lay down their arms
(attempts of Pierre Barrère and Jean Chastel, 1594) until the
Papal absolution of 1595. It was the Jesuits in particular who
were found to be at work behind the irreconcilable party, and
they were consequently banished from the kingdom.

Gradually however by their ability Henry IV and his ministers
—either old adherents, such as Maximilian de Béthune, Duc de
Sully, or Leaguers who rallied to the King's support, such as
Villeroy—brought the kingdom to a state of peace and began
to repair the ruin wrought by thirty-five years of civil war.
Everywhere the ill-paid troops of the different parties had lived
on the land, first plundering to live, then plundering for its
own sake, setting fire to houses, killing or carrying off cattle,
destroying crops or allowing their horses to feed on them. In
many regions in Dauphiné, Comminges, Périgord, Limousin, etc.
the peasants had formed leagues, devoid of religious distinctions,
to defend themselves against the men-at-arms and plunderers
of noble birth. "The people," said in 1595 the *députés* of the
country districts, "contribute payment, food, and strength;
they are beaten, robbed, and burnt, and are made to submit
to every kind of cruelty." Till the end of the reign there were
parishes where "the high roads, ways and paths were obstructed
by brambles, broom, and brushwood" and where wolves attacked
the passers by. The land was going out of cultivation as it had
done during the Hundred Years' War. The towns were hardly
less desolate and their industries were often ruined.

Henry IV had no desire to convoke the States General; the
assemblies convoked by the League had proved too dangerous.
But a gathering of influential men (*notables*), assembled at
Rouen (1596), considered plans for restoring the prosperity of
the kingdom—the construction of roads and canals, the regulation of trades, and the establishment of manufactures. The consideration of these matters was even handed over, from the year
1598, to the Council of Commerce, a more or less permanent body.

Meanwhile the war with Spain had recommenced. In March 1597 the Spaniards made a bold attempt to re-open the road to Paris and obtained possession of Amiens.

The situation grew extremely serious, owing to the fact that the Huguenot masses, who were discontented and sometimes severely treated by their former leader, refused to take up arms against the invader before having obtained guarantees. They raised disturbances in their assemblies at Loudun, Saumur, and Châtellerault; and threatened, since the Béarnais no longer acted as their protector, to appoint one for themselves. The cautious spirits of the party, Duplessis-Mornay and Odet de La Noue, kept their co-religionists loyal to the King, but demanded of him an edict, which, while maintaining and extending former peace edicts, should guarantee the rights of the Protestant minority. At last, on April 30, 1598, the King, by his "perpetual and irrevocable" Edict of Nantes, accorded his subjects of the reformed religion universal liberty of conscience, liberty to hold services in all places where they had been held for at least two years, civil and political equality, and guarantees in judicial matters; he conceded that the churches of the party should be organised into synods and assemblies, and accorded his Protestant subjects a hundred "cities of refuge."

The Edict put an end to the Wars of Religion. Three days later the Treaty signed at Vervins with the Plenipotentiaries of Philip II put an end to the wars which had been the logical outcome of the Italian wars. The Treaty of Vervins did no more in appearance than renew that of Cateau-Cambrésis. As a matter of fact, it marked the final ruin of the old Burgundian claims, as well as the renunciation of French claims to Italy. Above all it emphasised the checkmate to Philip II in his attempt to subject and dismember France. With this treaty began the decline of the power of Spain, which had already suffered from the defeat of the Armada.

It was thus that the 16th century, which had been near to seeing the irreparable ruin and dissolution of France, closed with a fresh triumph for centralised monarchy and with a treaty which paved the way for the foundation of French supremacy on the continent.

§ II. SEVENTEENTH CENTURY

Henry IV and Sully

By the Treaty of Vervins with Spain (1598), by those of Paris
(February 27, 1600) and of Lyons (January 17, 1601) with the
Duke of Savoy, by the Edict of Nantes imposed on Catholics
and Protestants alike, Henry IV hoped to procure security on
the frontiers with civil and religious peace at home for the
kingdom he had won by warfare and diplomacy. A period of
repose such as that from 1600 to 1610 is almost unique in the
experience of France in the 17th century. And to the contrast
between these years of fruitful peace and the troubled minorities
and long wars of Louis XIII and Louis XIV which succeeded
should perhaps be traced the illusions long entertained on the
government of Henry IV. It was not the reign of a constitutional and liberal sovereign, of a "good king Henry," prematurely
snatched from his subjects by the dagger of a fanatic, represented by 18th century philosophers as a model citizen king of
pacific habits, and contrasted by the historians Poirson and
d'Avenel with those bellicose and absolute monarchs, Louis XIII
and Louis XIV.

The rare and essential merit of Henry IV is that, after having
been for twenty years above all things a soldier, not merely
a captain and a leader of party levies, but a soldier in the firing
line and ever at the breach, he recognised and seized opportunities for making peace with external foes and between religious parties, in order, by means of the needful concessions,
to suspend the conflicts which were exhausting the blood and the
resources of the nation. "It is time," he said to the deputies of
Toulouse (November 3, 1599), "for us all drunk as we are with
war to grow sober at our own charges."

Such wisdom came easily to him, for he possessed a lucid and
balanced intellect absolutely free from prejudice and guided by
reason only. But Frenchmen at large were still under the sway
of that fever of passion which for forty years had been hurling
them at each others throats and even into the arms of the
foreigner. Recovery was only attainable by submission to an

authority inspiring confidence and respect. Henry IV sought and achieved before all else the restoration of the royal authority, of which he took an exalted view.

He never once called the States General of the kingdom, though he had promised to do so. The Assembly of Notables which he held at Rouen (1596) to obtain money was not renewed. The provincial Estates of Normandy, Burgundy, Provence, Languedoc, Dauphiné, and Brittany retained their right of meeting to vote and settle the apportionment of taxes. But it was with great difficulty that they kept the right of discussing their amount. Henry did not as a rule tolerate discussion. He took care to humour even his *Parlements*, to whom he had restored the right of remonstrance (1597), in order to avoid conflicts, but with a growing clearness of determination to be obeyed by them as by others. He dealt in the same way with the towns of the kingdom, which had preserved the municipal administration granted in the past, leaving them free to govern themselves, provided that they steered clear of a renewal of popular intrigues and outbreaks and that authority was retained in the hands of a small number of prominent burgesses, in most cases nominated by the royal officials. The constitution he gave the city of Amiens (November 3, 1597) contained the maximum of municipal liberties he would have granted, if he had had his way, to every city of his kingdom. By his edict of April 1597, all the craftsmen and tradesmen of France were placed under the obligation of enrolling themselves in the guilds (*corps de jurandes*), the supervision and taxation of which was reserved to the monarchy.

Next to the *Parlements* the aristocracy remained the chief obstacle to the restoration and extension of the royal power. In the provinces and towns where they claimed a life or even a hereditary interest in the government, princes of the blood and great lords had acquired in the civil wars and under pretext of religion such habits of independence that they played the rôle of sovereign princes, maintaining troops and officers at their charges and diverting monies from the royal exchequer. Henry had compounded with them rather than reduced them. He well knew the needs, the rapacity and the turbulence of the nobles, among whom he had recruited his comrades-in-arms, and who were ruined by the depreciation of the currency which diminished their resources, by the wars which tore them from their devastated estates, and reduced to live by their swords legitimately or otherwise. The peace and the justice of the kingdom were compromised throughout the reign by the brutality and excesses of this aristocracy, which Henry would have guided by the counsels of Sully and Olivier de Serres into sedentary habits and tastes and the care of their estates. The peasants were the chief victims, though the nobles did not escape. For duels were counted by thousands and rapes and even brigandage were frequent. From 1598 to 1606 there was a succession of conspiracies against the King himself with the support and encouragement—as later against Richelieu—of Spain—first that of Biron, Marshal of France and the King's own comrade-in-arms, who was compromised in intrigues both with the Duke of Savoy and Philip II and finally executed for treason. Then came in 1602 the plot hatched by the Count of Auvergne with his sister Henriette d'Entragues, the King's mistress, to whom he had been weak enough to promise marriage, a plot to which the Constable Montmorency and the Duke of Montpensier were privy; in 1603 and 1605 the intrigues of the Bouillons and the Turennes, Protestant leaders of Sedan and Limousin, and of Catholics like D'Epernon, supported by the German Princes, which all but plunged the country once more into foreign and civil war.

If Henry triumphed over all these elements of discord and strife, he did so by his own will-power, his activity, his ever watchful ability. He organised his power as he had won it by his own personal exertion. Not that he was not well served. In his letters he often used the expression "My good servants." Among these throughout his career Sully stands foremost, an intrepid soldier and a gentleman farmer, a convinced Huguenot and a practical politician, a vigilant quartermaster-general, and an expert and thrifty financier who built up again the fortune of his king and "his beloved country," while making his own. He held the posts of Superintendent of Finance (1596), Surveyor-General of Roads (1599), Superintendent of Fortifications and Buildings, Grand Master of Artillery, Governor of the Bastille (1602) and of Poitou (1604), and was created

Duc et Pair. Villeroy, his direct opposite and sometimes his rival, was an official by profession. He had been a grave and prudent minister to the last two Valois. He was always a Catholic, but never a fanatic. His fidelity to his legitimate king based on reason and duty was as great as Sully's founded on friendship to the king of his choice. The business of France, well served by his experience at home and abroad, was his exclusive business and his sole occupation. President Jeannin was an old Leaguer and a fervent royalist, whose ability completed in Holland the work of the Peace of Vervins. These with the Chancellor Pomponne de Bellièvre and Sillery were *bourgeois* devoted to work and order.

The valuable assistance which Henry had thus gathered round him did not, however, relieve him of the task of carrying out his work personally and as if it were a relaxation. "The attention given by this monarch," says Saint-Simon, "to every part of the government and the singular capacity he displayed in all is perhaps the highest praise he merited." And the same author has shown in a striking picture "the manner in which Henry IV governed, and which he owed entirely to the habits necessitated by his earlier life as a captain of party troops." His administration had no fixed centre or settled agenda for the year nor was it choked with documents and clerks, or divided into specialised commissions, ministries, and offices. Wherever he was—and he was perpetually on the move—the King consulted his council, which was more often than not reduced to his confidential ministers. He questioned, discussed, and decided.

This Gascon king with his gay humour in spite of infirmities, appreciating a smart word as much as a smart sword thrust, and women as much as play, had as lofty an idea of the duties and respect attached to his office as his grandson Louis XIV. He wished his court to be well attended and brilliant, and devoted to it almost a third of his revenue in salaries of servants, pensions to the nobility, upkeep of guards, entertainments, and buildings. The royal fêtes, ballets, masques, entries, and coronations contrasted by their brilliance and frequency with the wretched plight of a king who as late as 1597 was begging clothes of Sully, "being quite naked." He thought it only reason-

able that France in whose service he spent himself and which
was "under obligation to him," should furnish him with the
means to maintain his rank—the first, if he could make it so,
in Europe—and what he called "his house-keeping." His architects Du Cerceau and Métezeau prolonged the great gallery of
the Louvre as far as the Tuileries, and laid out splendid gardens.
They adorned his capital with the Hôtel de Ville, the Place
Royale (Place des Vosges) and with great manufactories for his
service. The château of Saint-Germain was continued, that of
Monceaux built and beautified. At Fontainebleau, Henry's
favourite seat—for he preferred country to town—the park
stocked with some 100,000 new trees and the canal with its
broad vistas were the principal ornaments of a luxurious residence, which more than thirty painters, such as Dubreuil,
Lerambert, Martin Fréminet and Pourbus, were decorating
with frescoes and portraits, and where the sculptor Jacquet of
Grenoble was erecting a stately chimney piece in the great
hall. This was the period when the Royal House called upon
the tapestry workers of Flanders and of the Louvre to found
the factory of the Gobelins which was to be its glory till the
end of the régime.

Once King of France, the modest King of Navarre was determined that his dynasty should reap in the eyes of Europe
the inheritance of the Valois and the Capetians. In allying
himself with Marie, a daughter of the Medici, he chose as Queen
of France a rich heiress whose dower was to contribute to the
brilliance of his court and his crown. In that dreary and ill-
assorted union he met with many mortifications. Marie de'
Medici, who was neglected and perhaps deserved it for her
cantankerous disposition, never adapted herself to the manners
of France or of the court, or to her husband's tastes. None
but Italians or things Italian could please her and her favour
was reserved for her Tuscan women, especially Eleonora Galigai,
"the queen of her heart," and her *cavaliere servente*, Signor
Concini. To punish her for falling so far short of his ideal of
a queen of France, Henry kept her waiting till 1610 for her
coronation at Saint-Denis, which took place only a few days
before the crime of Ravaillac.

Sully tells how Henry often came to him to console himself

for the vexations caused him by the Queen, at his residence in
the Arsenal. Throughout the reign this played the part of a War
Office, where the Grand Master of Artillery was accumulating
arms and munitions and adding yearly by his economies to
a war treasure hoarded in iron-bound barrels. In the eyes of
the King, and still more in those of his chief confidant, the
restoration and improvement of the army constituted the
essential condition for the greatness of the monarchy and for
its authority at home and abroad. The minister once complained that his master was spending on luxuries sums which
would have sufficed for the maintenance of 15,000 troops.
At the close of the reign the royal army had been raised at an
annual cost of four million *livres* from 20,000, the average
strength of armies of that day, to 50,000. It was composed
principally of infantry armed with muskets and pikes, of a
small cavalry force inferior, it is true, to that of Germany, but
supported by artillery and a siege-corps of engineers, to which
Sully gave special attention.

This minister owes his reputation—chiefly through the 18th
century economists, who made him the patron of their doctrines—
to his management of the finances, which were professedly
regulated by his solicitude for the people, the peasantry of
France. It must not, however, be lost sight of that he was
originally a noble not a financier or a legislator. He earned his
master's esteem in the years when the latter had to reconquer
France almost without means by his skill and zeal in procuring
money, "the sinews of war." In the years of peace he still
regarded the King's money over which he had charge as mainly
the sinews of the army and of military campaigns. On the other
hand it was natural in a country where the land was then
the principal wealth both of the State and of private persons,
when "ploughland and pasture" were "the two breasts of
France," that an intelligent administrator of the finances should
treat the tillers of the soil tenderly. His solicitude was kindly,
but not disinterested. With Henry he defended the peasants
against the pillage of men-at-arms, and the excesses of the lords
and the tax collectors. The burden of the *taille*, or direct taxes,
levied exclusively on them, was lightened by the reduction of
persons illegally exempt—by almost 40,000, it is said—and the

diminution so far as possible of the total amount of the tax.
Occasionally, when the crops were good, permission was granted
to the cultivators to export their wheat, so as to be able to
sell it at a higher price and "to pay their dues more easily."
The fiscal purpose thus always betrays itself in Sully's ordinances in favour of agriculture, whose burden was still so heavy
that in 1607 foreigners and many Frenchmen, Sully amongst
the number, pronounced the peasants "reduced to a state of
beggary incapable of bearing it."

The work of Sully was powerless to correct a defective social
system, powerless even to attempt this; peace and toil were
the true and only efficacious remedies for the miseries of the
people of France, so ruinous to the country and to the King
himself. One merit and no small one must be allowed to Sully,
and that is to have watched, without sparing himself day or
night, over the money exacted for the needs of the State from
these poor taxpayers. After having—as early as 1597—proceeded against and punished the malversations of the treasurers
and of the officers of excise and farmed taxes, verified and reduced the loans of all sorts out of which financiers had been
making money, and freed the royal domain of encumbrances,
amounting to 30,000 *livres*, he took care that all the receipts
should not be misappropriated by dishonest officials, but should
yield a clear annual balance of nearly two million over outgoings.
Stubbornly and bluntly he defended this *Épargne* against
courtiers and mistresses, and sometimes against the King himself, who could not resist his passion for gambling and buildings,
or the caprices of his entourage. The only expenditure Sully
approved was that which was useful to the army, such as the
improvement of the roads and of the canals—it was he who
founded the modern canal system of France—thus promoting
commerce and the progress of national production. He was a
vigilant and upright servant of the monarchy by the fact that
as steward to the House of Bourbon he was as attentive to its
interests as if they had been his own; and he thus served France,
exhausted by wars and disturbances, at a time when a Frenchman could not conceive of France as distinct from the monarchy.

Those twelve years of government were a period of fruitful
activity. The commercial and industrial towns repaired their

ruins. Factories were started again, foreign trade revived—
with Spain, with England, and especially between Marseilles
and the East. The middle classes had grown rich on the loans
contracted by the King and the nobility during the war. They
now chose to invest their savings in posts under government
and in the magistracy, which the crown multiplied—even under
Sully—in order to procure immediate resources. They wanted
these posts made hereditary, and this was granted them in
return for a tax of one-sixtieth on which Sully raised a loan of
a million *livres* from the financiers Paulet and Saunier (1601–6).
Henceforward these offices passed by will and were reckoned
in inheritances on the same footing as landed estates. These
middle-class savings flowed more and more into investments
which carried with them honours and social distinction. Already
at this time, Montchrétien, the first French economist, pointed
out with regret the taste of the French middle classes for
employing their activity, their sons, and their fortunes in offices
of this nature rather than in industry and trade, which they
regarded as speculative and less honourable. He rebuked them
and quoted the example of the Dutch and English in contrast
to their timorousness and vanity. His teaching was unheeded;
the whole century and the following ones only confirmed these
classes in their aspirations towards fortunes guaranteed by the
public service and towards honours and influence. Strong as
was the habit of saving in town society, the desire for display
promoted luxurious habits. Sully was indignant at this, because the purchase of objects of luxury abroad involved the
draining of the country to the extent of several millions of
currency annually. The King declared he would rather fight
Spain in three pitched battles than "all these fat *bourgeois*
and especially their wives and daughters." They attempted,
however, to organise the struggle against imported luxuries by
creating silk manufactures and introducing into France the
cultivation of the mulberry tree and the rearing of silkworms.
They sent for gold-thread spinners and glass blowers from Italy
and weavers of high warp tapestry, of Bruges satins, and of
fine linen stuffs from Flanders. These somewhat artificial efforts,
renewed later by Colbert, who was convinced, like all French
financiers of the time, that the wealth of a country consists in

the accumulation of specie, were not entirely lost. Neither did
the country stand to lose altogether by the importation of
foreign luxuries. French trade profited and French energies
were brought into play thereby. The men of Saint-Malo, Dieppe,
and Rouen who sailed in 1601 and 1603 for Newfoundland and
Canada in search of fish and furs and to found a new France;
the merchants of Marseilles who set up trading stations (*échelles
de commerce*) in the Levant under the protection of the *Capitulations* obtained in 1604 from Sultan Ahmed I by De Brèves,
the King's ambassador, did not hesitate to risk their lives and
fortunes in lucrative and durable enterprises. Their example
and their efforts, approved as they were by Sully, maintained
in the country for two centuries a current of economic life,
from which it was able to draw unforeseen reserves of strength
at moments of crisis determined by continental affairs.

Determined as Henry IV was "to be wise" after the Peace
of Vervins, his pacific policy was never a policy of abdication
or renunciation of the rôle in Europe which history has assigned
to France as against the Habsburgs and Spain, defeated indeed
but ever aggressive and insolent. On one side of his character
Henry IV was a warlike king, a king thirsting for glory, ambitious to be the first captain in Christendom, a powerful prince
capable of making Spain feel his strength, of increasing and
strengthening the kingdom. His advisers—Villeroy less than
the others, but Sully more than any—never ceased from dreams
of glory for their master. Already in 1600 they discussed with
him whether it would be opportune that he should be a candidate for the Imperial Crown. He declined, "the present state
of his affairs not warranting it." The "grand design" which
Sully attributes to the King in his *Mémoires*, of having planned
in 1610 the abolition of the Holy Roman Empire of the
Habsburgs in order to reorganise Europe on a new footing in
view of a crusade against the Turks with the most Christian
King at its head, is merely the *Surintendant's* own expression
of his personal dreams of a glorious future for the House of
France. But all his advisers were at one in pursuing what
Cardinal d'Ossat, Henry's envoy to Rome, called "the truth of
the salvation, safety, and greatness of the King, of his line and
of the crown of France."

It was, thus, this passion for grandeur and glory which determined the main lines of the royal policy. But it was not the
exaggerated passion of Louis XIV. It permitted itself "to be
governed by reason," and most often it was regulated by times
and circumstances and modified itself with them in detail as
regards men and things. Now events have rarely been more
complex and mutable, or statesmen more unstable, than at the
beginning of the 17th century, which was but a truce between
the struggles of the 16th and the Thirty Years' War. In order
to understand the continental policy of Henry IV it must be
followed year by year and almost month by month in connexion
with the manœuvres of parties in Holland, a change of reign
in England, the conflicts of the Italian princes, the ambitions
of the German princes, the schemes of the Habsburgs, the
quarrels of religious factions all over Europe, and even the an-
tagonisms of the French ministers, Villeroy always for peace,
Sully thrifty but desirous of war. It did not decide the victory
of the Bourbons over the Habsburgs, which was delayed another
fifty years. But it prepared the way for it by partial operations
which left enduring results. Among these were the acquisition
of Bresse and Bugey, ceded after an armed encounter by the
Duke of Savoy in exchange for the Marquisate of Saluzzo, the
independence of the United Provinces assured on the other
hand without war by the support and the negotiations of
France, whose envoy Jeannin obtained the signature of the
truce of 1609, with the possibility of territorial acquisitions in
the Catholic Netherlands (which were thus threatened both
from the north and the south), and finally the union of Henry's
own patrimony of Béarn and Navarre to the royal domain.

From 1607 to 1609 the conflicts of the German Catholics and
Protestants, which ten years later were to let loose the horrors
of the Thirty Years' War, imparted a more active character to
Henry IV's policy. In 1607 the Elector of Bavaria, egged on
by the Habsburgs, had fallen upon the Protestant city of
Donauwörth. The Lutherans and Calvinists of the Empire,
both princes and cities, thereupon formed the Evangelic
Union, which in 1609—on the advice of France—opposed the
schemes concerted between Spain and the Emperor in regard
to the succession of Cleves and Jülich. If once the fat lands

of the Lower Rhine fell into the hands of the Habsburgs
and their friends, Holland would be threatened, France kept at
a distance from the Rhine, the Spanish Netherlands fortified
and extended. It is intelligible that Henry IV encouraged by
Sully should have protested and armed himself, that by the
marriage of his daughter with a son of Charles Emmanuel he
should have assured himself of the support of Savoy, that he
should have solicited the help of the United Provinces and
promised to assist the Protestant Princes of Brandenburg and
Neuburg. Nevertheless the decisive enterprise on which the
King at first seemed resolved still hung in the balance in 1609
and perhaps—according to certain historians—would have been
arrested had not Henry rushed into war under the influence of
his infatuation for Charlotte de Montmorency, a mere girl. He
had married her to the Prince of Condé, who refused to play
the part of *mari complaisant* and fled to the Low Countries to
place her under Spanish protection and thence passed on to Milan
for greater security. Henry, according to this view, would have
armed France not to say all Europe to get the Princess of Condé
restored to him and the Prince punished—the Trojan War over
again with a difference, for in this case the part of ravisher was
played by the husband, and Henry IV at 55 hardly filled that of
the comely Paris. " All the benefits of the reign would have been
compromised by a moment of blind passion "—thus M. Mariéjol,
Henry's latest historian, thinks himself justified in writing—if
the King had not fallen on May 14, 1610, under the dagger of
the fanatic Ravaillac.

When, however, the acts of Condé immediately after the
event are considered—how on his return to France he plotted
to raise the provinces of the kingdom against the Queen Regent
and to hand over fortresses in Picardy and Normandy to the
Spaniards—is it so difficult to explain and justify the energetic
measures decided upon by Henry with his whole council against
Spain and the first prince of the blood who had become her
accomplice? The intrigues and plots of Spanish diplomacy in
Germany, in Italy, even in France, indicated to Henry the
dangers of the policy of the Habsburgs, who—especially at
Madrid and in spite of Philip II's failure—would not renounce
their schemes of domination, which would have been disastrous

for the future of France, for her internal peace and the security
of her frontiers. After a long period of patience and the time
requisite for necessary recovery, the hour appeared to have
struck for securing the permanent interests of the kingdom by
a fresh effort, the means for which had been prepared. Whatever
the extent of this effort might have been, it would assuredly
not have been the chimerical project which Sully ascribed to
his master and of which history has finally disposed. Henry IV
erected the French monarchy in the teeth of Spain. He would
not have imposed on it the task of a complete reshaping of
Europe. He would have been content that Europe should
escape from the grip of Philip II's successor, and should recognise that she owed her escape, as she did thirty years later, to
the ability and energy crowned by success of the most puissant
King of France.

Louis XIII and Richelieu

It was in 1614 that Louis XIII, Henry IV's successor, who was
barely nine years old at his father's death, was declared of age.
A boy of thirteen cannot govern a kingdom, and the legal majority
of the kings of France had been fixed at that age merely to
shorten the period of minorities, during which, "the royal
authority being suspended, the State relapsed into a kind of
anarchical republic." It was in reality only in 1624, ten years
later, that Louis XIII at the age of twenty-three began to reign
on the day when he placed at the head of his council Cardinal
Richelieu, the one man capable of assisting and guiding his
inexperience among intrigues and factions at home and the
complications of European politics.

This two-headed reign has greatly puzzled posterity and
historians, the reign of a minister of genius, all powerful and
jealous to excess of his authority, like Richelieu, and of a king
by no means lacking in military valour and moral qualities,
who "buried himself in modesty" to allow his minister to
govern, for it was the latter who was King of France during the
nineteen years which were decisive for the strength and greatness of the kingdom. It would seem that Louis XIV had already
faced the problem for his own guidance, when he wrote at the
outset of his reign that "nothing is more disgraceful than to see

the functions and the mere title of a king in different hands."
Saint-Simon, who conceived his *Parallel of the Three Bourbon
Kings* to throw into relief the merits of Louis XIII, "overshadowed by the glory of Richelieu," must certainly have discussed with his contemporaries a problem which has generally
been solved in favour of the Cardinal. M. Mariéjol, the latest
historian of this period, still calls Louis XIII "the illustrious
slave of the minister who had made him the greatest king in
the world." Yet there would appear to be some merit and a
certain grandeur in such a voluntary slavery.

The truth probably is that the bad influence both physical
and moral of Marie de' Medici on her son, who was brought
up in habits of laziness and in complete ignorance, and the
support extended for twelve years by the Queen-mother to
Richelieu, who was thus called upon to sustain the authority
and the greatness of the reign, determined both its failures and
its triumphs. Richelieu identified with his master may thus be
considered as the true successor of Henry IV in the development of the French monarchy.

No more striking contrast can be found than that between the
two men, between the Bourbon prince, the jovial Gascon with his
robust health, the proven hero of battles, camps, and pleasures,
the Protestant converted by reasons of policy, and the Churchman, the grandson of an advocate of no family who had married
his daughter to a scion of the lower nobility of Poitou, the consummate theologian, who for seven years had been absorbed
in the duties of his diocese of Luçon, the sickly student with
his sunken and pallid features. They had however one thing
in common which brings them together, that ambition which
turned a Huguenot party leader into the most Christian King,
and which after eighteen years of waiting gave Armand de
Richelieu, occupant of the least of the sees of France, the
highest offices in the Church and the State. The one succeeded
by his heroism in battle, the other by his skill in intrigue. But
Henry IV was an astute negotiator as well as a fighter and did
not fear to take part in theological debates; and Richelieu remembered, when it was needful, that he was a noble destined in
the first instance for the army. He donned the cuirass over the
priestly robe, and was to be seen at the head of the royal armies

at La Rochelle and the Pass of Susa in wars for the good of the kingdom. King and prime minister were equally ambitious; both thirsted for honours, offices, display, and power, both got all they could out of their success, but both paid France in the coin of vigorous effort exerted in her service.

To serve France their programme of government was in its main lines the same; to establish the King's absolute sovereignty, the theory of which was formulated by the juris-consult Lebret in 1632, and under it by persuasion, or if need be by force, to group all Frenchmen of every class, every party, every religion, so that the kingdom might derive from disci-pline and hard work the resources necessary to its security and to its position in Europe, in view of the aims and the plots of the House of Austria.

During the short time Richelieu was minister, November 1616 to May 3, 1617 (accepting, in order to gain the favour of Marie de' Medici, a secondary position, unworthy of him, as colleague of her favourite, Concini, Maréchal d'Ancre), he showed what were his views of internal and foreign politics. His career as a churchman, his talents, which had already brought him in the States-general of 1614 to the front rank of a clergy who tended rather toward ultramontanism, his friendship with Father Joseph, provincial of the Capuchins, and Father Bérulle, founder of the Oratorians, and his promotion to the Cardinalate in 1622, in no way foreshadowed the statesman whose political doctrines were to follow along the same lines as those of Henry IV, who, al-though he began as a militant Protestant, ended by becoming completely reconciled with the Holy See and its Catholic subjects.

It was no easy matter for the Cardinal in 1624 to achieve this union among Frenchmen, and above all this programme of working for the glory of the monarchy. The nobility of France, from the princes of the blood to the gentleman of low degree driven by ambition or poverty, immediately after the death of Henry IV began again the habitual cabals, plots, and attempts to stir up civil war. The first troubles were in 1612 when Condé and Soissons quarrelled with the Regent. In 1626 Richelieu found these same princes inciting the younger brother of Louis XIII to refuse the marriage proposed by his

mother with Mlle de Montpensier, and plotting civil war
with the Maréchal d'Ornano. It would take a volume to relate
all the intrigues which form the history of these sixteen years,
caused by the youth of the King, who, although married to
Anne of Austria in 1614, was for long without an heir or even
the wish for one. "It is in the Court," said Villeroy in 1611,
"that are engendered the fevers of Civil War, which afterwards
spread to the various parts of the State." From 1624 to 1631
it was the court, in which the women—Mme de Chevreuse, the
friend of Anne of Austria, the Princesse de Condé and the
Queen herself—gained more and more influence every day and
rehearsed the rôles of heroines of the Fronde, it was the court
that started a revolt at every moment and calls to arms—to
which the Cardinal replied with arrests, executions, and even
the exile of Marie de' Medici and Gaston d'Orléans to the Low
Countries.

It was indeed a real social evil that Richelieu succeeded in
repressing, though it was never completely cured. The birth
of the Dauphin in 1638, then of a second son at the end of the
reign, was a better remedy perhaps, the effect of which was
abruptly interfered with by the death of Louis XIII and
another minority.

On the other hand no one can deny to Richelieu the credit
of having put an end to the religious wars, which in 1612 were
about to break out again by the advice of the son-in-law of
Sully, Henri de Rohan, who was declared the leader of the
Protestants and supported by the republicans of La Rochelle.
The Edict of Nantes had granted to the Huguenots political
rights which might be said to be a guarantee of security, including fortresses, garrisons, the right of holding assemblies
which could send delegates to the King, all of which afforded
citizen and nobleman ready means of passing to armed conflict
should the Protestants think, or say, they were in peril. Neither
was this edict satisfactory to the Catholics, who in the Assembly
of Clergy of 1617 agreed with de Luynes in voting for the ruin
of the Huguenots, of their faith and of their places of worship.
War was started again in 1620 by the executions of Béarn,
which caused the Protestants of the south under the direction
of Rohan to revolt, each province arming as States within the

State. The Duc de Luynes had to admit defeat at Montauban, as had Louis XIII in 1621 at Montpellier, to the great chagrin of the Catholics, who had burnt a Huguenot temple at Charenton and who now placed all their hopes of revenge in the Cardinal. For the moment, Richelieu, who had only just come into power, would probably have preferred to keep to the Edict of Montpellier, which confirmed the Edict of Nantes, had it not been for the fact that the Protestant leaders (Soubise on the Atlantic coast and Rohan in Languedoc) incited the Protestants of the towns and countryside, sometimes against their will, to open revolt and to culpable alliances with foreign powers. When Richelieu had, by dint of obstinate energy, defeated them at La Rochelle and Montauban, he amended the Edict of Nantes by the Edict of Alais (1629), depriving the Huguenots of all rights which permitted them to make war, but leaving those which guaranteed freedom of worship and of conscience. Henceforth their security, like that of all other subjects, depended only on the King's benevolence. But the King in future would make no distinction between Catholics and Protestants, wishing for the temporal welfare of both alike. For Richelieu's plan of action in foreign politics, the essential lines of which he laid before his master on January 15, 1629, all the Frenchmen of France would not be more than enough.

To sum up this programme in one word, it was "a continuous plan to stop the career of progress of Spain," not of the House of Austria, as has been said in error, due to the vague language of the time which often applied this wide term to the Habsburgs of Madrid, the Kings of Spain. Indifferent to all losses, which in the end ruined the Spanish monarchy, the Count of Olivarez, minister of Philip IV, suggested to his master, who was blinded by the glamour of power, a policy of action and of influence, the success of which was helped by the Thirty Years' War. When the truce ended in 1621 Spain summoned the United Provinces, which for twelve years had been independent, to return once more beneath the yoke of their Catholic masters. These merchants who did not want war were forced to enrol themselves under the standard of the Stadtholders Maurice and Frederick Henry for a struggle which lasted more than twenty years, and which until the year 1629 seemed to favour the Spanish

armies commanded by Spinola. This general received in 1620
the order to occupy the Palatinate, which, captured from the
Protestants, handed over to the chief of the Catholic League,
Maximilian of Bavaria, and united to the Austrian possessions
of Bresgau and Alsace, became a perpetual menace on the
French flank.

In Italy the Spaniards were dominant everywhere; they were
masters of the Milanese and of Naples; thanks to the dependence
of Genoa and the lords of Tuscany they held the whole coast
from Liguria to Sicily; they were practically suzerains of the
Dukes of Tuscany, Parma, and Modena, and they caused the
Pope at Rome to tremble. Only three states resisted them:
Venice, where the Spanish envoy Bedmar organised a plot in
1618 to overthrow the Republic; Savoy, which defended itself
under still greater difficulties; and the Duchy of Mantua-Mont-
ferrat, to which the succession, open since 1612, was settled in
1617 by the treaty of Pavia, in spite of Spain's effort to gain
possession of it also. On the death of Vincent II (December 26,
1627), the succession was once more in dispute, and this time
Spain turned out the French claimant, Charles de Nevers, made
the Duke of Savoy adjudge to her the best part of the inheritance and tried to take possession of Mantua and Casale in
Montferrat (1628). If Philip IV continued this policy of expansion in Northern Italy, it was with a view to securing the roads
over the Alps and a way of access to Central Europe. It was
because of this design that the affair of the Valtelline (the
Catholic valleys of which were from 1621 to 1630 contested for
by Spain and the Pope against the Protestant Grisons) became
of international importance, as this country was of the utmost
importance to Spain in order to join up their Italian to their
German possessions.

Upon the chessboard of Europe, where the King of Spain
held such advantageous positions and had at his disposal infinite
resources, Richelieu aimed at keeping him in check, without
hoping to checkmate him. But his game was evident from the
first: the occupation of the Valtelline by French troops; alliances
with Venice and Savoy (January 1625); the expeditions of
Louis XIII to relieve Mantua, which was attacked by Gon-
salvo de Cordoba, and against the Duke of Savoy, who had

been forced into an alliance with Spain (March 1629); and another attack on Savoy in March 1630, which gave Pinerolo and Saluzzo to France and compelled Charles Emmanuel to humble himself before the victorious Louis XIII: these limited campaigns of the Cardinal left the ground clear in Italy for the future. When the Dutch appealed to France for protection against the oppression of the Spaniards, the Cardinal did not hesitate to furnish these Huguenots (by the Treaty of Compiègne) with pecuniary aid of more than a million francs. He negotiated with the Protestant leaders of Germany, Mansfeld and Christian IV (Sept. 1624), and supplied them with the men and money to reconquer from Spain the Palatinate, whose sovereign, the son-in-law of James I, then a refugee in London, was later to be the brother-in-law of Louis XIII through the marriage of Henrietta Maria to Charles I. And finally when Richelieu entered into relations with Gustavus Adolphus and caused him to invade Germany, his sole aim was to free the princes of Italy from the grip of the Habsburgs by means of the Swedish menace.

M. Fagniez, the historian of Father Joseph and the Cardinal, was entirely right when he wrote, "It is false to say that Richelieu had the intention of doing all the things that he did. He only had a rudimentary plan, which might according to circumstances either be rendered fertile or overthrown." Opposition to the progress of Spain depended firstly on the Spanish aims and secondly on the resources which France could at any given moment combine against her. This is evident from the Peace of Monçon (1626), when the Cardinal consented to make peace with Spain in order to disarm the Catholic party at the French court (March 1626), whilst in order to avoid friction with England and Holland he made terms with the French Protestants in the Peace of La Rochelle (February 1626). In 1628 the revolt of Rohan and the Protestants in the Cevennes after the taking of La Rochelle compelled Louis XIII to leave Italy in order to subdue them (April 1629). Again in 1630 the Cardinal was compelled to return from Italy, following the King, who was ill, in order to counter the intrigues of the two Queens at court, who were jealous of the Cardinal's authority and did their utmost to get Louis XIII to dismiss him. Until the year

1630 external or internal circumstances were almost always the decisive factor in the Cardinal's policy, who was governed by them just as much and even more than by his plans during the course of these critical years.

His work, like Sully's, was that of concentrating in the hands of the King (with the help of loyal and active collaborators— Champigny in finance, Claude and Léon de Bouthillier, Abel Servien and Sublet de Noyers) sufficient power to make him respected by Spain, to give cause for reflection to his enemies and confidence to his allies. The merit of the Cardinal was that he saw at once that the power of Spain was based on the maritime and colonial advantages of her immense empire, although somewhat lessened already by Dutch enterprise. "The sea," said he to the King in 1629, "gives access to all the king-doms of the world." In 1627 he had already taught France that she possessed everything necessary "for becoming strong at sea; wood and iron for the building of ships, the best ports in Europe, the keys to all navigable routes, an abundant popu-lation of sailors and seamen." With his uncle Commandant Amador de la Porte, the squadron-commander Isaac de Launay Razilly, and the bishops of Valençay and Sourdis, Richelieu (who in 1626 became *Surintendant* of Navigation and Com-merce) created almost entirely the French navy, which counted already in 1635 more than forty ships of the line, arsenals, sea-men recruited from the coastal regions, and cadres of general officers. He made great efforts to constitute an army worthy of the King and spent as much as sixty million *livres* a year, which would have been more profitably employed had Richelieu changed the system of recruiting which was left in the hands of officers, nobles who enriched themselves after the manner of the tax farmer at the expense of the King, who was badly served, and of the soldiers, who were badly paid, badly clothed, and badly fed, and who deserted *en masse*. In order to maintain the strength of the army it became necessary to have recourse to foreign soldiers, Swiss and German mercenaries, the Reiters and Landsknechts of the Thirty Years' War. The day came when the Cardinal hired an entire army all at once, the army of Bernard de Saxe-Weimar, in the same way as he turned to commanders trained in the school of Gustavus Adolphus or of the Stadtholders, before the day of Turenne and Condé. To him at least is due the credit for appointing civil administrators in control of the expenditure of the armies in order to get better results; these were the *intendants d'armée* who were (in conjunction with Sublet de Noyers and later le Tellier) the creators of the royal army in France, which was transformed in the middle of the 17th century. As the power of Spain decreased, the forces of France, organised by the care of the Cardinal, continued to increase in power until towards the end of the reign they were predominant at sea in the Mediterranean, and on land in Flanders and Alsace.

The plan which he had formed, differing greatly from that of Louis XIV, was not to arm the French monarchy for a campaign of conquest such as has been attributed to him, for example, the establishment at all costs of the natural frontiers of France. What he aimed at, and at the least possible cost, avoiding a long war whenever it was possible, was the security of the country, which could never be attained while Spain commanded in Europe. A cardinal of the Church of Rome, a very fervent Catholic, and, like Father Joseph, very desirous of reconciling all Christians in a crusade against the Infidel, he wished to avoid meriting the reproaches of the Holy See, of Urban VIII, who tried to persuade him not to make war, of the German Catholics, and of Italy, of having for the sake of ambition set fire to Europe. Hence his negotiations with the Emperor at Ratisbon in 1630 and with the chief of the Catholic League, Maximilian of Bavaria (with whom he made an alliance at Fontainebleau), and the armistice and Treaty of Cherasco granted in 1631 at the instance of the Pope. But at the same time he gained possession of Pinerolo by a treaty negotiated by Mazarin with Savoy, raised the siege of Casale, which remained in the hands of the Duke of Mantua, nor did he at first regret that the victories of Gustavus Adolphus and Frederick Henry made the Spaniards and Imperialists withdraw from the Rhine, from Alsace and Lorraine. He already had his eyes on Strasburg, the use of which in the hands of the King would be on the Rhine what Pinerolo was in Italy, what he called "doors opening into the states of our neighbours to enable us to protect them from Spanish oppression." His intention was evidently to fortify the frontiers of France with a barrier of States guaranteed against the Habsburgs and at length to establish the authority of France in a liberated Europe.

The victories of Gustavus Adolphus made the Cardinal's policy at the end of 1631 begin to veer in another direction. He brought Louis XIII into Lorraine at the head of 50,000 men, took Moyen Vic, and, the 6th of January 1632, considered with his master the advisability of declaring war on the Emperor. Two reasons decided him, the opportunity now offered to France during the distress of the Emperor and the German Catholics, of pushing on through Alsace to the Rhine, and the pretext furnished by the ambition and the power of Gustavus Adolphus of preventing triumphant Protestantism from spreading through the states along the Rhine. The influence of the Pope and of Father Joseph in 1632 caused the postponement of these plans of conquest and war against the Emperor. Gustavus Adolphus fell on the battlefield of Lützen, but his death was the price paid for a decisive Swedish victory, which decided France early in 1632 to make the supreme effort against the entire House of Austria. The plan which he submitted to the King at that date showed all the greatness of the Cardinal's ambition: the left bank of the Rhine with Alsace and a few strongholds on the right bank would give him a base of operations in time of war, and could be held as a pledge for any benefits France claimed when it came to making peace. In Flanders he negotiated with Holland for the occupation of Hainault, Artois, Tournai, Lille, and Douai, parts of Luxemburg and of the province of Namur, and the coast as far as Ostend. In Italy he definitely wished to be dominant at Mantua and Casale and in Montferrat, to unite to Pinerolo the neighbouring valleys and to turn this key to the Alps into a formidable fortress and arsenal, from which to keep an eye on the Duke of Savoy and Spain in the Po valley.

This programme was put into execution from 1635 to the death of Richelieu; he and Father Joseph (who was designated to be his successor) worked out in 1636 the diplomatic plan of action in Holland, Germany, and Sweden. This was the point of departure of a war of which neither the Cardinal nor his master saw the end. All the time that he was continuing this struggle (which was still very unequal and which began with the invasion of France by the Spaniards in 1636, when even the capital was threatened, and ended in the conquest of Alsace and Lorraine and Roussillon and the victory of Rocroi (1643)) Richelieu never ceased to negotiate, and was always ready to relinquish a part of his designs, even Lorraine, in order to lighten the burdens of his country. He bequeathed to his successors, who went too far, the policy of annexation to which Richelieu was led by the growing weakness of the House of Austria, but at the same time he gave as much care to the organisation of the kingdom as to its expansion.

His government gave to the crown he served absolute authority which was carried to the most extreme rigour, and the elements of a powerful administration on which it was able to count for the next century and a half. The nobles, incapable and unruly, were gradually exiled from the King's Councils and the important offices. They were also in some cases deprived of the governorships of provinces and towns, and in other cases were only able to retain them after having renounced the independence which such posts had hitherto carried with them. With the active and loyal collaborators whom he had chosen for himself, preferably from amongst the middle classes, and the intendants (chosen from amongst the *maîtres des requêtes*) whom he sent on missions to the provinces, he succeeded in establishing an administrative control over the army, navy, and finances which enabled France to support thirteen years of continuous warfare in spite of insufficient financial resources, which always showed a deficit. Never shackled by prejudice or formula, Richelieu always welcomed any initiative tending to increase the output of national energy or the domain of France. He aided Laffemas and Razilly in the organisation of commerce on a grand scale in the Mediterranean, Morocco, and the Antilles, granting the decree of 1629. A supporter of the Trading Companies, he made agreements with Champlain and his associates for the colonisation of Canada, with d'Esnambuc for that of St Christopher, La Martinique, and Guadeloupe, with Pronis and Flacourt for that of Madagascar. No one deplored more than Richelieu the indifference of the French *bourgeoisie* to commercial careers and the harm done to the nation by their preference for the classical education of the colleges and for public office. This great realist, although passionately interested in literature, the protector and head of the French Academy (founded in 1635) and the Maecenas, though at times a tyrannical and jealous one, of Corneille and Rotrou, understood as clearly as Sully did, or Colbert later on, the prime necessity of increasing the national money power, its wealth and capacity for work. Nothing throws more light on his work as a whole than the *Mémoires* drawn up at his dictation in 1628 by François Miron, Provost of the Merchants of Paris, exactly at the same time that he expounded to the Council his designs for foreign policy. By developing in the way we have shown, by absorbing his attention and the resources of the Crown, these designs militated against the projects he had formed for the national prosperity. But in spite of this, and to the honour of Richelieu, the reign of Louis XIII left France in possession of a portion of the advantages after which he had striven, and handed on to Louis XIV an army, a navy, and a system of administration, generals, intendants, and statesmen capable of taking from Spain and the Empire what remained to be acquired. And this very rule which had at heart the improvement and fertilising of the whole country, at the same time restored authority everywhere, pacified, regulated and policed French society, raising a rich harvest of great works and great men which redounded entirely to the credit of the second half of the century. Nothing was lost of what Henry IV had saved; everything was prepared for the power and greatness of Louis XIV and of France under his reign.

The Reign of Louis XIV

The greater portion of the 17th century in France coincides with the reign of Louis XIV, one of the longest reigns France has ever known, since the King ascended the throne in 1643 at the age of 5, and died in 1715—a reign of 72 years. "A reign," says Saint-Simon, "so long, so fertile and for so long glorious." As a whole it was the greatest period of the French monarchy, the one in which all the men of France, united in faith, gave themselves body and soul to a Bourbon King, invested by an inherited divine right with absolute power over the nobility, the supreme courts, and the people, happy to be governed and proud of the position held at that time in Europe by the nation associated with the greatness and power of a king who was envied and imitated by all other sovereigns.

And in this long stretch of 72 years what were the five years of the Fronde by comparison with the long civil wars of religion in the 16th century, or the fourteen doubtful and, though in a lesser degree, troubled years of Louis XIII's minority? The Fronde was a game played by children and women. It did great harm to France, which was desolated by disorder in the capital and in the provinces, by the pillaging and fighting of the soldiers, by famine and sickness. But it did no harm to the King in the hearts of his subjects. Although the King was a minor and incapable of maintaining his authority, it is noteworthy that from 1643 to 1648 his mother, Anne of Austria, the Regent, enjoyed "absolutely and entirely the free administration of the affairs of the kingdom," and, after having easily overthrown the *Cabale des Importants*, was for five years able to keep the administration in the hands of Cardinal Mazarin, designated by Richelieu and employed by Louis XIII as first minister. During these troubles of the Fronde the Regent on more than one occasion had only to show her royal offspring to his subjects in order to bring the men of France back to their duty. In 1651, as soon as he was declared of age, the revolts began to die down and the *bourgeois* of Paris already in 1652 displayed for the young King "a violent inclination beyond what the French ordinarily feel for their Prince," to use the words of one of these *bourgeois*, Guy Patin.

What we must from the outset notice in the long reign of Louis XIV is the way France was governed from 1643 to 1661, when its ruler was Mazarin, at first in conjunction with the Regent Anne of Austria, and then with Louis XIV after he had attained his majority—a government analogous to the two-headed rule of Louis XIII and Richelieu. "The Queen Anne of Austria," says Voltaire, "a regent with absolute power, made Mazarin the master of France and of herself." The binding force of this collaboration was the twofold weakness of this Spanish Princess who did not love work, and who did love Mazarin, to the extent of being perhaps secretly married

to him and at any rate of entrusting her son to him as to a step-
father. Between these three there was certainly affection and
confidence, upon which Mazarin founded his power and his
fortune, which were practically without limits.

With regard to his fortune we may mention that a number of
Italians after the end of the 16th century came into France and
had successful careers in financial affairs, in Church and State:
the Bonzis, who came from Florence and were installed as
bishops of Béziers, of whom the last was to all intent and purpose King of Languedoc and hoped to be Mazarin's successor;
the Gondis, lords of Retz, who made of the Archbishopric of
Paris a sort of family property, descending from the uncle to
the nephew, the famous opponent of Mazarin; the Orsinis from
Rome, who became related by marriage to the Montmorencys
and to the father of Mazarin; the Grimaldis of Genoa who
became Dukes of Valentinois; the Gonzagas of Mantua who
settled in the Duchy of Nevers; the financier Particelli of Milan,
who soon entered the administration of the finances, and became
the collaborator of Richelieu, the protector of Mazarin in Piedmont, *surintendant*, father-in-law of the Secretary of State La
Vrillière; and a great many others.

In the time of Louis XIII no one was surprised when Giulio
Mazarini, of a good Roman family, protected by the Colonnas,
provided by the Jesuits with a solid education and by Pope
Urban VIII with benefices, and nuncio in Paris, became in
1640 French envoy in Savoy and took the place of Father
Joseph at the side of Richelieu who bequeathed him to Louis XIII.
The favour of Anne of Austria then made him rich and, what
is more, very powerful, just as Richelieu had been. At his death
he was the greatest landowner in France; his wealth, valued at
a revenue of four million francs, was derived from his numerous
benefices, amongst which were the Abbey of Saint-Denis and
the Bishopric of Metz, and the Duchies of Nevers and Rethelois.
His estates were managed by Colbert, who was preparing himself
for the management of those of France and the King. His
palaces, his collections of books, paintings, and works of art,
have remained a part of the wealth of the nation. The highest
aristocracy, even the princes of royal blood, sought his alliance
by marriage with his nieces.

He governed entirely by diplomacy, in external as well as internal affairs. It was at once his strength and his weakness, as La Rochefoucauld has pointed out: "His views were narrow even in his greatest projects." No methods could be more different from Richelieu's than those he used to defend the royal authority, which he finally triumphantly established in 1660; no executions, no scaffolds, but prisons which were easily opened; no exiles, but on the contrary a consummate art in exiling himself from the court or the kingdom, in order to return as a conqueror; no haughtiness, no arrogance, but a methodical system of spying, to which his intimate personal note-books bear witness, in order to keep watch over his adversaries, their words, their intrigues; the subtlest dissimilation to throw them off the scent in his own intrigues; corruption to cause division amongst them, opposition of Princes to the Parliament, of the Princes amongst each other, Condé against Gaston d'Orléans. "Never was it more clearly seen," said Voltaire, "that politics consist of lies." This was the art of reigning which Mazarin, after practising it, taught to Louis XIV—"the royal talent for dissimulation," as the Abbé Choisy said. To keep the secret of his own plans and to learn the secret of others became the maxim of the King of France, and one recommended by Louis XIV in his instructions to his grandson the King of Spain as an essential rule of absolute government.

It was Mazarin's mistake that he neglected all other parts of ruling, which he abandoned to the ministers handed on to him by the government of Louis XIII, and who were at first put aside by the intrigues of Madame de Chevreuse and Beaufort: le Tellier, Secretary of State for War, Chavigny, Minister of State, and Loménie de Brienne, whose son, trained in the same school, married the daughter of Chavigny, Marshal de la Meilleraye, du Plessis-Guénégaud, Secretary of State, whose brother was Treasurer of the Épargne, Phélypeaux de La Vrillière, and three others, Abel Servien, Surintendant des Finances, his nephew Hugues de la Lionne, and d'Avaux, whose names were henceforth associated with all the glory of the reign. To these ministerial families, who from the time of Louis XIII to that of Louis XIV handed on to each other the administrative offices, Mazarin added only two: the Colbert family, who after Mazarin

were in charge of finance and diplomacy, and the Fouquet family
—Nicolas, *Surintendant des Finances*, for the help he gave him
against that unruly body the *Parlement*, the Abbé Fouquet who
was to Mazarin what Father Joseph had been to Richelieu, and
the Bishop of Agde, the Royal Almoner. These functionaries of
the monarchic state were fond of authority and conscious of their
position: le Tellier organised the military administration and
hierarchy and the intendancy of the army; the Secretaries of
State and the *intendants* "on mission" organised the administration of the provinces, thus continuing the work of Richelieu
and preparing for that of Colbert. But from lack of supervision,
they turned their offices into means of enriching themselves
and of establishing their children. Allied to each other by
marriages, ambitious for wealth and honours, they acquired
castles and land, and often confused the money of the State with
their own, since the Cardinal who employed them not only
tolerated this but set the example. Nicolas Fouquet was the
arch-type of these administrators who enriched themselves,
adopting a detestable system of State finance, reducing the
kingdom especially in time of war to living by loans and expedients, crushing the taxpayers with levies, of which the major
portion went to the profit of the financiers and the ministers,
their accomplices.

The Fronde was to begin with a revolt against the *surintendant* Particelli and his demands for money, and developed
into a revolution, as so easily happens if the State be in distress
financially, when the *Parlements* joined the movement. The
High Courts of Justice had been granted by the King the right
of registering the royal acts, decrees, treaties of peace, edicts
in religious matters, and of supervising education, the religious
Orders, and the police of Paris; and it is not surprising that they
should have attempted to discuss them, considering themselves
as helpers, rather than under the orders, of the monarch, as
the guardians of national tradition, the superiors of the Estates
General and the equals of ministers. The rank of nobility which
the members of the *Parlement* held by virtue of their office, and
the heredity of this office, which had become the rule since the
time of Henry IV, gave them, down to the end of the monarchy,
a haughty independence which prompted them to criticise the

government. The same themes upon which they dwelt in attacking Mazarin continued to serve them as texts later: the abuse of absolute power, the impoverished state of the taxpayer, the duty and right of the *Parlements* to resist the ministers for the sake of justice and the welfare of the people. The weakness of these arguments lay in the fact that in 1638, in 1648, and again later, these judicial bodies brought them forward against the fiscal edicts which tended to diminish their revenues by the creation of new offices or taxes on their possessions; that they interfered with the course of justice at the expense of the justiciables; and that by stirring up the feelings of the people, abetting the intrigues of the princes and their wives and mistresses and the invasion of the country by foreign troops, they aggravated the very ills for which they demanded remedies. Their right of control over the national finances, recognised as legitimate by Louis XIII in 1641 by a solemn declaration, which the negligence of Mazarin had rendered necessary, might have proved a precious safeguard for the crown. The civil war which they provoked served only to suppress this right of control throughout the entire course of the reign and to justify the abuses of the ministers and of the royal policy by the needs of public tranquillity. The diplomacy of Mazarin, who returned from exile as a saviour, cleverly turned the situation to account by forbidding the *Parlement* in the edict of 1652 to meddle in the affairs of the great nobles and princes or to take cognisance of the financial administration. He would have done better to take cognisance thereof himself; not even the Fronde could cure him of his negligence.

On the other hand his cleverness, his perseverance, and his flexibility were devoted to the interests of France in Europe, benefiting them in a durable and glorious manner. Under his direction French diplomacy won its most splendid successes (the Treaties of Westphalia and the Pyrenees, the League of the Rhine, and peace) and boasted its best servants (Lionne, Servien, d'Avaux, Chanut, the Duc de Grammont, Colbert de Croissy, Gravel). The genius of this Italian, cut out for a negotiator, contributed, just as much as the victories of Condé and Turenne to the superiority of France in the struggle begun in 1635 against the Habsburgs of Vienna and Madrid. His

policy, although thwarted by the defection of the Dutch who
treated with Spain (and without France) in 1648, by the disturbances of the Fronde which encouraged the resistance of
Philip IV, by the ambition of Charles Gustavus in the north,
and finally by the treason of Condé, the victor of Rocroi, who
became the last prop of Spain, retained for France the profits
of Richelieu's efforts: Alsace, Roussillon, Artois, Lorraine, the
fortresses of Flanders, Hainault, and Luxemburg. Mazarin was
able to replace Holland with England and to prepare the way
for the League of the Rhine by the Treaties of Westphalia,
giving France the position of mediator between the German
princes and procuring the same rôle for the King in the disputes
of the northern rulers.

If during this first part of the reign which is dominated by
him the policy of Mazarin can be criticised, it is chiefly because
it showed to an even more marked degree than that of Richelieu,
who allowed himself to be led into it, a tendency towards
conquest. The marriage of Louis XIV to Maria Theresa, arranged
at the Peace of the Pyrenees, was an earnest of further benefits
to accrue to France in the future, in view of the weakness of
Spain. It was not only benefits that France derived from this
succession; Mazarin left to the Bourbon not only a hope and
a temptation, but also a risk that France as the heir of Spain
might alarm all Europe. Already in 1647 Holland had fallen
away from its alliance with France, being afraid of her progress
in the Low Countries England had safeguarded herself by taking
Dunkirk. The Dukes of Lorraine and Savoy were plotting in
the Vosges and the Alps. In Germany they began to talk of
King Christian as a candidate for the empire which might have
disturbed the princes. In 1661 these were merely symptoms still,
but they would have been detected by a far-sighted and clear
policy. But it was to a young king only twenty-three years
old, handsome, energetic, impatient for action and glory, to
whom the dying Cardinal bequeathed these hopes and these
risks.

From the mere fact that Louis XIV wished to be his own
prime minister the conclusion has been drawn that in the
middle of the century a new reign began. As a matter of fact

there was at first merely a change of ministers in the same reign. Nothing is more artificial than the divisions, dictated by the superficial convenience of history, in the continuous life of society and government. Between the 9th of March, when Mazarin died, and the following day, when Louis XIV announced to the President of the Assembly of Clergy his intention of ruling, instead of merely being King, men and things did not change by a sudden transformation, which the King did not effect by declaring himself sole minister.

The members of the government on whom Louis XIV counted on this 10th of March—Lionne, le Tellier, Fouquet and Colbert—were not new men either, but all of them the habitual and most intimate collaborators of Mazarin. A restricted and secret group constituted during the whole reign what was called the *Conseil du ministère ou d'en haut*, the sole motive power of the King's action in internal affairs and more especially in foreign matters. This presidency Louis XIV reserved for himself with the exclusive right of carrying out all decisions. Spanheim has taken care to correct the mistaken notions of this personal government of Louis XIV, saying "When the government changed at the death of Cardinal Mazarin, and the King wished to govern *in his own person and by his Council.*" Thus with the help of these collaborators who had had experience under the preceding minister the risk of breaking the continuity in the conduct of affairs by this sudden resolution of an inexperienced king who was only twenty-three years old to take the place of Mazarin was lessened from the outset.

The King, moreover, had the qualities of a good minister. He had not the quick spontaneous intelligence, nor the cultivated and ingenious mind of his grandfather Henry IV, whom he hoped to equal and even surpass. He was also, as M. Lavisse has remarked, the great-grandson of Philip II, and from his Spanish mother, whom physically he greatly resembled, he derived a just sense of proportion and a well-balanced intelligence, which was neither brilliant nor vast, a taste for order and a very keen sense of his royal power and his rights. As a pupil of Mazarin, who by the way gave him very little classical education, he acquired (by practising those habits which for fifty years were the support of his government) great control over himself beneath an affected exterior of grace and dignity, profound dissimulation, a methodically organised system of spying, and above all the habit of constant application to business. The self-imposed labour of this king was his greatest virtue; exacting from his fellow-workers the same industry as from himself, he made of this the enduring foundation of the administrative establishment which, surviving his dynasty, has continued down to the France of to-day.

The trial and fall of Fouquet in September 1661, the only one of his ministers who had this fate, was without doubt due not only to his defalcations, but also to his pretensions to greatness, to his luxurious way of living, which gave umbrage to the King, and perhaps to his influence, which made the King anxious. The disgrace of the *Surintendant des Finances* was the last resort to which Louis XIV had recourse in order to concentrate in his own hands all the powers of government. Spanheim, speaking of the *Surintendant*, says: "Absolute and independent power was replaced, as in the case of the first minister, by the secret council, by a *Conseil des Finances*, which met twice a week in the Palace and was presided over by the King or by Villeroy. Louis XIV took pleasure in calling it the *Conseil royal*. This was essentially the Council of Administration of the monarchy."

In this way was completed the form of the royal government, which had been developing since the time of Henry IV, by the will of his grandson, who henceforward was the sole chief of his councils: the *Conseil d'en haut* in which were treated all the great affairs of state, as well for peace as for war; the *Conseil des Dépêches*, to which the four Secretaries of State came to make their reports as to the internal affairs of the kingdom for their respective provinces; and finally the *Conseil des Finances*. Sometimes, on exceptional occasions, the King took the opinion of larger committees, to which he summoned more people: Turenne, Condé, later the Grand Dauphin and his governor.

At the moment when things were arranged in this way, the two persons who apparently held front rank in these Councils were Lionne, Secretary of State for Foreign Affairs and the Navy, and le Tellier, Secretary of State for War for more than five years. Colbert had only just gained entrance to the *Conseil d'en haut*; before this he was a clerk to le Tellier and a mere *intendant des finances*.

While the King, aided by Lionne, directed high politics, all the glory of which he anticipated, le Tellier and Colbert, rivals in zeal and influence, organised the *personnel*, and established the rules and coordination of the various services upon which the monarchy, and later on France, founded the State. In the first place they trained their sons, associating them, roughly enough at times, with their methods. Le Tellier brought up Louvois but left to Louis XIV the flattering illusion that he had formed him; hence his own work was swallowed up for the most part in the achievements attributed by history to his son. Colbert scolded Seignelay and even administered correction with his hand, until his haughty nature, violent and at first inclined to debauchery, was bent to the duties and obligations of his office, the administration of the navy. They both found places for the men of their family, with no other help than their own favour, remaining masters of their work and using them for their own ends. In this way were established in the armies for war, in the provinces for finances and general administration, the intendants of the army and navy, commissaries of war, and intendants-general, who by regular correspondence with the central authorities linked up the army chiefs, the military and financial officers, the soldiers and the people of the towns and of the country. Saint-Simon (who collected and repeated the complaints of his fellows against the installation of these functionaries recruited from the parliamentary *bourgeoisie*) has described their career as almost as definitely regulated as that of the functionaries of the Roman Empire: youthful *maîtres de requêtes* waiting for an intendancy, provincial intendants waiting to be promoted to Paris as councillors of state, intendants of finance or commerce, provosts of Paris or even secretaries of state and controllers-general. By this hierarchy of men of trust of the same class as themselves and perhaps of their own family these two great servants of the King (who remained his own sole prime minister) worked out the central organisation of the army, the navy, and the State. Order, exactness, industry—this was their watchword, and given in such a way that it was understood and that the

zeal and discipline of the agents of the royal authority made
it felt from one end of the kingdom to the other. *Tout le monde
est devenu peuple* Saint-Simon bitterly complains. The whole
people was now really and completely in the hands of the King.
After Louis XIV there might once more be first ministers,
and they would have the whole of France at their disposal to
the same degree as Louis XIV had, and to a greater degree
than the ministers before his time.

It may cause surprise that their work, which in ten years
embraced the entire administrative activity of a great kingdom,
was able to imprint upon the nation such an enduring impression,
all the more so because it had for its object the glory and greatness of the Sovereign, ephemeral things, and for its consequence
things even more ephemeral—the rival family fortunes of the
men who constructed the work. Le Tellier and Louvois supervised the supplies of the army, cantonments, food, equipment,
and pay, stages and details of armament in immediate view of
a near campaign—the wars of Flanders and of Franche-Comté
announced to Europe after the death of Philip IV as the
overwhelming successes of a prince whom no one was in a
position to resist. After 1668 they did the same thing for the
campaign in Holland (the preparation of which was a masterpiece of sudden and concerted attack), when their zeal was
directed and upheld by the same hope of a brilliant triumph for
the great King over the Dutch who dared to oppose him. And
in spite of the opposition of Colbert and the marshals the
fortune of Louvois was at once made by thus serving the King's
greed for conquest and greatness.

Similarly when Colbert filled the royal coffers by confiscating
the wealth of the bankers, by retaking possession of the
mortgaged crown lands, by agreements with the tax farmers,
by the methodical collection of taxes, and rigorous supervision
of the accountants, it was to supply his master with means
(already assured in 1664) "to carry the glory of his name as far
as can be imagined."

Such modifications as were made for the benefit of taxpayers
in towns and country districts (reduction of taxes and duties
which fell only on the poor classes) were in no way inspired by
pity, and even less by a desire to adjust the unequal imposition

of the taxes. The anxiety to make the King rich, in order that he might be glorious and powerful, alone dictated to this hard-hearted financier (whose body had to be protected at his funeral against the anger of the people) measures which allowed, to the King's subjects, an "easier payment of the State charges." As early as 1670 Colbert drew the King's attention to the poverty of his subjects. In 1680 he maintained that the people were utterly ruined, of which fact evidence was given by all the letters he received from the provinces, from the intendants, the receivers-general and even the bishops. He did not succeed in the great purpose, which he formed in 1663, of opening up sources of revenue for the King equal to those which Holland, and Venice in the 16th century, found in trade, and which Spain derived from her colonies. Numerous and celebrated were the efforts of this minister to create in France manufactures of articles of luxury which would bring gold into the kingdom, to attract the world's commerce to the Atlantic and Mediterranean ports, to create Trade Companies equal to those of Amsterdam, and to develop colonies in Canada, the Antilles, and Madagascar. His doctrine (Colbertism, as it has been called) was that the greater the amount of money brought into the country by exchange with foreign countries and by the industry and ingenuity of its skilled workers, and the less sent out of the country for the needs of a nation which did not live in idle luxury, the more solid would be the foundation of the wealth of the country. "It is only the amount of money in a State that can affect its greatness and power," said Colbert; but listen to his conclusion: "You must restrict all the professions of your subjects to those which can serve these great designs, agriculture, trade, war upon land and sea." To make France work and fight in order that her King "might be lord of the earth"—such was the programme of Colbert, in realising which he profited no less than le Tellier in titles, revenues, castles, and land, in the brilliant establishments of his sons and daughters.

These famous *bourgeois*, made rich and illustrious by their services to the King, did indeed but share the general intoxication of the public of their time, who in the reign of the young god, amiable and victorious over all factions within and enemies

without, welcomed an era of prosperity and glory promised to
the whole nation. They performed their royal and national
task according to the law formulated by la Bruyère: "Everything prospers in a kingdom in which the interests of the State
are identified with those of the ruler." What Colbert aimed at
acquiring for the King was in part realised for the benefit of
France, the development of manufactures of luxuries, commerce with foreign countries, canals and ports, the organisation
of roads and transport, the police and whatever was new and
useful in a central administration, down to that monument of
French art, the Palace of Versailles, the Gobelins tapestries,
the treasure of the crown and of the nation, as well as the
masterpieces of Coysevox, Coustou, Rigaud, and Largillière.
The works of these men, like the monarchy of Louis XIV, was
perhaps better than their intention, which reminds one of the
phrase of la Bruyère, "Despotism leaves no room for patriotism;
interest, glory, and the service of the King take its place."
Spanheim, the Prussian envoy, has given the following verdict
on the unbridled passion for glory of Louis XIV: "It is his
great weakness, and fatal to the peace of Europe, whence springs
a great obstinacy in carrying out whatever he proposes, if he
thinks his glory and his honour are engaged, and to this he is
capable of sacrificing his real interests."

Louis XIV has himself admitted this and has pointed out in
his *Mémoire sur la Campagne de 1672*, the date when he allowed
himself to be carried away by ambitious enterprises, the effects
of which were felt during his whole reign after the first coalition
formed against France in 1673, and from the effects of which
France herself has suffered for centuries. "I will not justify
myself before posterity. Ambition and glory are always ex-
cusable in a Prince, and especially in a Prince as young and as
highly favoured by Fortune as I was." The war against Holland
was not merely, as Mignet narrow-mindedly argues, an episode
in the designs of Louis XIV upon the Spanish possessions in the
Low Countries, which were upset by the citizens of Amsterdam.
It was a plan of conquest, explained by the excessive confidence
of Louis XIV in his forces, in the weakness of his neighbours,
the docility of Europe, and the certainty of victory. "I am going
to travel in Holland," he wrote to Vauban, on April 8, 1672.

Similarly Marshal de Créquy went to Lorraine in September 1670, to reduce the Duke's country to utter obedience without listening to any negotiations, because it was "a very fine province to unite to the kingdom." Later it was Louvois who went to Turin to compel the Duke to furnish his master with four or five regiments. And finally, through the diplomacy of Lionne, an agent was procured, Prince William of Fürstenberg, who plotted with the German Princes, of Bavaria, Cologne and Brunswick, to enlist them in the service of France and prepare the election of Louis XIV to the Empire.

Germany then, just as much as Holland, felt the menace of the unbridled ambition of Louis XIV in the summer of 1671. "The action of France in Lorraine was the alarm clock of the Princes," wrote in 1671 the Austrian envoy to the Hague, Baron de l'Isola, in one of his numerous pamphlets (which gave birth to many others). "You will see," said he, "that the King coming from France will very soon annex the Rhine without striking a blow." Leibniz, who was in the service of the Elector of Mainz, wrote at this time his *Reflections on Public Security*, proclaiming the racial antipathy between France and Germany and appealing to German patriotism to oppose a purely German confederation to the ambitions of Louis XIV.

Lionne, more wary than Louvois (who advised his master to ignore the anger of Germany), at a council held at Dunkirk in May 1672, urged his master to postpone his attack upon Holland until the League of the Rhine was reconstituted, by which means Germany, discontented and uncertain, would be at the disposal of his ambition and of his generals. His suggestion was over-ruled; the Great Elector of Brandenburg, urged by the Grand Pensionary de Witt, abandoned the side of France 26th April 1672, in order to come to the aid of Holland which was in danger. In Berlin it was said, "The ruin of Holland would be the ruin of Germany."

These first efforts at resistance on the part of the Empire against the power of the great King gave great support in Holland to the party of national resistance incarnated in Prince William of Orange. The obstinate refusal of Louis XIV to listen to the proposals of peace from the burgher party (which the Prince repudiated) and his demands at the Congress of Cologne, helped the coalition which William of Orange succeeded in forming in August 1673 with Spain and the Empire. One year had barely passed before Turenne was reduced to defending the Rhine frontier against the Germans, while the people of Champagne trembled before the coming invasion, from which they were saved by the victory of Turckheim, celebrated in France and at Versailles in a way proportionate to the terror that had been felt. Louis XIV had preferred to run this risk rather than resist the temptation of conquering from Spain Franche-Comté and the fortresses of Flanders, and of establishing soon afterwards the superiority of his navy under Duquesne, and even of disputing the possession of Sicily.

The genius of Turenne and the intervention of the Swedes in Prussia, whither, at the price of being defeated at Fehrbellin (1675), they drew off the army of the Great Elector, allowed Louis XIV to "risk victoriously his glory and his good fortune." After the Peace of Nimwegen he seemed to be greater than ever, by reason of his superiority to this first coalition, which his excessive ambition had called into being. "He must have been formidable indeed," said Voltaire, "who suffered no greater misfortune than failure to retain all his conquests." Louis XIV was forced to offer peace to the coalition after having defeated it. He was, it is true, able to make his conditions, and to retain Franche-Comté, a large part of Flanders, and Philippsburg. But, after all, the chief success belonged to Holland, which Louis XIV wished to destroy, which very nearly was destroyed, but which had remained alive and intact and had forced her enemy to abandon Colbert's protective tariffs, and to take the place of Spain as the protector of the Catholics in the Netherlands by means of frontier garrisons at Charleroi, Courtrai, Audenarde, Ath, Ghent, and Limburg. To cover up this reverse, which would have cast a shadow upon his obstinate claim to give laws to Europe, the Great King dismissed his minister Pomponne. "Since he succeeded to Lionne," said he, "everything that has passed through him has lost something in the grandeur and strength that should be maintained in executing the orders of a King of France who is not unfortunate." What an admission and, at the same time, what obstinacy there is in such language!

The desire for fresh conquests and the fear of provoking
Europe to new wars, such were the motives which governed
Louis XIV after the Peace of Nimwegen. The policy of clandestine annexation, of *reuniting* to the royal domain by decrees
of the Courts of Justice, e.g. Metz and Breisach, was for a long
time attributed to Louvois. This unfounded opinion is due to
the fact that the diplomatic work of the Minister for Foreign
Affairs has never been studied. This was Colbert de Croissy,
for whom his brother the Controller-General had obtained in
1680 the office in succession to Pomponne, and who kept it
until 1696, handing it on to his son Torcy, who was minister to
Louis XIV up to the time of his death. "He had the misfortune," wrote Spanheim (of Colbert de Croissy), who was the
first to appreciate his penetration, his views, and his experience
of affairs, "to appear in the eyes of the people of the court and
of Paris to be less able and less enlightened than he really was."
Croissy, formerly President of the Supreme Council of Alsace,
then of the *Parlement* of Metz, was thoroughly conversant with
all the legal pretexts, which the condition of these provinces,
since the annexation, could furnish to his master's ambition;
the former collaborator of Lionne at Frankfort in 1657, an
envoy to the courts of Germany from 1659 to 1668, he was by
no means one of those who, at the French court, were inclined
to ignore, as was the case in 1672, the opposition of the rulers
of Brunswick, Hanover, Bavaria, and above all Brandenburg.
Without any further warfare this minister succeeded in obtaining more conquests for Louis XIV—Strasburg, Kehl, the
County of Chiny, Casale, Luxemburg and Chimay, which
Louvois hastened indeed to realise. His success was helped at
times by circumstances, for example, the Turkish threat at
the heart of the Empire in 1683, and the war of the Imperialists
in Hungary. But he was also hindered by other things, for
example, the affair of the *régale*, which dissatisfied the Holy
See, and above all by the Revocation of the Edict of Nantes,
which set on foot a new coalition at Augsburg in 1686 of
the Protestant powers stimulated by William III and the
Emperor.

The whole policy of Croissy is seen in the Peace of Ratisbon
in 1684, imposed upon the Emperor for ten years by the com-

plicity of the German princes, a provisional guarantee of new
conquests in addition to the advantages obtained at Nimwegen
and Münster, which Louis XIV and his minister still hoped, in
1688, to convert into a solid peace with Germany, another peace
which would redound to the greatness and glory of France.

If Spanheim (the servant of Brandenburg henceforward
estranged from France by the Revocation) may be credited,
such a peace was still not impossible at the end of 1688. It was
seriously compromised by the obstinacy of Louis XIV who
insisted on installing in the Electorate of Cologne the Bishop
of Strasburg, William of Fürstenberg, against the wish of the
Emperor and of the Pope, who favoured a Bavarian prince.
This time it was certainly Louvois who urged irreparable
measures, in spite of the advice of Croissy. "We shall pay
dearly for the peace we have enjoyed for five years," said he to
Louis XIV, who thought he could intimidate the Emperor and
the German princes by a haughty manifesto followed by the
devastation of the Palatinate.

Because he ignored Germany in 1672 Louis XIV saw a formidable coalition dispute all the glory and profit he expected
from the ruin of Holland. Eighteen years later (chiefly because
he had despised Germany, of whom he still hoped to get the
better by his power and skill), he saw a still more formidable
coalition raised against him in 1690. William of Orange was on
the point of realising the plan, formed after his marriage with a
Stuart princess and his intrigues with the Protestants of
England, of uniting England to Holland and of finding in this
alliance a more solid foundation than Holland alone could
furnish for a decisive struggle with the conquering ambition of
Louis XIV.

From this time on, indeed, until the year 1714, the history
of the end of the reign of Louis XIV is but one long effort, which
at certain times seemed hopeless, on the part of France, to
escape from the death-embrace of this coalition which was fatal
to the French navy (the first in Europe in 1685), which dismembered Canada, and which attacked victoriously the frontiers of Flanders, of the Rhine, and of the Alps. In order to
avoid this death-grasp Louis XIV negotiated with William III
in 1698 and 1699 a division of the Spanish Succession. He made

at this time some very fine speeches which bore witness to his readiness to recognise his mistakes and his willingness to recognise the superior power of the hand which struck him.

The truth is that neither the Spaniards nor the Emperor of Germany had agreed to the conditions of division suggested by Louis XIV with a sincere desire for peace. If France refused, the entire inheritance by the will of Charles II was reserved to the Emperor or to his sons who would not have been slow to claim it. To carry out the division would mean for France the prospect of a war against the Emperor and Germany supported by the whole of Spain and a part of Italy; could France count on the support of Holland and England, where, in spite of William III, the peace party remained dominant? To accept the Spanish invitation meant war also, but with the resources of Spain and Italy on the side of the Bourbons and the hope that the maritime Powers might perhaps remain neutral. Louis XIV decided for the latter alternative only after long deliberation with his ministers. There was some truth in the memorandum which he charged Torcy to address to the Powers, and in which it was urged that the gift of a French prince to Spain, whose integrity was thus guaranteed, "was not the equivalent in advantages for France of the dismemberment so long expected of this kingdom." Circumstance, which to the ancients would have seemed an avenging Fate, forced this monarch, who had been too fond of war and was now sorry for it, to adopt a policy which meant continuous warfare on land and sea for thirteen years.

Stress has often been laid on the mistaken policy of Louis XIV in occupying the fortresses of Flanders and especially in recognising the son of James II, thereby hastening the formation of the coalition against him; but it has not been sufficiently emphasised that the Emperor of Germany had invaded Italy in the spring of 1701, that, on 16th November 1700, he had consented to Prussia being raised to the rank of a kingdom, in order to make sure of the military support of the Hohenzollerns, and, at the end of the year, had invited the Electors of Saxony and Hanover to threaten the Rhine; it is also often forgotten that at the same time an agreement was reached between Holland and Scotland (then about to be united to

England) for the occupation of the Spanish colonies of Central
America. "There is no time to spare," wrote Louis XIV in
February 1701, "for sending to the Indies the ships which are
needed to assist the Crown of Spain. All the news from England
and Holland points to the fact that the chief design of the two
nations is to undertake enterprises in the New World." And
finally the Grand Alliance, formed at The Hague between
William III, Holland, and the Emperor, for the conquest of
the Netherlands and Italy, and the division of the Spanish
colonies, antedates by nine days the recognition by Louis XIV
of the Stuart Pretender (September 7–16). The responsibility
for this war (which was to bring the whole of Europe under
arms, and to extend to America) lies less with Louis XIV than
with the Habsburg Emperor who called Germany to arms in
order to fight with the Bourbons for Spain and Italy, or with
the Stadtholder who drew Holland and England into it by the
prospect of gain on sea and in the colonies. The result was later
on to prove to the Habsburgs and to Holland that the progress
of the Houses of Prussia and Hanover in Germany was no more
to the advantage of the one than the benefit gained for the
commerce and navy of Great Britain by the Treaty of Utrecht
was to the other.

It was to convince them of this that Louis XIV, with the
wise help of Torcy, worked during the last two years of his life,
during which period he probably best deserved the title of
Grand Roi which had been given to him by the flattery of his
courtiers in the middle of his reign.

The sufferings of his people (which, in 1709, reached the
extreme limit, and for which the political philosophers, Vauban
and Boisguilbert, proposed the necessary remedies), the disappointments of his policy which had been defeated by Holland,
his own domestic bereavements which left for his successor a
mere infant of three years, and the wisdom of age and of experience, had thoroughly cured Louis XIV of his love of glory
and of conquest. The instructions which he gave at this time
to his agents at the courts of Europe are worthy to rank with
those which he drew up, with the aid of Lionne, at the finest
moment of his reign. The accuracy of his information and of
his opinions, the clear, well-founded conclusions, and the logical

reasoning which links them together, constitute a complete account of the European situation and a model of a wise and fruitful diplomacy. The chief object of this diplomacy was, for the present, the maintenance of peace in Europe and on the French frontiers, saved from invasion as if by miracle at the battle of Denain. For the future, he made a remarkable attempt to bring the court of Vienna to an agreement in the interests of peace and of the continental powers, whose divisions only served the interests of England and the Princes of Germany, and tried to influence the Dutch by persuading them that by always following in the wake of the cabinet of London, and by disputing with Austria or France for the possession of Flanders, they were ruining their own country and exhausting it for the benefit of England. To realise these aims a longer reign would have been necessary, and in 1715 the reign of Louis XIV had already lasted 72 years. And who can say if Europe would ever have believed that the conversion of a glorious and ambitious king to wisdom and love of peace was serious and sincere? The French monarchy survived him only 74 years—about the length of his own reign. It was ruined, as he himself had nearly been, by a despotism fatal to France, by similar pretentions to greatness, fatal in a new age, for which the age of Louis XIV remained for Frenchmen of the time of Voltaire the inimitable model.

§ III.   EIGHTEENTH CENTURY

The Reign of Louis XV

Louis XV, like his great-grandfather Louis XIV, was destined to have a very long reign—1715 to 1774, nearly sixty years. On the other hand one cannot say that he ever ruled, except for five or six years at the most. At first he was prevented by his extreme youth, being barely five years of age when he succeeded to the inheritance of Louis XIV; it was only in 1733 that he reached the age at which his great-grandfather was able to take the place of Mazarin. By this time the entire government, which he professed to reserve for himself, had already been for seven years in the hands of his tutor Fleury, Bishop of

Fréjus. Fleury, who never held the title of First Minister, but merely that of Minister of State, discreetly took the place of the King at the head of the *Conseil d'en haut*, on which sat the Duc d'Orléans, Marshals de Villars, Huxelles, and Tallard, the Secretary of State de Morville, and in 1727 President Chauvelin. Up to the time of his death the Bishop, who later became Cardinal, disposed of the destinies of France, choosing his own collaborators. Then in 1743 there was a new outburst of good intentions, followed by a declaration from Louis XV, prompted, it is said, by Marshal de Noailles, that he was going to govern himself. He came regularly to the meetings of the Council but showed himself incapable of imposing his authority on Cardinal de Tencin, who was vexed at not succeeding to Fleury, on Marshal de Noailles, who was sure that he himself would succeed, and on the Ministers of War, Finance, Foreign Affairs, and the Navy. By the year 1747 this government was heading straight for anarchy and was only united by the influence of Madame de Pompadour, the King's mistress, who was in reality First Minister, at first in conjunction with Pâris-Duverney, then with Machaut and Cardinal de Bernis, and finally with the Duc de Choiseul, who remained principal minister, even after the death of the favourite, from 1758 to 1770. The reign closed with Madame du Barry as favourite, to whom certain courtiers in order to obtain office had suggested that she should continue the part played by Madame de Pompadour, but whose chief concern was to amuse the King in his old age.

To explain this reign we must first of all give the reasons, which are doubtless numerous, for all these contradictions in the character of Louis XV, the consequences of which determined the character of 18th century France. This King was a sickly child and as a young man his health was uncertain. He was married in an urgent hurry, so to speak, to Marie Leczinska just after a critical illness, which, coming on the top of several others, very nearly carried him off and left the country without a king. "Put no money on the King," said he himself in 1758 to a financier, "I'm told it isn't safe." He lived, if I may say so, with death staring him in the face, fearing and desiring, as a sick man will, everything that could evoke the reality of death. One might be tempted, after comparing the King's childhood with that of his mother and of his aunt, the Queen of Spain, to attribute it to heredity from the House of Savoy, if one did not remember on the other hand that poor invalid, the first Duc d'Anjou, Philip V, the heir and successor of the degenerate Habsburg race. The Spanish marriage and the Savoy marriage deprived from birth the heir of Louis XIV of that splendid strength for living and ruling which we must allow to his great-grandfather. The education of Louis XV was deplorable; the Duc d'Orléans offered him nothing but pleasure and a bad example. In order to get him away from the influence of the Regent, his governor, Marshal de Villeroy, and his tutor, the Bishop of Fréjus, avoided giving him any work, or anything tiresome. The King knew only adulation and flattery with regard to his person and his position, while his absolute power was put at the service of his caprices. He was *France,* as his last mistress called him. Nobody ever taught him, no one ever made him feel, what a great thing it meant, what obligations and what responsibilities it involved, for a man to be *France.* The historian who has most recently described his reign has come to the conclusion that "the principal cause of the ruin of the monarchy was the lack of a king"; I should prefer to say "the rule of a king who wished to reserve this function to himself and refused to exercise it." This fatal *régime* endured only through the devotion of the French to their monarchic faith, and the return at intervals of First Ministers, in fact though not in name, who were tolerated by their master and invested with the King's absolute power over his subjects. We are therefore inevitably compelled to study the reign in fragments, so to speak, which correspond to the various phases, resembling, in the way they succeed each other in this absolute monarchy, the succession of cabinets under a parliamentary *régime*—a resemblance which helps one to understand the fundamental viciousness of a government in which the defects of parliamentary government were added to those of absolutism at the expense of continuity of plan and national freedom of action.

The first years of the reign fall naturally into a division by themselves; the childhood and minority of Louis XV and the government of Philippe d'Orléans his uncle, provided for by the will of Louis XIV with certain reservations and instituted in 1715 by decision of the *Parlement*. This government is called "the Regency," as though there had been no other Regencies during previous minorities. It is spoken of as a separate period with its own manners and its own style. The Regency at the beginning of the century has been compared to the Directory at the end of it for the liberty or rather the license allowed to the French after two periods of excessive restraint, the one monarchic, the other revolutionary.

It must not however be imagined that the Regency of the Duc d'Orléans was a time of political liberty. Doubtless in order to obtain from the *Parlement* unrestricted sovereignty over the granting of offices and appointments Philippe d'Orléans granted to that body the right of remonstrance, and gave them to believe they would be allowed to take part in the government of the country. He also seemed to destroy the machinery of administration directed by the successors of Colbert and Louvois by creating Councils to take the place of the Secretaries of State, Councils of finance, of war, of internal affairs, and of foreign affairs. The novelty was not so great as was thought by contemporary opinion, that of Saint-Simon for example, such Councils having been called to deliberate on the affairs of the kingdom in the time of the late King, who presided over them. The novelty consisted in bringing into these Councils the aristocrats by birth and combining them with the parliamentary nobility and the high State officials, as was the case in Austria and England, and allowing them all to share in those advantages which under Louis XIV were reserved for a few ministerial families. This however lasted but a short time and produced nothing. All the useful work of these Councils was done by the official staff of the administrative offices and of the provinces, and as early as August 1718 this staff had their old chiefs back once more, the Secretaries of State, who alone were capable "of preventing a well regulated monarchical government from degenerating into anarchy." Neither was it very long before the Regent, impatient of the supervision of the *Parlement*, had recourse to *Lits de Justice*; and he arrested certain magistrates on August 26, 1718, in order to remind them that "the laws need only the sole will of the sovereign in order to become laws."

Although the King's minority had always previously been a time favourable to intrigues and rebellions, the minority of Louis XV was on the whole just as peaceful as if Louis XIV had continued to reign. The discontent of the men of the court of Louis XIV such as Huxelles, Villars, and Torcy, who were gradually pushed aside, and the opposition of the *Parlement*, gained no support from the public. At her court of Sceaux, the Duchesse du Maine, angered by the rigorous action taken against her husband, concerted with the Spanish ambassador, Cellamare, what looked like a conspiracy but was in fact merely a drawing-room intrigue. The Duc d'Orléans exaggerated the importance of it in order to compel the Spanish King to humiliate himself. All foreigners, including Cellamare himself, declared that the authority of the Regent, served by all the machinery of government set up in the preceding reign, was absolute. "France," said Law, "is a kingdom governed by one controller and twenty intendants."

But it was not the Duc d'Orléans himself who exercised the authority. For no later than the end of the year 1716 began the singular good fortune of his tutor the Abbé Dubois, who by secret diplomacy succeeded in making the Pact of Hanover, and later the Triple Alliance of the Hague (1717) to safeguard the joint interests of George I and the Regent. Since at this time between Philippe d'Orléans and the throne of France there was only the fragile frame of a sickly child of six, or the claims of the King of Spain, the Abbé advised his pupil to seek a guarantee in the *Renunciations of Utrecht*, which condemned the claims of Philip V, as opposed to England and the Elector of Hanover, who were likewise interested in the maintenance of these treaties definitely directed against the Stuarts. Upon this "solid foundation," Dubois, serving the ambition of a master who favoured his own fortune, constructed a diplomatic edifice made up of the acquiescence of the maritime powers and their ally the Emperor in the hopes of the House of Orleans. In 1718 he became head of the official diplomacy and employed his new office for the same ends that he had secretly pursued from the embassy in London. He did not even hesitate to engage in a war against Philip V and Alberoni, whom he accused of disturbing the peace of Europe, when they were only guilty of refusing to the Regent those concessions by which Dubois and England wished to pay the Emperor, at the expense of Spain and Italy, for the favour he showed to the fortunes of the House of Orleans. During these four years the Abbé Dubois, in the name of the Regent, became the master of French policy at the Palais-Royal and in Europe.

He had joined forces with the Scotchman Law, who in 1716 had come to offer to the Duc d'Orléans, embarrassed by the necessity of liquidating the heavy liabilities of the preceding reign, the resources of the credit system adopted more than a century before in Amsterdam and more recently in London. Law's Bank, later converted into the State Bank, which issued notes secured on the revenue of the great commercial companies to which he gave renewed energy (*Compagnie d'Occident* in 1717, *Compagnie des Indes et du Mississippi* in 1719), seemed at the time capable of wiping out the debts of the kingdom. "Such a prompt restoration of your finances wins the admiration of Europe," wrote Stanhope in October 1719 to Dubois, whom Law had helped to become Minister of Foreign Affairs and who helped Law to become Controller-General in January 1720.

"In France," said d'Argenson, "there are but two ministries, Finance and Foreign Affairs." With the help of Law and Dubois the Regent had the kingdom at his disposal. In 1720 he was called upon to choose between his two ministers. The defect of the one was the weakness of his system, with its too numerous notes secured on the wealth of the colonies and the great commercial companies, the return on which was too slow in coming in, while in addition to this there was the jealousy of the English at the unexpected prosperity. The defect of the other's policy was that the French discovered that in the end the friendship established at great cost between France and Spain had been sacrificed to the interests of the House of Orleans and the demands of England. Dubois, having become Archbishop of Cambrai, had sufficient influence over the Regent to hasten the ruin of Law and his enterprises with the help of England, and that in spite of the opposition of the Duc de Bourbon, who was interested in the system. But seeing the dangers of his victory he attempted to recover the friendship of

Philip by secret manœuvres, which were supported at Madrid by the court of Parma through the intermediary of Elizabeth Farnese. He suggested marriages between the Infanta Maria Anna and Louis XV, and between the Spanish princes and the daughters of the Regent. After six years of extraordinarily varied efforts he was lucky enough and clever enough to bring all the sovereigns of Europe to support his master's candidature for the French crown. Through the Stuarts, whom he helped in their distress at Rome, he obtained the Cardinal's hat. In 1722 the Duc d'Orléans protected him against all attacks on his fortune from the Palais-Royal. Just before the majority of Louis XV was decided upon (February 16, 1723), Cardinal Dubois restored (August 22, 1722) for his own benefit the office of First Minister, the Duc d'Orléans remaining *President des Conseils*, but binding himself to discuss no matters with the Secretaries of State except through the Cardinal. This was merely a precautionary measure on the part of Dubois in order to retain the power exercised by Mazarin before and after the majority of Louis XIV. For two years he was absolute master of the kingdom. The ambition and the indolence of the Regent relied on the devotion and activity of Dubois.

When he died in August 1723, the French nation did not ask for an account, nor did they from Philippe d'Orléans, who, after being Regent, was First Minister until the end of the year. And afterwards, from 1723 to 1726, there was no opposition to the function of First Minister being exercised by the Duc de Bourbon, who was advised to ask the King for it at once, before the Duc de Chartres, who might also have claimed it.

The ministry of Cardinal Fleury had at first the air of starting a new régime. This cunning old man, who considered he had a right to hanker after the success attained by Dubois under the protection of his pupil, said to his friend Walpole that there could never be another First Minister. At that time, in 1726, he was 74 years old; in 1722 he had raised no objection to the appointment of Dubois, nor in 1724 to that of the Duc de Bourbon. He made no secret of the fact that he was in favour of disgracing this Prince, when his incoherent policy involved France in a quarrel with Spain in regard to the cancellation of the marriage with the Infanta, in another with the court of

Vienna about the affair of Ostend, and was leading him on to undertake an adventurous war. Hiding his own ambition, at an age when the days of an old man should be numbered, he had it announced by the King himself that the administration would be conducted on the same lines as during the time when Louis XIV took the reins of government—no First Minister, no other Council than the *Conseil d'en haut.* "He will not take the title," said Horace Walpole, "but that will not prevent his power from being more absolute and more undisputed than that of Richelieu and Mazarin." It was hardly possible to foresee that, after an interval of a century, this septuagenarian would enjoy this authority for the same length of time as his illustrious predecessors. These fourteen years counted practically for nothing in the reign of Louis XV, and perhaps for the very reason that the King's influence was nil they were the most profitable to the country.

His contemporaries, and again recently M. Carré, have criticised the old Cardinal for having lulled France to sleep in order that he might in no way be disturbed in the enjoyment of his power. Others have criticised him for the English alliance and his friendship with Walpole, to which he sacrificed, for the same motive according to them, the interests and the dignity of the crown. But is it just to reproach Fleury for a policy of fruitful peace when Colbert is praised for advising, unsuccessfully, Louis XIV to pursue a similar policy?

It is to the Cardinal's credit that he kept peace from 1726 to 1731. The jealousy of the commercial nations against the Belgian Company of Ostend, the ambitions of the German princes, and above all the furious efforts of Elizabeth Farnese to establish her sons in Parma and Tuscany, interfered each year, indeed each month, with the pacific measures of French diplomacy. It was with still greater difficulty that the minister prevented France from taking part in the election of the King of Poland. All the court, humiliated at the marriage of the King to the daughter of a dethroned sovereign, demanded the crown for Stanislas Leczinski. Fleury was able to afford other satisfaction to the pride of France by the still popular means of waging a war against the Habsburgs, limiting it however in time and space. The result was the acquisition of

the Duchy of Lorraine granted in compensation for his disappointment in Poland to Leczinski, with right of reversion
after his death to the crown of France. The war lasted only
a little more than a year. When, in 1736, it broke out again
in the East against the Turks, who were threatened by
Russia and Austria, French diplomacy played a successful
part in the Peace of Belgrade, and from the Sultan, who had
strengthened his position in the Balkans, obtained *capitulations* favourable to the trade and influence of France in the
Levant.

The credit for this prudent policy is sometimes given not
to the Cardinal but to his colleague, the Keeper of the Seals,
Chauvelin, whose patriotic hatred, in conjunction with the
animosity of Elizabeth Farnese against Austria, was really
responsible for forcing the weak Fleury to adopt the resolutions
which benefited the kingdom. If it is difficult to determine the
precise share of the two ministers in this collaboration, there
is on the other hand no doubt about the energy with which
Fleury, on learning of the secret agreement made with Spain
by Chauvelin to compel Louis XV to continue hostilities against
Austria, obtained from the King the disgrace and exile of
Chauvelin. Persuaded, like Louis XIV, that the rivalry between
Bourbon and Habsburg no longer interested France now that
her frontiers were assured, and hoping that the alliance with
Spain, who had established the son of Philip V on the throne
of Naples, would prove to be the best guarantee of the peace
of Europe, he imposed this policy on the ministers, the King,
and France, and the credit for this cannot be denied him. And
when, in 1739, Spain and England were preparing for a naval
war owing to commercial rivalry and the refusal of English
ships to recognise the right of search, Fleury, in spite of his
love of peace and his friendship for England, promised to
Philip V without hesitation the support of the French fleet,
brought by Maurepas within the year up to the strength of
more than thirty ships.

Of the prosperity due to the peace arranged by Fleury, there
is still evidence to-day in all the commercial cities of France,
in Bordeaux, Nantes, Marseilles, Lyons, Dunkirk, Caen, where
the public monuments and the large houses of the wealthy

bourgeoisie, erected with the aid of the intendants and the architects, completely transformed the towns' appearance; in the French colonies, in America and India; in the great royal roads which Perronet, owing to the institution of forced labour in 1738, was able to construct for the convenience of commerce and of the citizens of France, and which were the envy of Europe. An obscure clerk of Parisian extraction who had made his mark as an administrator in Spain, Orry, supported by the body of intendants bequeathed by Colbert's administration, took up again, with the Cardinal's full confidence, the work of the great Controller-General, which had been interrupted by the wars of Louis XIV. Like Colbert and Sully he made no alteration in the conditions of levying the royal taxes, which continued to crush the people and to reduce the peasants to poverty for the benefit of the services of State, the luxury of the court, and the pensions of the courtiers. But, like Colbert, by supervision of the accountants and the strictest economy, he restored the royal budget to a state of equilibrium, balancing the accounts by anticipating the profits for the year from industry and commerce. The nation now responded better than during the 17th century to his lead. It had learnt to recognise since the time of Law the sources of wealth offered to its enterprise in the New World and especially in the Far East. The figures given later by Necker show that the value of French trade, which in 1726 amounted only to 80 million *livres*, in 1743 reached the sum of 308 millions, being quadrupled in the twenty years which correspond to the ministry of Fleury and the administration of Orry. From this came all the magnificence of the 18th century, which contributed to the spreading of French art and the reputation of her artists throughout the world at least as much as the patronage of Louis XIV.

It was the misfortune of the monarchy and the nation that, at the precise moment when society was abandoning itself to a life of pleasure and luxury, the political conditions, on which financial conditions depend, were abruptly changed by the unfortunate interference of Louis XV in the affairs of the kingdom.

In 1740 at the death of Charles VI, Emperor of Germany, his daughter Maria Theresa found herself threatened by a sudden attack by Frederick II in Silesia, and by the designs of the Elector

of Bavaria upon Bohemia and of the Bourbons of Spain upon
Italy. More than half engaged with Philip V in a war against
England, Fleury saw nothing to be gained in this war against
the House of Austria and a great deal of risk in undertaking an
expensive double war on land and sea. He immediately recognised the integrity of the inheritance of Maria Theresa, and
Louis XV replied at first to the courtiers who reproached him
for sparing the hereditary enemy, "When a great King does
not want war he does not have it." But tradition was stronger
than the advice of the Cardinal. The chief advocate was the
Maréchal de Belle-Isle, who won over the King by means of
memoranda written at Bourges by Chauvelin and discreetly
handed to the King by his *valet-de-chambre*, Bachelier. The beginning of it was the mission entrusted to Belle-Isle to go to
Frankfort and gain the Imperial crown for the Elector of
Bavaria, the one part of the paternal inheritance to which Maria
Theresa had no claim. There followed the coalition arranged at
Nymphenburg between all the Bourbons and Frederick II to
dismember the Austrian dominions, which resulted in 1742 in
disaster to the armies of France and of the Emperor she had
created. Yielding at last to the weakness of age accentuated
by his grief at such a ruinous war, Fleury implored peace from
Maria Theresa, and just before his death met only with the
shame of a refusal.

The French King and the nation welcomed the death of the
Cardinal as a remedy for the disasters of the adventure which
he had blamed, and whose success he had prevented through
the obstinacy of an old man incapable of understanding and
upholding the glory of a great nation. They were not at all
displeased, quite the contrary, when England and Savoy joined
their declared enemies. "The House of Bourbon," said Voltaire,
"was obliged, for the second time, to fight practically the whole
of Europe." A salutary challenge, since it made the brave and
intelligent young King decide at last to take into his own hands
the reins of government and the command of his armies, to
become the victor of Fontenoy and the conqueror of Flanders
and, like Louis XIV, to make the Dutch burghers tremble in
Amsterdam. It was left to posterity to calculate the cost of this
sterile conquest and glory, with the treasury empty, the people

crushed and trade suspended, while the colonies of America and
India were already endangered by the successful attacks of the
English navy. In the settling up after this war in 1748—"a very
stupid peace," by which the King's son-in-law, Don Philip, was
granted a petty kingdom in Italy, Parma and Piacenza—the
saddest part was the weakness of the King, in whom France had
thought to find the stuff of a new *Grand Monarque*. Tired of the
cares of government as soon as he took them up, tired also of
commanding his armies at the head of which he never again
appeared, Louis XV returned to his extravagant pleasures at
Versailles, where, in 1745, Mme de Pompadour appeared publicly
as his acknowledged mistress.

This personal intervention in his reign on the part of Louis XV
was materially and morally disastrous. The union of love and
trust between the King and his people, which had been the
strongest and surest support of the monarchy, was broken.
The King from Versailles now seemed merely the first among
those gentlemen who cared only for their own pleasures and
handed France over to the financiers. People talked of the
enormous sums spent on Madame de Pompadour, from seven
to eight million *livres* for buildings, four millions for the theatre
and fêtes, and the people of Paris in 1750 hissed this woman, who
was starving them, in the streets. During these years, when
the Controller-General Machaut dared to attempt to impose
upon the privileged classes the direct general tax of one-
twentieth, which was defeated by the *Parlement* and the clergy,
the luxury displayed by the nobles and the rich, in their dress,
their apartments and their following of artists and writers, was
greater than ever before. They must have known that this
luxury was no longer fed by the wealth of commerce, but by
the ill-earned gains of the financiers, who furnished supplies for
the war, and the usurious loans to the crown and to its ministers.
Orry was disgraced in 1745 for refusing to sign proposals made
by the brothers Pâris, the kings of finance and almost of the
kingdom. At this time the fable of the four cats became current:
the thin cat was the people, the fat cat the financiers, the one-
eyed cat the ministry, and the blind cat the King who saw
nothing and refused to see anything.

So towards the end of his reign Louis XV retired once more,

and the kingdom was governed by women, Madame de Pompadour and Madame du Barry, or rather in reality by the financiers. Two of them were at the bottom of the success of Antoinette Poisson—Lenormant de Tournehem, the lover of Madame Poisson, and his nephew Monsieur d'Étioles, married through his uncle's influence to Antoinette, and a protégé of Pâris-Duverney, *le général des farines*. The success of Madame d'Étioles in winning the favour of Louis XV firmly established the influence of Pâris-Montmartel, one of the first bankers of Europe and cashier to the royal army and navy. The financiers enriched at the expense of the poverty of the nation, living in a brilliant and luxurious style, winning over to their side the men of intelligence, who depended on them for their living, began definitely to wield more influence than the ruined nobility who cared only for their pleasures. "Pâris-Duverney," said d'Argenson in 1746, "does the whole work, in politics and in the army." These men were in a still stronger position when Antoinette, now known as Madame de Pompadour, became the King's mistress, and later, in 1755, his friend and practically First Minister.

The principal office of the Marquise was the supervision of the royal pleasure. Not only had she constantly to exert herself to keep the King amused by the intimate companionship described by Madame du Hausset, but also to organise his journeys and the functions and festivities of the court. In this ministry of Pleasures and Arts she was helped at first by Monsieur de Tournehem, then by his brother and pupil the Marquis de Marigny, and by an intimate circle of devoted friends, men of the world, who excelled in dancing, acting, music, and *jeux d'esprit*. She led a terrible existence, however, for the ministers were her creatures and had no other support but her. She had to defend Machaut, Controller-General, Keeper of the Seals, and Minister for the Navy, against the Comte d'Argenson, the King's friend, who opposed the minister's reforms because they threatened the interests of the clergy whose cause he espoused. She had to defend herself against the influence of the royal family, the Dauphin, and the King's daughters, indignant at the treatment of their mother and scandalised by the weakness of their father in giving her such an eminent position at court.

With the help of Puysieux she directed foreign affairs. She appointed the ambassadors, giving the embassy of Venice to a new-comer, l'Abbé de Bernis, who later became Cardinal and First Minister and had the highest ambitions, and the embassy of Rome to the Duc de Choiseul, who gained her favour by revealing an intrigue between the King and one of his relations.

These two men in 1754 easily came to an agreement in Italy with the Duchess of Parma, who resented being far away from Versailles and suggested to the Marquise a foreign policy which brought about a reconciliation between her and the royal family. Bernis was made minister, Choiseul was sent to Vienna to negotiate an alliance which gave Austria the hope of a war of revenge against Frederick II at the price of ceding the Netherlands to the royal family of France. The two Treaties of Versailles involved the kingdom in a new war, which Frederick II commenced in 1756 with the support of England, to forestall the attack of Maria Theresa by the occupation of Saxony. A seven years' war on land and sea, and in the colonies which it was to the interest of France, attacked in 1755 by England in America, in India, and on the ocean, to limit as much as possible; a disastrous war the irremediable gravity of which was obvious to Bernis after Rosbach. "The Austrian alliance," wrote Choiseul, who at least had the courage not to abandon the Marquise and the kingdom in this distress, "has made us neglect the naval war and the war in America which was the real war." Choiseul imposed úpon Austria a third treaty, in 1758, which compelled Maria Theresa to support France until she had taken her revenge on England. Then abandoning politics to his cousin, Choiseul Praslin, who in 1761 called on the King of Spain to help in accordance with the family compact, Choiseul devoted himself, while the war was still in progress, to restoring the army and navy, the essential instruments of national defence. The Marquise de Pompadour and the King were grateful to him for his activity and energy and forgave him the humiliating peace of 1763, which he could not avoid. France, humiliated and impoverished, could not forgive the monarchy for the shame and ruin brought about by this government. The *Parlement* took advantage of the discredit of the monarchy to encourage the nation to ask for an account, and, feeling sure of the support of the writers and of public opinion, showed almost as much impatience as during the Fronde to exercise control over the royal finances and administration.

The dispute between the *Parlement* of Brittany and the Governor, the Duc d'Aiguillon, and the Controller-General de Laverdy, which lasted nearly six years, was not favourable to the royal authority. And this was one of the reasons why Choiseul, who after the death of Mme de Pompadour became First Minister in her place, was disgraced in 1770. It was not the only, nor perhaps the chief reason. Regretting his inability to prevent the effects of the Seven Years' War, he did his best to repair them. From 1763 to 1768 he made a great effort to restore the forces on land and sea and to put renewed vigour into the French colonies. He thought that the Peace of Paris in 1763 could not finally put a stop to the future career of the kingdom in the colonies and at sea, and that by keeping peace on the Continent, and with the support of Spain, he could profitably intervene in the struggle between England and her American colonies. In 1770 a dispute occurred between Spain and England with regard to the Falkland Islands; the King Charles III obstinately refused to give in at the threat of war, and Choiseul considered, in spite of the opposition of Louis XV, that he was entitled by his direct relations with the King of Spain to pledge the support of France. He was abruptly exiled to Chanteloup, near Tours, on December 24.

After the disgrace of Choiseul, the reign ended with a decisive blow against the disobedient *Parlements*, which Louis XV authorised the Chancellor Maupéou to carry into execution in order to restore the much shaken royal authority. The edict of February 23, 1771, replaced the *Parlement* of Paris by *Conseils Supérieurs de Justice*, composed of judges appointed by the King with fixed salaries, put an end to hereditary office, and reduced the magistracy to its judicial functions. It was on the whole a final victory for absolute monarchy and a very easy one. The members of the *Parlement* admitted the defeat. "The nation," said Joly de Fleury, "looked on calmly while justice was destroyed." In reality the nation applauded, hoping for better justice after the annihilation of this privileged body, which opposed the King, nominally on behalf of the national

welfare, but as a matter of fact on behalf of their own interests.
Not that the public did not need protection. The luxury of the
court, the extravagance of Madame du Barry, Marie Antoinette,
the Comtes d'Artois and de Provence, and the pensions of the
nobles exhausted the taxpayers more than ever. Commerce
had been destroyed. In 1773 in Paris alone there were 2500
bankruptcies. The peasants crowded into the towns in order to
beg, and the citizens of the towns rebelled against it. There
was a general outcry against the Abbé Terray, the last Controller-General, or rather purveyor of the royal extravagance.
Revolution was talked of. Louis XV died on May 9, 1774. The
nation took hope once more and was faithful for another fifteen
years to the aristocracy and the ministers of a régime to which
it was devoted. "The King is dead, long live the King." For
the people of France the King was just as powerful as ever,
more powerful even, provided he understood his duty for good
and ill. But after Louis XV it was high time that good was done;
the ill had passed all measure and the invalid had apparently
come to the end of his patience and ability to suffer. "The
French nation," said Mirabeau later, "was prepared for the
Revolution much more by the sense of its sufferings than by
the progress of intelligence."

The Reign of Louis XVI

The fifteen years between the death of Louis XV and the
French Revolution were but a truce in the struggle of the nation
against the privileged classes, which were held responsible by
the people for the misery and the humiliation of the country.
This truce was the time allowed to the monarchy, the only
authority still undisputed, to find a solution of the crisis.
This must not be forgotten in judging Louis XVI and his
reign.

"The young King of France needs power and genius," said
Frederick II; who could measure the difficulty of the task of the
successor of Louis XV. But Louis XVI was before all things a
prince of weak will and mediocre intelligence. Very religious
and of strict conscience, he had a sense of duty and excellent
intentions. But from the first he was discouraged by the necessity of making an effort which he felt himself incapable of

making or sustaining. A great eater and a great hunter, he exhausted his energies in physical exercise like the Saxon Electors, from whom he inherited his somewhat heavy and entirely material nature. His whole government, the nominal responsibility for which he, like Louis XV, made the mistake of keeping for himself, was never anything more than a well-intentioned but futile attempt to understand and to act.

During the first years of his reign Louis XVI sought the aid of two principal advisers, the Comte de Maurepas and M. de Vergennes. The difference between these two men explains the different results in the King's internal and external policy. Maurepas, an old courtier, a sceptic, and a wit, incapable of seeing or of understanding the dangerous movement of popular discontent or the financial distress, led Louis XVI to have recourse to the usual expedients to pacify demands which he could not take seriously. He recalled the *Parlements*, appointed and encouraged Turgot, only to sacrifice him to the complaints of the *Parlement* and the court, when Maurepas advised that he should be replaced by Necker. The abandonment of Necker in 1781 was the final error of Maurepas and Louis XVI, who in 1787 was obliged to lay the balance sheet of the kingdom before the notables. On this day and by the mouth of the Finance Minister, Calonne, the truth, which for two centuries of absolute government had been kept hidden, was made clearly apparent—the inevitable necessity, in order to balance the national budget, of suppressing social inequality and of inviting the nation itself to pronounce its opinion on the privileges, the rights and the duties of the nobility, the *Parlement*, and the clergy.

Vergennes on the contrary, an experienced diplomatist, who had served his apprenticeship in the chief embassies, inspired only, like a faithful servant of France, with a zeal for the real interests of the realm, indifferent to court intrigues, opposed to the abuse of "reasons of State" and to any idea of vain glory or conquest, gave to the foreign politics of Louis XVI a direction to which the King, to his credit, adhered for thirteen years, faithfully devoted, in spite of the Austrian influence of Marie Antoinette, to this reliable servant of the Crown and his policy. Between the ambition of his brother-in-law Joseph II and the power of Prussia France remained neutral, guaranteeing at Teschen a European peace, which allowed her to concentrate, at the outbreak of the American Revolution, all her naval forces against the English pretentions to control the sea and monopolise trade. His work, which was crowned by the Treaty of Versailles in 1783, was one of the last successes of the monarchy. Louis XVI, through Vergennes, was also able to come to terms with England with a view to opposing the ambitious designs of Russia and Austria against the Turkish Empire, and to extend the commercial interests of France in the Black Sea and the Eastern Mediterranean. When Vergennes died in 1787, the French monarchy still held in the eyes of Europe the position, which her best servants had always tried to gain for her, of a power capable of making itself respected and of maintaining by her moderation and her prestige a balance between ambition and right, a peaceful régime less dangerous than the intrigues of "reasons of State" accompanied by violence.

At the very time when, in this same year, Louis XVI was unable through lack of the necessary means of action to come to the aid of the Dutch burghers against the conspiracy formed at the Hague by the Stadtholder with Prussia and England, Catherine II wrote to Grimm: "Louis XVI has application, good intentions, and a sense of right. If he allows these Georges and Williams to make a mess of everything he may say 'good-bye' to the consideration the French kings have enjoyed for two hundred years." And Joseph II, the brother of the Queen of France, gave the same verdict: "What a little time is necessary for a great State, possessing vast resources, to lose reputation, influence, and power through lack of order and a head of the State!"

It was not due to Austria, or to Marie Antoinette, the instrument of Austria, that Vergennes, who encountered incessant opposition from that quarter, was able up to the time of his death to maintain that consideration won for the monarchy since the day of Henry IV and Richelieu. Marie Antoinette moreover made another great mistake in living a life of pleasure and luxury and keeping up a court obstinately devoted to frivolous and ruinous occupations. Certainly her court at the

Trianon was very delightful; a taste for nature and a rather artificial simplicity, after the fashion set by Rousseau, gave to this elegant society, in spite of everything, a fresh and new charm, for whose enjoyment French art created the Louis XVI style under the protection of M. Angiviller, and produced work remarkable for harmony of line, delicate proportions, and a discreet use of antique decoration borrowed from Herculaneum and Pompeii. But it was a court that was always isolated in its luxurious retreat at Versailles, intriguing against those ministers who attempted to criticise or reduce its extravagance, unworthily occupied with trifling amusements, comedies, and songs at the edge of a precipice created by its own light-hearted indifference. Louis XVI, weak and submissive, was incapable of imposing the necessary remedies or of supporting those who pointed out the evils and dangers. It was the Austrian ambassador, Mercy-Argenteau, who gave Vienna this decisive warning: "The present government for disorder and rapine surpasses the late reign; it is impossible for this state of things to subsist for long without bringing about a catastrophe."

The nation was about to take a part through the States-General (1788–1789), which had not met since 1614, and which now called upon the Crown to cure the evils it had brought about or else leave it to them. It was no longer merely a request or a hope, it was a summons.

§ IV. THE CHURCH IN THE SEVENTEENTH AND EIGHTEENTH CENTURIES

Seventeenth century

The civil wars of the 16th century, which had devastated the country with all the excesses of anarchy and violence, and at the end of which, in 1600, the French returned once more to the royal authority as the only cure for their divisions and their sufferings, were caused and nourished by the heat of religious passions. The harm these passions and controversies did to the State was perhaps less than the harm done to the indi-

vidual conscience and to the Church. Cultivated men such as
Montaigne, Charron, Du Vair, and Gassendi turned aside from
dogma to seek in the wisdom of the Ancients (the Stoic, Epi-
curean, or Sceptic philosophers, with whose writings they were
familiar) lessons of reason and rules of life. They formed a
current of free-thought or "libertinage," as it was called in
those days, not a very wide but a deep current, which may be
traced all through the 17th century, in Saint-Évremond, Naudé,
the Vendômes and their circle, and Bayle, and from which
the following century derived its faith in reason. The greedy
and quarrelsome nobles and the higher *bourgeoisie*, who imitated and supplanted them, became accustomed to look upon
the goods and offices of the Church as the natural reward for
their services to the Crown. The Concordat of 1516 had granted
to the French King the valuable right of nominating bishops
and appointing abbots. The revenues of vacant sees were by
this means handed over to soldiers, women, and princes. Out
of fourteen archbishoprics there were sometimes six or seven
without a pastoral head, and the titular dignity was often held
by a mere child. The King installed one of his natural sons in
the See of Metz when he was six years old. Abbeys were distributed to favourites, royal mistresses, and even to Protestants.
With such heads it may well be imagined what the clergy must
often have been, ignorant, "shameless, debauched, drunkards,"
according to one bishop. The same may be said of the monks
and nuns who inhabited the convents and monasteries—those
hostelries where they lived a jovial life and kept good cheer.
And what an example for the faithful flock, whose indifference
was due to the degradation of the clergy. Religious worship,
which had been rendered difficult by the deplorable state of
the churches and the sacred vessels brought about by the civil
wars, had gradually ceased to be the prop of faith. The soul
was as empty as the temple.

The Reformation in attempting to cut away the parasitic
plants which threatened the very life of Christianity had
damaged the real roots. Even the people who had rallied round
Protestantism did not do so entirely from religious conviction,
but from interest and pressure also. It is said of certain towns
in Poitou that the women brought up their daughters to abstain

from religion up to the time of their marriage in order that they might be free to choose the new or the old faith according to the husband's convictions; the sons of the great aristocratic houses joined either camp according to the dictates of opportunity. Freedom of conscience, established by the Edict of Nantes, was apparently accepted by the, followers of both religions only on account of the universal lassitude resulting from the long civil disturbance and the troubled state of religion.

The sorry spectacle of a heresy established at the expense of Catholic unity, and of the concessions which the Church, in spite of the disapproval of the Holy See, had been compelled to make, stirred in the souls of those attached to the ancient faith a revival of mysticism, and a need for regeneration, sacrifice, and propaganda, which may be said to date from the earliest years of the 17th century. It is first noticeable amongst the women of the higher *bourgeoisie* in Paris who had belonged to the League and refused to join their husbands and brothers in accepting defeat: Madame de Sainte-Beuve, the sister of the Hannequins, the Bishops of the League, and above all Madame Accarie, the wife of one of the founders of the League, a disciple of St Theresa, whose cult she introduced into France in conjunction with the saint's translator, Jacques de Bretigny. She and her circle of mystics, André du Val, Pierre de Bérulle, ecstatic visionaries, were ripe for the instruction of St François de Sales who came from Geneva in 1602. The *Introduction à la Vie dévote*, that new *Imitation* for the use of the worldly, the *Traité de l'Amour de Dieu*, the foundation of the direction of souls, determined or supported many vocations at the beginning of the century which has been called "the century of saints" and compared to the early days of the Christian Church.

These holy women, numerous and active, were found in the ranks of high society, whether it was descended or not from the ancient aristocracy of the League—the Comtesse de Penthièvre, Marie the widow of the Duc de Mercœur, the chief opponent of Henry IV in Brittany, Catherine of Lorraine, Duchesse de Nevers, the daughter of Mayenne—and above all in two families, the Orléans-Longueville family and the Gondi family, some of them practising the virtues of asceticism while continuing to remain in the world, others entering convents as disciples and at the same

time acting as protectresses of the Apostles of the Religious Renaissance, whom they aided in founding new Orders or reforming
the old, in the practice of charity, and in the propagation of the
faith. Marie de' Medici, who cannot be compared to them for piety
or virtue, had at least the merit of supporting this apostolate,
to which her name remains attached just as that of Henry IV
is to the restoration of the country.

Finally in 1602 Villeroy, the very Christian minister of
Henry IV, who took from politics the time necessary for religious retirement, was able to write: "Never have I seen religion
more practiced among our people than at present. This is a
great consolation. Such ardour should be encouraged so long
as it does not go beyond the boundaries of the service of God,
which is so entirely in accord with the welfare of the State that
it is difficult to separate the one from the other." The greater
part of the nation therefore, as well as its chiefs, barely four
years after the Edict of Nantes, were disposed to follow the
guidance of these Apostles of a religious Renaissance brought
about by prayer, teaching and good works.

St François de Sales aided Jeanne-Françoise de Chantal to
found at Annecy (1610) and at Lyons (1615) the Order of *Les
Filles de la Visitation*, devoted to the service of the sick; M. de
Bérulle aided Madame Accarie in the installation of the *Carmelites* in the "Faubourg St Jacques," and Mme de Sainte-
Beuve obtained from Marie de' Medici a convent in the same
quarter for the *Ursulines*, an Order for unmarried ladies or
widows founded according to the rule of St Augustine, which
twenty years later counted sixty convents in the provinces of
France. Father Joseph de Tremblay, Richelieu's friend, and
from 1606 to 1611 Provincial of the Capuchins, whose ardent
activities he stimulated, persuaded the widow of the Marquis de
Belle-Isle (Albert de Gondi), Antoinette d'Orléans-Longueville,
to reform the Order of Benedictines at Fontevrault in accordance with the new rule of Calvary recognised by the Pope in
1621 and patronised by Marie de' Medici, the special feature
of which was prayer for the deliverance of the Holy Places.
It was at this time that Henry IV felt unable to refuse to Father
Cotton (Sept. 1603) permission for the Jesuits to reoccupy their
institutions from which they had been driven out by the *Parle-*

ments of Paris, Dijon, Poitiers, and Rouen, to reorganise their colleges and to found new establishments for teaching such as the Collège de la Flèche, the most perfect of those schools, to which the *bourgeoisie* began already to send their children. Father Mussart, a great friend of M. de Bérulle, established in 1601, in the Faubourg Saint-Antoine, the Franciscan Congregation of Picpus with the aid of the Comtesse de Rochechouart-Mortemart. In 1616 Marie de' Medici helped to found the Convent of *Les Filles Franciscaines de Sainte Elizabeth de Hongrie*, under the direction of Sœur Marie de Saint-Charles, who was consulted by ladies of the highest nobility, such as the Duchesse d'Angoulême and the Duchesse de Verneuil. Finally to the same circle belonged Port-Royal, the famous abbey, in the neighbourhood of Paris, of which the young Abbess Marie Angélique Arnauld, a disciple of St François de Sales, was with his advice reforming the Bernardines, and was later on to call upon Father Bérulle and his Oratorians.

In all these new foundations and reformations of abbeys there was the same inspiration, the same ardent faith, and a return to an inner spiritual life radiating from one central fire which was kept burning by St François de Sales, M. de Bérulle, Fathers Joseph and Mussart, their penitents and friends among the nobility and the *bourgeoisie* of Paris. These mystics and these pious women did not however think only of their own salvation and the joys of the communion of souls. They thought also of the necessity, imposed by the success of Protestantism, the disorders in the Church, and the canons of the Council of Trent, of propaganda and of the purification of conduct and the heart. Though they knew that true religion consisted in the transformation of the soul by inward piety and the creation of personality from the beginning, they also showed their intention of restoring the faith by means of these truths.

They concentrated their efforts on the priesthood and on the education of women and young men. Hence the foundation of that most important institution the *Oratoire* (1611), conceived by Bérulle, realised partly by him and partly by Father Condren, and originally intended to be not a Congregation but a centre for retirement and study, in order to arm the clergy with knowledge and faith for their fight against indifference,

error, and vice. To indicate the influence of this foundation,
which holds such a great place in the intellectual history of
France, it is only necessary to mention that St Vincent de Paul,
Olier the first head of the Seminary of Saint-Sulpice, Eudes the
founder of the Eudists, and the Abbess of Port-Royal, at the
outset of their careers all sought support, direction, and advice
from the *Oratoire*. It was to it that the zealous bishops and the
rich Catholics appealed for help in the organisation of seminaries
for priests in the provinces, which, hard as it is to believe, were
almost totally lacking and which were moreover promoted by
Olier of Saint-Sulpice, and Bourdoise and Compaing, disciples
of St François de Sales, at Saint-Nicolas-du-Chardonnet. After
this there sprang up innumerable Congregations and institutions devoted to the education of girls, *Les Filles de Notre-Dame*
at Bordeaux and Nancy, *Les Filles de la Croix* of the Order of
Ste Croix, *Les Hospitalières de Saint-Joseph*, and *Les Hospitalières
de la Providence*, devoted to the care of orphan girls.

It has been estimated that in 1626 there were 1500 convents
in France, and the greater part of them were foundations belonging to new Orders. The open spaces around all the principal
towns about this time became covered with religious houses,
the traces of which after 300 years may still be easily discovered, and in some cases the very buildings put to other
uses since the time of the Revolution. Of these new Orders
barely a quarter were given up to cloistered prayer, forming as it
were primitive cells; the remaining three-quarters threw their
doors open to the world in the form of poor-houses or hospitals,
kept up, at the instigation of Marie de' Medici, by brothers of
charity and especially the mendicant friars; or of houses for
study like those of the Oratorians, or the reformed Benedictines
of Saint-Vanne and Saint-Maur, or the Ursulines or the Cla-
risses; or of seminaries and Missions for France or abroad—all
instruments of that counter-reformation of which the plan
had been drawn up in Italy by S. Carlo Borromeo and which
was realised in France.

In this revival of monarchist and religious faith is to be found
the explanation of the interest taken by French Catholics of this
period in the Gallican Doctrines, which were brought forward
again in the writings of Pithou and Richer, and bitterly fought

over by the Jesuits and Ultramontanes on the one side and the
Parlement and the Sorbonne on the other. Gallicanism, opposed
to the Council of Trent, and including already several different
parties (the lawyers and theologians of the University of Paris
and bishops discontented with the independence of the monastic
Orders) was derived from a desire for national independence,
from confidence and sensitive pride in the intelligence and piety
of the French Catholics and in the direction and power in
religious matters of the most Christian King. It was distasteful
to the Holy See, which was anxious to guard the unity of the
Church; but it was agreeable to a great number of French
people who long remained as much attached to the idea of a
Gallican Church as to that of their monarchy, because they
saw in it the crowning glory of the moral greatness and unity
of France.

Twenty years had barely passed before it became apparent
that there were very great difficulties in the execution of this
work, the realisation of which had been striven for by the good
will of so many different and even opposing parties. If they were
all agreed as to the end in view, they differed as to the means;
should there be Orders attached to Rome, or bishops with their
clergy? zealous laymen, or the increase of religious Orders? Pope,
or King? The increase in monastic Orders which competed with
each other to their own undoing, and the growth of whose
power disturbed the Bishops of the Assembly of 1625, and on
the other hand the persistent apathy of the prelates of high
degree seems to have compromised the activities of this
Catholic movement of counter-reformation, which moreover
was conducted with too little co-ordination, or rather was left
to itself and the grace of God.

It was out of all this uncertainty that was born, in another
small group of mystics whose history has only recently been
revealed through the work of M. Allier and M. Rébelliau, the
Compagnie du Saint-Sacrement de l'Autel (1627). The founder,
Henri de Lévis, Duc de Ventadour, four years later separated
from his wife, who was childless, and built a convent for her at
Chambéry where she became a Carmelite, while he himself was
made a Canon of Paris. He still mingled with society, but in
conjunction with a Capuchin and his friend, the Abbé de

Grignan, he formed a project for constituting a Society of which
secrecy was to be the essence, with a very small number of
members, mostly laymen, united for the purpose of charity,
the care of the poor, combating immorality, impiety, and heresy,
the restoration of churches, the maintenance of missions and
seminaries, and, last but not least, influencing the powers of
Church and State. It was to be "a perpetual supervisor of all
that took place which might contribute to the glory of God."
As soon as it was constituted, this Society began to spread
in the provinces, at Marseilles, Poitiers, Lyons, Rouen, in
all nearly sixty towns, and until 1665 exercised an influence on
French society and the Church which was all the stronger
because it was hidden.

This pious enterprise was the signal for other and infinitely
more important manifestations of Catholic energy, which had
many things in common, though each had its own peculiar
characteristic—I mean the movements started by Saint-Cyran,
St Vincent de Paul, and Father Joseph. Duvergier de Hauranne, Abbé de Saint-Cyran, the friend and supporter of the
pious Mère Angélique, brought to Port-Royal the doctrine of
Jansenius, bishop of Ypres (1636), a doctrine which was soon to
be condemned by the Holy See. He found an atmosphere already
prepared by the Oratorians, who had accustomed the nuns to
fortify themselves with metaphysics and hard study. He immediately won over the brothers of Angélique, Arnauld d'Andilly
and Antoine Arnauld, a doctor of the Sorbonne, and his
nephews, Antoine Le Maître and Le Maître de Sacy, who all
belonged to that Parisian *bourgeoisie* which delighted in austere
practices and strong ideas, hated compromise and moral laxity,
for which it criticised the clergy and especially the Jesuits,
was confident of its own virtue, its charity, its zeal for good,
for truth, and for the regeneration of the Church. Mysticism was common to all the reformers, but Saint-Cyran and
the *Solitaires* of Port-Royal gave to it a solid foundation which
the others, such as St François de Sales and his disciples,
lacked; and this foundation was penitence, by means of which
Divine Grace is granted and continued. It was at once a source
of strength and of weakness, and the cause of the considerable
influence which they exercised through their somewhat arrogant

virtue and learning, and of the implacable enmity which they brought down upon themselves.

St Vincent de Paul on the other hand had only friends and admirers. In spite of Saint-Cyran's love for the poor, charity had not yet found its apostle. All the ardour and devotion to the work of comforting human misery that there was in this movement of religious regeneration was summed up and concentrated in the figure of this peasant from the Landes, who was the spirit of charity personified. Beginning as a tutor in great houses, notably the Gondi family, and the protégé of Cardinals Bérulle and Duperron, Vincent de Paul had no ambition for ecclesiastical honours, nor did the life of a mystic appeal to him. A modest country priest, in the Ain, he began there by forming a *Confrérie des Servantes des Pauvres*, which the Gondi family afterwards established in their domains and in Paris. In 1622 he went to Marseilles to comfort the sufferings of the galley-convicts. Between 1627 and 1632, at the *Collège des Bons Enfants*, he created the *Congrégation de Saint-Lazare* "for the religious education of the poor peasants of the fields," from amongst the members of which he drew the best disciples for his work. Soon after in the Marillac family, which like that of the Gondi was devoted to the Church, he met the admirable Mme Legras, a widow, who finally organised, in 1634, *Les Filles de la Charité*, and *Les Sœurs de Saint-Vincent de Paul*, whose devotion to the poor and the sick for three hundred years never relaxed. In 1648 he entrusted to them, with one of the most eloquent appeals ever known, "The Foundlings" (*Les Enfants Trouvés*). At 73 years of age he sent out his army of missionaries and sisters of charity through all the provinces devastated by civil war from 1648 to 1654 to combat the terrible sufferings of the poor people. By begging he collected the wherewithal to fight famine and disease. Truly during this tragic period, this minister of the unfortunate, officially recognised in 1651 by Anne of Austria, who admitted him to her Councils, was in the Governor of Saint-Quentin's words the "Father of his Country."

It is in no way derogatory to the greatness of St Vincent de Paul and his associates, and it is only just to the Port-Royalists, whose charity was somewhat thrown into the shade by their learning, to recall the work of a rival and competitor, a friend and disciple of the *Solitaires*, Maignant de Bernières, a magistrate of Rouen. This *procureur des pauvres* formed a committee of charitable men and in 1649 addressed to all Catholic magistrates his *Relations sur la Misère*, resulting at first in very great benefit, although this work was afterwards restricted by the severity of the Crown towards the Jansenists.

The influence of Father Joseph in politics has for long been more celebrated than his influence in religious matters, which has been brought to light by the researches of M. Fagniez. This historian goes so far as to say that he was the real founder of the missions which were at first devoted to the conversion of French Protestants, but which after 1628, when Gregory XV, under the influence of the Capuchin friar Girolamo da Narni, had founded the *Congrégation de la Propagande*, were sent out to the Mahomedans of the Orient, where the Jesuits had attempted unsuccessfully to establish themselves. Barely ten years later the Capuchin Missions of the Orient were flourishing at Constantinople, Smyrna, Aleppo, Beyrout, Bagdad, and Cairo. By the end of the 17th century they had developed still further and far surpassed in number and importance the Jesuit and Carmelite missions which later lent a hand in the propagation of Christianity. This was not the crusade against the Infidels for the deliverance of the Holy Land of which Father Joseph dreamed all his life long; nevertheless these were deeds, with enduring results, accomplished for the sake of their religion by Frenchmen who by their great missionary enthusiasm throughout the world—in America, Canada, Africa, Morocco, and Egypt, as well as in Asia—won for their country the title of "the eldest daughter of the Church."

The middle of the 17th century was truly one of the greatest epochs in the history of the French Church just as much as of the French monarchy, during which, with Pascal, St Vincent de Paul and Bossuet, all the forces of religion, propaganda, charity, thought, and literature were concentrated. The one thing which apparently was lacking was unity, and this depended upon the return of the "so-called" Reformers to the discipline and traditions of Rome.

The Edict of Nantes was revised after the revolt of La Rochelle and Languedoc in July 1629, when by the Peace of Alais it was established throughout the kingdom that "the diversity of religious sentiments, according to the expression of Antoine Arnaud, was not incompatible with civil and political peace." Richelieu, now a Cardinal and a friend of Father Joseph and Olier, was by no means of the opinion that such diversity was the ideal state of things, or that it must be considered final by the Catholics. The influence of time and persuasion might have done much, but he could not wait. Immediately after the Peace, Louis XIII ordered the Capuchins to convert the Protestant rebels, and he suppressed the subsidies to the reformed ministers and colleges. Moreover Richelieu thought that a solemn conclave of the ministers of both religions could bring about a reunion of the two Churches, which had been accepted already in principle by the pastors of the south and west. This policy of the Cardinal, who was compelled to give most of his attention to foreign affairs, while on the other hand the Protestants were worn out after so many years of civil war, had at least the advantage of giving the Protestants eight years of tranquillity and respite, during which they developed their material welfare and behaved like good and faithful subjects of the King (1631–1638).

But if Richelieu and the King were tolerant, this was not the case with those Catholics to whom tolerance seemed lack of zeal, and who, renewing their ardour from the very moment when the Peace of Alais was signed, bestirred themselves for the defence of their faith. In 1638 the *Compagnie du Saint-Sacrement* set to work all the secret influences they had with the King's Council, the *Parlements*, the ministers, intendants and bishops, to organise warfare against the Reformers, vexatious and clandestine warfare, with a view to destroying one by one all the privileges granted by the Edicts with regard to religious worship, preaching, the possession of churches, and holding Consistories. "It was," says the historian of this Society, "about the year 1645 that the annihilation of heresy began." Mazarin, however, who during the Fronde had tested the loyalty of the Protestants, granted them by the Declaration of St Germain (May 1652) a renewed confirmation of the Edict of Nantes. The Catholics did not lay down their arms. At the Assembly

of the Clergy in 1655 they showed their hand by their anger
and their exacting demands, setting forth the plans of the
Church against the members of the so-called Reformed Religion.
The government had to resign itself to the despatch of commissaries to the provinces in order to inform the Protestants
that their religion was only tolerated and to report on instances
of disobedience to the Edicts which were made the reasons or
pretexts of the persecution which was being prepared. Louis XIV,
by the advice of his Jesuit confessor and under pressure from
the bishops who were influenced by the Order in accordance
with the wishes of the Pope, although still somewhat restrained
by the fidelity of his Protestant subjects and Colbert's esteem
for their industrial activity, began, from 1660 on, to take arbitrary action against the Reformed Church. More than a
hundred churches were destroyed and the Protestant schools
were closed. National unity was to be achieved along the lines
desired by the devout Catholics and the mystics, who saw no
hope of salvation outside the Roman Church.

As soon as the State, forgetting its promises of tolerance,
consented to undertake the task, the destruction of a religion
became a possibility. To reach the individual conscience and
convict it of error was a more difficult matter, and not to be
accomplished by decrees of justice or violent executions.
Preaching, controversy, and example were the sole means and
these had been successfully employed by the Catholic missions
and doctors of the Church since 1620.

Port-Royal was devoted entirely to this work. "Jansen,
Saint-Cyran, Saci, Arnaud, Pascal," wrote M. Brunetière, "believed they were working for the same end as Vincent de Paul,
Olier, Bérulle. The Jansenist victory, after *Les Provinciales*,
fell little short of being in the 17th century the triumph of the
idea of Catholic Christianity." By its educational system, controversy, moral teaching, and literary works, Port-Royal influenced profoundly the whole of the 17th century. It was in
their little schools that Racine, Pomponne, and so many others
were trained; from the books of Nicole on *La Perpétuité de la Foi*
Bossuet derived his method of argument, and Bourdaloue the
grave and serious style of his finest sermons. Under this
influence, which from 1658 to 1668 was very great on the

educated classes, a great number of the Protestant nobility and *bourgeoisie* were brought back to the Catholic faith. The most notable conversion was that of the illustrious Maréchal de Turenne, who in 1661 had refused to accept the Constable's sword at the price of abjuring his religion. Jansenism had apparently absorbed all the forces of religious sentiment to concentrate them against heresy.

At the very time when Port-Royal was playing such an important part, the storm, which had been threatening for the last fifteen years, broke over the Convent of *la mère* Angélique, and her nuns were scattered by the whirlwind. Sainte-Beuve has related this dramatic story, the first act of which began with the Papal Bull *Cum occasione*, which, at the request of the Sorbonne and the bishops, condemned the Jansenist doctrine (May 31, 1653). The second act was the reply of Arnaud to the effect that the incriminating clauses were not in the book of Jansenius (1655) and the famous intervention of Pascal on the side of Arnaud with his *Provinciales*; the third act was the obligation imposed by the Assembly of the Clergy upon the nuns and the Jansenist bishops of signing a formal declaration to the effect that the condemned clauses were in the *Augustinus* (1661); the fourth act was composed of the hesitations and final refusal of the nuns who were dispersed in 1665; and lastly came the resistance of the Jansenist Bishop of Alet, Pavillon, supported since 1665 by a portion of the clergy, which seemed more serious to the government and forced it to make, through the agency of Lionne and the Papal nuncio, a patched up peace, September 28, 1668, without there being either victor or vanquished.

This quarrel following immediately after the Fronde of the princes and the *Parlements* was a Fronde in the ecclesiastical world. The Jesuits, who dreaded the increasing influence of the Jansenists, envied them their schools and their learning, while they hated the asceticism of the *Solitaires*, so contrary to the methods of their own order, and were artful enough to drive them to the heresy to which they were inclined by their dogmatic assurance, their polemical ardour, and their desire for martyrdom. The unpardonable sin of the Jansenists was that they had been *Frondeurs* not only in matters of religion

but in politics; they were more culpable on account of their
parliamentary origin and their relations with the great lords
and the great ladies than in their doctrines. Mazarin never
forgave them for having, in 1649, taken part in the revolt of
the *Parlement* and for being protected by the Cardinal de Retz.
Louis XIV declared that Mazarin on his death-bed advised him
to use all his authority against the Jansenists, adding that the
Church was threatened with a schism by men who were all the
more dangerous because they could be very useful. Cardinal
de Retz, from inclination or interest, favoured this new sect,
unless we prefer to say that they favoured him. The French
Crown was certainly afraid to silence the eloquent pen of the
Jansenists, but it imagined that they could be forced to abandon
their controversy regarding Divine Grace and continue only their
victorious attacks on Protestantism, in the same way as the
Parlements had been confined to their judicial functions and
the aristocrats to their court duties. But these ascetics had
nothing in common with the privileged classes, and in their
case the result was quite opposite. Protestantism was delivered
from its most redoubtable adversaries, while the Jansenist opposition did not disappear with Port-Royal. The whole century
was profoundly influenced by Jansenism.

Being deprived of the help of the Jansenists in 1671, from
this time onwards the implacable enemies of the Reformers,
the bishops and their faithful followers began to employ forceful measures, which, becoming daily more frequent and more
violent, especially after 1679, were the prelude to the Revocation
of the Edict of Nantes—offers of money, violence, abduction of
children, gradual destruction of chapels and schools, use of
military force, which began by order of the intendants in 1682,
and persecution of the pastors. It has been with justice pointed
out that when Louis XIV, in October 1685, signed the Revocation at Fontainebleau he had been convinced by the clergy,
Louvois, Mme de Maintenon, and the intendants, that the
majority of his Protestant subjects had been converted, and
that by one final and easy effort, directed especially against
the Reformed ministers who had been expelled from the
country, he could achieve religious unity and thereby gain
lasting glory. If it be argued that he was, to begin with, unable

to imagine that the whole Protestant population would abandon their homes and their commerce at the call of their exiled leaders preferring freedom of conscience to a tyrannical fatherland, that later he was annoyed by this exodus as by a criminal desertion fatal to the prosperity of the country, and that in order to prevent it he gave orders to his ministers for still greater severity, the answer is that there were very few Catholics in France who did not ratify by their applause the acts and decrees of Louis XIV, the conqueror of heresy. Bossuet and Nicole both adored the plans of the Almighty who was pleased to reveal by the dispersion of "our Protestants this mystery of iniquity and to purge France of these monsters." A philosopher like La Bruyère congratulated Louis XIV on having "banished a religion that was false, disloyal, and hostile to the monarchy."

The French, who were more and more inclined to believe that the greatness of the kingdom was bound up with the material and religious power of the King, were indifferent to the means employed in view of the results achieved by the Peace of Nimwegen and the Revocation. Daguesseau told Louis XIV that he should seek after that "two-fold spirit which forms great kings and great bishops." Gallicanism proclaimed alike in fact and law the triumph of these aspirations when the French bishops in the Assembly of the Clergy of 1682, provoked by the discussion of the Regalian Right, formulated the *Four Articles*, which declared that the King was independent of the Pope in temporal matters, that the nation had the right to defend its customs and constitution against the Holy See, whose infallibility, unless supported by the Councils of the Church, was not a part of Church dogma. The court of Rome, although it refused to agree to the decisions of the clergy of France, was obliged to wait for nine years, until January 9, 1691, to condemn, annul, and cancel the Four Articles which were the charter of Gallicanism.

In the Council of the King, who daily became more devout under the intimate influence of Mme de Maintenon, consulted at once as Queen and spiritual director, religious affairs became affairs of State. To these the King not only wished but felt compelled, by virtue of his Christian office, to give his personal

attention. By embarking on this policy, as he felt bound to do
more and more from this time on, the King stirred up opposition such as he no longer met with in political matters. And in
the end the Church suffered just as much harm as the Crown
from the constant need, after 1690, of resorting to the authority
of the Crown to settle internal disputes as to doctrine in which
too often influence played a part.

Henceforward the King was assisted by what might be called
a Ministry for Ecclesiastical Affairs, which became more and
more necessary as Louis XIV decided to give them more
attention. Up to 1685 such matters had generally been dealt
with by a *Comité de Conscience*, composed mainly of two persons,
the King's confessor, who was always a Jesuit (since 1675 Père
la Chaise), and the Archbishop of Paris, M. de Harlay, appointed
to this Committee through the influence of Père Tellier, the
predecessor of Père la Chaise. So long as Père Tellier lived
everything worked harmoniously, but with the arrival of his
successor in 1678 discord began, and little by little Père la Chaise
tried to monopolise the right of putting before the King the
names of candidates for benefices and ecclesiastical offices, on
which chiefly depended his influence and importance. On the
other hand it is difficult to-day to realise the important moral
influence wielded by the Archbishop of Paris, who was President
of the Assemblies and the "born leader," as they put it, of the
French clergy. The dispute about Quietism, which from 1695 to
1699 brought into opposition the two greatest churchmen of
the time, Bossuet and Fénelon, originated in the action of the
French clergy, who demanded that the Pope should condemn
the doctrine of Miguel Molinos, which had been tolerated
by the Holy See but condemned in France in 1678. It was
the Archbishop of Paris who instituted proceedings against
Madame Guyon, who had introduced this doctrine into France
and then into Saint-Cyr, and it was he who caused her to be
imprisoned in Vincennes in 1695. Père la Chaise on the contrary
seemed to encourage the resistance of Fénelon, the friend and
defender of Mme Guyon, as did Cardinal de Bouillon at Rome,
feeling that the King's interference in a question of doctrine
was not favourably received at the Papal court. It was M. de
Noailles, the successor of M. de Harlay (August 1695), who,

supported by the theology of Bossuet, took steps to have Fénelon's book in favour of Madame Guyon *Les Maximes de la vie intérieure* condemned. The court of Rome resisted nearly two years against pressure from the King and the clergy of France until the year 1699, encouraged in its opposition by Cardinal de Bouillon, who betrayed the King's orders and was punished for his disobedience by his disgrace without pardon. It was the Archbishop of Paris who had to pay the penalty for all this, when the King's confessor, annoyed because his consent was not asked when M. de Noailles was nominated, accused him before the King of being the accomplice of the Jansenists. "You have made your confessor a minister," said Fénelon to Louis XIV. "Bishops' quarrels," said the Princess Palatine, and she was not mistaken. It was a matter of grave consequence for the monarchy and for the Church that the Crown had to decide what was right and wrong in questions of dogma or discipline. The reign of Louis XIV did not close with the 17th century, and during the whole of the next century the French monarchy was entangled in religious disputes which revived the opposition of the *Parlements,* and caused the Catholic Church to lose a part of the advantages which it had gained during the 17th century by the growth of religion, of missions, of charity and Christian knowledge.

Eighteenth century

Jansenism, the Parlements, and the Crown. The 17th century was a great period in the history of religion as well as in that of the monarchy, while the 18th century, which was to end in a social, political, and religious crisis, is generally considered by contrast to be the period of the *philosophes*, the struggle between reason and religion and the institutions of the past, and the preparation, by literary attacks and propaganda, for the French Revolution. Without wishing to diminish the importance of the works of these 18th century writers, which Taine has perhaps exaggerated, I think that Rocquain (in *L'Esprit révolutionnaire avant la Révolution*) is nearer the truth when he says: "the change of opinion which produced the Revolution does not date from the *philosophes*. The entire century prepared the way for the catastrophe."

In the first year of the century Philip V took possession of the Spanish throne. One of the first things his grandfather asked him to do, in token of the alliance of the two crowns, was to order the arrest, at Brussels, of Father Quesnel, "the leader of Jansenism, a sect pernicious to the Church and to the State," and of his accomplice Father Gerberon (May 30, 1703).

After the peace of 1668 the Church of Rome had apparently ceased to attack the Jansenists. The Pope, Innocent XI, admitted that it was no longer possible to designate as Jansenists those "who had signed the formulary because they lived more austerely than other Catholics." Innocent XII was of the same opinion. The Jansenists, according to an expression of that time, "had made a submission of silence and respect to the decisions of the Church, with which the Church was satisfied." This external deference permitted them, through the influence of their virtues and learning, to re-establish themselves in the society of the 17th century. The *Oratoire* rallied to their methods of teaching, and continued their work. The Reformed Benedictines of Saint-Vanne and Saint-Maur adopted their scholarly methods. The principal prelates, and the most eminent for their goodness, protected them. And one writer has gone so far as to say that the "entire 17th century owed its severe morality and greatness to them."

There were however among the Jansenists certain men who could not accept this policy of mental reservation, upon which was based the compromise arranged in 1668, and were always ready to revolt against the Formulary; the Arnauds—the Bishop of Angers, who was censured in 1677 by the King for having denounced it, and the great Doctor Antoine Arnaud, who was threatened with imprisonment—and certain Oratorians like Desmares or Quesnel. As though he discerned that the chief danger to his friends came from Versailles rather than from Rome, on account of the King's bitterness against the Fronde, Arnaud decided to quit France and retired to Brussels in 1679, whither Father Quesnel followed him in 1681 and, after his death in 1693, succeeded to the leadership of the party. The transfer of the Jansenist capital from France to Belgium seemed to reassure Louis XIV, who in 1691 recalled to his Councils the minister Arnauld de Pomponne, and took into his confidence his son-in-law Torcy, the nephew of Colbert. The Jesuits were doubt-less indignant at this reconciliation of their adversaries with the King and the Holy See, but they felt helpless. Father Quesnel's book, *Les Réflexions Morales sur le Nouveau Testament*, a collection of pious meditations made at the *Oratoire* in 1671 and filled with the spirit of Port-Royal, became the handbook of the clergy, recommended by bishops, and familiar to the pious, even to Mme de Maintenon. "In 1693 it had a brilliant success at court and in the Church."

When in 1695 M. de Noailles, who in their eyes was tainted with Jansenism, became Archbishop of Paris, the rage of the Jesuits knew no bounds. Père la Chaise had not been con-sulted. Was the Church of France going to be officially handed over to the Jansenists or remain subject to the influence of their own Order? Henceforth they had only one idea, to force the prelate to declare himself, to choose between them and their enemies. The Jansenists made the mistake of lending them-selves to these tactics by their own conduct. "The designs of the Almighty seem extraordinary," wrote Father Quesnel joy-fully, when he heard of the appointment of the Archbishop. He imagined, and so did the extreme Jansenists, that the hour was approaching when from Brussels, with some support from Paris, which with its *curés* and parliamentary *bourgeoisie* re-mained a latent centre of Jansenism, their party would com-pletely conquer the kingdom. Racine, sent as envoy from M. de Noailles as early as August 30, 1695, in vain warned his aunt, the Superior of Port-Royal-des-Champs, that she must "guard against making too public a display of her eagerness and joy, which would only have the effect of preventing the Archbishop from carrying out his good intentions." From Brussels the Benedictine Gerberon published a book, which had remained in manuscript in the Jansenist archives, by the most uncom-promising successor of Saint-Cyran, his nephew Barcos, entitled *Exposition de la Foi Catholique touchant la Grâce et la Pré-destination*, 1696. This let loose a storm which gave the Society of Jesus the opportunity of forcing M. de Noailles to choose between the doctrine of the Church and the doctrine of Port-Royal.

Gerberon was in Flanders with Father Quesnel. It was quite

easy to suggest to Louis XIV that this revival of Jansenism
in the Netherlands was a new *Fronde* which would stir up
further disturbances and opposition in Paris with the complicity of the Archbishop. Père la Chaise and Fénelon, who
sought his revenge on M. de Harlay for the condemnation of
Quietism, did not remain idle; Gerberon and Quesnel were
arrested; the Jansenist archives were searched for compromising
documents, which were brought to the King. Some years later
Mme de Maintenon wrote to her niece that it had taken the
King "ten years, reading every evening, to go through the
papers seized in Brussels."

The rigorous measures adopted by Louis XIV with the idea of
preventing the outbreak of a religious and political insurrection
in Paris at the end of his reign started a revolt which lasted
for sixty years and of which the Jesuits were the first victims
and the monarchy the second. As early as the middle of 1703
Louis XIV urged the Pope to promulgate a new constitution
against Jansenism, a Bull "which should treat only of Jansenism and the obligation of the faithful to condemn it not
merely by a respectful silence but by a formal adhesion of
heart and mind."

The Bull *Vineam Domini* (1705) was the result; it was
welcomed with delight by the Jesuits, and Cardinal de Noailles
tried to forestall its effect by himself condemning beforehand
the policy of respectful silence adopted by the Jansenists. But
instead of putting an end to the eternal dispute regarding
Divine Grace, the promulgation of the Bull extended and
generalised the quarrel. The King was obliged to apply once
more to the Pope to overcome the resistance of Father Quesnel,
who had escaped from Belgium and taken refuge in Holland.
The response was the Bull *Unigenitus*, which set forth 101
heretical clauses contained in *Les Réflexions Morales* of
Father Quesnel, a book which had enjoyed the approval of the
French clergy for more than thirty years (September 8, 1713).

The heresies of the Jansenists had no interest for the *Parlement*. Moreover the *Parlement* no longer possessed the right
of remonstrance in political affairs. They remonstrated however
on religious questions not as regards matter but as regards
form, when this was contrary to Gallican customs, and under

cover of these formal objections the Jansenists were able to continue the quarrel as to questions of matter.

Through a secret memorandum of Fénelon we know something of the leaders and the main body of the Jansenist army which grew up in the early years of the 18th century in opposition to the Pope and the King: Cardinal de Noailles, and Cardinal de Coislin de la Tour, M. Duguet, the Superior of the *Oratoire*, numerous bishops, the students and masters of the Sorbonne, the Benedictines, Carmelites, many Recollets and Minims, the Lazarists, certain ministers of the crown, Pontchartrain and Torcy, the whole *Parlement* of Paris with its first President and its *Procureur-général* the eloquent, indomitable Daguesseau. The inferior clergy, the parish priests of Paris, of whom Noailles was the head, and who had to obey their passionate demands, actuated partly by the spirit of opposition habitual to Paris since the Fronde, and partly by compassion for the poor nuns of Port-Royal, whose home and tombs were destroyed by the lieutenant of police (1709–1711), refused to accept the Papal Bulls or the Royal Edicts. Jansenism, which had long been confined to the elect, at the death of Louis XIV was capable of exciting the feelings of the populace, of awakening in them a sense of their rights against the abuses of authority and of arming them for the defence of their convictions.

This transfer of Jansenism from the upper classes to less cultivated, more modest, and more ardent circles, has not been sufficiently noticed. It is usual to see only the society of great nobles and educated men, thanks to the authors of memoirs and other writers whom it is much easier to study, but these men gradually became detached from religious questions which bored them and at which they were more and more inclined to smile. The free-thinkers, or *libertins*, began once more to grow bold during these religious disputes of the end of the 17th century, which presented the spectacle of one and the same King revoking the Edict of Nantes and nearly causing a Schism with Rome, and then running the risk of another Schism with the *Parlement* on account of his submission to the Holy See. But at the same time that the *philosophes* were laughing at the quarrels of the theologians in the salons of Mme Geoffrin and Mlle de Lespinasse the Parisian populace were crowding into the cemetery of St Médard to the tomb of a mere deacon, a Jansenist, who died in the odour of sanctity in 1731, to witness the miracles wrought by his blessed remains. In 1749 similar crowds attended the funeral of the Jansenists to whom the Archbishop of Paris, Christophe de Beaumont, had refused the sacrament unless it was administered by orthodox priests. So great was the anger of the mob that Louis XV was threatened with murder by the hand of a second Ravaillac and took fright, and men talked of going to burn down the castle of Versailles erected at the expense of the people (1750). The Archbishop of Paris, who obstinately continued to refuse the sacraments and confession to the Jansenists, was insulted by the market-women, who wanted to drown "the man who refused the sacrament." A hundred of them mounted guard for a whole month at the house of the Jansenist priest of their quarter, who was interfered with by the police. The populace of Paris and in the provinces rose in support of the magistrates who sued the priests, friendly to the Jesuits, who defended the Bull *Unigenitus*.

The King railed against the *Parlement* and the *philosophes*, whom he considered responsible for all the disturbances at the end of 1753, but according to d'Argenson, "Everything is making for a great revolution, in the Church as well as in the government," and he adds, "it is all due to the Bull *Unigenitus* and not to the English Philosophy, which has affected barely a hundred philosophers in Paris."

On the other hand it must be pointed out that in Roman and Catholic circles a miracle, the visions of Marie Alacoque at Paray le Monial in 1690, had excited the public and led to the establishment of the new cult of the Sacred Heart of Jesus, recommended in 1731 by Languet, the orthodox Bishop of Soissons, and soon afterwards by the Holy See itself, in which the religion of love was coupled with a fierce hatred of heresy, be it Jansenist or Protestant.

When the *Parlement* arraigned the Jesuits, who by the bankruptcy of Père Lavalette were convicted of neglecting their religious mission in order to engage in commerce (1761), it was above all their doctrine that was denounced "as perverse, destructive of every principle of religion and even of probity, injurious to Christian morality, and pernicious to civil society." Was not this, after an interval of a hundred years, the revenge of Pascal who had been "outraged by the freedom with which the Jesuits undermined the most sacred rules of Christian conduct, attacking religion in the heart and depriving it of the very spirit which gave it life, saying that the love of God is not necessary for salvation"? *Les Provinciales* triumphed in the decrees of the *Parlement*.

The grandson of Louis XIV, at the request of Jansenist magistrates, expelled the Jesuits from his kingdom, suppressed their schools, handing them over to the Oratorians, and confiscated their possessions (1764–65), and soon afterward by the seizure of the Comtat Venaissin compelled the Papacy to suppress the Order itself in 1773. The Company, as Voltaire expressed it, "was stoned with the ruins of Port-Royal." The King had he been able to prevent it would have preferred not to procure this dangerous victory for the *Parlements*, to whom during the last sixty years the struggle against the Ultramontane party had given a pretext for sharing in the government of the State as well as of the Church. In 1765 he was obliged to assert his authority, in a *lit de justice*, over the Parliamentarians "who were aiming at making the nation a body separate from the monarchy, and claiming in the name of the nation part of the sovereign power." In 1771 he punished them; he suppressed the *Parlements* in their turn, to the great joy of the devout Catholics, who had overthrown Choiseul and put the Duc d'Aiguillon in power.

This double act of authority was not destined to benefit the monarchy, which had only worked for the *philosophes*, whose criticisms and doctrines after 1770 had more influence on public opinion than the royal authority. The growth of the philosophic spirit, which had as easy a task in pouring ridicule on these monkish quarrels as on the abuses of the *ancien régime* or the extravagance of the privileged classes, was not at all favourable to religion. In place of the ideal of royal authority and unity of the Church, each working for the benefit of the other, around which for nearly two centuries had rallied the majority of Frenchmen, the *philosophes* proposed not merely for Frenchmen but for the whole of mankind "an ideal of

Reason, Justice, and Liberty inspired by the recently discovered sense of human dignity."

They drew up the Declaration of the Rights of Man, of which one of the essential articles was freedom of conscience and the right of every one to practise and propagate the doctrines which were dear to him.

It would however be a mistake to suggest that the mass of the nation rallied round this philosophic programme during the reign of Louis XVI. Just as Frenchmen as a whole remained attached to the monarchy and could imagine no other possible form of government, so also they clung, whether Catholic, Jansenist, or Protestant, to some form of religion. However the report of the proceedings of the Assembly of the Clergy in 1786 calls attention to the fact that there was a falling off in the observance of Sunday and Holy festivals in Paris and in the provinces. And in the same year, the *Correspondance Secrète*, reporting a similar complaint, declares that indifference to religion was to be found among the masses. The national *cahiers* in 1789, which undoubtedly gave a faithful reflection of the national state of mind and were the "authentic will and testament" of French society of the *ancien régime*, show a desire to conserve the Catholic religion, to which the nation remained attached, in spite of the vices of the clergy, as a national form of worship, shorn of intolerance and servitude to the court and the privileged classes, and regulated by faith and morality.

§ V. THE FRENCH REVOLUTION AND NAPOLEON

General character of the French Revolution, 1789–1799

The French Revolution was neither a sudden impulse, nor an accident. It happened in conformity with the history of France, not in opposition to it. It did not interrupt but accelerated a progressive movement, which had been unduly retarded by circumstances and mistakes, and which was driven to violence by the antagonism of a bad policy. It achieved the physical and moral unity of France, which had been prepared and happily initiated by the kings. Its original aim was to destroy absolute rule and to establish liberty under a limited monarchy, after the English pattern. The failure of this endeavour brought about the establishment of a democratic Republic, which, under war conditions turned to terrorism, and after military victory became *bourgeois*, finally ending in the dictatorship of Napoleon Bonaparte. From the social point of view, the Revolution consisted in the suppression of what was called the feudal system, in the emancipation of the individual, in greater division of landed property, the abolition of the privileges of noble birth, the establishment of equality, the simplification of life, as well as in an unsuccessful attempt to organise popular education. The French Revolution differed from other revolutions in being not merely national, for it aimed at benefiting all humanity.

The Constitutional Monarchy, 1789–1792

France and her king. We presume that the reader has some idea of the unspeakable confusion of the Old Order in 1789, under a monarchy which had become as powerless as it was absolute. Partial reforms, such as those attempted by Turgot and Necker, were bound to fail. There was need of fundamental and general reform, in fact, of a revolution. The whole French nation had faith in the monarchy as the instrument for this complete regeneration. The reigning king, Louis XVI, was popular, in the first place, because he was the King, the hereditary leader, born to protect his people from their oppressors, and also because he had a reputation for goodness and kindness. When financial difficulties obliged him to summon the States General, which had not been assembled since the beginning of the 17th century, the French people greeted him with a unanimous cry of love and gratitude, expressed in the *cahiers* of resolutions and petitions which were prepared for this occasion. In simple confidence, the ignorant mass of the people expected that he would place himself at the head of the great reform movement, show himself to be king of the nation and not only king of a privileged class, establish a constitution, govern according to the laws, and grant the petitions of the *cahiers*, which were more moderate than radical in tone.

Unfortunately, Louis XVI was not equal to his task. He had

neither the genius of Henry IV, nor the pliant mind of his own
brother, the future Louis XVIII. He was not a stupid man, but
he had a narrow outlook. Being both feeble and obstinate, he
held it a point of honour not to relinquish any of the rights
inherited from his ancestors. His ideal was to rule despotically,
but benevolently. His wife, the Austrian Marie-Antoinette, encouraged him in his despotism, but certainly not in his benevolence, and she is partly responsible for his policy of resistance
to the people. The inadequacy of Louis XVI and the haughty
character of his wife were amongst the causes that contributed
to the extreme violence of the Revolution and its failure to
achieve all its aims.

**Oath of the Tennis-court. Taking of the Bastille. Municipal
Revolution.** If Louis, when the States General assembled, had
taken the part of the Commons against the two privileged
orders, he might have led the Revolution and strengthened the
Royal power by legalising it. He was urged to take this course
by Mirabeau, who proposed what he called a Royal Democracy.
But Louis turned a deaf ear to Mirabeau, as he had in former
days to Turgot. Under the influence of the queen and the court,
he foolishly took the part of the privileged classes. He supported the nobles, when they refused to vote as one Chamber
with the Commons, and he contemplated dissolving the States
General. The deputies of the Commons, assembled in a tennis-
court at Versailles, swore to resist despotism. After having
threatened them at a fruitless "Royal Session," the king was
obliged to yield: he agreed that the States General should be
formed into a National Assembly without any distinction of
orders, and in this case the Commons would have a majority.

This concession was only an apparent one; the king intended
to dissolve the Assembly. Troops were moved; Necker was
dismissed, and the Parisians, fearing a *coup d'état*, rose and on
July 14, 1789, seized the Bastille, a fortress and prison, which
seemed, as it were, a symbol of the iniquities of the Old Order,
or rather of despotism itself. The electors, who had been chosen
by Paris to nominate the deputies of the Commons to the States
General, formed themselves into a revolutionary Parisian
municipality; Louis was forced to give way; he went to the Hotel
de Ville, and bowed before the Revolution.

This kind of municipal revolution spread all through France
by some mysterious means, some sort of electric current, called
by contemporary writers "the great fear." Almost everywhere
and almost on the same day (generally the 29th or 30th of July)
a rumour spread in country districts as in towns that numerous
bands of armed brigands were approaching. Peasants and
townspeople, excited and trembling, rose, assembled, and armed
themselves. No brigands appeared. The wave of fear became a
wave of hope. They remained under arms, in volunteer bands,
which soon took the name of "National Guard." Revolutionary
municipalities came into being under the form of Committees,
which either joined the existing municipalities, or took their
places. The movement was not hostile to the king, whom the
people believed to be well-disposed to them, but misled by evil
counsellors. Some of the peasants at this time even shouted
"Long live the King," while they were attacking the châteaux.
But if it was not hostile to the king, it was not led by him; it was
spontaneous, popular, and national. This was the true, the real
Revolution, while the Revolution ordered by the Constituent
Assembly at Versailles, which is more celebrated in history, was
only a verbal one and less efficacious. But without the noble
declaration from a chosen few, would the mass of the people
have moved?

The Federations and National Unity. Contemporary writers
misunderstood this movement, which was truly and essentially
the Revolution. The partisans of the past, both in France and
abroad, grieved over the unhappy country, torn by anarchy, and
divided into thousands of independent municipal republics; it
seemed as though the end of the nation had come. In reality,
this was the beginning of a national organization, old and at the
same time, new: old, because it seemed like the resuscitation of
communal France of the 12th and 13th centuries; new, because
royal despotism had for long destroyed municipal life in France.
These revolutionary municipalities, regarded by superficial and
malevolent observers as independent and discordant units, were
animated as if by a centripetal force, which unified all their
efforts and directed them towards Paris. If national unity was
not the conscious and immediate aim of these Frenchmen who
rose at the time of " the great fear," their victory soon tended in

this direction, and, in less than a year, this was the result of their uprising.

How was it that people, then so little educated, who in country places did not even know how to write and read, were able to combine their unruly movements, so as to realise the political ideal which the kings had sought for centuries in the almost immediate unification of France, still split up into separate provinces? It was because these town and country people were guided and informed by a numerous and educated middle-class. There was no village in which there was not some well-read and book-possessing *bourgeois*, who spread abroad the ideas of Montesquieu, Voltaire, and Rousseau. Often it was this lettered *bourgeois* who had inspired, or even drawn up, the admirable parochial *cahiers*. He it was who in the municipal revolution possessed the feeling of nationality and enabled it to triumph.

The movement of French unification was begun almost at once by the communes, by means of "federations" and the National Guards. Ceremonies in honour of fraternity were held or oaths were taken at an altar of the country. At first, only a few communes of the same region or province united in this way; later inter-regional federations came into being, in which several provinces ratified the new patriotism. Such were, for instance, the federation of the Rhine at Strasburg, and the federation of Brittany and Anjou. All these federations were drawn to the historic capital, where they amalgamated, and, under the auspices of the Commune of Paris, on July 14, 1790, there was a great national federation in the Champ de Mars, when in the presence of the king the unity of France was established. France was no longer to be made up of separate people, such as the people of Provence, the Bretons, the Burgundians, the people of Franche-Comté: there was now to be one people only, the French people. By free consent, henceforth they were all one family, and swore an indissoluble friendship. That is why it was unbearable to the French, when Alsace and Metz were torn from France in 1871, and, for the same reason, there was so much joy when the people of Alsace and Metz were re-integrated in the French family.

Such is the origin of France as one nation, established by revolutionary means in 1790.

Establishment of Constitutional Monarchy. As these popular and communal movements manifested themselves, so the Constituent National Assembly translated the results into laws, attempting, however, to lessen as much as possible their very democratic character. As soon as the first episodes of " the great fear " insurrection became known, it was decided, in the night sitting of August 4, 1789, to bring out the famous decrees abolishing the principles of feudalism. Then the provinces, by the voices of their deputies, renounced their rights of self-government, in order to become merged in the equality of the kingdom of France. Instead of the old divisions (administrative, religious, financial, and military) which formed a hopeless tangle, the Constituent Assembly divided the country into 85 departments, a division which was not, as has been asserted, purely geometrical, but of which the limits were fixed by the authors, who were the deputies interested, after careful consideration of geography, history, needs, and customs. The division of France into departments was a most efficacious revolutionary measure. The old order of things was obliterated and no concerted counter-revolution was ever possible.

During this clearance of old notions off the ground on which the new administrative France was building, the Constituent Assembly was busy framing the Constitution, which had been asked for by the *cahiers* and which the French municipal insurgents demanded.

It began by drawing up a Declaration of the Rights of Man and of the citizen, in imitation of the analogous American declarations. In it were formulated philosophical principles, which were as much English as they were French, and had been expressed by Locke as well as by Rousseau; on these the new country was to be founded. Democracy and a Republic were the logical consequences of this Declaration of Rights. But the Constituent Assembly, which has so often been represented as extravagantly radical, achieved a work of prudent compromise, in accordance with public opinion. They had no intention of establishing a Republic, which the spiritual fathers of the Revolution had not sought, and which was only visible to the world in the form of a federation, which seemed incompatible with the French tendency to centralised unity. Moreover, the people were still royalist even in their most violent disturbances; they did not realise the weakness and disloyalty of Louis XVI, and, although they no longer expressed as much love for him as at the beginning of the Revolution, they still trusted him. None of the leaders of the majority in the Constituent Assembly was Republican, neither Barnave, nor even Robespierre.

The Constituent Assembly, then, not only supported monarchy, but the Bourbon dynasty, and the king, Louis XVI.

How was it possible to reconcile the old principle of the sovereignty of the king with the new principle of the sovereignty of the people, which was affirmed in the Declaration of Rights? The Assembly did not attempt this impossible agreement. It put two principles, the one mystical, the other rational, side by side in the formula: "Louis, by the grace of God, and the constitutional law of the State, King of the French." And, after that, they limited the power of the King strictly.

The other sovereignty, that of the people, was both organised and limited. The limitation consisted in the fact, that everyone was not called to exercise political rights. In order to be eligible to vote for the States General, it was only necessary to be entered on the roll of taxpayers, which, in 1789, meant almost manhood suffrage. The Constituent Assembly, less democratic than had been the absolute monarch, divided citizens into two categories—active and passive. The active citizens, who alone had a right to vote, had to prove that they paid in direct taxes a sum equal to the local value of three days' work. The electorate was in two grades. To be an elector of the second grade, a contribution equivalent to ten days' work was necessary, and the same in order to be eligible as a member of departmental, district, and municipal assemblies. Finally, to be eligible for the National Assembly, direct taxes equal in amount to a silver mark had to be paid, and furthermore a qualification from some sort of landed property was requisite. The philosophers had not demanded manhood suffrage; they did not believe that the poor and the ignorant could assist the cause of progress.

It was by this system based upon a property qualification, that the Legislative Assembly, which applied the Constitution, was elected. This Assembly held all the executive and financial power; it shared with the king the exercise of the right of peace and war. The administrative power of the king was in practice destroyed by the fact that all administration was entrusted to local assemblies, in which the king had no representative. The control over these assemblies which he could exercise through the Minister of Home Affairs was illusory. In avoiding despotism, the Constituent Assembly had run the risk of administrative anarchy.

However, a certain amount of political power was left to the king because, by the constitution, it was forbidden that the offices of minister and deputy should be held by the same person. Therefore, the ministers were his creatures, and not those of the Assembly. But this circumstance caused discord, and made sincere co-operation between the king and the Assembly difficult, thus weakening the monarchy and exposing it to greater dangers.

As to judicial power, it was entirely taken from the king and all judges were elected. Thus was realised Montesquieu's famous theory as to the separation of the three kinds of power.

Such was, on broad lines, the monarchical constitution, in which the Constituent Assembly tried with prudent calculation to realise the wisdom of the day, in imitation, partly of England, partly of America, but chiefly inspired by the ideas of French philosophers and adapting them to the circumstances.

The Social Revolution. A social revolution was effected at the same time as the political one, and one must not be separated from the other, or rather, they must be regarded as the same revolution under two aspects.

There were three "orders," that is to say three nations within the nation; the clergy and the nobles, who were privileged, and the third estate, which was the mass of the people, crushed by taxes, by dues, and by work, and as to part at least still in a state of servitude. The Constituent Assembly abolished all distinctions between the orders and there was now only one nation of equals. The nobles were suppressed, not only in their useful privileges but also in their honorary ones, and even titles of nobility were forbidden. A single code of laws replaced the hundreds of local codes. Testamentary rights were uniformly regulated and restricted, so that property was more divided. This division was hastened by the confiscation of the property of the clergy and the émigrés, which was sold. Extensive

properties were thus broken up. The number of small proprietors, which was already considerable at the end of the Old
Order, was much increased in this way. In what proportion?
An historical inquiry which has been begun on the subject has
not been yet completed.

The peasants were crushed by the feudal dues, the suppression
of which was the great social achievement of the Revolution,
the step which most completely changed the condition of individuals and things. We have seen that this suppression was
decided on, in principle, on the night of August 4, 1789, but
it was then neither complete, nor radical. Personal servitude
was absolutely abolished; there was not a single serf left in
France; some other dues were practically suppressed; most of
them were declared redeemable, but were maintained for the
time being. The shoulders of the people, especially of the rural
population, were only partly relieved of their burdens by the
decrees of August 4th.

For the workmen, the Constituent Assembly returned to the
policy of Turgot and suppressed the corporations, which, under
various names, had taken possession of and monopolised work,
and had ended by forming bodies of hereditary aristocracy.
Thus was given to the workmen the right of freedom to work,
which was their first desire, as it was their greatest need.
It was so much feared that these tyrannical guilds of the Old
Order should revive, that workmen were forbidden by law to form
any union amongst themselves, or to combine in order to raise
their wages, or to strike. Deprived of the right of combination,
they were treated as citizens of a lower order. This and some
other facts have caused it to be said that the French Revolution
was only individualistic. This is not so, but its first duty was to
emancipate the individual. This emancipation was effected by
a rallying of the French people into a nation, drawn together by
fraternal agreement and by a spontaneous movement. They
banded themselves together at the precise moment when they
became emancipated, but the hour for grouping themselves in
classes had not yet come; the idea of such groups was hateful,
because it recalled the Old Order.

Under the posthumous influence of Jean-Jacques Rousseau,
there was also the beginning of a revolution in habits, which

became simpler; and equality in dress, as in speech, became noticeable.

It must also be remembered that religious liberty was founded at this time, but Catholicism did not cease to be, in reality, the national religion. Or rather, the Constituent Assembly realised the politico-religious ideal of the kings, notably of Louis XIV, by the "Civil Constitution of the Clergy," by which, leaving only spiritual supremacy to the Pope, an autonomous "Gallican" church was created, of which the bishops and the vicars were chosen by the body of active citizens and paid by the nation. The Pope did not consent to this arrangement and there was a schism.

As to popular education, without which there is no true Revolution, the Constituent and the Legislative Assemblies had not time to organise it. They were only able to proclaim its utility and to sketch out plans for it.

The Working of the New Order. The constitution having been passed and established, it seemed as though the Revolution were over. But the resistance of the dispossessed orders, with whom were the king's sympathies, his lack of sincerity, his sufferings caused by his piety, when against the advice of his spiritual director he was obliged to sanction the Civil Constitution of the Clergy, the resolution which he then took to combat the Revolution secretly while declaring that he accepted it, the hatred of Marie-Antoinette for the Revolution and the "Patriots," these were the chief reasons why the new government could not work normally.

In June 1792, Louis threw off the mask. He fled to join on the eastern frontier a general and an army, on which he counted to bring about a counter-revolution. He was stopped at Varennes and brought back to Paris a prisoner, and his powers were suspended. There was a Republican movement in Paris and in the south-west, but it was quickly arrested, and the people were told that the king had been "carried away" by false counsellors. In this way the monarchy was preserved. There might have been a change of king, but that would have meant either the enthronement of the Duc d'Orléans, a man of commonplace type, or the regency of Marie-Antoinette, who was very unpopular. So they resigned themselves to replacing Louis on the throne and he continued to combat the Revolution in secret.

The politico-religious question became acute, because half the clergy, in obedience to the Pope, refused to enter the new Gallican church and were hostile to it; a religious civil war began. But the serious event, the event which opened a new revolutionary era, was the declaration of war against Austria (April 20, 1792). The king wanted this war, because he hoped thereby to regain absolute power. The advanced Patriots, those soon to be called the Girondins, led by Brissot and Vergniaud, wanted it, because they hoped that it would cause the Revolution to triumph, not in France only, but in the whole world.

This war, in which Prussia took part against France, opened with defeats. The people began to feel that the king was failing in his part as leader of the national defence. Although they did not know all that we know now, there was an impression, at least in the large towns, that he was playing the traitor. The people of Paris invaded the Tuileries on June 20, 1792, to give him a rough warning. When a threatening manifesto by the Duke of Brunswick, commander-in-chief of the enemy, appeared, a rumour spread that this manifesto had been inspired by the king and queen. On the 10th of August there was an insurrection which bore a national character, because there were concerned in it not only Parisians, but also people from Marseilles and from Brest; the Tuileries palace was taken by storm. The king took refuge in the premises occupied by the Legislative Assembly, was suspended from his functions, and shut up in the Temple prison with the queen and the dauphin.

The throne was vacant. This was not only the end of the constitutional monarchy, but also the end of the *bourgeois régime*, based upon a property qualification. The Legislative Assembly established manhood suffrage and summoned a National Convention to revise the constitution. The Revolution became more and more democratic.

As far as it was social and as far as the application of the decrees of August 4th was concerned, the Revolution was violent. The peasants, who had not the means to redeem the feudal dues which had been maintained (and these were the heaviest), generally refused to pay them. Here and there

occurred revolts, real insurrections, risings of peasants. After
the fall of the throne, the Legislature had to make some important concessions to the peasants and to suppress many dues
without indemnity.

The Democratic Republic, 1792–1795

Victory of Valmy and Meeting of the Convention. Under the
expiring Legislature, after August 10th, when France was for
some weeks in an uncertain political condition, no longer a
monarchy and not yet a republic, the Austro-Prussian army
advanced victoriously into Champagne. This invasion excited
the Parisians and made them furiously angry with the imprisoned royalists, in whom they saw accomplices of the invaders.
Bands of excited desperadoes repaired to the prisons, held mock
trials, and massacred many prisoners. These are known as the
September massacres; this bloody episode, which was made the
most of by all the supporters of the Old Order, has done
moral harm to the French Revolution in history. But
patriotism showed itself by voluntary enlistments, and by keen
enthusiasm. On Sept. 20th, 1792, at Valmy, the French army,
composed of old disciplined troops and volunteers under the
command of Generals Dumouriez and Kellermann, victoriously
stayed the invaders, who were forced to retreat and soon
evacuated French territory.

The National Convention met on the very day of the victory
at Valmy. Elected by manhood suffrage in two grades, it
numbered amongst its members the best of the old members
of the Constituent and Legislative Assemblies, and of former
administrators of departments and districts. They were young,
very young men, if one compares their ages with those of
politicians of the present day. Not one of the party leaders, not
one of the principal orators, had reached the forties. Saint-Just,
who had so great an influence, was only twenty-five. Their
youth explains the energy of the great Assembly which saved
French independence and tried, in the midst of war, to found a
democracy.

Establishment of the Republic and Execution of the King.
The National Convention abolished the monarchy on Sept. 21st;
the Republic was only established the following day; this form

of government was, as yet, neither popular nor well-understood. On the 25th, the Republic was decreed *one and indivisible*, in order to refute the objection of those who feared that a republic would dissolve the unity of France into Federalism. The Republic at once reaped the benefit of the victory of Valmy. It was loved and adored by the people, as having saved France when attacked by monarchical Europe. It personified the country and became the object of a religious cult; it had its martyrs.

The Convention constituted itself a court of justice to try Louis XVI. The papers found in the Tuileries proved beyond a doubt that he was in communication with the enemy. These documents were published in the newspapers and read and discussed in the popular political clubs (otherwise known as Jacobin clubs); they destroyed the popularity of the king and discredited royalty. Louis was condemned to death as being "guilty of conspiracy against public liberty and crime against State security," and was guillotined on Jan. 21, 1793. This regicide was formally authorised, and was inspired by the English example. The judicial murder of Charles the First haunted the minds both of the judges and of the victim.

The execution of Charles I did not kill royalist sentiment in England; it rather magnified it. It was not so in France: far from bringing a royalist reaction, the murder of Louis consolidated the Republic in the minds of men. It now appeared to be definitely established. When the peasants learnt that the Convention had guillotined the king, they believed and realised that the monarchy no longer existed, that there was a republic. The treachery of the king had changed the feelings of the towns; the defeat of the king, overcome and slain in Paris by the Republicans, showed the country folk that royalty no longer had power and took away its prestige. Henceforward, generally speaking, the French peasants ceased to be royalist, except in two or three provinces. When, in the following October, Queen Marie-Antoinette was condemned to death by the Revolutionary Tribunal, as being guilty of complicity with enemies without and within, her execution passed almost unnoticed; the people, recently so royalist in sentiment, seemed to have forgotten the monarchy. Never since then has the idea of a king again become popular in France.

The Revolutionary Government and the Terror. The National Convention had to frame a democratic constitution; this was done in June 1793, under the following circumstances. The Convention was divided into two parties: the Mountain, whose principal members were Danton, Robespierre, Saint-Just, and Marat; the Gironde, where Brissot, Vergniaud, Guadet and Barbaroux were eminent, and whose inspiring genius was Mme Roland, a woman of intelligence. The adherents of the Mountain wanted a dictatorship of the Paris Commune and the National Convention in this crisis of war abroad and at home. The Girondins wanted the government to go on as in normal times, and wished to reduce Paris to its proper share of influence, an eighty-third part, as one of them said. The wrangling between these two parties prevented the formation of the strong and united government which was required for national defence. A Parisian rising of May 31 and June 2, 1793, forcibly imposed unity on the Convention by the removal of the principal Girondins. Several of them fled and fomented in the departments of the west and south an insurrection against the coerced and truncated Convention. This revolt, insultingly called federalism by the Mountain, spread through about sixty departments, but the Ile-de-France, the old historic France, remained faithful to the Convention, which emerged victorious from this civil war. In order to disarm not only the hands but also the hearts of the insurgents, the Convention worked out and published a constitution, under which the dictatorship of Paris would be impossible; the executive power was feeble, and a system of referendums for the sanctioning of laws allowed the citizens of the departments to have the last word in everything which was decided in Paris. This constitution was ratified by a plebiscite, but the national danger becoming greater, the Convention did not bring it into force, but decreed that until peace came, the government should remain revolutionary.

This revolutionary government, which worked by dictatorial methods, called the Reign of Terror, was not a system but an expedient.

The Convention had complicated matters by declaring war against England and Holland, and then against Spain. The hostile attitude of these powers had caused the rupture. After the French had driven out the Austro-Prussians from their territory, they had conquered the whole of Belgium and the Rhine provinces, which they had even begun to annex by a system of popular consent, which had also enabled them to annex Savoy, the county of Nice, and Avignon, without doing violence to their principles. But although Prussia had almost severed her connexion with the coalition, when England entered the fray, the fortunes of war changed. The French were obliged to evacuate Belgium and the Rhine provinces, and they were threatened with a new invasion in March–April 1793. At the same time the serious rising in La Vendée, which was more religious than royalist, was a stab in the back to the Republicans. If the enemy from without succeeded in joining hands with the enemy within, with whom they were in alliance, the French Revolution was lost. The Convention, urged thereto by the Paris Commune and the Jacobin club, wished to prevent this junction and to save the Revolution by the Terror.

Under the name of Provisional Revolutionary Government, arbitrary institutions were improvised for the duration of the war, which were added and adapted to the constitution which had but lately been decreed by the Constituent Assembly and which still remained in force.

Since the 10th of August, the executive power had been entrusted to six ministers, forming a "Provisional Executive Council." Out of respect for the principle of the separation of powers, these ministers could not be chosen from the ranks of the Convention, and yet the Convention felt that it was essential for it to take the government into its own hands. It therefore established within itself a Committee of Public Safety, which under cover of watching the Executive Council in reality governed. Finally, at the end of a year, the Executive Council was suppressed and was replaced by Executive Commissions under the orders of the Committee of Public Safety. The real, but not nominal, chief of the first Committee was Danton, an impassioned orator, and a realist in policy. In the cause of national defence he made use not only of military but of diplomatic means. Although he succeeded in breaking up the federalist insurrection, he could not crush the Vendéan rising, nor preserve France from invasion. He was overthrown by the

Convention in the month of July 1793. A new Committee was elected, at the head of which was placed Robespierre, with his friends Saint-Just and Couthon. Carnot, called later the organiser of victory, controlled the war by land; Jeanbon Saint-André, by sea. La Vendée was quelled; the rebellious towns of Lyons and Toulon were taken. The Convention formed a strong army by amalgamating troops of the line with volunteers; the enemy was driven out of French territory little by little, after many vicissitudes; the war was carried beyond the frontier, and, in June 1794, by the victory of Fleurus the independence of France was secured.

Government by the National Convention depended upon those communes which had been the first focus of the Revolution in July and August 1789, and not on the departmental administrations. These, being artificially created, did not possess the national and unifying instinct, which at once rallied the communes (with the exception of two or three large towns) round the National Convention, as the inheritor of the centralising power of the monarchy. The Paris Commune was at the head of this patriotic concentration, in complete harmony with the Convention, since the Girondins had been got rid of; and the Jacobin club, which was the communal centre of propaganda, worked on the same lines. The other communes were quite in unison, nearly all of them having a Jacobin club affiliated to the Paris one, where workmen, or even sometimes peasants, might be seen side by side with the middle-class All these clubs inspired, directed, and regulated public opinion. There was a continual interchange of opinions, which drifted down to the country districts from Paris and returned to it. The central Jacobin club itself was stimulated by small clubs in the "arrondissements" (or wards), called sections, which were frequented by the workmen, all the more willingly because the Republic allowed them forty sous per day for this purpose. This agreement of the workmen with the middle-class democrats was called "sans-culottism."

By a decree of Dec. 4, 1793 (or as it was called in the new era, the 14th day of Frimaire in the year II), the Convention formulated this war legislation into a kind of provisional revolutionary constitution; municipalities were perpetuated as the

essential nucleus of national life, to the detriment of the departmental administrations, which were robbed of their principal
functions. By order of the Government, without any other
intermediate agent than the district, the municipality became
the essential administrative machinery and the Jacobin club
(called also the popular society) was admitted to an official
position of co-operation. To counteract the anarchical tendency
of the constitution which was still in force, the Convention
appointed a national agent with each administration. However
it had already secured its central authority by sending to the
departments, as well as to the armies, a great number of its
members, known as Representatives on Mission, of the nature
of travelling *intendants* and executive agents. Moreover, the
government received or, in many cases, took the right of
nominating the various administrations, which would normally
have been elected.

There was also in every Commune a revolutionary Committee
whose duty was to arrest suspects. If these police committees
were successful in cutting the thread of conspiracies, and in
preventing the enemies within from helping those without,
it was not done without acts of brutality and injustice, which,
if at the time they saved the Revolution, caused it to be exe-
crated in history.

The chief instrument of the Terror was the guillotine, to
which numerous persons of both sexes were sent by revolutionary
tribunals. The most celebrated of these was the Paris one, which
also had the most illustrious victims. It was a butchery of the
guilty and the innocent, not only of counter-revolutionaries, but
also of patriots, such as the Girondins, the eloquent Vergniaud, the
spirituelle Mme Roland; of democrats of the Mountain, rivals of
Robespierre, such as Danton, or the freethinking journalist
Hébert; finally of Robespierre himself, Saint-Just and their
friends. The prisons were full of suspects. It was indeed the Terror.

The object was attained in so far as the enemies of the
Republic, within as well as without, were conquered or paralysed.
The patriotic activity of the French, fiercely extended, saved the
independence of France.

The social evolution continued as before and quickened its
pace.

We have seen that some of the feudal dues still survived. When the National Convention wished to destroy the last remains of the Girondin sedition, and for this purpose to conciliate the mass of the peasants, it was decreed on July 17, 1793, that all feudal dues should be abolished without redemption or indemnity, thus sacrificing not only the properties of the nobles or the rich, but sometimes the only means of support of the poor. But nothing of the hated *complexum feudale* remained, and in this manner the heart of the peasants was for ever won over to the Revolution. The sale of national property, which had been confiscated from the clergy or the *émigrés*, continued to produce social and economic results under the revolutionary rule.

Social customs became even more uniform than they were in the days of the Constituent Assembly. The use of "thee and thou" established itself and became compulsory. Dress was still further simplified. Ultra-democratic people wore red caps, and clothed themselves in little round jackets called *carmagnoles*, and long trousers instead of breeches; sometimes they shod themselves with sabots, so as to give leather shoes to the soldiers.

During the Terror the politico-religious question showed itself in a new form. At the time of the Girondin sedition, some constitutional bishops opposed the Mountain. As that part of the clergy which had remained faithful to the Pope was openly hostile to the Revolution, the people associated the two parties of clergy in the same hatred, as being equally unpatriotic. In order to destroy such bad citizens as they deemed the ministers of religion to be, many advanced Republicans wished to destroy religion itself. This is what is known as the de-christianising movement, which sprung spontaneously from the popular societies, and geographically, from the very centre of historic France. Nearly all the churches were closed. A philosophic cult was organised, which was called the worship of Reason, because often a young girl personified Reason or Liberty. The Convention did not look on this movement with favour, but it was carried away. Robespierre and the Committee of Public Safety started a reaction, by substituting for the popular worship of Reason the official worship of the Supreme Being, of which cult Robespierre appeared to be the pontiff, and which was, or seemed to be, one of the instruments of his personal dictatorship. This worship gradually merged into the Tenth Day worship, which was neither more nor less than worship of the Country.

In this same period of the Terror, the National Convention attended to national education, as one of the essential things. Its Committee of Public Instruction prepared and passed laws of primary education, but they were hardly carried out at all, owing to the war. There were beautiful and instructive national holidays. The Committee of Public Safety, even at the most critical moments of the military operations, planned to improve Paris and France by the aid of the fine arts, but they had not time to obtain results.

The Thermidorian Reaction and the Executive Directory.

Fall of Robespierre and the Thermidorian Reaction. The continuance of the Terror, which had been instrumental in bringing about the successful national defence, became unnecessary and odious now that this success was attained. It may be said that the victory of Fleurus ruined the dictatorship of Robespierre, whom public opinion regarded as the personification of the Terror. All those who in the Convention felt themselves endangered by his ambition, made common cause against him. He was deposed at the sitting of 9th Thermidor, year II (July 27, 1794) and was sent to the guillotine with his partisans. The people of Paris, who had so much admired him, did nothing to save him. The Reign of Terror was over.

The rule of terror and of revolutionary government disappeared little by little. The last blow was given to it in the spring of 1795 by the treaty of Basle, by which the Convention made peace with Prussia and later with Spain. It was a glorious peace, as thereby France obtained indirectly a possibility of annexing in the future the left bank of the Rhine, including Belgium. The war with England and Austria continued, but no longer seemed to threaten grave danger. A Moderate majority was formed in the Convention, and there was a reaction, not only against the Terror, but against democracy. The Paris Commune, the Jacobin club, and the Revolutionary Committees were suppressed. The municipalities were deprived of their preponderance and the departments had their functions restored to them. It was the revival and triumph of the Girondin policy. In Paris two popular democratic insurrections were put down by force. The help of the proletariat was no longer required, as the enemy had been conquered. The Convention drew up a new constitution, known as that of the year III, in which manhood suffrage was replaced by a property qualification. "Thee and thou" disappeared, along with the manners of "sans-culottism." A *bourgeois* government was established. The former Terrorists were persecuted. The royalists began to lift their heads.

But in the Thermidorian period all was not reaction. More and more amongst educated Frenchmen, philosophy was taking the place of religion. The Tenth Day worship, or worship of the Country, was being organised. The Church was separated from the State, which became secular, a great innovation in the world. The different forms of worship became more evenly balanced and equal, more especially because of the schism which divided the Catholic Church. Freethought became organised. It had, as it were, an official position in the Moral Science section of the great National Institute, which was created by the Convention for the purpose of making "a living Encyclopaedia." As regards Education it was a time when plans were realised. The Convention enacted good laws of primary education and initiated normal schools. Unhappily, there were not enough teachers, and there was not time to train them. For the pick of the young men the Convention established Central Schools, which took the place of the old colleges, and which had this novelty that science was the basis of education instead of Latin. These schools worked with success until Napoleon destroyed them.

The Executive Directory. This was the name of the government which succeeded the Committees of the Convention, under the Constitution of the year III (1795–1799). The five Directors were nominated by the Legislature, which was divided into two sections: the Council of Five-Hundred, and the Council of Ancients. This was a return to the system of two chambers, which at first seemed a counter-revolutionary step.

It was a secular, moderate, and *bourgeois* republic. It came into being during a state of things, which was neither revolutionary nor normal. France was no longer invaded, and no longer in danger of destruction, as in the days of the Terror, but she was still at war with England and Austria. The royalist and Catholic rising was no longer raging; it had been crushed by military measures. But as yet there was not internal peace, and there were still here and there disturbances and sedition. The Constitution of the year III worked, but with some failures.

Up till now, only these failures have been chronicled, and nothing is celebrated in the history of the Directory, except some *coup d'état* by the Left or the Right. In reality, this period of four years was a time of realisation, of application of the political and social results of the French Revolution, which, after a crisis of destruction and disorder, calmed itself, realised its place, permeated life, established itself in minds and deeds, or rather, became changed into an almost regular evolution.

Municipal life had received a rational and practical organisation by an extension of its limits. The small communes were grouped into a single municipality, which was called *cantonale*; and by this means communal activity, the historical source of national activity, was stimulated, amplified, and intelligently improved. On the other hand, Paris was divided into several municipalities, and she, who had been the directing commune, ceased to be a commune. The head of the nation no longer directed the body of the nation. But the executive Directory had a commissary in each municipality and with each department. Centralised administration was established and bureaucracy already began to show itself.

The sale of national property continued and the economic results of a greater division of property were beginning to be felt, for instance in the improved cultivation of the land which formerly belonged to the clergy. The peasant was profiting by the suppression of feudal dues, and being less poor was tilling the land better. His only fear was lest the king should return with the Old Order and the feudal dues. This fear made him love the Revolution. Free labour began to give scope to new industries. The financial difficulties, of which we have spoken elsewhere in these pages, were being overcome. Enjoyment of life showed itself, after so many sufferings and so many troubles, after the horrible civil war and the dreadful invasion.

The beginning of the Directory was marked by the victories of General Bonaparte. He conquered Italy brilliantly and roused the French people to enthusiasm by his glory and his genius. This wonderful young man inspired France with a vision of world-domination, which was contrary to the principles of the Revolution. Nevertheless, these principles were loyally applied in the annexations which gave to France her natural and historical frontier, the Rhine. The Rhine provinces were only annexed with the free consent of their people, expressed in the form of a popular conference, of which the minutes still exist. Under the Directory was thus realised the territorial ambitions of the kings of France, within wise and useful limits. The independence of France was assured by this increase of territory, without compromising or threatening the independence of the other Powers. This was a great achievement, which was lost by the Napoleonic despotism.

It has been said that the Directory was a period of corruption. This is a legend invented by the enemies of the Revolution, who wish to discredit it by showing that it led finally to a relaxation of morals. The legend is founded on a few stories only. One of the Directors, Barras, was a man of loose morals; some contractors, enriched by the war, gave themselves to luxury and pleasure. But there is nothing to show that popular or *bourgeois* morality was any lower than it had been. In fact, one school of frivolity and dissipation had gone—the Court.

Whatever may have been said, political morality improved under the Directory, especially in the sense that a spirit of obedience to the laws became popularised. If there were *coups d'état*, they were not the work of the people in the street, but of the Government, or the legislative body, in the form of laws and without bloody encounters.

Conspiracies. Coups d'État. Wars. Causes of the Fall of the Directory. The reaction against the Terror still continued, while the scarcity of food in Paris made the communism of Babœuf popular with the working classes. Some democratic republicans formed a conspiracy with Babœuf, which was easily put down, because the French people as a whole were tired of revolutionary agitation and the peasants wished to enjoy in peace the advantages they had gained. Babœuf was guillotined, and for a lengthy period there was no more question of socialism. The anti-terrorist reaction encouraged the royalists; under the guise of moderate Republicans many of them were elected as deputies in the partial election of 1797. The Directory unmasked them, and by the celebrated *coup d'état* of the 18th Fructidor, of the year V, drove them out of the legislature, proscribed them and their partisans, and persecuted, or deported, many priests who were their accomplices, or believed to be such. Although the republican enthusiasm of the people was less keen now that the country was out of danger, they supported the Directory, for fear that the Old Order might return, and the country districts were decidedly anti-royalist. The partial elections of the following year were favourable to the democratic Republicans and hostile to the middle-class policy of the Directory, which annulled these elections by a *coup d'état*, which was a reversal of the previous one. The election of the year VII, held under the influence of the military defeats on the Rhine, gave a majority to the opposing Republicans of the Left. The Council of Five-Hundred forced two Directors of moderate views to resign and replaced them by two Democrats. These *coups d'état* gave an impression of instability and disorder to the external world, although, as I have said, they were only accidents.

They were political accidents brought about by military accidents. Russia joined the Austro-British coalition, and their armies advanced victoriously. Beaten in Germany and in Italy, the French were driven back to their own territory, while their best general, Bonaparte, was fighting in Egypt. France seemed to be threatened by another invasion. Learning this danger and seizing his opportunity, Bonaparte left his army in Egypt and landed in France to play the part of deliverer. He found the country already saved by the successes of Generals Masséna and Brune. The Council of Five-Hundred in this national danger had taken up the position of the National Convention. Some of the features of the Terror reappeared; for instance, the Jacobin club. The party of law and order was uneasy, and Bonaparte was able to present himself as a deliverer, not from the external enemy, who was already overcome, but from the democratic

Republicans, who were branded by the names of terrorists and monarchists.

Patriotism had gradually become corrupted; and Bonaparte had contributed to this corruption by holding up as an ideal to the army of Italy, not love of country, as in the days of Danton and Robespierre, but glory and pillage. French patriotism had ceased to be humanitarian, as it was formerly, and had become almost selfish. The tenacity of England in prolonging the war had given rise to hatred of England, which was encouraged by the French government. Militarism made its appearance. The army, which had been so submissive to the civil power in the days of the Committee of Public Safety, now intimidated or protected the government, which was only able to achieve its *coup d'état* of 18th Fructidor thanks to General Bonaparte and by the help of General Augereau. A Pretorian spirit was appearing.

After his return from Egypt, Bonaparte felt that he had become the hero of France, and that he was master of the popular imagination. He had only to come to terms with two of the Directors, one of whom, the celebrated Siéyès, was his accomplice and his dupe. The *coup d'état* of the 18th and 19th Brumaire, year VIII, when the Legislature was dispersed by soldiers, gave him the power. People were so accustomed to *coups d'état* that this proceeding shocked no one, and, with the exception of a few far-seeing Republicans, everyone ended by applauding it. People said that the Republic was going to be governed with a firm hand. The peasant felt protected from the return of the Old Order; the *bourgeoisie* felt protected against terroristic democracy.

Napoleon Bonaparte, 1799–1814

I have only a few pages in which to speak of Napoleon. It is, therefore, quite impossible for me to undertake even a summary account of his military operations. My English readers know them and I should not be teaching them anything new. But they know less of Napoleon as the organiser of contemporary France. In English (as indeed in French) books his civil genius has been less fully demonstrated than his military genius. Perhaps I shall best do what is expected of me if I show in what spirit and in what manner Napoleon Bonaparte sometimes realised, at other times thwarted, the ideals of the French Revolution, in what spirit and in what manner he sometimes destroyed or spoiled, at other times consolidated and developed its work. But even if I do not recount his wars and conquests, it is absolutely necessary to describe, if only in a few words, the spirit, the method, and the aim of his external policy.

External Policy of Napoleon Bonaparte. His external, like his internal, policy was in some respects only a continuation of the policy of the French Revolution, which itself frequently indirectly followed the policy of Richelieu and Louis XIV for the territorial aggrandisement of France, and her external influence.

The great aim of the kings of France was to acquire what are called the natural frontiers of France. The Pyrenean frontier had been acquired; the frontier of the Alps remained to be completed, and almost the whole Rhine frontier to be acquired. The Revolution had realised this aim by the application of its own principles. Proclaiming that it renounced all conquest by violence, it annexed Savoy, the county of Nice, the Rhine provinces, and Belgium, with the free consent of the annexed people. In order to preserve these gains and to guard these frontiers, which seemed indispensable to the security and independence of France, the executive Directory had surrounded itself with a circle of sister republics, which were morally subordinate. Bonaparte wished to replace these independent republics with vassal states, which he made later into dependent monarchies, which were in reality provinces of the French Empire, and to which he appointed his brothers or his generals as kings. If they showed any slight desire for independence, he recalled them, replacing them by some one else, or even, as in the case of Holland, annexing their State. His avowed aim was the preservation of the natural frontiers, and, if he could be believed, for this purpose he undertook the conquest of Europe and dreamed of world-conquest. England was the great and stubborn adversary to this design, and against her he waged a continual war, broken only by a truce of less than two years. Carried away by his genius, carried away by his victories, Napoleon lost his sense of possibility, as he lost his sense of justice. He crushed Prussia. He reduced conquered Austria to dependence by marrying Marie-Louise. He wished to enslave Spain and he used his strongest forces to succeed in this tyrannical design. Although weakened by the Spanish war, he desired to crush Russia, as he believed he had already crushed Prussia. The end must be the isolation or the defeat of England, who would not allow France to be great, and who could not be reached by means of the blockade, as long as she had allies in Europe. The Russian expedition was a disaster, the whole of Europe rose against him; after a grand resistance, he was finally vanquished, and forced to abdicate (twice over). Through this despot, France lost the natural frontiers which liberty had given her.

But Napoleon must not be regarded as a despot of the Old Order. His conquests broke chains and freed nations. Wherever he fought, he destroyed feudalism. He gave to the conquered the blessing of equality (if not of liberty), his admirable Civil Code, a rule of light and justice, a truly modern rule. The nations which he had tyrannically conquered were modernized by good organisation and entered on an era of well-being. The spirit of the Revolution, even if impaired or weakened, spread to them. When their kings returned, they could not restore slavery. If the name of Napoleon is popular all the world over in spite of all the bloodshed, it is because in him is seen the personification or the hero of the French Revolution, diffusing over the whole world the benefits of that Revolution.

If, as I believe, Napoleon deserves to be called a tyrant, it must be owned that he is a tyrant of a modern type. His conquests were not for the simple pleasure of conquering, but with the intention of making men happier. He belongs to the 18th century, to the Revolution. The whimsical paradox of those who called him "a Robespierre on horseback" was not altogether false.

Marengo, Austerlitz, Jena, Eylau, Moskowa, Leipzig, Montmirail, Waterloo, these celebrated battles, the names of which still live in the memories of men, can only be mentioned here, to recall the fact that the military genius of Napoleon was always great even in defeat. I repeat that I suppose these things to be common knowledge. I only pause to dwell on one point of great importance in the military and diplomatic history of Napoleon.

It is known that as First Consul he made peace with Austria

at Lunéville in 1801, and with England at Amiens in 1802. This was a general peace, and the end of a ten years' war. France and Europe were delighted; France, because she had secured her natural frontiers; Europe, because bloodshed had ceased. Why did this peace not last? Why did the war begin again so soon? Was it entirely the fault of Napoleon and his ambition? The historical importance of this question can easily be seen.

Apparently the English Parliament only accepted the treaty as a makeshift and a truce. Many Englishmen could not reconcile themselves to the definite idea of a state of things which gave France preponderance in Europe, left her in possession of Belgium and abandoned Holland, Italy, and, in a word, the whole of the Mediterranean to her influence. It was evident that the treaty once concluded, Napoleon would take all possible advantage of it, and would make all progress not forbidden by the treaty. When the English saw that he was annexing Piedmont, that he was preparing to place Switzerland and Germany under his protection, that he refused to make any commercial treaty with England, and that the prohibitive measures against English goods, which had been passed during the war, were still being kept in force by laws which permitted the government to raise or to lower tariffs, and to authorise or to prohibit imports and exports, there was a wave of indignation and uneasiness.

Let us add that the French Revolution was now personified by the striking figure of a great man, and the English aristocracy may have feared that its success might prove contagious, and might suggest to the English people the idea of, and the desire for, great social changes after the French pattern, more especially a change in the ownership of property.

We may be mistaken, but we in France are inclined to think that this unavowed anxiety and these Conservative fears were among the motives of the warlike attitude taken up by the British government.

Although Bonaparte carried out the treaty to the letter, the British government resolved not to put into execution one of the Mediterranean clauses, i.e. not to evacuate Malta, so as to prevent the command of the Mediterranean being held by France, and, at the same time, to draw out the evacuation of Alexandria as long as possible. In March 1803, the king asked

Parliament for supplies; it voted an increase in the navy and
passed other war measures. Bonaparte seems to have been surprised and vexed. He wanted peace in order to establish and
organise his despotic measures. It is true that, sooner or later,
his despotism would have led to war, in order to defend itself in
France against liberty, which peace would certainly have caused
to revive. But meanwhile Bonaparte wished for some years of
peace. He tried to prevent war by intimidation, by a threatening note, and by a "scene" which he had with the English
ambassador. This shows that he did not understand the English
character. At the same time that he was negotiating he
was making threats and granting concessions, some of them
material, going so far as to offer to leave Malta in British possession for ten years. But the British demanded that in addition
Switzerland and Holland should be evacuated, and that an
indemnity should be paid to the king of Sardinia. If we did not
understand them, neither did they understand us, as they
imagined that there was in France a party for peace at any price,
which, under the influence of Talleyrand, would force Bonaparte
to yield. They sent an ultimatum, which, considering Bonaparte's character, could not be accepted. The British ambassador
asked for and received his passports; and it was war. And what
a war! Its consequences still weigh heavily on the world.

Napoleon Bonaparte, then, was not entirely responsible for
the war. If it is objected that he would have made war when
it suited him, which after all is only a hypothesis, it must be
owned that Great Britain started a *preventive* war, which is very
serious, at the same time that she was irritating French opinion by
not carrying out the clauses of a treaty recently signed by her.
Here I have felt obliged to record the truth as I see it, in all friend-
liness to the British and in writing for them. It was not only the
ambition of Bonaparte which ruptured the peace of Amiens and
bathed the world in blood. It seems to me to be proved that at
this time he wished to postpone war. He was still reasonable
and it was his belief that England was the irreconcilable enemy
of France which excited his warlike genius and in the enthusiasm of victory led to his mad ambition.

Did he really hate England? No. This is proved by his
admirable letter to the Prince Regent of England, on July 13,

1815, in which he says: "I come, like Themistocles, to seat myself at the hearth of the British people: I place myself under the protection of its laws, which protection I claim from Your Royal Highness, as the most powerful, the most constant, and the most generous of my enemies." Thus he admired the British character, and Anglophobia, which he encouraged in France, was for him only an instrument of war.

Internal Policy of Napoleon. Under the Consulate and the Empire certain essential results of the Revolution continued to be realised and to develop, as if this government were only the continuation of the executive Directory. In particular, the suppression of feudal dues became in practice more and more irrevocable. To the peasant the Revolution consisted almost entirely of this suppression, which Napoleon assured to them, by saving them from a return of the Bourbons and the Old Order. Hence the popularity of this new leader of the State; his wars were forgiven by the peasants, because, although they lost their sons, they did not become impoverished, for the armies lived at the expense of the occupied countries. Comfort began to exist in the country. The sale of national property continued to divide up the land. Civil equality existed as established by the Revolution, and a good code of laws, inspired by eighteenth century philosophy, organised and applied this equality.

Political liberty ceased to exist, and it was in this that Napoleon did the work of counter-revolution. The Press was no longer free, and finally the Emperor arrived at making his police edit the few papers which were allowed to survive. No more freedom of assembly, no more clubs. The sovereignty of the people only remained under the form of plebiscite, like those by which, in 1793 and 1795, the people had accepted the two constitutions voted by the National Convention. A system of elections, first illusory, later of property-holders, resulted in Chambers, which were so annihilated by the Executive that it was possible for Napoleon to dictate a budget by decree. The financial power of the people, which had been one of the earliest and chief results, seemed to have been abolished. Individual liberty now scarcely existed, and under the name of State Prisons Napoleon re-established the Bastille. This suppression of liberty did not shock the populace in the country districts, nor even in the towns, who did not suffer in consequence. But it became hateful and intolerable to the *bourgeoisie*, who turned against Napoleon, when the fortune of war forsook him, and recalled the Bourbons.

The plebiscitary Republic, called the Consulate, and the plebiscitary Monarchy, called the Empire, can thus be described: the French people, who under the Revolution had hundreds of representatives (the deputies), now had only one representative, Napoleon Bonaparte. First Consul, then Emperor, he was the only representative of the French nation. He kept this character of representative even when he took the title of Emperor; even when, founding a new dynasty, he obtained by plebiscite the right to make his power hereditary. The people accepted the new monarchy, because it preserved the essential results of the Revolution, those which they valued, because it saved them from the return of the old monarchy, which they did not believe would preserve those results. The reinstatement of monarchical forms did not shock their republicanism, but struck them as a good joke at the expense of the Bourbons. The more firmly Napoleon made himself king, the more it seemed to the people that he was checkmating the king and consolidating the Revolution.

The Institutions of the Consulate and the Empire. Under the Consulate, as under the Empire, the same Constitution held sway, the Constitution of the year VII, dictated by Bonaparte himself; it only underwent two important modifications, the first in 1802, when the First Consul, originally elected for ten years, was elected for life; the second, in 1804, when taking the title of Emperor, his powers became hereditary. But from the beginning, Bonaparte, as First Consul, had received royal powers, wider than those which the Constituent Assembly had left to Louis XVI, the two other consuls having only consulting powers.

Napoleon was much more master than any of the Bourbons, even Louis XIV, had been, because of the centralisation which had been established by the Revolution after its clean sweep. The bands of this centralisation had been as it were fixed under the executive Directory, and Bonaparte had only to tighten them a little more and to hold the ends with a firmer hand. But under the Directory there were still elective administrative assemblies; under the Consulate and Empire these no longer existed. All administrative authority was entrusted to a prefect, nominated by the executive power. There were general Councils and Councils of the *arrondissements*, dealing specially with financial matters. There were also municipal councils. But these councils were likewise nominated by the Executive, as also all members of courts of law, with the exception of justices of the peace, and this exception was soon abolished.

How was it that the people so easily consented to be deprived of the right of electing its administrators and judges, which right had been conferred by the Revolution in 1790? It was because in the days of the National Convention, and subsequently under the Directory, this right had often been suspended by exceptional legislation. The people were already unused to exercising it and did not attach much importance to it. This right was all the more easily forgotten, because Bonaparte chose his prefects and sub-prefects very well, from a picked body of the political and administrative staff of the Revolution. Former Representatives on Mission, whose travelling authority had extended to several departments or armies, consented to become sub-prefects. Intelligent, active, public-spirited, and still attached to the Revolution, well supervised, well supported, they governed with justice and expedition, and were admirable when contrasted with the administrators of the Old Order, who were so dilatory and so unfair.

All this administration, for which France was then envied by the rest of Europe, led up to Napoleon Bonaparte himself, whose ministers were only advisers or clerks, who worked hard and efficiently prepared business for decision, and were always kept up to the mark by the master, the most indefatigable of workers, requiring little sleep. He personally brought order and energy into this administrative machine, so vast and yet so simple, which, as long as he guided it himself, worked without jar or accident, and with beneficent rapidity. This method of government was only mischievous because people became unused to liberty, because it deprived the French of the taste for managing their own affairs, and because it destroyed the spirit of initiative in individuals and in the communes. When the hand which held the reins was less skilled and less firm, this centralisation resulted in paralysis.

In Paris there were Assemblies, supposed to be national and elective, except the State Council, which was nominated by the First Consul. This State Council was the centre of his governmental and legislative activity. There, in the midst of eminent and competent assistants, were prepared, under the personal direction of Napoleon Bonaparte, his laws and great governing measures, and all important questions of home policy. He attended its meetings, he spoke at them, he showed his genius in intimate and extempore speeches, of which we find records in the Memoirs of State Councillors, such as Thibaudeau, or Pelet de Lozère, or in some Minutes, when the Civil Code was being prepared. Later, especially during the Empire, when his ambition became inordinate, he was annoyed by the wise advice of his councillors, and he feared the habit of submitting his extraordinary plans to private Councils, which he himself chose afresh for each occasion.

The projected laws, having thus been worked out by the Council, were then submitted to two Chambers, of which one was called the Tribunate, the other the Legislative Body. The Tribunate spoke and voted, the Legislature listened and voted, but without speaking. Above these Assemblies, a Conservative Senate had the task of preserving the Constitution by preventing any one from violating it. In reality, it had to be modified, and it was by Senatus-Consults that first the Consulate, and later the Empire, were established.

At first, these three Assemblies were nominated by dictatorial methods, but were composed of distinguished and experienced men. Later, the members were selected from what were called lists of notabilities, elected indeed, but including so many names that the election meant nothing. Thus, the list from the wards, whence came all the others, had to include one-tenth of the citizens of the ward. This was ridiculous and futile. When Napoleon wished to have the Consulate conferred on him for life, he conceded the reinstatement of elections for the National Assemblies to the *bourgeoisie*, who regretted their lost political liberty. There were electoral colleges, chosen by a complicated system of property qualification. But the electors did not directly nominate the senators, legislators, or tribunes. They nominated two candidates for each place and the Senate selected one of the two.

Working of the Consular and Imperial Institutions. The administrative institutions worked in the same way, without important changes, throughout the whole period of the Consulate and the Empire. The same cannot be said of political institutions. I have already said that a property-holding electoral system took the place of the illusory system of notabilities. It has also been recalled that Napoleon was appointed Consul for life, and then Emperor. There were other changes; the Tribunate, which had undertaken serious opposition, was purged, so as to eliminate the most distinguished members of the opposition; and under the Empire it was suppressed. As to the Legislature, which also showed some feeble desire for independence, it ended by being starved, that is to say, it was given hardly any laws to pass. Even the Budget was not referred to it.

The executive power only underwent nominal changes. When Napoleon became Emperor in 1804, it was a change in name only. Nothing was added to his real power, because nothing could be added, as he was already powerful. But this was the foundation of a new dynasty, the substitution of a monarchical system for the republican one, although the latter was nominally retained. In order to obtain the imperial title from the Senate, Napoleon made some apparent liberal concessions. Two Committees of the Senate were to watch over individual liberty and the liberty of the Press, but they were powerless and void. There was no liberty of the Press and hardly any individual liberty. By giving himself the power to add members to the Senate, the Emperor enslaved this Assembly, which did everything he wanted. He no longer governed by means of laws, but by Senatus-Consult and by decree. Each victory strengthened and developed his ambition. By the creation of the Legion of Honour, by the institution of a new aristocracy, by the pomp of a court which followed the etiquette of the Old Order, he restored to his own advantage the customs of the monarchy, and having recalled the emigrants, he utilised part of the old aristocracy, which seated itself obsequiously on the steps of his throne. The Bourbon claimant, Louis XVIII, seemed abandoned, forgotten, lost.

It was in the order of things both social and spiritual that Napoleon made the most serious changes, for the benefit of his dictatorship.

During the first two years of the Consulate, he firmly and cleverly applied the law of the separation of Church and State, which the Convention had established and the Directory had carried into effect. This policy had already almost become an integral part of life, to the great advantage of the State, which, by the equality and the competition of sects, remained secular and neutral, dominating and not dominated. By the Concordat of 1802, Napoleon destroyed this policy. He rendered the Pope the great service of suppressing the Schism which had divided French Catholics into two sects, ever since the civil constitution of the clergy. Catholic unity under the authority of the Pope was restored in France. The Catholic clergy received their stipends from the State. Napoleon, although an unbelieving philosopher, made an official profession of Catholic faith. All religious communities, except Protestants and Jews, were prohibited. A Deist sect, the Theophilanthropists, had been formed; it was now dissolved. The official Tenth Day worship disappeared. Freethought existed in organised form in the moral and political class of the National Institute; this class was suppressed. It was certainly not out of piety that Napoleon rendered these services to the Catholic Church. He wished to have the help of the Church and to subordinate the Pope. The Church helped him to become Emperor, but he was not master of the Pope, and when he wished to make the latter an instrument of his policy, he was met by resistance, in spite of imprisonment and violence. This resistance was aided by most of the French bishops, and as soon as the military disasters began, Napoleon had to yield, vanquished in this struggle with a spiritual force.

In the sphere of education, he followed an analogous policy. The Revolution had bequeathed to Napoleon a law of liberty. There were State and private schools. In the latter, which were mainly Catholic, a spirit of opposition was fostered. To overcome this, Napoleon gave a monopoly of instruction to an imperial university which was founded in 1808. All the private

schools were incorporated in it, under the control of an imperial
official, called Grand Master. But these private schools were
only nominally imperialised; the teachers and the spirit remained the same, while the number of pupils increased. In 1811,
Napoleon enacted the most violent measures against these
former private schools. But it was in vain; he could neither
tame nor suppress those hostile centres, to which the *bourgeoisie*,
irritated by his despotic methods, more and more sent their
children.

Public opinion under Napoleon. We know little about public
opinion under Napoleon. Nothing was known then, as there was
neither a free Press nor free right of assembly. It is, however,
certain that the bulk of the nation, especially in country
districts, remained faithful to the great man, in whom they saw
the follower or rather the upholder of the Revolution. By his
military victories, by the triumphs of his genius, by the romance
of his conquests, he intoxicated the imagination of men. It
seemed as though France lived only in him and for him. His
soldiers adored him and followed him everywhere, even in his
mad expeditions to Spain and Russia.

But the *bourgeoisie*, amongst which he was obliged to seek
his co-operators, gradually turned against him, in proportion
as his victories made him more despotic. The minutes of
political elections, which are in unpublished manuscripts, show a
continual development of the monarchical ideal amongst the
bourgeoisie. Thus, the candidates chosen by the electoral
colleges for the Senate are often disguised monarchists, and the
more tyrannical Napoleon became, the more there are of these
monarchist elections, not from love of the Bourbons, but from
love of liberty. It came to be said that the old dynasty, taught
by its faults and misfortunes, would know how to give to France
political liberty, similar to that which was instituted in 1789.
For this reason, when the military power of Napoleon crumbled,
the Senate proclaimed his deposition in favour of the Bourbons.
For this reason, the Legislative body, which had become Royalist
some time before, in 1814 hurried to offer the crown to Louis
XVIII.

§ VI. NINETEENTH CENTURY

The Restoration (1814–1830)

Louis XVIII gave to the French a Constitution which was an imitation of the English one; this was the Charter of 1814. The Restoration was an attempt to compromise between the Old Order and the Order which had resulted from the Revolution. The Old Order had as its symbol the white flag; the "legitimate" king considered himself as reigning by divine right and called 1814 the nineteenth year of his reign: the Chamber of Peers, an imitation of the House of Lords, was to form an hereditary aristocracy; finally, the Catholic religion again became the State religion. But the Charter recognised the equality of Frenchmen in the eyes of the law; the right of all to be eligible for public offices; liberty of worship, liberty of the Press; it created a Chamber of Deputies, who were chosen by the electors, beside the Chamber of Peers, who were nominated by the king. The great difficulty of the Restoration was to make this compromise between the principles of Old France and the principles of 1789 an enduring one; it was even more difficult to reconcile two groups of men in the governing class, on the one hand those who had held office under the Revolution and with Napoleon under the tricolour flag, and on the other the *émigrés* of the Old Order, who gloried in their steadfast fidelity to the Bourbons.

These difficulties, which were perceptible in 1814, were aggravated by the return from Elba. Napoleon presented himself as the champion of the people against the nobles, and of the army against the friends of foreigners; after having been accepted by France, he was overthrown at Waterloo. This episode of the Hundred Days made a breach between the *émigrés* and the men of Modern France. Nevertheless, the Charter remained and enabled the Constitutional Government to go on working until 1830.

The Charter had established civil, but not political, equality. In order to be an elector to the Chamber of Deputies, a payment of 300 francs in direct taxation was necessary; and to be eligible for election, a payment of 1000 francs. The two principal taxes were the land-tax and the *patente* or business-tax; thus the right to vote was chiefly in the hands of the landowners and big business men (manufacturers, merchants, bankers). There were hardly more than 100,000 electors and 16,000 eligible for election: the vast majority of the nation did not yet protest against this oligarchical rule.

The Chamber of Peers had no great prestige: twice over, in 1814 and in 1826, the kings allowed their ministers to create a "batch of peers," in order to assure a majority; this injured the assembly in popular estimation. The Chamber of Deputies became the scene of the great political struggles. The French parties have never been strongly organised and well-disciplined, like those of Great Britain or the United States: nevertheless, three parties can be distinguished in the Chamber; the ultra-Royalists, the constitutional Royalists, and the Liberals, or, in other words, the Right, the Centre, and the Left. The ultra-Royalists were the partisans of the Old Order, of whom the more intelligent, such as Chateaubriand in the Chamber of Peers, and Villèle in the other Chamber, accepted the Charter, on condition that special favour was shown to everything which recalled Old France. The constitutional Royalists wished to make the compromise between the Old Order and the New an effective one; their principal theorists, the "doctrinaires," had as their spokesman, Royer-Collard. The Liberals, who possessed great orators such as Benjamin Constant, Manuel, and General Foy, professed the principles of 1789: some accepted the Bourbons, provided that the Charter was respected; the others distrusted them, and regretted the Empire, or even dreamed of replacing the elder branch by the head of the younger branch, the Duc d'Orléans.

From 1814 until 1820, the power was in the hands of the constitutional Royalists, under two prominent leaders, the Duc de Richelieu, who felt the need of gaining modern France for the Bourbons, and Decazes, a new man and clever politician, who became the favourite of Louis XVIII. The Chamber of Deputies which was elected in 1815, nicknamed the "undiscoverable Chamber," was composed of ultra-Royalists, who favoured the White Terror (i.e. the popular movements carried out by the Royalists of the south) and the persecution of the adherents of the Hundred Days: Marshal Ney, for instance, was shot. Richelieu and Decazes persuaded Louis to dissolve this Chamber, and the new elections gave a majority to the Centre party. Richelieu, who was *persona grata* with Alexander I, obtained the liberation of French territory at the Congress of Aix-la-Chapelle. But the success of the Liberals at by-elections alarmed him and he resigned. Decazes continued his moderate policy, until the day when the assassination of the Duc de Berry, nephew of the king, by a revolutionary fanatic started a violent reaction, and the minister was obliged to resign his office.

The policy of the Right prevailed from 1820 to 1827. It was first led by Richelieu, whom the ultra-Royalists accepted for a few months as Premier; but soon they demanded a cabinet entirely composed of their friends, of which Villèle was head. A new electoral law, by virtue of which the electors who paid 1000 francs had two votes (this is the law of the "double-vote"), assured them a majority in the Chamber. The success of the Right exasperated the enemies of the Bourbons; the most violent amongst them, who had already formed secret societies, now, in imitation of Italy, organized the Association of *Carbonari*. It was composed partly of officers, worshippers of Napoleon, and partly of students, who conceived the idea of establishing a Republic. But all the attempted plots failed miserably; the Spanish expedition (1823), undertaken to restore the absolute power of Ferdinand VII, was an easily won success and was the means of absolutely reconciling the army and the monarchy. When Louis XVIII died in 1824, the Bourbons no longer met with any resistance.

Louis, lazy and sceptical, but witty and full of common sense, was succeeded by his brother, the Comte d'Artois, who became Charles X. This prince, who was stupid, obstinate, devout, and devoid of political sense, was beloved by the ultra-Royalists. They thought they could do as they liked, and Villèle, a hard worker and clever financier, but a timid politician, had not the courage to resist his party. By one law an indemnity of a thousand million francs was awarded to the *émigrés*, whose property had been confiscated; another law, half political, half religious, punished sacrilege by death; the government

proposed to re-establish the right of primogeniture, and totally
to suppress the liberty of the Press. These measures alarmed the
whole nation. They listened to the Liberals, who pointed out
that the Charter was menaced, and denounced the encroachments of the "priestly party," or the party, which in another
phrase of that time, favoured "the union of the throne and the
altar." The newspapers exposed the progress of the Jesuits
and the Congregation, a society chiefly composed of their old
pupils. The courts of law, resuming the Gallican traditions of the
ancient Parliaments, acquitted the newspapers who had used
this language. The whole of France applauded Béranger, the
song-writer, who celebrated the glories of the Republic and the
Empire. Some well-known ultra-Royalists, such as Chateaubriand, left their party and joined the Liberal opposition. The
elections, moreover, resulted in total defeat for the ministry,
and in 1828 Villèle had to abandon the power which he had held
for seven years.

A new ministry, led by Martignac, tried to return to the
policy of the Centre. But the Right became irritated by the
measures taken against the Jesuits, and the Left became
annoyed because insufficient concessions were made to it.
Charles X took advantage of these difficulties to dismiss the
ministry and to form a new and ultra-Royalist one, led by one
of his favourites, the Prince de Polignac, who was a mystic,
entirely devoid of any practical capacity (1829).

The external policy of the Restoration had remained prudent
and peaceful since 1815. It was only after an imperative man-
date from the Congress of Verona that France undertook the
Spanish expedition. At a later date, she intervened in the East
with England and Russia to save the Greeks; a French squadron
fought at Navarino, and a body of troops forced the Egyptians
to evacuate the Morea. The French ministers were hesitating
between an alliance with England or one with Russia: Polignac,
who wished for great successes abroad in order that he might
become popular at home, drew nearer to Russia, in the hope of
obtaining some territory on the left bank of the Rhine. At the
same time, against the will of England, he prepared an
expedition against Algiers to put down piracy and punish the
Dey, who had recently insulted France.

But the formation of this ministry had been regarded by the Liberal majority as a challenge. The Address of 1830, which declared that the Cabinet did not possess the confidence of the Chamber of Deputies, was passed by 221 votes. A very grave question thus arose. According to Louis XVIII and Charles X, the king could choose his ministers to please himself, and the Chamber could not reverse his choice: the Charter had created a constitutional Monarchy, but not Parliamentary control. According to the Address, the ministry should be in accord with the Chamber. Charles X dissolved the Chamber, but the majority of electors supported the cause of the 221. The king, encouraged by the capture of Algiers, let himself be persuaded by his ministers to violate the Charter, and he published the Ordinances of July 26th. But an *ordonnance*, issued by the king alone, was valueless when opposed to a *law*, passed by the two Chambers and promulgated by the king. Now, one of these ordinances modified the law which concerned the Press, and made it more severe; another modified the electoral law and diminished the number of electors. This was a veritable *coup d'état*; the Parisians replied by a Revolution.

It lasted three days, the 27th, 28th, and 29th of July. The young Republicans of Paris, former members of secret societies, on the 27th persuaded the workmen to follow them; arms were produced; barricades were erected. On the 28th, the insurgents seized the Hôtel de Ville and hoisted the tricolour flag, which brought them numerous recruits. Polignac had made no preparations for a serious battle; some regiments refused to fire on the people; only the Royal Guard, partly composed of Swiss, held firm to the end. But on the 29th they were driven out of the Tuileries and obliged to leave Paris. Charles X, who had remained inactive at Saint-Cloud, decided too late to make concessions; then, again too late, he abdicated in favour of his grandson, the Duc de Bordeaux. Finally, he had to submit, and left for Cherbourg, where he embarked. He died in exile six years later.

The July Monarchy (1830–1848)

During the three days, two revolutionary authorities had appeared in Paris; at the Hôtel de Ville, the aged Lafayette, the idol of the people, who saw in him the hero of 1789, was surrounded by the young Republican victors; in the house of the Liberal banker, Laffitte, there assembled numerous deputies, who resolved to offer the crown to the Duc d'Orléans. Lafayette, thinking France not yet ripe for a republic, persuaded his party to allow the establishment of the new royalty. The Duc d'Orléans went to visit Lafayette at the Hôtel de Ville, and for a few days kept the title of Lieutenant-General. The two Chambers, who were immediately summoned, revised the Charter, and on August 7 Louis-Philippe I was proclaimed king.

The Charter of 1830, as it is called, was only the Charter of 1814 amended, but it was founded on entirely different principles. The Old Order disappeared with the white flag, which was its symbol; there was no longer a "King of France," monarch by divine right, but a "King of the French," chosen by the Chamber. The hereditary aristocracy disappeared at the same time; the Chamber of Peers now consisted of life-members only. There was no longer a State religion; Catholicism was merely called the religion "professed by the majority of the French." All the governments since 1830 have kept the tricolour flag and have professed the principles of 1789.

The machinery of the Constitution was also changed. Parliamentary control was no longer contested; the fate of ministries depended on the vote of the Chamber of Deputies. Finally, this Chamber was elected by an extended suffrage: 200 francs in direct taxation must be paid to be an elector, 500 to be eligible for election. The number of electors under Louis-Philippe varied between 200,000 and 240,000; this was much less than the 700,000 voters given to Great Britain by the Reform Bill of 1832. The Legitimist nobility resigned all public offices, so as not to swear allegiance to the usurper; they retired to their châteaux, and held aloof; the reign of Louis-Philippe was therefore the reign of the *bourgeoisie*. This class not only chose the deputies, but was possessed of material force in the Garde Nationale, which had only played a secondary part under the Restoration, but which now became one of the fundamental institutions of France. In principle, every citizen had to serve in this armed force, which was charged with the maintenance of order and which elected its officers; as a matter of fact, the poor were eliminated by the regulation that each man should be equipped at his own expense and keep his arms in good order. The National Guard was the *bourgeoisie* armed.

Louis-Philippe was much superior to his two predecessors in intelligence and activity. He liked to manage everything himself and found it hard to acquiesce in the self-effacing rôle of a parliamentary monarch: above all he kept in his own hands the control of foreign policy, with the constant aim of maintaining peace and of causing himself to be accepted as an equal by the other sovereigns. Consequently, he came to be considered as responsible for everything which was done by the government; this was why a king, who was greatly loved by the electors, was hated by the enemies of the *bourgeoisie*, who made repeated attempts on his life.

The adherents of Louis-Philippe were divided, after 1830, into two parties: one, the "party of resistance," wished to establish order by force, and to make as few changes as possible; the other, the "party of movement," wished to re-establish order by gentler means, and proposed numerous reforms. Later, the first called itself the "Conservative party," and the second was called the "Dynastic Left." As these two parties were separated only by shades of opinion, questions of coteries and of personal rivalry held a great place in the debates of the Chamber of Deputies. As to the Chamber of Peers, public opinion took little notice of it, except at the times when (transformed into the Court of Peers) it tried cases of attempt on the king's life or crimes against the State.

The July monarchy had to fight two anti-dynastic parties, the Legitimists and the Republicans. In 1832, the Duchesse de Berry tried to stir up an insurrection among the Legitimists of the west, in favour of her son, the Duc de Bordeaux, whom she called Henry V, but the attempt failed miserably. Thenceforward, the Legitimist party confined itself to an opposition of the *salons*, preventing social intercourse between the court of

the Tuileries and the great houses of the Faubourg Saint-
Germain, and dissuading the European sovereigns from marrying
their daughters to the sons of the "king of barricades." This
party had in the Chamber one great orator, Berryer, who was
admired by all, but isolated.

The Republicans were much more formidable to the new king,
because they represented the democracy. At first, they were,
for the most part, cultured members of the *bourgeoisie*,
admirers of the Revolution, and dazzled by the victorious
struggle which it had maintained against Europe; they included the great journalist Armand Carrel, the chemist Raspail,
and Godefroy Cavaignac. But the party soon made numerous
recruits among the workmen of the great towns. At this time
the workmen were suffering terribly, both in France and in
England, and they could find no laws, either social or general,
to defend them; they joined the party which promised them
government by the people and the end of their sufferings. The
Parisian workmen, above all, who had just overthrown Charles X,
intended to take a part in political life. The Republicans told
them that a kingdom, which had been founded by one revolution, could be brought down by another. Thus broke out the
Parisian disturbances of 1832, 1834 and 1839, which were all
suppressed. After 1840, the Republican party gave up rebellions
and devoted itself to propaganda.

It would be erroneous to say that there was also a Bonapartist
party, but there existed a certain amount of Bonapartist sentiment. The Napoleonic cult, which was cherished by the poets,
historians, and artists, was encouraged by the Government
itself, when, in 1840, it caused the coffin of Napoleon to be
brought from St Helena and placed in the Invalides. After 1832,
when the son of Napoleon died in Austria, his nephew, Louis-
Napoleon Bonaparte (the future Napoleon III), regarded himself as the head of the family: twice over, in 1836 and in 1840,
he tried to stir up the army against Louis-Philippe, but without
success. In this way he at least advertised his name to the
people, who loved Napoleon as the symbol of the Revolution.

Finally, two parties made their appearance, not yet constituted, but which represented new tendencies: the Catholic
party and the Socialist party. The party of Liberal Catholics

originated with Lamennais, who exhorted the Catholics to separate themselves from the Legitimists, to defend the liberty of the people, and to demand the separation of Church and State. Being condemned by Rome, he broke with the Church; but his followers submitted, and the chief of them, Montalembert, became the leader of a party, which organised a violent campaign against the University and claimed liberty of education.

As regards Socialism, its first French theorists, Saint-Simon and Fourier, who were contemporaries of Robert Owen, were almost unknown to the people. But on the morrow of the July Revolution, the school of Saint-Simon had a moment of great brilliancy, till the school of Fourier eclipsed it. The workmen were ignorant of these theories and only knew that they were miserable; when the workmen of Lyons took arms in 1831, under a flag with the device "Live working or die fighting," they did not dream of socialism. About 1840, the new theorists, Louis Blanc, Cabet, and Proudhon adopted clearer, more aggressive, and more popular language, and their influence became powerful on the more educated workers. These listened above all to the militant democrats, Barbès and Blanqui, who organised secret societies with a view to revolution, and who established a link between the Republican party and the Socialist groups.

From 1830 to 1836, the new reign was greatly agitated by internal troubles. At the same time, foreign policy excited all the parties. At first it was believed that the Holy Alliance was about to take arms to restore Charles X. Then there was much interest in the revolted nations, the Belgians, the Italians, and, above all, the Poles. The French government helped the Belgians to free themselves, but only intervened timidly in Italy and abandoned the Poles. The leader of the party of resistance, the energetic Casimir Perier, declared that France did not want a warlike and revolutionary policy; when he died, his successors, Thiers, Guizot, and the Duke of Broglie continued his policy. They repressed the disturbances and took advantage of an attempt on the life of the king—that of the infernal machine— to pass repressive laws. All notable Republicans were either condemned to imprisonment or forced to leave the country. In 1836, peace at home and abroad seemed certain.

Then the dynastic parties became divided into numerous groups, the leaders of which, Thiers, Guizot, Molé, and Odilon Barrot, fought for power in the Chamber. This political confusion lasted until there was a grave foreign crisis. Mehemet-Ali, Pasha of Egypt and protégé of France, had just defeated the Sultan; the Tsar Nicholas, enemy of Louis-Philippe, came to terms with Lord Palmerston and brought in Austria and Prussia; and the four powers, leaving France isolated, signed the treaty of London (1840), which was aimed at the Pasha. Anger was great in Paris, where people spoke of fighting the new coalition and marching towards the Rhine; Thiers, then President of the Council, took military measures. But Louis-Philippe dismissed Thiers, made the Chamber approve the pacific policy of Guizot, and put an end to the Eastern crisis.

Guizot retained power from 1840 to 1848. Leader of the Conservative party, he wished to avoid political changes and to increase economic prosperity: the development of industries, which were protected by a very high customs tariff, and the construction of railways, as decided by the law of 1842, were the internal objects which interested him. Abroad, he wished to conclude an alliance with England, which was called *l'entente cordiale*, but various incidents, the quarrels concerning the right of search exercised by the English cruisers with a view to the suppression of the slave-trade, the claims of the missionary Pritchard, who was arrested at Tahiti, and the affairs of Morocco showed that this *entente* was not yet popular on either side of the Channel. Finally, a dynastic dispute, concerning the marriage of the Queen of Spain and her sister, caused variance between Louis-Philippe and Victoria, Guizot and Palmerston (1846). Then Guizot made advances to Metternich, to the great wrath of the French opposition, who blamed Austria for her tyranny in Italy and her threats against the Radicals in Switzerland.

While preserving peace in Europe, the Government afforded an outlet to French military activity in Algeria. After the fall of Charles X, the new monarchy had for a moment contemplated the evacuation of Algiers, and then had contented itself with the retention of some towns on the coast and the capture of Constantine. But the French remained blockaded in their possessions, which were frequently attacked by the natives, especially in the west, where the latter had found a remarkable leader in Emir Abd-el-Kader. Finally, complete occupation was decided on, and the governor-general, Bugeaud, was able to take the necessary strategical steps to conquer the whole of the Tell, to defeat the Moroccan allies of Abd-el-Kader at Isly, and unceasingly to pursue the fugitive Emir. The latter finally gave himself up.

However, hostility to the Conservative policy was growing in France. Louis-Philippe was regarded as responsible for it, and he lost his eldest son, the popular Duc d'Orléans, by accidental death. The king and Guizot were accused of neglecting the bulk of the nation, and of being interested only in the 240,000 electors, and of keeping these faithful to the ministry by corruption; some scandalous trials of peers, and of former ministers guilty of peculation, excited public opinion. The whole opposition demanded an increase in the number of electors; the members of the dynastic Left merely wished for a lowering of the qualification; the Republicans demanded manhood suffrage; but both united in defence of the principle of electoral reform. The agitation which was organised with this object in 1847 took the form of political banquets in all the large towns of France, and led to important results, all the more because there was a bad harvest and potato disease in France as in Ireland. But the king and the Premier refused all concessions, and prohibited a banquet in Paris, which had been announced for February 22, 1848. Disturbances therefore began on that day. On the 23rd, the National Guard, which had been summoned to restore order, greeted the king with cries of "Long live reform!" "Down with Guizot!" Louis-Philippe was alarmed and asked the minister to resign. This seemed likely to pacify every one, when a fusillade, which killed many in the crowd, roused the indignation of the workmen. On the 24th, the Government did not dare to put down the riots by force; Louis-Philippe abdicated in favour of his grandson, the Comte de Paris, and took to flight. The insurrectionists burst into the Chamber of Deputies; and a Provisional Government, appointed in the presence of the victors, proclaimed the Republic.

The Second Republic (1848–1852)

The Provisional Government was recognised by the whole country. This Government, which was to last until the convocation of a Constituent Assembly, consisted of a majority of moderate Republicans, such as the poet Lamartine and the scholar Arago, and a minority of Radicals, such as Ledru-Rollin, and Socialists, such as Louis Blanc and a working man. For two months Paris led a feverish life, stimulated by daily manifestos, meetings of clubs, and processions of armed workmen as National Guards. The Provisional Government, however, succeeded in maintaining its position without using force, and brought about some great reforms: the abolition of the death-penalty for political crimes, the abolition of slavery in the French colonies, the fixing of a maximum number of hours for a day's work and, above all, the establishment of manhood suffrage. This suffrage was in force for the election of the National Constituent Assembly, which met on May 4, 1848; it contained a large majority of moderate Republicans, most of them new men, knowing nothing of public life, and two minorities; to the Right that of the Conservatives, former Royalists who announced their adherence to the Republic, and to the Left, that of the "Social Democrats," who were also called the "Reds" because some of them wished to replace the tricolour by the red flag. The election of a moderate Assembly irritated the violent Parisian clubs, who on May 15 vainly tried to disperse it. The Revolution, however, had put an end to industrial activity; as Paris was full of workmen without work, "national workshops" were opened for them, where they were paid without doing much work; wrathful at the news that the Assembly was about to close these workshops, they revolted. The "June days" (21–25 June) ended after a desperate street-battle in the victory of the troops, who were commanded by General Cavaignac. The Assembly was able to complete the Constitution of 1848; it gave the legislative power to a single Assembly, elected by manhood suffrage, and the executive power to a President of the Republic, elected in the same manner. The election of the President was fixed for December 10, 1848. The moderate Republicans put forward General Cavaignac; but his opponent, Louis-Napoleon Bonaparte, was supported not only by the Conservatives, enemies of the Republic, but also by the workmen who were hostile to their June adversary and by the peasants who were attached to the memory of the great Napoleon. He was elected by 5,500,000 votes against 2,000,000 given to Cavaignac and other candidates.

Then began a great reaction, caused by the fear inspired by the Socialists, Communists, and "Reds." The Prince-President, as he was called, chose his ministers from the Royalists, amongst others, Falloux, who represented the Catholic party. The Legislative National Assembly, elected in 1849 in place of the Constituent Assembly, had a majority of 500 Conservatives, Legitimists, Orleanists, Bonapartists, and Catholics, all united against Socialism, and a minority of 200 Social Democrats, who called themselves the Montagnards, in memory of 1793. The party of Moderate Republicans was crushed. Before the elections, the President, in order to satisfy the Catholic party, had sent troops to Rome, where the Republicans were in the ascendant since the flight of Pius the Ninth; these troops were repulsed by Garibaldi. The Legislative Assembly approved the expedition; the minority provoked the Parisian rebellion of June 13th, which was at once suppressed. The President and the Assembly agreed to continue the expedition to Rome; the power of the Pope was restored. Internally, they multiplied repressive measures, and passed two great conservative laws: the Education law, called the "Loi Falloux," established liberty of education in such a way that it was specially to the advantage of the religious Orders; and the law of May 31, 1850, enacted three years' domicile before a citizen could be registered as an elector, and thus allowed three million voters to be struck off the roll, because the working population was at that time a very shifting one.

The agreement between the President and the Assembly did not last long. The leaders of the majority thought that they had found in the President an ignorant and docile person, who would allow himself to be led by them; they now perceived that the nephew of Napoleon was working for himself. The President placed at the head of his army, especially in Paris, generals devoted to his cause: afterwards to gain the workmen, who were irritated by the law of May 31, he proposed to suppress it; but the majority refused. Finally he brought about the *coup d'état* of December 2, 1851. His proclamations announced that the Assembly was dissolved, that manhood suffrage was restored, and that the President would remain Dictator, until the nation had been consulted by a plébiscite. The Conservatives in the Assembly attempted a legal resistance, but were arrested or dispersed; the Republicans tried to stir up the faubourgs to insurrection, but they were deterred by a short fusillade. In the same way, the attempts at resistance in various departments, especially by the Republican peasants in the south, found the army ready to suppress them. The plébiscite of December 20 approved the conduct of the President. Then began the systematic repression of the Republicans and above all of the "reds": in each department a "mixed commission," consisting of a general, a magistrate, and a prefect, sentenced them, without regular trial, to punishments varying from internment in a town to deportation to Algeria or Guiana.

During this time the Prince-President promulgated the Constitution of 1852, which established an arbitrary Republic. At the end of a few months it was modified in such a manner as to transform the Republic into an Empire. Another plébiscite approved this change and on December 2, 1852 the reign of Napoleon III began.

The Second Empire (1852–1870)

The Constitution of 1852 was copied from that by which France was governed under Napoleon I. The Emperor, who had been given the sovereignty by plébiscite, possessed all executive power, declared war, made treaties on his sole responsibility, and alone had the right to initiate legislation; the ministers depended entirely on him, did not form a Cabinet, and were not responsible to the Assemblies. As for the three Assemblies, the State Council, appointed by the Emperor, drafted all projected laws, while the Senate, composed of life-members nominated by the Emperor, supervised the working of the Constitution. Only the Legislative Body, elected by manhood suffrage, could have offered any opposition; but the Government insured elections favourable to itself by putting forward official candidates in all constituencies, by forcing the officials to support them, and by preventing the other candidates from holding public meetings.

The Legislative Body discussed and voted the laws, especially the Budget: but it was not yet allowed to hold long sessions, to publish the reports of its debates, or, above all, to vote amendments on any single part of the Budget; the credits of any minister had to be adopted or rejected as a whole. Finally, the Press was subjected, not only to the severity of Correctional Courts, but also to the supervision of the prefects; a paper which had received two administrative "warnings," could be suspended or suppressed.

In the early years of his reign Napoleon III showed intelligence and firmness. At home, he believed in having a very strong government, in suppressing political liberty, and endearing himself to the mass of the people by the increase of wealth and of work. Abroad, he wished to play a great part, to intervene in all important questions, and to bring about the triumph of a new policy, contrary to the treaties of 1815, and founded on the principle of nationality. This former conspirator always retained a taste for mystery; during the whole of his reign he carried on a secret diplomacy, often opposed to the official diplomacy, which depended on the minister of Foreign Affairs.

This arbitrary rule lent upon the police, which became very powerful, on the army, which again took the first place in Society, and on the Church, which was loaded with favours. On the contrary, the teaching body, consisting of school-masters and professors, was suspected of Liberalism, and was subjected to a real tyranny. The great majority of the nation profited by the economic development; the railways, the construction of which was pushed forward with much greater activity than ever before, transformed commercial life; the Paris Bourse became a powerful financial market. Finally, immense public works, directed by the prefect Haussmann, created in Paris wide, light, and airy streets, in place of the little narrow streets, where barricades could be easily erected. Abroad, Napoleon III allied himself with England during the Crimean War. The victory of the Alma was followed by the long siege of Sebastopol, which was ended by the successful assault on the Malakoff tower. At the Congress of Paris in 1856 Napoleon appeared as the arbiter of Europe.

The opposition of the Royalists was no longer powerful, since the clergy had abandoned them. The Republican opposition showed itself mostly outside France; the exiles living abroad, such as Edgar Quinet, Louis Blanc, and above all Victor Hugo, denounced the imperial despotism to the world. The attempt of the Italian Orsini on the life of the Emperor (1858) caused the law of Public Security to be passed, which led to further deportations without trial. The Republicans had succeeded in getting five of their number (out of 251) into the Chamber; the Five, as they were called, had two great orators, Émile Ollivier and Jules Favre, but their speeches did not reach the public. At the end of 1858 the absolute Empire seemed firmer than ever.

In 1859 everything was changed by the Italian war. Napoleon, who was formerly a Carbonaro, wished to drive the Austrians out of the Italian peninsula; after having come to an agreement with Cavour at the secret interview of Plombières, he took arms to defend Piedmont and won the victories of Magenta and Solferino; then, fearing an attack by Prussia, he stopped the war and signed the preliminaries of Villafranca. But it was too late to arrest the course of the Revolution in Italy; the Emperor allowed it to take its course, on condition that Savoy and Nice should be restored to France. The population of these provinces, consulted by a plébiscite, replied almost unanimously "yes." This was the apogee of the Empire (1860).

The Italian war brought about a change in home policy. The French clergy, seeing the Temporal Power of the Pope in danger, started a great campaign in favour of Pius IX; the Catholic party attacked the Italian policy of the Empire, and in many districts renewed their friendship with the Royalist party. At the same time Napoleon III suddenly announced his conversion to Free Trade and signed a commercial treaty with England (1860), thus causing discontent amongst the industrial workers who were Protectionists. As the opposition of the Right was becoming stronger, the Government sought for supporters among the Left. This was the beginning of an evolution, which little by little was to replace the absolute Empire by the Liberal Empire. The decrees of 1860 allowed the publication of the debates in the Legislative Body and enjoined an annual discussion on the Address. The Five could therefore make themselves heard throughout the country. Moreover, the desire for political liberty was increasing and when, in 1863, the Legislative Body was renewed, instead of an opposition of five, there was one of 35, amongst whom Thiers took the first place.

At this date, the foreign policy of Napoleon III seemed to be always fortunate. In Africa the Empire had achieved the conquest of Algeria and had begun that of Senegal: in Asia a French force was sent to protect the Christians of Syria from massacre, a Franco-British expedition punished the Chinese breach of faith and took Pekin, a squadron founded the colony of Cochin China; in Oceania, New Caledonia was occupied. The prestige of the Emperor, which was very great in Mahomedan countries, enabled him to continue the enterprise begun by Ferdinand de Lesseps, the Suez Canal, which was finished in 1869.

In 1863 misfortunes began, while the Emperor, stricken by illness, became more and more changeable and irresolute. The Polish Revolt in 1863 excited unanimous sympathy in France; Napoleon tried to intervene with the Tsar in conjunction with England and Austria, but this intervention had no other result than to destroy the amicable relations which had existed for six years between France and Russia. In Italy the Emperor, divided between the desire of befriending the new kingdom and of preserving Rome for Pius IX, promised to withdraw his troops on condition that the Italian capital should be fixed at Florence; but this compromise pleased no one. In Mexico, after having joined England and Spain in claiming an indemnity for the European victims of the civil wars, he continued, single-handed, an expedition to make the Austrian archduke, Maximilian, Emperor of Mexico; this expedition, which roused the anger of the United States, ended in the departure of the French troops and the death of Maximilian (1867). Moreover, Bismarck arrived on the scene; he made use of Napoleon's sympathy with Prussia and of squabbles between France and England, to deprive Denmark of Schleswig-Holstein. Afterwards, when he went to visit the Emperor at Biarritz in 1865, he was able to secure his neutrality during the war of 1866. Sadowa marked the arrival of a new great military power and the close of French preponderance. Napoleon attempted some clumsy negotiations on the subject of Belgium and was not even able to acquire Luxemburg in 1867. These checks were not compensated by the battle of Mentana (1867), where the French troops defeated Garibaldi, who was marching on Rome.

The authority of the Emperor at home suffered from these failures, which were mercilessly pointed out in the Legislative Body by opponents such as Thiers. A new military law, intended to strengthen the army, excited such discontent that they dared not enforce it; the Garde Mobile, which was meant to supply a territorial army, existed only on paper. It had been hoped to gain over the workmen by a law which gave them the right to strike (1864); nevertheless, all the militant workmen opposed the Government, became converted to Socialism, which had just reappeared, and joined the International Association of Workers, which had its headquarters in London. The youth of the *bourgeoisie*, more and more hostile to the Empire, applauded its new adversaries, the brilliant pamphleteer Henri Rochefort, and the great orator, Gambetta. And even in the Legislative Body a Liberal Bonapartist party was forming, which wished to change the Constitution. The elections of 1869 were a triumph for this liberal tendency.

For several years Napoleon III had been hesitating between the arbitrary policy, defended by his minister Rouher, and the liberal policy, supported by his cousin, Prince Napoleon, and recommended by Émile Ollivier, a former Republican who had rallied to the Empire. In the end the latter prevailed and became the leader of a new ministry (January 2, 1870): soon the Emperor agreed to the establishment of parliamentary rule, causing it to be ratified by a plébiscite, which affirmed it by a considerable majority. His foreign policy was equally vacillating: sometimes he was in treaty with Austria and Italy for an alliance against Prussia; another time he listened to the counsels of Ollivier, who desired peace, and who even proposed reciprocal disarmament to Berlin.

Then occurred the candidature of a' Hohenzollern for the throne of Spain; it was withdrawn, but the Ministry, urged thereto by the entourage of the Emperor, demanded guarantees for the future. Bismarck thus found the opportunity of publishing the telegram sent from Ems by King William of Prussia, altering it in such a manner as to make it appear that France had been insulted. The French Government fell into the trap, and the declaration of war was approved by the Legislative Body on July 14. Mobilisation was carried out amidst indescribable confusion. The slight check at Weissembourg (August 4), followed by the simultaneous defeats at Froeschwiller and Forbach (August 6), showed the military superiority of the enemy: soon, after three desperate battles, Bazaine was driven back to Metz, while MacMahon's army retreated towards Châlons. A new French Ministry obliged MacMahon to march towards Metz to relieve Bazaine; during this march the army was surrounded at Sedan. By its surrender on September 2, the Germans took 80,000 prisoners, including the Emperor. The news was known in Paris on the next day. On the 4th of September the people rose and invaded the Legislative Body without any resistance being offered: then they proclaimed the Republic.

The foundation of the Republic (1870–1875)

The Provisional Government formed on September 4 took the name of "Government of National Defence"; it consisted of most of the Paris deputies, presided over by General Trochu. He wished to remain in the capital, even during the siege, and he sent a delegation to Tours to govern the rest of France; its principal member was Gambetta. He and his assistants made a great effort to create new armies, with which they hoped to raise the siege of Paris. But the surrender of Bazaine set free large German forces. The new armies were composed of inexperienced soldiers, who were incapable of enduring for long the fatigues of war and the sufferings of a bitter winter. Even with good generals, such as Chanzy and Faidherbe, the Army of the Loire and the Northern Army were beaten; the Eastern Army, which had not succeeded in raising the blockade of Belfort, was obliged to retreat into Switzerland to avoid being captured. Paris had resisted much longer than had been expected; but the Paris army, in attempting to force the besieging lines, were beaten in the battles of Champigny and Buzenval; and famine compelled the town to capitulate. An armistice was concluded, so as to give France time to elect a National Assembly, which was to choose between peace and war.

Manhood suffrage showed itself hostile to the Bonapartists,

who were responsible for the war, and to the Republicans, who wished to continue it; the majority in the National Assembly was composed of Royalists, because they posed as partisans of peace. Thiers, who was very popular because he had opposed the foreign policy of the Empire, was elected in twenty-six departments, and the Assembly, which met at Bordeaux, made him President of the Republic. He came to Versailles to sign with Bismarck the preliminaries of a peace which robbed France of Alsace-Lorraine and imposed on her an indemnity of five thousand million francs. The final treaty was concluded at Frankfort in May 1871.

Civil war was added to invasion. The Paris workmen, exasperated by the sufferings of the siege, by the capitulation, and by the election of an Assembly which was hostile to the Republic, had supplied many adherents to a revolutionary party; the triumphal entry of the Germans into Paris put the finishing touch to their irritation. The disturbance of March 18, 1871, when the troops deserted their generals, made Thiers decide to leave Paris the same evening, and to transfer the Government to Versailles, where the National Assembly met. The revolutionaries, having become masters of the capital, elected a municipal council, the Commune of Paris, which for two months kept up the struggle with the Government of France. Finally the army entered Paris and, after a battle of barricades, suppressed the revolt, which was rigorously punished.

The President and the Assembly worked together to restore the financial position as so to pay the war-indemnity, and also to obtain the departure of the enemy. Thiers, who was very active in spite of his great age, was able to float vast loans with success, so that the liberation of French territory took place in 1873, before the date originally fixed. But the President and the Assembly disagreed over the definite form of government which should be given to France; Thiers, formerly a monarchist, thought that henceforward only a republic was possible; but the Royalist majority overthrew him (May 24, 1873) and appointed Marshal MacMahon President. It seemed probable that the monarchy would soon be restored in the person of the former Duc de Bordeaux, grandson of Charles X, who had taken the title of Comte de Chambord; the head of the house of Orleans, the Comte de Paris, went to visit him in Austria, and the two branches of the Bourbons became reconciled. But the Comte de Chambord, who had lived for forty years abroad and did not know France, declared that he would only accept the crown with the white flag, which was the symbol of return to the principles of the Old Order; whereupon the Royalist deputies realised that they must renounce any hope of the restoration of Henry V. The National Assembly hesitated for a year, unable to establish a monarchy, unwilling to establish a republic. But the partial elections had continued to increase the number of Republican deputies, and the whole of France demanded that the Provisional Government should end; some Conservatives joined the Republicans in the Assembly to pass the three constitutional laws, which taken together form what is called the Constitution of 1875. Legislative power is divided between the Chamber of Deputies, elected by manhood suffrage, and the Senate, elected by the delegates of the municipal councils. Executive power belongs to the President of the Republic, who is elected for seven years by the two Chambers combined (this joint meeting is called the National Assembly, or the Congress); he is not responsible and governs by means of ministers who are responsible to the Chambers. The Constitution can be revised, if it is so decided first by the Chamber and the Senate separately, and if the decision is afterwards ratified by the Congress. The revisions which have been made since 1875 have been only on points of secondary importance (particularly the electoral law of the Senate) and have not altered the general character of the Constitution, which is still in force to-day.

The Republic (1875–1914)

The first elections to the Chamber of Deputies (1876) gave a strong majority to the Republicans. But the Conservatives, who had on their side President MacMahon and a small majority of the Senate, did not despair of regaining power. On the 16th of May 1877, MacMahon, persuaded by them, dismissed his Republican ministers, and appointed a Cabinet of the Right, which obtained from the Senate the vote necessary to dissolve the Chamber, but in the elections the Republicans were again successful. The President yielded, and when the partial renewal of the Senate resulted in a majority for the Left in this assembly also, he resigned and was replaced by Jules Grévy (1879). All official power was now in the hands of the Republicans.

There followed a period of great legislative activity, in order to realise the political reforms which had been placed on the Republican programme. Laws established the right of meeting (1880), the liberty of the Press (1881), the liberty of professional syndicates (1884), and municipal rights (1884). Popular education was organised by making elementary education free and compulsory for all, and later, by deciding that all communal schools should be unsectarian and managed by secular teachers; religious instruction must be given by the ministers of religion outside the school (1882–1886). These laws came into force in spite of the heated opposition of the clergy and the Catholic party, called by its adversaries the *clerical* party. At the same time, France inaugurated a very active colonial policy, which gained for her Tunis (1881), Tonkin (1884), the Madagascar protectorate (1885), and numerous settlements in the regions of the Niger and the Congo (1883–5). On the other hand, she sustained a check in Egypt, where, after 1881, French influence was superseded by British influence.

During this period, the moderate Republican, or "opportunist" party had governed under the direction of Gambetta, who died in 1882, and of Jules Ferry; but the colonial expeditions, especially that of Tonkin, made Jules Ferry unpopular, and his party was beaten at the legislative elections of 1885 by the Radicals, whose leader was Clemenceau, and by the Conservatives. In the new Chamber, there were bitter political struggles, numerous ministerial crises, and finally, all the malcontents of the Right and Extreme Left gathered round an eloquent and ambitious general, Boulanger, who stood as the adversary of parliamentary rule; after a moment of great success, "Boulangism" was beaten at the legislative elections of 1889.

There was next a period of calm, which was helped by the success of the Paris Exhibition of 1889, and by the close of the agricultural and financial crisis, which had made things difficult for some years. Parliament conciliated the farmers and industrial workers by giving up Free Trade and returning to a system of Protectionist customs. Pope Leo XIII advised the French Catholics to support the Republic, a counsel which divided the Conservatives. The most important ministry of this time, led by Freycinet, concluded the Franco-Russian alliance, which was revealed to the world by the visit of the French squadron to Cronstadt (1891). The popularity of President Carnot, who succeeded Grévy, contributed to the consolidation of the Republic.

After this, working and social questions again presented themselves. French Socialism, quelled for some time by the suppression of the Commune, now reappeared; it was inspired by the theories of Karl Marx, and allied itself with international Socialism to celebrate the first of May. Financial scandals, such as the Panama one, brought it new recruits. While the violent Anarchists alarmed Paris by dynamite outrages, the political Socialists were successful in bringing into the Chamber at the elections of 1893 a group of about fifty deputies, led by some remarkable orators, Jules Guesde, Millerand, and Jaurès. They spread their ideas by constant propaganda; but the majority in Parliament rebuffed them and for two years upheld the ministry of Méline (1896–1898), who tried to unite the Centre and the Right and to consider, above all, the interests of the rural classes.

After 1898 political life was for some years dominated by the Dreyfus case. Captain Dreyfus had been sentenced to deportation as being guilty of delivering military documents to Germany. Some notable people, recognising that a judicial error had been committed, demanded the revision of the trial. As Dreyfus was a Jew, the anti-Semite group, at that time numerous and active, roused the clergy, officers, and Conservatives to oppose the revision; all the fighting members of the Right, united under the new name of "Nationalists," were *Anti-Dreyfusards*, while an increasing number of Republicans became *Dreyfusards*. The Nationalist movement became very violent at the time of President Loubet's election (1899). Then Waldeck-Rousseau, the former colleague of Gambetta and Ferry, formed a ministry of "Republican Defence," in which, by a novelty which then seemed very daring, he included a Socialist, Millerand. The Cabinet re-established order and passed a law which allowed liberty of association, while taking measures against the increase of religious Orders. As the policy of Waldeck-Rousseau was supported by the people in the elections of 1902, his successors continued the war with the monks, and the relations of the French Government with the Papacy became steadily worse. Finally the law of 1905 insured the separation of the Churches and the State.

About this time a change came in foreign policy. France had for thirty years shown great reserve in European affairs, but had founded a large colonial dominion; the successors of Jules Ferry had carried out the occupation of French Cochin China, the subjection of Madagascar, the unification of French West Africa, and of French Equatorial Africa. Some disagreements with England had resulted, and an armed conflict had almost broken out at the time of the Fashoda incident (1898). Meanwhile the Franco-Russian alliance became stronger, and rather intensified the distrust between France and Great Britain. As to Germany, she was satisfied with seeing the two Western powers on bad terms, and also satisfied at having brought Italy into the Triple Alliance, and of thus threatening France from the south-east, and she occasionally made perfidious advances to a nation which she regarded as negligible.

But conditions changed when Edward VII became king, and the Minister of Foreign Affairs was Delcassé, who held office for seven years (1898–1905); both realised the importance of the Franco-British Entente. The diplomatic agreement between the two countries in 1904 put an end to the chief causes of dispute, giving Egypt to England and Morocco to France. The reconciliation annoyed Germany, and provoked the visit of William II to Tangiers, which was as good as a challenge to France. As the latter did not want war, Delcassé left the ministry and the conference of Algeciras established international control in Morocco. Thenceforward German threats succeeded each other; the Casablanca incident (1908), when Germany demanded apologies which Clemenceau, who was then President of the Council, refused; the incident of Agadir (1911) followed by a compromise, where Germany made concessions in Morocco, in return for French territory ceded in the Congo; and the campaign in the whole of the German Press against the Foreign

Legion of the Colonial army. French diplomacy had, however, put an end to the differences with Italy, had strengthened the *entente* with England and had even succeeded, after 1907, in bringing about an Anglo-Russian understanding. But France remained frankly pacific, and reduced her standing army by the military law of 1905. Being rid of the Dreyfus case, since the *Cours de Cassation* had declared that the officer was innocent (1906), she was much occupied with working-class questions, and was applying a series of important social laws, dealing with such subjects as accidents caused by work, the length of the working day, and working-class pensions.

The increase in the German army, announced at the end of 1912, made it clear to the French nation, which was so eager for peace, that it was being more and more seriously threatened. In 1913, in spite of a heated opposition, the Chambers passed the new military law, which changed the two years' military service to three. This was a great sacrifice to impose on the people; the elections of May 1914 returned a Chamber which was divided on this question into two almost equal parties. They had just passed an important financial reform, the establishment of an income-tax, when, on August 4, the German aggression united all parties to save the country.

Social Conditions. The French population rose from 29 millions in 1815 to 36 millions in 1860, reached 37 millions after the re-union with Savoy, then fell to 36 by the loss of Alsace-Lorraine; in 1913, she counted nearly 40 millions. In 1815, the vast majority of the nation consisted of peasants, occupied chiefly in work on the land; for the last hundred years a slow but continuous movement, caused by industrial progress, has been attracting the country-folk to the towns. In the census of 1821, with the exception of Paris (713,000 inhabitants) there were only two towns with more than 100,000 inhabitants, Lyons and Marseilles; the census of 1911 showed, in addition to Paris (2,880,000 inhabitants), fifteen towns with over 100,000 inhabitants.

This change, however, has been much less accentuated than in England and Germany. More than half the French population lives exclusively by agriculture. A striking feature of the country is the division of property; this division is continually increasing, as was proved by the inquiry of 1908. French society thus possesses a firm foundation, which the numerous Parisian revolutions have not shaken. For long the peasants remained ignorant, indifferent to general politics, and only troubled when there was a question of interference with their property or of changing the land-tax. This inertia has much diminished in the last thirty years, especially since the development of elementary education; the peasants, who for long were distrustful of the Republic, have now assured its continuance by their votes. Their individualism kept them for long hostile to every kind of association; in this respect also, customs have gradually changed, and since the law of 1884, agricultural unions have grown up, which in 1914 comprised 1,029,000 members. Consisting chiefly of proprietors, these unions have been principally formed for the collective purchase of manures and machines; later, the local unions have formed themselves into district unions. In spite of their practical character, these associations have also exercised political influence in favour of a Moderate Republic. Agrarian Socialism has only found adherents in a small number of unions of workmen.

The noisy political part played by French workmen, for the greater part proletarian, is a contrast to the peaceable spirit of the peasants, who are mostly proprietors. The former dates from the revolution of 1830, which having been accomplished by the Parisian workmen, gave them the desire to take a place in the State; this coincided with a deplorable material situation, which was disclosed to the general public in 1840 by Villermé's inquiry. The militant workmen specially devoted themselves to secret societies and to riots, at a time when all unions and associations were punished as if they were crimes; the law of 1864 on strikes and the law of 1884 on unions permitted legal and public activity. Amongst the workmen in the large towns a struggle between two tendencies has always been noticeable: a political tendency, inclining them to join with the Radical middle-class in defence of a democratic programme; and a syndicalist tendency, leading them to form a "working class" apart, outside any middle-class party. The first tendency has generally predominated amongst the French workmen. For the last thirty years, the two tendencies have become reconciled and there has been a parallel development of socialism and syndicalism. Since 1893 socialism has set the example of the best organised, but not the largest, numerical party that there has ever been in France. As to syndicalism, it has grown slowly, for the French workmen are more refractory than the British to the regular payment of large contributions: but in 1914 the legally organised workmen's unions numbered 1,026,000 members, almost as many as the agricultural unions. The local syndicates have combined to form Labour Exchanges, or unions of syndicates of different trades in the same town, and National Federations, or unions of the syndicates of the same trade in the whole country. These unions have, in their turn, combined to form the General Confederation of Labour, which, organised in 1902, took over the direction of the whole syndicalist movement a few years later.

The tendency towards professional combination has, moreover, spread to all classes of society. Those employed in trade have copied the workmen; the various bodies of officials have formed "Friendly Societies," which are becoming more and more like unions. This transition from individualism to collectivism specially characterised the decade before the war of 1914.

The aristocracy, after the fruitless attempt made under the Restoration, has been forced to abandon the hope of playing a special political part. Its voluntary inaction under Louis-Philippe and its forced inaction under the Second Empire have ended in the ruin of its influence. Many of the nobles have, as great landowners, kept a real authority over their farmers or their tenants; but this ascendancy also has diminished in the last fifty years, for the peasants, feeling themselves freer, have been able fearlessly to express their old antipathy for the domination of the landlords.

Since 1830 it is the *bourgeoisie* which has governed France. Until 1848 the property qualification kept it in the position of a privileged class: since 1848 manhood suffrage has opened it largely to recruits coming from the workman and peasant classes. It therefore consists of various elements, with a single common feature, the education received in the Secondary

schools. Until about 1880, a young man of the *bourgeoisie* had
to learn Latin; since then this obligation, imposed by custom,
has disappeared. The lower *bourgeoisie* is numerous, thanks to
the French taste for the one-man business: it was for long
distinguished by its habit of preparing its sons for public offices,
which were attractive because of their regular work, assured
income, and the prestige they carried outside. The upper
bourgeoisie, which consists of the representatives of wholesale
trade, of manufacture, and of banking, has received a good
share of the wealth which has accrued to the capital and
revenue of France during the second half of the 19th century.
It remained opposed to the movement for professional combination much longer than the workmen; the trusts of America
and the cartels of Germany were without analogy in France
until the first years of the 20th century. Then the masters
followed the general movement, and associations such as the
Federation of Manufacturers and Traders, or the Committee of
Forges, have acquired an influence which, especially in economic
politics, is not negligible.

Feminism has not become an important article of political
programmes, as it has in Anglo-Saxon countries. The Rights of
Women were proclaimed by the followers of Saint-Simon and by
some Republicans, but without result. The feminist associations
which were formed later did not begin to combine their efforts
until 1903, under the influence of the National Council of Women.
A few partial results have been obtained: women engaged in
trade have become eligible to vote for the Courts and Chambers
of Commerce; a law passed in 1897 authorised women to serve
as witnesses to deeds, another (1907) gave the married woman
full control over her earnings. Above all, the organisation of
primary and secondary education for girls since 1880 has prepared the female sex to play a more important part than before.
But the claim for the right to vote at municipal and legislative
elections has found few partisans, even amongst women.

A final important feature of French society is the extraordinary
influence of Paris. In no other country in the world does the
capital exercise equal preponderance. All the revolutions made
in Paris up to 1870 were accepted by the whole nation; since
then, the growth of liberty all through France has slightly

reduced the political sway of Paris; Boulangism in 1889 and Nationalism in 1900, which were for a time successful in Paris, were rejected by the immense majority of the electors. But Paris still remains the centre of important trade, of the manufacture of luxuries, and of wealth; it remains the centre of intellectual life, of art, and of literature. Finally, it has maintained its direct power on the country, thanks to the centralisation established by the administrative system of France.

Administrative Institutions. The administrative machinery which was fixed by the Constituent Assembly and slightly modified by Napoleon, remained almost unaltered in the 19th century. The country is divided into *départements*; three were added after 1860 by the annexation of Savoy and Nice; there were three less after 1871 by the loss of Alsace-Lorraine; the total number in 1914, as a hundred years before, was 86. The departments are divided into *arrondissements*, the arrondissements into *cantons*, the cantons into *communes*. In 1814 the prefect governed the department: he consulted the General Council, which was composed of members living in the district, but chosen by the central Government. In the arrondissement was found the sub-prefect, not less docile to all orders from Paris. In the commune the Mayor and the Municipal Council likewise received their appointment from above, and not from the electors. The Government also appointed the judges, most of whom were irremovable: law-suits between the State and private individuals were tried before special courts, which might be suppressed at the pleasure of ministers, or by the Prefecture Councils in the department, or by the still higher authority of the State Council in Paris. An official could not be prosecuted by a private person before the ordinary courts, without the authorisation of the State Council.

Over against the ministers, who directed these officials, the Charter of 1814 and all subsequent Constitutions placed an elective Assembly, a Chamber of Deputies. On the other hand, there showed itself a tendency, which became daily stronger, to place in the department, arrondissement, or commune, a body chosen by the inhabitants in opposition to the administrator appointed by the central Government. Thence arose two important questions: in Paris, would the preponderance lie with the ministers, who were the heads of the executive power, or with the Chamber, which was invested with the legislative power? In local government, would the orders which came from Paris, or the wishes of the inhabitants, have most weight?

There was a great temptation for the ministers to make use of the officials to obtain elections favourable to their policy. Under all forms of government, the prefects and sub-prefects were considered as having a task at least as important as their administrative duties—that of preparing the legislative elections. From 1815 to 1848 the matter appeared all the easier, because the property qualification only allowed the electoral right to be exercised by a small minority. A deputy could be elected by 150 or 200 votes under the Restoration, by 300 or 400 under Louis-Philippe; only too often the prefects had the task of gaining by fear, by promises, or by corruption, some doubtful elector, who might decide the majority. It seemed as though the establishment of manhood suffrage in 1848 must put an end to the pressure of the officials. On the contrary, under the Second Empire it was stronger than ever: all administrative activity was employed in favour of the "official" candidates, whose names appeared on the white placards which were reserved for the announcements of public authority; the prefects replaced personal pressure on an individual elector by collective pressure on some commune, or some social group which was demanding a favour; finally, electoral constituencies were cut up in such a way as to swamp a Republican commune with villages which were inhabited by docile peasants. Since 1870 many ministers have still tried to have recourse to electoral pressure; but the development of public life, of the Press, and of political organisations have reduced almost to zero the influence of the prefects on the decisions of manhood suffrage.

In local government, the electoral principle spread after 1830; the General and Municipal Councils were nominated by the electors with a property qualification differing in value according to the importance of the commune. After 1848 universal suffrage was introduced. But the powers of these local councils remained very limited, and above all the central Government did not allow to Municipal Councils the right of choosing their mayor. Things did not change until after 1870; two laws especially, that of 1871 on General Councils, and that of 1884 on Municipal Councils, gave to local liberty a scope unknown since Napoleon I. To-day each department has still at its head the prefect, appointed by the ministers; beside him the General Council, elected for six years in the proportion of one councillor to each commune, holds at least two annual meetings and appoints a departmental committee, which represents it during the rest of the year. The arrondissement, which is much less important, is governed by the sub-prefect, and appoints the council of the arrondissement by universal suffrage.

The commune elects the Municipal Council by universal suffrage. The mayor, with the colleagues who assist him, is appointed by the Municipal Council, which chooses him from its members; he is both the agent of the central authority and the representative of the commune and is subordinate to the prefect, but depends, above all, on his electors. On most questions, the decisions of the Municipal Councils are final, if the prefect, after a month, makes no objection; the communal finances remain under the care of the prefects. In fine, the communal liberties have been much increased, without, however, extending so far as in the principal democratic countries of Europe. This system of autonomy seemed difficult to put into force, because out of the 36,000 communes of France 31,000 had less than 1500 inhabitants, and, amongst these, 16,000 had less than 500 inhabitants. Nevertheless, even the smallest of them have found a mayor capable of fulfilling his duties, sometimes with the help of a secretary, a paid official, who is generally the municipal schoolmaster.

Paris has kept a government of its own. After having had under the Second Empire a Municipal Council chosen by the Government, it possesses since 1871 an Elected Council; the city is divided into 20 arrondissements or wards and 80 quarters, and elects by universal suffrage a Municipal Council of 80 members, each quarter choosing one councillor. But this Council does not elect the mayor; the Government appoints the twenty mayors who administer the wards, and places above them the Prefect of the Seine and the Prefect of Police, who share the powers which would devolve on a mayor of Paris.

The Republican spirit has in the last thirty years spread to

institutions which seemed destined to combat it. Thus the State
Council appeared between 1815 and 1870 to be the instrument
of executive power and of centralisation. But in the last twenty-
five years it has become noted for the care taken to repress abuse
of power by officials or ministers; private individuals injured by
some arbitrary decision, mayors dissatisfied with the order of
some prefect, officials who consider that some ministerial
decision is contrary to the law, have found in this administrative
tribunal a security which no one would formerly have thought
of seeking there.

Religious Policy. Religious policy resolves itself into one
question, that of the relations between the Catholic Church and
the State. The Protestants, numbering about 640,000 in 1900,
and the Jews, from 60,000 to 80,000, form small minorities,
which, viewed as religious bodies, have played no political part.
As to the Catholic Church, for a century she remained subject
to the system which was instituted by the Concordat. Under
the Restoration, the clergy allied themselves with the Bourbons
against the champions of the principles of 1789; then the old
Gallicanism made its re-appearance. But all the governments
since 1830 have renounced divine right and the principle of a
State religion, and have invoked the principles of 1789; the
clergy, no longer having confidence in them, has turned towards
Rome, and the Gallican spirit has been superseded by the
Ultramontane spirit. The Liberal Catholic party, formed by the
disciples of Lamennais, attained its apogee in 1850, when it
succeeded in passing the education law; afterwards it divided
into two groups: that of the Right, led by Louis Veuillot, which
declared Catholicism incompatible with Liberalism, upheld the
authoritative Empire, glorified the *Syllabus* and applauded the
Vatican Council; and that of the Left, led by Montalembert, which
demanded liberty for the Church and for every one, accepted
democracy, and tried to persuade the Council to reject the
dogma of Papal infallibility. In spite of these differences, all
militant Catholics united in defence of the temporal power of
the Pope between 1860 and 1870; and in favour of the restoration
of the Bourbons between 1870 and 1873; hence a permanent
conflict between the Republican party and the Catholic party.
This conflict has remained one of the principal features of home

policy since 1875: the establishment of the secular and non-sectarian elementary school, the Government measures against the progress of the religious Orders, and the struggle caused by the Dreyfus case helped to revive it. After Leo XIII, who counselled support and conciliation, Pius X seemed to favour the irreconcilables. Subsequently the relations between France and the Papacy became worse; the protest made by the Pope against the visit of the President of the Republic to the King of Italy at Rome caused the suppression of the French Embassy to the Vatican. The law of 1905 abolished the Concordat and established the separation of Church and State. Necessary measures had been arranged to convey to Catholic associations the rich inheritance which had been amassed by the Church, but Pius X, contrary to the advice of the French bishops, forbade conformity with this law. The Catholic clergy since 1905 has thus been organised under the exclusive direction of the Pope; the system of separation has, moreover, been accepted without difficulty by the French nation, as has been proved by all the legislative elections since 1906.

The two principal Protestant bodies, the Reformed Church and the Lutheran Church, have existed since 1802 under the regulations which were instituted by the articles of Bonaparte, with pastors chosen by the faithful, and appointed and paid by the State. In 1830 the Government arranged a similar system for the Jewish religion and its Rabbis. The law of 1905 put an end to these links with the State; the Protestants and Jews accepted the new law without resistance, and created the "Associations cultuelles" prescribed by the law.

The Press. The Press has played a considerable part, in spite of the numerous laws promulgated against it up to 1881. Under the Restoration, newspapers, few in number and containing little matter, cost 80 francs a year to subscribers, and were not sold by single numbers; often a preliminary censorship was imposed. However, the great Liberal papers, the *Journal des Débats* and the *Constitutionnel*, made Charles X tremble, and the revolution of 1830 seemed a triumph for them. Under Louis-Philippe the Press, despite some repressive laws, always preserved the chief guarantee of its liberty, trial by jury. A bold innovator, Émile de Girardin, resolved to reduce the rate of subscription from

80 to 40 francs, making up for the loss by advertisements; he succeeded in founding *La Presse* under these conditions, but his example was not followed, and the papers remained faithful to their old customs. After the revolution of 1848, which gave rise to many ephemeral ventures, liberty of the Press entirely disappeared under the Second Empire. Most of the newspapers were suppressed, only one organ being left to each party of the opposition. The severity of the Government did not relax until towards the end of the reign. Nevertheless this period saw the accomplishment of an important advance by the Press: the foundation by a banker in 1863 of the halfpenny newspaper, *Le Petit Journal*, which supplied the necessary instrument for the political life of a democracy. Finally, the law of 1881, which is still in force, fixed the legal status of the Press, by ensuring it complete liberty. As a result, papers have multiplied, halfpenny as well as three-halfpenny papers. Up to 1870 the political Press was exclusively Parisian; the provincial papers only included local news and advertisements. Since then, things have changed, and the development of the telegraph, telephone, and motor, has facilitated the rise of a provincial Press which possesses some papers rivalling those of Paris.

Conclusion

The history of France since 1814 shows two periods which are absolutely different. From 1814 to 1870 no government could last more than eighteen years without being brought down by a revolution. Since 1870 half a century has passed, during which the Republic has been able to develop steadily and to found a democratic and liberal government. The War of 1914, which seemed likely to prove a formidable test for it, has strengthened it by showing that the institutions which were organised in 1875 have enabled France to face successfully the greatest of dangers.

BIBLIOGRAPHY

§ I. Henri Hauser, *Les Sources de l'histoire de France au xvie siècle*, 4 vols. 1906–1916. *Histoire de France*, ed. E. Lavisse, v. 1. *Les guerres d'Italie*, v. 2. *La lutte contre la maison d'Autriche* (by H. Lemonnier), 1903–1904; VI. 1. *La Réforme et la Ligue* (by J.-H. Mariéjol), 1904. *The Cambridge Modern History*, I.–III. 1902–1904. P. Imbart de la Tour, *Les Origines de la Réforme*, 3 vols. 1905–1914. P. Renaudet, *Préréforme et humanisme à Paris*, 1916. E. Doumergue, *Jean Calvin, les hommes et les choses de son temps*, 5 vols. Lausanne, 1899–1917. J. W. Thompson, *The Wars of Religion in France* (1559–1576), Chicago, 1909. L. Romier, *Les Origines politiques des guerres de religion*, 2 vols. 1913. E. Fueter, *Geschichte des Europäischen Staatensystems von 1492–1559*, Munich and Berlin, 1919. Victor Martin, *Le gallicanisme et la Réforme catholique, 1563–1615*, 1919. J.-H. Mariéjol, *Catherine de Medicis*, 1920. See also the *Revue du seizième siècle*.

§ II. *Histoire de France*, ed. E. Lavisse, VI. 2, *Henri IV et Louis XIII* (by J.-H. Mariéjol), 1905; VII. 1, 2, VIII. 1, *Louis XIV* (by E. Lavisse, A. de Saint-Léger, A. Rébelliau, and P. Sagnac), 1906–1908.
A. Poirson, *Hist. du règne de Henri IV*, 4 vols. 1869. M. Philippson, *Heinrich IV und Philipp III*, 3 vols. 1870–1876.
G. Hanotaux, *Histoire du Cardinal de Richelieu*, 2 vols. 1896. G. Fagniez, *Le père Joseph et Richelieu*, 2 vols. 1894.
A. Chéruel, *Minorité de Louis XIV*, 4 vols. 1879–1880; *Ministère de Mazarin*, 3 vols. 1883. Voltaire, *Siècle de Louis XIV*, ed. É. Bourgeois, 1890. A. Legrelle, *La diplomatie française et la Succession d'Espagne*, 5 vols. 1889. É. Bourgeois, *Manuel Historique de Politique étrangère*, vol. 1. 2nd ed. 1897.

§ III. *Histoire de France*, ed. E. Lavisse, vol. VIII. pt. ii.—*Le règne de Louis XV* (by H. Carré), 1909; vol. IV. pt. i.—*Le règne de Louis XVI* (by Lavisse, Carré and Sagnac), 1910.
Lemontey, *Histoire de la minorité de Louis XV*, 2 vols. 1832. É. Bourgeois, *Le Secret du Régent; le Secret de l'Abbé Dubois*, 2 vols. Paris, 1908. Jobez, *La France sous Louis XV*, 3rd ed. 6 vols. 1866–1873. C. Stryienski, *Le XVIIIe Siècle*, 1909.
Jobez, *La France sous Louis XVI*, 3 vols. 1877–1883. Cherest, *La Chute de l'Ancien Régime*, 3 vols. 1884–1887. P. de Nolhac, *La reine Marie Antoinette*, 2nd ed. 1899. É. Bourgeois, *Manuel Historique de Politique étrangère*, vol. 1. 2nd ed. 1897.

§ IV. *Histoire de France*, ed. Lavisse (see above, §§ II and III). M.-J. Picot, *Essai historique sur l'influence de la religion en France au 17e S.*, 2 vols. 1824. A. Rébelliau, *La Compagnie du St Sacrement*, in *La revue des Deux Mondes*, 1903; *Bossuet historien du protestantisme*,

2nd ed. 1892. C.-A. Sainte-Beuve, *Port-Royal*, 9th ed. 7 vols.
1888–1891. N. Puaux and M. Sabatier, *Études sur la Révocation
de l'Édit de Nantes*, 1886. L. Rocquain, *L'Esprit révolutionnaire
avant la Révolution*, 1878. Voltaire, *Siècle de Louis XV*, ed. Fallex,
1893.

§ V. In the few lines at our disposal it is impossible to give even a
summary bibliography. A. Aulard, *Paris sous la réaction thermi-
dorienne et sous le Directoire, Paris sous le Consulat*, and *Paris sous
l'Empire*, are important collections of documents in course of publication; see also by the same editor, *Recueil des Actes du Comité du salut
public*, 26 vols. The best elementary work is Ch. Seignobos, *Histoire
moderne de 1715 à 1815*, 1903.

For the Revolution read Michelet, whose account, though lyrical in
form, is solid and true. The most recent history is A. Aulard, *Histoire
politique de la Révolution française, 1798–1804*, 1901. Read also Acton,
Lectures on the French Revolution, 1910; the contemporary memoirs of
Mme Roland, 2 vols., ed. Cl. Perroud, 1905, Ferrières (Marquis de),
3 vols., 1821, and Thibaudeau (Comte), 1875; and the monograph on
Jeanbon de Saint-André by L. Lévy-Schneider.

For the Consulate and the Empire the great work of Thiers (20 vols.
1845–1862) is still the best. For the life of Napoleon read A. Fournier,
Napoléon I, Prague, 1882, E.T. by A. E. Adams, 2 vols., 1911; and
J. H. Rose, *The Life of Napoleon I*, 6th ed. 1913. The internal history
of his reign is still to be written. Read also Mme de Rémusat,
Mémoires, 3 vols., 1879–1880, E.T., 2 vols., 1880; Thibaudeau,
Mémoires sur la Convention et sur le Directoire, 2 vols., 1824.

§ VI. Ch. Seignobos, *Histoire politique de l'Europe contemporaine*, 1897.

P. Duvergier de Hauranne, *Histoire du gouvernement parlementaire en
France, 1814–1830*, 10 vols., 1857–71.

P. Thureau-Dangin, *Histoire de la Monarchie de juillet*, 7 vols., 1887–92.

Georges Weill, *La France sous la monarchie constitutionnelle (1814–48)*,
1912.

Georges Renard, *La république de 1848*, 1905.

P. de la Gorce, *Histoire du second Empire*, 7 vols., 1895–1905.

E. Zévort, *Histoire de la troisième République*, 4 vols., 1896–1901.

G. Hanotaux, *Histoire de la France contemporaine*, 4 vols., 1903.

A. Debidour, *Histoire diplomatique de l'Europe (1814–1878)*, 2 vols.,
1891; *Histoire diplomatique de l'Europe depuis le Congrès de Berlin*,
2 vols., 1916–17; *Histoire des rapports de l'Église et de l'État en
France de 1789 à 1870*, 1898; *L'Église catholique et l'État sous la
troisième République*, 2 vols., 1906.

Émile Bourgeois, *Modern France*, 2 vols. Cambridge, 1918.

CHAPTER II

THE ARMY

THE chief strength of the army which Charles VIII led into Italy in 1494 lay in the *gendarmerie* (men-at-arms). This had very nearly the same organisation as in the time of Charles VII and Louis XI. It was still made up of *compagnies d'ordonnance* containing so many *lances*, or groups of horsemen and bowmen (under Charles VIII one horseman and two bowmen went to a lance). The number of these lances varied from twenty-five to a hundred. The horsemen, with occasional exceptions, were recruited from the nobility. They wore complete armour and were armed with lance, sword, and mace. The *gendarmerie* therefore was still the heavy feudal cavalry which was called upon to throw its weight into the battle, at Fornovo (1495), for instance, and at Agnadello (1509), at the decisive moment. At the beginning of the 16th century, however, the improved use of fire-arms began to lessen the importance of this cavalry, which moreover remained very costly. Heavy cavalry, in fact, may be said to have been condemned the moment armour ceased to be bullet-proof, but its disappearance was slow. It figured still, though made considerably lighter, in the armies of Henry II, Charles IX, and even Henry III. New forms of cavalry had sprung up side by side with it; thus the Stradiots appeared at the outset of the Italian wars, drawn from the East, from Albania in particular, the ancestors of modern light cavalry; later, half-way through the 16th century, horsemen armed with the arquebus or the more recently invented and more manageable pistol gave the type to the cavalry of the line.

While cavalry was passing from the first to the second rank the importance of infantry proportionately increased. Foot-soldiers became a more and more numerous part of armies. As France itself could not supply enough, kings were fain to seek for them abroad, Louis XII in Germany and Switzerland, Francis I in Germany, Switzerland, and Italy. Like the mercenaries of former ages, these German landknechts

(*lansquenets*), Swiss pikemen, and Italian arquebusiers were recruited on his own account and responsibility by a captain, who,
when his company (*bande*) was formed, passed into the king's
service along with it. The king bore the expense. After the
campaign was over a few companies were retained, but most were
dismissed, much to the detriment of military discipline and of
the peace of the inhabitants. The men were enrolled afresh when
the winter was over. An ordinance of the year 1509, which restricted this cosmopolitan system of recruiting by aiming at
uniformity of establishment and command in the bands of foot-
soldiers raised in France, may be considered as the first step
towards constituting a national infantry. Francis I made a
slight advance in this direction when, in 1534, he ordered seven
legions to be formed in seven provinces of the kingdom, each
under a colonel's command and comprising six companies of a
thousand men with a captain, subalterns, and non-commissioned
officers. The captains were expected to find legionaries in the
provinces assigned to them as recruiting areas. The men were
exempted from taxation and received pay at the rate of 7 *livres*,
10 *sols* a month. Theoretically, they could rise from the ranks
and become captains or even be ennobled. But the system did
not yield very good results from a military point of view. Moreover, like the free archers whom it was meant to replace, it was
looked on with disfavour by the country gentry, who complained
that the peasants, once they were armed and freed from taxes,
became less subservient and more restive. It was difficult to
disregard this opposition, since the nobility continued to be the
foundation of all military power in the kingdom, the nursery
of leaders, and since, apart from the cavalry, it was beginning to
provide officers for the infantry. Six out of the seven legions
were organised and no more. The system of mercenary bands
with its medley of races, its drawbacks and abuses, remained
dominant.

Nevertheless it was from this archaic system that modern
infantry began to take shape, vaguely, it is true, but with some
clearly marked characteristics. The bands from Picardy and Piedmont, known as such, were the direct origin of the first regiments
of the army of the monarchy and gave their names to them.
Regiments and battalions, in word and in fact, date from the

first half of the 16th century. Under Francis I, and still more under Henry II, infantry preponderated; in the army which overcame the Three Bishoprics in 1552 the infantry numbered 30,000 as against 3000 mounted men-at-arms and archers. Shortly after they stripped off their defensive armour, which could no longer protect them against cannon or arquebus, and added to their offensive power the superiority which firearms conferred on them. Out of the 42,000 men of Francis I's legions it was provided that 12,000 should be *arquebusiers*, the rest pikemen. Under Henry II the proportion of *arquebusiers* in the infantry rises to a third or even half the total strength. For the arquebus after being kept in check for some time by the crossbow, which fired more rapidly, became a formidable weapon directly its mechanism was improved, and the spark-producing wheel-lock (*rouet*) did away with the slow process of lighting a fuse (*mèche*). Though still awkwardly handled the infantry's fire was to assume a growing importance in the fight.

The artillery made slower progress. During the Italian wars the French armies dragged along with them even beyond the Alps a relatively large number of guns of various calibres. The army which besieged Genoa in 1507 possessed 27 pieces, besides 50 arquebuses and 50 ammunition waggons. The army which won the battle of Agnadello brought 30 pieces into line. The artillery was already destructive enough to excite the wrath of the cavalry, decimated at a distance under their thick armour; but it remained heavy and unwieldly, best adapted to siege-warfare. It had not yet become an independent arm manned by specialised troops and with a rôle of its own in the fight. In the battle on level ground it was still of secondary importance. Besides, its cost was very great and the ruinous condition of the public finances could bear it less and less. This was probably the chief reason for the eclipse which the artillery suffered after Francis I and which lasted a long time. The army at Rocroy in 1643 had fewer guns than the army at Marignano or Pavia. For a whole century it was through the portable weapon much more than through cannon that gunpowder was to continue to revolutionise tactics.

In the midst of the general disorganisation caused by the wars of religion military power dwindled and sank to nothing. The

almost permanent state of civil war much restricted the scope
of recruiting for national purposes. The services of foreigners
were never more appreciated, but the lack of funds which was
common to both parties in the war prevented their being much
used. The fighting strength of both sides was reduced. It became
largely mere partisan warfare, and the bands engaged in those
battles whose names have come down to us are scarcely worth
calling armies. On the field of Arques (1589) 12,000 Protestants
opposed from 25,000 to 30,000 Catholics. The same year at Ivry
Henry IV had no more than 10,000 men to bring against
Mayenne whose total was only 20,000. After peace was made
Henry IV and Sully were forced by the sheer necessity of
economising to keep up the mere kernel of an army—the royal
household troops and five regiments of reduced strength, the
whole amounting to some 10,000 foot and horse. At the end of
his reign, when he was thinking of intervening in Germany,
Henry IV ordered reinforcements for the army, but his death put
an end to the plans he had laid down.

These plans were taken up again almost immediately by his
successor to meet the needs caused by the fresh outbreak of the
war of religion, and then for the struggle with the House of
Austria. The great designs formed by Richelieu in his foreign
policy were impossible to carry out without a strong instrument
of war. That minister accordingly set about forging such an instrument. As early as 1625 the strength of the army was increased
to 60,000 men. It went up to 140,000 or 150,000 in 1635–1640.
Several new regiments were created. Mercenaries were sought
for on a wider scale both in France and abroad, in Switzerland,
Germany, even Scotland and Ireland. Further, townships and
boroughs were called upon to furnish men whose pay and maintenance they had to provide for. In 1636, at the time of "the panic
of Corbie," the authorities went so far as to attempt a sort of mass
levy by indirect means, the shutting down completely or in part
of the industrial workshops, so that numbers of men would be
thrown out of work and induced to enlist. Men were most wanted
for the infantry, which had definitely become the most important
branch of the service. It now wore no defensive armour and
carried the musket, an improvement on the arquebus. There still
were pikemen, but fewer and fewer in proportion. The former

gendarmerie, still keeping the helmet and cuirasse but discarding the lance, had completed its transformation into heavy cavalry in the modern sense. Of the same order of troops were the *chevau-légers* armed with musket, pistol, and sword. The mounted troops, who, as occasion served, fought on foot and who later developed into the dragoons, date from this period. There was also some light cavalry. The growth of the artillery remained very slow. Only for sieges was it used to any large extent. The conditions of life were hard for troops, and much the same as they had been at the end of the Middle Ages. A campaign only lasted six months, as a rule, after which the army withdrew for the remaining six months into winter quarters. Then, according to the practice already referred to and which had become firmly established since the 15th century, part of the regiments were dismissed for economy's sake or they were reduced to cadres and to a depôt. The demobilised had to make a living as best they could. For those who remained there were no barracks. They were quartered in citadels and fortresses, or on the inhabitants. They were not always paid or fed regularly. So that, in spite of an almost barbarous system of punishments, they committed acts of violence and plunder and frequently deserted.

The royal army in the first half of the 17th century did not differ materially, therefore, from what it had been in the 16th. The basis of it was still mercenary troops raised, equipped, and armed by a captain who, according to the terms of his commission, then handed them over to the king, who defrayed the expense. What was new was that the king began to provide pay, clothing in the field, and rations. We must not conclude from this a real state of organisation among troops at the base and along the lines of communication. It was long before such was established. Nevertheless, a certain amount of order crept into the mass of waggons and carts, driven by servants, sutlers, and women, who followed in the wake of armies. Though sanitary measures were still unknown the bare outlines appeared of what was to become the service-waggon train. This progress was due to the *intendants d'armée,* created by Richelieu, chosen from the King's Council and invested with wide powers equivalent now-a-days to the direction of those branches of the general Staff which deal with supply, pay, and discipline. They had to ensure and check the carrying out of the king's wishes in all ranks from the lowest to the highest.

The monarchical army reached its highest glory under Louis XIV thanks to two great ministers, Le Tellier and Louvois, and thanks to the king himself, who was very clear-sighted where military problems were concerned and who brought to their study his sound qualities of concentration and good sense. Though they could not transform the whole of military organisation from top to bottom, even supposing such to have been their intention, for it would then have been necessary to transform also the whole political and social organisation, they were able by means of a series of reforms to introduce into it a large measure of order and efficiency.

The recruiting system was not changed. Captains continued to enlist their men. There was still a large proportion of foreigners. In 1688 the militia was created; drawn by lot from men between the ages of 20 and 40, equipped and armed by the parish, bound to drill on Sundays, the militia-men constituted a reserve intended to be used to fill up gaps among the fighting troops. Here once more after the free-archers of Charles VII, after the legions of Francis I, appears the conception of a national army, service in which was regarded as a public duty. But the time for its realisation had not yet come. At the beginning of the War of the Spanish Succession, Louis XIV thought for a moment of amalgamating with 57 regiments which he wished to reinforce an equal number of militia battalions. He changed his mind, however, and ordered a hundred new regiments to be raised by enlistment, staffs being found for them out of the establishment of existing regiments. The militia remained a considerable burden on the people, a burden which was to become grievous, yet it played and continued to play merely a subordinate rôle. The system of conferment of military rank also remained unchanged. Since the 16th century the method of purchase had been introduced. Men purchased their company or their regiment just as they purchased some civil practice; the king had the power merely to approve. This abuse would have been very difficult to uproot. Louis XIV and his ministers confined themselves to lessening its effects and giving some guarantee of advancement to officers who could not afford the rank of captain or colonel.

Another old and very serious abuse against which Le Tellier
and Louvois contended, without being able to suppress it, was
the use of "supers" (*passe-volants*), chance comers introduced
into the ranks for the day of the "show" (*montre*) or review,
and whose brief stay with the company enabled captains to
swell their pay-sheets unduly.

As against these partial failures some excellent results were
obtained. Le Tellier and Louvois made it their object to present
the king with a well-paid, well-equipped, well-armed, and regularly
rationed army. They succeeded. Rates of pay were revised and
fixed (at 5 *sous* a day for the infantryman). Measures were taken
for having pay-day at fixed dates and giving each man exactly
his due. In 1670 it became compulsory to wear uniform, which
took the place of the great diversity of dress still worn before
that date. The supply branch which was really created at
this time had special care bestowed on it. It included contracts
with munition-makers, dumps on the frontiers, and a system of
relays, transport, and ration supplies, and so did away with the
precarious dependence on local resources and substituted for it
a more or less stable supply of food. The good effects of this on
the moral of the troops gave the French army a real superiority.
But Le Tellier and Louvois were not so happy in their efforts to
establish a sanitary service worthy of the name. From 1674 onwards crippled soldiers found at the *Invalides* a refuge preferable
to that which the private enterprise of certain religious communities had hitherto offered them. But with the armies in the field
the condition of sick and wounded was still deplorable. The
sanitary service was long to remain the weak point in the French
army.

From the purely technical point of view the second half of the
17th century saw important reforms brought about. The arms
of the infantry were quite transformed by the introduction of
the firelock, which was an improvement on the wheel-lock. The
invention of the bayonet[1] by Vauban in 1687 caused the disappearance of the pikeman. The infantry regiment was now composed only of *fusiliers*, and of picked men, *grenadiers*, who had
just made their first appearance. In the cavalry the sabre com-

---

[1] This was the *baïonnette à aiguille*, i.e. needle-shaped, with no cutting
edge.

pletely replaced the rapier, and many mounted troops were issued with carbines, then first known. Both the artillery and the engineers had from the first been side branches of the service, in the hands of private individuals who contracted at their own risk for providing material and personnel, whether gunners or sappers. From this time onwards there were artillery troops, first a regiment of *bombardiers*, then twelve companies of *canonniers*. There was also an Engineers' Corps composed exclusively of *ingénieurs ordinaires ou extra-ordinaires*, i.e. of officers without men under them (with the exception of two companies of miners), but who none the less under Vauban were to play a highly important rôle, and in the 18th century were to contribute largely, on the theoretical side, to the improvement of the art of war.

In 1678 Louis XIV had nearly 300,000 men under arms: by whom were they commanded? After having rested during the 16th century with the sovereign himself, seconded by several *lieutenants*, the supreme command of the army in the field had passed through strange conditions at the time of the Thirty Years' War, when it was shared by two or three general officers who assumed it by turns in rotation. This mistaken practice was given up and replaced by what was known as *l'ordre du tableau*[1]. By this, if the commander-in-chief were incapacitated, his place was taken by his next in seniority. Among subordinate officers precedence of rank was revised and fixed. Louvois was anxious to have well-educated subaltern officers and with this in view he formed the Cadet schools in 1682, but the experiment had no lasting results. Nevertheless, the corps of French officers enrolled from the nobility, which was devoted to the king, clinging closely to military tradition, and, moreover, fairly quickly imbued, through camp life or through a few months' campaigning, with the necessary technical knowledge, maintained its superiority over the officers of other nations. Side by side with the command of operations the administrative branches asserted their importance, which was to prove great. At their head and at the centre of affairs under the king's minister was the Chief Secretary of State for War; at the theatre of operations were the *intendants*

[1] I.e. *tableau d'avancement*, the list on which officers were inscribed for promotion.

d'armée still invested with wide powers, the *commissaires des guerres* and their subordinates. To his immediate agents, to his *intendants*, Louvois demanded deference and, on occasion, obedience to be paid by officers of the highest rank, even by field-marshals. As he understood it, all officers, whatever their rank, ought to set an example of discipline.

During the fifty years which followed the death of Louis XIV military institutions in France did not undergo any important changes. Recruiting continued as before. The militia was re-formed in 1736, but recourse was occasionally made to it. No progress was seen in the matter of instruction or discipline. There were, however, two noteworthy improvements in arma-ment. About 1740 a musket with a steel ramrod, capable of firing two or even three rounds a minute and with 250 to 400 metres as its limit of effective fire, was adopted for the infantry, and, at the instance of a quartermaster-general named Vallière, some stout pieces for the artillery. These however were heavy and useless for shell fire, though they had been introduced with success into the other armies of Europe for use in siege warfare. Vallière's four-pounders could fire three rounds a minute, judging the elevation, for he would have nothing to do with tangent-sights.

The end of the reign of Louis XV and the reign of Louis XVI were marked by two attempts at far-reaching reform in military organisation. These attempts partially failed, primarily because of the opposition of the nobility who saw their privileges threatened, and partially succeeded, so opening up the way to the Revolution.

The first was made by Choiseul after the Seven Years' War. At the close of the year 1762 Choiseul undertook to reduce the strength of units and cut down the number of officers, which was far too large: in the last years of Louis XV for 163 regiments there were no less than 800 or 900 colonels on the active list with or without commands. Choiseul made improvements in administration and interior economy of units, gave a better status to captains, and paid attention to the instruction of young officers, and to discipline. He took a very important step in suppressing the proprietary rights of a captain over his company. These rights were transferred to the State. From that time onward a soldier enlisted in the king's name. The king took the full responsibility for his enrolment and maintenance. This was a great step towards a national army. Finally, in 1765, he substituted Gribeauval's type of gun for Vallière's. Thereby he endowed France with a light, powerful, and varied artillery, particularly well adapted to open warfare.

Though he had abstained from dealing with the question of purchase and had shewn special consideration for officers of noble birth, Choiseul had caused much discontent. His successors, the Marquis de Monteynard, the Duc d'Aiguillon, and Marshal du Muy, lessened the scope of his work without however obliterating it. The determination to reform showed itself once more in the Comte de Saint-Germain. This veteran soldier, who had retired after a brilliant career of home and foreign service, became Secretary of State for War in 1775. Eager for his task, he obtained the king's signature for as many as ninety-eight ordinances relating to his department in less than two years. He was anxious, if possible, through economy to increase the strength of the army without adding to the total cost, and ventured to tamper with that very expensive item, the king's household troops, suppressing some units and reducing the rest. He attacked the practice of purchasing promotion, and brought about the decision that in future vacant posts should lose a quarter of their *finance*, i.e. of the price they were estimated at, so that after four changes they became free of charge. This was positive proof that he was defending the lesser gentry against the nobles of the Court. In place of the Paris military college, to which only sons of the high nobility and of rich commoners were admitted, he established twelve military colleges in the provinces. This was favouring the same tendency. The whole constitution of the army was revised or transformed by the two great ordinances of March 25, 1776. One dealt with the regiment, the battalion, the company and its composition, the other with the question of corps, recruiting, remounts, military police, and discipline. Care of the men was one of Saint-Germain's chief preoccupations; he issued detailed orders for the billeting and rationing of troops. Yet he made himself unpopular with the men by certain rules relating to pay, punishments, and length of service. Though welcomed at first by public opinion he was in the end faced with an almost general opposition, which caused his fall. The leaders of it were the Court nobles, who could not forgive him for abolishing part of the king's household troops and for making certain irksome regulations, such as that requiring officers to be quartered near their men. His administrative reforms had been accompanied by useful technical changes. He it was who enabled Gribeauval to bring about the complete renewal of the artillery; and to him was due the formation of the first pioneers' corps, under the command of engineer officers.

Beside Saint-Germain the last three war ministers of the monarchy, the Prince de Montbarey, Marshal de Ségur, the Comte de Brienne, appear only as shadowy figures, particularly the first and last named. Ségur, whose intentions were good and who had to his credit useful innovations such as the introduction of light infantry, was conspicuous for signing his name to the edict of May 22, 1781. By this edict officer's rank was closed to all but accredited noblemen. A wave of protest arose in consequence, which swelled higher and higher till the year 1789. The story of Brienne's ministry owes its interest to the War Council which was instituted in October, 1787, to reorganise the army and was composed of eminent or distinguished specialists. It broke up without having completed its task which was made unnecessary by events. But it had the merit of raising a large number of difficult questions and suggesting on many points new and bold solutions, of which the military Committee of the Constituent Assembly took full advantage.

The period of three centuries which lasted from the wars in Italy to the Revolution saw the gradual development of modern tactics; but only the simplest outline of this development is possible here.

Down to the middle of the 17th century there was no perceptible change in the way in which operations in general or the battle itself were conducted. War was still a slow process, and dragged on from one siege to another. When at last a battle was fought, it still meant merely the shock of two masses rushing against each other. It was rare to find in any action the semblance of an intentional manoeuvre. From Fornovo (1495) to Rocroy (1643) victory was won by the cavalry charging the enemy's flank or counter-attacking him in front. At Marignano (1515) and Pavia (1525) the French artillery broke the enemy's lines, but these exploits were not followed up, for, as was said above, the straitened finances for many a long year forbade the use of a sufficient number of guns. A habit was formed among the infantry of alternating small bodies of pikemen and *arquebusiers* or musketeers, who gave each other mutual support and covering fire. This made the infantry more mobile, but it was not powerful enough yet to be the deciding factor.

Under Louis XIV as portable firearms improved the proportion of pikemen decreased. The more rapid and accurate the fire the more became the number of firers. The last battles of the 17th century, especially Fleurus (1690), are remarkable for the important place assigned to the infantry. It knew by that time how to deploy in long lines several ranks deep so as to ensure the maximum of fire effect. This by its influence on the final success or defeat now became the essential factor in the fight. But the infantry had to progress still further: it had to learn to open out quickly from the march to the attack formation. A bold first step was taken at the end of the 17th century, when intervals were left in the front line covered by musket fire at effective ranges. Then a long contention began between the supporters of the "thin" line or of "linear" order and those of "deep" order who had particularly in view the last phase of the fight and recommended attacks in massed formation. A halfway solution was found in 1764 by a great theorist, a forerunner of Napoleon, the Comte de Guibert. It may be summed up as the use of column for the march and of line for the fight. The use of this doctrine was made easier by the adoption of the "divisional principle," thought out by Marshal de Broglie in 1759. The army could be kept massed in columns which were easy to move so long as the moment for action had not yet come. Each *division* consisted of infantry, cavalry, and artillery, so as to be able to meet the first shock of the enemy without being overwhelmed, and so as to give time to the other divisions to come up. Thus, having become mobile and tactical, and having in its artillery parks the means of quickly overcoming obstacles, the French army was in a position to wage a new kind of warfare. The end of the 18th century was to witness this.

The thorough reform of the army, which was being prepared

for by so many political and social factors and which the monarchy had not brought about, was made possible by the Revolution and actual by the Constituent Assembly. The assembly quickly abolished the purchase of military promotion, which was thrown open to all by fixed rules. It gave continuous numbers to regiments instead of calling them after their provinces, now abolished. It reduced the number of generals and superior officers. It reorganised military law. Coupled with the oath of allegiance to the Constitution, which had to be taken by officers and soldiers alike, the object of these measures was to transform the royal army, without destroying it, into a national army. They were popular with the men and non-commissioned officers, but not so popular with the officers, the majority of whom favoured the *ancien régime* at heart. In 1790 and 1791 the army went through serious internal troubles, of which a series of insurrections among troops gave evidence. The march of events in the political world increased the discord in the various corps. Officers emigrated in large numbers, thus weakening the establishments of their units. The army, disunited and dwindling, seemed on the point of dissolution. But this very crisis saved it by eliminating the anti-revolutionary element among the officers. The Legislative Assembly and especially the Convention were thus enabled to devote themselves to its complete reconstitution. In 1794 and 1795 the French army, possessed of the military traditions which were kept alive by the old soldiers in it and strengthened by the influx of fresh national forces, reached a degree of power that it had never before known.

The Constituent Assembly's reforming activities had included no warlike scheme of territorial expansion. The Assembly had no intention of waging war abroad, and for keeping order at home it relied on the *National Guard* which had been formed spontaneously since 1789 all over France. But in June, 1791, the Varennes scare interfered with this resolutely pacific policy. Rumours of foreign intervention spread. The Assembly was forced to put the army on a war footing. Reinforcements were brought in amounting to 165 volunteer battalions, about 100,000 men, drawn from the National Guard. In almost all the departments this levy was carried out with genuine alacrity and even enthusiasm. But in the end, the threat of war having come to nothing for a time, it did not produce all the expected results. Only 83 battalions joined the army. At the end of the year 1791 it scarcely numbered 100,000 men. On April 20 following, war broke out with Austria and Prussia. The Legislative Assembly decreed fresh levies of volunteers between May and July, 256 battalions in all, without mentioning numerous independent bands. The campaign began with reverses but ended happily with Valmy, Jemappes, and the conquest of Belgium. The beginning of 1793 saw a fresh decrease in numbers, caused in the main by the return home of many volunteers, just at the moment when the beginning of hostilities with England and Spain made the need of men more urgent. A great effort had to be made. The result was what was known as the levy of the 300,000, which took place on February 24, 1793. All unmarried or childless men from 18 to 40 were called up, if the number of volunteers proper were insufficient, and choice was made among them either by lot or by the votes of their fellow-citizens.

This levy caused difficulties and in some cases revolt; the best known example was the insurrection in Vendée. The country, however, was in extreme danger and the land of Liberty had suffered invasion. Then the revolutionary government, in spite of the repugnance they felt for what we should to-day call compulsory and universal military service, resolved on drastic action. This was not exactly a mass levy, such as popular meetings demanded with more zeal than discernment and which was for practical reasons impossible, but a system of requisitioning, without allowing substitutes, all unmarried men who were more than 18 and less than 25 on August 23, 1793. This measure added some hundreds of thousands of men to the forces during the years 1793 and 1794 and kept the army up to full strength. French territory was set free, and the Netherlands and the left bank of the Rhine were conquered and the Coalition were forced in part to accept the peace of Basle.

Austria and England, however, still remained in the war, which was not yet over. On coming to power at the close of 1795 the Directory was confronted with a serious situation. As a result of losses, and particularly owing to the large number of absentees on furlough or deserters, in the course of the preceding few months the army had dwindled from 1,100,000 men, the 1794 total, to less than 700,000 and the parade-states showed scarcely more than 400,000. The Directory intervened energetically. In less than a year more than 100,000 men rejoined the colours. But though an improvement, this was not sufficient; the evil was great and needed more than palliatives. Moreover the large reserve of men created by the requisitioning in 1793, which had not been renewed, was the current source of supply and was beginning to fail. In the autumn of 1798, at the moment when the Second Coalition was forming, the Directory were obliged to pass the conscription law subjecting to active service for five years, no longer exceptionally but permanently, every young Frenchman on reaching the age of twenty. Special laws were to fix the classes to be called up. At the end of the Directory on the 18th Brumaire the five classes were complete and in working order.

These summary outlines are enough to indicate all that is covered by the well-known term "a volunteer of the time of the Revolution." Literally this term is only applicable to the men who joined in 1791; later on there were some more true volunteers, but in diminishing numbers. In 1792 and the first months of 1793 the levies for the so-called volunteer battalions were made up largely either of the victims of the recruiting sergeant, men who had sold themselves, or else of those who had been chosen by lot or by vote. In other words compulsion had come to stay, and was confirmed first by the requisitioning of August 23, 1793, and then by conscription itself. The "volunteers of the Revolution" are not a myth, but they have been regarded as more numerous than they really were. Left to themselves the peasants and workmen in the mass would have remained inert. To get them to move the energetic action of a central power was needed and also those district and municipal councils, those popular political clubs which were throughout France in 1793 and 1794 the rallying points of the Revolutionary spirit.

What use did the army make of this crowd of men who joined up or were conscripted from 1792 to 1799? A certain number of them, but relatively few, went into the cavalry or into special branches of the service such as the artillery or engineers. Throughout the Revolution the cavalry kept up to a surprising degree, not the ideas, but the appearance and traditions of the *ancien régime*. Though numerous new units were formed, often only

temporary it is true, its strength remained limited. Voluntary
enlistment was still of primary importance to it. The artillery
and engineers were less exclusive, but could not without risk, in
view of their technical needs, open their doors too widely or too
soon. A more serious drawback to the artillery's development
than lack of men was the lack of guns and horses. The needs of
the infantry on the other hand were easily satisfied. An increase
in the manufacture of uniforms and small arms was all that was
wanted. And there were practically no limitations. The greater
part of the men raised between 1791 and 1793 and later by conscription were absorbed into the infantry.

Until the spring of 1793 the men who joined as volunteers
remained together in battalions bearing the name of the departments from which they came and commanded by officers of their
own choice. On the other hand the old regiments still existed
and went on recruiting. So that there were two infantries with
different constitutions, and whose spirit up to a certain point
was different. The drawbacks of this dual system were not slow
to appear, and as early as 1793 the Convention ordered an amal-
gamation. Two battalions of volunteers and one of old soldiers
were grouped together and fused into one "half-brigade." This
process was slowly carried out in the intervals between battles
and was completed in the course of 1794. It had excellent results.
Instead of what were in some cases mere skeleton units much
over-staffed, there were now in these half-brigades the less
numerous but stronger units of the armies of the Rhine or of
Italy, units which combined the solidity of the old line regiments
with the dash of the younger volunteer battalions. These "blue
coats" have left behind them in legend and history an imperish-
able memory.

It is a mistake to think that the victories of the Revolution
were won, as has often been stated, by improvised soldiers.
This was never the case, even at the beginning. At Valmy
and Jemappes there fought side by side with the old army
some volunteer battalions which had already seen more than
a year's service. In 1793 the new formations were very far from
being led at once against the enemy. Before starting on the
march they had had several weeks' drill and when they reached
the camps their training continued. No doubt insufficiently

trained men were led on occasion into the battle. But these experiments turned out badly, and were not repeated. From 1793
onwards as a matter of routine all fresh levies were led first
into fortified positions in the second line, into camps and depôts,
from which they were allowed only to go forward when they had
the requisite knowledge of drill and musketry. In 1794 and 1795
the armies had seen war-service and included a noteworthy proportion of veterans, which increased still further under the
Directory.

Apart from this real renovation of the infantry what technical
novelties had the Revolution to shew? The uniform had changed
little, in cut if not in colour. Arms had changed little: the small
arm in use was still the "1777 model," and the guns those of
Gribeauval. But what had not been seen hitherto was the extraordinary increase in the manufacture of arms. It is difficult to
imagine the unprecedented efforts needed at a time when
machinery was only in its infancy, when communications were
slow, when man's manual labour or animal traction were the
only motive power, to clothe, equip, lodge, feed, and provide with
stores, munitions, rolling stock, and horses this series of armies
posted on the frontiers from the North Sea to the Pyrenees. In
this consisted a very extensive side of the Revolutionary
government's military accomplishment, a side which may have
left no very brilliant trace in history but which is none the less
of the liveliest interest.

The higher command offers two peculiarities during the period
of the Convention. First, the state of tutelage in which generals
were kept by the government. Closely watched, constantly
threatened with dismissal or worse, they had to carry out, just
as it was, the plan of operations transmitted to them from Paris
in the name of the Committee of Public Safety by that great
master of the art of war, Lazare Carnot. Secondly, an original
institution, that of government representatives with the armies
in the field. These members of the Convention were sent in
varying numbers (three or four or even more) to the various
armies and were invested with unlimited powers. Besides the
general supervision of the commanding officers' actions their
highest function consisted in seeing to the maintenance of discipline, of the military and of the revolutionary spirit among

the troops, and the proper working of the administrative services
at the base. Some of the missions they fulfilled have remained
famous in history, for instance that of Saint-Just and Le Bas,
carried out with inflexible severity, to the armies of the Moselle
and of the Rhine in November and December, 1793. It is now
proved beyond a doubt, after all the heated discussions to which it
has given rise, that the action of the government representatives
with the armies was from 1793 to 1795 one of the determining
causes of success in the national defence. After they had disappeared the civil power interfered with more timidity in the
conduct of the armies. The troops gained more and more the
mentality of professional soldiers. Their leaders showed a tendency to emancipate themselves and to have a policy of their
own, like Bonaparte in Italy. War itself became a war of conquest and plunder. The way was prepared for that military
dictatorship which the first Revolutionary assemblies had
dreaded and which victory was to set up in earnest.

Once master of France, Napoleon Bonaparte had the glory of
re-establishing universal peace by the treaties of Lunéville and
Amiens. But war soon began afresh and was to last ten years
interrupted only by short truces. To face the needs of a long
struggle against the rest of Europe men were needed and yet
again more men. Conscription must provide them. Directly
he was in power Napoleon made use of the law of 1798.
Soon the use degenerated into abuse. In 1806 he began to
anticipate the legal age, calling up young men who were not
yet twenty; in 1808 he recalled classes which had already served;
later he took the weaklings. The finding of conscripts was
what most taxed the powers of the imperial administration.
The rights of individuals were not respected; men who had redeemed themselves three or four times over (for substitutes were
allowed) were forced in the end to join. Exhausted by such
repeatedly forestalled levies the country acquiesced less and less
readily. Defaulters and deserters, already frequent during the
Revolution, increased beyond belief under the Empire. In 1804,
in peace-time, when there was as yet no particular reason for
weariness, the police arrested no less than 25,000 deserters
from the land forces; how many escaped is unknown. In the
last years so much resistance was shown that we find regi-

ments only receiving 10 or 5 per cent. of the conscripts detailed to them; the others had run away. The severest orders were issued in vain. Thus the *communes* were held responsible for any deficit in their contingent's numbers, and bailiff's men were lodged with the parents of defaulters. These however were backed up by the people and often by the government officials (there were frequent cases of complicity on the part of the authorities) and either remained hidden or joined with others to form armed bands which fought the police. Some idea of the burden laid on France can be formed from the fact that conscription between 1800 and 1815 affected about 3,000,000 men, more than half of whom died of wounds or sickness.

This exhaustion of the overbled generations, these hecatombs of slain, are the dark side of military history under the First Empire, the side on which stress has been laid by few historians. They prefer to treat of a much more attractive subject: the Grand Army. The Grand Army! The mere name calls up a whole legend of glory. It was first used in August, 1805, when the troops collected against England at the camp at Boulogne marched off to Germany to attack the third Coalition. From 1805 to 1814 it was given in the course of his campaigns to the army commanded by Napoleon in person; it disappeared in 1814, for the name would have been disproportionate if applied to the small numbers brought into line during the campaign in France; the French army at Waterloo was known as the Army of the North. The Grand Army had therefore no permanent existence, and, officially, it never included more than a part of the Emperor's forces. Yet it has become the habit in everyday speech to lump together under the name Grand Army the whole of the French troops under the First Empire: we propose to conform to this habit in the following pages.

The Grand Army, particularly at first, from 1805 to 1807, was in outward aspect very like the armies of the Revolution. The regiment had been restored as an infantry unit. The distinction between infantry of the line and light infantry remained. In each regiment beside the company of grenadiers, which had existed more than a century, there was now another picked company of *voltigeurs* (scouts) for rapid marches and attacks. The uniform had changed very gradually. The *shako* took the place of the republican cap, and trousers of breeches and long gaiters. The infantryman's arms remained the same. The cavalry had been reorganised. Remounts were improved. But, as before, it consisted of heavy cavalry for the charge and for pursuit, line cavalry able to fight on foot, light cavalry for reconnoitring. The artillery, already much increased, was to reach the proportion of four guns to a thousand men. It still used Gribeauval's guns with a type of howitzer. Beside the artillery were the engineers including companies of sappers and miners and of bridge-builders. The transport had become a branch of the service. From 1807 onwards the troops employed on the service-waggon train were formed into battalions. The administrative branches had likewise been developed. Efforts, which proved insufficient, had been made to improve the sanitary service. Lastly, to complete this summary picture, mention must be made of the Guard, the celebrated Imperial Guard, whose total strength increased from 11,000 men in 1805 to 100,000 in 1813, and which, with its grenadier regiments, its *chasseurs à pied*, its horse grenadiers, its *mamelouks*, its artillery, and even its sailors, was a perfect model on a reduced scale of the whole Grand Army.

From 1807 to 1815 the very numerous reforms in detail of which the Grand Army was the object did not perceptibly change its general organisation. What varied a great deal, however, was its total strength. This was between 200,000 and 300,000 men from 1805 to 1807; in 1809 it increased, and in 1812 it rose to 600,000. It was reduced to less than half in 1813 and in 1814 fell below 100,000, to rise once more to 125,000 in 1815. The considerable growth shown in 1812 is due to the presence to the extent of 50 per cent. of foreign contingents furnished by the united countries (Belgium, the Rhine Provinces, Switzerland, Italy, Illyria), the vassal states (the Rhine Confederacy, the kingdom of Westphalia, Holland, Italy, Naples) or allied states (Prussia, Austria), and by one nation, Poland. The armies of the Revolution had included foreigners (the Batavian legion, etc.) but never in so large a proportion. This exaggerated cosmopolitanism is a peculiarity of the Grand Army; all the languages of Europe were spoken by it, except English.

At least as interesting as the variations in the numbers and types of an army are its variations in quality, when these can be ascertained. Successive inquiries, made at the time and handed down to us in precious records, tell us that in the summer of 1805, six months before Austerlitz, 43 per cent. of the troops in the Grand Army had seen active service; in some cavalry regiments 77 per cent.; in many infantry regiments two-thirds of the men and nearly all the officers and non-commissioned officers. No comment is necessary on these figures. These were the years of Eylau, Austerlitz, Jena, Friedland. The Grand Army reached at that time the height of its destructive power. At Wagram, in 1809, the quality of the troops was distinctly less good: there were many more young soldiers. In 1810 and 1811 much labour was spent on reinforcing, instructing, and training the army with a view to the invasion of Russia. From information relating to establishments in July, 1811, we can deduce that most of the officers and non-commissioned officers were still war-experienced at that time; but far from 43 per cent. of the men. In the retreat from Russia the Grand Army literally melted away. What was left of the foreign troops returned home. At Mainz in February, 1813, the French infantry could not muster more than between 6,000 and 7,000 men. In three months Napoleon succeeded in reconstituting an army considerable at least in numbers and capable of winning the battles of Lützen, Bautzen, and Dresden. But the predominance of conscripts in it made its staying power small. Then followed Leipsic. During the winter of 1813–1814, the Emperor tried to improvise a fresh army as he had done in the preceding spring, but he failed. It was with the remnants of the army of 1813, with some troops returned from Spain, 90,000 men in all, and only 50,000 of these under his direct command, that he held out against the 500,000 men of the Coalition army which was invading France. On his return from Elba Napoleon found the army in a better state than it had been in since 1812. Thanks to the large numbers of returned prisoners of war, most of whom had seen some fighting, it contained nearly 200,000 men. This number was doubled by the 1815 conscription. With these forces Napoleon might have tried to begin the 1814 campaign over again. He preferred to march against the Anglo-Prussian army in Belgium before it could be joined by the Austrians and Russians. After Waterloo the remains of what had been the Grand Army was driven over the Loire by the invaders and there finally dismembered.

Under the Empire peace was constantly used to prepare for war. Napoleon possessed a surprising knowledge of the state of distribution of troops, their positions, the contents of arsenals, etc., and gave himself up unremittingly to the work of organisation, seconded by his two war ministers (for he had two). The moment the campaign was about to begin he fixed on the units which were to compose the armies, and named the marshals and generals who were to take command. These were former officers of the republican armies on the Rhine and in Italy, almost all of them soldiers of fortune, most of them excellent subordinates devoted to the Emperor, who heaped honours and riches on them, until the years of misfortune came when weariness crept over the Emperor's Staff and was one of the causes of the final ruin. Then communications and dumps having been planned out the armies started on the march.

The Grand Army, which has left such a war-like reputation behind it, did not possess all the military virtues. Courage, endurance, confidence in its leader, that omniscient genius in whose footsteps victory followed; these it had. But in discipline it did not shine nor even in drill. Recent research has proved that even in 1805 the drill of the Grand Army was not more than passable in comparison with foreign armies. What interfered with discipline was in the first place a tradition of independence, with a trace of the republican spirit in it. Secondly the system of promotion on the spot, in the same unit, may have given cohesion to the whole, but it gave rise to a harmful familiarity between the superior and his subordinates, with whom he had just been on equal terms. Last, and not least, Napoleon's methods of warfare interfered with good discipline. The severe trials he frequently imposed on his troops' endurance resulted in a loosening of the bonds of discipline, and his principle that war should feed war had its advantages for the Staff, but was distinctly bad for the moral of the army in that it incited to marauding and plunder. The Grand Army suffered in the highest degree from these evils. Even in 1805 and 1806 in the course of operations it presented the appearance of a solid kernel of an army surrounded as it moved along by a cloud of pillagers, many of whom rejoined at once when the battle began. An eye-witness who was struck by the sight of it said of the Grand Army's march on Vienna in 1809 that it was like "the rout of an advancing army." In Russia, in 1812, laggards and men left behind became so numerous that the army was to some extent paralysed in its movements.

A theory once commonly accepted held that the revolutionary army's methods of fighting differed fundamentally from that of the armies of the *ancien régime*. A contrast was drawn between the systematic slowness and the limited objectives of warfare under the monarchy and the large concentrations and decisive bayonet charges which characterised war in the days of the Revolution. But it is now recognised that the revolutionary army's tactics proceeded directly from those of the 18th century. If the Revolution increased the offensive spirit of the army, this army none the less owed its existence to the material and theoretic progress made in France since the Seven Years' War. In 1789 the principles and the means of the new methods of warfare were already conceived or created. They were at first used clumsily enough. Their full value came out later as a startling revelation. The great date in the history of the art of war in the periods of the Revolution and Empire was the date of Napoleon's command in Italy. The battle of Montenotte on April 12, 1796, presents, in a small frame, a picture containing all the essential features of the great battles of the Empire. What was war as Napoleon conceived it? It is not possible to treat this large question here, even summarily. Some general hints must suffice. Whereas, but for rare exceptions, the divisional system caused poor results in the hands of the unskilful generals of the Revolution by scattering their forces, Napoleon carried the use of it to perfection. Once he had got on to the enemy's lines of communication or retreat so as to force him to fight in unfavourable conditions he marched towards him with his divisions (from 1805 onwards with his army corps or groups of divisions) disposed on a wide front. Then at the right moment he gave the order to close in (*réunion de l'armée*) and concentrate for a frontal attack or a turning or enveloping movement which was to prove decisive. This kind of warfare requires exceptional qualities of speed and calculated boldness of action. In the battle itself he made his own peculiar use of the artillery, concentrating it to destroy part of the enemy's line, and of the cavalry to pursue and complete the rout of the defeated. He won and kept the supremacy for the French army until the time when his enemies, learning from their disasters, discovered the necessary parrying measures and found means to retaliate effectively.

From Waterloo to the war of 1914–1918 a century elapsed, during which the question of military organisation never ceased in France to be of primary importance. Recruiting was still the main problem. In its reaction against the Empire the Restoration desired peace and reduction of armaments. Conscription was abolished and the strength of the volunteer army, including the Royal Guard, only amounted to 240,000. Even this total, however, could not be maintained. In 1818 compulsory service, with limitations, was once again made law. Volunteer enrolment remained but was completed by virtual conscription. Each year young men of twenty drew lots to provide a contingent of 40,000 for active service. Substitutes were allowed. In 1832 this contingent was fixed at 80,000 and the length of active service at seven years. The army had a total of about 500,000. The law of 1832 remained in force under the Second Empire. After Sadowa there dawned the possibility of a war with Prussia. The French army, weakened by its losses in the Crimea, Italy, and Mexico, and through the abuse of *exonération*, by which a sum of money could be paid to the State instead of providing a substitute, could only muster 300,000. Accordingly, the imperial government through Marshal Niel, then War Minister, drew up a scheme of universal compulsory service. Numbers were drawn by lot and each contingent was divided into two, half serving five years in the army and four in the reserves, and half going first into the reserves and then into the *Garde nationale mobile*, a kind of territorials. By this means it was hoped to obtain a total of 800,000 men, either on the active list or in the reserves. Public opinion, however, thought the burden too heavy. The law was passed, but with a serious modification: the second half of the contingent was not called upon to serve in the reserves. This docked the army of 250,000 men in the first battles of the Franco-Prussian war. After it, in 1872, compulsory universal service was established, this time without opposition. Numbers were again to be drawn by lot, and the yearly contingent to be divided into two categories: those who served for four years and those who served for one year. The men were then to pass according to their age and category into the army reserves, the territorial army, or the territorial reserve. This law of 1872 laid the lasting foundations of the general organisation of the army under the Third Republic. Further laws modified it. The period of active service was reduced to three years in 1889, to two years in 1905, and went back to three in 1913, and, further, all exemptions were disallowed. It may be said that since the beginning of the 20th century, the principle of the Nation in arms is in full force in France.

Material changes of capital importance have taken place during the same lapse of time. The formation of special units for Africa like the *Zouaves, tirailleurs, Algerians,* and *Spahis,* the changes in uniform and many like questions, must be passed over in silence. We need only compare the flintlock musket with the repeating rifle, and the bronze muzzle-loader with the quick-firing steel gun to realise the changes in armament. These changes, however, like the strategical and tactical innovations of the same period, are not specifically French. Since the middle of the 19th century, and particularly for the last thirty years, the study of the technical problems of war has been common to most countries of Europe, and, even if we had the necessary space at our disposal, the solutions which have been found to these problems could not suitably find a place in an account of the French army.

BIBLIOGRAPHY

Army of the Ancien Régime. L. André, *Michel Le Tellier et l'organisation de l'armée monarchique,* 1906. J. Gébelin, *Histoire des milices provinciales* (1688–1791), 1881. L. Mention, *Le Comte de Saint-Germain et ses réformes,* 1884. Louis Tuetey, *Les officiers sous l'ancien régime,* 1908.

Army of the Revolution and the Empire. A. Chuquet, *Les guerres de la Révolution,* 11 vols. 1886–1896. Lt-Col. Hartmann, *Les officiers de l'Ancien Régime et la Révolution,* 1910. P. Caron, *La Défense nationale de 1792 à 1795,* 1912. Gén. Colin, *L'éducation militaire de Napoléon Ier,* 1900, and *Les transformations de la guerre,* 1911; by the same author, and by numerous other officers a series of works of great value in the *Publications de la Section historique de l'État-major de l'Armée,* from 1890 to 1914.

It is impossible to give here a list of even the most important authorities. See the chapters on the army in the *Histoire de France*, ed. Lavisse, vols. v–ix, and in the *Histoire de France contemporaine*, by the same editor, with the bibliographies attached. See also the *Bibliographie des travaux publiés de 1866 à 1897 sur l'histoire de la France depuis 1789*, by P. Caron, 1912, and the annual bulletins of the *Répertoire méthodique de l'histoire moderne et contemporaine de la France*, which are in continuation of it.

CHAPTER III

THE NAVY

1. *Italian wars*

INSTEAD of seeking, like his ancestors, a normal increase of territory, Charles VIII launched out into hazardous undertakings inherited from the house of Anjou—the conquest of the kingdom of Naples and the restoration of the Eastern Empire. For these distant expeditions he had at first no more than twenty-one vessels, divided among the admiralties of France, Brittany, Guyenne, and Provence. This weakness was made up for by the support of the Genoese navy and its bold *condottieri*, who had just become illustrious by the discovery of the New World. The naval victory of Rapallo on September 8, 1494, opened the way to Naples, which Charles VIII entered, only to return immediately to France.

The victor, Louis Duke of Orleans, when he mounted the throne as Louis XII, did not forget that he had been a sailor. At his invitation, admirals, provinces, and loyal towns reinforced the royal fleet at their own expense; beside the *Grande Louise* and *Catherine*, given by admirals de Graville and de La Trémoille, were arrayed the *Charente*, and the ships of Bordeaux, La Rochelle, Brest, Rouen, Dieppe, Orleans, and, above all, the ship of Morlaix, *La Cordelière*.

Driven from Italy in spite of the exploits of Prégent de Bidoux off Gaeta, Naples, and Genoa, the French were at war with a formidable League called "Holy," because the Pope supported it. Italian, Spaniard, English, and Imperial ships were putting to sea from all sides. The French fleet retired on Brest, on August 10, 1512, closely followed by Admiral Howard. *La Cordelière* was covering the retreat. Surrounded and riddled with shots, she grappled Knyvet's ship the *Regent* and blew up with her. Rather than surrender, "the valiant and virtuous Breton," Hervé de Portzmoguer, had put a match to the powder magazine, immortalising a name which legend has distorted into Primauguet.

Howard was bottling up the rest of the French squadron in the entrance to the harbour of Brest, when Prégent de Bidoux arrived from the Mediterranean with his galleys and took him in the rear. A brisk engagement in the creek of Blancs-Sablons, near Conquet, ended in the defeat and death of the English admiral on April 25, 1513.

2. *The war between France and Islam*

On the occasion of his triumphal entry into Naples, Charles VIII, discounting the future, had donned the ceremonial costume of the Eastern Emperors, with the sceptre and orb. His policy was henceforth frankly directed against Islam. In August 1499 the squadron of Guy de Blanchefort, supported by the Venetian fleet, sustained the shock of the Ottoman fleet in the straits of Lepanto, where, in later years, Don John of Austria distinguished himself; it only broke off the fight, after a battle lasting a fortnight, because its Venetian allies retreated.

Two years later, Louis XII gave to a new squadron the definite mission of regaining Lepanto and Modon from the Turks. Its leader, Philippe de Clèves de Ravenstein, admiral of the kingdom of Naples and of Jerusalem, was the author of a learned manual on strategy. None the less he failed in the attack on Mitylene, which he had intended to make a naval base to blockade the Dardanelles. In imitation of Louis XII, Francis I planned a crusade in which he would use his youth and strength to make war "for the honour and glory of God our Saviour against the enemy of His faith." Prégent de Bidoux attacked the island of Sainte-Maure and the magnificent roadstead of La Coupole at Bizerta; in 1517 Pero Navarro bombarded El-Mehdiah, and Christophe Le Mignon, called Chanoy, was killed in 1520 during a landing at Beyrout. By these attacks on Islam Francis I gave himself a claim to the empire. His candidature was set aside, and the defeat of Pavia obliged him to renounce his policy and sign a treaty with the Sublime Porte, in order to keep the balance of power in Europe. The Capitulations of February 1536 guaranteed political pre-eminence in Turkey to

France; in fact, in order to help to defend the coasts, the Mussulman fleet of Barbarossa wintered in Toulon harbour.

3. *Rivalry with Charles V*

France was in danger. Her little ally in previous wars, Castile, had become inordinately powerful by successive additions of territory and now threatened France everywhere. The vast empire of Charles V was supported by the Pope and the King of England. Marseilles had twice to repel the attacks of imperial troops, in 1524 and in 1536. The mobile defence was directed by one of the most eminent seamen of the time, the Genoese Andrea Doria, whose nephew, Filippino, in 1528 won the naval victory of Cape Orso. But the great seaman was alienated by the imprudent conduct of Francis I, and he passed to the service of Charles V, whereby France lost the mastery of the seas. An expedition directed against England in 1545 only resulted in exposing the weakness of the admiral, Claude d'Annebault, formerly master of the royal boar-hounds.

Convinced of the necessity of "being on the sea at least as strong as his enemies," Henry II organised two squadrons of oared ships, galleys in the Mediterranean, row-barges in the Atlantic, always ready for action, "all and each time that they were required, either in the east or in the west, without further delay than the necessary time to transport the crews from one sea to the other." These sixty war-ships, under the orders of energetic leaders such as Leone Strozzi and Paulin de La Garde, more than once gained the ascendancy over Andrea Doria or the English, so much so that for a short time Corsica became French, and after two centuries of occupation Calais was taken from England (1558).

4. *In search of a Colonial Empire*

France had left the beaten tracks of the Old World to seek for fortune beyond the seas. After two preliminary explorations, Jacques Cartier, a native of Saint-Malo, led a party of colonists to Canada in 1541; his seamen wore a uniform of the royal colours, black and white. The expedition was a failure, owing to a mistake which rendered it ridiculous. The diamonds and gold which he thought he was bringing back proved to be pebbles and copper; and "as false as a diamond from Canada" passed into a proverb. The work of colonisation, resumed by one of Catherine de' Medici's pages, Troilus du Mesgouez, was not successful until the time of Henry IV, under Samuel de Champlain.

Access to distant lands was denied France by the Portuguese and Spaniards in virtue of the famous bull of Pope Alexander VI, which settled the boundaries of their spheres of action in the discovery of the world. Any foreigner discovered beyond the "Peace Lines"—the tropic of Cancer and the meridian of the island of Hierro—was treated as a pirate; the Protestant colonists, who were led to Florida by Ribaut and Laudonnière, were massacred as such in 1565. In vain did the shipowner of Dieppe, Jean Ango, demand the freedom of the seas; the protests of Francis I did not go beyond a witty speech: "The sun shines for me as much as for the others; I should like to see the clause in Adam's will which excludes me from a share in the world." Spain upheld its veto and thus provoked the reprisals which under the name of Navigation Acts, in England under Cromwell and in France in the time of Colbert, reserved intercourse between the metropolis and the colonies to the national flag.

As for the Portuguese, they forbade access to Brazil, which however the French claimed to have discovered before Cabral, and whither the *Espoir* of Honfleur repaired in 1503 as to a country visited for "many years" by the Bretons and Normans. The French founded there numerous colonies; the island of St Alexis near Pernambuco was occupied by Dupéret in 1530; Rio de Janeiro became in 1555 the "Antarctic France" of Villegagnon; and São Luiz de Maranhão was founded in 1612 by a brother of Richelieu. Each time the Portuguese drove them out. A great armed expedition sent by Catherine de' Medici in 1582 did not even arrive at its destination. Its leader, Filippo Strozzi, had in his pockets the brevet of "Lieutenant-General of the land to which he was going," which was Brazil; defeated and slain at the Azores by Alvaro de Bazan, he carried to the grave the "secret of the Queen."

On the road to the East Indies, the expeditions of the *Grand Anglais* in 1527, the *Sacre* and the *Pensée* in 1529, remained isolated attempts which sailors of Saint-Malo in one case,

Normans in another, wished to repeat in the time of Henry IV and Louis XIII, but without succeeding in establishing any durable settlement in the Sunda Islands.

France was then suffering to the point of exhaustion from the wars of religion, the outbreaks of which recurred from the reign of Francis II till that of Louis XIII. As a result of these fratricidal struggles, the State navy fell to two vessels under the League and to one under Henry IV. "In truth, the French are no good on the sea," said hastily Marshal Vieilleville. But Captain Beaulieu-Persac showed that there was no truth in this. With Henry IV's only ship of the line he destroyed the whole fleet of the Tunisian pirates near La Goulette (1609).

A reaction was brought about by a terrible lesson, the necessity under which the monarchy found itself in 1625 to beg for the help of a Dutch and an English squadron to repress the rebellion of the seamen of La Rochelle. The four provincial admiralties (France, Brittany, Guyenne, and Provence) were suppressed and in October 1626 all naval power was concentrated in the hands of a new officer, the "Grand Master and Superintendent of the navigation and trade of France." The Grand Master was Cardinal Armand Du Plessis de Richelieu.

5. *Richelieu, Grand Master of Navigation*

Great-grandson of Vice-Admiral Du Chillou, who founded Havre, grandson of a ship's captain, son of an owner of second-hand ships, who bought the remains of the fleet which was beaten at the Azores, Richelieu inherited a love of the sea. He proved it in 1627 by organising the defence of the Ile de Ré against Buckingham's fleet, and the following year by his blockade of the port of La Rochelle. Callot's engravings have popularised this famous siege, in which the Cardinal constructed the mole of La Rochelle and reinforced it by a double line of mobile defences, both to prevent the egress of the besieged and to bar the entrance of the port to the English. The besieged were forced to surrender.

"To guard against all injury and to inspire fear on all the seas," Richelieu thought it enough to maintain "forty well-armed ships and thirty galleys"; squadron leaders named according to the titles of the four abolished admiralties commanded them, after their equipment in the military ports of Havre, Brest, Brouage, and Toulon. The general of the galleys was stationed at Marseilles. France asked Holland for engineers of naval construction and for vessels. But the finest vessel of the period came from a Breton ship-yard; the *Couronne*, two hundred feet in length from the flag-staff at the stern to the figure-head at the bow, carried its flag two hundred and sixteen feet above the keel.

As navy and colonies were complementary one to the other, a number of colonies, sure of support from the national fleet, came into existence between 1626 and 1642 on the shores of the Atlantic Ocean and the Indian Ocean, in Canada and in Acadia, which was called New France and New Guyenne, in the Antilles and the Bahamas, in Senegal and Madagascar, called at that time Oriental France. For a short time Spitzbergen was called Arctic France. Divided up from Sallee to the Niger between Chartered Companies, French Western Africa came into being—on the map. For hardly was the French colonial Empire planned than it felt the formidable shock of the Thirty Years' War.

6. *The Thirty Years' War and its consequences*

In order not to allow her north-eastern allies, the Palatines, Danes, and Swedes, to be crushed by the House of Austria, France, "with leaden steps," abandoned her neutrality. She made herself the champion of the little nations oppressed by the Empire or by Spain. To free Italy from the domination of Spain, to create a "free state" for the Catholic Netherlands, and to contain the Empire on the Rhine, all these war-aims showed the genius of the master-spirit which conceived them. Richelieu also foresaw the *entente cordiale* with England; if his negotiations had been successful, the "Auxiliary League," planned in 1636, would have shortened the war, by cutting off Spain alike from Italy, from the Netherlands, and from her colonies; Richelieu wished to abandon the care of the Atlantic to the British fleet and to reserve the Mediterranean for the French. But he could count only on the support of the Dutch.

Nevertheless, such was the importance of naval supremacy on

the course of continental events that the successive blows of the
naval victories at Guetaria and Genoa (1638), of the Dunes
(1639), and of Cadiz (1640), caused the fall of Spanish rule in
Portugal and Catalonia. France's great seamen at this time were a
churchman and a youth. The victor of Guetaria, Henri d'Escou-
bleau de Sourdis, Archbishop of Bordeaux, in August 1641
gave battle near Tarragona to an enemy four times his superior
in numbers and retired without the loss of a vessel. He was
nevertheless disgraced. "Would to Heaven that I had made a
similar retreat," said his adversary, Gianettino Doria, "my
fortune would be made for ever." The victor of Cadiz repeated
his performance near Barcelona in 1642 and near Cartagena in
1643. This young man, Armand de Brézé, who succeeded to the
title of Grand Master of Navigation and to Richelieu's heavy
task, ended his short career in a blaze of glory. He was killed on
June 14, 1646, off Orbetello while victoriously opposing the
galleys of Spain, Naples, and Sicily, the galleons of the Plate
fleet, and the terrible squadron of Dunkirk.

After him, the Grand Mastership was assumed by the Queen,
Anne of Austria, and the post of General of the galleys by
a child. With the exception of a bold demonstration by the
Chevalier Paul in view of Naples, which followed a short
insurrection of the *lazzaroni*, the navy lost all offensive spirit.
As a result, in the treaty of Westphalia Spain refused to
disarm; in fact, she found an ally in France herself. The civil
troubles of the Fronde armed our sailors against one another.
The conquests in Italy, in Spain, in Flanders were lost by
this disruption; the heroism and disinterestedness of a handful
of sailors, of the Chevalier Paul, son of a laundress of Marseilles,
of Captain Des Lauriers, who blew out his brains and sank his
galley rather than be captured by Gianettino Doria, and of *Le
Lion Couronné*, which gave battle near Formentera to the
whole fleet of Don John of Austria, second of the name (June
17, 1651), could not avert the fall of Piombino, Porto Longone,
Tortosa, and Barcelona. Dunkirk, only just conquered, fell the
day after a relieving squadron was intercepted by the English
(1652). But here Cromwell's support reversed the situation six
years later; and the help of an English fleet was instrumental to
the victory of Turenne in the Dunes. France and Spain, equally

tired of the war, ended it by a marriage which was arranged
between Louis XIV and the Infanta Maria-Theresa (1660).

7. Colbert, First Minister of the Navy

The two last Grand Masters of Navigation, César de Vendôme
and his son, the Duc de Beaufort, allowed the navy to fall into
the state of "a paralysed body, without hope of cure." Neither
"the man who had belonged to every party without having made
himself of importance to any," nor the "King of the Halles,"
who owed his favour to the Fronde, possessed enough authority
to reform it. Salvation came to the navy from the son of a
cloth-merchant of Reims, who from being a simple intendant
in charge of maritime affairs in 1661 was promoted in 1669 to
the position of Minister of the Navy and the Colonies. This was
Jean-Baptiste Colbert.

He found twenty vessels; he left in 1683 two hundred and
fifty-eight, with a strength of 53,200 men and 1200 officers. In
place of the odious Press-gang system, which embarked sailors
by force, he instituted so flexible a system that it is still in
use: "Maritime Registration," with the division of the men
registered into classes, automatically assured the supply of
crews. A very marked distinction between military duties and
administrative duties assigned the former to the admiral of
France, his two vice-admirals, and the squadron leaders; the
latter to the minister, the intendants, and the commissaries.
A seniority list served as a safeguard against arbitrary appointments; the selection went by merit, which the intendants
reported to the minister. Prizes for naval construction, schools
for naval cadets, schools of gunnery, sick pay allowances supported by deductions from pay, the reform of hydrography
with the help of three new institutions (*Académie des Sciences,
Observatoire*, and *Service Hydrographique*), the art of Lebrun,
Girardon, Puget, and Caffieri placed at the service of naval
construction, the genius of Vauban devoted to the organisation of arsenals, maritime legislation fixed in 1681 by an
"eternal monument of wisdom and intelligence"—such was
the work of Colbert.

The Minister was in addition an inspirer of energy, a "Prime
Mover." He tried to animate all the world; "application,

industry and zeal" was what he demanded. But from want of suitable men the choice of leaders did not at first do justice to the soundness of his principles; Louis XIV showed himself "much disgusted with naval affairs," and the sequel will show the reason.

8. *Naval campaigns in the reign of Louis XIV*

A succession of mortifications attributable to the Duc de Beaufort, the failure of the occupation of Djidjelli in 1664, the negative campaign of 1666 against the English, the fruitless Candia expedition in 1669, where the duke was killed in a rash sortie against the Turks, marked the termination of the Grand Mastership of Navigation. The Admiral of France, who replaced the Grand Master, was a baby, an illegitimate son of Louis XIV. It was a mistake to delegate his duties to a Lieutenant-General of land forces, promoted to the rank of Vice-Admiral.

Before he was seasoned and accustomed to naval manœuvres, the Vice-Admiral, Jean d'Estrées, found himself face to face with a great seaman, De Ruyter. At Solebay (Southwold Bay) on June 7, 1672, he fought under the orders of the admiral, James, Duke of York; at Schooneveldt, the year after, also on the 7th of June and at Texel, on August 21, he was under the orders of Prince Rupert, who had a squadron twice as large as that of the French. At Solebay, Ruyter, coming up, "like a torrent," surprised the allied fleet at anchor, and only the vigilance of the *Aeolus*, commanded by Captain Cogolin, averted a disaster. The allies improvised a vigorous defence with the first vessels which could be got under sail; in this action the French flagship, the *St Philip*, had 67 killed and wounded. At Schooneveldt, off the coast of the Netherlands, the situation was reversed; the Dutch were attacked by a "shock" force, detached from the squadrons of Rupert, d'Estrées, and Spragge. Tromp changed his ship three times and was only disengaged by De Ruyter: "We risked everything in order to apply the naval forces of the king advantageously. Only one fire-ship remained out of nine." The brush of Van de Velde has chronicled all the phases of the battle of Texel, hour by hour. Jean d'Estrées, who was at the head of the fleet, did not succeed in piercing the line of the enemy, so as to turn it and take it between two fires. Driven

by the wind, he left Rupert to struggle with Ruyter and Banc-
kert and, when evening fell, missed the opportunity of falling on
the harassed Dutch fleet. A violent statement by his subordinate, the Marquis de Martel, emphasised this neglect and
put an end to the combined efforts of the French and the English.

The defection of an ally was aggravated by the addition of
numerous adversaries, Spain, the Empire, etc. It was then that
the French navy reached the height of its glory. Regenerated by
Colbert's efforts, it experienced nothing but success. Marvellous
paradox! "The greatest captain ever seen on sea," according
to the avowal of Colbert, suffered the humiliation of a bloody
defeat at the hands of a single French vessel. Ruyter attacked
Fort Royal of Martinique with a force of 5000 men; it was defended by 161 sailors and militiamen. On the night of July 20,
1674, his assaulting columns, crushed by the defenders of the
place, caught in a slanting fire from the guns of the ship, *Les
Jeux*, were forced to re-embark with heavy losses. Jean d'Estrées
crowned the work begun by Captain d'Amblimont; in two
campaigns in March and October, 1677, he destroyed the fleet
of Admiral Bincks at Tobago and blew up the fortress. But as
he was sailing to Curaçao, to occupy this other Dutch island, his
squadron in the darkness ran on to the reefs of the Islands of
Birds, where they almost all went to pieces.

The naval war was decided in Sicily. Messina, having
revolted against the Spanish domination, called for French help.
With six vessels, Jean-Baptiste de Valbelle ran the blockade,
then passing in front of the squadron of Louis-Victor de Morte-
mart, Duc de Vivonne, he took Enrique de Bazan and Melchior
de la Cueva between two fires: they were beaten at Stromboli
on February 11, 1675. The Spaniards called De Ruyter to the
rescue; the French sent "the Turenne of the seas," Abraham
Du Quesne. After a first encounter near Alicuri on January 8,
1676, a furious duel started between the two great sailors in sight
of Etna on the following 22nd of April. The Lieutenant-General
who acted as second in command to Du Quesne, Guillaume
d'Alméras, died while fighting De Ruyter, but the latter was
mortally wounded. His weary squadron, reinforced by the
Spaniards under Diego de Ibarra, took refuge under the ramparts
of Palermo, where on the 2nd of June, Vivonne, Du Quesne, and

Tourville inflicted a final defeat; ten ships and three thousand of the enemy perished in a gigantic fire.

9. *Second Hundred Years' War*

The reaction against the protectionist policy of Colbert and De Seignelay culminated in the war of the Augsburg Confession, a business war—as it is called by an eminent Cambridge professor, J. R. Seeley—waged in the interests of the English and Dutch merchants, whose trade was imperilled by the union of France and Spain. But the varying allies on each side being subtracted, it was England and France who found themselves face to face in a gigantic rivalry, the stakes of which were the French colonial empire, or rather, the world. Opening with the English Revolution in 1688, this second Hundred Years' War did not end until 1815 after the French Revolution and the Empire.

The situation was excessively grave for France. She espoused the cause of King James II, who had been driven from England on account of his militant Catholicism; the stadtholder, William of Orange, proclaimed king under the name of William III, had behind him all Protestant England, the Netherlands, the adherents of the Augsburg League, the Empire, Spain, nearly the whole of Europe, and finally the Protestants who had been driven from France by the reversal of the Edict of Nantes. Only Catholic Ireland was faithful to the banished king; Châteaurenault conveyed him thither with a small army, evading the cruising squadron of Admiral Herbert, which he forced to turn aside to Bantry (1689). The year after, Herbert, in command of the Anglo-Dutch forces, tried his strength near Beachy Head with the "greatest seaman there had been for a century," i.e. Anne-Hilarion de Cotentin de Tourville. The loss of seventeen ships obliged him to take shelter in the Thames. In 1691, in the celebrated campaign out at sea, Tourville played with Russell, luring him out to the open sea and exhausting him, without offering him the smallest chance of attack.

But Colbert's son and the inheritor of his ideas, Seignelay, was dead. The new Minister of Marine, Louis de Pontchartrain, lacked experience; he left to the Intendant-General, Bonrepaus, the initiative of a plan of disembarkation in England, which

was adopted by Louis XIV. The troops were concentrated at La
Hogue in Cotentin. "Tourville, as a man who understood his
business, represented that it was not possible to hold the sea in
the presence of an enemy whose fleet was three times as strong
as his. The Secretary of State, becoming impatient, persuaded
the King to give an order written with his own hand that
Tourville was to attack....The battle of La Hogue will be an
eternal monument to the danger of entrusting the affairs of war
to folk who understand nothing about them." Having only
twenty thousand men against forty-two thousand, forty-four
ships of the line against ninety-nine, Tourville did not hesitate
to engage on the 29th of May, 1692, off Barfleur. While Nesmond outsailed the Dutch under Van Almonde, so as to prevent
them from getting clear, and while Pannetié's three ships made
off to the south, drawing Shovel's squadron after them in pursuit, Tourville attacked with fury the centre commanded by
Russell. At nightfall he was master of the position, having only
seventeen hundred men out of action as opposed to five thousand,
and not a ship sunk, while the allies had lost two, in addition
to nine fireships. Then followed disaster; for want of a naval
port which would serve as a point of support in the Cotentin,
the French ships dispersed; three, one of which was the *Soleil d'Or*,
which had carried Tourville, were burnt opposite Cherbourg,
six at Tatihou, six at La Hogue. James II beheld with consternation the ruin of his hopes. Louis XIV, frustrated, thought
no more of invasion. Tourville received orders to make the
Mediterranean his rallying-point, where his junction with
d'Estrées would ensure France's mastery of the sea; on the way,
in June and July 1693, he put Admiral Rooke to flight at Lagos
and captured a very large convoy.

A similar victory inspired the French with a new method of
warfare until the treaty of Ryswick (1697), the method which
characterised the War of the Spanish Succession (1701–1714)—
privateering warfare. *L'Art des Armées Navales*, published by le
Père Hoste, De Tourville's chaplain and mouthpiece, was, as it
were, the last will and testament of Squadron Warfare, the
last echoes of which were heard at Vigo, when Châteaurenault's
squadron was burnt by Rooke (October 1702), and at Velez
Malaga, where the Admiral Comte de Toulouse did not succeed

in pushing to its full extent the advantage gained over the Anglo-Dutch fleet (August 24–25, 1704).

10. *Privateering warfare*

Privateering warfare alone seemed compatible with the increasing weakness of the royal navy: "By renouncing the vain ambition of great naval armies which can never be suitable to us," said Vauban, "and using the King's ships partly for privateering, partly in squadrons to support them, we should give the English a great fall." In this kind of warfare the "furia francese" excelled. French Levantines had been seen giving battle to the whole Ottoman fleet during the war of Candia; the Chevalier d'Hocquincourt, in 1665, in a fight in which Tourville began his career, with a single vessel put to flight thirty-six Turkish galleys; and Gabriel de Thémericourt at Nio with two frigates held his own against fifty-four galleys of Capoudan Pasha (1668).

The Filibusters of the Antilles were similar to the Levantines of the Greek Islands. Of various races, French in the island of Tortuga, English in Jamaica, they carried the spirit of combination so far as to call themselves the Brethren of the Coast. If there are sceptics "inclined to regard the historian as a romancer," wrote one of these Brethren of the Coast, "I do not advise these gentlemen to read the life of the filibusters, where everything is extraordinary"—everything, from the exploits of Monbars the Exterminator against the Plate fleet, or of Nau the Olonnais against Havana, to the campaign of the Welshman, Henry Morgan, against Panama in 1671, or of Massertie, a native of Bordeaux, in 1687, in the Pacific Ocean.

In the European seas, the hero of this kind of warfare was Jean Bart. Grandson of the celebrated Jean Jacobsen, who blew up his ship rather than surrender to eight enemies, son, brother, and cousin to a legion of pirates or corsairs of Dunkirk, Jean Bart, in 1679, forced his entry into the aristocratic navy of the king. Ten battles and eighty-one captures enabled him to obtain a brevet as "Lieutenant on a ship of the line." Further exploits gained for him in 1694 the rank of commodore; in company with Forbin, a Provençal of old family, who returned from Siam with a foreign title of admiral, he spread abroad such

terror that the allies were obliged to detach a score of vessels
to blockade Dunkirk, without any result. Commerce-raiding,
directed by officers of the royal navy such as Nesmond,
Coëtlogon, and Renau, became a real industrial war, which
caused the English a loss of eight hundred million *livres*.

Duguay-Trouin, a native of Saint-Malo, twenty-four years of
age, in 1697 boarded the ship of a Dutch rear-admiral; then in
1709 he escaped from the grip of fifteen British vessels, and at
the entrance to the Channel carried off four vessels of the first
rank, one of which, the *Devonshire*, perished in flames with more
than a thousand men; and in 1709 he gained a patent of nobility
by a total of five hundred ships of war or trading vessels captured.
He set the seal to his glory on September 21, 1711, by his
attack on Rio de Janeiro, where the Portuguese had given
shelter to his adversaries; the capture of the town inflicted on
them damage to the amount of thirty million *livres*.

A year later, Cassard of Nantes, of whom Duguay-Trouin said
modestly that he was the best seaman of the period, inflicted
fresh blows on the Portuguese by the capture of Santiago in the
Cape Verd Islands, on the Dutch by the conquest of Surinam,
Essequibo, and Berbice, and on the English by the ruin of St
Kitt's and Montserrat.

The Béarnais Ducasse rendered even finer services. He
gained a commission as ship's captain by defeating Admiral
Codrington at Guadeloupe (1692), the cross of St Louis at the
capture of Cartagena by Pointis (1697) and the rank of American
commodore by a long fight off St Martha, where he put Admiral
Benbow to flight. The War of Spanish Succession turned the
gallant corsair into a convoyer of galleons, which he succeeded
in escorting safely, sometimes to Pasajes, sometimes to La
Coruña. Philip V made him a knight of the Golden Fleece, and
the honour was well deserved. For the English were masters of
the sea. The gold which thus eluded them helped to finance the
last battles of a disastrous war. Spain was ruined, France was
defeated at Ramilies, Oudenarde, and Malplaquet, but she made
a last effort at Villaviciosa and Denain; and this enabled her to
make an honourable peace at Utrecht.

11. *Naval Decadence under Louis XV*

Since then, since the naval battle of Malaga, "there has been no naval army," wrote the Naval Secretary, M. de Valincourt, in 1729. A minister, Phelypeaux de Maurepas, replaced the oligarchical rule of the Naval Council, instituted under the presidency of Admiral the Comte de Toulouse. "This young man, aged twenty-four, of good sense, but who does not know the colour of the sea, nor how a ship is constructed, will shut himself up with four clerks, who know no more than he, and will issue instructions for the fleet, if it is possible to have one. By such means has the navy of France fallen little by little into decay." The minimum effective force of the fleet, fixed at sixty vessels, was far from being attained in 1748, when the English fleet consisted of two hundred and sixty-eight ships of war. The War of the Austrian Succession, in which France took the part of Spain, while England supported Maria-Theresa, gave France the feeble support of the Spanish fleet.

To save the French colonies, two squadron-leaders sacrificed themselves; La Jonquière, opposing 436 guns to 944, gave battle to Admiral Anson, who was waiting for him near Cape Ortegal, on May 14, 1747; and, though he succumbed heroically, part of his convoy reached its destination, Canada. In the same way, the Antilles convoy escaped, thanks to the sacrifice of Des Herbiers of the Étanduère, who lost six out of eight ships in the battle of Cape Finisterre on the following 29th of October. In the Indian seas, Mahé de La Bourdonnais was more fortunate. With a single ship of the line and eight "Buoys loaded with artillery"—meaning thereby the ships of the French East India Company—he defeated the squadron of Admiral Peyton at Negapatam on July 6, 1746, and forced Madras to surrender. A foolish quarrel between him and the Governor of France's Indian settlements, Dupleix, brought him as a recompense a cell in the Bastille. The war ended in 1748 with the treaty of Aix-la-Chapelle, which returned everything to the *status quo ante*.

Nevertheless, the French colonial empire was growing in importance, and hence excited British covetousness. In India, Dupleix, by a very active policy, and by armed intervention on behalf of native claimants, had established French suzerainty over the Carnatic and the Deccan, French authority over the coast of Orissa, and French influence over the Great Mogul. The islands of France and Rodriguez and the Seychelles were so many steps to India.

In America, the thirteen colonies of New England became annoyed by the activity which the French displayed in their rear, by increasing the number of their forts between Louisiana and Canada. In June 1755 an army of Americans deported the Acadian colonists; another force was beaten by the French Canadians on the Monongahela. The English fleets of Boscawen and Hawke were called to the rescue. The Seven Years' War began.

A reversal of alliances placed France on the side of Austria against Prussia and England. The diversions of the British fleet at Cancale, Cherbourg, and Saint-Cast were of service to the armies of Frederick II by obliging the French to keep troops on the coast. After a fortunate start (the capture of Port Mahon by La Galissonnière), the French navy gave way before a force four times as strong. The squadron of La Clüe was destroyed by Boscawen at Lagos (August 18, 1759) and the squadron of Marshal de Conflans was cut to pieces by Hawke in the fight at Quiberon in the following November. At the end of the war, France had lost fifty-six ships and twenty-five thousand prisoners; it was the greatest naval disaster that she had experienced since the battle of Sluys.

The cost of defeat was the loss of her Colonial Empire, in spite of the help which, bound by the Family Compact, Spain had finally given her. Louisburg in Acadia, besieged by Boscawen, capitulated. The breach opened in New France became wider when Wolfe's army arrived outside Quebec; the death of the brave Marquis de Montcalm on the plains of Abraham decided the fate of the colony. On September 8, 1760, Montreal, the last strategical position of France, surrendered. In the Antilles, the cowardice of the governor, Beauharnais, and of the commodore, Bompar, allowed Dominica, Grenada, St Lucia, Tobago, and Martinique to fall into Rodney's hands. Of France's American colonies only Louisiana and St Domingo remained untouched. Senegal, Guinea, and the magnificent Empire planned by Dupleix in India were taken from her. She kept only

Mascarenha and five small ports in India, which were assured to her by the treaty of Paris in 1763.

12. *Voyages of discovery*

Having no longer a colonial empire to defend, French seamen went in search of a new one. They were very late in penetrating into the Pacific, because the Spanish monopoly forbade all foreign commerce. The "Compagnie Royale du Pacifique" was not formed until 1698 by a native of Saint-Malo, Noel Danycan de Lépine, and by a Parisian, Jourdan de Groussey. It was planned for trade with "uninhabited islands, beyond those occupied by the Spaniards," notably California, then regarded as an island. The islands of "Malouines" (Falkland) and "Danycan" (Sea Lion Island), near the Straits of Magellan, the coasts of Chile and Peru, the small islet of "La Passion" (Clipperton), reached on April 3, 1710, marked the stages of the operations, whose terminus was Lower California. Trublet, a seaman from Saint-Malo, even received from the Spanish viceroy of Peru in 1704 the rank of "Capitan de mar y guerra," because he held his own against the celebrated English seaman, William Dampier. But by the treaty of Utrecht Louis XIV was compelled to forbid his subjects to engage in the fruitful trade of the Southern Seas.

It was in the Malouines Islands that the son of a Parisian notary, Bougainville, former lieutenant to Montcalm, attempted to establish the colonists driven from Acadia after the disastrous treaty of Paris. But scarcely had the colony begun to prosper than in 1766 the Spaniards demanded the evacuation of the island, and the English occupied it. Bougainville then undertook his famous voyage round the world, in which he was to visit and describe, long before Pierre Loti, the enchanting life of Tahiti, the New Cythera. The Navigator Islands, the Great Cyclades or New Hebrides, the Louisiade archipelago, Port-Praslin, and Bougainville Island in the Solomon archipelago were his principal stages before his return by the Moluccas to Saint-Malo. A little later, in 1772, a Breton, Kerguelen, discovered the islands in the south of the Indian Ocean to which he gave his name and which still belong to France.

The three voyages of discovery of James Cook greatly excited men's imagination, and popularised the idea of the Pacific Islands to such an extent, that a noble emulation spurred the French on to follow in his footsteps.

In 1769 Surville reached the land of the Arsacides and New Zealand, where Marion-Dufresne was massacred three years later. Richery, only a naval ensign, reconnoitred the points where forts should be placed, the Ridang islands near Siam, Turan in Cochin China, Manilla, Haïnan, etc.

Finally, a great navigator, known by his expedition to Hudson Bay, Jean François de Galaup de La Pérouse, a native of Albi, received a mission to link up the various itineraries of Captain Cook with each other. His instructions were drawn up by Louis XVI himself; the king was much interested in geography, so much so that the Bibliothèque Nationale still preserves maps drawn by his hand. Doubling Cape Horn, La Pérouse gained the north-west coast of America, where he took the bearings of Port des Français and Cenotaph Island before Vancouver; from Monterey in California he proceeded to Macao, drew up the hydrography of Japan, where the northern strait still bears his name, and then despatched the notes of his discoveries to Paris from Kamschatka on September 7, 1787; then by way of Samoa, where his lieutenant, de Langle, was massacred, he reached Botany Bay in Australia, and wrote a last letter to the minister on the 7th of February 1788. After that, there was silence.

The Provençal Bruni d'Entrecasteaux was sent in search of him: he was the man to whom in 1787 Ensign Richery had entrusted the account of his explorations; he left Brest in 1791, and for two years he cruised the Australian seas, the strait which bears his name, the Papuan archipelago in prolongation of New Guinea, to which he gave his name (Bruni Island), the seas round New Caledonia, and New Zealand. He found no vestige of La Pérouse. However, in the distance he perceived an island which he named Recherche Island (Vanikoro) without reconnoitring it further; there had occurred the scene whose mystery he was seeking to unravel.

Long afterwards, in 1827, the English captain Dillon was surprised to see a sword-guard in the island of Ticopia and learnt that it came from two large wrecked vessels, whose crews had perished fighting with the natives of a neighbouring island. The guard of the sword bore the initials of La Pérouse. In February 1828, Dumont d'Urville discovered the remains of his predecessor's two frigates under the waters which break against the reefs of Vanikoro.

13. *The War of American Independence*

When the worthy Benjamin Franklin came to ask French help in the name of the American rebels, a cautious and veiled support in the way of arms and munitions was given under the name of Beaumarchais. Then on February 6, 1778 a treaty of amity and commerce bound France to their cause. The recovery of her navy under Choiseul, Sartines, and, soon after, the Marquis de Castries, enabled her to come into line against England. The plans of the naval operations were the work of the Director of Ports and Arsenals, Claret de Fleurieu, who for fifteen years under various ministers before the Revolution ensured a spirit of continuity to the French navy.

Imbued with the idea that "defensive warfare does not suit the French, that it humiliates the nation, depresses courage, and destroys energy," Fleurieu proposed "a plan of offence, to attack the English in different parts of the world," a strategical plan which resulted in the dispersal of the French naval forces and the impossibility of striking a decisive blow. The "perfect battle," demanded by the Comte de Broglie in order to "end the war by one blow," had taken place off Ushant on the 27th of July 1778 between d'Orvilliers and Keppel; it had no decisive result. But it was a success for the little French navy to have checked its formidable rival. The support of the Spanish fleet, guaranteed by the treaty of Aranjuez on April 12, 1779, had been no help. The interminable delays of Cordova had a disastrous effect on the crews of Admiral d'Orvilliers, who arrived before their allies. Seven thousand sick on board and hundreds of deaths prevented any invasion of England. The French wished at least to retake Gibraltar. Eliott (afterwards Lord Heathfield) offered a heroic resistance to the floating batteries invented by Colonel d'Arçon and supported by eighty

ships and gunboats; shortly before the arrival of Admiral Howe
a red-hot ball exploded the floating batteries, closely pressed
against each other. Gibraltar, which had been invested since
1779, remained the property of England (1782).

In a secondary theatre of war there took place a duel pal-
pitating with interest. "A fiery character," who prided himself
on "making war, and not paying court," Suffren-Saint-Tropez,
sent to help the Cape Dutch and the Sultan of Mysore in India,
had saved the former by outsailing commodore Johnstone and
throwing his force into disorder near Praya in the Cape Verd
Archipelago. And now there succeeded without a pause the
blows of a bitter struggle between Suffren and Vice-admiral
Hughes, who was defending India. Taken between two fires,
maltreated at Sadras (February 17, 1782), and robbed of two
vessels at Provedien (April 12), Hughes regained the advantage
at Negapatam, where the French lost eight hundred killed and
wounded (July 6). But at Trincomalee he was not able to dis-
lodge Suffren, who had established himself in a commanding
position (September 2), and at Goudelour, on June 20, 1783,
he abandoned the scene of battle. None the less he prevented
Bussy, formerly Dupleix's lieutenant, from resuming the epic
contest. "It is dreadful to have four times succeeded in destroying the English squadron and to find it still in existence !" sighed
the conqueror. In fact, Suffren, a quarrelsome fellow as well
as a man of genius, was in every occasion badly obeyed by
those of his captains whom he had bullied, or who were jealous
of him.

However, in the principal theatre of war, the proverbial skill
of the British navy was keeping decision in suspense, in spite of
the bravery of the rebels helped by Lafayette's volunteers, when
there arrived on the scene the twelve ships of the Comte d'Estaing,
vice-admiral of the seas of Asia, Africa, and America. Howe had
to leave the waters of the Delaware in order to cover New York.
D'Estaing forced the passage of Newport, which was enveloped
by American troops under Sullivan, and destroyed six frigates
and corvettes at anchor (August 9, 1778). Two other English
squadrons were announced. D'Estaing met one at Santa Lucia,
a French colony, which his lack of decision allowed to fall into
the hands of Admiral Barrington. But he redeemed his hesita-

tion by his impetuous attack on Grenada, a British possession, which he was about to carry by storm, when Byron's squadron appeared. Byron, taken under the fire of the Georgetown forts, which he did not know to be in French hands, had four ships disabled; the French vice-admiral would not "have allowed them to escape had he been as good a sailor as he was a brave man" (July 6, 1779). But he was an old officer of land forces, more familiar with methods of assault than with naval man-œuvres; he was seriously wounded on October 18, while attempting to carry Savannah, the British base of operations in Georgia.

Very different was the Comte de Guichen, a seaman almost seventy years old, who allowed Rodney to exhaust his strength, without gaining any advantage, in three battles near the Antilles. In 1780, the arrival of a corps of the French army, with Ternay's division, gave the American Government the valuable support of regular troops, but did not bring about an immediate decision. And why? The Lieutenant-General of the French troops, Jean-Baptiste de Vimeur de Rochambeau, wrote without disguise: "Nothing without naval supremacy." A lucky blow gave it to France. The Comte de Grasse, slipping through the Bahama Channel to baffle the British cruisers, appeared in force at the mouth of the Chesapeake on August 30, 1781. Washington and Rochambeau were besieging Lord Cornwallis in Yorktown. Admiral Graves, even when reinforced by Admiral Hood, could not relieve the pressure. The French mastery of the sea rendered the issue inevitable. Yorktown capitulated on October 19 with an army of eight thousand men. The Independence of the United States was an accomplished fact. A defeat made no difference. Attacked off Les Saintes by Rodney's thirty-seven ships on April 12, 1782, the Comte de Grasse bravely resisted the attack with thirty ships. But his flagship, the *Ville de Paris*, tackled by ten opponents, was reduced to three unwounded sailors and to guns without charges, which could only be loaded with ladles, and had to strike her flag; four more ships succumbed. This victory palliated for British pride the enormous losses suffered by her trade and the loss of the American colonies, which was sanctioned by the treaty of Versailles in 1783.

14. *From the "Vengeur" to the Continental Blockade*

The Revolution of 1789 shattered the mainspring without which a navy is nothing—discipline. Insulted by the sailors, the Commandant of the Arsenal at Brest resigned; the Governor of Toulon and his Major-General were hanged by mutineers; at St Domingo, at Réunion, on the coast of India, at Quiberon, everywhere a spirit of revolt breathed among the crews and even reached the expedition of Bruni d'Entrecasteaux in Oceania, which was sent to find La Pérouse. The absence of official support, the suspicion which attached to their aristocratic origin and which weighed heavily on them, spread discouragement through the ranks of the naval officers, already disinclined to welcome the new ideas. Two-thirds of them were reported as "absent without leave," after a review held at Brest in January 1792. They had left the country. The minister, La Luzerne, had set the example. They died in exile or in the landing at Quiberon, when, with the aid of the British fleet, they attempted to lend a helping hand to the "Chouans" and were surrounded by Hoche.

France's naval unpreparedness synchronised with the moment chosen by the Convention for the declaration of war against England (February 1, 1793), thus blindly helping the coalition which was seeking to destroy her, Austria, Prussia, and Sardinia. A representative of the people sent to Brest to revive courage in the navy succeeded in doing so by terrorism. But although Jean-Bon Saint-André was able to impose comparative discipline, he could not make up for inexperience. In the battle on the "13th of Prairial" or of Finistère (June 1, 1794), Villaret-Joyeuse and Howe had equal forces; yet the French lost 5000 men and only put 1148 of the enemy out of action, because of the want of skill of the gunners and the faulty manœuvring of the leaders. Six of the vessels were surrendered; the seventh, the *Vengeur du Peuple*, riddled with shot from three adversaries, allowed herself to be sunk rather than strike her flag. Half of the crew perished.

A report by Barrère gave an epic character to the exploit of the *Vengeur* and the act of Captain Renaudin, and held him up as an example to seamen. They required encouragement. The year before, the English had been allowed to occupy Toulon, whence they removed or destroyed twenty-three vessels and frigates, when they left the town under the fire of Bonaparte's batteries (December 18, 1793).

When Vice-Admiral Truguet was appointed to the ministry of Marine in 1795, he reconstructed the staffs with all the former naval officers who had not left the country—Brueys, Latouche, Villeneuve. And from the defensive he passed to the offensive.

Simultaneously with the action of Bonaparte and Moreau against the Austrian Empire a direct attack was to be developed against England. Carnot had planned it; Hoche was to carry it out. His twenty thousand men were to invade Ireland and raise an insurrection there. But the Channel had to be crossed. British territory was safeguarded more by stormy weather than by the fleet; the squadron of Morard de Galle was dispersed. A renewed attempt with the help of the Spaniards and the Dutch was foiled by two energetic admirals. At Cape St Vincent on February 14, 1797, Jervis attacked Cordova, who retired to Cadiz and remained there for three years. Duncan inflicted a crushing defeat on the Dutch admiral De Winter at Camperdown on October 11. With only a thousand men, General Humbert landed in Ireland, where he covered himself with glory in a campaign of eighteen days, before his surrender on September 8, 1798. Bompard's division, despatched to help him, was captured almost in its entirety. The French abandoned the idea of invading England, for which object Forfait had prepared a flotilla of gunboats. The soldier who had condemned it as being impossible without the mastery of the sea was Bonaparte.

He agreed with the old idea of Suffren's day, to which the seamen, Truguet and Villaret-Joyeuse, remained faithful, the ruin of England's empire in India; but he presented it under a new aspect: "an expedition in the Levant would threaten Indian trade." The victor of Arcole and Rivoli himself undertook the conduct of the expedition. Bonaparte landed in Egypt without hindrance, where the Battle of the Pyramids would have destroyed the power of the Mamelukes, had not Nelson discovered the French squadron moored in the bay of Aboukir on August 2, 1798. One of his columns slipped between the shore and the French line of ships, which a second

column took between two fires. It was a disaster for the French;
they lost eleven out of thirteen ships, and six thousand men;
Admiral Brueys perished on board the *Orient*, which was
blown up. The consequences of the defeat of Aboukir were
incalculable; Bonaparte, cut off from France, beheld the appearance of a new enemy, who was no longer held in check, namely
Turkey. A crushing offensive drove the Turks out of Syria; but
for want of a fleet, Bonaparte failed outside Acre; he was
obliged to fall back on Egypt, and then to return to France. For
want of a fleet, Egypt, abandoned to its fate, was also lost to
France. Perrée's division was annihilated by Nelson in February
1801. Ganteaume, eagerly pursued by Keith, could not land
Sahuguet's troops at Alexandria. Linois, attacked in the bay
of Algeciras by Saumarez on July 6, resisted victoriously, even
capturing a vessel; but his adversary took a striking revenge on
the 12th, by destroying three magnificent Franco-Spanish three-
deckers. On September 1, Menou surrendered in Alexandria.

Bonaparte returned to France at a critical moment. The
monarchies had formed a coalition against the young republics
which had issued from the Revolution, against the French,
Batavian, Cisalpine, Ligurian, Roman, and Parthenopian
Republics. Souwarow's Russians came to help the Austrians
and their fleet reinforced the British admiral, Duncan, for a
landing in the Netherlands. Disasters were succeeding one
another, when Bonaparte, put in power as First Consul on the
18th Brumaire, 1799, retrieved the position; the victory of
Marengo induced Austria to ask for peace on February 9,
1801. A confederation signed with the Northern States under
the name of the Armed Coalition turned the European coalition
against England. Nelson took the initiative, and by an attack
on the floating batteries of Copenhagen in April forced Denmark
to secede from the confederation. The Brest fleet, closely blockaded, could not leave the harbour. Only the Boulogne flotilla,
reorganised by Latouche-Tréville, inspired the British with so
much fear that they detached Nelson to deal with it. England
with 202 ships as opposed to 39 was mistress of the seas;
Bonaparte dictated laws on the Continent. Victory was in the
balance between them, and the Peace of Amiens, May 27,
1802, could only be a truce, which gave the French time to

resume contact with their small colonial empire: with
St Domingo, where General Leclerc did not succeed in sup-
pressing the rebellion of the negroes; with Louisiana, which Spain
returned to the French and which they handed over to the
United States; with the Colonies in the Indian Ocean, whither
General Decaen was sent; and with Oceania, which Captain
Baudin explored and where he founded some settlements.

A year after the Peace of Amiens war was resumed. A formidable flotilla of two thousand flat-bottomed boats, able to
run ashore without injury, was assembled at Boulogne to
attempt invasion; praams loaded with heavy artillery, gunboats,
and pinnaces manœuvred in squadrons and divisions under
the high command of Bruix. But powerless to break through
the British cruisers, they waited until the fleet of ships of the line
opened a way for them. If Neptune would lend him his trident
for three days, Napoleon, as we must now call him, hoped to
put "an end to the fortunes and existence of England."

In this instance, Neptune was represented by the admiral of
the Toulon squadron, who, after raising the blockades, and
rallying the Atlantic divisions one after the other, was to force
an entrance of the Channel. But after a feint on the Antilles to
draw off our opponents, Villeneuve did not succeed in reaching
the French Atlantic ports; driven back to Spain by Calder, he
was blockaded in Cadiz in company with the Spanish admiral,
Gravina. When he attempted a sortie, urged thereto by a
threatening message from Napoleon, he ran into Nelson on
October 21, 1805. The battle of Trafalgar was decisive. When at
the mast of the *Victory* rose the signal "England expects that
every man will do his duty," Collingwood bore down on the
French line, which he cut in two, and then turned parallel with
the rear-guard in such a manner as to envelop it. Nelson fell
upon Villeneuve, whom he crushed with the converging fire of
several ships; after a desperate struggle, in which the *Redoutable*,
commanded by the intrepid Lucas, lost six hundred men in
trying to disengage him, the *Bucentaur* struck her admiral's flag;
Villeneuve was a prisoner. The *Achille* had blown up; the battle
was lost; seventeen French and Spanish ships out of thirty-three
fell into the hands of the English. But the English mourned
their victory; their great man, Nelson, was dead, his spine

shattered by a ball from the *Redoutable*. The disaster of the allies did not end with the battle; the four vessels of Dumanoir's division, while attempting to escape, ran into Commodore Strachan on November 2; he captured them off Cape Ortegal.

Napoleon replied to Trafalgar with the thunderbolt of Auster-litz. England's allies, the Emperor and the Tsar, felt the wrath of the lion robbed of his prey. A year later Jena and Austerlitz subdued Prussia; Eylau and Friedland inclined Russia to peace. It was then that Napoleon, master of the Continent, king of Italy in his own person, and king of Holland and of Naples in the person of his brothers, launched against the mastery of the sea that formidable engine of war which was formerly conceived by Philip the Fair—the Continental Blockade. The Decree of Milan of December 17, 1807, declared every vessel which had allowed the visit of an English ship, or had made a voyage to England, to be a lawful prize. The Blockade became extended to the New World, where the United States, indignant at the searching of their ships by British cruisers, who impressed their crews, combined with the French in 1812.

The Emperor hoped to strengthen the effect of the Blockade by privateering. But his divisions had fallen one after the other into the meshes of the net spread by the British squadrons. Leissègues was beaten by Duckworth at St Domingo (February 6, 1806); Willaumez was forced to take shelter in the Chesapeake; Linois, on his return from the Indian Ocean, where he had inflicted a loss of thirty million *livres* on enemy commerce, was captured near the Canaries by Burlase Warren (March 13, 1806). A stronghold, defended by five hundred guns, became the base of operations of frigate-captains and bold privateers, Bourayne, Bergeret, Motard, Épron, and Robert Surcouf, who, with a hundred and thirty men, boarded and captured the *Kent*, which carried a crew of four hundred and fifty. This stronghold was the Ile-de-France, whence General Decaen commanded the possessions in the Indian Ocean, Bourbon (then called Bonaparte), Madagascar, and the Seychelles. His defeat on December 2, 1810 by an avalanche of disembarking troops, which amounted to 23,000 British and sepoys, caused the loss of all the French colonies, including those of Holland, which had passed into French power, the Sunda Islands, the Dutch Indies, and Cape Colony. The battle of Grand-Port, in which four British frigates were captured or destroyed by Hamelin, Duperré, and Bouvet in the preceding August, was the swan-song of the French navy.

In any case, could the Continental Blockade bring about a solution? No. It carried its own sentence of death. The restraint which it imposed on the nations irritated them and detached them from the French cause. In Portugal, where the house of Braganza was declared to have forfeited its claim, and in Spain, where Napoleon had installed his brother Joseph, England found a breach in the blockade, which was enlarged by her fleets and her troops in alliance with the insurgents; the surrender of the French troops at Cintra and Baylen in 1808 sounded the first knell of the imperial power. The Emperor's brothers, Joseph, Louis, Jérome, lost the Spanish, Batavian, and Hanseatic territories respectively, foot by foot. A final mistake, the Russian campaign, finished the disastrous work of the Spanish war. That alliance of injured interests and unsatisfied rancour, the sixth coalition, was aimed against France. Napoleon retreated step by step. After the retreat from Moscow there followed Leipzig and the French campaign. Napoleon succumbed under the invasion which developed on all sides. There was a return to the offensive in the fiery adventure of the Hundred Days. Waterloo brought down the Colossus for ever. In the duel between the sea and the continent the sea had conquered. In the island of Elba, as at St Helena, Napoleon remained its prisoner. "Whoever is master of the sea has a great thoroughfare on the land" was said two centuries earlier by Isaac de Razilly, the inspirer of Richelieu. Of the highly prosperous colonies in the time of Louis XIV, the second Hundred Years' War left France only the wreckage; Guiana, Senegal, the Lesser Antilles, Réunion, and a few small settlements in India.

15. *Foundation of a new Colonial Empire*

War had robbed France of a colonial empire, peace was to give her a new one. The naval victory of Navarino, in which Admiral de Rigny, in conjunction with the British fleet, fought the Turco-Egyptian fleet (1827), marked the beginning of a spirit

of agreement with England, the consequences of which were
fruitful. The two nations in concert mapped out possessions
among the cloud of islands in the Oceanic seas. A series of
voyages round the world, which were initiated in 1817 by
Desaulses de Freycinet, former companion of Baudin, by
Duperrey, Dumont d'Urville, and Dupetit-Thouars prefaced the
occupation of Tahiti, the pearl of the Pacific, by the last-named
(1843). In default of New Zealand, occupied in 1840 by England
a few weeks before the arrival of a party of French colonists,
France obtained New Caledonia, where the massacre of some
of Admiral Febvrier Despointes's sailors was the pretext for
annexation (1851), and later, the Marquesas, the Gambier, the
Touamotou, and the Society Islands.

By the taking of Saigon in 1859 Admiral Rigault de Genouilly
hoisted the French flag on the Asiatic continent. The illustrious
Admiral Courbet enlarged the possessions by his victories over
the Annamites and the Chinese, by the capture of Thuanan
and Sontay, and by the destruction of the Chinese fleet at Fu-
Chow. Indo-China became a French possession. The task was
hardly completed when the admiral, worn out by fatigue, died
on board the *Bayard* (1885), having richly deserved the national
funeral which he received from his country.

The Third Republic witnessed a magnificent expansion of the
colonial work begun under the Royalty and the Second Empire,
since the day when the Algerian expedition in 1830 had sounded
the knell of the powers of Barbary. The protectorate of Tunisia
in 1881, and that of Morocco more lately, has bound the fate of
Northern Africa to the fortunes of France. On the Atlantic,
Benin and the Congo have been added to Gabun, Dahomey to
Senegal. The feelers of the three French African possessions,
Northern, Western and Equatorial Africa, converge towards
Lake Tchad. On the other side of the continent, Madagascar,
definitely conquered, has gained the Comoros and Réunion as
satellites. Obock on the Red Sea has been joined to Djibouti.

The task of the navy being ended, and the work of conquest
having been carried out by its marine fusiliers and marine
infantry, the exploitation of this vast empire has passed into
other hands. The Colonies passed under the control of an Under-
Secretary in 1889, and then to an autonomous Ministry. Need

I add that the navy has performed its duty valiantly in all the wars, in the Crimea, in the bombardment of Bomarsund against the Russians, at Vera Cruz against the Mexicans, and at the siege of Paris against the Germans?

They have had to study the numerous problems presented to our workshops by the invention of steam, of quick-firing guns, and of high explosives. The construction of an armoured frigate, the *Gloire*, by the engineer Dupuy de Lôme in 1859 was a revolution. But in the contest between armour and guns, the employment first of the torpedo, then of the submarine, seems to have inclined the scale in favour of the latter by rendering the best defensive arms uncertain; and in the construction of submarines France has had some real masters, Zédé and Laubeuf. In the midst of incessant evolution of naval means one element has remained unchanged, testifying the solidity of the institutions of the Great Century. The administrative mould —ministry, naval register, naval pensions—has not varied since the days of the greatest minister whom France has ever known—Colbert.

BIBLIOGRAPHY

Ch. de La Roncière, *Histoire de la Marine française* (in process of publication), 1906–1920: Vol. III. *Guerres d'Italie.* Vol. IV. *En quête d'un Empire colonial: Richelieu.* Vol. V. *Guerre de Trente Ans: Colbert.*

For the period after 1683 there is no general history of the rival maritime nations based upon the numerous sources, written and printed. But whether from the point of view of the philosophy of history, or from that of anecdote, the following recent works may be read with profit: J. R. Seeley, *The Expansion of England*, 1883; French translation by Baille and Rambaud, 1885. Henri Malo, *Les Corsaires dunkerquois et Jean Bart.* 2 vols. 1908–1913. Lieut. Castex, *Les idées militaires de la marine du xviiie siècle: De Ruyter à Suffren.* 1911. E. W. Dahlgren, *Les relations commerciales et maritimes entre la France et l'Océan Pacifique (commencement du xviiie siècle).* Vol. I. 1909 (based on original documents). V. Brun, *Les Guerres maritimes de la France: port de Toulon.* 2 vols. 1885. M. Loir, *La Marine royale en 1789*, 1892; *Le Vengeur* (based on documents in the *Archives de la Marine*), 1892. O. Havard, *Histoire de la Révolution dans les Ports de Guerre.* 2 vols. 1911–1913. E. Desbrière, *1793–1805. Projets et Tentatives de Débarquement aux Iles britanniques.* 4 vols. 1900–1902; *La Campagne maritime en 1805: Trafalgar.* 1907. M. Dubois, *Un siècle d'expansion coloniale.* 1900.

CHAPTER IV

ECONOMIC AND SOCIAL LIFE

§ I. PROVINCIAL ECONOMY (16TH CENTURY)

At the close of the 15th century great changes occurred. The New World was discovered and made demands on the activity and often on the avidity of the French, as of all the nations of Western Europe. Then for the first time since the Crusades, France, freed from the burdens of the Hundred Years' War, and revived by the peaceful reigns of Charles VII and Louis XI, ventured beyond her own frontiers, engaged in grandiose wars, and attacked Italy. Her horizon all at once became extended to the whole of the Mediterranean and to the Atlantic Ocean.

Nevertheless, although the French outlook became enlarged by its contact with the Italian Renaissance, the social economy showed no revolutionary change. Throughout the 16th century France reaped no benefits either from the discovery of America, or from the European exploitation of India and China. No doubt some bold Frenchmen carried out brilliant explorations: Jacques Cartier of Saint-Malo in Canada between 1534 and 1541; Roberval of Picardy, also in Canada; Admiral de Villegagnon in Brazil in 1555. Moreover, Francis I took an interest in the Canadian expeditions, which were mainly financed by Jean Ango, the patriotic shipowner of Dieppe. But the lack of co-operation between Jacques Cartier and Roberval prevented any French colonisation of Canada, and the French explorers were not consistently supported by the king, whose European policy obliged him to make concessions; furthermore public opinion was slow to accept the new conditions of the world and looked to the Mediterranean and the southern countries, which had been the cradle of civilisation, rather than across the Atlantic to the virgin lands and vast icy solitudes of North America; finally, after the long struggles with the House of Austria under Francis I and Henry II, France under the later Valois was engrossed in the tragic wars of religion, in the war with Philip II of Spain, and in the material and moral reconstruction of the country.

And if France could not then expand externally, as was suggested by the three seas with which she is surrounded, neither could she renew her economic activity. There was no great transformation in trade in spite of the foundation of Le Havre de Grâce in 1519, nor in industry notwithstanding the development and capitalist concentration of silk-weaving at Lyons; and agriculture made no progress, although the process of forest-clearing and the cultivation of new land had increased production. France continued to subsist almost entirely on her soil; and her wheat, her wines, and her salt defrayed the cost of the raw materials and manufactured produce of foreign lands: spices from Portugal, silken stuffs, brocade, velvet, glass, lace, jewels, and arms from Italy. The peasant thus paid for the articles which many nobles and even *bourgeois* who had been enriched by trade caused to be brought from abroad for their apparel, their pleasures, and the adornment of their sumptuous houses, or for the magnificent town-halls and fine churches, which were erected or altered after the Renaissance style.

The social economy of France was less that of a great state than that of a sort of federation of provinces. The lack of roads and canals, the multiplicity of tolls and provincial customs, the mediocre importance of industry and maritime trade, the weakness of credit, which nevertheless had made a start, especially at Lyons under the influence of Florentine and Lombards, all this imparted a very different character to French economic life than that possessed by those of Italy or the Low Countries, which had come under the influence of the Renaissance.

§ II. NATIONAL ECONOMY FROM 1600 TO 1750

However, France was attempting to shake off the provincial system of the Middle Ages and to aspire to the idea of a national economic system. But policy was regarded as more important than economy. It was indeed necessary that France should take form, that she should have settled frontiers and a strong and centralised government, so that she could develop in security and transform her social economy.

From the time of Henry IV a new system gradually became established side by side with the former one; Henry IV, Sully, Laffemas, later Richelieu and the economist Montchrétien, finally and pre-eminently Colbert, defined it and put it into practice. From Sully to Colbert in spite of some divergent details there was perfect continuity of views. All these statesmen and economists were passionately interested in national welfare and were anxious that France, at last delivered from her enemies and from internecine warfare, should resolutely set to work to use the best methods in the economic struggle between nations.

Richelieu and Colbert were amazed at the object-lesson given by the wealth of the Dutch, "who, strictly speaking," wrote Richelieu, "are only a handful of people confined to a corner of land where there is nothing but water and meadow-land, and who nevertheless supply almost all the nations of Europe with the greater part of their necessities." Colbert was struck by the fact that of the 20,000 vessels carrying all the commerce of Europe there were between 15,000 and 16,000 Dutch ships, almost all the rest sailing under the English flag. Compared with this vast fleet, what were the six hundred French ships? "But," said Colbert, "the number of these European vessels cannot be augmented, for the amount of trade available cannot possibly be increased, inasmuch as the population is always equal in number in all the States, and consumption is always similarly equal." In order to take a place in general commerce it was therefore necessary to divert some from other nations. It was necessary to increase production, to purchase little abroad, and as much as possible to manufacture requisites at home; above all to sell a great deal; thus would be amassed a goodly share of the world's gold, which, according to Colbert, is almost a constant quantity. To attract gold to France it must be taken from those who were detaining it. This is "a money war," said Colbert. It would be all the fiercer, because, according to the view held by Colbert and his contemporaries, all that they wished to acquire, ships, trade, and gold, is limited in quantity in the world.

In order to conquer they must work with all their might. In a kingdom where all respect was paid to noble birth and official position, where all manual labour was regarded as servile, and trade was deemed derogatory, it was essential to restore agriculture, industry, and commerce to public esteem. After Richelieu, Colbert devoted himself to this task. "We must," he wrote to the King, "reduce all the professions of your subjects as much as possible to those which may be useful to these great schemes. These are agriculture, trade, warfare by land and by sea. If your Majesty could force all your people to these four kinds of profession, it would be possible for you to become master of the world." This was a new sort of language to be addressed to a king who by tradition and education had eyes only for the army, war, and foreign policy. Thus was formed the mercantile theory which had already made progress in Italy and the Low Countries, and whereby the greatness of Venice and Antwerp had been established.

To apply it an entirely new system had to be devised. Up till then the economic system had been founded on "privilege." Agriculture, or to speak more exactly, landed property, was founded on the seignorial system, according to which the lord who granted any land to a husbandman demanded from the latter a number of irksome dues, either in money or in kind. Industry and commerce had as their base the "corporation," the monopoly which placed the means of work and the actual right of working in the hands of the "master" only, in virtue of his ownership. This system, by its meticulous and tyrannical regulations of trades, limited the number of masters in each guild and of the workmen and apprentices of each master; it thus hindered production and could only supply a restricted market. The mere limitation of markets necessitated tolls and provincial customs, which were defensive measures against the markets of neighbouring provinces.

On the contrary the system now to be established tended, in spite of vicissitudes and even serious set-backs, towards freedom of labour. As regarded agriculture it would end theoretically, if not in the abolition, at least in the diminution of seignorial dues, and already at the end of the 18th century, in law and sometimes in fact, in the abrogation of certain dues, such as forced labour. As regarded industry and commerce it no longer recognised either guilds or masterships or statutes; it favoured the free exercise of activity, of mechanical invention, and consequently of production, with a view to a constantly expanding market. It tended to the suppression of all internal hindrances, provincial customs, and tolls; it no longer regarded France as a federation of provinces separated by custom-house barriers, but as one realm which should be governed by the same laws. In anticipation of the day when the ideal commercial system should be established internally, Colbert intended that it should be almost completely realised externally; in foreign eyes the kingdom of France was to form an almost homogeneous whole, protected and defended by strict tariff laws. Freedom of labour at home, protection of French products and occasionally even prohibition of foreign manufacture, such was the new system in its principal features, and especially in its tendencies. It was not to replace the old one, but to be added to, and established on it.

The new economic system was born in the 17th century in the days of Sully and Laffemas, but it came to its greatest development under Colbert; it made fresh progress in the 18th century, and then became more and more imbued with the spirit of liberty, which was the very reason of its existence; and at the fall of the old monarchy, it went so far as to extend its liberty to relations between France and foreign countries, contrary to Colbert's plan. It thus relegated more and more to the background the old system of guilds and red-tape, which had continued to exist, and which actually attained its perfect form of codification at the very height of the 17th century; but it was dying slowly, unable to survive.

Agriculture and the Peasants. It is impossible to ascertain even approximately the division of land between the different classes of society in the 17th century. But we know that side by side with the great properties of the Church and the nobles, which often included 1000, 2000, or even 3000 *hectares*[1], in the north, east, and west, and in the Central Massif, there existed a large number of small properties, peasant holdings, especially in the fertile territory of Flanders, Alsace, the Loire valley, the Garonne valley, Béarn, etc., and in the vineyard country. It is nearly certain that the progress of rural property

[1] A *hectare* is nearly 2½ acres.

was almost completely arrested during the second half of Louis XIV's reign, which was entirely occupied with wars. It is only during times of peace and prosperity that the division of the soil can continue.

Among the various modes of tenure some, such as lease by champerty (*champart*) and lease by ground-rent, amounted to a transfer of the property, on condition of some monetary payment, or due in kind; others only granted a very short lease or a lease of uncertain length which could be cancelled at the will of the owner, or at the death of the holder of an ecclesiastical living. The former were favourable, the latter unfavourable, to the tenants and hence to agriculture.

Land was leased out in return for rent in money, often for rent both in money and in kind; but most commonly it was farmed co-operatively, generally in equal shares; not only the nobles but also the *bourgeois* and rich peasants leased land for rent or on co-operative terms. The latter system (*métayage*) does not encourage the labourer to work really hard; it is an antiquated method of cultivation, specially prevalent in the centre and the south.

Fettered by the meshes of the seignorial system—which nevertheless was gradually becoming relaxed by negligence—and above all shackled by red-tape and the co-operative system, agriculture in the 17th century remained much what it had been in the 15th and 16th centuries. Henry IV's government made efforts to raise it. Sully took pleasure in asserting that "Husbandry and pasture are the two breasts of France," and these were not idle words. He gave his support to Olivier de Serres, who taught the method of "collecting silk" (1599) and wrote the *Théâtre d'Agriculture* (1600), which ran into several editions. He encouraged the draining of marshes in "Little Flanders" of Médoc, which was carried out by Bradley, a Dutchman; he reduced the *taille* from twenty to fourteen million francs, revised the exemptions from taxation, so as to increase the number of those liable, and remitted arrears; he declared cattle and tools to be exempt from seizure (1595), restricted sporting rights, and tried to restore to the village the possession of their commons, which had been usurped by the nobles. In 1610 Henry IV was much perturbed by the pillaging of soldiers. "If my people is ruined," he said, "who will support me?"

Richelieu's government, which paid so much attention to trade and the navy, took no interest in agriculture and the peasants; it did not prepare for distress, and when the weight of misery provoked serious riots, such as those of the Va-nu-pieds in Normandy (1639), they were cruelly suppressed. Nor did Colbert concern himself greatly with agriculture; absorbed in the mercantile theory he considered industry and commerce before all else. It was therefore not surprising that agriculture, neglected by the government, abandoned in some places to the scantily productive system of the great ecclesiastical or seignorial properties, subjected in others to the methods of peasant holding, routine-bound, and exhausted by the triple exactions of the nobles, the Church, and the King, should have made no progress subsequent to the beneficent efforts of Henry IV and Sully.

The system of triennial rotation of crops was still followed; the first year winter cereals (wheat, rye, and meslin); the second year spring crops (barley and oats); the third year fallow ground. Moreover this was only carried out on good ground. There was no culture of artificial grasses, which alone restores to the soil the chemical substances which the cereals have exhausted; consequently few cattle and little manure. Much land remained waste, especially after the great wars of Louis XIV. The forests were ill attended to and few seedlings were planted. Cattle were badly looked after and cattle-disease was terribly rife; meat was often of indifferent quality.

Nevertheless the crops of wheat, barley, and oats, and the produce of the vines generally supplied the wants of the population, which was about twenty million; in good years there was actually a surplus produced, and then exportation, which alone gives its full value to corn, was allowed; it was forbidden whenever the government foresaw an indifferent harvest, and corn was then imported from the Mediterranean countries (Sicily, Barbary, and Turkey) and from the north (Danzig). In order to increase the all-important cultivation of wheat, and to supply bread to the towns, especially Paris, which soon revolted if there was any shortage of food, Colbert waged war on the vine; his

successors imitated him and vines were rooted up. Some intendants, such as Bégon of La Rochelle, opposed this measure. In
1731 the King's Council forbade any new vineyards to be
planted and those which had been two years out of cultivation were not to be reclaimed without special permission under
penalty of a fine of three thousand livres. No doubt this order
was not everywhere enforced.

In spite of the wars, thanks to the high prices of produce at
critical times, rural landowners were able to live and sometimes
even to become rich. A real rural *bourgeoisie* of *laboureurs* and
farmers on a large scale came into being under Louis XIV and
made steady progress during the 18th century; it was these
"cocks of the parish," always ready to escape fiscal burdens
themselves and lay them on the poorer classes, against whom
Colbert and his intendants were constantly struggling, often
in vain. But beside these privileged members of the landed
classes there existed in misery a vast army of very small holders,
who, unable to live on the produce of their land, carried on
some industry or trade, and of day-labourers or poor *brassiers*,
who had no other resource than to hire themselves out to the
laboureurs and large farmers; a very dense army, especially in
Normandy, Brittany, Maine, and Poitou, where they included
four-fifths of the rural population.

In 1707 Vauban wrote in his *Dîme Royale*, "When I say that
France is the most beautiful kingdom in the world, I am stating
nothing new; it is a well-known fact; but were I to add that it
is the richest, no one would believe me, to judge from appearances." Agriculture was indeed suffering severely. "The country districts," says Vauban, "return a third less than they
returned thirty or forty years ago." "Most of the inhabitants,"
wrote the Intendant of Bordeaux in September 1708, "have
not wherewithal to sow their land." The Intendant of Champagne said in 1697: "During the five and a half years that I
have had the honour of serving in the province of Champagne,
I have seen poverty increasing every year." In 1694 the Bishop
of Montauban declared that every year four hundred people
died of starvation in his diocese. According to an official
inquiry made in Orléanais and Maine in 1687 the peasants
slept on straw, and had no furniture and no supplies; if many

ate buckwheat, many others lived on "the roots of heather boiled with barley-meal, or on oatmeal and salt." There was no exaggeration in La Bruyère's picture of peasant life. France really seemed to have become "a great desolate hospital, without food," as Fénelon said in his letter to the King.

The prevalence of rural distress gave rise to insurrections. They were frequent in the days of Colbert; they occurred in Bourbonnais and above all in Brittany in 1679, on account of new taxes (on stamped paper). At the end of Louis XIV's reign riots became a chronic evil in the kingdom, which seemed at the point of dissolution. "The fear of lacking bread has stirred up the people to frenzy," wrote the Controller-General Desmaretz, in 1709, during and after a terrible winter, "they have taken arms to seize corn by violence; there have been insurrections in Rouen, in Paris, and in almost all the provinces; they have waged a species of war, which only ceased while they were busy with the harvest."

Misery caused strange disturbances. When unrest showed itself in one district, this was enough to spread panic quickly throughout the whole of a large province. This was the case in 1703 almost on the same day, from the 28th to the 29th of September, in the Camisard districts of the Cevennes, in Castrais, Albigeois, and the plain of Toulouse. These alarms were a sure sign of the misery of the times, of the general insecurity and discouragement.

Industry and the operatives. The organisation of industrial or commercial labour—industry and commerce are closely linked—tended to develop the guild-system, and to transform free trading into the *jurande*, a trade-guild to which admission was obtained by oath. In 1581 and 1597 royal edicts enjoined this transformation, which was to be subject to the King. These edicts, which were essentially fiscal, were not indeed everywhere fully applied, even in the time of Colbert, who revived them in a more imperative manner. But many trades hitherto free were turned into guilds and their statutes were confirmed by the King, in return for financial contributions. Moreover many trades in becoming changed to sworn guilds did so, not because they were compelled, but because of the utility of an organisation which ensured to customers a good quality of goods and because of the increasingly great influence of the Parisian statutes.

However all trades were not included in the corporative system. First of all, in country districts the few trades carried on by a small number of artisans escaped the system by force of circumstances, although the towns soon wished to force them to comply. Then in towns many small trades remained free; only the more important were subject to the *jurande*, such as those concerning food-supply, apparel, construction, and "indispensable trades," which affected the purse and life; those of goldsmiths, locksmiths, surgeons, and apothecaries. Finally there were towns in which trades were generally free; among the most important of these was Lyons, in opposition to Paris, the city of the old statutes of Étienne Boileau; also the Burgundian towns, Dijon, Beaune, etc., which in imitation of Lyons succeeded in preserving their liberty for at least a great part of the 17th century.

In all these trades, whether free or bound by oath, home industry generally predominated; the small employer and master of the trade worked at home with a restricted number of workmen. The baker, the butcher, the locksmith, the goldsmith, or the weaver, was generally a master on quite a small scale, whose status differed in no way from that of his men; home industry brings people together.

In contrast to these family businesses there developed after the days of Henry IV large undertakings, often collective, either for manufacture, or, as will be seen, for commercial transport and the exploitation of distant countries; these companies and societies had wider horizons. Private companies under some personal name, limited companies, above all joint-stock companies, collected the capital of merchants, magistrates, and even nobles, and strove to divert towards business on an extensive scale some part of the wealth usually employed in the purchase of Hôtel de Ville stock or of crown offices. These companies avoided the red-tape of the unproductive guild-system and in this sense it may be said that they enjoyed liberty. Thus there was a tendency to replace the rigid machinery of the old traditional guilds by the more flexible, freer, and more ingenious machinery of companies, in which the merchant, ensconced in his counting-house, or the magistrate established in his official post could take part.

Henry IV created royal factories; in the first rank was the tapestry factory of the Savonnerie in Paris. Colbert multiplied factories; France was no longer to be dependent on foreigners. And as in spite of all the royal edicts of several centuries luxury could neither be banished nor restrained, superfluities must be manufactured at home; lace, glass, mirrors, fine tapestries, cloth of gold, and cloth of silver, etc. By all sorts of means Colbert tried to attract to France the clever craftsmen of Italy, especially of Venice, and of Holland; he addressed inquiries to ambassadors, made them scour foreign countries, and worried them with a tenacity, backed by arguments and hard cash, which ensured success. He summoned Mignard and Lebrun, the most eminent French artists, to superintend the manufacture of tapestries at Les Gobelins. Above all he encouraged the development of the textile industries—which were then much the most important—the trade in linen, silk, tapestry, and especially cloth. Cloth of ordinary and of fine quality was manufactured in great quantity from the wools of France, and specially of Spain, the Levant, and the northern countries. The factories of Languedoc worked specially for exportation to the Levant, whose market Colbert wished to seize from the English and Dutch; there were many in existence before his time, but he founded new ones. These were all in a brilliant but illusory position, as they had no other support than the State. Several of these royal factories were owned by the King; most of them belonged to individuals, or to private companies under the patronage of the King. Here for the first time there worked together operatives by the hundred. At the end of the 17th century the factory at Saptes near Carcassonne employed as many as six hundred men; about 1715 the factory of Van Robais at Abbeville had fifteen hundred men working in the same mill, ordinary workmen, foremen, inspectors, and directors—a perfectly ordered hierarchy.

But the most widespread method of work was neither that of the family workshop, nor that of the large modern factory, but that of home-work. At Le Puy-en-Velay, Darnetal, and the villages round Rouen, in Picardy, Flanders, and Brittany, etc.,

workmen and workwomen, and field-labourers who were idle
in the winter season, worked the raw materials which the large
manufacturers and the wholesale town-merchants supplied to
them each week. Usually in the small towns and villages the
workmen or peasant-workers fell into dependence on the manufacturer or the trading capitalist. Thus the manufacturers of
Rouen and Lyons, Lille, etc., rose to great positions, and in
cases where circumstances were favourable they generally
amassed fine fortunes, which were capable of being employed in
vast maritime adventures and large banking transactions.

Work at home, work in great factories and workshops which
foreshadowed the modern era, often even work in family workshops in various towns and in various industries, all these
avoided the rule of the trade-guilds. But in constructing a new
system which, freed from the red-tape of the former system,
might seem inevitably to be based on the ideal of complete
liberty, the absolute monarchy created royal privileges in favour
of the great manufacturers. It was by new privileges and by
royal protection which entailed police, regulations, and taxation,
that the State combated the former economic system. And it
is a curious fact that at the very moment when Colbert was
attempting to universalise the sworn guild, he ruined it by his
great privileged factories.

Colbert felt in fact that the time had come when France
should embark on great industries. There was abundance of
capital which had been accumulating for centuries; labour
was not lacking either in town or country; division of labour
which had started in certain industries, such as that of wool,
was becoming accentuated. The great creative minister watched
over his work. In order that only goods which were in demand
at home and abroad should be produced, Colbert regulated the
manufacture of cloth, linen, silk, etc., with extraordinary
minuteness—so many threads to the warp and woof, such a
length and breadth per piece—and he sent special inspectors as
well as the ordinary surveyors to supervise the execution of
his orders. He protected these budding industries from the
formidable competition of more advanced nations, England and
Holland; it will be seen that the tariffs of 1664 and 1667 defended French manufactures against similar foreign ones by

means of heavy taxes. This was a necessary step. The policy indeed gave rise to many diplomatic conflicts and wars, especially with Holland. But it succeeded in creating great industries in France.

These prospered in spite of the meticulous regulations and the resultant taxation. Cloth-weaving, linen-weaving, silk hosiery, stocking-weaving, the hat-trade, lace, paper-making, tapestries, mirrors, glass-works, metallurgy, etc., all were in full swing about 1680. The magnificence of the tapestries from the factories at Beauvais and Les Gobelins is well known, as also the achievements of the glass-works at Saint-Gobain, and the delicacy of the point-lace of Alençon and Chantilly.

But hardly were the French industries established than they suffered an eclipse between 1685 and 1715 as the result of the great and often unsuccessful wars of Louis XIV, which interfered with foreign trade and decreased home consumption, and of the revocation of the Edict of Nantes and the exile of about two hundred thousand Protestants from the west and south, who transferred their activities to England, Holland, Prussia, and all parts of Germany. Cloth-weaving declined in Champagne and Flanders; silk-weaving in Lyons, Tours, Nîmes, and all other parts; the linen-trade especially in Normandy; the hat-trade in Normandy; finally in all parts there was a decline in lace-making, paper-making, tapestry-weaving, and fisheries. Only industries necessary for war were maintained or even developed—metallurgy, the manufacture of weapons and munitions, the weaving of cloth for the troops. Finally new industries made their appearance, such as the cotton goods and printed calicoes of Rouen, Marseilles, and Lyons.

After the peace of Utrecht, industry, which in spite of unfavourable circumstances had struggled to maintain itself, resumed its activity. The coal and iron mines which were in working during the 17th century only supplied local consumption, and the ironworks of Hainault, Berri, Nivernais, Forez, and Dauphiné were obliged to have recourse to wood, or to send to Sweden and England for large quantities of ore and coal. Now the mines were being worked with greater method. About 1730 new mines were opened at Anzin near Valenciennes and at Carmaux in Albigeois. Ironworks increased in number. New mechanism was brought into play. Many foreign workmen and several manufacturers came to settle in France, as in the time of Colbert. Individual initiative was busy everywhere, in spite of the regulations, which were more severely enforced than ever before, and the heavy taxation on imports and exports, of tolls and internal customs. And increasingly active and conscious of its power it demanded thoroughgoing reform and above all liberty. A new era was in preparation.

Capital assumed an ever-increasing influence on manufactures and especially on the cloth-trade, silk-weaving, and printing, which require a considerable floating capital. In the silk-trade, the "master-workers," or *canuts*, of Lyons, small masters working with their companions, were falling more and more into dependence on the "master-merchant," who supplied the silks, gold thread, and designs to the master-workers. In Lyons two hundred master-merchants controlled the silk industry, for it was they who invented the beautiful stuffs, commissioned the new designs and the rich or delicate colours, in fact ruled the market. In the cloth-trade the master-weavers of the town and the workmen and workwomen of the country districts worked for the master-merchant-manufacturers of Lille, Rouen, etc. The same thing occurred in the printing-trade at Lyons and Troyes. The evolution towards capitalist concentration, which in the cloth-trade began at the height of the Middle Ages and in the silk and printing industries in the 16th century, progressed rapidly in the 18th century with the influx of capital and the growth of credit. Small isolated industries, such as the woollen factories of the Cevennes and the Pyrenees, and the silk-factories of Comtat, Tours, and Nîmes were endangered. The large factories found an abundant supply of labour in the country districts, and as well as men, they attracted women, who were paid half-rates, and even children. The great modern factory was already in being.

The abundant supply of labour kept wages at a very low level. In the 17th and 18th centuries the wages of artisans were inadequate, if we consider the cost of necessaries—in Rouen at the beginning of the 18th century a pound of wheat was worth a sou in an average year. Vauban calculated that the artisans in large towns, cloth-workers, hat-makers, etc., usually earned twelve sous, sometimes fifteen sous or over, and he concluded that the average was twelve sous. Thus food-prices having risen, especially after 1693, wages had really fallen. The operatives demanded higher wages to meet the greater cost of living. And the struggles between masters and men, which were present in the social life of the Middle Ages, became ever more frequent and more bitter. Combinations of workmen, coalitions of masters, strikes, violence, appeal to public authority, such was the uninterrupted course of the class warfare. From 1539 the printing-trade was disturbed by perpetual strikes; the journeyman printers in 1571 declared themselves "the real printers, as they did the hardest and greatest part of the work of printing," while the masters were only merchants "supplying the materials, plant, and instruments." Nor were strikes uncommon in the cloth and the silk trades. The insurrection of the Lyons silk-workers in 1744 was terrible. Striking was made a misdemeanour punishable by law; it was even suppressed by armed force. The Lyons strike of 1744 led to executions by hanging and to sentences of penal servitude in the galleys.

In order to wage war on capital which paid them only enough to escape starvation, the workmen combined in secret associations. These spread to all the towns and were affiliated to each other. They were called *compagnonnages*. The workmen (*compagnons*) travelled from town to town, certain of finding a welcome everywhere. Moreover the working population of several towns was very fluctuating during the 17th century and became even more so; at Dijon there were natives of every province; they called themselves by the names of their districts—Languedoc, Bordelais, Breton, Picard, Champagne, Lorrain—they agreed in opposing the masters, demanded increases of wages, went away if their demands were not satisfied, and continued their journey through France.

In their turn the masters formed secret associations to resist these claims. These also were illegal; but they escaped suppression by the public authority more easily than did the *compagnonnages*; moreover the royal or municipal authority was on the masters' side, as a strike was considered a misdemeanour. The object of these associations was to prevent the rise of wages, even when the cost of living had risen, and to bring about a fall in wages if possible. These alliances between masters explain the low rate of wages in the 17th and 18th centuries.

In fact if we examine the general history of French industry between 1600 and 1750 we see that the corporative system, which was supported by the State, was nevertheless ruined by the State: large industries sprang up owing to the efforts of Henry IV and above all of Colbert, and they increased in spite of wars and the abuses of the system of regulations. Industries were scattered all over the kingdom; their concentration in certain regions only came in the coal and iron age of the 19th century. But although there was geographical dispersion, there was in certain industries (cloth, printing, and silk) a capitalist concentration, and a predominance of the merchant over the master-worker. Finally industrial life was not yet independent of agricultural life; on the contrary they were always closely associated. The workmen were often agricultural peasants who, unable to live entirely on the produce of their land, worked at weaving in winter, while their wives and daughters span wool and flax, or made lace. There was close solidarity between town and country.

Commerce. Commerce advanced at the same rate as industry. After the time of Henry IV the commercial horizon enlarged in an extraordinary way, and progress, which had been delayed by the foreign wars and the wars of religion, became rapid.

And first, internal commerce increased along with peace and security. Plant was improved. Canals were made; the canal of Briare between the Seine and Loire, which was begun in 1605, was finished in 1640; the canal of the Two Seas between the Atlantic and the Mediterranean from Toulouse to Cette, undertaken under Colbert's direction by the engineer Riquet, was opened in 1681; the Orleans canal in 1692; the Picardy canal between the Oise and Somme from Chauny to Saint-Quentin in 1738. Several rivers were rendered navigable for ships, or at least for rafts; but in general the navigability of streams left much to be desired, and navigation was still artificially hindered by tolls; however Colbert began to reduce the number of tolls, and this work, which he brought to a successful conclusion on the Seine, was extended to the Loire in 1702. But Vauban's plan, which affected a hundred and ninety rivers, was far from being realised. Roads were improved by the State and by the provincial States of Languedoc and Burgundy, but they were nevertheless often in a very bad condition, especially during the wars; even the causeways of the suburbs of Paris were in bad repair.

Internal commerce benefited greatly by the reform of custom house dues. Before Colbert's day there were as many custom house zones as there were provinces. Although Colbert did not succeed in realising the commercial unity of the kingdom, which was specially opposed by the great provinces that had been united to the kingdom since the 15th century, he at least managed to establish a whole district in the centre of France to which goods could penetrate freely; this was known as the "Five Great Farms," because the customs dues for import and export were farmed out to five societies of " farmers." Outside this zone there lay a second zone: the provinces regarded as foreign, Brittany, Guyenne, Languedoc, Provence, Franche-Comté, Flanders, and Artois; goods were not admitted from the first to the second zone, or *vice versa*, except on payment of duties; moreover all the provinces forming this zone were separated from each other by customs. Finally certain provinces or districts of recent acquisition, Alsace, the Three Bishoprics, Sedan, and the district of Gex, to which must be added the four free ports, Marseilles, Bayonne, Lorient, and Dunkirk, carried on trade freely with foreign countries, while their trade with France was hampered by customs; these provinces were practically like foreign ones. There were thus still many hindrances to internal trade. This state of things interfered specially with the transport of corn, and the famines, so frequent in some districts while there was abundance elsewhere, were caused by these provincial dues and the habits of isolation and selfishness which they encouraged in the provinces as much as by the lack of good communications.

Internal commerce was carried on through the great valleys (Seine, Loire, Rhône, etc.) and easy thoroughfares (the passes of Poitou, Lauraguais, and Burgundy). Certain routes, such as that from Lyons to Roanne between the Rhône and the Loire, assumed great importance in the 17th century.

After the reign of Henry IV foreign trade became much more active; trade by land with the neighbouring countries (Spain, Italy, Switzerland, Low Countries) and above all sea-borne trade. At this time regular relations with America, India, and China became added to the traditional dealings with Spain, the Levant, Italy, the Netherlands, the Hanseatic towns, and England. Sea-borne trade became the most important. But France, having only light products to export, had only a few ships; she made use of Dutch and English vessels and was obliged to pay enormous freights. Henry IV, Richelieu, and Colbert tried to free France from this irksome and costly dependence. "There is no kingdom," said Richelieu, "so favourably situated as France and so rich in all the means of making herself mistress of the seas. To attain this object we must observe how our neighbours behave, we must form great companies, force merchants to join them and grant important privileges, as is done by foreign nations." It was thus by great companies supported by the State and granted monopolies in various parts of the world that the creators of national economy planned to give to France that place in the world to which she was entitled and whereto she was destined by all the history of the brave populations of her coasts. Richelieu realised what might be expected from the adventurous districts of the west, whence his family had sprung and where he had been bishop. He roused the energies of the Bretons, and of the people of Poitou and Saintonge, and pointed to the New World; he wished to make colonisation attractive to the nobles, and in 1629 he decreed that maritime commerce on a great scale was in no way derogatory; finally he lavished immense care on the navy, the natural protection of sea-borne trade. Colbert returned to the policy of Richelieu, which was neglected by Mazarin, and built a new mercantile marine and a navy.

It was impossible to compete with the Dutch and the English without protective tariffs. The Surintendant Fouquet had already placed a tax of fifty sous per ton on Dutch vessels entering a French port. Colbert retained this tax and moreover in 1664 he imposed taxes on foreign manufactures, cloth from Holland, England, and Spain, silk stockings, beaver hats, tapestries from Antwerp and Brussels. Then, as the French manufacturers still complained of foreign competition, he increased the 1664 tariff, doubled and even occasionally trebled the import taxes on cloths, and on silk, cotton, and above all woollen stockings; finally he forbade the importation of Venetian glass and lace, under the penalty of a fine. But this course was not without danger. The Grand Pensionary of the United Provinces, John de Witt, who in vain sought to obtain concessions, said: "There remains only the path of retaliation," and prohibited the importation of French wines and brandies. Threatened with such reprisals, France was obliged to yield; in 1674 the 1664 tariff was conceded to England; at the end of the war it was even granted to Holland, and the tax of fifty sous per ton was suppressed in 1699. During each war indeed—and in the 17th century war was a chronic condition—commercial relations ceased, and foreign nations sent to Portugal, Spain, and Italy for salt, wines, brandies, and fruit, instead of procuring them from Nantes and Bordeaux.

In order to create commercial companies, leaders of expeditions, ships, and capital were requisite. France was not lacking in great sailors and clever and determined explorers; Samuel Champlain, Cavelier de La Salle, Père Marquette, and later Dupleix, André Brue, François Martin. All these celebrated names showed that the spirit and desire for colonisation were then at their height among the French. Naturally ships were offered by the whole seaboard. Nor was capital lacking; but the King absorbed a part of the national savings by his continually increasing taxation, his incessant multiplication of offices, and his repeated loans. There did not seem to be enough money left for the support of great enterprises, or rather, capitalists were wanting in boldness, having been accustomed to invest money in stocks and official undertakings, which returned a safe six per cent. Furthermore, many merchants who had made fortunes, but were held in low estimation, disgusted with the heavy taxation and bureaucratic arbitrariness, gave up trade and bought an office; or, if they still carried it on, their children left it. Thus in order to find money it was necessary to conduct an efficient propaganda; the King placed his name at the head of the lists of shareholders in trading companies.

These commercial companies created in Canada by Henry IV

and Richelieu, and by Colbert in the West Indies, East Indies, North America, Northern Europe, the Levant, Africa, etc., were all failures. One after another Colbert saw his companies disappear; his successors, Pontchartrain and Desmaretz, had the same unfortunate experience. The same causes must be assigned to this persistent failure. First of all the individualism of the merchants; each man wished to carry on his business personally and mistrusted great enterprises which monopolised trade. Then the scarcity of money; not that there were no rich merchants, but these were exceptions. The sums invested in the companies were quite inadequate. These were not national undertakings—the privileged class and almost all the *bourgeois* directed their attention elsewhere—but only those of a few merchants and bankers. Finally, in the 18th century, the government gave no support to its companies, which were altogether lacking in breadth and steadiness of outlook when compared with the patient English and Dutch companies; it is notorious that the East Indian Company, which under the direction of Dupleix might have given France an empire, repudiated its director and received no help from the King, who left the way open to the English Company, which was powerfully supported by its government.

Notwithstanding all these failures, French commerce had become transformed and extended since the days of Henry IV. Henceforth it included Muscovy, Persia, Ethiopia, the Pacific Ocean, China, and India. The activity of the French in China and the Pacific Ocean was truly remarkable; in 1714 twenty ships sailed for the Pacific.

Marseilles, whose Chamber of Commerce, created in 1600, exerted great power, was becoming more and more enriched by trade with the Levant, of which it held the monopoly, Levantine produce being subject to a tax of 20 per cent. in other ports. As we have seen, it was also becoming a manufacturing town, which increased the export freights received from the Rhône valley. The ocean ports, Dunkirk, Rouen, Nantes, La Rochelle, and Bordeaux held the right of trading with the islands of Santo Domingo and the Antilles. Nantes, La Rochelle, and Bordeaux were being transformed into great markets of colonial produce (sugar, cocoa, coffee, tobacco, indigo, and cotton) for

France and part of Europe. Privileged companies conveyed negroes from the west coast of Africa to the islands. Bordeaux and Nantes made their fortune by this traffic in "ebony" and by the importation of colonial produce and the refining of sugar, especially after the peace of Utrecht. These ports and Rouen attracted foreigners: Flemings, Dutchmen, and later men from the Hanseatic towns. Lyons was pre-eminently the place of exchange. It was too the metropolis of the silk-trade and possessed the privilege that all silks imported to France were obliged to pass through Lyons, where they paid taxes, to the great discontent of Tours and Nîmes. Finally Paris, a city of luxury and pleasure, was also a banking centre, where there were great accumulations of capital; this was clearly seen by the fever of speculation which was roused by the "System"; great bankers controlled credit there; in the foremost rank of these were Crozat and the Protestant Samuel Bernard, who at the close of Louis XIV's reign were bankers to the embarrassed royal treasury.

Thus everywhere, even in times of war and under the system of regulations, individual initiative asserted itself. It is evident that the encouragement given by Richelieu and Colbert had not been fruitless. But subsequently there had been an excess of taxation and regulations. Colbert's system was therefore keenly criticised; the deputies of the Council of Commerce, which was re-established after Colbert in 1700, protested against the abuses of the monopolist companies, and against the exorbitant duties on foreign manufactures, which caused reprisals injurious to the districts of the west, south, Champagne, and Burgundy, who had their wines and brandies left on their hands. They declared that the interests of agriculture and trade were sacrificed to those of industry. "We must," said the deputy of Languedoc, "abandon M. Colbert's maxim which asserted that France could get on without the rest of the world, and who even wished to force foreign countries to have recourse to us. This was contrary to nature...." The government was already contemplating a more liberal policy, and Desmaretz was inclined to conclude commercial treaties. Several were signed at the beginning of the 18th century with the Netherlands, the Austrian Netherlands (Belgium), and with Prussia, and there was a serious but fruitless attempt to come to commercial agreement with England. There was a reaction after 1715. Protection and regulations revived. Criticism became more acute.

§ III. ATTEMPTS AT REFORM (1750–1789)

Economists now began to make their appearance. Boisguilbert in his *Détail de la France* and Vauban in his *Projet d'une dîme royale* had expressed criticism of the economic and fiscal system. Now it was no longer isolated economists, but two schools which came into being between 1750 and 1760. It was the turning-point of the age; between 1746 and 1763 there appeared the principal works of Quesnay, the Marquis de Mirabeau, Montesquieu, Rousseau, and Condillac, also the *Encyclopédie*.

The principle common to the writings of this period is that of liberty—liberty of thought, political liberty, economic liberty. The economists insist only on economic liberty. No State intervention. Above the State Nature must rule. Above the positive laws and variable regulations of sovereigns there are natural laws, physical or moral, "established by the Supreme Being, immutable and irrefragable, which are the best possible laws.... All these laws exist eternally and implicitly in a natural Code." They form "the essential order of Society" and are a "legal despotism." The State must respect this order. The "natural rights of man," which are older than human conventions, cannot be violated without crime; these rights are liberty and property. When the State protects these natural rights, then production, consumption, and population will increase; the strength of the nation will grow in a manner hitherto unknown.

Among these economists the physiocrats, who recognised the dominating power of the natural laws, specially encouraged agriculture; they were led by Quesnay. The others, sometimes called plutocrats, attached greater importance to industry and commerce; at their head was Vincent de Gournay, Intendant of Commerce. Quesnay asserted that "the value of industrial work resulted from a change of form and not from the addition of a substance," that only agriculture gives net proceeds (*produit net*); this is what remains after the agriculturist has reimbursed his advances in seed, manure, upkeep of buildings and of implements, and has taken his fair profit. The agriculturist lives on this profit, but landowners who do not cultivate their own land, gentlemen, clergy, nobility, "officials," merchants, manufacturers, even the State, are "sterile"—they only live on the net proceeds, on that which exceeds the unimpeachable share of the cultivator. Efforts must therefore be made to increase these net proceeds, which are the only real wealth. They must be given their full value, by allowing internal circulation and the export of corn; the higher the price of corn, the more anxious will be the cultivator to sow more. Quesnay's views thus led to free trade.

Gournay and his followers asserted that industry and commerce were no more sterile than agriculture; in these the methods of working add a real wealth to the mass of riches. Liberty alone enables them to live. Abolish trade-guilds, prohibitions, and all hindrances to labour, said Gournay and his disciples. "Give them free play."

The doctrines of Quesnay and Gournay, which were very different, became reconciled and gradually welded into the same result in the minds of writers and statesmen; Turgot reconciled them by the liberty which he gave to agriculture, industry, and commerce. Meanwhile between 1750 and 1760 the new ideas, protected by Mme de Pompadour, found favour in the sight of many administrators; on Gournay's side, who was one of the four intendants of Commerce, there was first Trudaine, President of the Council of Commerce, and later his son Trudaine de Montigny. It was the two Trudaines and Gournay who, in the midst of conflicts initiated by themselves, attacked the system of regulations, opposed monopolies, and ended in 1764 by ensuring free trade in corn abroad as well as at home within the kingdom.

Agriculture. Agriculture was now honoured. "Agricultural Societies," which were founded in all the provinces, the provincial Academies, intendants, and provincial states, in accordance with the orders of the economists and the government, recommended new crops; especially artificial grasses (clover, lucern, etc.), and oil-seed, as well as potatoes and turnips, to prevent land lying fallow, to improve the soil, and in consequence the wheat crops. They also paid attention to increasing the number of cattle. Great landowners, such as La Rochefoucauld-Liancourt on his fine estate of Liancourt, which was visited by Arthur Young, and La Chalotais near Rennes, themselves set an example. But the directions of the government and the intendants and even these good examples did not succeed in drawing the peasants from their routine. It was only in Flanders, which was already in advance of the rest of the kingdom, that artificial grass-land developed greatly. Elsewhere progress was generally small. However the breeds of animals were improved by cross-breeding with Spanish (merino sheep) and English strains (Durham cows).

Forests were cleared and marshes drained. The government encouraged these undertakings by exemption from taxation (1764–1768). In Brittany and Lorraine there was remarkable activity in thus bringing new land into cultivation. The dunes and *landes* of Gascony were planted with pines, principally under the direction of the engineer Brémontier.

Many commons were divided, especially after 1770, in Picardy, Normandy, Marche, Auvergne, and the country near the Pyrenees. But the rich sought to take the greater part, whence arose frequent and bitter social struggles. Should the division be by head, or by household, or else according to the amount of taxes paid, or the property already held by each? The first two systems favoured the poor and were preferred by the government and the intendants. "When some kind of property is given to those who have none, they become attached to their possessions and settle down as heads of families and citizens." In accordance with this governmental theory the edict of 1773 about the commons of Artois prescribed an equal share to each head of a family, one-third being reserved according to custom for the lord of the manor. But elsewhere other systems prevailed, more in conformity with the wishes and habits of the inhabitants of the commune; the land was then divided between the landowners and taxpayers, in proportion to their holdings and contributions, as for instance in certain villages of Auvergne, contrary to the views of the government and the intendant.

These divisions, clearings, and drainings, and the working of laws of succession, especially in the districts where perfect equality was customary (Touraine, and Anjou), where property was divided equally between all children of the non-noble class, led to a greater division of the land. It also appears that as a result of the increasing price of corn and other produce, which enabled them to amass wealth, the peasant holders, *laboureurs*, and large farmers were buying land from the nobles and the *bourgeois*, especially in the Central Plateau. In Limousin, Auvergne, Berri, Touraine, as well as in Laonnois, Artois, and Normandy, this process was pretty sharply accentuated.

This division of land was not however intense enough or rapid enough to keep pace with the growth of the population, which increased from nineteen millions at the beginning of the 18th century to twenty-four or twenty-five millions in 1789. It did not provide land for the class of day-labourers, or *brassiers*, who became even more numerous than in the 17th century.

If we add the high rents, which more and more debarred the poor from working the land, and the suppression by means of enclosures of common-land and of the right to glean after harvest, especially in the east; the frequent abolition by the nobles of the right of access to the commons which they had usurped, or a third of which they had seized either in accordance with the right of *triage* or contrary to this right; the fact that it was difficult, or rather impossible, for the small holder to send his cow or his goats to graze on the usual pastures or in the seignorial forest; the formation of large farms by the disrepair of buildings on small farms, and the control of these great properties by a restricted number of people in the north, Ile-de-France, Normandy, and Maine; the increase in royal taxation; the burden of tithes on wheat, wine, vegetables, and increase in the number of animals; the demands of the landlords, or their agents, who after a century of neglect were claiming the full payment of seignorial dues, and even the arrears of twenty-nine years, and were proceeding to compile *terriers*, in which were recorded all the indebtedness of the tenants, all the cost of which, trebled in 1786, was charged to the cultivator; the threefold fiscal exactions of the king, the clergy, and the landlord, which robbed the cultivator of 34 to 40 per cent. of the revenue from his land, to which must be added the amount of the rent; finally the high cost of provisions and of all commodities; all these factors combined to make the condition of the small holder, small farmer, *métayer*, and agricultural labourer increasingly wretched. To crown their misfortunes there were very poor harvests, as the result of floods in 1787, drought in 1788, and a hailstorm on July 13, 1788, which laid waste the western part of France. In Nantes the price of a pound of wheaten bread of the first quality rose to five sous; in 1761 it had been one sou, five deniers. In Paris the rise in the price of bread was continuous; at the end of 1788 a four-pound loaf cost eleven or twelve sous; in January 1789 it cost fourteen sous, and in February it even touched fifteen sous. These were real famine prices if we remember the relative value of money in 1789. The poor peasants suffered greatly, as also did the poor people in towns, all the more because there was an industrial crisis which kept many workmen idle.

The government had hardly done anything for the peasants. That Turgot had wished to modify the seignorial system is proved by the pamphlet which he commissioned Boncerf to write on the drawbacks of the feudal dues in 1776. All that was done was that in many districts a money tax was substituted for forced labour. The landlords and their agents opposed these humanitarian tendencies and increased the unpopularity of feudalism. Consequently riots broke out in all parts; in Provence, Brittany, Burgundy, Guyenne, in the *généralités* of Paris and Orleans, etc. At Bourg-de-la-Seyne, near Toulon, the peasants were assembled by the ringing of the bell and destroyed the office where the town-dues were collected. In the ports and great markets of Brittany everything was in disorder. "The germ of sedition is in the hearts of the people," wrote the Intendant de Molleville in 1788 to Necker, "not against the government, but against the nobles and great landowners, who are accused of hoarding great quantities of corn." At Plancoët people spoke of "crushing the *bourgeois* and gentry." Rural revolution was at hand.

Industry. Industry became transformed, especially after 1770, less by the liberal doctrines of Gournay and Trudaine, than by mechanical inventions. Machinery made its appearance; the reign of steam began. The example was set by England in 1760; but in addition to the influence of the English industrial revolution, which was considerable, French science and the inventive genius of the workmen also contributed to the prosperity of manufacturers.

Manufacturers from Great Britain brought new inventions. In 1752 Holker, an Irish engineer, installed improved cotton-looms at Rouen. Alcock, an English engineer, established hardware factories at Roanne and Charité-sur-Loire. Wilkinson, the Welsh "ironmaster," built a factory on an island of the Loire below Nantes, where he cast heavy cannon, which were afterwards bored by a machine worked by steam. All these men were followed by English workmen.

In France, Vaucanson of Grenoble, who became celebrated in 1738 by the invention of automatic figures, a flutist playing tunes, etc., invented various machines, a weaving-loom and a silk-throwing mill. In 1779 Cugnot constructed a carriage moved by steam, and in 1776 the Marquis de Jouffroy navigated the first steamboat on the Doubs. The Parisian clockmakers, Berthoud, Lepaute, and others made fine clocks and timepieces, such as the famous clock in the Council-Chamber at Versailles. And in tapestry, furniture, and fashions, many "creations" were produced by the taste, the grace, and sometimes the genius of our artists. However, the lead taken by England in the great industries was very striking.

The French manufacturers attracted clever foreign workmen; besides the English, there were the Genoese, who manufactured damask, Italians, Turks, Greeks, Dutchmen, etc. But the French manufacturers lost more than they gained. The foreign governments, realising the superiority of the French artisans in all industries which demanded talent and taste, succeeded about 1780 in decoying away many of the workmen from Les Gobelins, Sèvres, and Lyons. It was above all countries without industries, such as Spain and Russia, which tried to attract the French workmen; but it was manufacturing countries, Germany and Switzerland, who had already reaped great advantage from the influx of the Protestant manufacturers and workmen driven out by persecution. There were agents paid to entice men; amongst them were the brothers Rulhière, who were in the pay of the King of Spain; they were tried in France and sentenced in default to the galleys for life and to be pilloried for three market-days with a scroll bearing these words: "Guilty of transferring industries to foreign lands and of seducing workmen."

About 1760 industry, supplied with better plant, made fresh strides. The government now established few factories under royal protection; privileges and regulations lapsed automatically; it was no longer necessary to maintain them at all costs in a country where industries were developing themselves and where customers had learned the quality of goods by experience. The corporative system, already moribund, was vigorously attacked. The first skirmish was in 1762, when by a decree in Council country artisans were authorised to manufacture any kind of material. Great resistance was offered by the town guilds of Lille and Amiens. During the time between 1763 and 1764 freedom of trade gave prosperity to the manufacture of cloth and flannel at Roubaix and Tourcoing, two large villages close to Lille. But the inhabitants of Lille, supported by the intendant and by influential people in Paris, succeeded in averting the menace, and the factory at Roubaix succumbed without however improving the position of Lille. Then in February 1776, the fatal blow fell; by an edict passed under Turgot's direction, art-guilds and trade-guilds were abolished in Paris and theoretically in the provinces. At last liberty of labour was assured to the country districts. But Turgot fell; the guilds were re-established, rearranged, and diminished in number, which foreshadowed their approaching end. The edict on the liberty of labour in country districts was no longer attacked even in Flanders (1777); Roubaix resumed the manufacture of flannels; in 1786 70,000 pieces of material were produced by this agglomeration of 5000 inhabitants.

In 1786 French industries, revived by the liberty which was being gradually introduced into all commercial organisations, by the influx of capital, the inventions of technically clever artisans, the interest shown by all classes of the nation, even by the nobles, of whom many, such as the Marquis de Solages, proprietor of Carmaux, had embarked on great enterprises, seemed to be in a brilliant position hitherto unknown. They were widely scattered throughout the kingdom, but already showed a tendency towards the formation of manufacturing districts; Lyonnais, Forez, and Nivernais; Normandy, the north, Lorraine, Alsace, to which must be added Languedoc, in which the textile industry had been artificially supported since the time of Colbert. Lyons, Rouen, Amiens, and Marseilles were the great labour centres. In these places there existed old traditions of work, supplies of capital and labour, and easy communications with the outside world. Other centres came into existence in the 19th century, or were developed in such a manner as to appear new creations, such as Roubaix; but these old homes of French manufacture will always remain among the most important.

After 1750 various industries developed greatly; cotton-spinning and weaving, calico, which was imitated from India, prints, and muslins, which became increasingly fashionable in town and at the court of Marie-Antoinette; manufacture of cut-glass, especially in Lorraine, which is rich in very fine gritty sand, at Baccarat (1764); metallurgical works in Hainault, Lorraine, and Alsace, where there was much iron, much wood, and already more coal to be had. Some industries which had flagged between 1730 and 1740, such as silk, now revived, thanks to royal protection and to Marie-Antoinette, and Lyons now displayed her full splendour. The paper-trade, which had also declined at the beginning of the 17th century, made progress both in Angoumois and Auvergne, on whose clear rivers there had long been paper-mills, and also in Dauphiné and Vivarais (Annonay), which possess an abundant and suitable water-supply. Finally ship-building prospered when France reconstructed and maintained a fine fleet which, under the command of Grasse and Suffren, proudly carried the flag with the *fleur de lys* from America to India; the fisheries and sugar-refining in the Atlantic ports and the towns on the Loire shared in the progress of sea-borne trade.

The evolution towards capitalism which had begun in the large industries continued and was helped by free labour; workshops were larger; industrial concentration became accentuated but was not yet universal; work at home for long still predominated in country districts.

The condition of the workman was still somewhat precarious.

It was perhaps even worse because of the higher price of necessaries especially after 1770, as wages had not increased at all. Even in the best privileged factories a workman hardly earned enough to live, and he worked for thirteen or fourteen hours a day. Some masters, such as the brothers Montgolfier of the paper-mills of Annonay, treated their men fairly; but almost all, as was remarked by the inspector Roland de la Platière, took cruel advantage of the condition of the artisan. Therefore we no longer find authority invariably arrayed on the master's side in the struggles between masters and men, as we did in the 17th century. It negotiated, if not with the suborners at least with the workmen who were deserting. Trudaine refused to inflict corporal punishment on workmen who left their factory, as he said this contract was a civil act, which could be submitted to the courts of justice. "It is a principle," he added, "that in France workmen are not slaves and are only subject to their own conventions."

After 1787 the condition of the workman deteriorated along with industrial conditions. At the moment when industry arrived at its height the liberalism of the government brought about a grave crisis. In 1786 to consolidate the Peace of Versailles, the minister Vergennes signed a commercial treaty with Sir William Eden representing Great Britain; this indeed favoured the importation into England of French wines, brandies, and vinegars, but was injurious to French manufactures, which were not yet in a position to compete with the English industries, better supplied with plant, coal, and iron, and working at cheaper rates. Cottons, woollens, and hosiery were on both sides subject to an import tax of 12 per cent.; English hardware, steel, iron, and copper goods were admitted to France on payment of a 10 per cent. duty on their value. This was the death sentence of the metallurgical industry, which had been so carefully fostered in France. And as English cottons and woollens were admitted to France at the price of their declared value, which was much less than their real value, the 12 per cent. duty fell to 8 per cent. or even less; so that this was also the death-sentence of all the textile industry. After 1787 many factories and works in the north and east were no longer able to dispose of their goods and closed down;

others carried on a precarious existence. In the north, the tradition for long survived that men should be employed to unfold, brush, and refold the pieces of material so as to prevent moth getting in. Many workmen emigrated; a large number went to Paris and swelled the army of malcontents. Both the industrial crisis and the agricultural crisis helped the revolution.

Commerce. Commerce revived under the influence of liberty which encouraged the spirit of initiative, and was also helped by a better planned system of transport.

Appliances were improved. Means of control and unification were created; such as government engineers and the School of Civil Engineering between 1750 and 1754. This was the work of Trudaine, "who was entrusted with the control of roads and bridges" after 1743, and of Perronet, director of the Engineering School from 1747. They made new roads, but money was lacking; only a few millions a year were devoted to roads. At that time the forced labour of the peasants—detested, it is true, and commuted about 1770–1780 by many intendants to a money tax—supplied France with the finest roads in Europe. There were few canals and these were private property granted by the King. It was only in 1775 that the government contemplated taking over canals as a public service. Then great plans made their appearance. Little came of these grandiose schemes; the Franche-Comté canal to connect the Rhône and Rhine was begun in 1783; the canal of Burgundy to link the Seine and Saône by the Ouche and the Armançon was undertaken in 1777, etc. The navigability of rivers made no progress; on the contrary, owing to the negligence of riparian owners, and the lack of buoys, ships could no longer come so high up the Seine, Aube, Clain, Loire, etc. On the map the system of rivers and canals made a great show; but owing to bad upkeep and to its being in the hands of guilds of careless and lazy boatmen, it was not as useful as it should have been. Water-transport, so advantageous nowadays, was then only the exception. The new roads, in spite of their frequently indifferent condition, afforded a singular activity to cartage and transport, which was finally farmed out by the State. Turgot developed this service by ordering everywhere the establishment of diligences, which went twice as fast as the coaches and cost less. Their average rate was four kilometres an hour, for the roads were often bad, especially in winter. Further the cost of transporting passengers and goods fell a little.

Foreign trade increased and attained unknown prosperity. Liberty brought about this miracle. By 1769 there were no more privileged companies; the East Indian Company, which had had such a brilliant future after Law and his re-organisation, was suppressed. Trade with India became free. A new Indian Company was indeed created in 1785 and companies for dealing in African negroes were established in 1777 and 1784; but with these exceptions commercial liberty reigned.

The West Indian trade expanded. This was now much the most important; it surpassed by far the Levantine trade, which was languishing, as the cloth of Languedoc was less and less in demand in the Mediterranean. Sugar, coffee, indigo, tobacco, and cotton accumulated in the docks of Bordeaux, Nantes, Lorient, Le Havre, Rouen, and Marseilles; in 1789 the annual value of these imports was 185 million francs, and in exchange the West Indies bought brandy and manufactured goods to the amount of 77 millions. The opulence of the great shipowners and merchants of Bordeaux and the Atlantic ports dates chiefly from this period, and these towns now assumed the appearance which they have to-day. Bordeaux commissioned Gabriel to lay out her fine Place Royale and to build her Custom House and Stock Exchange; Ollivier was chosen to decorate the ceilings of several of the rooms in the Exchange (this master-colorist after his return from Spain worked there for two years); and the architect Louit to design the Theatre, the finest in Europe after that of the Court. The Quai des Chartrons along the picturesque crescent of the river, and the Cours du Chapeau Rouge then received their final shape and beauty. The town was increasingly frequented by Dutchmen, and men of Lubeck and Hamburg settled there in greater numbers after 1740. The *bourgeoisie* of Bordeaux lived luxuriously and without counting the cost; Arthur Young was astonished at the good living. But many of these great *bourgeois* also appreciated intellectual pleasures. Journu in his house on the Cours du Chapeau Rouge collected pictures, amassed a fine library, in which the works of Montesquieu, Voltaire and Rousseau predominated, and possessed a splendid collection of maps, marine instruments, and animals of every country. This was not a solitary instance. Intellectual culture there accompanied wealth.

The brilliant condition of French trade continued. After the treaty of 1786 English goods were imported into France in large quantities; French wines, brandies, and vinegars sold better than before; only the merchants and many proprietors of vine-yards congratulated themselves on a treaty which helped commerce, but ruined French industries. The principle of liberty applied too soon and in too abstract a manner did not produce entirely good results.

Nevertheless, although French society was permeated by the new ideas, there still existed privileged classes, persons, and "orders," provinces, districts, or towns, and commercial companies. There remained "districts almost like foreign ones" and free ports; the economic privileges of Lyons and Marseilles; the Indian company; and finally the trade-guilds. And none of these privileged individuals were any more willing to relinquish their monopolies than were the nobles and bishops, whom they so bitterly attacked, to renounce their fiscal privileges or their offices and pensions.

§ IV. THE REVOLUTION AND THE ACHIEVEMENT OF NATIONAL ECONOMY

In 1789 the French demanded above all things the abolition of the fiscal privileges, either pecuniary or honorary, granted to the clergy and nobles. They also claimed, at least for the most part, freedom of trade and of industry, and the suppression of all the privileges to which provinces, towns, and corporations remained firmly attached. No doubt among these twenty-four million French people there were some divergent interests and opinions; the peasant was struggling specially for the affranchise-ment and possession of his land; the workman for his wages and the maintenance of his unions, which were his only weapon of defence; the *bourgeois*, and especially the cultured *bourgeois*, for the control of power; but as a whole, *bourgeois*, peasants, and operatives were all united against the privileged orders by common interests and sentiments.

Reforms. Liberty, equality of rights, and property were proclaimed "natural rights," in conformity with the doctrine of Quesnay and Turgot, by the "Declaration of the Rights of Man" (August 26, 1789). These principles ruled the economic and social work of the Revolution.

Freedom and enfranchisement of land became the motive power of the rural classes. If the *bourgeois* brought about the political revolution to their own advantage, it was actually the peasants who began the economic revolution. In July 1789, after the taking of the Bastille, they rose all over France, destroyed a number of court-rolls, and pillaged the châteaux. The *bourgeoisie* became alarmed. On August 4 the National Assembly was forced to recognise the accomplished fact; it proclaimed the abolition of the seignorial system. In reality it only suppressed without compensation those rights which were degrading to human beings (servitude, forced labour, etc.), monopolies of markets, and fairs, and of courts of law, and ecclesiastical tithes; most of the really important seignorial rights were declared redeemable, especially all those which directly referred to land; quit-rents, champerty, and ground rents. Although some peasants bought these rights, more did not, especially as the State was just then offering a quantity of land for sale. They were indeed allowed by law to prove that they were not bound to pay these dues in return for a grant of land; but they had no means of furnishing this proof. Therefore in 1790 and 1791 there were fresh rural disturbances, especially in the centre of France. After August 10, 1792, another step in the abolition of the seignorial system was taken; real rights were still redeemable, but the landlords had to prove that these payments were due in return for a concession of land by presenting the original title-deeds of the contract. Now in many cases these deeds had been lost or destroyed in the peasant risings, and it was impossible for the landlord to produce this proof without searching in the archives of the Chamber of Accounts to find a copy of the original contract. Under the revolutionary and democratic government of July 17, 1793, the last stage was reached; all seignorial rights were abolished without compensation; original title-deeds were actually to be burned. Thus there were no more tithes or seignorial dues. The tenant, without loosening his purse-strings, became full proprietor of the land which he cultivated; all old contracts were broken; it was an immense revolution, which was not imitated in the 19th century by the various European states, monarchical and feudal, who contented themselves with the redemption of dues in accordance with the methods of the Constituent Assembly.

The division of land progressed rapidly. The revolutionaries wished to wipe out the enormous national debt and to multiply the number of small holders. They therefore declared ecclesiastical property to be national property (November 2, 1789, and various decrees in 1790) and also confiscated the properties of *emigrés* (1792), and offered them for sale. Church property was estimated at about three milliards of francs (£120,000,000); and the property of *emigrés* at two and a half milliards (£100,000,000). Church property was alienated after the closing months of 1790, and the best lots were sold during the following year; the land of the *emigrés* was put up to auction after August 10, 1792. All through the Revolution these sales continued; this is one of the most essential facts of its history. There were various modes of alienation to suit circumstances, the needs of the Treasury and the depreciation of paper-money. But as a whole conditions always favoured purchasers. The decree of May 14, 1790, which offered Church property for sale, only demanded 12 per cent. of the price down and granted the purchaser a delay of twelve months. By repeated extensions this decree remained in force until January 1, 1794. Farms were fairly often sold as a whole. Many peasants therefore in Laonnois and elsewhere clubbed together to obtain possession of a large holding, which they subsequently shared. The numerous sales of whole farms explain how *bourgeois* from the towns, who were wealthy or comfortably off, and penniless speculators were originally enabled to buy more properties and houses than the peasants, who specially wanted small lots. The property of the *emigrés* was to be divided into small lots of two, three, or at most four *arpents*, i.e. one or two hectares[1] (August 14, 1792); although this order was very often dis-

[1] An *arpent* varies according to the district from a third to a half of an hectare.

regarded, the parcelling out of these properties, which were chiefly in the country, enabled the peasants to make up for the fact that they had often been outbidden in the sale of Church lands. However many large properties belonging to *emigrés* were not sold, especially in Brittany, or, as in the north, they passed into the hands of men of straw, who returned them later to their original owners.

It is now impossible to fix the amount of national property which fell respectively into the hands of *bourgeois* or peasants. No doubt in many cases poor country folk were able to buy small plots and build themselves a house and make a little garden; the number of landowners increased. But it was above all rich and moderately wealthy people in town or country who bought the national property. In fact most of them were *bourgeois*, for there had been for about a century a real country *bourgeoisie*, composed of large *laboureurs* and large farmers. They and the lawyers, doctors, notaries, and town officials were the people who profited by these great dealings at the expense of the Church and the nobles. And they acquired land and houses at small cost. They made their payments to the State in paper currency which was always depreciating; their successive instalments decreased in real value, so that they ended in acquitting their debt with a sum three or four times less than the original purchase price. By the end of the Revolution some of them obtained an estate at the price of a cow.

The State was seriously affected. The National Debt was not wiped out. The increase in the number of small holdings was only partly realised. The poor found themselves the victims of legislation which had not given these their fair share; they received very little but the common-land, the division of which was declared compulsory in 1792, but was made optional according to the wishes of the communes in 1793. However in 1793 and 1794 they were protected by Robespierre, the Committee of Public Safety, and the Convention, against the greed of the large farmers and wealthy rural owners by means of the *maximum* law, which taxed wheat and the chief necessaries of life. But after the fall of Robespierre, the cupidity of the landowners and great merchants succeeded in obtaining the suppression of the *maximum* (December 1794) and the liberty thus restored to the corn trade coincided with a deficient harvest and caused an exorbitant rise of prices inflicting terrible suffering on the poor in town and country, which ended in riots in Germinal and Prairial III, under the cry of "bread and the Constitution of '93"; these revolts were soon quenched with the blood of the last Montagnards.

Thus even in '93 the Revolution did not give land to every one. It always considered the individual right of property as a natural right, "inviolable and sacred." Having suppressed corporate property (of the Church, Crown, etc.), it strengthened the rights of property, which were not attacked except in the case of those who had emigrated, and in default. There was never any suggestion of the division of property, or of the agrarian law; the death penalty was even decreed for those who suggested such a step (March 18, 1793); Robespierre himself said that "absolute equality was a dream."

Liberty of labour, that principle so dear to economists and philosophers, was not proclaimed in 1789. The Constituent Assembly was then absorbed in reform of the land laws, policy, and administration. But, as soon as all privileges were abolished, the manufacturing and trading *bourgeoisie* was at last obliged to renounce its privileges, which in a regenerate world were no longer justified. Thus on March 2, 1791, trade-guilds and "all professional privileges of any kind" were suppressed without debate. "From the following first of April according to law any person was to be free to carry on any business or exercise any profession, art, or trade, which he thought good." Thus was established the system of free competition, which encourages individual initiative to the highest degree. This initiative had certain rights which by law must be respected: the right of invention. "It would be attacking the rights of man in their essence if an industrial discovery were not regarded as the property of its discoverer" (decree of December 31, 1790). Consequently patents for inventions were instituted on May 14, 1790.

Freedom of trade was established. First internally. Provincial customs, which the centralised monarchical government had allowed to remain, were abolished (November 2, 1790); custom houses were relegated to the frontiers, and thus Lorraine and Alsace were included in the kingdom. Colbert's dream of fiscal unity for France was realised at a blow. Henceforth according to law corn could and should freely circulate throughout the whole realm. But custom is stronger than law; and fear of famine and selfishness caused corn to be hoarded in many well-supplied districts at the expense of more necessitous provinces. All the taxes which were so many fetters on trade and industry —trade-marks on iron and leather goods, tolls, town-dues, duties on wines—were suppressed in 1791. Free trade with foreign countries could not be established without great injury to French manufactures, as the treaty with England had shown. A protective tariff was fixed (March 15, 1791); import taxes on foreign goods remained at the rate of 10 or 12 per cent. as in Eden's treaty, but as many as thirty-four articles were prohibited and there were export taxes on eighty articles, especially on wines. The export of corn, so often allowed since 1764, but suspended in 1789, was forbidden, in spite of the theories of economists, for fear of famine. There were no more free ports; no more facilities for warehousing; on many points the principles were more rigid than those of Colbert, in excessive reaction from the disastrous consequences of the too liberal and advanced policy of 1786.

The general state of war, especially after 1793, strengthened yet more this national exclusiveness. A large quantity of French produce (bread, meat, wool, cotton, iron, copper, etc.) was kept for France, then at war with almost the whole of Europe. The importation of goods from countries at war with France was prohibited. The Navigation Act of September 21, 1793, reserved the coasting-trade from one French port to another for French ships. French ships were allowed to import to France, or French colonies, foreign commodities and produce, in competition with the ships of the countries from which these commodities were derived, "if the officers and three-quarters of the crew of foreign ships were of the country under whose flag they sailed." By a French ship was understood a ship built in France or a French colony, owned entirely by Frenchmen, and whose officers and three-quarters of whose crew were French. Thus foreigners could only import the produce of their own country to France. This decree was specially aimed at England. The Americans, who were friendly to France and provided wheat, received preferential treatment; they were allowed to trade freely with the French colonies on the same footing as the French.

By all these great reforms, which had long been in preparation, the work wrought by monarchical France throughout centuries was brought to completion. A definite shape was given to the national economic system. Henceforward it was animated by the spirit of liberty and helped by territorial unity and still more by uniformity of weights and measures, which was decreed by the Convention, but which was only very gradually put into practice in the 19th century. Free labour and free trade opened a new era in the history of French activity.

The Result. The full effects of such a revolution were not felt at once. Everything was upset by the war which lasted almost without a break for twenty-three years, from 1792 to 1815. And yet even in 1800 at the time when the *bourgeoisie* and the peasants were clamouring for a strong government which should end war and the general insecurity, and ensure them the enjoyment of their new rights and new property, there could already be seen many social and economic benefits resulting from the Revolution.

There were many more landowners in Doubs, Meurthe, Moselle, Nord, in fact everywhere. Furthermore estates were much smaller. Many large estates had disappeared. In Indre in 1800 there were no estates large enough to require four ploughs, very few requiring three. In Cambrésis, a wide plain of oozy limestone, where there had been great abbeys, instead of properties of over two hundred hectares there were estates of between twenty and a hundred hectares, and most of them were between twenty and twenty-five. Many small properties sprang from the division of common-land; in Meurthe there remained only 4238 *arpents* of the 18,108 which existed in 1789; there was a similar state of affairs in the departments of Doubs and Moselle. The division of land was becoming accentuated and was causing injury. "Rural properties," said the Prefect of Haute-Vienne, "are too much divided. Each plot of land in the first class does not contain, taking one with the other, more than 42 ares[1]. A strip of land of three hectares generally contains eighteen or twenty small distinct plots."

[1] 100 ares = 1 hectare.

The land was attracting capital; the industrial crisis and paper currency encouraged this tendency, which continued under the Consulate. The Prefect of Haute-Vienne complained of this passion for acquiring land, which "should be combated"; and he said it would be well to direct the attention of the rural population towards the manufacturing industries. Moreover capital did little for the cultivation of the land.

As properties were more sub-divided, the holdings became too small to enable the owners to make a living merely from the produce of the land. The number of peasants who carried on some industry in addition to labour on their land was greater than in 1789.

The number of workmen seems to have decreased. The relative scarcity of agricultural labourers resulted in high cost of labour. The wages of day-labourers were nominally increased by a quarter; in reality they were only proportionate to the general rise of necessaries. Workmen's wages were higher in towns than in the country. There were however exceptions. These wages were easily paid by the landowners, who were enriched by the high price of necessaries; the cost fell on the consumer.

The condition of the rural population was much improved. Hence during the Revolution the rural population increased at the cost of the towns; in the country security and work could be found.

There was also evident improvement, sometimes in houses, furniture, and clothing, and often in food. In Limousin, where formerly the people lived on chestnuts and buckwheat and drank only water, now almost every family occasionally bought butcher's meat, and "salted a pig for the year's consumption"; part of the butter, eggs, and cheese formerly taken to market was now eaten at home; more wine was drunk. The agricultural labourer too was better nourished. "The day-labourer in the country," said the Prefect of Moselle, with some exaggeration indeed, "has reaped all the benefits of the Revolution." Nevertheless dwellings still left much to be desired. In 1803 there were not perhaps in the whole of the department of Moselle thirty farmhouses which were properly built; there were no sheepfolds; the stables and cowsheds were small and insanitary.

So it was in Meurthe and Eure. Begging seems to have decreased; many vagrants whom the great ecclesiastical establishments had accustomed to live on alms, now found work.

Between 1792 and 1815 agricultural development was chiefly
hampered by enlistment and conscription. In Eure alone
between 1791 and the year VIII 21,720 men were taken for the
army out of a population of 400,000. The Prefect of Gers said
that conscription had had a fatal influence on agriculture.

In fact, while the Revolution had enriched the *bourgeoisie*, by
giving it a more established position as regarded land, it had
also improved the condition of the rural population, definitely
founded a rural *bourgeoisie*, given life to the country districts,
and increased the number of small holders, the class which
supplies born soldiers to the country when in danger.

The Revolution exercised a much less beneficial influence on
industry and commerce. Although various manufactures working for the army were prosperous—an immense effort was made
by a crowd of factories in Paris and in the departments under
the direction of the Committee of Public Safety and of scientists
collected by Prieur of the Côte d'Or—industry as a whole
languished, as was shown by an inquiry made in the year V in
the departments of Nord, Pas-de-Calais, Moselle, etc. Lyons,
which in 1788 had over nine thousand looms working, had in
the time of the Directoire only three thousand. General trade,
which thanks to colonial produce had at first been maintained
and which improved in 1792, attaining a total of 1732 million
francs, fell to 533 million in 1799.

Thus the working classes were far from having benefited as
much from the Revolution as the rural population. Many
operatives were unemployed. In Paris the municipality opened
charitable workshops, the traditional remedy; these employed
19,000 men in October 1790; 31,000 in January 1791; then the
Constituent Assembly, fearing disturbances, disbanded them
and sent them to make roads in the departments. Even trade-
unions were forbidden on the same grounds as the masters'
guilds; contracts to work were to be freely made between
masters and men (June 14, 1791). According to law this put
both sides on an equal footing; but actually it placed the workmen in the power of the employer at times when work stopped.

The men were dissatisfied and insisted on combining. They were in the front ranks in July 1791, and August 10, 1792, in Germinal and Prairial III, on the occasion of the "days of revolution."

The working class, which was not yet a very distinctive class —we have seen that it was generally half operative, half rural— nevertheless benefited greatly by the liberty of labour and the abolition of guilds, and above all by circumstances. By the *maximum* decree of September 1793, wages were increased 50 per cent. compared with those of 1790, while the price of prime necessities was only increased by a third. In fact during the Terror the workmen could eat till they were satisfied, and they even lived well. They could indeed at that time impose their own conditions. Later, when the rule of the property-holding *bourgeoisie* succeeded the revolutionary government, they fell back into the condition which had obtained in 1791 and which was in fact the same as it had been under the old system.

Thus on the ruins of the upper classes, the clergy and nobles, there rose to power, not the workmen, whom their *bourgeois* masters left in the same condition and whose secret associations they wished as usual to destroy so as to have the men at their mercy, but the peasants, who benefited as to their property by the suppression of a hundred million of tithes and at least a hundred million of seignorial dues, who acquired a quantity of land belonging to the Church, the *emigrés*, or common-land, very cheaply, and who up to at least 1793 sold their provisions and cattle at unhoped for prices; and finally and above all the *bourgeoisie*, already wealthy, which in spite of the decline in industries and trade had still more enriched itself, like the peasants, by the national property, and had obtained political power, thus assuming responsibility for the future of France.

The exclusiveness of national economy after the Revolution. Social economy in the 19th century developed along the lines laid down by the Revolution. Protection, which started in 1791 and was aggravated by the war in 1793, continued at first in a moderate form; later during the great struggle between France and England it ended in prohibition under a phase of unparalleled violence—the Continental Blockade.

France was no longer France, but the vast French Empire,

comprising eighty million subjects; and for this reason
Napoleon's policy, which would at once have ruined a small
state, was enabled to survive some years in this Empire and the
great Confederation of European States which obeyed him. The
two deadly enemies suffered equally. At one time the French
Empire prospered. The blockade caused the creation of various
industries, such as the manufacture of beet sugar; it stimulated
the spirit of invention : Philippe de Girard invented a machine
for spinning linen and Jacquard of Lyons another for silk
weaving. Antwerp, Ghent, and on the left bank of the Rhine
Aix-la-Chapelle, Crefeld, etc., became flourishing; from the
right bank of the Rhine the manufacturers hastened to
migrate to the left bank, which was French territory, so as to
enjoy the advantages and markets of this great state. The
Rhine towns, Mayence and Cologne, carried on a trade double
or treble that of the former Prussian state. But meanwhile
Marseilles, Bordeaux, Nantes, Rouen, and Le Havre were languishing. Then followed the crisis of 1810–1811. It was only at
a very high price that the French manufacturers were able to
obtain raw materials, which were detained by the English, or
which came from distant lands, and they could only produce
costly goods. When there were good harvests, the consumer was
able to pay. But when bad harvests came, the consumers in the
Empire could not purchase all the industrial output, which was
too abundant and too dear, and the manufacturers could not
dispose of it outside Europe because English ships were block-
ading the French coast. Napoleon indeed lent millions to the
manufacturers embarrassed by their stores of goods; but this
was only a precarious expedient in a general condition which
could not fail to become aggravated. Trade dwindled to an
alarming extent, especially in 1813 and 1814; it fell from the
1806 standard of 933 million francs to 605 and 585 millions. This
was an alarming decline, especially when compared with the
1789 figures, when the general trade of France had surpassed
a milliard of francs. However new channels for credit were
established, among the foremost being the Banque de France
(1800), which in 1803 was granted the exclusive right of issuing
promissory notes to bearer, payable in gold and at sight, and
which rendered great services to Paris, Lyons, and Rouen by

discounting commercial bills; but the best institutions are powerless when the whole economic system rests on such slight foundations.

National economy continued its course assisted by protective tariffs until 1860 or even later.

During this long period of nearly half a century, which was a time of peace, economic activity was intense. Then indeed there appeared and developed fully the benefits derived from free labour and the Revolution. Every kind of energy was inspired by all the various economic and social doctrines, those of the orthodox school (Jean-Baptiste Say), and above all those of the socialist school of Saint-Simon, with which were associated many engineers and scientists full of initiative, such as the Pereiras.

Agriculture made great strides between 1815 and 1860. Land was cleared; virgin land was brought into cultivation; the *landes* and forests decreased; arable land increased in extent. Artificial grassland was developed. Potato culture increased as it had done since about 1670, above all after the famines of 1816 and 1817, especially in Alsace and Lorraine. Cattle increased and were improved. The high price of wheat and provisions, insisted on by the great landowners and former *emigrés*, and attained by protective legislation analogous to the British corn-laws, and by the sliding scale, kept the agricultural population in the country districts, especially under the Restoration. Rural life remained what it had been in the 18th century and was intimately associated with industrial labour. Population increased in the country districts. This increase was most rapid between 1820 and 1825; there were still, as in old days, many families of five, seven, ten, twelve, or even more children. Thus were compensated the heavy losses of man-power on the battle-fields of Europe during twenty-three years. After 1850 agricultural progress seemed arrested. Industry and industrial wages, which were higher than agricultural wages, caused a large number of rural workers to hasten to the towns; in all parts, the north, Lorraine, Alsace, etc., rural labour was obtainable for industrial work in great abundance.

Industry was completely reorganised. Machinery was master everywhere, occasionally to the great discontent of the operatives, who, as in England, broke the machines. Henceforward there was a continual struggle between machinery and hand-labour. And machinery led to division of labour and specialisation, in preparation for industrial concentration, to the advantage of large factories.

About 1850 there was a great revolution in transport. Railways, which were often promoted by the followers of Saint-Simon, such as Émile Pereira, Michel Chevalier, and Professor Perdonnet of the École Centrale, altered all the conditions of economic life; in 1847 there were already 1931 kilometres of railroad open to traffic. The State farmed out the railways on a 99 years' lease to great companies of shareholders who worked under state control. River-navigation was improved; canals were made; that of Burgundy, begun under Louis XVI, was opened in 1832; that of Nivernais, undertaken in 1784, was finished in 1843; that of Berri in 1841; those from Nantes to Brest, and of Ille and Rance in 1842; those from the Marne to the Rhine and from the Rhône to the Rhine in 1853. In 1847 the navigable length of canals was 3750 kilometres. This revolution in transport hastened the evolution towards industrial concentration, facilitated the influx of raw materials and labour to the centres of industry. The progress of coal and iron extraction, especially in the centre of France, also gave a powerful stimulus to geographical centralisation of industry.

Trade, which had languished during the wars of the Empire, now rapidly revived. After 1827 special trade (import and export) regained all the ground it had lost since 1789 and rose to a milliard of francs. Between 1837 and 1846 general trade rose to over 2,100,000,000 francs, and between 1847 and 1856 to 3,175,000,000. Banking was making rapid progress; in addition to the Banque de France there were a number of great private banks, such as Ouvrard's under the Restoration and Lafitte's under Louis-Philippe. Bankers contributed greatly to the Revolution of 1830 and arrested it on the slippery path of Republicanism to form a *bourgeois* republic, the tool of a small number of privileged people; then under the Second Empire several great banking establishments were founded (*Crédit foncier, Crédit mobilier,* etc.), which helped to centralise financial operations.

Contemporary era (from 1860 to our own times). The contemporary era opens with the year 1860. France was then at the height of her prosperity, economic, political, and colonial. She was the arbiter of continental Europe. After 1830 she established a colonial empire to replace that of which she was deprived by Great Britain in the 18th century, and of which in 1860 Algeria, Guinea, and Cochin China were the essential foundations. The protective tariff, successfully assailed by Michel Chevalier and the free-traders, and the sliding scale for corn both disappeared, as the British corn-laws had already disappeared. In January 1860, a commercial treaty with England fixed the maximum import duty from 1864 onwards at 25 per cent. of the value. This important treaty was followed by others, which caused rapid progress in the import trade. Railways, which had been begun in 1838, were already highly developed. Gold became increasingly abundant owing to the exploitation of the Californian mines and the growth of national wealth; discounting and banking operations in mortgages and commercial loans were much more common and more easily arranged.

The prosperity of France continued to increase. In spite of the defeat of 1870, which cost two of her finest provinces and over ten milliards of francs, without taking into consideration the irreparable loss in human lives, France under the Third Republic set to work patiently, bound up her wounds, loyally discharged her formidable debt of five milliards which she had promised to the victorious enemy, freed her territory from occupation in three years, obtained magnificent harvests from the land, and once more found in agriculture her principal industry.

Agriculture became industrialised, especially in some districts. Gradually almost everywhere specialisation of crops became the rule. The four million landowners on a large or moderate scale appreciated the need for this change, and so did even many of the 4,835,000 peasant holders enumerated in the census of 1881. In Normandy, even in the district of Caux, the land was often given up to pasture instead of to wheat; in Lower Languedoc there were only vineyards; while elsewhere, in Beauce, Picardy, and Flanders, cereals and sugar-beet predominated. Notable progress was made in the actual method of cultivation; a number of agronomists studied the selection of seeds; in the first rank were Vilmorin of Paris and Florimond Déprez of Cappelle near Orchies (Nord). In addition to animal manure (cattle and especially sheep), chemical manures were used (nitrates from Chile, phosphates from Picardy, Algeria, Tunis, and since 1919, Alsace). But notwithstanding the example set by a number of great landowners many small peasant holders remain wedded to routine. Moreover they often wish to produce a little of everything on their land, according to the custom of the ancient Romans and the precepts of Columella; and in consequence the average of wheat-production to the hectare in France is only given in statistics as seventeen hectolitres[1]. But this figure is entirely fictitious and cannot serve as a basis for comparison with foreign agriculture. Actually in every part of France where wheat is sown in any great quantity, over twenty hectolitres per hectare are obtained; in the northern district at least thirty to forty hectolitres; and on great model farms, such as that of Déprez at Cappelle, over forty.

Agriculture has passed through many crises; from 1882 to 1886 cryptogamic diseases destroyed a great part of the vines; on various occasions, especially at the beginning of the 20th century, the sale of wine at a loss caused serious social disturbances, particularly at Hérault, which is given up to monoculture; even wheat, which fetched twenty-five francs a hectolitre in 1875, was threatened by American competition, which could supply it at twelve or thirteen francs, carriage included. But French agriculture has succeeded in outliving all these serious dangers. The vines affected were torn up and new ones, either French or American, were planted. The depreciation of wine has not lasted; it is long since a litre of wine could be had in Hérault for ten centimes. Finally a duty of seven francs per quintal[2] was placed on wheat by a vote asked for in 1892 by M. Méline for the protection of French agriculture. This tax, paid by the consumer, was imperative; France is preeminently an agricultural country and a land of small-holdings; the agricultural population represents 47 per cent. of the whole population. In this France differs greatly from Germany and England.

[1] A hectolitre = 2·75 bushels.   [2] A quintal = about 8 quarters.

As usual industry made much more rapid progress than agriculture; the manufacturer is often a speculator who shrinks from no risk, and moreover scientific inventions bring about changes of plant and of all kinds of work. Since 1860 we live still more in an age of coal and iron. Industries became concentrated in districts which are rich in coal; first in the centre (Forez, Lyonnais, and Nivernais), then in the north; in 1885 the quantity of coal yielded by the mines of the north (Anzin, Lens, Marles, and Courrières) was greater than that of the mines in the centre (Commentry, Blanzy, Saint-Étienne, Decazeville, etc.); in 1914 the mines in the north yielded twenty-seven million tons; those in the centre thirteen millions. In addition to the metallurgical factories of the centre (Le Creusot, Commentry-Fourchambault, Vierzon, Bourges, etc.) there sprang up the workshops of Fives-Lille, and in the district of the Scheldt and the Sambre those of Hautmont, Denain and Anzin, and Blanc-Misseron, which manufacture machinery, engines and material for railways. At the end of the 19th century, and especially from 1895 to 1900, Lorraine, which was developing the extraction of iron at Briey, in its turn became a great manufacturing district; the victory of 1918 restored the iron mines of Lorraine which were annexed in 1871 by the Germans; there also lies the richest ferriferous basin in Europe, and to feed the great furnaces of Briey, Longwy, and Hayange there are the coal-fields of the la Sarre close by, which have been assigned by the treaty of Versailles to an association of the mining companies of the north of France, which suffered from the enemy's devastations. Finally the discovery and exploitation of rich beds of iron in Lower Normandy at the beginning of the 20th century and especially during the Great War have created a new metallurgical district in and round Caen. Coal attracts all the industries which require motive power; thus as well as metallurgy textile industries have developed in Forez and Lyonnais, and above all in the north, where they are of long standing, and finally in Lorraine and Alsace. Water-power supplied by the mountain-torrents is in course of altogether transforming all the region of the Alps (Savoy and Dauphiné) and is making the district of Grenoble and Voiron an industrial centre, in anticipation of the day when, under its impulse, the Pyrenean region and the Central Massif, which are still asleep, shall awake, and with the help of the mighty Rhône a great part of eastern France shall be the scene of a marvellous activity.

Beside this movement of geographical centralisation, the reign of machinery has accentuated the tendency towards industrial concentration; large factories have become multiplied; those affording occupation to over fifty workmen absorb 45 per cent. of industrial labour (not including transport). But large factories have not destroyed little ones. Over 500,000 factories, employing from one to four men each, give occupation to over 800,000 men. The large establishments of ready-made clothing give out work to be done at home. And if the small workshops are threatened, motive power supplied by small electric motors is in course of saving them.

Finally, trade, which after 1880 remained stationary for some years, has not ceased increasing in spite of the protective tariffs of 1881 and 1892. General trade made a marked advance after 1897; it rose to eleven milliards of francs and between 1907 and 1909 to nearly fifteen milliards. Credit has advanced along with national wealth. Like industry, it has become more and more centralised in Paris; but special banks have been founded in the great economic regions, at Lyons, in the east, and the north, and a tendency towards decentralisation has shown itself.

At the beginning of the war in 1914 France was at the height of her prosperity. In spite of the adventurous investments which she had made in Panama, South America, and Russia, France was then, according to a recognised formula, the "banker of Europe" and of the world. Money was plentiful. The gold reserve of the Banque de France was the largest in existence. The rate of interest was 3 per cent.; the city of Paris even borrowed at 2 per cent. The north, east, south-east, and Normandy were all making enormous industrial progress. And at the same time agriculture, the principal French industry, the foundation on which rest her prosperity, her military power, and her independence, with its millions of solidly established workers, was making obvious progress and becoming slowly but surely industrialised.

It is specially the *bourgeoisie* and the rural landowners who have profited by all this economic movement; the Great War has enriched a small number of *bourgeois*, especially manufacturers, and many peasant holders, who have paid off their debts to the *Crédit foncier*. But the operatives have also reaped some advantage. They enjoy more liberty than formerly. Their right to strike was recognised in 1863. In 1884 they were allowed by law to form unions. Syndicalism has continued to spread; it has its centralised organisation; the *Confédération Générale du Travail* is a real power. There is now a working class, conscious of its strength and its rights. It has gained much by the war of 1914. Wages have greatly increased; while the pay of officials has been doubled, that of the workmen has been trebled, quadrupled, sometimes quintupled. The operatives of to-day often live much better than many clerks, officials, and above all, gentlefolk, whose incomes are now inadequate. Their leaders have often forced them into great strikes, and even into a general strike against the capitalist *bourgeoisie* and against the nation. These attempts failed in 1919 and 1920 and they have very little chance of success in a country where wealth is much sub-divided and where there are a large number of small rural landowners, who are hardworking and conservative.

By the war ten of the richest French departments have been laid waste wholly or partially. The enemy blew up the shafts of the northern mines with dynamite (Lens, Courrières, Aniche, Anzin, etc.), destroyed and pillaged the workshops and factories of Lille, Armentières, Denain, Cambrai, Saint-Quentin, etc.; destroyed farms and even cut down fruit-trees in the Somme region. In addition to this, 1,400,000 Frenchmen were killed in the war, most of whom were cultivators of the soil; and several hundred thousand more were disabled; a total of two million French men, young, and among the best of the nation, whose strength has been lost to France. And it is well known that the birth-rate in France has been declining ever since 1860. There are therefore a number of problems to be solved regarding the economic reconstruction of France. But no lofty-minded Frenchman can fear for the future of a country which in 1914 succeeded in arresting on the Marne and decisively defeating the most formidable army in history and thus ensuring final victory to the Allies. Notwithstanding the extent of her losses

France will recover. Thoroughly reconstructed, she will remain a great land of agriculture and of small landholders; possessing the iron-mines of Lorraine, Normandy, and Algeria, she will be able to become the greatest metallurgical power in Europe; she will still be the home of good taste and of art. With the immense resources of her colonial empire still undeveloped, she will be able to become more and more independent of foreign countries for raw materials. It is the hope of the historian that, when she becomes wealthier than she has ever been before, she may not fall into materialism, but that she may remain, as ever since the 17th century, the great Light of the West.

BIBLIOGRAPHICAL NOTE

The economic and social history of France is still to be written. The student must therefore consult, in preference to the older works of Levasseur or d'Avenel, the more recent books and articles which have been based on the documentary evidence of the archives, especially the articles in the *Revue d'histoire moderne* (1899–1914), the *Revue historique*, the *Revue d'Économie politique*, the *Révolution française*, the *Revue du Nord* (Lille), the *Annales de Bretagne*, the *Revue d'Histoire de Lyon*, the *Revue napoléonienne*, the *Annales de Géographie*, etc.; he should also consult the *Histoire de France* edited by E. Lavisse. Some documents have been published by the Government, principally on the Revolution (sales of national property, the working of iron, abolition of the seignorial *régime* in France, Savoy, etc.). The economic study of this period is organised for the whole of France by departmental Committees and a central Committee.

CHAPTER V

THE FINANCE OF THE *ANCIEN RÉGIME*

WITH the progress of civilisation money has played an ever-increasing part in determining the destinies of nations. Few factors have contributed more to the development of princely power than a well-filled purse, whilst poverty or mismanaged resources have been a frequent source of weakness to a State. How the State gets its revenue is a question affecting every citizen, and oppressive taxation has brought about the downfall of governments. The most catastrophic event in modern history, the French Revolution of 1789, owes its origin in large measure to the vicious financial system of the *ancien régime*; and it is very tempting to speculate on what might have happened in the great eighteenth century struggle between England and France for world-power, if France, possessing as she does a most thrifty peasantry and a large part of the most fertile soil of Europe, had had her resources carefully husbanded. Historical values can never be measured in terms of x and y, but though the precise effect of money matters on national life may be difficult to estimate, it is certain that a more accurate understanding of the past can be gained from an historical survey of national finance.

1. *The Legacy of the Middle Ages*

Taxation is a by-product of civilisation. In early times, the leaders in war reserved for themselves large blocks of a conquered territory and were expected to pay for the upkeep of the Government from the proceeds of their estates. Of direct taxation there was little, though several of the taxes of the *ancien régime* can be traced as far back as the Roman occupation of Gaul. It was to his landed property that the ruler had mainly to look for his revenue, and though much of the royal domain was in the course of time alienated to magnates, the Crown usually retained certain rights—e.g. military service—which were directly or indirectly valuable sources of revenue. From early times also the King possessed rights of purveyance and pre-emption which enabled his servants to commandeer, at a price fixed by themselves, all requisites for a journey; as often as not prices were fixed at considerably below market-value, and even then creditors found no little difficulty in getting payment.

The French Crown possessed also very ancient and valuable mineral rights. Salt duties existed during the Roman occupation, and the *gabelle*, or salt tax, was a main source of the income of the State till the Revolution. On iron, steel, lead, copper, silver, etc., the Crown took toll, usually to the extent of 10 per cent. of the output, and if neither the landlord nor the tenant of property containing minerals exploited them, the Crown was entitled to do so and retain the whole of the profits. Stone and marble quarries were taxed, the usual rate being 5 per cent. of output, and from the minting of money considerable gain was made, especially in hard times; for the kings of France, like the kings of England, not infrequently debased the coinage.

One of the worst legacies of Mediaeval to Modern France was the duties on goods, vehicles, cattle, and persons in transit. Not only were customs duties collected at the ports on imported goods but local tolls also were a regular feature of the economy of the Middle Ages. Tolls had to be paid for the use of rivers, roads, and bridges, and for the privilege of offering goods for sale at fairs or in public market-places. Some of these duties were purely local and the proceeds were the property of a town or a private individual, but in other cases the Crown took a share. Naturally, the adding of duty to duty made goods very dear and prevented one part of France from trading with another. Internal tolls were abolished in England in the later Middle Ages, but they survived in France till the Revolution and are seen in part in the town *octrois* of to-day. Their survival was one of the chief causes why France took so long to develop into a nation-state.

Lastly, the Middle Ages bequeathed a whole host of rights of all sorts and descriptions; they can be characterised as the usual attributes of a mediaeval king, and for the most part were feudal in origin. They included feudal escheats, wardships, reliefs, fines, confiscations, etc.; the aids collected for the king's ransom, for the knighting of his eldest son, and for the marriage of his eldest daughter; the *régale*, or right to the revenues of a vacant bishopric or abbey; the *droit d'aubaine*, or right to the goods of deceased foreigners; the *droit d'épave*, or right to take possession of lost goods or animals; the *droit de varech ou de naufrage*, or right to goods washed ashore from a wreck; and many such rights. From fines in the Courts of Law and from quasi-judicial acts such as the registration of title-deeds considerable revenues were obtained.

Such were the main sources of royal revenues when modern French history began. All of them were domain revenues; they had never been in any way subject to Parliamentary grant or control.

2. *The Central Financial Authority; its weakness*

Where Parliamentary government exists to-day, there are to be found three main divisions in the financial system: (1) the preparation of the Budget and its sanction by the National Assembly; (2) the collection and expenditure of national income according to the principles decreed by Parliament; and (3) the audit of accounts by means of which Parliament ascertains whether or not its commands have been observed. These three divisions existed under the *ancien régime*, though there was no French Parliament to check the Monarchy. The King's Council received estimates of the cost of the upkeep of the governmental departments and issued decrees for the raising of the necessary revenues; no monies could be paid legally from State funds without the King's signature; and every superior official responsible for the handling of national monies was, as a matter of course, subject to having his accounts examined and audited by the *Chambre des Comptes*. The analogy between the financial system of the *ancien régime* and that of to-day must not, however, be pressed too far. There was nothing of the modern thoroughness about the French Monarchy. The entire system was rarely, if ever, fully in force. No complete review of the yearly income and expenditure was ever to be had; and no law precluded the King from incurring a debt or assenting to the payment of monies not provided for in the Estimates. Indeed, if the King agreed to a particular charge, no further sanction was required from him, even though the charge was repeated year after year; and in actual practice, in spite of Sully's attempt to stop the custom, a wide range of recurrent expenditure was met year after year by the local Treasuries without reference to the central government. This is the main reason why nobody ever knew what it cost to run the machine of state.

3. *Privileged Immunities from Taxation*

In the finance of the *ancien régime* there was nothing universal, nothing uniform. No tax hit all Frenchmen alike. Everywhere there existed local immunities and individual and class exemptions, the owners of which were strong enough to frustrate all attempts at reform.

The way in which the Monarchy was built up helps largely to explain some of the fiscal anomalies of the pre-Revolutionary period. Hugh Capet was lord of the Ile-de-France. His successors gradually, in the course of centuries, built up the French Monarchy. Provinces from time to time were brought under the control of the Crown, and, as the price of incorporation with the Monarchy, were often able to secure financial privileges or the maintenance of local customs. For certain fiscal purposes France was almost as much a bundle of states as was contemporary Germany. No better illustrations to the point can be given than the differences between the *pays de taille réelle* and the *pays de taille personnelle*, or than the widely differing salt tax, the rate of which varied from district to district. The Provincial Estates were very tenacious of their privileges, and many a project of financial reform broke down in the face of their particularism.

Quite apart from these territorial privileges, there were personal and class privileges. Frenchmen were divided into privileged and unprivileged. The former category included the clergy and the lay nobility, and many commoners, thanks to their wealth, were able to purchase "privilege," whilst exemption from taxation was also attached to numerous offices. The privileged were normally the richest persons in France and the result of their immunity was that a very large proportion of the wealth of the nation contributed next to nothing to national needs. The Church formed a self-governing body outside the ordinary tax-collector's range, the theory being that the spiritual administrations of the clergy were an adequate contribution to the upkeep of the State. Yet the Church owned between a quarter and a third of France. It is true that from time to time the Church made "free gifts" to the King, and the clergy were liable to special war-taxes, such as the *dixième* and *capitation* instituted by Louis XIV, but they always compounded by lump sums and invariably paid far less than laymen. The great command over capital possessed by the Church and the ease with which it could borrow money enabled the clergy to bargain for very advantageous terms with the State, which, in the 18th century especially, was always unable to meet liabilities and was ever willing to satisfy present necessities by mortgaging the future. Further, the higher ranks of the clergy were always strong enough to pass on to the parish priests the greater part of the contributions of the Church to the State.

The lay aristocracy were subject to many of the domain duties, but they were exempt from most of the ordinary direct taxes, and especially from the most objectionable, the *taille*. Their duty to the State lay in fighting for it, and doubtless this was not an unfair share of the burdens of citizenship at a time when wars were frequent. The *taille*, in fact, was originally levied on those only who did not serve in the Army. When privilege did not give a wealthy individual legal exemption from taxation, his social importance generally secured it for him, at least in country districts, for he was able to over-awe or cheat the ignorant local tax-collector.

It can hardly be surprising, under the circumstances, that the Monarchy was almost invariably in want of money. What the Treasury lost as a result of the privilege system it would be idle to guess, but there can be little doubt that the bankruptcies of the 18th century might have been avoided if all citizens had been made to contribute, according to their means, to the necessities of the State. The *ancien régime* was, in fact, strangled by the privilege system.

4. *The Tax Administrative System*

A rapid growth of Royal power in France followed the close of the Hundred Years' War in 1453. Before the century had come to an end, France was united under its Valois kings. Taxation, which had hitherto been mainly feudal in character, became permanent, general, and, to a degree, national, and attempts were made to improve the administration. Under Francis I reforms were introduced with the object of centralising control over the royal revenues. The *Trésor de l'Épargne*, renamed the Royal Treasury in 1662, was set up in 1522; the famous *Cour des Aides*, which had jurisdiction in suits relating to tax-revenues (as distinct from domain-revenues) was established in 1543; and the Crown took away from provincial governments the right of appointing local tax-officials. From the reign of Francis I also there was a regular head of the Finance Administration; generally this power was given to an official called the Superintendent of Finance or Controller-General of Finance, though occasionally control was vested in a Board. When the 16th century opened, there existed some ten *Recettes générales* or local Treasuries, to each of which was paid in the tax-revenues of a certain area. The several *Recettes* worked independently of one another, and it was by no means unknown for the same bill to be paid by more than one of them. It was mainly to prevent such abuses that the *Trésor de l'Épargne* was established. Francis I ordered that strictly local expenses only were to be paid by the provincial *Recettes*; all other bills were to be presented at *L'Épargne*. Local financial administration was reorganised and France was redivided into 16 *Généralités*, a number which was subject to fluctuation until in 1789 there were 22.

Each *Généralité* had its own Treasury, and the chief officials had to be resident. The head official, the Treasurer-General, had to prepare and send to Paris, at the beginning of each financial year, a statement of the probable revenues of the *Généralité*, and, at the close of the year, an actual balance sheet. The former was a guide to show the Crown what income it could expect to obtain from the area, whilst the Treasurer's final accounts had to be audited by the courts. Staff increased with time. Often increased *personnel* was necessitated by the expansion of business, but very often indeed posts were created simply in order that they might be sold, and even the highest were duplicated and triplicated for no other reason than this.

The *Généralités* were divided into a number of *Élections*, which in turn were subdivided into parishes. As soon as the King's Council had decided on the amount of taxation to be levied, the Treasurer of the *Généralité* was informed of his quota, and he then split up the sum as he thought fit amongst the *Élections*. In each *Élection* there was a Controller and a Select Council of local men (*Élus*), who arranged what each parish had to contribute. In theory, the sum at which the parish was assessed depended on the supposed wealth of the village, though in practice grave anomalies were found. The actual assessment of individuals was made by parish collectors, who were personally responsible, till Turgot's days, for the payment of the sum fixed for their parish. There were generally four of these parish collectors, and the work was so odious that the male tax-payers had to be made to take the office in turn. As often as not, the collectors could neither read nor write, and normally there was in each parish a regular clerk (*greffier de la taille*) who set down in writing the assessments made by the collectors. But the vagaries of the clerk, who often took it upon himself to alter the assessments, were so scandalous that Henry IV allowed the collectors to select whom they liked as their clerk.

When the parish collectors had completed their assessments, their lists had to be approved by the council of the *Élection*. On each list had to be shown the names of all residents exempted from the tax, the names of the tax-payers together with the sum at which each person was assessed, and the total sum which the parish had to pay. It was open to the Controller to see that no man was treated unfairly, and that the collectors did not take more than they were entitled to collect. As soon as the list had been approved by the District Council, it was sent back to the parish collectors who proceeded forthwith to get in their taxes. There thus existed the machinery for a sound, equitable system of national taxation.

Every taxpayer had the right to appeal against the assessment made on him by the parish collectors. In the first instance, an appeal would be taken before the council of the *Élection*, and if the complainant was not satisfied with the verdict, he could take his case to the *Cour des Aides*, until Henry IV, in order to prevent people from ruining themselves by costly lawsuits, made the decision of the council of the *Élection* final for all small amounts. In practice, appeals against assessments were numerous; often the sum at issue was not more than a few *sous*, but the lawyers did their best to encourage complaints, and one of the reasons why reform was so long delayed was that the lawyers, standing to lose by any improvement, placed every obstacle in the way of change.

5. *The Absence of Constitutional Checks*

The Estates General, the French National Assembly, never attained the power over national finance which was possessed by the English Parliament. In fact the Estates General did not meet between 1614 and 1789. The French *Parlements*, however, which were incorporated societies of lawyers, exercised certain negative powers of control over taxation. In order to become law, a Royal edict, whether dealing with finance or not, had to be registered by the *Parlements*, and the *Parlements* assumed the right to refuse registration, but it was not till the 18th century was well advanced that the lawyers maintained their claim. Hitherto, the Crown had always been able to overcome opposition by a *lit-de-justice*, or Royal Session; for registration could not be refused in the King's presence. Normally, therefore, there was no check on the Crown, except such as nature placed upon its caprice. The Crown was bound by no rules, and from time to time the Monarchy plunged into wild orgies of expenditure, adopted all sorts of financial expedients to get money, and on several occasions in the 18th century had to repudiate liabilities by actual bankruptcy.

6. *The* Taille

Of all the taxes of the *ancien régime* the study of the *taille* is the most important. If a Frenchman living prior to the Revolution had been asked which tax he would most like to escape, his answer would without doubt have been the *taille*. The *taille* was a property tax; it was paid by the unprivileged classes only, and to be liable to pay it was a social stigma. All manner of subterfuge was adopted to escape it, and complaints against it would fill a library. It was not that the total amount of the *taille* was really excessive; in truth, it amounted to only a very small percentage of the income of France, but the exemption of the privileged classes, combined with the vicious methods of levying the tax, created a rankling sense of injustice which has made the name of *taille* synonymous for all that a tax should not be.

As has been stated above, the actual assessments on individuals were made by the parish collectors. These men, having personal knowledge of all their neighbours, might have been expected to apportion the quota of the village with reason and equity. The assessments, however, were not based on a statement of income, as is done in the case of the British income tax, but were, it seems, as often as not based on appearances or prejudice. If a person seemed to be prosperous, his *taille* was increased; consequently nobody liked to appear to be as well off as he really was. The richest man in the village, said a very important official in 1709, would not dare to kill a fowl except at night, for if he did it openly, his taxes would be increased. Under such a system of taxation it is obvious that nobody was likely to try to improve his property.

It seems, also, that on the one hand the collectors favoured their friends, and on the other hand took their opportunity of paying off old scores against their opponents in the village. But this might be expected in any village economy. A far worse evil was the escape from their share of the *taille* by the influential and well-to-do commoners, who used all the resources in their power to intimidate or cajole the collectors into assessing them at less than their fair share. Often a rich commoner had property in several villages; in such cases, he could elect to be taxed in one only, and he would indeed be a foolish collector who drove away from the village his wealthy neighbour by enquiring too closely into the amount of property held and assessing the neighbour fairly. For if the rich neighbour elected to be assessed elsewhere, the whole of his share of the village *taille* had to fall on the other inhabitants, the village quota being fixed without regard to the number of taxpayers.

Moreover, to pay taxes promptly was to court disaster, for it was sure to bring a heavier assessment in subsequent years. It was quite a normal occurrence for taxpayers to be two or three years in arrears with their payments. In fact, it was common knowledge that it paid better to delay payment until distraint orders had been issued by the courts and even to bear the expenses of a prosecution rather than to pay the taxes as they fell due. Nobody was interested, except the National Treasury, in prompt payment. Indeed, the shoals of lawyers and law officials were particularly anxious for no change of system to be made, because if payments were made when due, there would be less litigation and therefore the lawyers would lose part of their incomes. Under the circumstances, the cost of collection of the *taille* was all out of proportion to the proceeds of the tax, and in places must have amounted to fully 50 per cent. of what the Government received. The lawyers in every way encouraged suits, and the law provided almost limitless opportunities for litigation. A taxpayer could sue the collector or even the whole parish for an overcharge of a few *sous*; he could bring an action against a neighbour whom he alleged to be under-taxed or wrongly exempted and so on; and the courts usually gave their verdict for the plaintiff so as to encourage litigation. What with the lawyers and the officials the peasant must have had a most unenviable existence. But on one occasion at least the peasant scored. The *Élus-Généraux* of Burgundy and the *Cour des Aides* of Dijon quarrelled, and the peasants of Ricey-Bas, on the borders of Champagne and Burgundy, took advantage of the trouble not to pay a single sou of *taille* from 1780 to 1784.

The village tax-collector was in a most undesirable position. He was the butt of everybody. His wealthy neighbours did their best to terrorise him; if he favoured them, other villagers could prosecute him and perhaps ruin him with law costs. If any taxpayer defaulted, the collector had to find means of making up the deficit. If he did not pay into the District Treasury the full quota of the village, his own property could be distrained upon. His work was bound to make him unpopular, and it is no small wonder that every effort was made to evade the post. It is even alleged that a main cause of the depopulation of the villages in Auvergne in the 17th and 18th centuries was that so many men ran away to the towns rather than serve as *taille*-collectors.

The evils of the *taille* were felt worse in country districts than in the towns; worse in the *pays d'élection* than in the *pays d'état*. The government always preferred not to deal directly with taxpayers, and was generally prepared to strike a bargain with any form of local authority which could take the onus of tax-collecting from the revenue officials. Such organisations were able to compound by the payment of lump sums and would be free to make their own arrangements for the distribution of the *taille* amongst the taxpayers. Some of the towns, for example raised money to pay their taxes by levying *octroi* duties on goods coming into the borough. Other municipal authorities raised their quotas by calling on the several guilds to provide a specified sum, the guild officials in turn dividing up the tax amongst their members.

France was divided into *pays de taille personnelle* and *pays de taille réelle*, but in a few districts, of which Paris was one, the *taille* was partly *personnelle* and partly *réelle*. Where the *taille* was *personnelle*, it was attached to persons; where it was *réelle* it was attached mainly to particular parcels of land. The latter always had the reputation of being far less arbitrary than the former, and Colbert and several other ministers proposed to substitute it everywhere for the *taille personnelle*. In the *pays de taille réelle*, all that had to be done, when the amount to be raised was known, was to divide the sum by the number of acres subject to the *taille*, and the share of each contributor was known. Land once free from the *taille* always remained so, no matter if it passed into the possession of a commoner; similarly, in theory at least, land subject to the *taille* was always so, even if a noble bought it. The obvious advantages of the *taille réelle* were that the basis of assessment remained the same from year to year and there was no place for the personal caprices of the village collector. It certainly seems that the *taille réelle* was preferable to the *taille personnelle*, but it was not without serious imperfection. The richer classes could usually manage to evade payments due from *taillable* land which came into their possession, and it was frequently difficult to prove what land was and what was not subject to tax, because so many district records were lost, mutilated, or falsified in the course of years, and there was a general tendency for the number of taxable acres to diminish steadily. The result was that in some places, as for instance round Montauban, the *taille* became so heavy that the owners abandoned their land and let it go out of cultivation. Instances are on record showing that local authorities tried to check rural depopulation by offering land *taille*-free to peasants for a period of years on condition that they restored it to cultivation.

A complete organisation existed for no direct tax but the *taille*, and almost invariably when new taxes were found difficult to collect, they were converted into "supplements" of the *taille*, if only for the simple reason that the *taille* machinery could squeeze a modest sum from a class powerless to resist the government. In course of time the supplements actually amounted to about half of the *taille* proper. Some of them, especially those of military origin[1], were far preferable to the original burden, but in other cases, as when the *capitation* was converted into a supplement of the *taille*, a monstrous injustice was done, for the unprivileged classes alone were made to pay[2].

7. *The* Capitation

Towards the end of Louis XIV's reign, in 1695, the government, at its wit's ends to find funds for the prosecution of the war, instituted a special war tax called the *capitation*. Peace was made in 1697, but when war broke out again in 1702, the *capitation* was revived, it being announced that as soon as peace was made the tax would be discontinued. Far from this happening, the *capitation* existed as long as the *ancien régime*, though all trace was lost of the principles on which it had originally been based.

---

[1] E.g. the *taillon* supplement was substituted for the right of the Army to commandeer provisions.

[2] The following figures give an approximate idea of the yield of *taille*: under Charles VII, about 1,800,000 *liv.*; under Louis XI, about 4,800,000 *liv.*; under Henry III, about 24,000,000 *liv.*; in 1660, about 33,000,000 *liv.*; in 1680, about 41,000,000 *liv.*; in 1786, about 45,000,000 *liv.* It must, however, be borne in mind that the accounts of the Monarchy are very unreliable: the student will also realise that figures convey only a most imperfect idea of values.

According to the intention of the government in 1695, all subjects of the king, privileged as well as unprivileged, except persons whose *taille* amounted to less than 40 *sous*, were to be liable to the new imposition. Thus, only the lowest stratum of society was to be exempted. The *capitation* thus introduced a new principle into French finance; it was the first attempt of the Monarchy to make the whole body of citizens, irrespective of social standing, contribute, in proportion to their wealth, towards the upkeep of the State. Frenchmen were to be ranged in one or other of 22 classes, according to their wealth, every member of a class paying a fixed sum which varied from 2000 *liv.* per annum for persons in the first category down to one *livre* which individuals in the last group had to contribute.

There was reason and justice in the scheme, but lack of organisation rendered failure inevitable. There existed no direct-taxation machinery other than that of the *taille*, and the *taille* did not fall on the privileged orders, which the *capitation* was expressly designed to hit. The State at the time was always on the verge of bankruptcy, or actually bankrupt. To get money quickly was always necessary: it was impossible to wait for it till new administrative machinery could be devised and put into action, with the result that the original principles were abandoned without a serious effort to put them into practice. The *capitation*, like the English income tax, was capable of becoming progressively aggressive, and it was most unfortunate that the State failed to maintain the proposals of 1695.

From the outset the government showed itself willing, such was the need for ready money, to accept compoundings, and the Treasury officials even brought pressure to bear on local organisations to compound. When an organisation had compounded, its own officials assessed its members. The State was thus saved trouble, and the taxpayers concerned avoided a too close enquiry into the amount of their wealth. The French clergy agreed to make an annual payment of four million *livres* as their *capitation*, and later, in 1710, secured permanent exemption by the payment of a lump sum of 24 million *livres*. Many towns and provinces also compounded. In some towns the municipal authorities assigned to each guild a specified part of the composition sum and left the guild officers to tax their members. In other towns assessments were based on the rental value of property occupied. In those country districts where the *taille* was *personnelle* the *capitation* was converted into a supplement of the *taille*. In the *pays de taille réelle*, since the *taille* was attached to land and not to persons, the existing *taille* machinery could not be used. It was therefore necessary for new assessment lists to be made up, and though the assessors were changed annually, a good deal of unfairness became evident. "Pierre ménage Jean afin que celui ait les mêmes égards lorsqu'il est cotisateur." The contributions of the upper classes in the country districts were assessed by the *Intendant*, who was assisted by a local gentleman, but often at so small a sum as to give practical exemption. The upper classes in fact were determined not to be subject to direct taxation and the Government of Louis XIV was not strong enough to coerce them. The original idea of grouping citizens into classes completely disappeared and as often as not the *capitation* depended on official caprice. "In Béarn no privileged person, whatever he was worth, paid more than 250 *liv.*; in Pau, no *bourgeois*, however rich he might be, more than 12 *liv.*"

Though those who had compounded during the war escaped their fair share of taxation, the State got on even terms with them in 1715 by declaring void all compoundings except in the case of the clergy, but not refunding any part of the composition fee. The Government broke faith, it is true, but it is only fair to add that the *capitation* had been imposed for the period of the war only, and if compounders had calculated on this basis, no very great injustice was done. The needs of the State were great, and it was imperative that an attempt should be made to increase the revenue at the expense of the well-to-do, even if this could be done only by having recourse to new compoundings. At times, as for example towards the close of the Seven Years' War, serious efforts were made to extend the range of the *capitation*, with what success may be gauged from the fact that whereas Louis XIV got from it from 25 to 30 million *livres*, Louis XVI, just before the Revolution, derived a trifle over 40 millions only, in spite of the great rise in prices in the 18th century.

8. *The* dixième *and the* vingtième

The *dixième* instituted by Louis XIV in 1710 was, like the *capitation*, a special war tax. In few wars in which France has been engaged have the stakes at issue been more momentous than in the War of the Spanish Succession. In 1709 the battle of Malplaquet had opened the gates of France, and, under the circumstances, it might have been expected that the upper classes would gladly have contributed to the necessities of the State; yet Saint-Simon called the *dixième* everything that was bad, and his fellow *privilégiés* did their best to escape it.

The *dixième* has been called "the fairest, even the only fair tax" of the *ancien régime*. It was to be an income tax imposed on all incomes, from whatsoever sources they were obtained, and it was to fall on privileged and unprivileged alike. In actual practice, however, the new tax was levied almost exclusively on incomes derived from real estate. Trade and industry so far escaped the duty that in 1789 the *vingtièmes d'industrie* amounted to approximately $2\frac{1}{2}$ per cent. only of the 57 millions which the tax brought in to the Treasury, the *vingtièmes des biens-fonds* producing roughly 97 per cent. of the total yield.

Income tax has always been most difficult to collect in France. Even to-day the French government finds it almost impossible to put such a tax in force; in 1710 it was still more impossible. Owners of real estate were called upon to make a return of their average annual income, and special officials were appointed to travel round the country-side to check the returns. Some property owners made out returns, others refused, and wherever there was opposition, it can be taken for granted that the lawyers were stimulating resistance. None the less, the story of the *dixième* is one of the few bright pages in the history of French finance, because the original principles on which the tax was based did not die out, and the piecemeal progress of their application in the 18th century had by 1789, though perfection was still far from being realised, laid the foundation stone of an equitable financial system.

The immediate difficulty of the Administration in 1710 arose from the fact that there had never been a valuation of French property or a census of French incomes. If the original principles of the *dixième* were to be applied, of necessity new assessment *rôles* would have to be made for the whole of France. To do this in the middle of a great war was out of the question; and the Treasury, living as it was from hand to mouth, very soon expressed its willingness to accept compositions, as it had done in the case of the *capitation*. The French clergy, for example, compounded at eight million *livres*, on condition that they should for ever afterwards be exempted from the *dixième*. Provinces and towns also compounded, though they were not allowed to purchase perpetual exemption. Aquitaine compounded for 1,280,000 *liv.*, Lyons for 650,000 *liv.*, Brittany for 1,200,000 *liv.*, Strasbourg for 41,000 *liv.*, and so on. To accept compositions was certainly a safe way of getting money, for it was found exceedingly difficult to obtain returns of income, and, where they were forthcoming, little reliance could be placed on them. Where officials made the assessments, corruption was rampant; and in almost every locality payments fell into arrears, the nobles and lawyers being notoriously bad payers. As events proved, the *dixième* produced in Louis XIV's reign an annual revenue of about 22 million *livres* only, a sum which was probably less than one-third of what it ought to have brought to the Treasury; it is significant that a company of tax-farmers are stated to have made an offer of 60 million *livres* per annum for the right of farming the *dixième*.

When peace was made in 1714 the *dixième* was dropped, but in 1733, during the War of the Polish Succession, and again in 1741, during the War of the Austrian Succession, it was revived, in each case expressly as a war-tax for the duration of the war. In 1749, however, it was found impossible to discontinue war-taxation, and in that year, the *vingtième* was instituted on the lines of, and to take the place of, the *dixième*; but the *vingtième* was to be a permanent tax, and the income obtained from it was to be used for the cancellation of the National Debt. Machault, who was in charge of finance at the time, sternly set his face against compoundings; he intended, by abolishing all exemptions, and by reorganising and rendering effective the tax administration to obtain as much revenue from the *vingtième* as had previously been obtained from the *dixième*. This was quite possible, because in actual fact large numbers of wealthy people had by some means or other evaded payment of the *dixième*. France, however, lacked that strong executive which was essential for the enforcement of Machault's proposals. Little help could be expected from Louis XV, who chose the smooth path of surrender rather than encounter the resistance of his courtiers and mistresses. Machault, as was usual with ministers hostile to the courtiers, had to go, but he did not by any means fail wholly: his administration was so vigorous that so long as he was in power the *vingtième* yielded a good deal more than half of what the *dixième* had produced. He had made a step forward in the right direction and his work outlived his fall.

During the Seven Years' War two additional *vingtièmes* were imposed. France was again engaged in a life and death struggle with Britain for the dominion of the Atlantic and for colonial power. None the less, everything possible was done by the privileged interests and especially by the *Parlements* to prevent the raising of funds. The second *vingtième* (1756) secured registration from the lawyers only after the Crown had made considerable modifications in its original edict. Nothing can serve to show more clearly the weakness of the Monarchy between 1750 and 1770 than the obstinate resistance of the Church, the lay aristocracy, and, above all, the *Parlements*, to the *vingtièmes*. It is unfounded criticism to say that the opposition of the *Parlements* to these taxes was actuated by constitutional sentiments; it was not; the *Parlements* were motived solely by a desire to escape burdens which they hoped to make the unprivileged bear. In the years between 1750 and the Revolution, again and again, the *Parlements* prevented a more equitable distribution of the national burdens. Whilst posing as the protectors of the nation against the caprice of an absolute monarchy, and often giving voice to constitutional sentiments which contemporaries applauded, they were the true arch-stone of the privilege system.

The Government had exactly the same trouble in 1759 over the registration of the third *vingtième* as it had had over the second, and again obtained registration only on terms—concessions which weakened the control of the Crown over popular imagination and by so doing prepared the way for the excesses of the Revolutionary period. In 1761, the registration of the edict for the continuation of the third *vingtième* had to be bought by the Crown by the expulsion of the Jesuits, between whom and the *Parlements* there were perpetual feuds. In 1763, when Bertin, the finance minister, tried to introduce essential reforms, the *Parlements* went so far as to arrest the messengers carrying the royal orders to the provinces. Royal messengers could travel only with armed escorts. Again, however, Louis XV gave way. Bertin's plans were abandoned. Changes in the financial system became impossible; new assessment schedules were forbidden by the *Parlements* and examination of old schedules was made useless because the *Parlements* insisted that no person's tax should be increased! The *Parlements* were in fact masters of the Crown.

From 1771, however, after Maupéou's *coup d'état*, matters improved. The Abbé Terray imparted great vigour to the administration of the *vingtièmes*. A real measure of success attended his efforts at securing new assessments on the privileged classes: persons who had never paid a *sou* to the *vingtième* found themselves amerced. The upper classes knew no bounds to their wrath. In Normandy and elsewhere open rebellion was threatened by the nobles, but Terray stood firm and the opposition collapsed. His successors carried on his work. The number of new assessment *rôles* steadily increased and the revenue grew year by year. It was a misfortune that the *Parlements* were allowed to revive, for they again took up the banner of privilege and in the last few years of the *ancien régime* denied absolutely the actual right of the Crown to levy general taxes without the consent of the Estates General, "which alone were competent to alter rights of property." There was the same old trouble over the registration of royal edicts, and Calonne, in desperation, was prepared even to sacrifice the *vingtièmes* in return for a tax payable in kind and varying according to the fertility of the soil, from $\frac{1}{20}$th to $\frac{1}{40}$th of the produce of the land, provided that no class should be exempted. He even told the Notables that those who did not contribute towards the needs of the State could expect no protection from it, and just before he was driven from power he frankly told the King that it was impossible for the Government to exist unless the privilege system was abolished, and everybody, without regard to class distinctions, made liable to national taxation. Calonne perhaps more than any finance minister of the *ancien régime* has been vituperated, but he at least tried to open the eyes of the Court to the dangers of the existing system of taxation. His successor, Brienne, after a vain attempt to get the consent of the *Parlement* to a modified form of Calonne's financial proposals, secured an extension of the *vingtièmes*. But the end was now near. The storm of Revolution was about to burst and to sweep away privilege and *Parlement* alike, but though with Old France the name of *vingtième* disappeared, the general principles on which it had been based survived, at any rate in part, in the *contribution foncière* of the Revolution period.

The story of the *vingtième* reveals several important factors. In the first place, it shows that the Government could not overthrow the privilege system; that the administration, whilst realising that direct taxation levied on all classes alike was essential for the very existence of the State, was impotent to effect reform, and that the privileged classes were so selfish that they preferred to ruin the State rather than sacrifice their class immunities. In the second place, the ignominy to which the Crown was put in its struggles with the *Parlements* for registration of edicts undermined every vestige of respect and authority for the Government, for again and again the Crown had been flouted. Unable to raise the revenues necessary to pay its way, and unsheltered by that halo of respect and power which is at bottom the basic force of all government, the *ancien régime* was bound to collapse, even had there been no causes of revolution other than financial ones.

9. *The* gabelle

The most ancient, the best hated, but at the same time the most productive for the Treasury of all French indirect taxes, was the *gabelle*, or salt tax. Salt was a State monopoly. Yet there was nothing uniform in the perception of the tax; there was no sense of justice in its incidence, and the rate of the duty varied from province to province. For the purpose of the salt administration France was divided into six groups of districts. Where the duty was highest, in the *pays de grandes gabelles*, salt cost in Louis XVI's reign 12 or 13 *sous* the *livre* as a rule; in the second group, the price was from 6 to 8 *sous*; in the last group, which was exempt from duty, the price fell to 1 *sou* or even less. Further, it was obligatory for everybody over eight years of age in the *pays de grandes gabelles* and some other districts, to purchase annually 7 *livres* of salt for domestic purposes; if salt was wanted by the peasant for curing meat, or if a manufacturer wanted salt for industrial purposes, extra quantities had to be bought.

Within the higher-taxed areas, there often existed privileged districts and privileged persons, who were entitled to rebates or duty-free salt. The existence of these special privileges, the wide variation in prices from province to province, and the fact that often there could be no kind of natural frontier between provinces where the maximum duty was levied and provinces where the duty was small naturally led to smuggling. It is obvious that smuggling could be very profitable, and in spite of very stringent *gabelle* laws, people of all classes engaged in the illicit trade. Priests assisted smugglers by allowing smuggled salt to be concealed in churches, and even nunneries, into which *gabelle* officers could enter only if accompanied by a judge and a priest, were favourite store-houses of smuggled salt. The very officials of the *gabelle* administration were not above being bribed to connive at the "trade," often preferring a bribe to the risks of an encounter with the smugglers. None the less, when smugglers were caught, they were treated with exceptional barbarity. At Saumur, for example, the salt prison was a veritable, permanent Black Hole of Calcutta. Nothing, however, could stop smuggling. The greater part of the inhabitants living near a "salt frontier" seem to have been directly or indirectly connected with the traffic. They bade defiance to the law; they lived in a constant state of war with the law; the law bred criminals; the moral effect of the *gabelle* system was perfectly deplorable. Perhaps nothing can illustrate better than the history of the *gabelle* the pernicious effects on society of an inequitable tax.

10. *Douanes, aides, enregistrement, tabac*

Of the important sources of royal income, other than those already mentioned, the chief were the customs, excise and stamp duties, and the tobacco monopoly.

In pre-Revolutionary France considerable revenue was raised by taxing goods imported from abroad (*douanes*). Little is heard of such duties except when a Colbert makes wide or startling changes, because their incidence is indirect. Such taxes must, however, help to determine the price of the taxed goods and normally must come ultimately from the taxpayers' pockets. Any import duty levied on an article of necessity hits more heavily the working classes than the rich, but the *ancien régime* was virtually self-supporting so far as articles of prime necessity were concerned, and the customs duties fell therefore mainly on the classes which were not on the margin of subsistence. *Douanes* were collected, not only at national frontiers, but many of the ancient provinces of France also retained till 1789 their old customs frontiers, so that even French-manufactured goods in transit from one part of France to another might have to pay duty two or three times, whilst local duties (*octrois*) were a regular feature of mediaeval municipal economy. It not infrequently happened, especially in maritime regions, that foreign goods brought by sea paid so much less tax that they could be sold at a lower price than similar French-made goods brought overland from a native factory. French producers might thus be excluded from their natural market by their tariff system. At the same time, it must be mentioned that quite a large list of goods of primary importance were taxed at the first frontier only and their circulation was then free in the whole of France, and, moreover—for one never finds uniformity under the *ancien régime*—certain provinces annexed for the most part after 1600 and including Alsace, Lorraine, Franche-Comté, and the Three Bishoprics of Metz, Toul, and Verdun, could trade with foreign states without payment of French customs duties.

The *aides* comprised a large number of excise duties, such as those levied on playing-cards, oils, leather, etc., but by far the most important of them all were the taxes on liquors. Liquors were liable to a truly amazing number of duties which differed in name and amount from place to place. Le Trosne, a writer well known to French economists, says that not in his whole lifetime could a man get to know all the ins and outs of the taxes on liquors. For the most part, the liquor taxes were purely local and the proceeds were retained by local authorities, but in part of north-central France they were the property of the Government. It is completely out of the question to give even a brief account of the *aides* in such a short survey of French finance as this is.

Enregistrement consisted mainly of duties payable on successions to property and on the registration of important documents such as contracts, declarations on oath, and legal acts. The Treasury in Louis XVI's reign received normally some 40 million *livres* yearly from such duties, which can perhaps be characterised as the most equitable of all the financial burdens of the *ancien régime*. So little objection, in fact, could be raised by the Revolutionaries in 1789 that whilst repudiating the name of *enregistrement* they retained the old officials and in 1790 reorganised the registration laws. No tax of the pre-Revolutionary period was collected with less friction from the nation as a whole, and none was more capable of expansion along wise lines. Thanks to successive improvements, the tax under the First Empire brought in over 100 million *livres* a year. Of the *enregistrement* administration before 1789 it can be said that no governmental organisation in France had reached a greater stage of perfection. The laws might be and were very complicated, but the officials knew their work, so well in fact, that it was said to be hopeless to attempt to argue with the Administration; "les profanes sortent [du bureau d'un receveur d'enregistrement] presque toujours ahuris et mécontents."

Tobacco was, and is to-day, a State monopoly in France. In the very early days of tobacco smoking, the Government was content with a customs duty of 3 *liv.* per kilogramme, but in 1674 a State monopoly was established, and as tobacco came more and more into general consumption, the revenue from its sale steadily increased. When the monopoly was first instituted, it produced a revenue of 500,000 *liv.*, but by the close of Louis XIV's reign this sum had increased to about 2;000,000 *livres* annually. In the 18th century, especially in the second half of it, tobacco smoking increased rapidly, and by 1789 the financiers who were farming the monopoly were paying for this privilege an annual sum of 30,000,000 *liv.* to the Treasury.

11. *Tax-farming*

Wherever possible, the *ancien régime* farmed the taxes. The right to collect a particular tax, or the whole of the taxes of a district, or groups of taxes, was let to financiers who paid the Treasury a lump sum at stated periods and then made the most of their bargains. It was the rule, rather than the exception, for the Government to be unable to satisfy its creditors and the financiers were able to make very advantageous terms, whilst the Treasury preferred regular payments at regular intervals to irregular payments at irregular intervals. How much the tax-farmers obtained from the taxpayer it is impossible to say, but it was common knowledge that in the 18th century some of the financiers were making over a million *livres* per annum each. Whether these large profits were due mainly to efficient organisation or to extortion, or partly to both, it is incontestable that the Treasury did not obtain as much as it should have done, but from time to time the tax-farm leases were revised, and sometimes sold by auction, the State always insisting on an increased price as a condition of the renewal of the lease. Most of the taxes, including the *gabelle*, the customs duties, registration duties, various domain rights, and the tobacco monopoly were let out to farm.

12. *Chronological survey*

Though the *ancien régime* was brimful of financial abuses, it must in fairness to French administrators be stated that contemporary continental Europe almost everywhere presents a similar state of affairs. The explanation is that the importance of a sound financial system was only rarely realised, and the great men of the day turned their attention to more attractive branches of the administration, such as diplomacy. Two statesmen only, in the days of the Monarchy, were worthy of being called finance ministers—Sully and Colbert. Turgot had great ideas, but his tenure of office was too short for his work to be of much practical value. From the standpoint of sheer financial genius, no greater name is to be found than that of John Law, a Scotsman whose financial schemes, thanks mainly to developments over which he had no control, produced such a crash during the Orleans Regency. Necker enjoyed great contemporary popularity, which his work little merited.

Sully came into office in 1597. The preceding century had witnessed a long series of wars, foreign and civil, and the State debt was enormous. Francis I had left a debt of about 40 million *livres*; by 1597 it might well have been 300 millions, but nobody knew to what it really amounted. The financial administration was utterly wasteful and corrupt. Probably not more than 25 per cent. of the taxes paid by the people reached the Treasury; and to meet current expenditure the Government was ever borrowing at ruinous rates of interest.

Sully's first object was to wipe out the annual deficit, to make the Government solvent. His main weapon was administrative reorganisation. He did not attempt to abolish the existing *tailles* and *gabelles*, though he realised their injustice, but he imposed two new taxes only, the *pancarte*, a tax on goods taken into towns for sale, and the *paulette*, by the annual payment of which officials could make their posts hereditary. The *pancarte* roused so much opposition that it was speedily cancelled, but the *paulette* remained in force till the Revolution and by strengthening the position of the lawyers did much to make possible the resistance of the *Parlements* to the Crown in the 18th century. Nor did Sully increase existing taxes. Yet he converted the deficit into a surplus and there was a reserve of 30 million *livres* in the Treasury when he left office. That he had succeeded so well was due partly to his limitation of privileged exemption from taxation, partly to his forcing holders of State bonds to prove their titles (for forgery was not rare), partly to his policy of refusing to meet current expenditure by loans, partly to his efforts to foster French agriculture and to the King's encouragement of French trade and industry, but above all to his close personal scrutiny of tax-officials' accounts and to the absence of a big European war between 1597 and 1610.

After Henry IV's death, France was in an anarchic condition

till Richelieu restored order in the realm, but though the cardinal is a giant in political history, he did nothing of any consequence to carry on Sully's financial work. His foreign policy involved France in vast military enterprises which started her on her path to glory and ruin. Neither Richelieu nor Mazarin did anything to improve the economic life of France and by 1660 nearly all Sully's work had been undone.

From the standpoint of actual achievements, Colbert was without doubt the greatest of French finance ministers. He found chaos and debt everywhere; yet within four or five years so successful were his improvements that without the help of any extra tax—some taxes were actually decreased—Colbert could pay his way. His greatest work lay in his increasing the taxable wealth of France. His policy was to make France a great commercial and manufacturing nation. Foreign artisans were encouraged to plant their industries in France; Frenchmen were helped to extend their businesses; the King himself insisted, as far as possible, on the use of exclusively French-made goods in the royal household; trade companies were formed to develop French over-seas trade; by the abolition of certain internal *douanes* free trade in a large central area in France was established; transit of goods was facilitated by the construction of canals; and foreign manufactures excluded by high tariffs. He stopped the system by which the taxes of certain areas had been assigned to individuals, the *Partisans*, in return for loans. The *Partisans* had been utterly unscrupulous, and Colbert established a tribunal to deal with them, and forced them to refund to the Government enormous sums. He made the Intendants attend to their financial duties and diminished, but did not abolish, privilege. He took over direct control of the collection of taxation, and to obtain a clear statement of national finance he had the financial reports of the local treasurers codified into a single document, a rudimentary Budget; he cancelled debt where titles were questionable, by simply repudiating it, and he arbitrarily reduced the rate of interest.

Colbert's reforms, however, were not lasting. Louis XIV plunged France into a mad orgy of wars and consequently enormously increased the debt. Not content with this, in 1685 he revoked the Edict of Nantes and by so doing he destroyed much of Colbert's work, for a large part of French industry had been carried on by Huguenots. Expelled from France, they took their skill with them to Holland, to England, and to Prussia, and helped to provide the wealth which was one of the main decisive factors in the 18th century wars.

At Louis XIV's death French finance was again in an appalling condition. To give even an approximate idea of the debt is impossible; as a rough indication, 2000 million *livres* may not err greatly. The country was flooded with paper-money, continually depreciating in value and on an average not worth more than 20 per cent. of its face-value. Trade was at a standstill and agriculture languishing. Not only had current revenues been exhausted, but the income for several years ahead had been heavily anticipated. On several occasions there had been outbreaks of revolt in Louis XIV's reign against financial oppression; at his death there was every sign of a popular upheaval.

The task of the Regency was, therefore, tremendously difficult. In the closing years of *le grand Monarque* there had been two great repudiations of State debts—a polite way of labelling bankruptcy—and the coinage on several occasions had been debased. Bankruptcy, total or partial, was openly advocated as the only possible method of saving the State. Public opinion was certainly not averse to bankruptcy. The Regency Council, however, would not face this: it preferred to deal piecemeal with liabilities, but it none the less acted very drastically. One of its first measures was the reduction of the rate of interest on most classes of State bonds to 4 per cent., whilst it cancelled some 40 per cent. of arrears of interest due to creditors and also a large class of bonds. A large, but fictitious, gain was made by debasing the coinage. A special *Chambre de Justice* was set up in 1716 to enquire into the methods by which individuals had come into possession of State bonds, with the result that on one pretext or another more than 200 million *livres* were cancelled. The brothers Pâris held an enquiry into other paper and drastically cut down the capital by amounts varying from 5 per cent. to 80 per cent.; another 300 million *livres* approximately were thus wiped out. The Regency thus relieved itself of a large portion of Louis XIV's debts; whilst the remainder was

for the most part consolidated and was to bear interest at 4 per
cent. only.

The Regency, also, in 1715, withdrew the privilege of exemption from the *taille* from those who had recently obtained
privilege. Large reductions were made in the military and
naval establishments, and locally, though only very occasionally
with success, attempts were made to change the method of
assessing the *taille* so that this tax should be more equitably
distributed. Local tax-officials were forced to keep detailed
accounts showing in what currency payment had been made,
and to furnish fortnightly financial statements to the Treasury.
For long it had been common for the revenue officials to be
money-lenders also. The Treasury had never objected to this
practice, for the chief officials had often advanced loans to the
Treasury as well as to the taxpayer at interest, for the Government was ever in need of ready money. It was not unknown
for the officials to lend the King his own money, money received
by these very officials in payment of taxes. The fact that taxes
were habitually in arrears made for all sorts of abuses, for the
Crown never knew when or what taxes had been paid. Coins of the
same face-value, thanks to the monetary changes of the period,
differed much in real value, and the tax-officials regularly paid
to the Treasury the baser coins. The fortnightly statement
instituted by the Regency did much to check the financial
juggling of the local officials and was as real an economy as the
decrease in the military and naval establishments.

It was during the Regency that France experimented with
the schemes of John Law, a clever Scot from Edinburgh, who
had studied finance in many lands. He held that France was
languishing because of an inadequate supply of sound currency.
He had seen how stable bank notes were in England and
Holland and he proposed to create in France a great State
bank, backed up by all the resources of the State, with power
to issue unlimited credit. With stable credit, French business
would, he argued, rapidly recover and the country become so
prosperous that deficits and debts would speedily vanish. The
Regent was strongly attracted to "the system," but his Council
demurred, so that Law, instead of establishing a State bank,
had at first to be content with the sanction given him to found

a private bank. But this bank flourished exceedingly. Its notes were accepted universally, even by the State in payment of taxes. The notes were convertible into specie at sight at the bank at a fixed price; business houses took up bank paper freely and such general confidence was felt in the institution that in December 1718 Law's private venture was made into a State bank.

The second part of Law's system was a gigantic venture into State socialism; the Government was to control all trade and industry in the interests of the nation. Law's first step was to float the *Compagnie d'Occident* to exploit French possessions at the mouth of the Mississippi. The capital of the company was fixed at 100 million *livres*, divided into 200,000 shares of 500 *liv.* each, and was readily subscribed. Then, one after another, the French China and India Companies, the tobacco monopoly, the Mint, the tax farms and the National Debt were taken over by the Company. For each additional venture fresh capital was raised by public subscription, and so great was the eagerness to buy Law's stock that the Rue Quincampois, his Paris head-quarters, was literally besieged by would-be share-holders. A veritable mania for speculation set in; stock rose to fabulous prices, the 500 *liv.* share reaching 15,000, 16,000, and even 18,000 *liv.* All classes from dukes to lackeys engaged in the gamble. Nothing that Law could do could check the speculation mania, which he well knew could end only in disaster. When realisations began, the crash came, suddenly and violently. The very steps which the Government took to restore confidence served only to increase the desire to sell; the market was glutted with stock; prices fell with amazing rapidity, and thousands of Frenchmen were utterly ruined. The trading schemes thus collapsed, and the bank was overwhelmed by the disaster.

Without doubt the evil consequences of the system outweighed the good. Law had hoped to replace all the varied and fluctuating State paper by a uniform issue, constant in value. He had accepted State paper in payment for his shares and by so doing had largely achieved this desirable end for the time being. For a moment he had given France a stable currency and it is remarkable how great a fillip this gave to French trade.

He had, however, issued paper far in excess of requirements, and the rapid expansion of the currency, without a corresponding increase in production, sent prices up and produced a fictitious appearance of wealth; an age of extravagance set in which long outlived the system. Certain trades, however, more especially the building trade and agriculture, benefited permanently; workers got higher wages; many debtors were able to discharge their debts; and the State took advantage of the situation to buy out the holders of sinecure offices. If Law had succeeded in substituting a State organisation for the tax-farms, the millions of profits which the financiers reaped yearly would have been saved to the taxpayer. By his failure, however, French credit received a terrible blow, and for generations Frenchmen preferred to hoard their savings rather than entrust them to banks.

On the famous Pâris brothers fell the difficult work of liquidation. They reduced the debt to some 1½ milliards, with an interest charge of some 50 million *livres*. Then they set to work to increase State revenue and decrease expenditure, but their methods roused such a storm of opposition that an outbreak of rebellion was probably averted only by their dismissal (1727).

Fleury, who at first made considerable headway towards a national balance, was forced during the Polish War into all manner of expedients. Few purchasers of *rentes* could be found, but single-life annuities and *tontines*, a form of annuity spread over several lives, found ready buyers. The total amount of a *tontine* annuity was fixed and was paid in full until all the subscribers were dead, the last survivor thus getting the whole *tontine*. Premium bonds were instituted, and during both the Polish and the Austrian Wars were found very attractive, issues being almost invariably over-subscribed. Money was borrowed also, as in Louis XIV's reign, through the Provincial Estates, whose credit was better than that of the State. By these methods funds were obtained for the wars, though efforts to increase the tax-revenue met with very indifferent success.

The financial history of the period from 1750 to 1770 is characterised by the conflict between the Crown and the *Parlements* over the *vingtièmes*, with the consequent complete undermining of royal authority in France, and by the wanton and criminal lavishness of Pompadour and her court. The Crown lost every atom of respect; no pen picture can adequately depict the folly and extravagance of the royal household. Such enormous debts were piled up that the Abbé Terray had really no option but to admit bankruptcy. He realised the utter impossibility of meeting liabilities and saw that the only way to financial order lay in a general clearance of the accumulated debts of the past. Contemporaries cursed him and historians in the past have been too prone to condemn him for the bankruptcy. Terray, however, had a great many constructive ideas, and the course he took was probably the only one possible if his other proposals were to be a success. He wanted a clean slate to start with, and he then intended to pay his way. He bluntly told the King that there could be no end to financial disorder until the royal household was more economical. He did much to improve the *vingtième* system; his reorganisation of the *capitation* at Paris made the amount of tax payable depend on the rental of property occupied—a very useful reform. He squeezed every possible *sou* out of the tax-farmers, and when he had to stoop to old abuses he exacted his price. At best, he meant well; at worst, he did better than most of his predecessors or successors.

Turgot, Terray's successor, was a physiocrat[1]. He had a brilliant program of reform, but held office only 20 months (1774–5), and had therefore no real chance of testing his schemes. In spite of his physiocratic principles, he stopped the free export of corn because it was helping to make bread excessively dear in France. He abolished the *contrainte solidaire* by which the deficit in the *taille* of a parish could be surcharged on the chief taxpayers. He aimed at replacing the *corvée*, forced labour on roads, by a general tax. He wanted to abolish all fetters on trade and industry, especially the trade guilds and the provincial *douanes*; he tried hard to force economies on the royal household; he continued the improvement of the *vingtième* system and intended eventually to abolish all privileged exemptions from taxation; and, in accordance with physiocratic doctrines, he hoped eventually to substitute a single tax on land for all the varied and irksome taxes then existing. His

---

[1] See above, pp. 261 f.

plans were far-reaching and ambitious, and it has even been
considered that, had they been put into operation, the Revolution might have been averted, though Vauban, over a half-
century earlier, had cried that the financial system was so
corrupt that not even the angels in heaven could amend it.
Against Turgot were ranged the Queen, the courtiers, the
Parlements, and the whole gamut of *privilégiés*; they all had
good reason to hate reform and Louis XVI yielded to their
clamour for Turgot's dismissal.

Necker, Calonne, and Brienne followed in turn. No French
finance minister has ever had half of Necker's popularity. He
was hailed as a genius, but rarely, if ever, has public confidence been more misplaced. Necker was a man of unbounded
ambition and egoism. As for financial policy, he had none. He
certainly effected a few reforms along lines indicated by his
predecessors, but he refused to sacrifice his popularity by raising
by taxation the money necessary to meet current liabilities. To
pay for the American War, his plan was to borrow, always to
borrow, at no matter what rate of interest. So attractive, in
fact, were his loan-issues that even foreigners subscribed.
His ministry was a veritable rake's progress. His "financial
statements," which influenced public opinion so largely in his
own day, contain many inaccuracies, and modern criticism has
shown that his figures are quite unreliable. Yet so great was
his popularity that he probably could have raised all the taxes
necessary to place the nation's finance on a sound basis, but he
preferred to mortgage the future so that he could remain in
office, and by so doing helped to force on the Revolution.
After his downfall Calonne and Brienne attempted reforms,
but the day had passed for partial measures to be effective.
Provincial assemblies had for some time been discussing the
situation and here and there had actually been putting into
practice better methods of taxation, but what was required was
not merely local improvements, but something far wider in
scope, an equitable, truly national, financial system. It needed
a national upheaval to overcome the hosts of privilege and the
appalling waste of the Court: that upheaval came in 1789.

BIBLIOGRAPHY

R. Stourm, *Bibliographie historique des finances de la France au dix-huitième siècle*, 1895; *Les finances de l'ancien régime*, 1885. L. Bouchard, *Système financière de l'ancienne monarchie*, 1891. Léon Say, *Dictionnaire des finances*, 1889–1894. M. Marion, *Histoire financière de la France depuis 1715*, 1914; *Les impôts directs sous l'ancien régime*, 1910. L. de la Vergne, *Les Économistes français du xviii⁰ siècle*, 1870. C. Gomel, *Les causes financières de la Révolution*, 1892–3.

Of the abundant contemporary literature, the following may be cited as of special interest:

Sully, *Œconomies Royales*. Colbert, *Lettres, Instructions et Mémoires*, ed. Clément, 7 vols. 1861–1863.
Boisguilbert, *Détail de la France*, 1697; *Le Factum de la France*, 1707. Vauban, *Projet d'une Dîme royale*, 1707. G.-F. Le Trosne, *De l'administration provinciale et de la réforme de l'impôt*, 1779. Turgot, *Œuvres*. 9 vols. 1808–1811. J. Law, *Considérations sur le numéraire et le commerce*, etc. All these are reprinted by E. Daire in *Économistes-financiers du xviii⁰ siècle*, 1842–1846.
Necker, *Compte rendu présenté au roi*, 1781.

Abundant material for original research exists at Paris in the *Archives nationales* and the *Bibliothèque nationale*, whilst many of the Departmental Archives contain equally valuable documents.

There is no work in the English language on the general history of French finance, but A. J. Sargent's *Economic Policy of Colbert*, 1899, and A. McF. Davis' *Historical Study of Law's System*, Boston, 1887, deal with important periods.

CHAPTER VI

LAW

THE term *Droit*, which is difficult to translate, has various meanings in French. It denotes (1) the whole body of laws, whether *written* or *customary* (*objective law*); (2) the *science* of law, which considers these laws in their historical aspect; (3) the *art* of law, which makes practical use of them; and finally (4) the power, with which from some particular point of view some definite person is invested by law (*right*). Taken in the first sense, which is here paramount, law is the term applied to the whole body of legislation publicly enacted with some human sanction, regulating all the manifestations of human activity in every rank of social life. Hence everything which appertains to public or private life is subject to law—government, administration, family life, property, labour, industry, and commerce. But as life—whether it be political, domestic, or economic—is continually changing, it follows that law—the rule of life—is also, like life, constantly being modified.

The history of French law from the Renaissance to our own times is consequently bound up with the history of France itself. For many centuries the aim of both was unity; of France under the guidance of the King, of French law under the guidance of the King's legal advisers, the "jurists." Having made use of Roman law to build up for the King of France a power independent of Pope or Emperor, the jurists skilfully enabled the King's courts gradually to prevail over those of the nobles, and gave to the royal ordinances, which were applicable to the whole of France, priority over the variations of local laws. The monarchy had striven to give to France a unity, supported but limited by the Church, based on right divine, but without a constitution to protect the individual, the King's subject, from the caprices of arbitrary government. This unity was assured to the country by the Revolution, which had shaken off all religious influence, on a basis of national sovereignty, after it had solemnly declared that the source of authority lies in the will of majorities, and that the limitations of that authority are in the natural and inalienable rights of the man and the citizen. Legality took the place of arbitrariness, liberty that of authority, and equality that of hierarchy. The diversities arising from the arbitrary rule of an authority superior to the nation were henceforth succeeded by the unity caused by the regularity of an authority derived from the nation and limited by Nature. The numerous excrescences of a parasitic legislation, encumbered with puny, dead, and dying branches, were uprooted. On the cleared space there sprang up a sturdy growth of new institutions, vigorous with liberty and equality. Much fresh and elaborate legislation came into being which, too systematic, exaggerated, and hasty, over-shot the mark. A new era began with the Consulate and the Empire—that of adjustment; a process which was retarded in political affairs by the mild relaxations of the Empire and the belated reaction of the Restoration, but which was fairly rapid and steady as regards non-political legislation. It was recorded in Codes which spread throughout Europe almost as quickly as they were promulgated, and which were more lasting than the Emperor's victories, for they did not retire with his armies. If French law ceased to be a system of political and civil liberty, yet under all the various forms of government it remained a system of economic liberty and domestic equality. Since the opening of the 19th century, it has been the persistent tendency of French law, the evolution of which from the very beginning and in its broad lines has never ceased to be the expression of the national genius, to restrain excess of power by the Constitution and to compel the State to observe the law by the exercise of an independent justice. French public law being thus re-established on a sure foundation, the enactments of the Napoleonic *Codes et Lois* have been gradually brought into harmony with the evolution of a society which, inspired by the gentleness of human pity and by a great effort at solidarity, increasingly seeks after absolute justice.

§ I. THE ANCIEN RÉGIME

Public Law

From the 15th to the 18th century France was tending towards unity, in absolute ignorance of equality, and without in any way attaining either political liberty, whereby the individual shares in the exercise of government, or civil liberty, that bundle of indispensable rights which is expressly guaranteed against the arbitrary abuse of power.

Political Liberty. The France of old days had certain fundamental laws: interdiction of any hereditary division of the kingdom, which was transmitted from male to male in order of primogeniture, to the exclusion, not only of women, but of heirs in the female line (nullity of the Treaty of May 21, 1421; Edict of 1717); inalienability of the Crown dominions (Edict of Moulins, 1566); independence of the temporal power as regards the spiritual power (Declaration of the Clergy, March 16, 1682, drawn up by Bossuet, and proclaimed a law of the State by the Edict of March 23, 1682). But these were laws which contained no safeguards either for the nation, or the individual; France had "fundamental laws," but she was in need of a constitution.

The King, in his conflict with the rival influence of the nobles, frequently sought the support of the nation. He applied to the States-General (elected by the three orders—nobles, clergy, and third estate—and united in the chief town of the territorial division, the bailiwick, in a single assembly) for *aide* and counsel (in old French *aide* means a tax). But although the assent of the States-General was necessary for the imposition of a new fiscal charge, it was not requisite for the continuance of previously established taxation. At Tours in 1484 the States-General expressed views which surprised the King; they declared that the monarchy was a "dignity," and not a hereditary right; that the people included all the subjects of the King, and that the States-General had a right to vote the taxes and to meet at regular intervals. Alarmed at this attitude, the King thereafter was reluctant to summons the States-General; they were only assembled at long intervals (1506, 1560, 1576, 1588, 1614), when they gave expression to some interesting grievances in their *cahiers*, which resulted in useful legislation. After 1614 they were not convoked again till 1789. Even the Assemblies of Notables,

composed of representatives of the three orders directly chosen
by the monarchy, were not summoned between 1626 and 1786,
although the King preferred to have recourse to them, since they
were appointed by him. Finally in the provinces recently united
to the Crown there were still maintained the Provincial Estates,
which, in their own province, had the same rights as the States-
General. But the King suppressed them, except at the extremi-
ties of the kingdom, and controlled them through his own officers,
namely the intendants of Justice, Police, and Finance, who were
utilised by Richelieu and organised by the Code Michaut, serving
their purpose until 1789.

From an administrative point of view the municipal organisation established under the feudal system was no more capable
of resisting royal authority than the seigniorial organisation.
The intendants supervised the administration alike of the towns
and of the "communities of inhabitants"; these might not
go to law without the intendant's authorisation; an authorisation from the King was necessary if they wished to borrow, sell,
or buy. On the other hand municipal officers were no longer
freely elected by the towns; they were appointed by the intendants or elected under their direct influence. The municipal organisation of 1784 was not extended to the country
districts.

On the other hand the Church threatened to limit the royal
power. The Clergy formed a privileged order, possessed great
estates, and preserved their own jurisdiction, which was recognised by the State. Finally, secular law, accepting some of
the regulations of canon law, inflicted civil death upon members
of religious communities. But, in virtue of the universal *royal
protection* which the King claimed over the churches and religious houses of the kingdom, any action brought against the
Church which touched her property came within the province
of the temporal courts, and not under ecclesiastical jurisdiction;
moreover, ecclesiastical property was subject to the same taxation as the other estates in the kingdom, amongst which was the
tenth which the King demanded from the Assemblies of the
Clergy, especially after the Concordat of Leo X and Francis I
in 1516. After the Contract of Poissy (1561) the Clergy, like the
Pays d'États, but more freely and more completely, voted and

sanctioned the taxation for which they were liable, and decided disputed claims as to its imposition. Originally the ecclesiastical courts were competent to try the clergy; but gradually the royal judges divested them of this right, either when the crime was a very serious one (privileged cases) or when the matter dealt with an ecclesiastical benefice presented by the King. The jurisdiction of the Church over the laity from the threefold point of view of marriage, wills, and misdemeanours quickly disappeared before the royal jurisdiction (Ordinance of Villers-Cotterets, 1539; Edict of 1695). Finally the rights, laws, and franchises of the Gallican Church (Royal Declaration of 1682) laid down three principles: (1) the temporal power is entirely distinct from, and independent of, the spiritual power, (2) the Pope has no absolute authority over the French clergy as regards discipline and temporal matters, (3) the King has legitimate authority as to discipline and temporal matters over the Church of France; councils may not meet there without the permission of the King, who has the right of supervision over associations and religious communities, with power to suppress and forbid them when he considers them dangerous, and, in order to give effectual force to his regulations, to appeal to a secular court.

Those of the King's councillors, who, having studied Roman law (*leges*), had received the name of "legists" (*legistae*), sought in the Roman legislation the model of an absolute monarchy, devoid of liberty, but perfectly centralised. The ruler is in possession of sovereign power as analysed by Jean Bodin in his *Six Livres de la République* (1576). The sovereign has no superior. Sovereignty, which by its nature is indivisible, appertains to the King alone. In vain a school of jurists—the *Monarchomachi*—which included François Hotman, the author of the *Franco-Gallia* (1573), sought to limit the royal power by making the French monarchy a representative one, subject to the authority of the law; Bodin's views prevailed. In vain the States-General tried to assert themselves; they were no longer summoned. In vain Fénelon and Saint-Simon demanded the reinstatement of the Provincial Estates; it was not until the days of Turgot and Necker that a vast scheme of elected municipal and provincial assemblies made its appearance; and then it was an expression of local rather than of political feeling. It mattered little that

sovereignty allowed no rights either to the nation or to the
individual. The main point was that it strengthened the royal
power so as to enable it to crush all rival powers.

Civil Liberty. Supported by the Roman theory of sovereignty,
the King acknowledged no other claimant to the attributes of
absolute power in the kingdom. War, taxation, and justice, the
consequences of sovereignty, all were to be in the King's hands
alone. At the end of the 15th century private warfare ceased. After
the time of Charles VI no one could without *lèse-majesté* question
the King's right to impose taxation, for Roman law conceded it exclusively to the Emperor. New taxes having once been voted by
the States-General or the Provincial Estates, custom transformed
them from provisional to permanent measures. Indeed, under
Louis XIV the monarchy imposed taxation on its sole authority; the seigniorial *taille* was replaced by the royal *taille*, subject
to regulations which differed in the *Pays d'États* (Brittany, Burgundy, Languedoc, and Provence) and the *Pays d'élection*; there
followed later the capitation-tax (1695) and the *dixième* (1710–
1717), converted after 1749 into the *vingtième*. Besides these there
was the salt-tax (a tax on consumption), while the seigniorial
taxes became reduced to tolls, market-dues, and escheatage, and
to the legal costs and other dues levied when feudal property
changed hands. Thirdly, supported by Roman law, the King
declared himself the supreme dispenser of justice. He established in the 13th century the *Parlement* of Paris, a judicial body
detached from the *Curia Regis*, which was rendered necessary
by the increase of business and the complexity of law; he
created and placed above the provosts and petty bailiffs, who
were inferior magistrates, the jurisdiction of the high bailiffs
of the north and the seneschals of the south (pending the appointment of Presidial Courts by Henry II); he reduced the seigniorial
courts to a subordinate position, thanks to the Roman institution
of Appeal, which was unknown in feudal law; finally, as the
source of all justice, he claimed the right to try a case in his
own courts, when royal interests were involved (royal cases),
these interests, however, being bound up with the "common
weal of the kingdom." But, in delegating the exercise of justice
to his courts, the King did not part with the rights; he reserved
them. Hence a whole chain of consequences; the claim for

cognisance by the King's Council, notwithstanding protests by *Parlement*; trial by commissioners, a special court of law, always appointed in political cases, in spite of lively objections by the States-General; the *proposition d'erreur*, which enabled the decisions of the Supreme Courts to be set aside and suppressed by causing their decrees to be contested before the "Masters of Requests" of the King's household (this was the origin of the power of appeal to the King's Council, which was established in the 17th century to deal with violations of ordinances and customs); the *lettres de grâce* used in penal matters to remit or modify a sentence; the *lettres de justice*, applied in civil matters to give rights to suitors which were recognised by Roman law but not by the customary law; and finally, an extreme inference from reserved rights, the *lettres de cachet*, letters from the King—not subject like others to the control of the Chancellor, but simply invested with the King's seal—which ordered imprisonment without trial and excited protests from the States-General, *Parlements*, and public opinion.

Criminal cases were tried secretly in the absence of the accused; the judge was bound to accept proofs, not according to his conscience, but by a narrow and artificial system of legal evidence; the testimony of two witnesses was taken as certain proof, whatever might be the innermost conviction of the judge. The object of a trial was rather to establish the guilt of the accused, who was not allowed an advocate, than to elicit the truth. Punishments were arbitrary and cruel; when life was forfeit, property was forfeit; the death penalty was accompanied and aggravated by torture—quartering, the stake, the wheel. The galleys were particularly brutal. There was neither civil liberty, nor even humanity; the royal penal laws had to be severe that the royal peace might be secure. The criminal legislation of 1670, influenced by Pussort, is remarkable for harshness and inflexibility.

As yet the guarantee arising from a divided authority, which is a safeguard against tyranny, as pointed out by Montesquieu in his *Esprit des Lois* (II, iv), did not exist. The *Parlements*, which were supreme courts entrusted with the administration of justice, shared in the legislative power by means of the registration of ordinances. From this they deduced the right of remonstrance, which forced the King to issue *lettres de jussion* to break down

their resistance, and, if they still persisted, to have recourse to a
lit de justice, a solemn session which he personally attended to
enforce his will. Moreover by the *arrêts de réglement* they shared
in the administration of the kingdom; no distinction was made
between police and justice. Under the Supreme Courts, the
royal judges, provosts, bailiffs, and seneschals, were the administrators, to whom the King granted jurisdiction. The chief
agents of the royal government, the intendants, could sit in all
the royal courts of their district, even the Presidial Courts and
Parlements, except that of Paris, and preside over them. In
spite of the existence of the *Cours des Aides*, which dealt with
disputed taxes, claims relating to the *dixième* and the *vingtième*
were assigned to the intendants. In Alsace, where these courts
never existed, all disputed claims as to taxation were in their
hands.

If the judge was irremovable and consequently independent,
it was an accidental security which those amenable to justice
owed to the purchase of offices. Nevertheless the municipal
spirit preserved liberty intact. An edict of 1563, displaying
the germ of a principle in the regulation of fairs, created a
special body of judges, elected by the merchants, to try commercial cases. Commerce and industry, at first defended by the
corporations of masters and wardens, were later oppressed by
them; the edict of 1776, for which Turgot was responsible, attempted to free them, but without success.

At the close of the *ancien régime*, France, with a few unimportant exceptions, enjoyed neither political nor civil liberty.

Nor did she know the meaning of equality; there were in the
nation "Orders," that is to say, a hierarchy. The nobles expiated
their crimes on the scaffold, the common people by hanging; the
nobles were amenable in the first instance to the courts of the
bailiwick in civil matters; in criminal cases nobles and clerks
were amenable only to Parliament. In the States-General, when
the Third Estate addressed the King, its spokesman knelt; those
of the clergy and nobles stood. Ecclesiastics and nobles were
exempted from the principal direct tax; like the seigniorial
taille, the royal *taille* only affected the non-nobles and the serfs;
although the capitation tax should have been levied on all subjects of whatever quality and condition, the clergy escaped it

altogether, and the nobles in part. The nobles refused to make the return necessary for the *vingtième*, a universal tax on income; the salt-tax should have been imposed alike on all, nobles, clerks, or non-nobles, but certain provinces were exempt, the *pays rédimés*. Thus in ancient France, there was no political freedom, but royal power; no civil liberty, but arbitrary authority; no equality, but inequality.

To eradicate the last vestiges of feudalism so as to establish direct royal authority over the people and to create French unity, such was the goal aimed at by the monarchy. Everything was subordinated to unity. And yet, just as feudalism was not yet entirely destroyed, so unity, for which the monarchy strove, was not completely attained; from the administrative point of view, because of the difference between the *Pays d'États* and the *Pays d'élections*; from the judicial point of view because of the number of supreme courts—*Parlements* of Toulouse (1430), Bordeaux (1460), Dijon (1477), Rennes (16th century), Metz, Besançon, Tournai (17th century), Rouen, Nancy, Pau (18th century); from the point of view of private law, because of the great division of the kingdom into provinces in which the customary law obtained and those in which the written law obtained.

Private Law

The great judicial division of the kingdom, starting from the west, followed the northern boundaries of Saintonge, Perigord, and Limousin and ended at the district of Gex, leaving out almost the whole of Auvergne, but including Forez, Lyonnais, Mâconnais, and Bresse. To the north of this line the provinces were *pays de coutume*, to the south *pays de droit écrit*—with a few isolated districts, such as Alsace in the zone of customary law. On both sides Roman law was applied, and customs were prevalent. Nevertheless the systems differed greatly. In the provinces of written law, Roman law was the common and general law; in the others, where the monarchy had been careful to have the unwritten laws officially reduced to writing (Ordinances of Montils-lès-Tours, 1453), the common law of Paris (1510), broadly interpreted by a jurist of great capacity with a powerful and daring mind, Charles Dumoulin (1500–1566), was gradually superseding all others. Its regulations were developed by Guy-Coquille (16th century), Loyseau, Lebrun, and Ricard (17th century). In 1770 Bourjon tried to unify the unwritten law on the basis of the Parisian form under the significant title of *Le Droit commun de la France et la Coutume de Paris*. But written law was unfavourable to the civil unity of the kingdom.

Inspired by Colbert, Louis XIV issued Ordinances which were really Codes; in 1667 on civil procedure; in 1669 on woods and forests; in 1670 on criminal procedure; in 1673 on commerce by land; and in 1681 on the navy. But these were texts of public law, except for commerce, where community of practice had caused a spontaneous growth of common law on land for the fairs or markets; at sea in *Le Consulat de la Mer*, *Les Règles d'Oléron*, and *Le Guidon de la Mer*.

However great was the tendency of private law towards unity so as to avoid conflicting legislation in home affairs, mixed questions, raised by the statutes and resolved by Dumoulin according to the nature of legal analogy, by D'Argentré with a leaning to territorial law, provoked fresh controversies and fresh conflicts. In such matters France did not dare to interfere until the time of Louis XV, and then only on a very few points by three Ordinances, for which D'Aguesseau was responsible—on donations (1731), wills (1735), and entails (1737).

Nevertheless amidst the persistent variety of legislation some common features became apparent. All that part of private law which impinged on public law was the same for the whole kingdom, but not that relating to individuals and estates. As a result of the essentially unequal political condition of individuals there existed innumerable civil inequalities. Any one born out of the kingdom, *alibi natus*, or, by contraction, *aubain*, lived a freeman and died a serf. The *garde noble* differed from the *garde bourgeoise* in having a wider application; the survivor of a husband and wife who were noble had a right to a *préciput*; the inheritance of a noble was regulated after a different manner from that of a non-noble. The King abolished servitude on the Crown-lands (1779), but dared not suppress it on seigniorial properties. Feudal tenures, like individuals, were noble, non-noble, or servile. Other tenures were created after the pattern of the feudal ones; as for instance the tenure by perpetual lease, where the tenant possessed a real and inalienable right to the land, and the tenure where the lessor reserved a rent—a long lease with a ground rent and the right of planting. Non-feudal tenures might be established on every kind of land; feudal tenures only on noble land (a fief), or on free land (*alleu*). Burdens on non-feudal lands might be extinguished by prescription; burdens on feudal lands could not. Besides feudalism, which influenced the condition of persons and estates, the Church, against which the State defended itself by the edict of 1749, limiting the amount of property which could be alienated from descendants (*mortmain*), had an important influence on the condition of persons. The monks, united in communities, enjoyed many social and political advantages, but they were individually deprived of civil life; their *profession* imposed on them a kind of *civil* death; they could neither marry, nor receive legacies, nor succeed to their parents, nor make a will; if they did not dispose of their property before taking their vows, their next-of-kin succeeded them as though they were really dead. Difference of religion troubled or destroyed the civil life of non-Catholics. In the heart of France Jews held a position somewhat akin to that of serfs. After the Revocation of the Edict of Nantes in 1685 all legislation was based on the fiction that in the kingdom there were now only Catholics. All the King's subjects were bound to enter their marriages and the birth of their children in registers of civil condition kept by Catholic priests; marriage, for all, was to be a permanent indissoluble union; every one was to be brought up in the Catholic faith. Consequently Protestants were deprived of civil rights; their marriages were irregular, their children were bastards deprived of all right to their inheritance, whom the King brought up in his own faith because he stood in place of a father; divorce, which their religion allowed in certain cases, was forbidden by law. For them there was no personal liberty, no paternal power, no property, until the time when the edict of 1787, without permitting them the free exercise of religion, restored to them a civil condition.

In a monarchy of which the principle is the honour and greatness of the family, on which rests the honour and greatness of the State, the individual is of no account, but disappears before the family, to which he is sacrificed according to the all-powerful will of its head. For, in the King's eyes, the family is like another kingdom, which must not be dismembered, but increased; a body, whose stability must not be injured by any inferior admixture. Marriage is the foundation of the family, and the family is of so much importance to the State, especially a monarchical one, that the King took care to maintain its power, by placing the establishment of the new family under the joint control of the old family. In the Middle Ages the King left the regulation of marriage to the Church. But the wish to encourage morality by facilitating marriage caused the Church, in this instance, to support the individual against the family. The King intervened to take the part of the family against the individual. He declared, by means of his jurists, that marriage was not merely a sacrament subject to canon law, but a contract subject to civil law. Although they did not recognise the binding force of the provisions of the Council of Trent (1563) about the formalities of marriage, the King adapted its essential rules to his own use (publication of banns; presence of the parish priest; solemn witness to the exchange of vows, in accordance with the Council of Trent, but following the Gallican form, which was the real foundation of the marriage ceremony). The Church allowed marriage without the consent of the parents. The King, by the Ordinances of Blois (1629 and 1639), required the consent of both parents, and, failing these, of grandparents; if this were dispensed with, there was abduction, regarded by royal jurisdiction as akin to rape, and nullity of marriage, not to mention the disinheritance of the child who had been guilty of want of respect to his or her parents.

In a monarchy which did not allow women to succeed to the throne, it was natural that even a single woman was debarred from managing a business for any one. In a monarchy where the sovereign was absolute, the husband in married life necessarily effaced the personal competency of his wife by his conjugal authority. In the interest of the family she was not allowed to be surety for her husband, nor to surrender in his favour the *hypothèque* (a kind of mortgage) which secured her inalienable dowry. In the provinces of customary law, with the exception of Normandy, it was otherwise; here mercantile influence came into play, and, having created communal liberties, associated the wife with the

business activities of the husband. Though the married couple
retained their own property, as a result of the influence of the
family, they possessed a common fortune, which was constantly
increased by their work and their savings; this was the *régime
de la communauté*, established as soon as the customary law was
officially codified, and subject to modification, although, after
the 16th century, in the interests of the family and of third
persons it was impossible to modify a settlement made at the
time of marriage. By the written law, which was more in
sympathy with the monarchical spirit than the customary law,
within which germinated those principles of equality and liberty
which were manifested later in political law under the Revolution, the son was placed, as in Roman law, under the absolute
power of his father. While in the customary law "paternal power
had no place," in the written law the *patria potestas* remained the
same as in the code of Justinian; in the provinces of customary
law, domestic authority belonged both to father and mother,
was exercised in the interest of the children, and was only a
kind of "natural guardianship"; in the provinces of written
law, paternal authority sprang, as in Roman law, not from marriage, but from relationship in the male line (agnation), and
women were excluded. The sons of the family remained indefinitely in tutelage with their children until the death of the
head of the family; or until their formal emancipation. They
could neither make a will, nor borrow money, nor be a valid
security for any reason whatever. They possessed no sort of property, except what they earned by their personal efforts (*pécule*);
any property which came to them otherwise (*biens adventices*)
was administered and enjoyed by their father. The fear of being
injured as regarded the paternal inheritance, or even in some
cases disinherited, placed them in their father's power and
absolutely destroyed their liberty.

Both in the provinces of customary law and in those of written
law bastards were considered by morality and by law as re-
probates. Even if they were recognised by their father, they
remained in their position of inferiority, unless they were raised
from it by the legitimation which followed the marriage of their
parents. Investigation as to paternity was allowed, but its only
result was to obtain the costs of confinement for the mother and

aliment for the child. Bastards could neither inherit from any one, nor bequeath anything; their property lapsed—like flotsam —to the Crown.

In a juridical conception, in which the family played so great a part, succession was arranged in such a manner as to insure the integrity of the inheritance. In the provinces of written law the *patria potestas* resulted in the right of the head of the family to dispose freely of his property; heirs were appointed by his will, according to his pleasure; and, although the freedom of bequest was restricted in certain particulars, this was only to prevent abuses. Children were bound to receive their legal share, a third or a half of the paternal fortune; the father could dispose of the remainder as he chose, giving or bequeathing it to relatives, or to strangers, or using it to the advantage of *one* only of his children. In customary law, which preserved traces of its Germanic origin, the heirs were fixed by law. Here the individual, even its head, was of no importance compared with the family, which was the real and perpetual owner, and which had to be protected in itself and in the person of each of its members. In contradistinction to written law, which, owing to the favour with which a will was regarded, tended more and more towards inequality and the concentration of property, in perfect agreement with monarchical principles, customary law tended towards equality and the division of property among the members of the whole family. Written law, inclined to generalise like the Roman law from which it was derived, regarded the inheritance as a single whole, which came under the same regulations. Customary law, more concrete, more specialised, recognised various kinds of inheritance; real estate, acquired property, personal property; three differing inheritances in one. Inherited property received from ancestors must remain in the family, while the individual might dispose more freely of land which he had acquired by his work and his economy, and of personal property, which in those days did not possess great value (*res mobilis, res vilis*). For the protection of the family and above all of the children, the customary law created the reserve of four-fifths of personal possessions, applicable to family property, adding to it the Roman *légitime* of one-half the property of the deceased, while the power of favouring one child was forbidden. Finally,

there came in a distinct system of inheritance for the possessors
of noble lands; it was, like the customary system, founded on
the law, but, like the Roman system, it tended to inequality and
the concentration of property. Having originated in military
and political conditions which no longer existed, it was maintained and fortified by aristocratic pride. Although daughters
were excluded from succession, and the eldest son received all
or almost all the inheritance, it was no longer in order to render
to the sovereign lord the costly military service; it was to shed
on the family a glory and splendour hitherto unknown. And
if, to a daily increasing extent, in the families of the nobles and
even of the rich *bourgeois*, entails and settlements by contracts
were increasing the inequalities of inheritance and concentrating
ancestral fortunes in one man's hands, it was in order to blason
the greatness of the house in the person of its head.

Until the close of the *ancien régime* the nation actually lived
on the land and for the land. Laws mostly relate to the family
and to property. Economic relations, dealing with personal
estate, hold only a secondary place in legislation as in society.
Canon law, which forbade loans on interest, was evaded by
the settlement of ground rents, which brought the economic relation of personal property into the category of landed property.
Bills of exchange, which are a commercial instrument, were developed by degrees in the markets, fairs, and then in the large
towns, but were not negotiable between one town and another.
Merchants had their special judges. The Ordinance of 1563,
framed by Michel de l'Hospital, established the jurisdiction of the
judges and consuls of Paris, for "the public weal and the lessening of cost, and for divers other merchants, who should deal with
each other in good faith, without being bound by the subtleties
of laws and ordinances." In the Ordinance of March 1673,
Louis XIV, after recalling his efforts to make commerce flourish
in his kingdom, declared that he considered it necessary to draw
up regulations "capable of ensuring against fraud those who
buy and sell in good faith and of guarding against the obstacles
which keep them from their employment owing to the law's
delays." In this Ordinance bills of exchange are developed,
while bankruptcy leaves much to be desired.

At the close of the *ancien régime*, the juridical system derived

from many sources, and varying according to districts, individuals, and estates, was tending towards unity. Colbert,
D'Aguesseau strove after it; the philosophers, Voltaire, Diderot,
and Linguet claimed it; Bourjon, like his predecessor Dumoulin,
sought to deduce the common law of France from the custom
of Paris. In 1789 the *cahiers* of the States-General demanded
the unification of civil legislation. But France is an aggregation
of nationalities. The survival of feudalism, the maintenance of
the power of the Church, the persistence of various nationalities
in the same kingdom, led to the retention of many privileges
and to a confusion favourable to social inequality, and incompatible with the establishment of national unity. To attain
national unity, it was necessary to discard the differences which
kept back the monarchy, break with the Church, which was still
a State within the State, and blend all the provinces, even the
most distant ones, into one nation. Not only had royalty, imbued with absolutism, inequality, and severity, failed to give
to France laws of liberty, equality, and humanity, under a
limited monarchy, but in spite of all its efforts, it had not succeeded in giving her unity, either from the political, or civil
point of view, for unity cannot be attained without liberty and
equality. But all these, all alike desirable, were to spring up
simultaneously, as soon as the King, too feeble an instrument
of unity, was replaced by the Nation.

§ II. THE REVOLUTION

Public Law

The Revolution hailed the Nation as Sovereign. The Nation
is the collective body of men who in the State exercise the will
of the people. In contrast to the former Sovereign, the King,
the new Sovereign, the People, found in the very origin of its
power the principle limiting that power. "The aim of every
political association is the preservation of the natural and indefeasible rights of Man; these rights are liberty, property..."
(*Declaration of the rights of man and the citizen*, August 26, 1789,
art. 2). If "the law is the expression of the general will" (*ibid.*
art. 6), it is "on the condition of respecting the fundamental
rights of man." "Any society in which rights are not assured

has no constitution" (*ibid.* art. 16). Henceforth in France there was an end of government at any one's good will and pleasure; for "government by police," i.e. by arbitrary procedure, was substituted government by law (*Rechtstaat*), in which authority proceeded only from the law and was only exercised within the bounds set by the Constitution. Thus in the first three Constitutions (September 3–14, 1791; June 24, 1793; August 22, 1795) are laid down the two fundamental bases of the new public legislation: on one side, political liberty, i.e. the participation of the citizen in the exercise of power; on the other side, civil liberty, i.e. the limitation of the sovereign power by the natural and indefeasible Rights of Man.

Political Liberty. The Constitution of September 3–14, 1791, which retained the King as the first official of the kingdom, the Constitution of June 24, 1793 (never put into force), which appointed a council of twenty-four members invested with executive power, and finally the Constitution of 5 Fructidor, year III (August 22, 1795), which created a Directory of five members, all assigned only a subsidiary part to the executive as opposed to a legislative body consisting of a single Assembly in 1791 and 1793; and in the year III, of two Chambers (the Ancients and the Five Hundred). Ministers had no authority under any of these Constitutions; they sank soon to the position of agents of secondary importance, who were appointed and dismissed at the will and pleasure of the executive without any reference to Parliament. There was no collaboration between the two powers—the legislative and the executive. The former very soon gained the ascendancy over the latter; the Convention became all-powerful, and by the Constitution of the year III the executive was powerless in the face of assemblies which were only overthrown by the *coup d'état* of Brumaire because of their disagreement.

France, which was a Monarchy until 1792, and subsequently a Republic, did not, under these successive Constitutions, cease to be a nation in which authority under all its forms was derived from the people. By the Constitution of 1791, all citizens of over twenty-five years, who had been domiciled in the canton for six months, and who paid in direct taxes a sum equal to the value of three days' work, had a vote and were named *citoyens actifs*. They met

in the chief place of each canton in *Assemblées Primaires* to
nominate to the second grade, according to particular conditions
of taxation and property, those electors who, collected in *Assem-
bleés Electorales*, selected the deputies, administrators, and judges.
In place of the old divisions of France—governments and generalities—there came into being one single and identical division,
adapted to all requirements, the department (Decree of December 22, 1789), itself divided into districts by the Constitution
of 1791, and into cantons by that of 1795. The Constitutions of
1791 and 1795 entrusted the administration of the departments
and their subdivisions to bodies elected by the electoral assemblies, which the executive could neither appoint nor dismiss, but
only suspend individually after appeal to the Legislative Body.

Judicial unity was, like administrative unity, founded on the
basis of the national sovereignty; the purchase of offices was
abolished and the judges were elected by those amenable to the
courts (Law of August 16, 1790); the "active citizen" and the
electoral assemblies nominated them; the King was bound to
appoint them. The lowest grade of the judicial hierarchy, the
juge de paix, who tried petty cases and arbitrated in important
ones, was elected for two years by the *Assemblée Primaire* of
the canton; he was moreover assisted by four Notables selected
by the same assembly from among the active citizens of each
municipality. Above these judges was the Court of Appeal
corresponding to the wider electoral division, the district (1791);
it was composed of five judges, elected by the electoral assembly
of the district, until 1795, when, districts being abolished, two
departmental courts, one civil, the other criminal, were established, consisting of judges elected every five years; while the
police-courts, of which there were at least three to each department, were presided over by the judges of the civil court and
justices of the peace, and were thus also elected. Finally, higher
still, was the *Cour de Cassation*, created (Decree of November 27 and December 1, 1790) in close relation to the Legislative Body, so as to preserve the unity of legislation, and composed of members elected for four years by the electoral assemblies of the departments. Moreover, it was not merely through
their elected representatives that the citizens participated in the
administration of criminal law, but directly and personally by

serving on the grand jury or the common jury (Law of September 16–29, 1791); for the twofold British protection of
liberty—the grand jury and the common jury—now passed into
the French judicial system. Similarly the National Supreme
Court, formed to try all the crimes and misdemeanours in
which the Legislative Body was prosecutor, was not only composed of four Grand Judges chosen by lot from the members of
the *Cour de Cassation*, but of a jury of twenty-four grand
jurors.

Civil Liberty. The first French constitutions recapitulated
all the declarations of the Rights of Man and of the citizen;
these declarations, inspired by those of the United States of
America, not only assured political liberty, as demanded by
Rousseau in his *Contrat Social*, but also civil liberty, i.e. those
rights which appertain to man as man, and, contrary to Rousseau's views, limit the power of the general will, i.e. of the law,
the instrument of the majority.

The ancient maxim "All punishments are arbitrary in the
kingdom of France" was, in the Declaration of 1789, replaced
by the new axiom "No man may be punished except by virtue
of a law established and promulgated previous to the crime and
legally applied" (art. 8). Every man was presumed to be innocent
until he was found guilty. All procedure was to be public and oral
from the examination onwards (Decree of September 16–29,
1791); it ensured complete liberty to the defence; legal proofs
were to yield to moral proofs; the law only required the jurors
to give expression to their positive conviction. The Penal Code
of the Constituent Assembly (September 25, 1791) enumerated
and limited punishable acts and the corresponding penalties.
Under the Convention the *Code des délits et des peines* of 3 Brumaire, year IV, drawn up by Cambacérès and Merlin, was inspired
by the system of 1791, which it regulated and defined; the safeguards granted to the defence were multiplied, all formalities
minutely described, and it was declared that questions put to
the jury were to be exactly framed so as to require the answer,
yes or no.

In the administrative order the individual was protected
against arbitrary proceedings. Not only did he elect the administration, but he could appeal against its acts to the King,

to the councillors, or to the ministers, who decided the question subject to the right of appeal to the Legislative Body.

But this liberty was granted only to the individual. The Revolution, fearing excess of corporate power, denied it to communities (Chapelier Law of 1791). The civil liberties promised by the early Declaration of Rights were purely individual; none of them possessed any collective character; the wider liberties of freedom of assembly, association, and education were not yet conceded; only the primary steps, personal liberty (*habeas corpus*), sanctity of the home, liberty of conscience and worship, liberty of labour, appear in the Declarations. To make a sure foundation for liberty, it must be established on property, which by the Declarations was stated to be one of the Rights of Man; hence, property was freed from all the restrictions with which it had been surrounded by the old laws. The feudal system was abolished; serfdom was suppressed; every man became free as soon as he trod the soil of France (Decree of September 22, 1791). The Convention (Decree of 16 Pluviôse, year II) abolished slavery in the colonies and conferred all the rights of a French citizen on the emancipated negroes.

Political equality. Equality was included among the Rights of Man. It was placed after liberty in the Declaration of Rights in 1789, but before it in 1793, and with it formed the fundamental basis of the new laws. Henceforth (Decree of August 26, art. 14) citizens had the right to verify, either personally or by means of representatives, the need for public taxation, to give a free consent to it, to examine the use made of it, and to determine its amount, assessment, recovery, and duration. Henceforth the great principle of "no taxation without representation" was to be applied to the taxes imposed to replace the old indirect taxes (salt-tax, internal customs, *octroi, aides*), of which the land-tax on the partition of property was the basis, as it was also of the various taxes on personal property. Measures were thus taken to make equality the basis of taxation. Similarly as regards the heavier burden of military service; whenever the enlistments on which the regular army depended were found inadequate, the law of 19 Fructidor, year VI, established compulsory military service alike for all, by creating military conscription. Nevertheless political equality was not complete. The

Constitution distinguished between *active citizens*, who had the vote, and *passive citizens*, who had not, because they paid lower taxes. The Constitution of 1795, although it did not demand a property qualification, also debarred wage-earning servants from voting. The Constitution of 1793, which was never applied, was democratic and not *bourgeois*; it established universal suffrage.

Private Law

When the Revolution founded sovereign authority on the Nation One and Indivisible, it necessarily established the principle, to which the monarchy had already tended, of the uniformity of legislation, not only public, but private, throughout France. "There shall be drawn up," said the Constitution of 1791 at the end of its first article, "a Code of civil laws common to the whole kingdom." But the Revolution brought about not only the unification of Civil Law, but its transformation.

In the first place as regards human beings, the philosophical ideas whence it proceeded led to the assimilation, at least from a civil point of view, of the foreigner to the native; "the *droit d'aubaine* was abolished" as contrary to the principle of fraternity, which should bind together all men (August 6, 1790). Then the exclusively lay conception of the State, which led to the suppression of the religious orders (Decree of February 13–19, 1790), and the obvious exaggeration of Gallicanism shown in the civil constitution of the clergy (July 12–August 24, 1790), made the registration of personal status a civil act, and the exceptional legislation passed in 1787 for the Protestants became the common law. This was the logical consequence of the separation of Church and State, and moreover was the best means of securing respect for liberty of conscience (Law of September 20–25, 1792). Finally, the fundamental ideas of liberty and equality which governed the new public laws inspired the constitution of the new legislation as regards the family, property, and contracts.

The Revolution by secularising marriage was able to reject its indissolubility. The philosophers—Montaigne, Montesquieu, Voltaire—had attacked its perpetual character. The Revolution, adopting their views, pronounced marriage to be dissoluble in the name of liberty; "when free to separate, husband and wife will be all the more bound." Divorce, "the source of mutual consideration," was allowed in three cases: for stated causes (madness, desertion, emigration, as well as adultery, slander, and cruelty), by mutual consent, and, on the application of either husband or wife, for incompatibility of temper (Law of September 20, 1792). Mere separation—a false solution—was rejected as contrary to nature and liberty.

Revolutionary legislation, zealous for freedom, limited paternal power, regarding it as a kind of domestic monarchy, as an image of royal despotism. Inspired by the philosophy of the 18th century, the Legislative Assembly abolished perpetual paternal authority, ending only with death or emancipation, such as still existed in the provinces subject to written law. The consent of parents to the marriage of their children now became necessary only up to the age of twenty-one. The right of disinheriting disappeared, and, the disposable share (that part of the estate which might freely be disposed of) having been reduced, the father of a family found himself deprived of any means of a pecuniary nature by which to influence his children. The right of correction, so highly developed under the *ancien régime* that the imprisonment of a son was allowed up to any age, was henceforth, by an application of the idea of liberty, subjected to the decision of a family council. Childless persons could obtain a child by an act of the will, by virtue of adoption—an institution of Roman origin, which appealed to the men of those times, because of the sensibility which it implied in the adopter (Law of 26 Germinal, year II).

The right to property springs from the right to freedom. Property must be free like the individual, or to be more exact, the individual must be free to dispose of his property. The *retrait* (i.e. the right of buying back land sold by its proprietor) of various kinds (seigniorial, by persons of the same lineage, conventional, etc.) was abolished, especially because it threatened to interfere with the sale of the national property confiscated from the *émigrés* (Law of May 13, 1792).

Although the Roman principle of the transfer of property by consent was recognised in dealings between two parties—the result of preference for the principles of the customary law—this transfer could only affect a third party, i.e. others than the contracting parties, by virtue of publication prescribed by the law of

11 Brumaire, year VII, which compelled all acts relating to the transfer of property or of real estate capable of being mort-gaged to be transcribed in a register *ad hoc* kept by a special official, the keeper of mortgages. Invading the realm of contracts, liberty abrogated the old canon law forbidding loans on interest (October 2, 1789), thenceforward depriving the various procedures employed to defeat this prohibition—the settlement of annuities, charges on estates, contingent annui-ties—of most of their utility. Finally zeal for the liberty of the individual led the Constituent Assembly to forbid im-prisonment for debt (March 1793). In the name of equality the civil status of women, at least unmarried ones, became ap-proximated to that of men; the Velléien Senatus-consult, which was in force in the provinces where the written law obtained, did not permit women, whether married or single, to manage a business for another; the Revolution put an end to this disability as regards single women. In the name of equality, the natural child, whom religious and aristocratic pre-judice had reduced to a kind of pariah in the family, was granted the same right as the legitimate child; the privileges of legitimacy seemed to have as little justification as those of nobility. While the Revolution required of natural children that they should prove their filiation by voluntary recognition or notoriety (Law of 11 Brumaire, year II), it placed the natural child not born of adultery on the same plane as regards succession as the legiti-mate offspring (Law of June 4, 1793, and 5–12 Brumaire, year II). On even stronger grounds, in the name of equality, the Revolution was determined to equalise the position of le-gitimate children in the family. Not only was its first care to abolish the privileges of the male, and the right of primogeniture, but by the great law of succession of 17 Nivôse, year II, the Revolution also proclaimed, with retrospective effect to July 14, 1789, that in the devolution of an inheritance, taken as a whole (according to Roman law) without distinction drawn from the origin of the property (as in common law), all children should share alike, while by the regulation enacting that, failing any descendant, the estate must be divided in two equal parts, one for the paternal, the other for the maternal line, property became parcelled out among a great number of people. Thus

from the equality of Man the Revolution deduced the limitation of fortunes. The right of making a will—an act of liberty
contrary to the equality desired by the law—was only recognised
with difficulty, after violent attacks in the Constituent Assembly,
and was then limited to a tenth if the deceased had heirs in
the direct line, and to a sixth if there were collaterals; and this
insignificant amount could not even be assigned either to a
living person, or by will to one of the heirs by virtue of a
special gift (*préciput*).

But although the new legislation was essentially favourable
to individuals, to whom it distributed property of as stable a
character as it could, and in as many fragments as possible, it
remained absolutely mistrustful of associations in which the
"orders" could reorganise themselves, or of endowments on
which great and solid patrimonies could be established, which
might some day serve interests contrary to the State. Revolutionary legislation, which favoured individualism, was hostile to
corporate bodies, which it dissolved, and to endowments, which
it condemned. "As the destruction of every kind of association
among citizens of the same state and profession is one of the
fundamental bases of the French constitution, it is forbidden to
re-establish these under any pretext or any form whatsoever"
(Chapelier Law of June 14–17, 1791). In order that "the land
may not belong to the dead but the living," the Law of May 6,
1791, inspired by Turgot's celebrated article in the *Encyclopédie*,
abolished endowments, that is to say, the application, in per-
petuity, either by living persons or by will to a single object, of
a patrimony.

§ III. THE CONSULATE AND THE EMPIRE

At this period French juridical institutions assumed their
definitive shape both in public and private legislation, though
from the political point of view they were still in a state of
transition.

Public Law

The Consular constitution of 22 Frimaire, year VIII, and the
Imperial constitution of 28 Floréal, year XII, alike attempted
a compromise between the authority of the *ancien régime* and
the liberty of the Revolution. The authority which Bonaparte

could not claim by divine right he necessarily sought to obtain from the sovereignty of the nation, but he proclaimed it only in order that behind this imposing semblance the Head of the State might have scope for greater activity. "Trust must come from below, authority from above," says Sieyès. The suffrage was almost universal. The electors were those citizens who were over twenty-one, and who had resided more than a year in the country, always excepting hired servants. But this was only apparent. These citizens elected a tenth of their number, whose names appeared on a list from which were selected the public officials of the commune; the citizens registered in the communal lists of a department in their turn elected a tenth of their number; those formed the departmental lists, from which the public officials of the department had to be selected. Finally the citizens on the departmental lists elected a tenth of their number; this formed the list of those eligible for public national appointments. Thus while this edifice had for its base an almost universal suffrage, it gradually became narrower. Moreover the electors who drew up the three lists had only a right of nomination. As "authority comes from above," the Senate—self-recruited—selected from the national list the legislators, tribunes, and the consuls and judges of the Supreme Court, while the First Consul selected the departmental officials from the departmental lists, and the district officials from the communal lists. And although the Senatus-consult of 16 Thermidor, year X (August 4, 1802), modified this system in some details, it maintained it in principle; the rights of the electors were actually less than in the past; in the electoral assemblies of the district and department, the elected members became real permanent officials; moreover the First Consul was empowered to add ten or twenty members, according to circumstances; finally, only those most heavily taxed could be elected to the departmental assembly. The Empire retained this system with only very slight modifications (Senatus-consult of 28 Floréal, year XII, May 18, 1804). There remained, therefore, only a few empty phantoms of manhood suffrage.

The legislative power became subordinated to the executive. The Legislative Body, which by the Constitution of the year VIII passed laws without debating them, was a "body of mutes"; the Tribunate, which discussed the drafts of laws presented by the government, could only attack or defend them before the Legislative Body, and in 1807, being in the way of the Emperor, it was suppressed. The *Sénat Conservateur*, which was entrusted with the maintenance of the Constitution by annulling any anti-constitutional measures submitted to it by the Tribunate, neglected its duties, even when Bonaparte disregarded the provisions of the Constitution that declarations of war and treaties of peace must be introduced, debated, and promulgated like laws, and be then presented in the first place to the Senate itself. Finally, in home affairs the Emperor did not hesitate to assume legislative powers, deciding by a simple decree matters which could only be dealt with by way of law.

Thus the violation of political liberty, already noticeable in the Constitution of the year VIII, became aggravated under the Constitution of the year XII. The violation of civil liberty, begun under the Constitution of the year VIII, which no longer contained any "declaration of rights," became complete under the Empire. Nevertheless at this time modern France assumed, from the legal point of view, certain of the features characteristic of its modern structure; from the centralisation which under the *ancien régime* had superseded feudal and local decentralisation, the Revolution had passed to total decentralisation, placing the general interests of the nation in the care of the communal administrations. There was now a strong reactionary movement against this system, and under the Consulate and the Empire there was absolute centralisation; the Head of the State appointed the district Councillors and the general Councillors, the Prefects and the Mayors of the large towns; the Prefect appointed the Mayors of the other communes and the municipal Councillors.

But even as the tendency towards centralisation and unity became accentuated, so the work of codification, which had formed the chief object of monarchical concentration and subsequently of the reforming activity and levelling spirit of the Revolution, was resumed with untiring energy in all branches of the law. "I shall appear in history with my Codes in my hand"; "My true glory is not in having won forty battles; Waterloo will efface the memory of my victories, but my Civil

Code will live for ever." These words of Napoleon at St Helena show what importance the drawing up of the Codes possessed in his eyes.

The Codes

The unification of Civil law, which neither the Old Monarchy nor the Revolution had attained, was achieved by the ambition of one man. On 24 Thermidor, year VIII (August 13, 1800), Bonaparte appointed a Commission to prepare Civil Codes. With true eclecticism he called to this Commission men from the south learned in the written law, Portalis and Maleville, and men from the north acquainted with the common law, Tronchet and Bigot de Préameneu. Bonaparte took an active part in the general discussions of the Council of State. Under his direction the Civil Code not only attained unity, but to a great extent brought about a successful fusion of the two fundamental sources of internal law—custom and Roman law. From the customary law he derived the legislation on the disability of the married woman, marital authority, the community of goods between husband and wife, and many regulations as to succession; from Roman law he borrowed the laws relating to property, the general rules of obligation, and the dowry system. In accordance with the principle of liberty in matrimonial agreements, the contracting parties might choose between the marriage laws of the north— community of goods and its variations—or those of the south, the system of dowries. Child of the Revolution, the Code Napoleon retained the spirit of equality, but it discarded all the idle visions and violent measures of the Revolutionary Assemblies. Neither reactionary nor revolutionary, it aimed at progress, but avoided rashness.

In the organisation of the family it maintained the separation of the civil State and religious creeds; the registration of the forms of the civil State were no longer entrusted to a minister of one of the various religions, but to a public official representing the commune; marriage was henceforth not a sacrament recognised by law, but a contract. In the organisation of property and the regulation of inheritance, the Code scrupulously respected the ideas of equality introduced by the Revolution; testamentary liberty no longer allowed an advantage to be given to the eldest son;

each child had its legal share, of which it could not be deprived
by will. Civil liberty was protected by the declaration which
forbade a contract of hired service by which any person could
be bound for the term of his natural life; his services could only
be hired for a limited period (art. 1780). The Civil Code favoured
the circulation of property by forbidding agreements rendering
land inalienable in the hands of the owner (substitution); it
gave a wide application to the revolutionary system of equal
shares, and favoured the subdivision of property; but it kept
the married woman in a position of disability, the child in a
close dependence on its parents as regards marriage, and the
natural child, "an irregular heir," in a definitely inferior position
to the legitimate child, as to patrimony; in illegitimate connexions
inquiry as to paternity was prohibited. On many points the
family regained the importance which it had held under the
old laws; the rights of the family—so absolute as to be irksome—
overshadowed individual liberty; the rights of the husband, as
"head of the family," reduced the legal independence of the
wife to a formidable extent. Bonaparte's imperious will planned
the family and the household on the strongly hierarchical model
of the State. Finally, as other nations had not followed the
generous example of the Revolution in abolishing the *droit
d'aubaine*, by article XI of the Civil Code he re-established the
disability of aliens, especially as regards inheritance, subject to
diplomatic reciprocity.

When the *Code Civil des Français* had received shape by the
Law of 30 Ventôse, year XII (March 21, 1804), which combined
in a single Code of 2281 articles the thirty-six laws of which it
was made up, the impression produced was considerable. Furthermore, additional Codes came to complete it: the Code of Civil
Procedure (January 1, 1807); the Commercial Code (January 1,
1808); the Code of Criminal Law and the Penal Code (both on
January 1, 1811). But these four Codes are greatly inferior to
the Civil Code. The Code of Civil Procedure, with its costly procedure, long delays, and superannuated forms, calls for simplification. The Commercial Code, which for the most part only
repeats the regulations of 1673 on commerce and of 1681 on the
merchant service, is obviously inadequate, and when it departs
from its models, as in the new regulations with regard to bank-

ruptcy, it is ill-conceived; Colbert's legislation, which is over two hundred years old, remains as an obsolete survival, now that commerce is constantly and rapidly changing. The Code of Criminal Law is old-fashioned, the system of punishment established under the Empire being much too severe and inflexible. But with the Codes the whole juridical structure of French life becomes more or less complete. Henceforward it can only develop within the limits imposed by the legal formulae of the Codes, reserving, however, its right to mitigate what is too severe, and to enlarge what is inadequate in these formulae.

§ IV. FROM 1814 TO OUR OWN TIMES

Public Law

After the fall of the Empire in 1814, France entered until 1870 on a long period of political instability—first reverting to the monarchy only to return to the Republic, then to the Empire, and finally to the Republic; but this political instability was in strong contrast to the stability of its institutions, which, both in public and private legislation, retained their fundamental features and improved them in more than one particular by a process of gradual evolution.

Notwithstanding the reversion to the monarchical system in 1814, and to Conservative ideas in 1875, France has remained faithful, though not without a struggle, to the great principles of 1789, strengthened and vitalised by experience. Manhood suffrage, affirmed by the Constitution of 1793 and established by the Constitution of 1848, makes the principle of national sovereignty a reality, which will only be perfected on the day (still distant) of female suffrage. The present Constitution, which is made up of the three laws of February 24 and 25, 1875, and of July 16, 1875, combines both revolutionary and monarchical features. Parliamentary authority and the collective responsibility of ministers ensure the control of the government by the will of the people, expressed by a Chamber of Deputies entirely renewed every four years. But the danger inherent in the representation of the people by a single Chamber, in the name of the revolutionary principle of the unity of the popular will, is averted by the counterpoise of a second Chamber. In 1884 the

Conservative Senate of 1875 was rendered democratic by the abolition of permanent senators (75 out of 300) and by the variation in the number of senatorial electors in each commune according to the size of its population. The President of the Republic is elected for seven years, but tradition has imposed upon him a strictly self-effacing rôle, and never since 1877 has he exercised the right of dissolving the Chamber. The Republican form of government, which was long opposed and only tried as a provisional experiment after the fall of the Second Empire (1870), was finally adopted in 1884, after the second revision of the Constitution of 1875. The constitutional machinery, thus formed of elements taken from the various historical types of government, was so solidly constructed that it was strong enough to withstand the ordeal of the Great War without the slightest mischance.

The Consulate and the Empire had greatly centralised the administrative government. But, after having retained this system under the monarchy of divine right, France, from 1830 onwards, returned by stages to decentralisation; in 1831 the general Councils became elective, and in 1833 municipal Councils followed suit. The Second Empire tended rather to less concentration than to less centralisation; it increased the powers of local representatives of the State, not those of bodies independent of the State. Napoleon III, however, decentralised in 1861 and again in 1867, when new legislation decreed that matters within the competency of prefects should henceforth be within the competency of the general Councils. After the fall of the Empire, the movement towards decentralisation became accentuated by the laws of August 10, 1871, concerning County Councils, and of April 5, 1884, on municipal government, when mayors became elective, except in Paris, which has its own form of government.

Under the Consulate and the Empire the administrative government had assumed special privileges, which it gradually relinquished. In order to protect it from the encroachments of the ordinary tribunals, the law assigned to special and purely administrative courts—the Council of Prefects and the Council of State—the hearing of cases in which the Administration was a party; by the Constitution of the year VIII, art. 75, an action of the governed against the government was subject to a preliminary inquiry by the Council of State. But after 1870 the suppression of the preliminary authorisation of the Council rendered an official amenable to common law in any action in which he could not give an administrative character to the case. Moreover administrative jurisdiction, created to protect the administrator against the encroachments of the magistracy, does not hesitate to defend legality against administrative arbitrariness, and gradually abolishes the old maxim—"the State, which is the source of the law, is above the law."

The *Tribunal des Conflits*, created in 1848 and reorganised in 1872, composed of members taken partly from the State Council, partly from the *Cour de Cassation*, has gradually reduced administrative privilege by developing the principle of equality for all, governors and governed, in the eyes of the law. The "right of appeal against the abuse of power," an original creation of French jurisprudence, compels the government to pay the most absolute respect to the law, lest its enactments should be nullified. No procedure guarantees the respect of Parliament for individual rights, as in the United States; but private rights which entered into French public law with twofold force, derived from the old texts and from custom, are guaranteed on the one hand by the courts of law and on the other by the administrative tribunals, and have become more and more developed and extended; hence individual liberty, the inviolability of the domicile, the right to work, freedom of trade and of industry, the inviolability of property, and liberty of thought established by the Law of 1905 on the separation of Church and State. To these individual liberties complementary liberties have been added; freedom of the press (which is safeguarded by the jury system), freedom of education, right of assembly, and liberty of association.

The institution of a jury in criminal cases, the appointment for life of the judges in inferior courts and courts of appeal, the existence of a *Cour de Cassation* charged to try cases of violation of the law, ensure impartial respect for law. Finally it is a principle that no one can be deprived of his natural judges, although in great crises the *état de siège* (Laws of 1849 and 1878) substitutes courts-martial for the civil tribunals and individual liberty is suspended. The Penal Code of 1810, founded on the utilitarian principle of intimidation, was too severe; certain penalties have been gradually abolished, first the capital penalty

for political offences (1848), then outlawry (1854); finally supervision by the police was superseded by expulsion from France
(1885); the plea of "extenuating circumstances," barely admitted in police cases in 1810, and introduced into criminal
cases in 1824, was widely extended in 1832, when the penal code
was revised; henceforth the judge might modify the sentence
according to the gravity of the case and the moral perversion of
the criminal. The amendment of the criminal by punishment,
which the Code of 1810 had never contemplated, now became
one of the main principles of the penal law. If really incorrigible,
the criminal is *relégué*; but for a first offence, he may be pardoned
if, after five years, there has been no repetition of the offence
(Bérenger Law of March 26, 1891). The age of majority in criminal
matters has been advanced from sixteen to eighteen, and a
special court for children has been established. These are all
real advances.

From the point of view of criminal procedure, the Code of
1808 called for numerous modifications. The special Courts of
arbitrary jurisdiction disappeared after 1830. At the Assizes,
at which the jury decide on the degree of culpability and the
extenuating circumstances, the magistrates only pronouncing
on the details of procedure and the application of the sentence,
the summing up of the presiding judge was suppressed in
1881 out of regard for the rights of the defence. Besides the
right of quashing a sentence for violation of the law, a special
safeguard against any error by the judge is provided by an
extension of the procedure for revision. In 1808 it was only
admitted in criminal matters and during the life of the condemned man, but in 1867 it was extended so as to clear his
memory, even in police cases, but only under very limited conditions; since June 8, 1895, it has been extended so as to include
all possible cases. Not only does revision grant moral reparation
to an innocent man, but since the law of 1895 it assures him a
pecuniary reparation for judicial error in the form of damages.
Finally the law of December 8, 1897, although it does not yet
admit cross-examination at the preliminary examination in
criminal cases, allows the defending counsel to be present at
all examinations, to have access to the evidence, and to interview
his client even if he is in close confinement.

Private Law

In the realm of private legislation, more than one reform, long prepared by jurisprudence, has been introduced into our laws. Manners and customs exercise a profound influence on law. During the course of the 19th century there was a great change in French customs. The authority of the family decreased, the independence of the individual increased. Divorce, which was abolished in 1816 under religious influence, was definitively introduced in 1884. Although legal separation exists as well as divorce, the law of June 6, 1908, grants even to the guilty party the right of converting a separation into a divorce. The laws of 1896, 1907, and 1919 show a persistent tendency to weaken the conditions and formalities of marriage as regards the consent of parents, the necessary residentiary qualification, and the insistence on twofold publication.

Under the influence of the same spirit of individualism, which permeates social life and legislation, the condition of the married woman has improved. In 1893 a legally separated woman was granted all her civil rights; a woman living on her own earnings may not only belong to a benefit society without her husband's consent (1898) and join a trades-union (1920), but may invest her savings in a savings-bank and withdraw them (laws of 1881 and 1895); a woman carrying on a profession distinct from that of her husband may, for a pecuniary consideration, alienate the property acquired by the proceeds of her work, and may even engage in a law-suit without his consent in any question pertaining to her rights under the act of 1907. Henceforward, the working-woman, the woman engaged in business, the female barrister or doctor, are emancipated from the traditional rules which governed our old law. Further, to repair an unpopular injustice of the Civil Code, which sacrificed the wife to the family, the law of March 9, 1891, grants to the surviving party the right of usufruct in the estate of the predeceased. The lot of the child born out of wedlock, formerly sacrificed to the superior interests of the legitimate family, has been appreciably ameliorated. Not only are affiliation proceedings, which were forbidden except in strictly exceptional cases by the Civil Code, now permitted more frequently, but the rights of natural

children have been increased since 1896; the natural child is a
real heir, possessing a right to his share. Moreover, in cases of
divorce a child who is not the husband's may be legitimised by
the marriage of the woman with the co-respondent after she has
been divorced for adultery. Finally the family, which is losing
its authority over the individual, is also losing its own force and
power; from the legal point of view it is becoming more restricted. To enable the State to bear its ever-increasing burdens
more easily, the Financial Act of December 31, 1917, limited to
the sixth degree the right of succession in cases of intestacy, which
the Civil Code granted to the twelfth degree.

As regards landed property legislation subsequent to the Civil
Code has effected great reforms, but the compilation of a new
register of landed property, estate by estate, with compulsory
registration of every transfer of property, or of any concession
of real ownership, is still needed.

As regards personal property, to which the Code only attached
a very secondary importance, the legislature has voted many
laws between 1872 and 1902, both to assist the owners of lost or
stolen documents, and to protect the property of the legally
incompetent (1880); laws also have been passed for the regulation of trading companies (1867–1893).

Under the influence of the new conditions of labour, there has
been an enlargement of the old individualistic and narrow
conception of contract and tort. The Law of April 9, 1898,
recognises the liability of the employer towards the workman, commensurate to the risks of accidents arising from his
employment; the establishment of trades-unions (1884), whose
scope has been extended by a new law (1920), has introduced
a new type of contract—the collective contract—which re-
establishes the equilibrium between two parties of unequal
strength. Moreover, recent legislation enables any one who, from
ignorance or necessity, has accepted too hard conditions to
demand a revision of the contract. Finally, when the system
of insurance came into being, especially life assurance, which
was not foreseen by the Code of 1804, case-law intervened
to protect the insured against unreasonably severe clauses.
Judicial theory co-ordinates the efforts of jurisprudence to
adapt, from a growing sense of justice, the rigour of the

written law to the increasingly complex emergencies of life.

On the whole, law is becoming less hard and inflexible, more humane and adaptable. In commercial law the old severe legislation relating to bankruptcy has been modified by the law of March 4, 1889; judicial liquidation offers to the unfortunate debtor the relief of a partial bankruptcy.

Since the disability of aliens was re-established by the Civil Code French law has granted them all but a few private rights of little pecuniary importance; it has even gone so far that, to induce families who have lived for some generations in France to regularise their position, it has granted French nationality to children born in France of foreigners themselves born there (Law of June 26, 1889). But French law still maintains, especially in matters of civil procedure, certain precautionary measures and marks of suspicion as regards foreigners, foreign laws, and foreign judges. Numerous treaties, notably with Belgium and Switzerland, have, in this matter, modified legal severity. Finally the French decree of 1913 on the civil status of French and foreign inhabitants in the French zone of the Sherifian Empire denotes a marked advance in the direction of compromise between conflicting laws.

BIBLIOGRAPHY

Brissaud, *Manuel d'histoire du droit français*, 2 vols. 1898–1903. A. Esmein, *Cours élémentaire d'histoire du droit français*, 14th ed., ed. Pr. Génestal, 1921. E. Glasson, *Histoire du Droit et des Institutions de la France*, 8 vols. 1887. P. Viollet, *Précis de l'histoire du droit français*, 3rd ed. 1905. F.-A. Isambert, *Recueil général des anciennes lois françaises*, 29 vols. A. Esmein, *Cours élémentaire d'histoire du droit français de 1789 à 1814*, 1908. Merlin, *Répertoire de jurisprudence*, 5th ed. 18 vols. 1827. Ph. Sagnac, *La législation civile de la Révolution française (1789–1804)*, 1898.

Le Centenaire du Code Civil, 1904. Planiol, *Traité élémentaire de droit civil*, 8th ed. 3 vols. 1920–21. Colin and Capitant, *Cours élémentaire de droit civil français*, 3rd ed. 3 vols. 1920. Garsonnet and Cézar Bru, *Traité théorique et pratique de procédure civile et commerciale*, 3rd ed. 1912. Lyons and Caen, *Manuel de droit commercial*, 13th ed. 1922. Thaller, *Traité général de droit commercial*, 1907–1914; *Traité élémentaire de droit commercial*, 5th ed. 1916. Thaller and Pic, Percerou, Josserand, Ripert, Huvelin, De Lapradelle, Hémard, *Traité général de droit com-*

mercial, 19 vols. (in course of publication). Pillet, *Principes de droit international privé*, 1903. Weiss, *Traité de droit international privé*, 6 vols. 2nd ed. 1913. Valéry, *Manuel de droit international privé*, 1915. A. Esmein, *Éléments de droit constitutionnel français et comparé*, 7th ed. revised by H. Nazard, 2 vols. 1921. L. Duguit, *L'État*, 2 vols. 1901–1903; *Les Transformations du Droit public*, 1913; *Les Transformations générales du Droit privé depuis le Code Napoléon*, 1912; *Manuel de Droit Constitutionnel*, 3rd ed. 1918. A. de Lapradelle, *Cours de Droit Constitutionnel*, 1912. R. Carré de Malberg, *Contribution à la théorie générale de l'État*, 2 vols. 1920–21. M. Hauriou, *Précis de droit administratif*, 8th ed. 1914. A. Berthélemy, *Traité élémentaire de droit administratif*, 9th ed. 1921. E. Garçon, *Code pénal annoté* (in process of publication). R. Garraud, *Précis de droit criminel*, 11th ed. 1912; *Traité théorique et pratique de droit pénal français*, 6 vols. 1898–1902.

J.-B. Sirey, *Recueil général des Lois et des arrêts*. D. Dalloz, *Jurisprudence générale*.

CHAPTER VII

EDUCATION AND LEARNING

§ I.   1494–1660

DURING the thirty years which followed the expedition of Charles VIII to Italy the intellectual energy of France was chiefly devoted to that revival of learning which is known as Humanism. The first leader of the movement was Robert Gaguin (1433–1502), General of the Order of the Trinitarians, who, down to his death in 1502, did much to promote the study of Latin authors and the practice of Latin composition. A new phase was introduced by the printer and publisher, Josse Badius Ascensius (1461 or 2–1535), who greatly increased the production of Latin works and promoted the cause of humanistic education by writing "familiar commentaries," and by editing and printing improved grammars and other manuals. Meanwhile within the University of Paris Jacques Lefèvre d'Étaples (Faber Stapulensis) (c. 1455–1536) had reformed the whole study of Aristotle and had introduced great improvements into that of mathematics and the other subjects of the Quadrivium. But he was an imperfect Greek scholar and the development of Greek scholarship in France was mainly the work, carried on in the face of great difficulties, of Guillaume Budé (1468–1540). He had already made himself a sound scholar when the coming of the Italian humanist, Girolamo Aleandro, to Paris (1508) gave a real impetus to the movement. Aleandro lectured there for four years (1509–1513) with great success, trained pupils to carry on his work, and encouraged the printing of Greek books. French Humanism also owed much to Erasmus, who after the publication of the Aldine edition of his *Adagia* (1508) exercised a marked influence in France. He kept the balance even between Christian and pagan antiquity, believing that the moral seriousness of the best pagan literature made it a fitting instrument of Christian education.

The publication of Budé's *De Asse*, two months after the accession of Francis I, established his reputation as one of the leading humanists of Europe. But Humanism had now to reckon with the growing animosity of the Sorbonne, caused by the spread of the Lutheran doctrines and by the sympathy at first accorded to them by the majority of the French humanists. It was not till the year 1529 that Budé and his cause triumphed with the foundation of the Royal Professorships for Hebrew, Greek, and Mathematics. The provincial universities followed the lead of Paris: Trinity College at Lyons, the College of Guienne at Bordeaux, and the new University of Nismes, all successfully adopted the new methods of study. Lyons vied with Paris in the printing and translating of classical authors, and provided a martyr in the person of the printer and scholar, Étienne Dolet (1509–1546), who was burnt on a doubtful charge of heresy in 1546.

The enthusiasm of the age for learning is best represented by François Rabelais (c. 1495–1553 or 4), who in his *Gargantua* (1534) unfolds a scheme of humanistic education modelled in its broad outlines on the practical experience of Vittorino da Feltre and his successors in Italy. Its two most remarkable features are the large proportion of time allotted to physical exercise and the care taken to train the powers of observation. Another feature, common to the age, is its encyclopaedic character.

But with the accession of Henry II universal learning began to give place to specialism, and in two of the departments of knowledge, classical scholarship and jurisprudence, France now took a decided lead. In Greek scholarship the chief names were Adrien Turnèbe (1512–1565), Jean Dorat (c. 1502–1588), both notable editors of Aeschylus, and Henri Estienne (1528–1598), who issued from his press at Geneva eighteen first editions of Greek authors, nearly all of his own editing, but whose greatest work was the *Thesaurus Graecae Linguae* "still unsurpassed as a Greek lexicon on a large scale." Latin scholarship could boast of Denys Lambin (1516–1571), a brilliant editor of Lucretius, Plautus, and Cicero, and Marc-Antoine Muret (1526–1585), the foremost Latin stylist in Europe.

The leading Hebraists were François Vatable (d. 1547) one of the first royal professors, and Sanctes Pagnini (c. 1470–1536) an Italian by birth, who made his home at Lyons. Oriental studies—Hebrew reckoned as a classical language—particularly Arabic, were represented by Guillaume Postel (1510–1581), a man of multifarious learning and strange opinions. In Jurisprudence the greatest names are Jacques Cujas (1522–1590), who edited the *Corpus Iuris* in the true spirit of humanism, Hugues Doneau (1527–1591), who aimed at a philosophical conception of the Roman law as a whole, and François Hotman (1524–1590), whose chief work, the *Franco-Gallia*, is a notable contribution to historical knowledge, establishing as it does the German origin of the Franks. The Protestant diplomatist Jacques Bongars (1554–1612), a man of many-sided learning, who had been a pupil of Cujas, also did good service to historical studies by publishing, the year before his death, a collection of contemporary writers on the French crusades under the title of *Dei gesta per Francos*.

Of greater importance than any of these scholars both in the history of education and in that of general thought was Pierre Ramus (1515–1572), the descendant of the noble Flemish family of La Ramée, but the son of a day-labourer, who rose from humble beginnings to be Principal of the College of Presles. This bold and practical reformer, who had startled the University of Paris by his opposition to the time-honoured logic of Aristotle, was appointed in 1551 to the new royal professorship of eloquence and philosophy and made a great reputation as a brilliant lecturer. His *Dialectique* (1555) was the first philosophical work written in French; it marks his interest in the vernacular and his endeavour to dispossess Latin from its stronghold as the sole language of education and learning. In 1562 he addressed to the king a far-reaching project for the reform of the university, and in particular of the abuses arising from the undue multiplication of professors, the corresponding increase in fees, and the grave defects in the teaching of the higher faculties. As a remedy he proposed that a limited number of professors in philosophy, mathematics, law, medicine, and theology should be appointed and paid by the state, while the teaching in Arts, that is to say in grammar, rhetoric, and logic, should still remain in the hands of the colleges. He thus, more than two centuries in advance, drew that line of demarcation between secondary and higher education which was adopted after the Revolution. But the time was not yet ripe for his reforms, and, even if it had been, the religious wars which had already broken out when he proposed them would have prevented their realisation. He himself perished in the massacre of St Bartholomew, a victim, it is almost certain, to the jealousy and hatred of a brother-professor.

Two years after the massacre another Protestant scholar, Joseph Scaliger (1540–1609), who had fled to Geneva, returned to France. Combining a mastery of Greek and Latin with wide learning, a strong critical sense, sureness of method, and con-structive power, his is the greatest name in the history of French classical scholarship. His edition of Manilius (1577), which is practically a treatise on ancient astronomy, was the prelude to the great work of his life, the creation of a scientific system of ancient chronology embodied in his *De emendatione temporum* (1583) and *Thesaurus temporum* (1603). But when the latter, his master-work, was published he had left France to become a professor at the new University of Leyden (1593). After his departure the most learned man in France was Pierre Pithou (1539–1596). He was little of a Greek scholar, but an excellent Latin one, and we owe to him four *editiones principes*, among them that of Phaedrus, and the first important text of Juvenal and Persius. He also published various texts of medieval historians. The special aim of Isaac Casaubon (1559–1614), who returned to France from Geneva in the year of Pithou's death and who, for ten years, was one of the royal professors of Greek, was, in Mark Pattison's words, "to revive the picture of the ancient world." His editions of Athenaeus, Theophrastus, and Strabo have never been superseded.

But these last three scholars stood almost alone. The effect of the massacre upon classical scholarship in France was disastrous, and the condition of the kingdom during the next quarter of a century was fatal to learning generally. In the *Satire Ménippée* (1594) the University of Paris is represented in the burlesque speech of its Rector as empty of scholars and professors, while in place of Greek and Latin the class-rooms resound with the lowing of kine, the braying of asses, and the grunting of pigs.

In his project for the reform of the university, Ramus had

chiefly concerned himself with the superior Faculties, but in that of Arts also, though the teaching was efficient and well-organised, there was plenty of room for improvement. Ramus had 'humanised' logic, but logic still occupied too large a place in the curriculum. The pedantry of scholasticism had been to a large extent abolished, but Humanism had introduced a pedantry of its own. It had developed a strong tendency to stuff pupils with undigested knowledge, to make them, in Rabelais's words, "abysses of learning," and thus to fill their heads instead of training their characters. Montaigne, who was educated on humanistic lines at the new College of Guienne from the age of seven to that of thirteen (1539–1546), looked back with strong disapproval on his early training. The well-known essay (I. 25) in which he gives an account of it is, with the preceding one, a lively criticism of the education of his day, and at the same time an exposition of his own views. His central idea is that the object of education is to train the mind rather than to fill it—in other words, character rather than learning. He has been criticised for a want of sympathy with the pursuit of knowledge for its own sake, but it must be remembered that he is thinking chiefly of young nobles, who, at the age of fifteen or sixteen, would probably take up the profession of arms, and whose education therefore ought to be largely practical, including travels and intercourse with living men or with the great characters of history. Like Rabelais, he is not so much concerned with the academic education of students destined for the learned professions as with the upbringing of men of affairs. Thus his scheme, like Rabelais's, is the old individualistic training of the days of chivalry with its insistence on physical culture, but penetrated with the humanistic ideas of the Renaissance. There is, however, this difference between the two schemes, that, while Rabelais's ideal is a highly accomplished prince of the Italian Renaissance, Montaigne's is a shrewd and open-minded man of the world, not far removed from the *honnête homme* or well-bred gentleman of the 17th century.

One of the first measures taken in hand by Henry IV after his acknowledgment as king was the reform of the University of Paris, and as the result of a Commission appointed for the purpose new statutes were promulgated in 1600. The reforms most needed were those concerned with discipline and the organisation of the teaching in the higher Faculties. The changes in the character of the studies chiefly affected the Faculty of Arts, or in other words secondary education. This was made more thoroughly classical, and while a place in the new programme was given to Greek, it was made the chief business of the students to read, speak, and write Latin.

In spite of these reforms the university did not recover its ancient prestige. This was largely due to the rivalry of the Jesuits, who, having been expelled from France in 1595, were recalled in 1603. In 1618 they reopened the College of Clermont —after 1682 called the College of Louis-le-Grand—which they had more than half a century before established at Paris. Their revised *Ratio studiorum*, which they issued only a year preceding the reform of the university, followed the same severely classical lines in secondary teaching. The chief differences were that, while in the university the explanation of authors played an important part, the Jesuits insisted more upon written work, especially upon translation and composition, and that, while the university favoured the reading of whole authors, the Jesuits used extracts which had been carefully prepared in the moral and religious interests of their pupils. The popularity of Jesuit colleges, which in 1626 numbered fourteen with over 13,000 pupils in the province of Paris alone, was due to the combined efficiency and mildness of their discipline, to their care for the health and physical well-being of their pupils, and to the pains they took to make the life attractive. The result was that the sons of the nobility and the well-to-do *bourgeois* flocked to their colleges. Among their most distinguished pupils were Condé and his brother Conti, Luxembourg, Descartes, Corneille, Molière, and Bossuet.

Jesuit teaching had two grave defects. The first, which it shared with the university, was the making of Latin the sole basis of education, to the complete neglect of the vernacular. The second was the exaggerated importance attached to style and language, as compared with what they called "erudition." Both these defects were remedied in the teaching of the Oratory, which, founded by the Cardinal de Bérulle in 1611 as a seminary for the education of priests, undertook in 1623, by order of the

Pope, the secular education of children. The work rapidly grew; numerous colleges were founded, and that of Juilly, about twenty miles N.E. of Paris, which was regarded as their model establishment, attracted the young nobles in large numbers. The chief features of their education were that in the lower classes, up to the fourth inclusive, French, and not Latin, was the medium of instruction, that history was taught in French throughout, and that under the inspiration of Descartes special attention was given to mathematics, natural science, and philosophy. The Oratory was fortunate in its professors, chief among whom were Father Lamy, whose *Entretiens sur les sciences* appeared in 1683, and Father Thomassin, who published various *Methods* of study from 1681 to 1693. It also produced a great philosopher and writer in Malebranche, two distinguished pulpit orators in Mascaron and Massillon, and the founder of biblical exegesis in France in Richard Simon.

The same sound principles which guided the education of the Oratory were put into force in the famous Little Schools of Port-Royal some twenty years later. There were, however, certain differences. Less attention was paid to history and geography, to mathematics and natural science, though none of these studies was neglected. On the other hand the French language and literature were studied with greater thoroughness and for their own sakes, the pupils being taught to write French partly by translation from Latin and partly by reading French authors.

This care for the vernacular language shown by Port-Royal and the Oratory marks a fresh stage in the long struggle with Latin which had been going on ever since the reign of Francis I, and in which the *Deffence et Illustration* of Du Bellay (1549), the *Dialectique* of Ramus (1555), the three treatises of Henri Estienne (1565–1579), the *Discours de la Méthode* (1637) and the *Lettres Provinciales* (1656) were so many victories for the French language. A similar crusade had been started in England by Roger Ascham and Richard Mulcaster, while later in Germany Martin Opitz had played the part of Ronsard and Du Bellay.

At the same time the importance of Latin was fully recognised by the Little Schools. A wide range of authors was read, and the old-fashioned grammar of Despauterius was replaced by the

Nouvelle Méthode of Claude Lancelot, one of the chief teachers of Port-Royal. "Themes" or Latin essays were preferred to Latin versions of French passages, and—admirable provision—the making of Latin verse was confined to boys who showed a taste for it. Lancelot also wrote a new method for Greek and a *Jardin des racines grecques*, and in the higher classes the principal Greek authors (with the omission of Aeschylus and Plato) were read. It was to Lancelot that Racine, the most illustrious pupil of Port-Royal, owed his admirable knowledge of Greek literature and his profound sympathy with the Greek spirit. But the pupil who best reflects the spirit of Port-Royal is Sebastien le Nain de Tillemont (1637–1698), the modest and profoundly learned historian of the Roman empire and the first six centuries of the Christian Church.

The influence of Port-Royal education was out of all proportion to the number of its pupils. The Little Schools, from their definite organisation in the Rue Saint-Dominique d'Enfer to their dispersion in 1660, only existed for fourteen years, and at no one time did the number of their scholars exceed fifty. But their spirit has permeated the theory and practice of French education down to the present day. It is due to Port-Royal that in no country in the world is the study of the vernacular for its own sake so much honoured as in France. The Port-Royal *Logic*, mainly the work of Antoine Arnauld, and not published till some time after the dispersion of the Schools, has remained in use down to our own times. The reforms which Rollin, Arnauld's friend and admirer, introduced into the University of Paris were but partial and timid copies of Port-Royal methods. The teaching of the vernacular was introduced by La Salle into the education of poor children, and by the Abbé Fleury, a pupil of the Jesuits, into that of the young Princes de Conti.

One of the results of the Catholic revival in France was that learning was diverted from pagan to Christian studies. This was largely the work of the Jesuits, who realised that, if they wished to control Christian thought, they must produce rivals to Scaliger and Casaubon. They succeeded so far, that several members of the society produced epoch-making editions of Greek and Latin Fathers and other Christian writers: Fronton Du Duc (1558–1624) of Chrysostom, Jacques Sirmond (1559–1651) of Sidonius

Apollinaris and a number of ecclesiastical writers, Denys Petau (1583–1652) of Synesius and Epiphanius, Philippe Labbé (1607–1667) of several Byzantine historians. Petau also wrote an important chronological work, *Doctrina temporum*, while Labbé, who with Petau was the chief Jesuit contributor to historical knowledge, edited several volumes of a great work on the Councils. Jesuit training also produced Nicolas Rigault (1577–1654), the editor of Tertullian and Cyprian, Charles Du Fresne, Sieur Du Cange (1610–1688), the great lexicographer of medieval Latin, and Pierre-Daniel Huet (1630–1721), Bishop of Avranches, founder of the Academy of his native town of Caen and editor of the celebrated Delphin classics, who spent the long evening of a life devoted to study in a Jesuit house at Paris and bequeathed to their Society his considerable library.

At Leyden, as a young man, Huet met Claude Saumaise (1588–1658), who occupied Scaliger's chair. His chief work, *Plinianae exercitationes*, shows enormous erudition, but he had neither judgment nor literary tact, and the last four years of his life were disfigured by his gladiatorial controversy with Milton on the subject of Charles I. His contemporary, Nicolas de Peiresc (1580–1637), who lived at Aix in Provence, was remarkable for his rich collection of books, manuscripts, and other precious objects, and for his intimate relations with all the men of learning of his day.

§ II. EDUCATION FROM 1660

Under the *ancien régime* France possessed a score of universities of varying degrees of efficiency, but in the 17th century all fell below their ancient level. The *petites écoles* of Paris multiplied and flourished during the same period; most of them were boys' schools under masters, some were girls' schools under mistresses. In 1672 they taught reading, writing, calculation by counters and by "sums" ("le calcul tant au jet qu'à la plume"), Latin grammar, catechism, and the Office of the Mass. They closely resembled the English "petty schools" of that time, serving the double purpose of preparatory and purely elementary instruction. Some of these Parisian schools, *Parlement* notwithstanding, kept their pupils beyond the stipulated age of nine and began the teaching of the second liberal art, rhetoric. It is not surprising that the *grandes écoles*, or grammar schools, which should have been the intermediary between the *petites écoles* and the university, disappeared from Paris, while they survived elsewhere.

Instruction of the humblest type was supplied in a great variety of ways. Parish schools, founded by the Church in early days to ensure the universal teaching of the Faith, sometimes added rudimentary instruction in reading and writing to the elements of a purely religious education. An abortive royal *ordonnance* of 1698 called for the establishment in all parishes of schoolmasters and mistresses to teach "all children of both sexes the chief mysteries of the catholic, apostolic Roman religion...as also to teach reading and even writing to all who need them." Failing other funds, the cost was to be borne "by all the inhabitants." Private teaching and private schools of a very modest sort were common in centres of population. Where a scriveners' guild existed, the teaching of writing and summing was a recognised function of these men of the pen.

It seems to have been customary in northern and eastern France to organise local charity by means of a bureau conducted by a voluntary association (often of ladies) or by the town council, and to maintain an almshouse and a public teacher for the children. Charity schools for the destitute existed throughout urban France; their first object was religious and moral education, the latter including the teaching of a simple handicraft, such as spinning. Occasionally reading and writing were added. In the 17th century a great number of religious communities of women sprang up to give a religious education to poor girls. These French charity schools may be compared with the much later English "schools of industry"; like them they coped with, but failed to abolish, the ignorance and hooliganism which often characterised the children and youths of the town population of both countries. The dominant place assigned to religion in these schools and in their successors was based on the principle that religion was, in essentials, education; knowledge or skill were incidental and dependent on time and opportunity. The teachers' qualifications were frequently few and always of a very modest kind; reading, writing and a little summing usually completed the secular list, although not all possessed them. Such teachèrs were selected, after some trial of their ability, by the *curé*, sometimes aided by the local notables, sometimes by the parishioners in public meeting. They drew a fixed stipend, received school-fees in money or in kind and shared casual church fees when they assisted the clergy in the church services.

Thus the machinery of primary instruction appears to have been fairly extensive, but its efficiency was seriously hindered by the lack of qualified teachers and by the unwillingness of some to forgo their children's wages or to pay fees. One of the first to attempt a remedy was Charles Démia, arch-priest of Lyons, to whose official charge the parish schools of that diocese were committed. By exhausting his own patrimony and by successful appeals to the lay authorities, Démia was instrumental in founding (1666–1668) in the great diocese of Lyons an organisation which set up and conducted schools for the poor of both sexes, an *école de travail ou d'apprentissage*, and (1672) a seminary for preparing teachers. The last seems to have come to an end with his death in 1689; the committee and its school, or schools, were still at work in 1790.

The man who gave France a body of trained, elementary schoolmasters sufficiently numerous to meet the demands of the greater part of the country was St Jean-Baptiste de La Salle (1651–1719), canon of Reims, his native city. Here in 1684 he founded his Institute of the Brothers of the Christian Schools[1], a lay congregation devoted to the work of elementary school teaching. At first a purely local institution, it became national in range before its founder's death; at the date of his canonisation (1900) its labours were world-wide, its 15,000 members giving gratuitous elementary education to more than 300,000 boys.

During the first twenty-five years of its history the Institute devised, always in response to the need of the hour, new types of school which place La Salle and his *Frères* in the front rank of pioneers. The heart of the Institute's work was, and still is, the gratuitous education of the very poor; the typical school of the Brothers taught religion and the "three R's," sometimes

---

[1] This Institute is frequently confused both by French and English writers with the "Brothers of the Christian Doctrine" *vulgo* "les Ignorantins," a teaching community founded in 1592 by César de Bus.

adding geometrical drawing and a manual trade. The traditional practice sanctioned by authority was to teach French children reading from the Latin Psalter, not for the understanding of the Psalms, but as an easy introduction to the reading of the vernacular. The saint's good sense was illustrated by his insisting that the boys of his schools should begin to learn reading, not in Latin, but in their own tongue, a sensible reform previously introduced by Port-Royal.

Using present-day terms, it may be claimed that La Salle devised (1) a school (1699) which was at once Sunday school, continuation school, and trade school, in which on Sundays and holy days two hundred Parisian youths of the poorest, roughest, and most turbulent kind were taught the "3 R's," drawing, and a simple handicraft; (2) a higher primary school (1705) teaching the vernacular and another modern language, mathematics, drawing, music, book-keeping; the course of studies expanded as years passed, but always remained "modern" in character; (3) a reformatory school (1709–1715) for intractable and criminal boys, where much was made of geometrical drawing, engineering (not all the pupils were poor or criminal), wood-carving, carpentry, locksmithery, and building. A training seminary for country schoolmasters was one of the Institute's earliest experiments (1684). Religious training and instruction were integral parts of the work in all these schools.

The Institute encountered much opposition in its early days, particularly in Paris, where its schools were regarded as contravening the immemorial jurisdiction of the *Scolasticus*, the *chantre* of Notre-Dame, and as contrary to the vested interests of the guild of writing masters. The legal right of any parish priest to open a charity school was not always accepted as a justification for the presence of the Brothers in a parish, and the founder had to suffer in consequence. Six years after La Salle's death his Institute received formal papal recognition and at once entered upon a period of great expansion. Just as the Jesuits were virtually in possession of the secondary education of France, so were the Brothers of the Christian Schools in virtual possession of the elementary sphere, a position which they maintained till their temporary suppression in 1792, only to be revived by the First Consul in 1803 and received into greater favour.

In the late 16th century young noblemen did not resort to schools or universities, but received instruction in *académies*, where the old chivalric education was maintained and supplemented by the study of modern history and languages, and of mathematics especially in relation to military engineering. Educational theory greatly interested French writers of the 17th century and much of their thought concerned the courtly or princely upbringing which it was the object of the *académies* to direct. Writing of that kind came naturally from the tutors of royal or noble pupils but was by no means confined to them. Bossuet, Fénelon, Claude Fleury, La Bruyère all contributed; Nicole (of Port-Royal), Jean de Tavannes, and the Marquise de Lambert were also of the number. In their several ways these all urge that education is more than instruction and that instruction limited to the language, literature and history of the two ancient civilisations was too narrow for Frenchmen who had a part to play in public affairs.

Bossuet took infinite pains to give his pupil, the Dauphin Louis, an almost encyclopaedic range of study, redeeming it from smattering by making usefulness, as a reigning sovereign might think of it, the discriminating principle amongst studies. Mathematics, physics, anatomy, geography, and, above all, French history were included, subjects ignored by European schools in general. Fénelon did his best to nullify the autocracy of Louis XIV by the principles with which he imbued the king's grandson, "le petit Dauphin." *Télémaque*, which began by being a prince's political *vade-mecum*, continued a long career as a text-book of literature for French children and an exercise-ground for foreigners in French.

Fénelon's reputation as an educational writer rests upon his *Traité de l'éducation des filles* (1687), a work written, like the contemporary *Some thoughts concerning education* of John Locke, for the immediate use of a particular family. The thread running through the book is the preparation of women for the part which they play in society. Fénelon believed that intellectual sloth, romanticism, and a craze for theology were characteristic feminine defects; there would seem to be a touch of personal reminiscence in this last. These weaknesses he would correct by a moral rather than by an intellectual discipline. The appropriate studies for girls were religion, the Bible, Church history, spelling, hand-writing, French grammar learned by the careful practice of speech and, for practical purposes, simple arithmetic. Neither French nor English schools invariably made it their business to teach these things at that date. As these girls were in later life to preside over their husbands' *châteaux*, they should understand rural economy, know the chief principles of judicial and civil administration, how to establish "petty schools" and home industries and other means of succouring the poor. A girl who had the necessary taste might study eloquence and poetry, music, and painting; but precautions must be taken lest their emotional character overwhelm the student. The same distrust of poetry, romance, and stimulation of the feelings generally appears in the otherwise liberal discussion of girls' education contained in Mme de Lambert's *Avis d'une mère à sa fille* (1728).

The claim that women possess a right to culture, which Mme de Lambert puts forward in her *Réflexions nouvelles sur les femmes*, should be contrasted with the following sentence from Fénelon: "Keep young girls within the customary limits and teach them that, with reference to knowledge, their sex should have a modesty almost as scrupulous as that which is inspired by a horror of vice." The passage might be matched from most books, French or English, which discussed the subject during the 17th and, particularly, the 18th centuries. Its sentiment helps to explain the futility into which girls' education sank in the period which followed.

A much less cultured upbringing than that depicted by Fénelon as suitable for a nobleman's daughters was carried out at Saint-Cyr, the school which Madame de Maintenon established in 1686 and kept up till her death in 1715, visiting it almost daily, sometimes herself "taking a class." Madame de Maintenon's *Entretiens sur l'éducation* (1696) and *Lettres sur l'éducation* (1705) exhibit the author as well-balanced, shrewd, amiable, sincere, in short, the typical *bourgeoise*, to whose practical good sense and indomitable courage France is so deeply in debt. It is the type which Saint-Cyr was meant to cultivate.

On the general question of the *instruction* of girls, Saint-Cyr shared contemporary public opinion. "*Bourgeoises* must be brought up as *bourgeoises*. There is no question of adorning their minds; they must be taught their duties to the family, obedience to their husbands, the care of children....Reading does more harm than good to young girls....Books make intellectual pretenders ('beaux esprits') and arouse an insatiable curiosity[1]." "Women never but half-know, and the little they know commonly makes them proud, disdainful, tatlers, disinclined to solid things[2]."

At first Saint-Cyr showed no distrust of the assumed emotional nature of its inmates. Dramas were played under the guidance of Racine and Boileau to distinguished audiences, who were moved to enthusiasm by the girls' acting. But the effect upon the girls themselves was soon thought to be so detrimental that the plays were given up, with the consequence that the study of letters in the school suffered a set-back.

The pupils numbered 250 of all ages up to twenty, "jeunes filles nobles et pauvres," whose fathers had served their country; they were admitted on the king's nomination and of course were educated gratuitously. All were trained to use their hands and to practise household management. On its intellectual side, the course comprised the rudiments of religion and learning, the French language, music, dancing, drawing, and a very superficial acquaintance with history, geography and mythology. But the intellectual was its less important side. The alternatives assumed to be open to the girls on leaving were marriage or the convent; the great aim was to fit them for either by means of a moral training which would root in them the ideal of duty.

A girl was not nominated unless there were at least four degrees of *noblesse* on the father's side; Saint-Cyr might therefore be considered one of those *académies* which gave to persons of rank a more suitable instruction than any which university or school then gave. But its limited intellectual range is in marked contrast with that of the *académies* and even with that which Fénelon recommended for girls of birth. Saint-Cyr achieved with great success the type of education which both France and England then believed to be the most appropriate for most

---

[1] Compayré, *Histoire critique des doctrines de l'éducation en France*, etc., vol. I, p. 363, quoting the *Entretiens* and the *Lettres*.

[2] *Id.* p. 364.

girls; and it did this without lapsing into the triviality which so often satisfied its contemporaries. To modern eyes the curriculum seems altogether wanting in liberality of outlook; yet the girls who, at home or in the convent, followed equally meagre studies taught on similar principles, grew to be the brilliant women of the *salons* and of public life. Nor must we fail to appreciate the fact that these closely restricted studies were but a part, and not the most important part, of a true curriculum, an ordered mode of life, whose purpose was not merely to inform but to educate in the most comprehensive sense. It might be fairly objected that in our day of multifarious knowledge in the schoolroom we tend to forget education, when the whole value of the school is attributed to the knowledge it confers. The intellect and the will are one person and the object of education is the person, not the conferment of knowledge or of skill alone.

The prolonged struggle between the Jesuits and the French nationalists closed in 1764, when Louis XV proscribed the Company, the *Parlements* leading the attack. In 1773, Pope Clement XIV in one and the same decree loaded the Society of Jesus with praises and announced its suppression. In some important particulars the Jesuit education had long been out of date. A curriculum virtually confined to Latin rhetoric and mediaeval philosophy could not satisfy a society amidst which experimental science and inquiry directed to all fields of life were obviously opening new vistas. The quantity of talking and writing about educational theory during the 18th century was enormous; nearly all started from the experiential psychology of Locke, which, when made known to Frenchmen by Voltaire, became an accepted pre-supposition of philosophy. Condillac and Helvetius turned it into a psychology of sensation, pure and simple, with consequences visible in the educational theorising of d'Alembert, Diderot, La Chalotais, President Rolland, and the revolutionaries of all shades who followed them.

The *tabula rasa*, which Locke assumed was an accurate figure of the new-born intelligence, justified a faith in the almost unlimited possibilities of instruction rightly conducted; Condillac's unintended demonstration (in the person of his pupil, Ferdinand, Louis XV's grandson) of the unsoundness of this belief does not appear to have struck his contemporaries. The claims of positive as distinct from verbal knowledge were strongly pressed by this new school of thinkers; mathematics, physics, experiment, modern history, geography and languages were conspicuous in their programmes.

In Rousseau's *Émile* (1762) the breaking away from the old paths sometimes leads to roads singularly un-French. The training of the senses, the encouragement of handwork, the supervision of the child's unfolding powers are, after Locke, only the common form of the period. But the exaggerated value attributed to feeling and sentiment at the expense of reason, and the confusion between a wary observance of what physical law renders expedient and the obedience which moral law enjoins are Rousseau's own. Neither of these is French; nor is the exaggerated individualism of the *Émile* in accord with French opinion or practice. Abel Faure goes so far as to say, "*Émile* was widely read in our country, much admired or vigorously combated, but nobody dreamed of putting it into practice. The germs of life which it contained were fertilised by foreigners" (*L'Individu et l'Esprit d'autorité*, p. 140). But Rousseau's principles were frequently cited in the Convention, and *Émile* certainly added to the ferment in thought and speech concerning education during the revolutionary period. It was a starting-point for speculation throughout Europe, which sometimes passed and still passes into practice; it is hard to tell whether it has effected more good or more harm in that field.

A book more immediately and, from some points of view, more profoundly influential in France was associated with the struggle against the Jesuits. Louis-René de Caradeuc de La Chalotais, *procureur général* of the *Parlement* of Rennes, had impeached the Company in his *Compte Rendu* etc. of 1762. In the following year he published an *Essai d'éducation nationale*, which asserted that education should be national, State-controlled, free from clerical direction, and that, as a necessary consequence of its national character, public instruction should include the teaching of moral and civic duty. Religious instruction was a function of the home and of the priest. These principles were taken for granted or pushed to their ultimate conclusion by speakers and writers of the Revolution; they were adopted by French liberalism and to-day are the foundation of the *école laïque*.

La Chalotais' prayer was that the king would reform the *collèges*, that is, the secondary schools; he had no care for the public instruction of the people at large, as to the inexpediency of which both he and his admirer, Voltaire, had no doubt. La Chalotais declared that the *Frères de la doctrine chrétienne* "had ruined everything by teaching reading and writing to folk who should only learn to draw and to handle plane and file, which they no longer desired to do....The good of society requires that the learning of the people should not extend beyond their business." To which sentiment Voltaire replied, "I thank you for proscribing study amongst ploughmen. I, who cultivate the soil, make a request for labourers, not for tonsured clerks." A similar opinion was emitted about that time by Voltaire's patron, Frederick the Unique.

Old France possessed extensive machinery for the conduct of public education of all grades, the lowest not excepted. Much of it was under the control of the Church; and general opinion, being strongly convinced that education should be religious in character, approved of the arrangement. Municipalities and private enterprises supplemented the work of ecclesiastical bodies. According to Villemain's *Report to the King on Secondary Instruction*, made in 1843, the proportion of children who received secondary instruction in 1789 was 1 in 31, while it was only 1 in 35 in 1842. In the latter year there were 358 *collèges* having 40,091 pupils, of whom 7567 were wholly or partially exempt from fees; in 1789 the numbers were respectively 562, 72,747 and 40,621. Bursaries, free tuition, and low fees were the administrative response to a demand for education which came (on the evidence of La Chalotais, a hostile witness) from ploughmen and mechanics "who send their sons into the *collèges* of small towns where living is cheap." When Condorcet commissioned Romme to estimate the cost of executing the scheme of public instruction, which the former laid before the Legislative Assembly in 1792, Romme reported that the cost "would not exceed that of the former establishments," which he set down at 24,300,000 livres.

The reports made in 1791–2 by Talleyrand, Lanthenas, and

Romme complain, not of the absence of provision for culture, but of the want of co-ordination amongst institutions devoted to that object, and of the encouragement afforded to super- stitious beliefs and anti-republican sentiment. They note the great number of existing schools, colleges, and universities, of independent chairs established in Paris and elsewhere for the advancement of science, of letters, and of the fine arts, the liberal supply of technical instruction in civil and military engineering, the army and navy, the academies and similar corporations for encouraging learning of all kinds, the numerous libraries and collections of maps and of scientific apparatus. Calès told the Convention in July 1793 that "the towns swarm like ant-hills with religious houses" for the education of girls; and boarding schools for the same purpose, under similar direction, existed in the country.

The complaints of these official reports were directed in part against educational inefficiency, in part against political principle. Primary schools, in which "the most indigent" were instructed, were said to be insufficient in number in country districts, and subservient everywhere to the Church, the *collèges* were not progressive but pedantic, the numerous privately founded scholarships and the places of higher education ministered to the privilege of a caste. "None of the old institutions," said Romme, "can be preserved, their forms are too discordant with our republican principles and too remote from the present state of our knowledge." From this sweeping condemnation he excepted the Collège Royal (now the Collège de France), which he held up as a model for the proposed new institu- tions.

Projects on national education, literally innumerable, were brought before the Convention by corporations and by indi- viduals. The majority aimed at giving to the State the monopoly once possessed by the Church, "republican morals and civics" replacing religion. All aimed at rendering a minimum of in- struction generally accessible and giving it gratuitously. Compulsion was favoured by the extremists only, who urged it in the supposed interest of equality amongst citizens; their opponents more than suspected that it would be used to make the government supreme. These schemes however were destitute of any reliable statistical basis, they lacked funds and, above all, they failed to win public sympathy.

Very early in its history the Convention adopted the policy of placing education under government control. In December 1792 it decreed the confiscation of the property of all educational establishments; in the following August all academies and societies, chartered and endowed by the State, were suppressed, the *Académie des Sciences* only excepted. The intention of these acts was to prepare the way for the assumption by the State of the functions of the bodies thus attacked. It was in dealing with advanced instruction and the encouragement of learning and culture that the educational policy of the Revolution obtained its few successes. But the successes consisted in enlarging and bringing under one administration existing institutions devoted to higher education, rather than in creating new. The schools of applied science, military, naval, and engineering, civil as well as military, were united in one great school "of public works"; one of the last acts of the Convention was to complete the organisation of the *École Polytechnique*, as the school was then called, by adding to the numbers of its scholarship-holders and making the entrance examination more severe. The same policy brought into association those various academies which, under the former *régime*, had fostered letters, arts and science; the result is extant in the *Institut de France*. Special schools to give professional instruction in law, in medicine and in other branches of applied science were established, and a beginning was made in training teachers in "normal schools." The names of Lakanal, Daunou, and Fourcroy are connected with these measures.

But in public instruction, as the term is usually understood, the Convention achieved little indeed. It launched grandiose schemes for•schools, both primary and secondary, though it eschewed the latter word as being "aristocratic," "a sanguinary outrage on the principles of equality," and called them "central schools." Yet the majority of French parents obstinately preferred schools of the old order and neither the anti-clerical policy implied in the new schools nor the expressed intention to use them for political propaganda commended them to the bulk of the people. The Lakanal law of 27 *brumaire, an* III (Nov. 17,

1794) permitted private persons to set up schools on condition that they were open to official inspection. Fourcroy, reviewing the situation in 1802, declared that a "multitude of private schools" had sprung up in the interval; these chiefly taught mathematics in preparation for the *École Polytechnique*.

It was evident that the attempted control of the schools by the Executive had failed. Lakanal's report to the Convention on the scheme for "central" schools (February 1795) not only deprecated the aristocratic term "secondary" school, but also explained that the schools proposed were for "young citizens excepted by nature from the ordinary class," the latter, being "common minds whom nature has not destined to genius," going to the primary schools. This seems an even more "sanguinary outrage" on equality. Later in the same year, Daunou was preaching the liberty of the teacher. Fourcroy, reporting under the Consulate, threw over the central schools as of "little use," and replaced them by *lycées* giving a liberal education through ancient and modern letters, mathematics, and physics. He urged local authorities to establish and maintain schools, the Government being too poor to do more than assist, and he gave a welcome to private schools. The true course of morals, he held, consisted in the example of the teachers' lives, the ordered lives of the pupils and the wise and constant occupation of their time.

This was not all sincere, but it was all symptomatic. The plan which Fourcroy was then merely outlining was to be completed on very autocratic principles when the First Consul became Emperor. Bonaparte gave early tokens of his policy, and in no quarter were these more evident than in education. Some five months after the supersession of the Directory, a censorship of the theatres and of the press was instituted which steadily grew more severe till in 1811 (Bonaparte became Emperor in May 1804) both press and theatre were reduced to being mere State instruments. In 1803 the Convention's *Institut de France* was so re-organised that the section of moral and political sciences disappeared and its interests were distributed amongst four sections, physical and mathematical sciences, French language and literature, ancient history and literature, fine art. Fourcroy's law of 1802 was a first step towards Government control of public education.

The Emperor took the next step by creating a corps of teachers, all under State control, characteristically seeking his model in the Company of Jesus. The Imperial University, instituted by a law of May 1806, which was supplemented by a decree of March 1808, was a corporation which included all public teachers of youth from the primary school upwards. Only members of its faculties (letters, science, law, medicine, theology) could conduct schools, and all schools, private schools included, were through their teachers within the university's jurisdiction. Each of the sixteen regions of French territory which was the seat of an appeal court was also the seat of an academy, that is, a body of teachers of all grades under a rector, who was assisted by an academic council and academic inspectors. The sixteen academies, with a council and grand master at the head of affairs, together formed the Imperial University. Schoolmasters were members of the faculties of letters or of science; some academies also contained faculties, teachers, and schools of law (twelve in all), or medicine (five in all), or both. Throughout the university the teaching was based upon the Catholic religion and fidelity to the Emperor and to the Napoleonic dynasty, the safe-guard of French unity and of the constitution.

As with the Jesuits, the university's operations were in fact confined to secondary and higher education. The decree of March 1808 promised measures for recruiting and training teachers of primary schools; but no State funds reached these schools. Their supply and maintenance were left to local authorities and to private persons or bodies, especially to the Brothers of the Christian Schools, who, having returned to France in 1801, had forthwith actively engaged in the work.

By the Concordat of 1802 it was agreed that there should be but one liturgy and one catechism used in all the Catholic churches of France. By 1806, in spite of the clergy and of Rome, the catechism had been shaped by the French Government. It made loyalty to Napoleon and his dynasty a virtue and pronounced "worthy of eternal damnation" those who failed in this duty. It is scarcely surprising that the megalomania of Napoleon and the policy which set up the Imperial University bore the seeds of opposition within themselves. On the collapse of the Empire less than half the secondary education of France was being given in purely public schools. Thirty-six *lycées* with 9000 pupils and 368 municipal *collèges* with 28,000 pupils were in effect rivalled by 1255 private institutions educating 40,000 pupils[1]. Again, the new system failed to secure the adhesion of the people; indeed, the first Grand Master, Louis de Fontanes, appears to have been an active sympathiser with its clerical opponents.

Certain concessions to freedom had had to be made even in the Concordat and in the decree founding the university; Napoleon's administration of public instruction was a series of unsuccessful essays to nullify these. The principle of Lakanal's law of 1794 was part of the university constitution; families and religious *congrégations* were permitted to open schools under the sanction and inspection of the university authorities. But when public opinion and the sympathies of the inspectors and officials favoured these private schools, inspection and terms of university membership were not likely to be exacting. It was to little purpose that regulations tried to hamper these schools by compelling their senior pupils to attend the nearest *lycée* or *collège* for some of their studies; excuses were readily found and accepted. By the Concordat the bishops retained their seminaries for the education of candidates for holy orders; as students of theology were exempt from conscription, the seminaries became popular, although the increased number of their students did not mean an equal increase of the candidates for orders. It became necessary to open preparatory schools, *petits séminaires*, which were even more popular than the bigger institutions. The Government in vain attempted to reduce the number of seminaries, *grands* and *petits*, or tried to confine their privileges to *bona fide* theological students, or endeavoured to render the clerical schools partially dependent upon neighbouring *lycées* or *collèges*, where these lacked the full complement of pupils. Much red-tape was manufactured for these purposes between 1802 and 1803, but the seminaries evaded its meshes.

Yet this relative want of success does not mean that the Imperial University was bound by its nature to fail, because alien to French ideas. In the larger sense, it did not fail; the

---

[1] Pariset, *Cambridge Modern History*, vol. IX, p. 128.

administration of public instruction in France to-day cannot be understood apart from the organisation of the University of France, which in essentials is the Imperial University. By a second thought, the Restoration preserved it, merely changing the persons and the particular objects of its policy; there was, perhaps, greater freedom of teaching under the government of its originator than under those of Louis XVIII and Charles X. Its survival under different forms of government, absolute, constitutional, democratic, proves that this great administrative system is congenial to the French mind, to its feeling for logic and for the inherent solidarity of living, active, human society.

From the Revolution of July 1830 to the beginning of the Second Empire in December 1852, French "politics" revolved chiefly about public instruction. The issue was whether the Church, with the strongest ultramontane leanings, or the State, represented by the university on its more public side, should exercise control. It was a losing fight for the university; but the extreme, reactionary behaviour of the clerical party, aided by the eloquence of men of genius and supported by a genuine religious revival amongst the people, laid the foundation of that bitter hostility which found expression under the Third Republic in Gambetta's "Le clericalisme, voilà l'ennemi!"

The appointment under Louis XVIII of a Royal Council of Public Instruction was an intimation of change quickly followed by an *ordonnance* to the effect that the watchwords of the teaching body were to be "religion, the monarchy, legitimacy, and the charter." The bishops regained their ancient standing as directors of education for their respective dioceses. Private schools were excused from sending their pupils to complete their courses in public schools. Parish priests were permitted each to receive three or four theological students who were to be exempt from the regulations governing private schools, in other words, from university interference. The *École normale supérieure* (founded in 1808–10) and the Faculty of Medicine, being regarded as strongholds of anti-clericalism, were temporarily suspended. Between 1815 and 1820 fifty thousand francs had been voted annually for primary schools; this derisory grant disappeared from the budget in the latter year. England at that date was spending nothing from State funds on education. In 1824 France set up a ministry of public instruction; the first minister was a bishop. An *ordonnance* of 1829 made grave changes in the secondary curriculum. The first place was given to religion. *Philosophie* (that is, the highest class in the *lycées*) saw its course enlarged by the addition of various branches of science, which were to be taught in *Latin*, thus at once diminishing the opportunity for the study of classical authors, hindering the teaching of experimental science, and making it easier to teach scholastic philosophy. History was removed from the studies of *Philosophie* and *Rhétorique* (the class next below), while from the third down to the sixth classes that subject was assigned one hour only per week, the pupil's part being to memorise "clear and precise summaries" of each lesson.

In this struggle for the control of the machine, its true motive power was apt to be forgotten; no great, permanent advance in education was made between 1830 and 1852. But primary instruction was once more organised whilst Guizot was at the ministry of public instruction. By the law of June 26, 1833, each commune, or group of sparsely peopled communes, was required to maintain a school. The teachers were to be State servants. Poor pupils were to be taught gratuitously; those who could were to pay fees. Attendance was not obligatory. All communes of more than 6000 inhabitants and every *chef-lieu de departe-ment* (county-town) were each to possess a higher primary school, teaching the common applications in daily life of the elements of physical and natural science, geometry, drawing, surveying, singing, history, and geography, that of France especially. The courses were to be adapted to local conditions. This provision of the law of 1833 took effect but slowly; the higher primary school under direct public control almost came to an end under the Falloux law. During Guizot's ministry science courses became the rule in all classes of secondary school, and in 1838 modern languages were made obligatory in the communal *collèges*, the secondary schools below the rank of the State *lycée*.

The university and the purely public schools were slowly yielding to clerical persistency. In 1830 the Brothers of the Christian Schools were teaching 87,000 French children; in 1847 the number stood at 175,000. A petition in favour of granting

liberty of secondary instruction secured 80,000 signatures in
1846; next year a similar petition numbered 140,000 adherents.
The Church demanded "freedom of instruction," which, in
concrete terms, meant the abolition of university monopoly,
and exemption from the requirement of degrees, or of certificates
of having studied in a *lycée* or *collège*, which was laid upon
private teachers and members of the *congrégations*. The clerical
party urged these measures on the ground that the teaching of
the university was immoral, anti-Christian and subversive of the
social order; the spread of "liberalism" and the general unrest
throughout Europe were regarded as additional reasons for
curbing or suppressing the alleged teaching.

The Falloux law of March 1850 secured the triumph of this
policy. Dupanloup thus enumerated the victories assured by
this law. The *petits séminaires* were liberated from university
control, teaching *congrégations* hitherto proscribed or ignored by
law secured admission to the educational system as constituent
members, degrees or *certificats d'études* were not required from
teachers, and generally the university's monopoly was lost.

It had in fact passed to the ultramontanes. The dominant
position in the Council of Public Instruction and in the academic
councils was assured to ecclesiastics, some of whom were not
university teachers and might not possess university degrees.
Before and after the enactment of the Falloux law, there had
been changes in the university personnel: fixity of tenure was
gone and the teachers and inspectors who had hitherto formed the
academic councils were swamped by the newcomers. Private
schools, including those conducted by *congrégations*, might be
inspected from the point of view of morals and hygiene; their
instruction could only be inspected to ensure that it was not
contrary to law. Membership of the ministry of an authorised
cult qualified a man to teach; a nun's letters of obedience were
equivalent to a certificate of capacity, and the regulations seemed
to anticipate that most girls would be taught by nuns.
Lacordaire[1] called the law the Edict of Nantes of the 19th
century; but it emphasised, if it did not create, a breach in the
national life. Some Frenchmen reflected that this breach was

---

[1] M. Arnold, *A French Eton*, has an account of Lacordaire's school at Sorèze
as it was in 1859. See also his *Schools and Universities on the Continent*.

instigated by an alien corporation in whose interest it was chiefly maintained. The point should not be overlooked in connexion with the anti-clerical measures of a later time.

But this law was not altogether contentious. It required that in drawing up courses for the *lycées* and *collèges* local conditions should be considered. Encouragement was given to the publication of books which might be usefully employed in Sunday schools, works' schools, almshouses, in courses of public lectures. *Salles d'asile* (infants' schools), schools for adults over 18, schools for apprentices over 12 were recognised. While the communal chest and school fees were to find most of the pay of the *instituteurs* and *institutrices* (the names by which primary school teachers had been known since 1791–2), the State guaranteed a minimum stipend of 600 francs yearly.

Victor Duruy, who stood for the policy of La Chalotais, became Minister of Public Instruction in June 1863, and the Falloux law received its first set-back. In spite of opposition from ministerial colleagues and those engaged professionally in education, Duruy tried to laicize public education by developing the State organisation of primary schools, by introducing the State education of girls (hitherto the business of religious communities almost exclusively) and by increasing the lay element amongst teachers. The examination called the *agrégation* (which may be compared with an examination for fellowships in British universities) was again made a necessary qualification for the senior posts in the *lycées*, thus abolishing a clerical privilege. The restoration of classical studies to their former place in secondary and higher instruction, and of *Philosophie* (the French "Sixth Form") to its earlier character and content, the introduction of history later than 1815, were parts of the same policy. The institution of school libraries, of courses of lessons and lectures for adults, of training courses for women secondary school teachers, the introduction of physical training and of economics into the courses, the establishment of research laboratories and of the teaching of applied science, were also measures of the Duruy ministry. It failed in its attempt to create a purely modern type of instruction, literary and scientific; teachers were very hostile and parents indifferent to the project.

The events of 1870–1871 led to much discussion of public education, which was complicated by the quarrel between the executive and the clerical party, a quarrel that led to the adoption of the principle that in religion the State must be neutral. The Third Republic completed the State system which had been forming for nearly a century. In primary instruction the policy was to make such teaching gratuitous, universally accessible and compulsory; the policy was rendered effective by laws passed in 1881, 1882, and 1886 respectively. The principle of religious neutrality was applied *à outrance* by the law on associations of July 1901, which a year later completely severed the congregations from the work of education and so closed some 2500 schools and charitable institutions.

In 1881 *salles d'asile* were replaced by *écoles maternelles* for children between the ages of two and six. Compulsory attendance now begins on completion of the latter age and is obligatory till thirteen, except that pupils who, after the age of eleven, pass the examination for the *certificat d'études primaires élémentaires* are exempt. In addition to the "three Rs," primary instruction comprises very careful teaching of the mother-tongue, the teaching of object-lessons, singing, drawing, hand-work, and some history and geography. Moral and civic lessons also are integral parts of the course; a former Minister of Public Instruction, M. Georges Leygues, describes these as inculcating "le patriotisme, la liberté, la justice, la République" (*L'école et la vie*).

The studies prescribed in the primary school for the four years between seven and eleven are virtually identical with those of the *divisions préparatoire et élémentaire* which, during the same period, precede the secondary instruction of the *lycée*. To that extent France may be said to possess a "common school,"rightly named primary rather than elementary. Above the primary school, but in no relation with *lycée* or *collège*, is the higher primary school (of four sections) with a three-year course covering the years from 11 or 12 to 14 or 15. The general section may be regarded as continuing the primary school studies, with mathematics and a modern language added. The first of its three years is common to all four sections; on the completion of this first year pupils either remain in that section or pass to one of the other sections, commercial, industrial, agricultural. Naturally, no one school has all four sections; beyond the general section organisation is conditioned by local needs. Where there is no higher primary school, a *cours complémentaire* of one year may be added to the courses, *élémentaire, moyen, supérieur* of the primary school, which are followed between the ages of seven and thirteen. As is the case with this type of English school, most of the pupils, boys and girls, fail to complete the full three years' schooling. Tuition is gratuitous; some of these schools are boarding schools, payment being exacted for board and lodging. Scholarships assist children from the primary schools to attend the higher primary schools as well as the *lycées* and *collèges*, which also are wholly or partially boarding schools. As in the secondary, so in the primary school field, local authorities cooperate with the State in financing and conducting education. Adult courses, evening lectures, and popular libraries belong to the administration of primary instruction.

While the primary school policy was being developed, government turned its attention to the re-establishment of universities as distinct from the University of France, the hierarchy of teachers and administrators originated by Napoleon. A process extending from 1885 to 1896 first formed the faculties of that University into separate corporations, each with a legal status; next, the faculties in each academic district received a like status, thus making possible local universities of two or more faculties, that is, of letters, of science, and of one or more other faculties. Finally, the separate and largely autonomous universities were constituted. The University of France consists of seventeen academies, Algiers being one, named from the towns which are the official seats of their rectors and academic councils; sixteen of these are universities in the ordinary meaning of the word. The State pays the teachers, maintains scholarships, provides equipment; in 1913 its contribution exceeded one million pounds sterling. Tuition is gratuitous in all French institutions of higher education, universities included. There is no system of residential colleges. Degrees are awarded on the results of State, not university, examinations; for these candidates may prepare where and how they will. Each university confers many kinds of diploma, one of the most recently created and best known outside France being that of *Docteur de l'Université*.

But the higher education of France is by no means limited to its universities. The various institutions maintained for that purpose by the State, by municipalities and by private bodies are far too many to be even named here; they cover all forms of knowledge, "pure" and "applied," of technology and of art. The Collège de France and the École nationale des Chartes are eminent amongst these great places of learning and of culture; both are in Paris, with whose university neither is associated.

The greatest educational change wrought of late has been in the studies of the *lycée* and *collège*; it dates from 1902. The earliest years of the Third Republic witnessed a long controversy between the partisans of the older type of classical education, or of modern literary and scientific culture, and of those who regarded a more direct preparation for a professional career as the main business of the secondary school. In the meantime those who preferred State predominance in public instruction noted that the *écoles libres*, controlled chiefly by the *congréga-tions*, were proving very successful rivals of the State *lycées* and the communal *collèges*. At the opening of this century, the *écoles libres* numbered 439, one hundred in excess of the other secondary schools. Apart from the parents' preferences, con-tributory causes to the difference were the facts that boarding fees were fixed and high under the State, variable and low, or very low, under the *congrégations*, and that pupils of the *écoles libres* received assistance with reference to their future careers, which the less elastic State schools did not give. French thought concerning education is, and always has been, very sensitive to the distinction between education and instruction; official programmes and individual thinkers have constantly emphasised it. Yet paradoxically the State schools since Napoleon's day have employed very able instructors, the *professeurs*, while they have entrusted the moral and more purely educative part of the *lycéen's* school-life to a relatively inferior body of men, the *répétiteurs*. The number of full boarders has decreased in recent years; yet it still contains a considerable part of the pupils in *lycées* and *collèges* and those who do not board spend a long day under school discipline. The professors of the *lycées* are probably unrivalled as capable, learned schoolmasters of highly cultivated minds; yet by common consent the State system appears to develop a uniform type amongst pupils at the individual's expense.

Like ourselves, perhaps even more than ourselves, the French have made examinations play a great part in their system. Every course, primary, higher primary, secondary, institutional or university looks to a public examination, usually of a severe sort. The *baccalauréat* examination closes the secondary course and opens further courses and professional careers to the successful. Its content and standard have necessarily figured in all discussions on secondary education; teachers, pupils, and studies have all felt the constraining power of this examination. There is a growing disposition to make the examination depend upon the teaching by encouraging the collaboration of teachers and examiners and by taking into account a pupil's record, his *livret scolaire*, when assessing the final result. After many experiments, there is now but one *baccalauréat* awarded, irrespective of the branch of study followed by the pupil in the secondary school.

France, Germany, Italy, and England were all debating public education when the twentieth century opened. In England discussion was limited to the very important but purely administrative problem, how to set up a national system; in the other three countries the question was how to adapt curricula to the life of to-day in schools already existing. Germany and Italy reformed their secondary schools in 1901; after an exhaustive parliamentary inquiry during 1898–9, France, in 1902, laid down courses for secondary schools which, in spite of some fundamental changes, maintained the tradition, as old as Roman Gaul, of making the rhetorical study of the Latin language and literature the staple of education for most boys. Beginning about the age of eleven, the full secondary course occupies seven years, divided into two cycles of four and three years respectively. The first cycle (classes 6e up to 3e) consists of Division A, classical, in which Latin is obligatory but Greek optional, and Division B modern or scientific, with no Latin or Greek, modern languages supplying the humanist matter. A *certificat d'études* is awarded to those who successfully complete the course; some pupils then leave school. To avoid the mistake of confining a pupil within an unsuitable division, passage from A to B, or *vice versa*, is possible. The second cycle (classes *seconde, première, philosophie*) is divided into four branches: A, Latin, with Greek; B, Latin, with a study of modern languages carried beyond that of the first cycle; C, Latin, with a similar study of science; and D, modern languages and science, but no Latin. French occupies an important place in the work of all the classes from 6e to *première*; the study of the mother-tongue and of its parent, Latin, is and long has been the distinctive feature of French education. It has left its mark on all written and spoken French for more than two hundred years past; it has made all Frenchmen sensible of the vitality of Latin civilisation, their debt to it and the obligation to hand it down unimpaired to posterity.

In some *lycées* there is a *branche courte* lasting two years; the programme of studies is determined locally, but the general idea is to give instruction in applied science. Although very like the higher primary school in purpose, its roots are in the first cycle of *lycée* or *collège*. It is a concession to the demand for "real" or "useful studies," which disposes boys, or their parents, to prefer branches B, C or D, before A.

The public instruction of girls above the primary school is not sixty years old in France; while Duruy was Minister he recognised certain secondary courses of three years' duration, which proved so successful that in 1880 *lycées* for girls were established. The courses, of five years' duration, are literary and mathematical. Girls' *lycées* are winning their place in French life; some observers think they are the brightest feature of the country's education. Certainly they have no lack of excellent material in French feminine mentality.

§ III. LEARNING FROM 1660

Among the signal services rendered to France by the great minister Colbert, not the least was the encouragement of learning. The two chief French Orientalists of the 17th century, Barthélemy d'Herbelot (1625–1695) and François Petis de la Croix (1653–1713) were among the recipients of his favour and patronage; they were appointed professors at the Collège de

France in the same year (1692), d'Herbelot of Syriac, and Petis de la Croix of Arabic. In general learning the foremost man of this time was Colbert's librarian, Étienne Baluze (1630–1718). He not only made his patron's library one of the finest in Europe, but he collected largely on his own behalf—his manuscripts numbered 1500—edited numerous texts, and published several substantial volumes on subjects connected with French mediaeval history.

His love of learning brought him into close relations with the Benedictines of Saint-Maur at Saint-Germain-des-Prés. Their splendid series of monuments was inaugurated in 1655 by Dom Luc d'Achery with the first volume of his great *Spicilegium*. He handed on the torch to Jean Mabillon (1632–1707), perhaps the greatest of all these princes of learning, who is represented by his immortal *De Re Diplomatica* (1681) with its noble motto, *Scientia veri justique vindex*, his edition of St Bernard, and his *Acta* of the Saints of his Order. He had worthy successors in his pupil, friend, and biographer, Thierry Ruinart, in Denys de Sainte-Marthe, the editor of *Gallia Christiana*, in Martène and Durand, the two companions of the famous *Voyage littéraire*, and above all in Bertrand de Montfaucon (1655–1741), the editor of Athanasius and Chrysostom, the compiler of the *Bibliotheca Bibliothecarum*, and the author of *L'Antiquité expliquée* (1719), of which 1800 copies were sold in two months, and *Palaeographica Graeca*, which laid the foundations of Greek palaeography. The next generation was represented by Dom Rivet, who began the *Histoire littéraire de la France*; Dom Bouquet, the first editor of the historians of Gaul and France; and Dom Clément, who is chiefly famous as the editor of a new edition of *L'Art de vérifier les dates*. He died at the age of eighty in 1793, the year after the suppression of the great abbey which had done so much for learning. It is significant that after the publication of the last volume of Montfaucon's Chrysostom (1738) the Benedictines abandoned the ecclesiastical field for that of French history and literature. Notable work was also done for the national history by the Academy of Inscriptions (both collectively and by individual members), by the Dominican, Father Lelong, who published in 1718 his great *Bibliothèque historique de la France*. The study of classical archaeology was ably promoted by the travels, writings, and liberality of the Comte de Caylus (1692–1765), and that of numismatics by the Abbé Jean-Jacques de Barthélemy (1716–1795), the author of the *Voyage du jeune Anacharsis en Grèce*.

The Revolutionary era was not favourable to learning. Napoleon was too great a statesman to ignore its importance, but his autocratic methods hampered its free development, and his own inclinations were rather towards science than towards what is usually known as learning.

However, in the year of his first downfall, a notable piece of work was accomplished by the publication of a new volume of the *Histoire littéraire de la France*, that great undertaking which had been begun by the Benedictine, Dom Rivet, but which had been interrupted since 1763. It was now resumed by a group of laymen with Pierre Daunou (1761–1840), an ex-Oratorian, one of the most learned men of his day, as editor. Fellow-workers with him, and successors, were Claude Fauriel (1772–1844), Joséph-Victor Leclerc (1789–1865), Paulin Paris (1800–1881), Émile Littré (1801–1881), Barthélemy Hauréau (1812–1896), the historian of scholastic philosophy, Ernest Renan (1823–1892), Léopold Delisle (1826–1910), Gaston Paris (1839–1893), and Paul Meyer (1840–1917). Of these Gaston Paris vitalised the study of French mediaeval literature by the warmth of his sympathy and the charm of his style, while Delisle and Meyer did incomparable service as editors of mediaeval texts; in the same field worked Natalis de Wailly (1805–1886), the editor of Villehardouin and Joinville, Francisque Michel (1809–1887), who published the first edition of the *Chanson de Roland* (from the MS. in Bodley's library) and many other mediaeval texts, and Léon Gautier (1832–1897), who besides his classical edition of the famous *Chanson* thoroughly explored the whole field of the *chansons de gestes*. Lastly Joseph Bédier (*b.* 1864), both by his teaching and by his published work, has inaugurated a new and fruitful era in mediaeval studies. Celtic studies have been worthily represented by Henry Arbois de Jubainville (1827–1910).

Gaston Paris, Delisle, Meyer, and Gautier were all closely connected with the École des Chartes, which, planned by Napoleon and founded in 1821 for the study of palaeography and the older

French literature, developed later into a training-school for historians. To this school belonged Gabriel Monod (1844–1912), whose influence as a teacher was far-reaching and who did much for the study of historical sources, and Achille Luchaire (1846–1908) the chief authority for the history of the 12th and 13th centuries.

But the organisation of the critical study of history dates back to François Guizot (1787–1874), who, as Minister of Public Instruction, founded the *Société de l'histoire de France* (1834) and began the publication of the great collection of the *Documents inédits* (1835). Before this he had made his mark as a historian, partly by his lectures at the Sorbonne, but chiefly by the publication of his *Histoire de la Civilisation en Europe* (1824) and his *Histoire de la Révolution en Angleterre* (1826–27). Looking in history for guiding ideas, he found them in the structure of society and he studied man chiefly as a social organism. This being his aim, it was natural that reason and analysis should take the place of emotion and colour. Similar qualities, allied to a greater regard for artistic presentation, inform the sober and careful political histories of François Mignet (1796–1884), whose *Histoire de la Révolution* appeared in the same year, 1824, as Guizot's first work. On the other hand Mignet's friend and fellow-Provençal, Adolphe Thiers (1797–1877), shows in his great *Histoire du Consulat et de l'Empire* (1845–1862) a remarkable talent for arranging and controlling large masses of facts, and for presenting them in a style, which, however open to criticism in detail, has the artistic simplicity essential for so long a narrative.

Alexis de Tocqueville (1805–1859) was a political thinker rather than a historian. In his *De la Démocratie en Amérique* he investigated the problem of reconciling democracy with liberty in the spirit of calm judicial inquiry, and the same spirit animates his later work, *L'Ancien Régime et la Révolution* (1850). Numa-Denys Fustel de Coulanges (1830–1889), after writing a brilliant work, *La Cité antique* (1864), which is a model of artistic construction and lucid exposition, adopted a more scientific method, based on laborious research, and applied it to the early history of French institutions in volumes which revolutionised the whole study of the subject—*Histoire des institutions politiques de la France* (1875–1892). Paul Viollet (1840–1914) carried on this side of Fustel's work; Albert Sorel (1842–1906) in *L'Europe et la Révolution française* (1885–1904) studied the revolutionary period from the diplomatic side; and Pierre-Émile Levasseur (1828–1912) for nearly half a century made contributions of great importance to the history of the working classes, and wrote much on other economic subjects. Among living historians may be mentioned Camille Jullian (*b.* 1859), the historian of Gaul, a pupil of Fustel de Coulanges, and Charles Diehl (*b.* 1859), who has given new life to Byzantine studies. Political economy has been ably represented by Paul Leroy-Beaulieu (1843–1916). The chief authority on the geography of France has been Paul Vidal de la Blache (1845–1918), while the researches of Rodolphe Dareste de la Chavanne (1848–1912) in comparative law have covered a large field of ancient and modern jurisprudence.

Apart from her own literature and history, the field in which French learning achieved the greatest distinction during the last century was that of Oriental studies. The pioneer was Abraham-Hyacinthe Anquetil-Duperron (1731–1805), who brought back from India in 1762 nearly 200 manuscripts, chiefly Zend and Sanscrit, and whose translation of the *Avesta* (1771), though it has the inevitable defects of pioneer work, had the merit of introducing the religion of ancient Persia to Europe.

But the real inspirer of modern Oriental studies, not only in France but throughout Europe, was Antoine-Isaac, Baron Silvestre de Sacy (1758–1838), who, in 1822, with Abel Rémusat, founded the *Société Asiatique* with the *Journal Asiatique* for its organ. He knew many languages, but he made a special study of Persian, and above all of Arabic. Of his pupils, to whom he was a constant inspiration, Joseph Reinaud (1795–1867) chiefly devoted himself to the study of Arabic geography and history; Armand Caussin de Perceval (1795–1871), professor of Arabic at the Collège de France for nearly 40 years, wrote on early Arabian history; William MacGuckin, Baron de Slane (1801–1878), an Irishman by birth, translated into English the celebrated biographical dictionary of Ibn Khallikán; Albert de Biberstein Kazimirski (1808–1887), besides important work in Persian, published an Arabic-French dictionary, which has become a classic; and Joseph Garcin de Tassy (1794–1878), a

Persian and Arabic scholar, took up at the suggestion of his master the study of Hindi and Hindustani, in which he did brilliant work. Charles Defrémery (1822–1883), Casimir Barbier de Meynard (1826–1908) and Stanislas Guyard (1846–1884), who died young, combined Persian with Arabic and worked in more or less the same field as Reinaud. A new line was opened up by A. Pavet de Courteille (1821–1889) in the study of eastern Turki, the original language of the Turks.

Joseph Halévy (1827–1917) travelled for two years (1869–1871) in Yemen, where he collected and deciphered numerous Sabaean inscriptions; Hartwig Derembourg (1844–1908), a pupil of Reinaud, worked in the same field and also published the Arabic text of the autobiography of a Syrian emir, Usama Ibn Munkid, who lived during the first century of the Crusades. François Woepcke (1826–1864), who was a mathematician as well as an Arabic scholar, and whose early death at the same age as Guyard was a great loss to Oriental studies, translated into French (1851) an Arabic treatise on Algebra by Omar Khayyám. Sixteen years later the famous Quatrains of the astronomer-poet were made known to Europe by J.-B. Nicolas, French consul at Resht, who published a Persian text with a literal prose translation.

Ethiopic studies have been represented in France by Antoine d'Abadie (1810–1897), a native of Dublin, who spent twelve years in Abyssinia.

As regards the other Semitic languages the chair of Hebrew, Chaldee, and Syriac at the Collège de France was held for many years by Ernest Renan (1823–1892), who began his literary career with his brilliant *Histoire générale et système comparé des langues sémitiques*, and who was the originator and chief inspirer of the *Corpus inscriptionum semiticarum*. Paul-Rubens Duval (1839–1911) was distinguished both in Syriac and Aramaic; Jules Oppert (1825–1905) may be said to have founded Assyriology; and Charles-Simon Clermont-Ganneau (*b.* 1846), like Renan and Oppert a professor at the Collège de France, has done excellent work in Semitic archaeology.

Jean-François Champollion (1790–1832) shares with the English physicist, Thomas Young, the honour of being the first to decipher Egyptian hieroglyphics. Many years after his premature death François Mariette (1821–1881) founded in Egypt a great school of archaeology and his successor, Gaston Maspero (1846–1916), carried on with great energy the work of translation and publication.

In 1815 the first European chair of Sanscrit was founded at the Collège de France for Antoine de Chézy (1773–1832). He had a brilliant successor in Eugène Burnouf (1801–1852), who in his too short life rendered incomparable services to the study both of Buddhism and Zoroastrianism. Auguste Barth (1834–1916), also made an important contribution to our knowledge of eastern religions in his *Religions de l'Inde* and in his bulletins on the same subject. He has worthy successors in the same field in Émile Senart (*b.* 1847) and Sylvain Lévi (*b.* ˙1863).

Persian studies owe a great debt to Étienne Quatremère (1782–1857), professor for thirty years at the *École des langues orientales vivantes*, founded by the Convention for political and commercial purposes in 1795 and reorganised in 1838. His colleague at the Collège de France, Jules Mohl (1800–1876), left a monumental work in his edition with a translation of the *Livre des Rois* of the Persian poet, Firdawsí, and a brilliant pupil in James Darmesteter (1849–1894), who added largely to our knowledge of Zoroastrianism, and as the result of travel in Afghanistan went far to prove that the language of the Avesta is the ancestor of modern Afghan. Charles Schefer (1820–1898), Quatremère's successor, was a great collector of rare Persian and Arabic MSS. and a translator of Persian historical narratives, but in knowledge both of Persian and Arabic he was inferior to Hermann Zotenberg (1836–1894), Keeper of the MSS. at the Bibliothèque Nationale. The Comte de Gobineau (1816–1882) obtained an insight into the oriental character such as few have possessed; his *Les Religions et les Philosophies dans l'Asie Centrale* (1863) and *Trois ans en Asie* (1859) are classics. Lastly Marcel Dieulafoy (*b.* 1844) has carried out important excavations at Susa and is the author of a great work on early Persian art.

The pioneer of Chinese studies in France was Joseph de Guignes (1721–1800) whose great work, *Histoire générale des Huns, Turcs, Moguls et autres Tartares occidentaux* was published in 1756–1758. He had a distinguished successor in Abel Rémusat (1788–1832), but the first thoroughly well-equipped Chinese scholar was Stanislas Julien (1799–1873) who translated many Chinese works, notably the *Life of Hsüan Tsang*, a travelled priest of the 7th century. In recent years the chief representative of Chinese studies in France has been Édouard Chavannes (1865–1918), who died before his great and varied knowledge had borne full fruit. His chief work, left unfinished, was the translation of the great history of Ssŭ-ma Ch'ien. An archaeological expedition which he made to northern China in 1907 had important results.

Classical studies did not greatly flourish in France during the first half of the 19th century; the best scholars of that period were of German origin, notably Carl Hase (1780–1864) who edited for Didot the great Greek *Thesaurus* of Henri Estienne, and his associate Frederic Duebner (1802–1867), who also edited numerous volumes of the *Scriptores graecorum librorum*, and Henry Weil (1818–1909) whose admirable work in the field of Greek tragedy and wide-spread influence were honourably recognised in the *Mélanges* published on the occasion of his eightieth anniversary.

Useful work was also done by archaeologists, such as Philippe Lebas (1794–1860), William Waddington (1826–1894), the statesman and diplomatist, who studied the epigraphy and numismatics of Asia Minor, the many-sided François Lenormant (1837–1883), and Georges Perrot (1832–1914), whose great *Histoire de l'Art grec* was completed in ten volumes in the year of his death.

The foundation of the French School of Athens (1846), followed by that of Rome in 1873, did much to promote the study of archaeology, while the *École pratique des Hautes Études* (1868) gave a strong impulse to classical studies generally. One of its founders was Michel Bréal (1832–1915), the author of the famous *Essai de Sémantique* (1897), who quickened the study of comparative grammar and philology by his rare intelligence, and by his happy blending of the scientific with the humanistic spirit. His chair at the Collège de France is worthily filled by Antoine Meillet (*b.* 1866).

During the last thirty years classical studies have made great progress in France. Their chief living representatives are Louis Havet (*b.* 1849), who has done excellent work on Latin texts, especially on Plautus, Émile Chatelain (b. 1851), whose special province is Latin palaeography, Théophile Homolle (b. 1848), famous for his excavations at Delphi, Delos, and elsewhere, Maurice Croiset (b. 1846), the historian of Greek literature, René Cagnat (b. 1852), who has contributed so largely to our knowledge of Roman Africa, Ernest Babelon (b. 1854), the accomplished numismatist, Solomon Reinach (b. 1858), who rivals, with greater accuracy, the many-sided industry of François Lenormant, and his brother, Théodore (b. 1860), remarkable both as historian and philologist, and Henry Omont (b. 1857), the distinguished palaeographist, who is on the commission of the *Histoire littéraire* and is as much at home with French manuscripts as he is with Greek and Latin ones. The brilliant career of Charles Graux (1852–1884), who especially distinguished himself in Greek epigraphy, was cut short by his early death.

Theology, too, in its various branches has been worthily represented by Samuel Berger (1843–1900), who did excellent and durable work on the Vulgate, by Albert Réville (1826–1906), who published four volumes on the *Histoire des Religions*, and by the Abbé Duchesne (1843–1922), sometime Director of the French School at Rome, whose great edition of the *Liber Pontificalis* appeared in 1884–1889, and who has since then devoted himself to the early history of the French Church. His pupil Alfred Loisy (b. 1857), starting from the foundations of solid learning, has been carried by his inquiries far beyond the bounds of orthodoxy. If not actually the creator of Modernism he is at least its most conspicuous figure.

We see from this brief and imperfect survey that during the last hundred years the greatest achievements of French learning have been on the whole in Oriental studies and her own mediaeval literature, and that after the Restoration historical studies, which had greatly languished during the second half of the 18th century, made a fresh and vigorous start. In other departments, though good work was done, the advance for a time was not so striking. But when France had shaken off the discouragement and depression caused by the Franco-German war she began to organise every branch of learning on sound and scientific lines. For the last five and twenty years her research work has been the admiration of students; and the École des Chartes has, in some respects, furnished the best historical training in Europe. French learning has proved that it can be patient, industrious, and thorough, and it has in addition clarity of thought, sureness of method, and that power to distinguish the important from the unimportant which is the sign of true critical insight. Above all, true to the traditions of Descartes and Pascal, of Malebranche and Montesquieu, it knows how to make itself intelligible to the unlearned as well as to the learned, to the layman as well as to the expert. It adores reason, it abhors jargon, and in its endeavour to be scientific it does not cease to be literary.

BIBLIOGRAPHY

F.-E. Buisson, *Dictionnaire de Pédagogie*, 1880–1882 (historical and biographical notices in the first edition only). G. Compayré, *Histoire critique des doctrines de l'Éducation en France*, 2 vols. 2nd ed. 1880. J. W. Adamson, *Pioneers of Modern Education, 1600–1700*, Cambridge, 1905. K. A. and G. Schmid, *Geschichte der Erziehung*, II 2–IV 1, Stuttgart, 1889–1896.

A. Douarche, *L'Université de Paris et les Jésuites*, 1888. P. Lallemand, *Histoire de l'Éducation dans l'ancien Oratoire de France*, 1888. A.-E.-A. Perraud, *L'Oratoire de France aux xviie et xviiie siècles*, 1865. H. C. Barnard, *The Little Schools of Port-Royal*, Cambridge, 1913; *Port-Royal*, Cambridge, 1918. J. Carré, *Les Pédagogues des Port-Royal*, 1887. T. Lavallée, *Œuvres de Mme de Maintenon*, 8 vols. 1854; *Histoire de la Maison royale de Saint-Cyr*, 1856. C. Rollin, *Le Traité des Études* in *Œuvres*, ed. Letronne, 1821–1825.

G. K. Fortescue, *List of the contents of three collections of books, pamphlets, and journals, in the British Museum, relating to the French Revolution*, 1899. V.-C.-O. Gréard, *Législation de l'Instruction primaire en France depuis 1783*, 3 vols. 1874; *L'Éducation des Femmes par les Femmes*, 1886; *Éducation et Instruction*, 4 vols. 1887. E. Allain, *La Question d'Enseignement en 1789 d'après les Cahiers*, 1886. L. Liard, *Histoire de l'Enseignement supérieur en France, 1789–1893*, 2 vols. 1888–1894; *L'Université de Paris*, 1909.

A. Croiset and others, *Enseignement et Démocratie*, 1905. F. E. Farrington, *The public primary school system of France*, 1906; *French secondary schools*, 1915.

     See also French tracts relating to education, 1830–1852 (Catalogue of the British Museum), and Special Reports on Educational subjects (Board of Education), vols. I, II, VII, VIII, 1896, etc.

Comte de Franqueville, *Le premier siècle de l'Institut de France*, 1895.

CHAPTER VIII

LITERATURE

§ I. SIXTEENTH CENTURY

IT is impossible to give a definite date for the beginning of modern French literature. The most that can be said is that the transition from medieval literature to modern took place under the influence of the Renaissance spirit. What then was this spirit? It was a spirit of restless energy, of eager curiosity, of revolt against authority and tradition, of free inquiry into long-established doctrines, of insistence on the rights and claims of the individual, of desire for beauty and colour in life, of belief in the goodness and dignity of man. But all these symptoms are vague, elusive, and difficult to trace. A more recognisable characteristic of the Renaissance is the revived study of Greek and Latin literature, or, as it is usually called, Humanism. Further, the country in which the Renaissance spirit first manifested itself in a marked degree, and in which Humanism first made a substantial progress, was Italy. Thus the expedition of Charles VIII to Italy, which historians with some reason have fixed on as marking the beginning of modern French history, is also an important date in the history of French literature.

Literature, however, was slow to respond to the new forces that were set in motion by this event. In 1494, under the dominating influence of the *grands rhétoriqueurs*, it was still thoroughly medieval in character, and for the next thirty years it still remained medieval. But the expedition of Charles VIII, and still more the occupation by Louis XII of the Duchy of Milan for twelve years, did much to prepare the soil. The leading men of France, princes and nobles, prelates and ministers, were captivated by the stately beauty of the Italian palaces and gardens.

A few even were able to appreciate the artistic treasures which were the pride of the Italian cities, or to profit by intercourse with Italian humanists. At the same time Italian scholars and artists came at the invitation of Charles VIII or Louis XII to France, and encouraged by guidance and example their French brethren to follow in their footsteps.

It was not only from Italy that the Renaissance spirit in France derived nourishment and stimulus. Another pervading influence was that of the Low Countries. Among the pioneers of French Humanism there was a large sprinkling of Flemings. Josse Badius, scholar, printer, and publisher, who did so much for both the elementary and the higher study of classical literature, was born at Ghent. Jacques Lefèvre, the *doyen* of French scholars as well as of French reformers, was born at Étaples, one of the towns on the Somme which Louis XI had ceded to the Duke of Burgundy. But chief of the scholars who came from the Low Countries to France, and who helped to mould the forces not only of French Humanism but of the whole French Renaissance, was the great Dutchman, Erasmus. From the publication of the second and enlarged edition of his *Adagia* (1508) onwards, he exercised an ever-increasing influence on French scholarship and thought and literature. When Rabelais in a memorable letter addressed him as *Pater mi humanissime*, he was but expressing the feelings of the whole band of French humanists from Budé downwards.

During the reigns of Charles VIII and Louis XII, while learning steadily advanced, literature remained stagnant. One man alone rose superior to his training and his traditions. He was a Netherlander in the service of Margaret of Austria, JEAN LEMAIRE (1472 or 3–*c.* 1515) of Belges or Bavai in Hainault. Though by no means free from the faults of his contemporaries, he had what they lacked—imagination, a poet's feeling for movement and harmony, and a natural gift for narrative and descriptive prose. He had too a considerable share of the versatility, the love of beauty, and the humanism which are characteristic of the Renaissance spirit. In verse he was the master of both Marot and Ronsard, while his chief prose work, *Les Illustrations de Gaule*, of which the first book appeared in 1510, had a still more illustrious student in Rabelais.

The Early Renaissance

The accession of Francis I was full of promise for the growth
of the new spirit, for by training and education he was a child
of the Renaissance, and, though his intelligence was superficial
and his character unstable, he had a real regard for learning and
letters. Thus to the influence of Italy and Humanism there was
added a third influence, that of the Court. In his dispensation
of patronage the King was greatly helped by his sister, MARGARET
of ANGOULÊME (1492–1549), the wife first of the Duc d'Alençon
and then of the King of Navarre. She was a Latin, Italian, and
Spanish scholar, and a facile writer of both verse and prose.
Her verse only rises on rare occasions, under the impulse of
mystical fervour, to real poetry, but her prose charms us by its
modern air of ease and good breeding. The actual stories,
however, of her *Heptameron* are greatly inferior to the conversations with which they are interspersed. These not only show
much insight into character, but they give an interesting picture
of the intellectual and social atmosphere of the age.

Among those who profited by the Queen of Navarre's patronage and protection was the poet CLÉMENT MAROT (1496 or 7–
1544). Born at Cahors, but of Norman stock, he made his *début*
by presenting to the young king a poem, of which the title
Le Temple de Cupidon was suggested by two pieces of Lemaire's.
He had less learning and less of the Renaissance spirit than his
predecessor, but he had the advantage of being a Frenchman
by birth as well as by speech and culture. Attached to the
household first of Margaret and then of the King, aided by his
native tact and good sense, he gradually threw off the pedantry
and provincialism which were among the fundamental causes of
the absurdities of the *rhétoriqueur* school. Yet it was not till
about the year 1524 that he began to write in a really natural
vein. From that time his poetical powers steadily matured, and
in 1532 he published the first collected edition of his poems,
under the title of *L'Adolescence Clémentine*. Meanwhile he had
become a Protestant and the last ten years of his life were
chequered by persecution and exile. After two winters at Geneva,
where he worked out his translation of the Psalms, he died in
obscurity at Turin in 1544.

In Marot's work medieval and Renaissance sympathies are happily blended. He remains faithful to many of the medieval forms of verse, but his *chansons* (*Qui veult avoir liesse*) and *rondeaux* (*De sa grande amye*; *Au bon vieulx temps*) have a clarity and artistic finish which are rare in medieval work. Though he had no Greek and little Latin, he followed with considerable success Martial in epigrams, Virgil in eclogues, and Ovid in elegies. Together with his songs and *rondeaux* his Epistles, in which he is largely influenced by Horace, are his most characteristic work; the two addressed to the King, *Pour avoir esté derobé* and *Pour le delivrer de prison*, are masterpieces of their kind. Nor must his Psalms, of which he translated forty-nine, and which became immensely popular with his fellow-Protestants, be forgotten. They represent a serious and not unsuccessful attempt to introduce a more elevated tone into French lyrical poetry, and they reveal Marot as a skilled metrist, an inventor of many new forms of strophe. Ronsard built largely upon Marot's foundations; the loudly heralded reforms of the *Pléiade* were not so novel as their champions proclaimed.

The year (1532) in which Marot published his collected poems saw also the appearance of *Pantagruel*. Its author, FRANÇOIS RABELAIS (*circ.* 1495–1553 or 4), the son of a licentiate of law, who owned several small properties in the neighbourhood of Chinon in Touraine, had been in turn a Franciscan friar, a Benedictine monk, and a medical student; he had taken a degree of bachelor of medicine at Montpellier, had lectured there with success on Hippocrates and Galen, had moved to Lyons, and just before the publication of *Pantagruel* had been appointed physician to the hospital of that city. His studies had by no means been confined to medicine. He had ranged over the whole classical field, and had acquired large stores of humanistic learning; he was familiar with French and Italian vernacular literature; he was keenly interested in architecture and music; and he had a considerable knowledge not only of anatomy and physiology, but also of zoology and botany. Like most of his fellow humanists in France, he at first sympathised with the new religious doctrines, but he had been alienated by the affair of the Placards and by the publication of Calvin's *Institution*, with its virtual negation of the Renaissance principles of free inquiry and individualism. He continued, however, to interpret the less fundamental doctrines of the Catholic Church after his own fashion, and his writings contained passages which the Sorbonne eyed with disfavour, and which made the publication of them a delicate and risky business. Thanks, however, to the protection of his patrons, Cardinal Jean Du Bellay and his brother Guillaume, he was saved, if not from persecution, at any rate from the stake. In the service of the Cardinal he paid three visits to Rome, while in that of the elder brother he spent from two to three years at Turin.

He had many distinguished men among his friends, all of whom valued him as a man of great and varied learning, an eminent physician, a delightful companion, a *bon vivant*, and a wit. They also knew him as the author of a popular and amusing book. It is by this book that he is immortal.

The publication of *Pantagruel* was followed by that of *Gargantua*, which treats of the life and adventures of Pantagruel's father, in 1534. A Third Book appeared in 1546, and a Fourth in 1552. The authenticity of the posthumous Fifth Book has been frequently discussed. The evidence goes to prove that it is substantially Rabelais's work, but that it is very far from being in the form in which he meant it to appear. Much of it is unfinished and unrevised, and some of it he had probably rejected on second thoughts as unsatisfactory. It is only of the last fifteen or sixteen chapters that we can say with confidence that they were definitely intended to take their place in the great work, possibly, but by no means certainly, as its conclusion.

The framework of *Gargantua* and *Pantagruel* is a burlesque romance of chivalry in the form of a giant-story. But Rabelais has allowed himself complete freedom in the execution, and in *Gargantua* the giant element is far less prominent than in *Pantagruel*. In many respects *Gargantua* is the most attractive of all the books. It contains the celebrated account of the hero's education, which is conducted mainly on humanistic lines, but which has this novelty that it provides for the development of the pupil's powers of observation, and for the training of his body by physical exercise. The longest section of the book is a narrative of the war between Grandgousier and his neighbour, King Picrochole. Founded on a legal dispute in which Rabelais's father, together with other riparian proprietors, was engaged with one Gaucher de Sainte-Marthe, physician to the abbess of Fontevrault, it becomes the occasion for an admirable satire on schemes of universal conquest. In the course of the narrative we make the acquaintance of that delightful person, Friar Jean des Entommeures. The abbey of Thelema, which Gargantua gave him leave to found as a reward for his services, is an ideal picture of cultivated society as it presented itself to Rabelais's imagination. *Pantagruel*, the earliest written of the books, is the most medieval; there is much in it that is dull and much that is coarse and repulsive. But the noble letter of Gargantua to Pantagruel contains the germ of the educational system sketched in *Gargantua*, and the book introduces us to the great character of Panurge. In physical appearance this worthy is the complete antithesis of Falstaff, but, like Falstaff, in spite of his many ignoble qualities, he inspires us with sympathy, almost with affection, and, like Falstaff, he seems to grow in his creator's hands.

In the Third Book the framework of a giant-story is abandoned, and from this point a certain unity is given to the work by the quest of Panurge, with the view of ascertaining whether, if he marries, his wife will prove faithful to him. The conduct of this allegory is the occasion for many delightful episodes, of which perhaps the most amusing is that of Judge Bridoye, who gave his judgments according to the fall of the dice. This book as well as the Fourth is distinguished from the earlier ones by the frequent introduction of short stories, in which Rabelais shows himself a master. The Fourth Book, which moves in a breezy atmosphere of adventure, and testifies to Rabelais's interest in geographical discovery, narrates the voyage to the Divine Bottle, diversified by many incidents, of which the most humorous are the encounter of Panurge with the sheep-dealer and the visit of the travellers to Bishop Homenaz in the country of the Papimanes. In the Fifth Book we have the episodes of the Ringing Island and the Furred Cats, and in both the satire is more bitter and more heavy-handed than is Rabelais's wont. But in the concluding chapters he gives us of his best. The impressive termination of the quest and the parting exhortation of the Priestess Bacbuc show that under the mask of laughter Rabelais had a deep and serious philosophy—a philosophy founded on a robust optimism, and on an unshakeable belief in the goodness of God and in the high destiny of man.

Potentially Rabelais is the greatest of French prose-writers; his prodigious vocabulary, his unfailing ear for harmony, his command of clause-architecture, his imagination, his energy and gusto, gave him a command of his instrument that has never been surpassed. But he lacked discipline, method, and self-restraint. He was too individual to become a good model, and though he had imitators he did not found a school. Moreover, in his later books he is reactionary rather than progressive; harmony and not the need for clear expression determines the order of his words, and this betrays him into an exaggerated use of inversion and other archaic forms of syntax.

According to a contemporary who was well qualified to judge, French prose owed much to Herberay des Essarts, the spirited, if unfaithful, translator of the first eight books of *Amadis de Gaule* (1540–1548). But the man who taught French prose to reason as well as to narrate and describe was the great Protestant leader, JEAN CALVIN (1509–1564). He was the first French writer who was really logical, for his aim was not to charm, but to expound and convince. He was a humanist before he was a religious reformer, and he had learnt from Latin models lessons of terseness, lucidity, and precision. In his earlier writings he often Latinises both in the order of his words and in the structure of his sentences, but he gradually shakes himself free from this habit, and in his later work he succeeds in imparting the great qualities of Latin to a language which is thoroughly French and almost modern. The difference between his original version of the prologue and first seven chapters of the *Christian Institution* (1541) and the later version which he made in 1560 gives the measure of his development[1]. But even in the earlier period, when he is not translating from Latin but is writing original French, as in the two letters known as the *Traité des*

---

[1] For the remaining chapters of the work he made a fresh translation of the additional matter only.

superstitions (1543) and in the two other pieces which deal with the so-called Nicodemites (1544 and 1545), he uses very few Latinisms. All three treatises are masterpieces of vigorous and searching polemic.

It is not only in his style that Calvin shows his logical mind. The *Institution* is, as has been said, the first French book written on a regular plan. In its original Latin form, published in 1535, it contained only six chapters, but in the second Latin edition (1539), from which the original French translation was made, these were expanded to seventeen, and the matter was more than trebled. In the eighth and final Latin version, which appeared in 1559, considerable further alterations and additions were made, and the work was divided into four books and eighty chapters. The four books correspond to the four divisions of the Athanasian Creed. The subject of the first is God as Creator and Sovereign Ruler of the world; of the second, God as Redeemer; of the third, the means of Grace or God the Holy Ghost; of the fourth, the Church. The execution of this plan is worthy of its conception. Every paragraph testifies to the lucid and logical mind of the writer.

BONAVENTURE DESPERIERS (*c.* 1510—1544) is coupled by Calvin with Rabelais as one who, after welcoming the preaching of the Gospel, had rejected it with contempt. Of an artistic and impressionable temperament he was the disciple in turn of Marot, Rabelais, and Margaret of Navarre. But he did not lose his individuality. In two or three of his poems he touches a spiritual note that was new in French poetry; his anti-Christian *Cymbalum Mundi* (1538) owes nothing to anyone except Lucian, and his *Nouvelles Recreations et Joyeux Devis*, published, many years after his death, in 1558, reveal him as a *raconteur* of the first order. He tells his stories with a pregnant and business-like brevity that reminds one of Maupassant. But they are as joyous as those of the modern writer are sad. Yet Desperiers' end was equally tragic. He became insane and died by his own hand, in the same year·(1544) and possibly in the same month as Marot.

Except Desperiers, Marot left no disciples of genius. There were, however, at the time of his death, a few poets of some individuality and independence—Mellin de Saint-Gelais, who represents Italian influence, and who is credited with having introduced the sonnet from Italy to France; Antoine Heroet, whose chief work, *La parfaite amye* (1542), is a dignified but prosaic exposition of the philosophy of love; and Maurice Scève, the author of *Delie* (1544), a series of barely intelligible *dizains* addressed to an imaginary mistress. These two latter, both of whom owed much to Margaret of Navarre, are generally classified as belonging to the school of Lyons, but as a matter of fact Heroet had little or no connexion with that important literary and intellectual centre.

The Mid-Renaissance

During the reign of Henry II the influence of the Renaissance, especially of the Italian Renaissance, was at its height. This was partly due to the nationality of the Queen, Catherine de' Medici, but more to the intercourse between the two countries which, in spite of wars, had been going on ever since the expedition of Charles VIII. Italian artists and men of letters found a ready welcome and lucrative posts in France; Frenchmen went to Italy to study art and collect manuscripts. Yet under this Italian influence the French spirit, as always, when fanned by foreign breezes, retained its independence and individuality.

The two outstanding intellectual features of the reign are the supremacy of France in classical scholarship, and the flourishing condition not only of the greater arts of architecture, painting, sculpture, and stained glass, but of every minor art that helped to minister to the beauty of the home. It is these two influences—art and humanism—which largely determined the character of the literature.

In the first year of the new reign, if not earlier, the eminent Hellenist, Jean Dorat, was appointed Principal of the Collège de Coqueret at Paris, where he had among his pupils PIERRE DE RONSARD (1524–1585), Jean Antoine de Baïf, and JOACHIM DU BELLAY (1522–1560), all young men of good family. Fired by their teacher with an enthusiasm for Greek poetry, they conceived the design of investing French poetry with the same dignity and with consciousness of its high calling. They accordingly published a stirring manifesto written by Du Bellay, entitled

Deffence et Illustration de la Langue Françoise (1549), in which they urged their countrymen to confer lustre on the French language by writing poems on the model of the Greek and Latin and Italian masterpieces. Then, adding example to precept, Du Bellay published a volume of sonnets, and Ronsard a volume of odes. The arrogance of their prefaces and the novelty of their verse provoked strong opposition from the older school, till Ronsard, who was recognised from the first as the leader of the revolutionary forces, was induced to conciliate his chief antagonists by tactful flattery and to abate something of his lofty programme. Accordingly, he abandoned Pindar for Horace and Anacreon, and the conventional insincerities of Petrarchism for the natural language of the heart. By 1555, when he published his *Continuation des Amours*, mainly addressed to a new mistress, Marie, the new school was firmly established. Its reign lasted for exactly fifty years.

Its adherents were at first known as the Brigade. From these Ronsard gradually formed a select band, which, reaching the number of seven by the admission of Remy Belleau, he compared to the Alexandrian Pleiad, and the name, first used by way of metaphor, passed into common usage. The remaining three, besides Ronsard, Du Bellay, Baïf, and Belleau, were Pontus de Tyard, Estienne Jodelle, and another whom tradition names as Dorat, but who more probably was Jacques Peletier.

In 1560 the seal was set on Ronsard's reputation by the publication of his collected poems in four volumes. He now became the official poet, not only of the court, but of the nation, and numerous benefices which the King conferred on him brought him fortune as well as fame. Hitherto his poetry had been completely pagan, but in his *Discours*, partly didactic, partly polemical, he became the champion of catholicism. Of personal religious feeling he had little or none, but as a patriot and a loyalist he regarded militant protestantism as a serious menace to the nation. After the accession of Henry III, who already had his favourite poet in Desportes, he retired from court (1575) and lived chiefly in the country at one of his abbeys. In 1578 he published a carefully revised edition of his poems, which contained with many other new pieces the famous *Sonnets pour Hélène*. The remaining seven years of his life were devoted to further revision and expurgation of his works. He died at his priory of Saint-Cosme at Tours in 1585.

Ronsard's remarkable versatility is shown by the great variety of his productions. They were not all equally successful. His Pindaric odes, his Petrarchian sonnets, his unfinished epic *La Franciade*, were foredoomed to failure, and in nearly all his long poems his inspiration tired without his perceiving it. But if you take the best of his sonnets and lighter lyrics, of his elegies and poems of an elegiac character, of his *Discours* and other pieces written in a more or less familiar tone, and if you add to these the finest passages from his hymns (modelled on the Homeric hymns and those of Callimachus) you can make a volume which for the high level of its inspiration and execution may compare with a similar selection from the greatest poets. It is simple truth to say that no poet, except Victor Hugo, did more to raise the tone and add to the resources of French poetry. He found her a simple maiden; he transformed her into a princess. Recognising that great poetry demands a heightened language and a noble harmony, he enriched the poetic vocabulary by various methods, and he carried on the work of Lemaire and Marot, not merely by inventing a large number of new metrical strophes, but by reforming the rhythm of the individual line. If he lacked depth of passion and an outlook on the infinite, he had warm and quick feeling, a genuine love of nature, the power to create a picture, and in his shorter pieces consummate craftsmanship. His high conception of his art, his patriotism, and the seriousness with which he handled the great commonplaces of life, saved him from being the mere leader of a poetical school. It is as a great national poet that he is honoured in France to-day. The history of his literary fame is a singular one. Soon after his death his world-wide reputation began to decline. From 1630 he was completely forgotten for two centuries. Then Sainte-Beuve re-discovered him, and from that day to this he has steadily increased in favour. He is now not only honoured but he is widely read.

Du Bellay's poetical endowment was less rich than Ronsard's; he had neither his creative imagination, nor his metrical science, nor his devotion to his art. His first attempts in verse were cold and artificial imitations of other men's work, and it was not till he visited Rome as secretary to his cousin, Cardinal Du Bellay, that he discovered the true bent of his genius. The ruins of the ancient city inspired him to write the *Antiquités de Rome*, but even in this volume there are only a few sonnets that are original in thought and first-rate in execution. His first real masterpiece was *Les Regrets*, a sonnet-sequence in which he records in simple and sincere language his personal thoughts and feelings, his melancholy and nostalgia, his indignation at the corruption of the Roman Curia. It was followed by *Divers jeux rustiques*, a volume of short lyrical pieces, many of them translations or imitations, but nearly all stamped with the delicate grace which is so characteristic of the French genius. The best known is the inimitable *D'un vanneur de blé*.

To his note of intimacy and his note of delicate distinction he added *esprit* and a gift for irony. His *Le poète courtisan* (1559) is one of the earliest regular satires in the French language. It was almost his last poem; he died suddenly on the first day of the year 1560.

Outside the Pléiade itself the two most interesting figures are Olivier de Magny, who died young, a year before his friend Du Bellay, and who is in many respects a typical product of the Renaissance, and *la belle Cordière* of Lyons, Louise Labé, who wrote love sonnets, rough in execution, but burning with the glow of passion.

Du Bellay's appeal to his countrymen to write tragedies and comedies instead of moralities and farces was responded to by Estienne Jodelle (1532–1573), who in the autumn of 1552 produced the tragedy of *Cléopâtre* and the comedy of *Eugène*. As first attempts they both show promise; the chief character in each is not a mere puppet, but an active agent in life's drama; there is truth and passion, and therefore pathos, in the utterances of *Cléopâtre*, while the characters of the comedy are fairly successful as contemporary types. But *Cléopâtre* is a succession of dramatic lyrics rather than a true drama, and *Eugène* moves in the conventionally immoral atmosphere of the medieval farce and *conte*. *Cléopâtre* is modelled on Seneca, and it was the misfortune of French Renaissance tragedy that Seneca, who had no sense of dramatic action, and whose plays were almost certainly written for the recitation room, and not for the stage, continued to be the model of Jodelle's successors. It was a further misfortune, which confirmed its undramatic character, that it had no association with a regular theatre or experienced actors. The solitary Paris theatre, the Hôtel de Bourgogne, confined itself to the production of mystery-plays and farces, and the new classical drama had to be content with performances by raw amateurs in colleges or châteaux. The result was that ROBERT GARNIER (1545–1590), the chief writer of Renaissance tragedy, produced plays which, thanks to their style, had a great literary success, but which are as devoid of action as Jodelle's first experiment. *Les Juives* (1582), which is rightly regarded as Garnier's masterpiece, has a really tragic note, but the only one of his plays which makes any pretence to dramatic action is the romantic tragi-comedy of *Bradamante*.

Comedy had rather a different fate. *Eugène* owes very little to Plautus or Terence, and in fact differs from a medieval farce chiefly in being a complete drama instead of a single scene. But soon Italian comedy became the dominating influence, with the result that observation of life and character, which is the basis of true comedy, was neglected for the ingenious working out of a complicated plot. The stock characters are wholly conventional, and there is a complete indifference to morality. The most productive writer of Renaissance comedy was PIERRE DE LARIVEY (c. 1540–c. 1611), but his plays, which are all translations or adaptations from the Italian, show no regard for the requirements of the stage. Their one merit is their language, which is colloquial, natural, expressive, and amusing, the language of true comedy. The high-water mark of Renaissance comedy, however, is reached not by Larivey, but by ODET DE TURNÈBE (1553–1581), a son of the great Hellenist, whose solitary production, *Les Contents*, has other merits than those of style. Two of its characters are really alive, it has a moral atmosphere, it is national in tone, and it is to some extent a serious study of manners.

The Late Renaissance

The French Wars of Religion, which alternated with longer intervals of peace, had at first no adverse effect either upon learning, or literature, or art. But the massacre of St Bartholomew gave a sudden check to learning and art, and greatly changed the complexion of literature. It became more serious, more thoughtful, more national in form and sentiment. There was a reaction from the prevailing Italianism, which found expression in three treatises (1565–1579) by the distinguished Hellenist, Henri Estienne. Prose was produced in a larger measure than poetry, and poetry took on a prosaic tone.

In 1573, the year before Ronsard retired from the Court, two new poets made a first appearance, PHILIPPE DESPORTES (1542–1606) with a volume of Court poetry, SALLUSTE DU BARTAS (1544–1590) with *La Muse Chrestienne*. They represent the two channels into which the poetic stream divided. Desportes, a Catholic and a courtier, was in high favour with Henry III, who showered on him rich benefices. In spite of the reaction against Italianism he was a frank and skilful plagiarist of Italian models. His poetry is more of the head than of the heart, but he is not wholly without feeling, and his songs, of which the most famous are *Rozette, pour un peu d'absence*, and *O Nuit! jalouse Nuit*, have real merit.

Du Bartas, who was a Protestant country gentleman, represents the protest of his party against the frivolity and immorality of the Court poets. His long poem on the Creation, *La Semaine* (1578), was received with enthusiasm by his fellow-Protestants, and in the translation of Joshua Sylvester became highly popular in England. He united to his moral seriousness a rich and lofty imagination, but he lacked taste and self-criticism. Though his poem as a whole is a failure, it has fine passages, especially those which are inspired by his love and intimate observation of country life.

His fellow-Huguenot, AGRIPPA D'AUBIGNÉ (1552–1630), is a far more important figure. Fighting was his element, and for twenty years he never spared himself in the service of the Huguenot cause. He wrote with the same impetuosity with which he fought. After sonnets and odes in the manner of the Pléiade, and an epic which was even a greater failure that *La Semaine*, he began in 1577 a long poem in honour of the cause which was so dear to him. Though the completed work, entitled *Les Tragiques*, was not printed till 1616, it circulated in manuscript as early as 1593. It is sometimes called a Huguenot epic, but it is more accurately described, in the author's own words, as a poem in seven *tableaux*. Though no *tableau* is successful as a whole, all contain some magnificent passages, especially the second (*Princes*). The description of the young man (evidently D'Aubigné himself) arriving at Court, of Henry III's *mignons*, and of Henry III himself, are admirable examples of indignant satire. D'Aubigné was doubtless as close a student of Juvenal as he was of Tacitus, and he has all the concentrated energy, the lofty declamation, and the descriptive power of the Roman satirist, coupled with greater sincerity.

His chief prose work, the *Histoire Universelle*, though it dates in intention from 1577, was not finally completed till after the death of its central figure, Henry IV, and was not published till 1616–1620. In spite of its title, and of its author's attempts to embrace the history of other countries, it is in reality a Huguenot narrative of the Religious Wars of France. But Huguenot though he is, D'Aubigné writes with a high sense of the historian's duty of impartiality. He is scrupulously fair to opponents and it is interesting to compare his impartial summing up of the character of Henry III in the *History* with the satirical portrait of *Les Tragiques*. Other good character-sketches and some admirable summaries of the political situation testify to D'Aubigné's psychological bent, and his narratives of scenes and events in which he himself played a part are extremely vivid. He also wrote a regular autobiography (*Vie à ses enfants*), which was not printed till the eighteenth century. It is a concise and on the whole trustworthy record of a singularly adventurous life.

If the Religious Wars acted adversely on the production of poetry and drama, they gave a direct impulse to prose. It was "this school of treason, inhumanity and brigandage" which drove Montaigne to the retirement of his library; it was the struggle of parties which called forth a succession of vigorous and well-written pamphlets culminating in the *Satire Ménippée*; it was Monluc's wound, it was Brantôme's fall from his horse, it was La Noue's imprisonment, which moved them to beguile the tedium of forced inactivity by recording their opinions and experiences.

BLAISE DE MONLUC (*c.* 1503–*c.* 1577), a *Maréchal* of France, whose chief feat of arms was his eight months defence of Siena, led the way. His models were the Du Bellay memoirs and the *Commentaires* of François de Rabutin; but while these are military histories and no more, Monluc, by introducing the personal element, stamped his memoirs as literature. He was nearly seventy when he began to write them—without any experience of writing, but with the reputation of an admirable *raconteur*. His style is a conversational one, but it is the style of a man who has a natural gift for clear and vivid speech. From his book emerges the portrait of a born leader, brave, vigilant, resourceful, but pitiless to his Huguenot opponents, whom he regarded as rebels rather than as heretics—for he himself was but a lukewarm Catholic—quarrelsome, self-seeking, and vain. *J'ay esté tousjours glorieux: aussi suis je Gascon.*

Monluc's friend PIERRE DE BOURDEILLES, ABBÉ DE BRANTÔME (*c*. 1540–1614), did not write regular memoirs, but his biographies of great captains and noble ladies, which occupied him during the last thirty years of his life, contain a large autobiographical element, and if he often fails in portraying the character of those about whom he writes, he at any rate reveals his own. Much of the interest of his book is in the numerous digressions and the amusing stories which he culls freely from various sources. He is no moralist; he merely reflects like a mirror the more trivial and scandalous features of the Court of his day. He sees nothing blameworthy in his age; even the fashionable duels, bloodthirsty and treacherous, meet with his approval, and he has an elaborate disquisition on the economic advantages of the Religious Wars.

It is to Brantôme's credit that he was an intimate friend of FRANÇOIS DE LA NOUE (1531–1591), surnamed *Bras-de-Fer*, one of the most capable, high-minded, and tolerant of the Huguenot leaders. Only the last of his *Discours politiques et militaires* (1587), which gives an account of the first three religious wars, can be described as memoirs, and even here he keeps his own personality in the background. The rest are moral or political essays, written in a clear logical style, which marks him as of the school of Calvin.

Possibly both Brantôme and La Noue were led to authorship by the success of a remarkable book which had appeared in

1580—Montaigne's *Essays*. The author, MICHEL DE MONTAIGNE (1533–1592), was the son of Pierre Eyquem, a country gentleman of Périgord. After being educated on humanistic lines at the new college of Guyenne at Bordeaux, he studied law at Toulouse and became a Councillor of the Bordeaux *Parlement*. A memorable, but too brief, friendship with a brother-magistrate of lofty principles and some literary promise, Estienne de la Boétie (1530–1563), had a beneficial and lasting effect upon his character. In 1568 he succeeded to his father's château and estate: three years later he retired from public life and for the next nine years, with occasional intervals, he occupied himself with reading his favourite authors and writing his *Essays*. They were published in two books in the spring of 1580, and soon afterwards their author set out for a prolonged tour through Switzerland, Germany, and Italy, returning home in November 1581 to fill the office of Mayor of Bordeaux. In 1588 he brought out a new edition of his *Essays*, with a Third Book and six hundred additions to the First and Second Books. On September 13, 1592, he died of quinsy. Three years later Mlle de Gournay published a fresh edition of the *Essays*, based on a copy of the 1588 edition which Montaigne had carefully prepared for the press, and which now exists in the public library of Bordeaux; the additions amounted "to a third more than the preceding impressions." This practice of continually adding to his essays must be carefully borne in mind in considering the development of Montaigne's thought. His mind was unusually supple, receptive, and progressive; and consequently the opinions expressed in his earlier essays often differ widely from those which he held later. It must be remembered too that he writes as a poet, and not as a professional philosopher. Careless of consistency, he gives full rein to his imagination and the impression of the moment, and his philosophy of life is all the more instructive because it reflects with rare sincerity the mental growth and development of the man.

His earliest essays were but modest experiments, differing only from the popular *Lectiones* or *Leçons* of his day in that the anecdotes were taken from modern historians, such as Guicciardini and Du Bellay, as well as ancient. In the essay, *Que philosopher est savoir de mourir* (I. 19) he successfully attempted a higher flight, but still without much originality of thought. His favourite author at this time was Seneca and the essays were coloured by the mitigated stoicism of that philosopher. But he now found a more congenial guide in Plutarch's *Lives* and *Moral Works*, reading both in the famous translation(*Lives*,1559; *Moral Works*, 1572) of JACQUES AMYOT (1513–1593), who had risen from humble beginnings, and after a hard struggle at the University of Paris, to be Grand Almoner of France, and Bishop of Auxerre. A sound and competent Greek scholar, he achieved his rare success as a translator by combining fidelity to the sense of his original with equal fidelity to the genius of the French language. Where Plutarch is concise, Amyot is redundant and picturesque, and where Plutarch is obscure, which is not unfrequently, Amyot expands him for the sake of clarity. Moreover, like a true artist, he was always learning, and no writer of the sixteenth century, not excepting Calvin, did so much to develop French prose in the direction of logical thought and artistic construction.

Plutarch, whose writings, thanks to Amyot, acquired an unique influence in France, not only detached Montaigne from stoicism but, what was more important, helped him to develop his originality and to give free play to his inborn interest in moral questions and the study of human character. About the year 1576 Montaigne entered upon a new phase of thought. He read Sextus Empiricus, struck a medal in honour of the Pyrrhonist philosophy, and had sceptical texts and mottoes carved upon the beams of his library. Under this new influence he wrote part at least of his longest essay, the *Apology for Raimond de Sebonde* (II. 12). Much of it is highly rhetorical and much purposely paradoxical, but from rhetoric and paradox emerges the important thought, that we only know phenomena, and that all human knowledge is merely relative. This phase of acute scepticism passed away, but it helped to develop Montaigne's naturally critical spirit.

We now come to the most original and characteristic feature of the *Essays*, Montaigne's portraiture of himself. At first he only proposed to draw a portrait for his friends to hang in a corner. Then it occurred to him that every man, however humble and undistinguished, was a type of humanity, and that the study of one's own character was the best starting-point for the study of mankind. So boldly claiming that on this subject he is "the most learned man alive," he deliberately makes himself the centre of his book. In the Third Book he gives full play to his design. The essays *On Vanity* (III. 9) and *On Experience* (III. 13) are rich in details of his life and character; indeed his confidences are sometimes carried beyond the limits of discretion, and he allows his imagination and his language a more than permissible licence. But it is a mistake to ascribe this to moral dilettantism. Montaigne was never deaf to the call of conscience or duty, and in the first essay of the Third Book (*On Expediency and Honesty*) he upholds their claims with firmness and eloquence. But it is to the concluding pages of his last essay (III. 13) that we must look for the final word of his philosophy. He had explored the moral systems of the ancients; he had studied human nature, partly in history, but, above all, in himself; and his conclusion was that every man must shape his moral life —with due regard to conscience and duty—in conformity with his own nature. He could admire the lofty idealism of martyrs and ascetics, but to his mind "the fairest lives were those which were regulated after the rudimentary human pattern." The great aim was "to enjoy loyally one's own being." He looked back on his past life with cheerfulness and gratitude—and without repentance. Had he to live it over again, he could not do better, for he could not "mend his faculties." The sentiment is unchristian, as is much of the whole essay (*On Repentance*, III. 2) in which it occurs. Yet according to the standard of his age Montaigne was a good Catholic both in belief and practice. But religion was for him, as for the majority of his contemporaries, a thing apart. It did not influence his daily life or his morals, just as it found no place in his scheme of education.

One of the chief attractions of Montaigne is what Emerson calls his "invincible probity." He may have his little vanities and pretences, but his book makes upon us a general impression of transparent candour and sincerity. As he claims in his preface, *c'est un livre de bonne foi.* Moreover, his digressions, his anecdotes, his varying moods, his very desultoriness, all help to make him a delightful companion. His style is that of the sixteenth century, drawn-out, ill-balanced, and illogical, but rich in images, richer than that of any French writer, whether of verse or prose, excepting Victor Hugo. Further—and this perhaps is its greatest quality—it reflects as in a mirror the changing moods of the man.

Montaigne had no sympathy with Protestantism, but his humane nature inclined him to a policy of tolerance. Being also a convinced royalist, he was in complete sympathy with that *politique* party which preferred the unity of the State to the unity of religion, and which had Jean Bodin, the author of the *Six Livres de la République*, for its philosopher. Two years after Montaigne's death it produced a brilliant pamphlet in *LA SATIRE MÉNIPPÉE* (1594), the work of several individuals who had been living in Paris under the sinister shadow of the League. In form this is a burlesque account of the sittings of the Estates which were held at Paris during the year 1593 to determine the succession to the throne. But, while the idiosyncrasies of the various speakers are happily caricatured, they are compelled, as in a Palace of Truth, to declare their real sentiments, their greed of place and profit, their subordination of the public interest to their private advantage. The last and longest speech, said to be the work of the distinguished scholar and historian, Pierre Pithou, is put in the mouth of the Sieur d'Aubray, the representative of the Third Estate. It differs from the rest in not being a caricature, but a serious harangue, couched in language which often rises to real eloquence, on behalf of the rightful monarch, Henry IV.

The twelve years during which Henry IV, having secured external peace by the Treaty of Vervins and internal peace by the Edict of Nantes, laboured, with the able help of Sully and his other ministers, at the great task of reconstruction, are among the most fruitful and memorable in the history of France. The literature of the reign, which is one of transition from the imagination of the sixteenth century to the reason of the seventeenth, closely reflects the need for repose and order and recuperation. Order is represented by PIERRE CHARRON (1541–1603), who, in his *La Sagesse* (1601), tries to reduce to a classified system the inconsistencies of his master, Montaigne, and after establishing in his First Book the natural depravity and vanity of man on the authority of the *Apology for Raimond de Sebonde*, proceeds in his Second Book to reconstruct morality on the basis of man being naturally good. Here he is largely copying GUILLAUME DU VAIR (1556–1621), first President of the *Parlement* of Aix, and afterwards Keeper of the Seals and Bishop of Lisieux, who in the stormy times of the League wrote three treatises, the longest and most important being *De la constance et consolation ès calamités publiques* (written 1590), in which he preaches to his countrymen a message of hope and encouragement, based on the principles of a Christianised stoicism. He also supported his fellow-*politiques* and royalists by his eloquent speeches, and wrote an interesting *Traité sur l'éloquence française*.

The same seriousness, the same regard for this moral basis of life, is shown in the later poetry of JEAN BERTAUT (1552–1611), Bishop of Séez, the official poet of the reign of Henry IV. Though Boileau, in a well-known line, has coupled him with Desportes, and though there still clings to him a breath of the imaginative spirit of the Renaissance, he is really a forerunner of Malherbe, strict and careful in language and versification, with a preference for the Alexandrine even in his lyrical poems.

Very different in character from Bertaut's grave and correct verse are the brilliant and careless satires of MATHURIN REGNIER (1573–1613), a native of Chartres and a nephew of Desportes. His earliest work is written under the influence of Juvenal and Horace, of Ariosto and Italian Burlesque. But in the Fifth Satire, though it owes much to his spiritual kinsmen, Horace and Montaigne, he is really himself. Other fine satires are the Eighth (an imitation of Horace's *Ibam forte via sacra*), the Ninth, which contains the famous counter-attack to Malherbe's onslaught on the Pléiade, and above all the Thirteenth (first published in 1612), with its celebrated portrait of Macette, to which the creator of Tartuffe evidently gave a careful study. Regnier is on many counts a thorough representative of the sixteenth century, of its individualism, its imagination, its vividness, its zest for life and pleasure. He has too the merits and defects of the poetic school which he championed with such spirit. He lacks constructive power; his best work is in short bursts of inspiration, and he borrows freely, not only from Latin,

Italian, and Spanish writers, but from his masters Ronsard and Desportes. Yet in his concise and vigorous style, in his firm and manly versification, in his accurate observation of life and character, he is a herald of the seventeenth century.

HENRY IV, of whom Regnier might have drawn a superb and sympathetic portrait, had little time for reading, even if he had had the inclination. But he had a natural gift for expression, and his brief notes, dashed off for the most part between saddle and supper, are characteristic of the man. They are written in the style which Montaigne loved—*tel sur le papier qu'à la bouche court et serré* and *soldatesque*. The two men, indeed, had much in common, and the evening which the King spent at Montaigne's château, preparatory to hunting in his host's forest, must have been memorable indeed.

During the last years of his reign there appeared, within a year of one another, two works which had a wide and remarkable influence on French society. The earlier of the two, *L'Astrée* (1607), will be noticed later, but this is the place to mention the *Introduction à la vie dévote* (1608), which happily combines in its style the picturesque richness of the sixteenth century with the clarity of the seventeenth.

Its author, ST FRANÇOIS DE SALES (1567–1622), a Savoyard by birth, and Bishop of Geneva from 1602, spent the greater part of that year at Paris, where partly by his preaching and partly as a spiritual director he exercised a great and beneficial influence on the work of religious revival which was being actively carried on in that city by a group of devout men and women. He impressed upon them that a true religious life could be lived in the world as well as in the cloister, but that constant and rigid self-examination, with the help of a spiritual director, was needed. Such help François de Sales himself, with his deep piety and remarkable insight into motive as well as character, was well qualified to give. Among his penitents were Marie de Chantal (St Fremyot de Chantal), the grandmother of Mme de Sévigné, the Mère Angélique (Jacqueline Arnaud) of Port-Royal, and Mme de Charmoisy, with all of whom he corresponded on spiritual matters after his return to Geneva. His letters to Mme de Charmoisy were expanded into the world-famous *Introduction à la vie dévote*, in which all his great qualities as a director

of souls find expression. Eight years later he published his
Traité de l'Amour de Dieu (1616), which is practically a treatise
on mysticism. On this difficult subject he keeps well within the
bounds of sobriety and good sense, but in the view of later
developments one can detect in all his writings a certain tendency to quietism and an almost feminine sweetness of tone,
which needed to counteract it the philosophical thought of
Cardinal de Bérulle and the active charity of St Vincent de
Paul.

§ II. SEVENTEENTH CENTURY

The preparation for the Classical Age

The literature of the reign of Henry IV forms a transition
from the sixteenth to the seventeenth century. Similarly the
whole first half of the seventeenth century, or more precisely,
from the peace of Vervins (1598) to the death of Mazarin (1661),
is a period of preparation for the great classical age of Louis
XIV. From this literature four names stand out as pillars of
classicism—MALHERBE, who prepared the way for classical
criticism and determined the form and harmony of classical
verse; DESCARTES, who supplied a philosophical basis for the
authority of Reason; CORNEILLE, the creator of classical
tragedy; and PASCAL, the creator of classical prose. Other
shaping influences were the salon of Mme de Rambouillet, which
organised society, the *Académie Française*, which organised
literature and language, and the Catholic revival, which reconstructed the religious life of France and made the classical
age definitely Christian.

But in spite of these great outposts of classicism, literature, as
a whole, was not yet classical. The authority of the leaders was
far from universally recognised. Malherbe gained an easy
victory over his opponents, but there still remained rebels to
his rule. The tragedies of Corneille were followed by the sentimental tragi-comedies of his brother and Quinault. Mme de
Rambouillet's salon was succeeded by that school of *préciosité*,
the salon of Mlle de Scudéry. The age of the Catholic revival
was also the age of the *libertins* or free-thinkers. The authority
of Reason which Descartes did so much to uphold could not

restrain either the hero-worship and love of adventure which filled the romances of La Calprenède and Mlle de Scudéry, or the tasteless burlesques of Scarron and D'Assoucy. In fact to such an extent did Reason abdicate her authority, that during the whole eighteen years of the rule of Mazarin the classical ideal was almost entirely forgotten, and bad taste rioted unchecked. Thus when the school of 1660 began its campaign on behalf of classicism it had to reconquer ground which had already been won and lost, and it had to fight against the united forces of Pedantry and Burlesque and *Préciosité* with the *Académie Française* at their back.

The first representative of the classical spirit was FRANÇOIS DE MALHERBE (1555–1628). A Norman by birth, he came to Paris from Aix, where he had chiefly resided since manhood, in 1605. In the same year he quarrelled with Desportes and subjected his poetry to a searching criticism, which he extended to the whole of the Pléiade school, including Ronsard himself. So successful was his attack that by the close of the reign of Henry IV he had gained a complete victory. This was due to various causes; firstly to the decline of the old school, both in vitality and in public favour, secondly to the need of the new generation for order and discipline, and thirdly to the positive and arrogant temper of Malherbe himself. This "tyrant of words and syllables" was primarily a critic of language. The three qualities on which he most insisted were clearness, precision, and purity, and his standard of purity was usage—the usage of polite society. But all these qualities belong to prose as well as to poetry, and it was Malherbe's defect that he recognised no distinction between prose and poetry save rhyme and metre. His own poetry is such as you might expect from his precepts. His style has the clarity, precision, and polish that he demanded from others, though to Englishmen it seems hard and metallic and wanting in imagination. His versification is manly and dignified, and proved a splendid instrument for the classical drama. But his abiding merit is that he introduced a critical spirit into French literature. The Pléiade had trusted too much to inspiration; Malherbe proclaimed the need of self-criticism and discipline.

When Malherbe came to Paris in 1605, polite society, to which he appealed as providing a standard of pure language, can hardly be said to have existed. The want was, to some extent, made good when Catherine de Vivonne, daughter of the Marquis de Pisani and a high-born Italian mother, and wife of the Marquis de Rambouillet, withdrew from the Court in 1607, and received her friends in her own house, which she reconstructed with a view to making its apartments better adapted to intimate conversation. Her salon was soon frequented by men and women of distinction, but its most flourishing period was from the death of Malherbe (1628) to the outbreak of the Fronde (1648). In forming her salon Mme de Rambouillet had certain distinct social aims in view, of which the chief were refinement and the raising of the intellectual standard of conversation. To this end she admitted literary celebrities on a footing of equality with the leaders of fashion, and thus society became literary and literature became social. In her promotion of refinement she was greatly assisted by a book of which the First Part appeared in the very year (1607) of her retirement from the Court, and the last in 1627. The book was *L'Astrée*, the work of HONORÉ D'URFÉ (1567–1625), a gentleman of La Forez, who had been a militant Leaguer, but who had dedicated his work to Henry IV. Modelled on the *Diana* of Jorge de Montemôr and influenced by Tasso's *Aminta* and Guarini's *Il pastor fido*, this pastoral romance, of which the absorbing topic was love—honourable love—but which relieved its discussions on every possible aspect of the soft passion with adventures after the manner of *Amadis*, had a prodigious influence in France. It began to be highly popular after the publication of the Third Part in 1619, but from 1628 to 1660 its influence was at its height.

It set before the society which assembled in the Blue Chamber an ideal of love, which, if it sometimes expressed itself in high-flown language and empty gallantry, was a vast improvement on the soulless sensualism of the later Renaissance. During the last eight years of the reign of Louis XIII (1635–1643) the most brilliant of members of this society were Condé, then the Duc d'Enghien, and his sister, Geneviève de Bourbon, the future Duchesse de Longueville; La Rochefoucauld and Saint-Évremond, both to win renown in the world of letters; and VINCENT

VOITURE (1598–1648), the son of a wine-merchant of Amiens, who in spite of a fitful temper and freaks of outrageous impertinence made himself indispensable by his invention and wit, and his skill in organising entertainments. He published nothing in his lifetime, but his carefully written letters and his *vers de société* testify to his *esprit*, and have assured him a modest place in the history of French literature.

JEAN GUEZ DE BALZAC (1597–1654), though he never set foot in the Blue Chamber, corresponded assiduously with several of its *habitués*. His elaborate letters, stilted and pompous in style, differ only in length from his *Dissertations politiques*, the first four of which are addressed to Mme de Rambouillet. They were collected from time to time in volumes, and even before publication were read aloud in the Blue Chamber. Balzac had common sense and critical acumen as well as learning, but, apart from his services to French prose, of which more hereafter, his chief importance is that by inspiring French society with an interest in antiquity, especially in Roman antiquity, he contributed greatly to the development of the classical spirit.

If the Hôtel de Rambouillet with its literary conversations and discussions assumed something of the air of a literary tribunal, the Académie Française has retained almost to the present day its original character of a club. Its origin was in this wise. About the year 1629 some eight or nine men of letters used to meet at the house of one Valentin Conrart and discuss familiarly the latest news, public affairs, or literature. This went on for three or four years, when Richelieu, hearing of their meetings, and recognising with the far-reaching vision of a great statesman what an advantage the organisation of literature would be to France as a world-power, proposed that they should become an incorporated body, meeting regularly and under public authority. Reluctantly, but inevitably, they accepted Richelieu's proposition. The first regular meeting was held on March 13, 1634; in February 1639 the number of forty was completed. They included practically all the chief men of letters of the day. The most active member was JEAN CHAPELAIN (1595–1674), author of *Sentiments sur le Cid*, which established his reputation as a critic, and of an epic, *La Pucelle*, which, though unreadable, failed to shake his position as "the head of the French Parnassus."

The year 1637, in which the Letters Patent of the New Academy were registered by the *Parlement* of Paris, saw the publication of the most epoch-making book which had appeared since the beginning of the century—the *Discours de la méthode* of RENÉ DESCARTES (1596–1650). Written in French instead of in Latin, and in the form, not of a set treatise, but of a personal narrative, it won the attention of the ordinary educated reader. Philosophy had left the lecture-room to converse at ease in the market-place. Descartes's work as a philosopher will receive due attention in a later chapter; his influence on literature demands a word here. It is true that in his glorification of reason, in his re-establishment of order and unity in the world of thought, he was merely carrying on the same work as his contemporaries. But on many of the writers of the classical age his influence was direct.

The philosopher Malebranche and the theologian Antoine Arnauld were alike his enthusiastic disciples, and both the Oratory and Port-Royal welcomed his philosophy as a buttress against scepticism. Even Pascal and Bossuet followed him up to a certain point, though they both recognised that the setting up of human reason as the one criterion of truth must in the end prove fatal to the claims of the Christian religion. Another work of Descartes's, the *Traité des passions* (1649), made a special appeal to his contemporaries, for by its orderly arrangement and careful analysis it helped to stimulate and solidify the growing interest in psychology. In his insistence on the power of the will to control the passions and on that of the reason to distinguish good from evil as a preliminary to the exercise of the will, he was merely reducing to a system ideas which the drama of Corneille had already made familiar.

To be in a position to appreciate the great work which Corneille accomplished for the French drama, we must go back a little. We have seen that Renaissance tragedy, though it attained to considerable excellence in point of style, was lyrical and rhetorical, but undramatic. This dramatic element was supplied by ALEXANDRE HARDY (*c.* 1572–1631 or 2), who for more than thirty years was employed as a playwright by an actor-manager, named Valleran Lecomte, the lessee since 1599 of the Hôtel de Bourgogne, but he had a born instinct for drama and he understood the requirements of the stage. His early tragedy of *Mariamne* gives a good idea of his powers. Unliterary though it is, it is dramatically far superior to the productions of Garnier and Montchrestien. The principal characters are drawn with some feeling for psychological tragedy; the action of the play is determined by their passions; there is a real conflict of will between them; and the interest is sustained to the end.

About the year 1610, Hardy, at the bidding of his manager, abandoned tragedy for tragi-comedy or irregular drama, and this kind of play, in which the unities were thrown to the winds and improbable incident took the place of character, held the field for the next twenty years. From 1629 to 1634, there now being two Paris theatres, there was a sharp struggle between the partisans of the classical and the irregular drama. The victory of the former was largely due to the success of Jean Mairet's tragedy of *Sophonisbe*, which is sometimes spoken of as the first example of classical tragedy in France. But dramatically it shows little advance on the tragi-comedies of the period, and though greatly superior to Hardy's *Mariamne* in style, it is inferior to it as drama.

PIERRE CORNEILLE (1606–1684), the true founder of French classical tragedy, was born at Rouen, and, after being educated in the Jesuit college of that city, was called to the Bar and presented by his father with two legal sinecures. Shy and unattractive in society, he was extraordinarily receptive of every current phase of thought and literary influence. Malherbe, *L'Astrée*, Spain, the salon of Mme de Rambouillet, Balzac's dissertations on the Romans, the question of Grace, the controversy on the unities, Stoic philosophy, the glorification of will and reason, the cult of military heroes, the interest of society in politics, all contributed to the fashioning of his drama. He began his career with a comedy, *Mélite* (1629 or 1630), in which he struck out an entirely new line. In place of the unliterary farce, generally coarse and indecent, which was patronised by the Hôtel de Bourgogne, he presented at the rival Paris theatre a new kind of comedy, written in an easy, graceful, and pointed style, perfectly decent and without any comic element. The language "imitated the conversation of polite society," and the influence of *L'Astrée* is unmistakable. The only theme is love, and the only psychology is that of the tender passion. But in *Mélite* and its successors, of which the best is the latest, *La Suivante* (1633 or 1634), we have the germ of social comedy. They attempt to portray real life and contemporary society.

After his four great tragedies Corneille returned to comedy, and in the winter of 1643–44 produced his comic masterpiece in *Le Menteur*. He had by this time realised that, if comedy was to compete with farce, it must be comic. So his new play, except for a single scene, is comic throughout. Its charm and gaiety, its brilliant and vivacious style, make us forget its unreality. If the hero, Dorante, is a caricature, he is, at any rate, a delightful one, and if the incidents by which the plot is worked out are more or less improbable, they lead to scenes of genuine comedy.

The *Cid* (winter of 1636–37), like *Le Menteur*, is founded on a Spanish original, and, like that play, it captivates us by its radiant charm. It is the first classical French tragedy, and this by virtue of the fact that Corneille has grasped the two fundamental principles upon which the Greeks founded their drama, the necessity of action, and the importance of developing the action, not from without, but from within; not mechanically, but by and through the characters. Thus in the *Cid* each individual act is the result of character, and by these acts, which are firmly linked to one another by a logical chain, the plot is worked out to its *dénouement*. Judged by the stricter classical standard of later plays, the *Cid* has certain defects. The Infanta is a superfluous character, a survival from the lyrical tragedy of the sixteenth century. There are other lyrical elements, and there is an epic element in the long narrative of the Cid's victory over the Moors. The unity of place is not strictly observed, and the unity of time is only maintained by crowding an impossible number of incidents into the twenty-four hours.

The recognition of the unities forms an interesting chapter in the history of French classical drama. In *Cléopâtre* Jodelle calls attention to the fact that the action takes place between sunrise and sunset, but he is less particular about the unity of place. Garnier and Hardy both observe the unities with a certain

latitude. Then during the reign of tragi-comedy they were more
or less forgotten till the controversy between the partisans of
classical and irregular drama revived the question. The supporters of the unities based them either on the supposed
authority of Aristotle or on the theory of verisimilitude, which
held that the length of the action should approximate to that
of the performance, but no one put forward the true argument
in their favour, that they make for concentration. However,
the classicists prevailed, and their leader, Chapelain, in the
Sentiments sur le Cid interpreted Aristotle's "revolution of the
sun" in the sense of "from sunrise to sunset."

In the interval of three years which elapsed between the *Cid*
and his next tragedy Corneille had opportunity to digest
Chapelain's criticisms and generally to meditate on the principles
of his art. The result was that he produced in *Horace* (1640)
a play which conformed to the strictest rules of classicism.
Moreover, he went to Roman history instead of to Spanish for
his subject, and this practice he continued in his five succeeding
tragedies. *Cinna, ou La Clémence d'Auguste* (1640) was, Corneille
tells us, generally regarded by his contemporaries as his masterpiece, but that position is rightly assigned by most modern
critics to *Polyeucte* (winter of 1642–43). Apart from its many
and obvious beauties, no play of Corneille's shows so careful
a study of normal humanity. Sévère and Pauline, and, on a
lower plane, Felix, are all drawn with a more delicate brush
and with more feeling for light and shade than is usual with
Corneille. He never again reached so high a mark. In his later
plays he showed an increasing fondness for complicated and improbable plots, mostly founded on political intrigues, and gave
evidence of his versatility by experiments, of which the most
successful is *Nicomède* (1651), a tragedy which has nothing tragic
about it, but which has well-drawn characters, including the
comic one of Prusias.

In 1662 he came to live at Paris, where he produced plays,
more or less successful, till 1674, but he was embittered by his
jealousy of the growing fame of Racine. He also wrote a series
of criticisms on his plays, entitled *Examens*, and *Trois Discours*,
which are rather ingenious pleadings on behalf of his own
practice than dispassionate inquiries into the principles of

dramatic art. But if his judgments are often partial, his ideas are always interesting, for he was a great playwright with an instinctive knowledge of stage construction.

His style has the same logical character as the construction of his plays. It is not imaginative, but it is always clear, dignified, and expressive, and at its best it is of transcendent merit. His *belles tirades qui font frissonner* stir the blood as with a trumpet call.

The Cornelian hero has been described as a "superman," but it is only Corneille's later heroes—Héraclius, Nicomède, Sertorius, Otho, Surena—who deserve this description. The earlier heroes, even Polyeucte, achieve a mastery over their passions after an inward conflict. Their fault is that they are not really tragic. The true tragic hero—an Oedipus, a Hamlet, an Othello—is tripped up by some flaw in his character to become the sport of destiny.

The interest in political intrigue and conspiracy which is so prominent a feature in some of Corneille's plays—*Cinna, Héraclius, Nicomède*—gives life and colour to the *Memoirs* of PAUL DE GONDI, CARDINAL DE RETZ (1613–1679). Though not written till after 1671—they did not appear in print till 1717—they belong virtually to the period covered by his narrative (1643–1655). Retz has been over-praised, both for political wisdom and for insight into character. He was never more than a skilful but unsuccessful party leader, and though he has a remarkable gift for hitting off the portraits of lesser men, he fails with really great men like Richelieu and Condé. But his talent for vivid and picturesque description is undeniable, and he writes with the careless and well-bred ease of a man of the world, and the racy vigour of the age of Louis XIII.

The decline of Corneille's art after *Le Menteur* was partly due to the bad taste which prevailed in French literature from the death of Richelieu to that of Mazarin. It is an age of dull epics, written under the delusion that a knowledge of literary rules can supply the place of inspiration and genius; of trivial and tiresome burlesques, of which the chief exponent was Paul Scarron (1610–1660) with his *Typhon* (1644) and *Virgile Travesti* (1648); of comedies by Scarron and Thomas Corneille in which the true comic spirit introduced by the great Corneille was contaminated by the same element of burlesque; of tragi-comedies by Thomas Corneille and Quinault, with their complicated plots and super-refined sentiment; and lastly of the interminable romances of La Calprenède and Mlle de Scudéry, which provided subjects for these tragi-comedies. Only the romances demand a word or two of further mention. All were descendants of *L'Astrée*. The *Polexandre* (1629–1637) of Gomberville had changed pastoral romance into heroic romance; La Calprenède with *Cassandre* (1642–1645) and *Cléopâtre* (1647–1659) gave it an historical background; Mlle de Scudéry, with *Le Grand Cyrus* (1649–1653) and *Clélie* (1654–1660), while retaining the historical background and the heroic adventures, returned to the analysis of sentiment. But her historical background was a mere pretence; her characters under transparent disguises belonged to her own day. The chief *habitués* of the Blue Chamber figured in *Le Grand Cyrus*, while *Clélie* was a transparent representation of her own Saturdays.

It was at these Saturdays, which date from 1653, that *préciosité* reached its full development. It is the fashion to identify *préciosité* with the whole movement towards refinement and intellectual conversation inaugurated by Mme de Rambouillet. But against this view we have, first a definite statement that the term *précieuse* had in 1656 recently come into vogue, and secondly the fact that only the germs of *préciosité* can be found in Mme de Rambouillet's salon during its palmy period. It is not till just before the death of Louis XIII that we can detect symptoms of positive disease. In *Clélie* the *préciosité* is clearly marked, not only by the tone of sentimental gallantry but also by the numerous "portraits" and conversations. The "portraits" are far too flattering to be true to nature, but the conversations, which many years later were published separately, show good sense and considerable power of psychological analysis.

On January 23, 1656, when *Clélie* was still running its course, when *La Pucelle* was on the eve of publication, and when *Timocrate* was about to be played to a crowded house for six months, there appeared as a small pamphlet of eight quarto pages the first Provincial Letter. Its author, BLAISE PASCAL (1623–1662), was born at Clermont, the capital of Auvergne, where his father was President of the Cour des Aides. In 1631 his family moved to Paris, and about ten years later to Rouen, where, under the influence of two Norman gentlemen, he became an ardent Jansenist, and converted all his family to the same austere and logical creed. He had little book-learning, but at the age of sixteen he had shown his rare genius for mathematics by writing a work on conic sections, and in 1647–48, his experiments on the nature of a vacuum[1] won the admiration of learned Europe. Jansenist though he was, he did not disdain the pleasures of society, and in 1652 and 1653 he lived at Paris, where he read Montaigne, visited the salon of Mme de Sablé, and made the acquaintance of the Chevalier de Méré and other free-thinkers. Then, on November 23, 1654, in which year he had presented to one of the scientific academies several important mathematical treatises, he had a species of trance or ecstasy, which gave him the certainty of intense conviction and confirmed his desire to separate himself from the world. In January 1655, in obedi-ence to the orders of his Jansenist director, he left Paris for Port-Royal and took up his abode with the Solitaries, without however becoming a member of their community.

The intimate connexion of Port-Royal with Jansenism had begun in 1636, when Jean Du Vergier de Hauranne, Abbot of Saint-Cyran, the friend of Cornelius Jansen and of the Arnauld family, became spiritual director to the monastery of Port-Royal of which Jacqueline Arnauld, La Mère Angélique, was Abbess. In 1640 Jansen published his famous *Augustinus*, in which in the name of St Augustine he attacked the Pelagian and semi-Pelagian doctrines of Grace.

In 1653 the Pope issued a Bull condemning five propositions, which were said to be contained in the *Augustinus*. This brought into the field Antoine Arnauld, a disciple of Saint-Cyran, whose *La Fréquente Communion* (1643) had had a wider influence than any book of devotion since the *Introduction à la vie dévote*. He in his turn was condemned by the Sorbonne, and Pascal wrote the first Provincial Letter in his defence. The other seventeen Letters appeared at intervals up to March 24, 1657, and in May of that year they were collected and issued by a French publisher.

---

[1] For Pascal as a mathematician and a physicist see chapter XIV.

The enthusiastic praise which Mme de Sévigné gave to the "Little Letters" has been echoed by many generations of readers. The irony and dramatic skill of the earlier letters, the force and eloquence of the later ones, and the lucidity and sincerity of all, are uncontestable. At the present day those which deal with the question of Grace and the controversy between Arnauld and the Jesuits (i–iv, xvii, xviii) have less interest than those which are concerned with the wider question of Jesuit casuistry and direction. Though Pascal writes as an advocate, and therefore presents only the bad side of his opponent's case, and though he was a born fighter and a hard hitter, he was an honourable fighter, and he had collected his facts with scrupulous care. All the efforts of his opponents have only convicted him of two or three inaccuracies and of a few cases of unfair presentation of his authorities. It is only a partial answer to his indictment that the manuals of casuistry were written for confessors and not for their penitents, and that the use made of them depended upon the individual confessor or director. The fact remains that the general system of Jesuit direction was based upon a sham morality. François de Sales had taught that you can remain in the world and be a good Christian; the Jesuits tampered with the code of Christ in order to reconcile it with that of the world. The best justification of the Provincial Letters is the change that they brought about in Jesuit methods of direction.

After beginning a nineteenth letter, Pascal suddenly abandoned the attack and began to put into execution a design he had formed of writing an Apology for the Christian religion, with the object of confuting not only heretics but also atheists and free-thinkers. He spent a year in reading the Scriptures and the Fathers, especially St Augustine, and in arranging his thoughts. But in the middle of 1658 his health, which had always been delicate, became much worse and, though he was not confined to his room, or even to his bed, he was rendered almost incapable of any application. During the last four years of his life, however, he used to write down or dictate anything that he thought might be serviceable to his design, using "any scrap of paper that came to his hand." When he died, on August 19, 1662, all that was found of his intended work were a number of fragments, erased and altered, and often barely legible. These were put into order by his family and his friends of Port-Royal and published in 1670 as *Pensées de M. Pascal sur la religion et sur quelques autres sujets.* But in this edition there were many omissions and alterations, and in 1842 Victor Cousin called for a faithful text. This has at last been given us by Molinier (1879), Michaut (1896), who follows the order of the manuscript, and Brunschvicg (1897); and the last editor has rendered further service by publishing a photographic facsimile of the fragments.

Any attempt to reconstruct with certainty the design of Pascal's intended work and to arrange all the fragments in an order corresponding to that design is foredoomed to failure, and accordingly modern editors have for the most part adopted an arrangement of their own. But we are not wholly without indication of what was at least Pascal's original plan. In the spring of 1658, shortly before he was incapacitated for serious work, he explained to his friends for the space of two hours the line of his intended argument, and the substance of his exposition, as reported by one of his listeners eight years afterwards, is preserved in the preface written by his nephew, Étienne Périer, for the Port-Royal edition of the *Pensées*, and more fully in the *Discours* of Filleau de La Chaise. Further, some of the fragments contain headings or notes on the order and arrangement of the work.

Pascal began his exposition by pointing out that neither metaphysical proofs (like those of Descartes) nor proofs from the works of Nature (like those of Grotius) appeal to the ordinary man, who can only understand moral or historical proofs. So beginning with moral proofs he sketched his celebrated picture of the dual nature of man, of man in his misery and man in his greatness. The picture with its striking contrasts could not fail to rouse the free-thinker from his apathy and to dispose him to further inquiry. Pascal then sends him to the philosophers, to find that both sceptics and dogmatists are wrong, the former in ignoring man's greatness, the latter in ignoring his misery. The study of religions leads to no better results; some are already dead, others are ignoble or ridiculous. The inquirer is in despair, when Pascal directs his attention to a particular people, whose history, laws, and religion are set forth in an unique Book. Here begins the historical proof. The inquirer will find in this Book a solution of the various problems that have perplexed him In the Redemption of man by Jesus Christ and in the beauty and moral grandeur of His life and teaching, the contradictions of human nature can alone be reconciled.

Such in rough outline was Pascal's original design, though he doubtless modified it during the four years which elapsed between his exposition of it and his death. We also know from some of the fragments that letters and dialogues were to form part of the completed book, and we may even conjecture from the analogy of the *Provincial Letters* that he intended to give it in part a quasi-dramatic form. Lastly, it must be remembered that, as we are expressly told by Étienne Périer, some of the fragments have nothing to do with the Apology.

The four great prose-writers of the sixteenth century were Rabelais, Calvin, Amyot, and Montaigne. Rabelais has the creator's joy in developing the resources of a new instrument; Montaigne varies his language with every movement of his changing thought; Calvin seeks before all things to be clear in order to convince; Amyot combines clearness with picturesqueness in order to produce a work of art. The chief prose-writer of the reign of Henry IV, Cardinal Du Perron, substituted for the imaginative style of the sixteenth century one of greater plainness and more logical precision. But he excelled chiefly in the oratorical period, and what French prose needed was a general standard of style to serve as a model for the ordinary writer. The way was prepared by Malherbe, but as a prose-writer he lacked finish; he could not compose a perfectly-balanced period. French rhetoric still awaited its professor. He appeared three years before Malherbe's death in the person of Balzac, and it is to Malherbe's credit that he at once recognised his merit.

Balzac is a master of the formal qualities of style, but he is always a professor of rhetoric. He mouths commonplaces and empty generalities as if he were uttering novel and profound truths; he revels in hyperbole and high-flown compliment; he is for ever on stilts; he is an "author" not a "man." Pascal had read the chief Jansenist works, including the *La Fréquente Com-*

munion of Arnauld, whose clear and cogent reasoning is expressed in well-balanced and harmonious sentences. He had also read Balzac and Montaigne, and with his usual insight he must have noted the merits and defects of both. He would have agreed with Bossuet that Balzac with all his formal excellence was too affected and constrained to be a good model, and he would have learnt from Montaigne that "style is only a manner of thinking," and of feeling. Thus, his logical and analytical mind, his intellectual sincerity, his habit of accurate observation, his deep and ardent conviction, all combined to find expression in a style, which is simple, lucid, and precise, which is tense with restrained emotion, and which has the movement and passion, if not the imagery, of great poetry.

The Classical Age

The classical idea dominated French literature throughout the seventeenth and the eighteenth centuries, but the true classical age is confined to the reign of Louis XIV, or in a more limited sense to those central and glorious years of his reign which extend from 1661, the year in which he began his personal government, to 1688, when his power began sensibly to decline. In November 1659, Molière produced his first experiment in social comedy, *Les Précieuses ridicules*. In 1660 Boileau published his first satire. But the "school of 1660" had to fight many battles and win many victories before it obtained complete recognition. It was strong, indeed, in the support of the *bourgeois* public, of the best judges among the nobles, and of Louis XIV himself. But the *Académie* remained hostile, and it was not till 1673, just before Molière's death, that it opened its doors to Racine, and it was not till eleven years later that it admitted Boileau and La Fontaine.

A link between the generation of Corneille and that of Racine is formed by the three illustrious friends, La Rochefoucauld, Mme de Sévigné, and Mme de La Fayette. All had frequented Mme de Rambouillet's salon; La Rochefoucauld's *Maximes* are largely based on his experiences during the Fronde; Mme de Sévigné was a pupil of Chapelain, a friend of Retz, and to the end of her days a staunch partisan of Corneille; Mme de La Fayette's second novel was a Scudéry romance in miniature.

FRANÇOIS VI, DUC DE LA ROCHEFOUCAULD (1613–1680), the head of an ancient and distinguished family of Poitou, was at an early age involved in the political intrigues of the time, playing Cinna to Mme de Chevreuse's Émilie. During the Fronde, under the influence of a new mistress, the Duchesse de Longueville, he threw in his lot with Condé and the rebellious nobles, and fought with bravery, but signal ill-success, in that ridiculous and self-seeking cause. Disillusioned and morose, he settled down at Paris in 1656, and in the salon of Mme de Sablé shaped and re-shaped with the help of her criticism his immortal maxims. The first authorised edition (1665) contained 314 maxims; the sixth, the last published in his life-time (1678), 504. Other maxims, including *Réflexions diverses*, were added later. La Rochefoucauld's view of life is strongly coloured by his own experiences. His maxims on love and jealousy, on passion and intrigue, on ingratitude and disloyalty, on flattery and duplicity, on pride and vanity, reflect his disillusionment, his bitterness, his regrets over his early career. Many are inspired by his own self-love; it consoles him to think that the success of others is due rather to good fortune than to superior merit (LXI). The first maxims give the key-note to the rest. We are told at the outset that "what we take for virtues are often nothing but a collection of diverse actions and interests," and then follow three maxims on that *amour propre* or self-love which La Rochefoucauld declares to be the mainspring of most of our actions. The maxims are not all at the same high level; some are obscure, some are a mere jingle or mosaic of words, some are commonplace, and some by reason of their brevity are but half-truths. But the majority show great penetration and what is called knowledge of the world, which means knowledge of a certain section of society. Few will accept La Rochefoucauld's book as a true portrait of human nature, but even the most modest reader may be helped by it to a better knowledge of his own character. The maxims which relate to society and conversation have a special interest, for they present us with the conception of an *honnête homme*, that characteristic product of the seventeenth century, as formulated by a man whose natural good breeding had been polished in the salons of Mme de Rambouillet and Mme de Sablé. La Rochefoucauld's ideal was the *honnête homme* rather than the Christian, but though there is little reference to Christianity in his book, except the maxim that "Humility is the true test of Christian virtues," there is nothing in it that is at variance with Christian teaching. In fact the governing idea of the natural depravity of man is thoroughly Jansenist, though, as has been said, with the Redemption left out. The style of the *Maximes* is beyond praise; it has those qualities of precision, brevity, polish, and simplicity—that last achievement of art—which are the glories of the classical ideal.

The evening of La Rochefoucauld's days was cheered by the friendship and society of Marie de La Vergne, MME DE LA FAYETTE (1634–1693). She was well-educated, highly intelligent, enterprising, and resourceful, reserved but sympathetic, and above all absolutely sincere. But her health was delicate, and the mysterious failure of her married life had left her bruised and melancholy. As early as 1662 she published a novel, *Mlle de Montpensier*, in which she substituted for romantic adventure and high-flown sentiment an attempt to portray life as she knew it. Then, after a partial return to romance in *Zayde* (1670), she repeated her original experiment with far greater success in *La Princesse de Clèves* (1678). There had been earlier novels of a realistic character: Sorel's *Histoire comique de Francion* (1622), a picaresque story of rogues and adventurers; Scarron's *Roman comique* (1651–1657), a loosely-constructed story of strolling players; and Furetière's *Roman bourgeois*, the character of which is indicated by the title. But, except for *Mlle de Montpensier*, the *Princesse de Clèves* was the first novel which faithfully portrayed the aristocratic life of the day. Moreover, though psychological analysis, especially in relation to love, was not in itself a novelty, it was the first novel to employ psychological analysis as the sole source of its interest. It also differs from the romances of La Calprenède and Mlle de Scudéry in being very short and in containing few episodical stories. There are only three characters of any importance, and these are types rather than individuals. M. de Clèves is the type of a high-minded and honourable husband, and M. de Nemours, who in the pages of Brantôme appears as a rather brutal Don Juan, is softened down to the type of an accomplished man of the world who has had many love affairs. Mme de Clèves has

more individuality, and that by reason of the same straightforward and clear-thinking sincerity which distinguished her
creator. By virtue of this she makes passion yield to duty. She is
thus a true sister of Corneille's Pauline; but her inward struggle
is developed with a subtlety and accuracy of analysis worthy
of Racine. Mme de La Fayette is eminently of her time. Though
her narrative relates to the last year of the reign of Henry II,
and though she keeps closely to historical fact, so far as her
authorities represent it, the atmosphere and tone are those of
the Court of Louis XIV. In her power too of eliminating everything that is unessential and of subordinating the particular to
the general; in her disregard of local colour and physical details;
in her clea., easy, unpretentious, but perfectly finished style,
she is wholly of the school of 1660.

Besides the faithful La Rochefoucauld, a frequent visitor to
Mme de La Fayette's house, with its charming garden, in the Rue
Vaugirard, opposite to the Petit Luxembourg, was MME DE
SÉVIGNÉ (1626–1696), her friend for more than forty years.
Marie de Rabutin-Chantal was left an orphan at the age of seven,
and, after an excellent education, married in 1644 the Marquis
de Sévigné, of an old Breton family. Left a widow in 1652, with
one daughter and one son, she lived for two years in retirement
at Les Rochers, repairing the breaches which her husband had
made in his estate. Then she returned to Paris, educated her
children, especially her daughter, with the greatest care, introduced her at Court, where her cold, statuesque beauty was greatly
admired—she was, declared her cousin Bussy, "la plus jolie
fille de France"—and married her in 1669 to the Comte de
Grignan, head of an ancient family of Provence and soon afterwards appointed its Lieutenant-General. The separation from
her adored daughter, which took place in February 1671, was
a heavy blow to Mme de Sévigné, but it made her the greatest
letter-writer of France—perhaps of the world. For though she
was incapable of writing a dull or an uninteresting letter, those
to her daughter are the best because they are the most spontaneous. She could write to her, as she could not write to Bussy
or Coulanges, without fear of her letters being shown to the wrong
people.

In the sixteenth century Estienne Pasquier (1529–1615),

under the influence of Latin and Italian models, introduced the epistolary art as a definite form of literature into France. His letters on various subjects, addressed to the public rather than to his nominal correspondents, were published in part in his lifetime. His example was followed by Balzac, *le grand épistolier de la France*, and Voiture wrote letters which were certainly meant for more eyes than those of their recipients. Letters play an important part in *L'Astrée* and its successors, and, as we have seen, Pascal intended to make use of them in his *Apology*. But with this epistolary art Mme de Sévigné has nothing to do. Her letters are genuine letters, the natural expression of a mother's love for her daughter. Yet their very artlessness is the prime source of their artistic charm, for they reveal with limpid candour the rich and varied nature of the writer—her warm heart, her clear intellect, her vivacious wit, her prejudices and her tolerances, her wide charity and her lack of sensibility, her love of society and her feeling for nature, her appreciation of the pomp and gaiety of the world and her enthusiasm for austere religious teachers like Nicole and Bourdaloue. But if she herself is the principal figure on her stage, it is peopled with many characters, most of whom only exist for us by virtue of the life with which she has endowed them. Lastly there is her style. If she did not write for the public, she wrote at least to please herself and her daughter, and both were excellent judges. Thus it is the style of one who writes rapidly and spontaneously, but who takes a pleasure in writing—of one who has been well-trained in the use of her native language, but who, not being a professional writer, can take liberties with her vocabulary and her syntax. Above all she excels all her contemporaries, except La Fontaine, in the faculty of picturesque and vivid description.

In contrast to this aristocratic group, who, if they published their writings, published them either anonymously or under the name of a literary godfather, was the *bourgeois* group of La Fontaine, Molière, Boileau, and Racine, who, in 1664 and 1665 frequently met either at Boileau's lodgings or at the taverns of the *Mouton blanc* or the *Croix de Lorraine*. The five years from 1664 to 1669 are perhaps the most glorious in the whole annals of French literature. They witnessed the production of *Tartuffe* and *Le Misanthrope*; of *Andromaque* and

Britannicus; of La Fontaine's *Fables*, Boileau's *Satires* and La Rochefoucauld's *Maximes*; the preaching of Bossuet's finest sermons, and the *début* of Bourdaloue. Yet throughout these years of splendid performance Boileau and his friends were fighting hard against the forces of obstruction and bad taste; Molière was struggling for the public performance of *Tartuffe*; Boileau was waging a relentless warfare in his *Satires*.

NICOLAS BOILEAU (1636–1711), called Despréaux, was the son of a registrar of one of the Paris courts. His main work as a critic may be divided into two periods—a period of attack (1660–1668), comprising *Satires* I–IX, and a period of construction (1669–1677), during which he wrote *Epistles* I–IX and the *Art poétique*. During the first period his criticism was personal; it was based upon instinct, good sense, and the hatred of a *sot livre* rather than upon any system or principles. The great majority of the writers whom he pilloried are unknown at the present day, except to professed students, but when he attacked them they had on their side reputation and success. They included Quinault, Mlle de Scudéry and her brother, La Calprenède, the Abbé Cotin, and above all Chapelain, who was not only the head of the French Parnassus, but was Colbert's chief adviser in the delicate task of bestowing pensions on men of letters. In his earlier days Chapelain had done good service in the cause of the classical ideal, but his inordinate vanity had impelled him to swim with the stream, and he was now a frequenter of *précieux* salons and an active opponent of the new school. To attack so powerful an individual required considerable courage, but it did not daunt Boileau. In 1666 he published the first edition of his *Satires* (I–VII), and in 1668 he drove the attack home with his Ninth Satire, *ce terrible abatage de réputations* (Lanson), in which hardly one of his opponents escapes punishment and Chapelain is held up to eternal ridicule in some of Boileau's finest lines.

During the next six years Boileau was chiefly occupied with his *Epistles*. Then in 1674, a month or two after Chapelain's death, he published a new edition of his works, which included the *Art poétique*, the code of the new school. It embodies certain main principles, some of which are definitely stated in the poem, while others may be gathered from Boileau's other writings or from the general practice of his school.

1. The works of the ancients have obtained a universal and lasting reputation. This is a strong proof of their excellence, and it is due to the fact that they deal with eternal truths and that they represent nature at first-hand.

2. The moderns must tread in their footsteps and in their turn must study nature at first-hand.

> Jamais de la nature il ne faut s'écarter.

But they must represent the universal and permanent, not the exceptional or transitory. To guide them in their choice they have Reason—the Reason of Descartes, the faculty which distinguishes truth from falsehood, and which is almost equivalent to good sense.

> Aimez donc la raison; que toujours vos écrits
> Empruntent d'elle seule et leur lustre et leur prix.

3. Another lesson to be learnt from the ancients is the importance of style and perfect workmanship. The first secret of style is to think clearly.

> Avant donc que d'écrire apprenez à penser.

But this must be followed by self-criticism and repeated revision.

> Soyez à vous même un sévère critique.
> .   .   .   .
> Polissez-le sans cesse et le repolissez.

The truth and importance of the first and third of these principles are beyond dispute, but the second principle is too narrow and too rigid. Firstly, reason and good sense alone will not account for the highest flights of poetry or creative imagination, neither for an Ariel nor for a Caliban. The transitory and the ignoble cannot be banished altogether from literature. Molière found in the passing fashion of *préciosité* matter for eternal laughter, and Boileau himself showed in *Le Repas ridicule* and *Les Embarras de Paris* that his practice was wider than his theory. Secondly, Boileau interpreted "nature" in a much narrower sense than the ancients. He limited it to human nature, and to human nature of the Court and the town.

But perhaps the greatest defect of his art of poetry, and the

cause of its cramping effect upon French literature down to the
Romantic revolt, was his rigid demarcation of *genres*. For
instance, in spite of Molière and La Fontaine, he ignored prose-
comedy and verse-fable, because these were unknown to the
Greeks and Romans.

Boileau lacked the imagination which can divine what the
eye has never seen. But he could think in images and he could
present from memory a singularly clear and effective picture
of physical things. Hence, as M. Lanson has admirably
pointed out, it is in realistic descriptions such as those of
Le Repas ridicule (*Satire* III), *Les Embarras de Paris* (*Satire* VI),
and his serio-comic poem, *Le Lutrin*, that he comes nearest to
being a poet.

On the other hand, with the exception of the tribute to
Molière in the *Épître à Racine*, his *Epistles* are his weakest work.
For in that age of psychologists and moralists he was not a
psychologist and only a superficial and perfunctory moralist.
His one intellectual interest was literature, and for that he had
a real passion. He hated the author of a *sot livre* as a personal
enemy, and his strongest verse is inspired by that hatred.

JEAN-BAPTISTE POQUELIN, called MOLIÈRE (1622–1673), was
forty-one and the author of *L'École des Femmes* when he made
Boileau's acquaintance, and though he rose to still greater
heights in high comedy, he made many successful experiments
on lines which Boileau disapproved. The son of a well-to-do
Paris upholsterer, he received a good education at the fashionable Jesuit College of Clermont, and then in spite of the opposition of his family insisted on becoming an actor. After two years
of failure at Paris his company tried their fortunes in the provinces (1645), and after a period of hard struggle attained, under
Molière's able management, so large a measure of success that
in 1659 they ventured to return to the capital. During this
period of apprenticeship, Molière only wrote two comedies, the
earlier of which, *L'Étourdi*, modelled closely on Italian lines,
revealed him as a brilliant writer of dramatic verse and as
exceptionally prolific in comic invention. With *Les Précieuses
ridicules*, his first piece after his return to Paris, half-farce and
half-comedy, he gave a foretaste of that social comedy which
he so finely illustrated in *L'École des Femmes* (1662), and which

he brought to perfection in *Tartuffe* (1664) and *Le Misanthrope* (1666). The success of *L'École des Femmes* brought him many enemies, and during the ensuing years till January 1669, when he at last obtained permission to play *Tartuffe* in public, he had, like Boileau and Racine, to battle against powerful opposing forces. *Le Misanthrope* and the three plays of 1668—*Amphitryon, George Dandin*, and *L'Avare*—all bear traces of depression and spiritual conflict, for in addition to the attacks of unscrupulous enemies he had to bear the burden of ill-health and domestic trouble. In *Les Femmes savantes* (1672) we return to a serener atmosphere, but with *Le Malade imaginaire* (1673) the shadow reappears. It was the shadow of impending death. The end of the fourth performance was nearly reached, when Molière had a sudden seizure, and, though he struggled through his part, he died at his house in the Rue Richelieu less than an hour later.

Molière had an unrivalled genius for comedy. He was far from blind to the tragic issues of life, but he realised that tragedy and evil often have a ridiculous side, and it was this side which roused his creative imagination. Thus *Tartuffe, Le Misanthrope, George Dandin, L'Avare*, and *Le Malade imaginaire*, all potential tragedies, become in his hands true comedies.

We laugh alike at Tartuffe and Harpagon, whom we loathe, at Alceste, whom we love, and at George Dandin and Argan, whom we pity. For Molière had the humorist's power of sympathising with those whom he ridicules and he can see the ridiculous side of those whom he admires. There is a touch of the ridiculous even in Don Juan, that wonderful portrait of a *grand seigneur* of Molière's own day, who in spite of his bravery and his bravado is hateful and in some respects contemptible. But Molière's characters appear differently to different people, and most have been the subject of eager discussion. There can be no stronger proof of their truth to nature. They are neither mere types nor mere exhibitors of a single humour; they have the individuality and complexity of living men and women.

Molière's interest in plot was in inverse ratio to his interest in character. His plot only serves to provide his play with the necessary framework and to bring out his characters. It is sometimes an old plot; sometimes a new one of his own invention, and then it is the simplest imaginable. He cared as little for his *dénouement* as for his plot, but he had to end his comedy some-how. So he had recourse to hackneyed and mechanical devices, which seem all the more mechanical by contrast with the natural development of the rest of the play. But it is a mistake to suppose that he did not understand the art of dramatic construction. In *L'École des Femmes* and *Tartuffe*, comedies which he conceived and built up at leisure, the construction is admirable. Every act is the natural outcome of the agent's character, and one act follows another in a logical sequence. Even in *Le Misanthrope*, which has been described as a mere succession of *tableaux*, there is a closer connexion between the scenes than is generally supposed.

Within the limits of comedy Molière showed the versatility of a true artist. Besides his great comedies he wrote to please the king several *comédies ballets*, which include *L'Amour médecin, Le Mariage forcé, Le Bourgeois gentilhomme*, and *Le Malade imaginaire*, a *comédie galante*, a *comédie pastorale héroique*, and in collaboration with Corneille and Quinault the *tragédie-ballet* of *Psyché*. *Don Juan* is a romantic drama, *Amphitryon* is a mythological comedy written in *vers libres*, the charming *Le Sicilien* is the libretto of a comic opera. But after his experi-ments Molière always returned to the type of comedy which he had created for the modern world—the social comedy of character. For he was before all things an observer of man in his social relations, and especially as a member of that primitive and natural social unit—the family. The vices that he attacked were chiefly anti-social vices—religious hypocrisy and atheism in *Tartuffe* and *Don Juan*, social insincerity in *Le Misanthrope*—or vices and lesser evils which tend to disintegrate the family—avarice in *L'Avare*, neglect of household affairs in *Les Femmes savantes*, undue influence of a spiritual director in *Tartuffe*—and as the indispensable condition of healthy family life is a suitable marriage, he is never weary of protesting against the sacrifice of daughters to the selfish aims of parents. He even looks unfavourably on all unequal marriages, whether in point of age or in point of station.

He was no idealist. He would have agreed with Montaigne that "the fairest lives are those which are regulated after the ordinary human pattern." But he was an eminently sane and healthy moralist, attentive to the calls of conscience and duty and to the claims of his fellow-men. Like Rabelais and Montaigne he made common-sense his touchstone. In the name of common-sense his Aristes and Cléantes and Béraldes protest against the follies of their relations, and the valet Sganarelle against the atheism of Don Juan. His delightful maid-servants, his Dorines and Nicoles and Toinettes, are the very embodiment of laughing common-sense. His morality may seem to some wanting in elevation, but he was a writer of comedies, and common-sense is the soul of comedy.

Some critics, notably La Bruyère and Fénelon, have objected to his style, and it is easy to find blemishes both in his language and in his versification, the result of haste and negligence. But he wrote for the stage, not for the study, and often when he is ungrammatical or involved he is so purposely, in order to be more dramatic. His style at any rate is the joy, not only of all actors and theatre-goers, but of all readers who have any dramatic imagination.

JEAN RACINE (1639–1699) was only twenty-three when he first met Molière and Boileau, so that he was young enough to come under their influence. Boileau regarded him with pride as his pupil, but possibly Racine owed a greater debt to Molière. Left an orphan at a tender age, and brought up by his grandparents, he was educated, first at the College of Beauvais on Port-Royal lines, then, for three years (1655–1658), at Les Granges de Port-Royal, where he had four remarkable teachers in Nicole, Lancelot, Hamon, and Antoine Lemaître, and finally at the College d'Harcourt at Paris. Port-Royal imbued him with Jansenism and with an ardent love of Greek literature. But for some years his Jansenism remained in abeyance, and having abandoned the idea of taking Orders he embarked on a literary career, received a pension for an ode, and produced two plays, *La Thébaïde* and *Alexandre* (1665). The latter closely follows the Cornelian pattern, except that Alexandre is a lover before he is a hero. This gave him a clue to his true line, and his first masterpiece, *Andromaque* (1667), was based on a conception of tragedy which differed widely from his predecessor's. There followed *Les Plaideurs* (1668), a clever comedy, the idea of which is borrowed from the *Wasps* of Aristophanes, *Britannicus* (1669), *Bérénice* (1670), *Bajazet* (1672), *Mithridate* (1673), *Iphigénie* (1674), and *Phèdre* (January 1, 1677). Then, partly in disgust at the tactics of his opponents, but mainly on religious grounds, under the influence of his old friends of Port-Royal, he retired from the stage, married a young woman, who never read a line of his work, but who was an excellent wife and mother, became a model head of a family, was appointed with Boileau historiographer to the king, and played the courtier's part at Versailles with the approval of so difficult a judge as Saint-Simon. Then at the request of Mme de Maintenon he wrote two plays, *Esther* (1689) and *Athalie* (1690), for her school-girls of Saint-Cyr. *Esther*, which is admirably written, but which is little more than a highly skilful arrangement of the Bible story, proved highly successful, but intrigues and other causes prevented the production of Racine's greatest tragedy at Saint-Cyr. It was played twice in Mme de Maintenon's apartments at Versailles, and twelve years later in the Versailles theatre, but it was not produced at Paris till 1716.

Racine, with his intimate knowledge of Greek literature, realised that a classical tragedy demands simplicity of action, and in *Andromaque* and in all his succeeding plays he put this principle into practice. The plot of *Bérénice* is founded on five words of Suetonius—*Titus Berenicem dimisit invitus invitam*—and even where there is a background of political intrigue as in *Bajazet* and *Mithridate*, the essential plot may be stated in a few sentences. In this Racine was following Molière, from whom he also learnt to "portray men after nature," instead of heroes after his imagination. So, while accepting the classical tradition that tragedy deals with princes, he made his princes like ordinary men, and banishing all declamation from his style approximated it to that of *Le Misanthrope*. But while Molière's strength is in the portrayal of character, Racine's lies in the analysis of passion, and chiefly, if not entirely, of the great elemental passions of love, jealousy, pride, and ambition. These he studies in many forms, choosing for their display characters of a simple and ordinary type, who, by reason of their rank and environment, are free to develop their passions without external restraint. Hermione, Agrippine, Néron, and Roxane are at heart

commonplace, even vulgar criminals, caring for nothing but
their own selfish aims. Pyrrhus and Achille are violent and
energetic lovers; Oreste and Xiphares are resigned and melancholy lovers. Monime, Bérénice, and Iphigénie, who subordinate
passion to duty, are types of womanly virtue; Andromaque
and Clytemnestre of maternal devotion; Acomat (superbly
drawn) and Narcisse, of cool calculating ambition. Agamemnon's
ambition is more ordinary and more vacillating. Mithridate is
at once a great king fighting for the freedom of his country, and
an elderly, suspicious, and tyrannical lover. Phèdre appeals
strongly to our imagination and our sympathy, but apart from
her great passion, which is portrayed with marvellous insight
and delicacy, we know nothing of her.

In *Athalie* Racine's method is different. Here he forsakes
the analysis of passion for the creation of character, and
with a master's hand he draws Athalie, the great queen,
criminal, ruthless, courageous, and capable, who is presented to
us at the moment when remorse and a remnant of feminine
feeling are beginning to weaken her resolution; Joad, the great
ecclesiastic, the born leader of men, with his superb faith, his
knowledge of human nature, and his inspiring eloquence;
Mathan, a more vulgar Narcisse; Abner, the honest but stupid
soldier, who is like clay in Joad's hands; Josabeth, with her
woman's fears and her maternal love; and the child Joash,
with his royal spirit and his trusting obedience. But *Athalie*
is not only remarkable for the individuality of its characters;
it shows a feeling for spectacular effect hitherto unknown in the
French classical drama. The Priests and armed Levites, the
Queen's soldiers, the chorus of young girls, the Temple of Jerusalem, and above all the thrilling moment, when at Joad's cry,

> Soldats du Dieu vivant, defendez votre roi,

the scene changes to the interior of the Temple—all make
an appeal to the imagination through the senses which it is
impossible to resist.

The praise of Racine's style is on every critic's lips. A
foreigner may fail to appreciate its more subtle beauties,
whether of language or of harmony, but he can at least admire
its pregnant clarity, its elegant precision, and its musical
cadences. To speak of it, however, as great poetry is a misnomer.

Indeed for the purpose of Racine's art, which is the analysis of passion in simple and ordinary characters, a poetical style would have been out of place. It is only in *Athalie* that we sometimes feel the want of a higher flight.

JEAN DE LA FONTAINE (1621–1695) made the acquaintance of Racine, whose distant cousin he had married, in 1659, when the younger man was a student at the College d'Harcourt and the elder was writing occasional poetry for his patron, Nicholas Fouquet. He was born at Château-Thierry in a house which the Germans destroyed in their retreat in 1917, and after reading first for Orders, and then for the Bar, settled down to an indolent life of literary *flânerie*. In 1665, when he was well on in the forties, he published a volume of *Contes* from Boccaccio and Ariosto, which revealed an admirable gift for verse-narrative. At last in 1668, when he published six books of *Fables*, his genius found its true bent. Five more books appeared in 1678–79 and the Twelfth and last in 1694. Till the end of 1692 he had led the life of a man of pleasure, but a severe illness brought about his conversion, and no one questioned its sincerity. An egoist in the sense that he never did anything that he disliked, he had some charming qualities, some of which do not usually go with egoism. He was easy-going, unambitious, candid, warm-hearted, sincere, and among the things he liked was taking trouble for the sake of his friends.

The classical Aesopic fable, even when versified, is brief, dry, and prosaic, and the story is told for the sake of the moral. La Fontaine tells the story, poetically and dramatically, for the story's sake, and he appends the moral almost as an afterthought. In making this transformation he was helped by two sixteenth-century writers. Marot suggested to him the right tone, as he had already done for the *Contes*, and a certain Guillaume Haudent, master of the choristers at Rouen, whose verse-rendering of Aesop was published in 1547, showed him that the fable might be treated in a lively and dramatic fashion. But his achievement was mainly due to his own genius. He had a genuine love of animals and nature, and both at Château-Thierry and in the neighbourhood of Paris he observed them in his lazy unmethodical fashion. Moreover, like that other *bonhomme*, Corot, to whom M. Lafenestre has so happily compared him, he was

an artist to his finger-tips. He was a master of technique and he
took infinite pains with his work. Further, like Corot, though he
painted after Nature, he stamped every picture with the impress
of his own individuality. To speak of his fables as pictures is
something more than a conventional metaphor. *Cela est peint* says
Mme de Sévigné of *Le singe et le chat* (IX. 17), and if we ask ourselves why some of the fables in Books VII.–XI., which contain so
many masterpieces, are less perfect than the rest, the answer is
that they fail to call up a picture. La Fontaine paints with few
strokes because he can see into the heart of things and seize
their characteristic quality. "Demoiselle belette au corps long et
fluet," "le héron au long bec emmanché d'un long cou," "aller
son train de sénateur," of the tortoise; "caracolant, frisant l'air
et les eaux," of the swallow; "faisant la chattemite," of the cat.
What more is needed? There are no elaborate descriptions of
Nature, but a perfume of the country pervades his whole poetry.

> Des Lapins, qui sur la bruyère,
> L'œil éveillé, l'oreille au guet,
> S'égayaient, et de thym parfumaient leur bouquet.

La Fontaine's animals are real animals so far as their outward
appearance and habits are concerned, but he has invested them
with the moral nature of human beings. He is, in short, a
moralist like his great contemporaries, and his opinion of man is
no more exalted than theirs. *Les Compagnons d'Ulysse* (XII. 1)
is at one with Boileau's Eighth Satire and with the speeches of
Alceste and Philinte in the opening scene of *Le Misanthrope*.
But La Fontaine combats folly and vice, not with stern indignation, but with the gentler weapons of irony and humour,
and Rousseau and Lamartine, to whom humour was denied,
found him hard and unfeeling. Yet no one has written more
tenderly of friendship. *Les deux pigeons* (IX. 2) and *Le corbeau,
la gazelle, la tortue et le rat* (XII. 15), the latter dedicated to
Mme de la Sablière, under whose roof he lived for twenty years,
are two of his very finest fables. Love your friends; Help your
neighbours; Trust in God; Work hard—these four maxims may
be said to constitute the sum of his simple morality.

If his animals represent human nature in general, they also
stand for the society of his own day. Taine has brought this
out with his usual fertility of illustration, but with too great

insistence on details. It is true, however, that La Fontaine has grouped his animals in a sort of social hierarchy which corresponds more or less to that of his own age. The lion is not Louis XIV, but he is an absolute monarch, studied from the only model with which La Fontaine was familiar. *Les animaux malades de la peste* (VII. 1) and *Les obsèques de la lionne* (VIII. 14) are biting satires on royalty.

Of the charm of La Fontaine's style much has been said. It is a happy blend of the medieval with the classical spirit, of the picturesqueness, quaintness, and malice of Gaul with the grace, moderation, and perfect workmanship of Greece. And he is a master, not only of style, but of versification. His rhyming may be faulty, judged by strict standards, and he may violate mechanical rules, but his handling of the *vers libre*, in which the ordinary reader sees nothing but a capricious arrangement of unequal lines, is "the last word of the most learned and complicated art." For the rhythm changes with the thought, and the whole poem is composed of rhythmical units, or strophes of unequal length, which represent the paragraphs of a prose narrative, or, it may almost be said, the scenes of a drama.

A characteristic feature of the age of Louis XIV was the popularity of sermons. The chief seasons for preaching were Advent and Lent, when the churches were thronged. When Bourdaloue preached on Good Friday, 1671, people sent their lackeys, writes Mme de Sévigné, on the previous Wednesday to keep seats for them, and the crowd was *à mourir*. Of the preachers who drew these enthusiastic audiences two stand out head and shoulders above the rest—Bossuet and Bourdaloue.

JACQUES-BÉNIGNE BOSSUET (1627–1704) was born at Dijon of a family of magistrates. After studying the humanities and theology at Paris and taking Orders he spent six active years at Metz in preaching and controversy. Summoned to Paris in 1659, he preached there for ten years with unbroken success. In 1669 he was appointed Bishop of Condom and, a year later, tutor to the Dauphin. In 1681, his pupil's education being completed, he was nominated to the see of Meaux. From 1688 to his death in 1704 he was absorbed partly in the work of his diocese and partly in various controversies on behalf of the Catholic Church: against the Protestants (*Histoire des Variations des Églises Protestantes*, 1688); against the stage (*Maximes et Réflexions sur la Comédie*, 1694); against Fénelon and quietism (*Relation sur le Quiétisme*, 1698); against Richard Simon (*Défense de la Tradition et des Saints-Pères*). His six great funeral orations were delivered from 1669 to 1687. It was for the benefit of his pupil, the Dauphin, that he wrote his *Discours sur l'histoire universelle* (1681), his *Politique tirée de l'Écriture sainte*, and his *De la connaissance de Dieu et de soi-même*. The two latter were not published till after his death, as were the *Élévations sur les Mystères* and *Les Méditations sur l'Évangile*, in which his imagination soars to some of its most lofty flights.

Bossuet is with Burke the greatest of modern orators, and for the generality of readers he is this chiefly by virtue of his funeral orations. They have the true spirit of classicism: they rise from the particular to the universal; they are not mere panegyrics of individuals, but religious meditations on life and death and eternity. Even in those on Condé and Henrietta of England, in which the personal note is more prominent, and which for that reason affect us more powerfully than the others, topics like the rebellion of Condé and the sudden death of Madame are the occasion for general meditations on loyalty and death. Similarly the oration on the Princesse Palatine, who like Condé had been a doubter, contains an eloquent attack on the free-thinkers of the day. Bossuet's sermons show the same oratorical power, the same dynamic quality of movement, the same rich imagination. The sermon *On Death* vies with the oration on Henrietta of England, those *On Providence* with the oration on the Princesse Palatine. The great sermon *On the Unity of the Church*, which Bossuet preached before the General Assembly of the Clergy in 1681, is a magnificent appeal, by one whose Gallicanism was beyond question, for more conciliatory action towards the Head of the Church.

Bossuet's passion for visible unity made him a vehement opponent of Protestantism, and like the great majority of his contemporaries, Vauban and Saint-Simon being honourable exceptions, he applauded the revocation of the Edict of Nantes, though he reprobated *dragonnades* and other violent methods of repression. But he had a powerful weapon in his pen, and his

Histoire des Variations des Églises Protestantes was regarded as
the most effective attack that had yet been made on the Protestant position. By a sound historical instinct he took his facts
solely from Protestant sources, and in his choice of those sources
he showed a more critical spirit than is often allowed to him.
Noteworthy also are his portraits of Luther, Calvin, and Melanchthon. The *Discours sur l'histoire universelle*, the greatest of
his non-oratorical writings, consists of three parts: a chronological abridgment of universal history down to Charlemagne, a
commentary on religious history as set forth in the Old and New
Testaments and a commentary on the rise and fall of empires.
The earlier epochs of the abridgment are naturally out of date,
but the later ones, from Cyrus to Charlemagne, may still be
read with profit. The narrative sweeps on like a large flowing
river, and one cannot sufficiently admire the historical insight
with which Bossuet seizes upon the salient events of each epoch.
The second part, to which he himself attached great importance,
has been largely invalidated by the results of modern scholarship,
but the third part has a special interest because it sets forth and
applies that which formed the central idea of Bossuet's philosophy—the dogma of Providence. His theory, which is almost
identical with that of Rabelais, has been greatly misunderstood
by unfriendly critics. It does not exclude secondary causes; it
recognises the long chain of cause and effect that constitutes
history, and the initiation of great movements by men of
exceptional genius. But it insists that events and men alike are
under the control of a Supreme Ruler.

With his love of order and authority Bossuet regarded all
independent thought in matters of faith as heretical. Thus he
looked with equal distrust on the quietism of Mme Guyon and
the Biblical criticism of Richard Simon. Detecting in both alike
a danger to orthodoxy, he attacked them with his usual vigour
and confidence. But failure to comprehend his opponent's case
resulted in a certain want of charity. In Fénelon, the champion
of Mme Guyon, he had an antagonist who could brook defeat
as little as himself, and whose subtle and complex nature
irritated and perplexed his more simple one.

Bossuet is recognised as one of the greatest masters of French
prose, and that not so much by reason of his higher flights as by

the even excellence of his more level passages. He combines force with clarity, dialectical power with concrete imagination, and he writes with the majestic ease of one whose knowledge of his instrument is so perfect that he can afford an occasional blemish.

LOUIS BOURDALOUE (1632–1704), a Jesuit, was born at Bourges; like Bossuet, he came from a family of magistrates. In 1669, the year in which Bossuet was appointed to Condom, he preached his first course of sermons at Paris, and he continued to preach there till his death thirty-five years later. Preaching and confessing were his whole life. Seeing that he was as austere in the pulpit as he was in the confessional, his enormous popularity speaks volumes for the attraction which moral questions and psychological analysis had for the society of his day. Like Bossuet he attacked special vices with uncompromising boldness, especially those of the court and society. But his sermons were more severely practical than his predecessor's; he addressed himself more to the individual sinner, and he introduced a larger element of actuality. Extravagance, gambling, failure to pay your bills, mercenary marriages, evil-speaking, hypocrisy, impurity—these are some of his topics and they at once suggest *Don Juan, George Dandin, Le Misanthrope, Tartuffe*. But it was not only his actuality but his psychological penetration, the fruit of his experience as spiritual director, which fascinated his hearers. They talked of his "characters" and "portraits," and they found in them personal allusions of which the preacher had never dreamed.

In an age of Reason it was his "design," he said, "to convince the reason." He has none of Bossuet's passion and imagination; but his feeling for movement and his power of continuous development stamp him as a true orator. In his sermon *Sur la Médisance* he alludes with irony to the *Provincial Letters*, but there is no greater tribute to their efficacy than the stern and austere morality of this "most Jansenist of Jesuits." The sermon *Sur la Pénitence*, in which he defends his Society from the charge of relaxing morals, is unsurpassed as a moral tonic.

NICOLAS MALEBRANCHE (1638–1715) was a pupil first of the Paris University and then of the Oratory, that broad-minded school of humanism and philosophy. His work as a philosopher will be discussed in a later chapter, but he is entitled to a place

here as being with Berkeley the most fascinating of all philosophical writers, and as second only to Bossuet among the prose-
writers of his day. The secret of his style is that, abhorring jargon
and pedantry, he writes with absolute simplicity and sincerity.
Of his chief work, *De la Recherche de la Vérité* (1674), the Second
Book, on the Imagination, is most read to-day. It contains the
well-known chapter in which he criticises Montaigne. The great
Essayist's self-portraiture, his scepticism, his inconsistencies,
even his imagination, the beauty and vivacity of which his critic
acknowledges, were all alike distasteful to the humble Christian
priest, who, like his master Descartes, regarded Reason as the
supreme human faculty.

Malebranche conducts his search after Absolute Truth on
psychological lines. The headings of his first three parts—the
Senses, the Imagination, the Understanding—are just what one
would expect in a treatise on Psychology. Nor does he ever forget that man is a moral being. His method is a testimony to the
solidarity of aim and thought which is so striking a feature of
French classical literature. Of the ten writers who best represent
the great period from 1661 to 1668 it may be said that all except
Boileau, who is more interested in books than in men, are both
psychologists and moralists. Even Mme de Sévigné, who would
not have claimed to be either, had as her special favourites
Nicole and Bourdaloue. Secondly, all these writers are observers
at first-hand; they go direct to Nature.

> Maintenant il ne faut pas
> Quitter la Nature d'un pas

wrote La Fontaine after the performance of Molière's *Les
Fâcheux*, thirteen years before Boileau enunciated the same
doctrine in his *Art poétique*. Thirdly, they all use their observation of particular instances for the discovery of general truths.

Nor do they agree less in their artistic principles. Whether in
the sermon or the fable, whether in tragedy or comedy, whether
in the brief maxims of La Rochefoucauld or the long metaphysical treatise of Malebranche, you find the same love of order,
the same respect for the authority of the ancients—even when
it is disregarded—the same careful attention to form and style.
In the matter of style there is, as Sainte-Beuve has noted
with his usual insight, an appreciable difference between the

older and the younger writers. There is more imagination, more individuality, more savour, a richer vocabulary, a greater freedom in the treatment of grammar and syntax in La Fontaine, Molière, Mme de Sévigné, and Bossuet. There is greater purity and precision, a more absolute correctness, a more finished perfection (though in this quality La Fontaine is their equal) in the work of Bourdaloue, Mme de La Fayette, Boileau, Malebranche, and Racine. La Rochefoucauld, who was eight years senior to La Fontaine, is an exception. Though he had imagination, he makes a sparing use of images, and the special character of his art renders precision and finish indispensable. But he did not begin to write his maxims till 1659, or two years after the publication of the *Provincial Letters* in a collected form. If you couple with this the fact that, when the first Letter appeared, Bossuet, the youngest of the older group, was twenty-nine, and that Bourdaloue, the eldest of the younger group, was only twenty-four, it is tempting to conjecture that the difference in style is partly due to the work of Pascal. In any case the difference is not a profound one. All the ten are masters of style. But the supreme masters are La Fontaine, Bossuet, Malebranche, Racine. These are the great enchanters; and one secret of their enchantment is that their style is always the interpreter of their thought. The dress never conceals the figure; the artist never makes us forget the man.

The transition to the Eighteenth Century

The year 1688, says Saint-Simon, marks "the apogee of the reign of Louis XIV, the height of his glory and prosperity." This is particularly true of the literature. After 1688 the great writers of the school of 1660 wrote little or nothing. La Bruyère, who published his *Caractères* in March of that year, begins his book with *Tout est dit*, and, though an ardent classicist in spirit and sympathy, alike by his style and by his manner of observing human nature, he inaugurates a new era. Fénelon, another lover of the classics, was as much an individualist in literature as he was in religion and politics. Massillon's note in the pulpit is very different from Bossuet's and Bourdaloue's. The comedies of Regnard and Dancourt are on a lower plane than those of Molière. Bayle, whose *Pensées sur la Comète* appeared as early as 1682, and

Fontenelle, whose *Dialogue des Morts* was published a year later, are something more than forerunners of the eighteenth century —they are actually of it.

But even more significant of the change that was coming over French literature was the "Quarrel between the Ancients and the Moderns." It arose out of a poem entitled *Le Siècle de Louis le Grand*, which CHARLES PERRAULT (1628–1703), now best known as the author of the *Contes des fées*, read before the *Académie française* in January 1687. He extolled the age of Louis XIV as superior even to that of Augustus, and having roused a storm of indignation in the classical camp, he stated his reasons at length in the *Parallèle des Anciens et des Modernes* (end of 1688). He was answered by Boileau in his *Réflexions critiques sur Longin* (1694), a flank attack discourteous in tone and not very convincing in argument. In 1697 Perrault completed his *Parallèle* with a fourth part and the first phases of the "Quarrel" were closed by a conciliatory letter, in which Boileau acknowledged the superiority of the age of Louis XIV to that of Augustus in tragedy, comedy, and the novel. The effect of this controversy on the future development of French literature will be considered in the next section. Here it is sufficient to point out that one result of it was to free literature from the tyranny of the ancients. Even Boileau admitted that they were not the only models, and that the famous "rules" were not immutable. It was the application to literature of that Cartesian doctrine of criticism which Bayle and Fontenelle had already applied to religion.

JEAN DE LA BRUYÈRE (1645–1696), a Parisian by birth, was whole-heartedly on the side of the Ancients, and in his *Caractères* he ostensibly took Theophrastus for his model. The attention that he paid to form and style proclaimed him of the school of Boileau, and, like the great writers who immediately preceded him, he took for his subject Man. But in two important respects he was a Modern, pointing forward, instead of back. Firstly, he was an observer of manners and conduct rather than a student of character. His portraits, not only of imaginary persons, such as the hypocrite (Onuphre), or the book-collector, or the tulip-grower, but also of real individuals—La Fontaine, Corneille, Fontenelle (Cydias)—are drawn from the outside.

They present the external man with faithful accuracy, but they do not penetrate to his soul. The method is thus the exact opposite to Racine's, who gives us souls without bodies. But it was the method of the future; it inspired not only the comedy of Regnard and Dancourt and Lesage, of Dufresny and Destouches, but it was also the foundation of the eighteenth century novel.

Secondly, La Bruyère was an innovator in style. In the matter of vocabulary, construction, order, harmony, polish, French prose, he says, had well-nigh reached perfection; it only remained to *mettre de l'esprit*. And by this he meant that the writer should put more of himself into his style, that he should be more of a conscious artist, and that his aim should be *bien définir et bien peindre*. It was in pursuance of this double aim which, it may be noted, was precisely that of Flaubert, that La Bruyère gave so sharp an outline to his portraits, and added to them, so to speak, a touch of colour. Further, the artist in him led him to introduce great variety into his style, both in vocabulary and construction. He does not shrink from the *mot propre*, nor even from the technical term. He relieves the long oratorical phrase of Pascal and Bossuet with the short broken phrase which was to become that of the eighteenth century. He is thus the precursor of Montesquieu and Voltaire.

"Sa figure," says Sainte-Beuve, "appartient à deux siècles. Il termine l'un: on dirait qu'il commence et introduit l'autre." Yet as the artist who conceals his art is greater than the artist who does not, competent French critics rank La Bruyère, original and interesting writer though he is, a little below the greatest masters of French prose.

FRANÇOIS DE SALIGNAC DE MOTHE-FÉNELON (1651–1715), whose sympathy with Greek literature was equal to Racine's, but who preserved a courteous and dignified neutrality in the Quarrel, was the younger son of a noble family of Périgord. Thus, unlike the great majority of the writers of the reign of Louis XIV, he was a *grand seigneur* and a southerner. As a spiritual director, as tutor to the Duc de Bourgogne, as Archbishop of Cambrai, he did noble work, and his writings are little more than by-products of these activities. Three of these, however, have become classics. The best-known, *Télémaque*, written for the

Duc de Bourgogne, but not published till 1699, is a *pastiche* of Homer, Virgil, the Greek tragedians, and other ancient authors, but the skill with which the story is managed and a certain power of characterisation show that Fénelon had in him the makings of a novelist. His descriptions of scenery, and his accounts of battles and hand-to-hand fighting are conventional and unconvincing; the real interest of the book lies in the expression of his political views and particularly in his insistence on the duty of a monarch to promote the welfare of his people. It is in these political disquisitions that his fluent and graceful style becomes the natural expression of his warm heart and clear brain.

His *Traité de l'Éducation des Filles* (1687), timid though its programme of studies seems to-day, has a historic importance, for it marks the beginning of female education in France. Written with good sense and feeling it shows a real appreciation of woman's character as well as a belief in education generally.

But on the whole the *Lettre sur les occupations de l'Académie* (1714) has of all Fénelon's writings the greatest interest for the modern reader. It is the fruit, not of deep or long thought, but of an enlightened, cultivated, and independent mind, which judges for itself and not in accordance with any theories of criticism. The admiration for La Fontaine and Molière (in spite of the criticisms on the latter's style), the complaint that the rules of versification are too strict, the plea for a richer vocabulary—"On a appauvri, desséché, et gêné notre langue"—and for greater simplicity in French poetry, are some of the more interesting *obiter dicta*. But in all Fénelon's writings three-quarters of the interest is in the light they throw on his own complex, contradictory, and fascinating character. It is for that reason that possibly, as M. Lanson suggests, his real masterpiece is his vast correspondence. Certainly nowhere else, whether the letters are addressed to his family or to strangers, whether they are concerned with mundane or spiritual matters, do we get a better idea of the seductive charm of the man—no saint, but a great gentleman, a warm and sympathetic friend, an unrivalled spiritual director, and a true Christian.

In his posthumously published *Dialogues sur l'Éloquence* Fénelon criticises the pulpit oratory of his day with some severity. One of his criticisms, aimed specially at Bourdaloue, was that evangelical doctrine was made subordinate to moral pictures. The criticism applies less to Bourdaloue than to JEAN-BAPTISTE MASSILLON (1663–1743), a native of Provence, who was appointed Bishop of Clermont in 1717, and whom good judges regard as marking the decline of pulpit oratory. He might fairly have replied to Fénelon that at least under the Regency, when he preached his *Petit Carême*, the censorship of morals was the most pressing need. His inferiority to Bossuet and Bourdaloue lies rather in the fact, that he lacks their noble simplicity, that he has the rhetorician's tendency to exaggeration and artifice and the abuse of *esprit*. In his sensibility and his optimism, in his dislike of war and his belief in the natural goodness of man, he foreshadows the eighteenth century.

Comedy also declined. Only portions of Molière's mantle fell upon his successors. JEAN-FRANÇOIS REGNARD (1655–1709), a Parisian, inherited his gift for boisterous and exuberant gaiety, and *Le Légataire universel*, which some critics regard as his masterpiece, is a farcical version of *Le Malade imaginaire*. A higher type of comedy is represented by *Le Joueur*, which attempts seriously to portray manners and has two characters, both owing something to Molière, of some individuality. Regnard writes admirable verse, careless indeed, and incorrect, but easy, vivacious, and picturesque. FLORENT-CARTON DANCOURT (1661–1725), on the other hand, wrote the great majority of his forty-seven comedies in easy and familiar prose. He makes no attempt at a regular plot, and no pretence of a moral purpose. His world is one of fools and knaves, but with this limitation he gives us by means of well-chosen types and clever observation of fashions and manners an excellent picture of the *bourgeois* life of his day. As a rule he is at his best in one-act plays, but *Les Bourgeoises à la mode* (1692), in five acts, of which Vanbrugh's much-praised *The Confederacy* is an inferior imitation, is one of his more successful pieces. His rapid and indolent sketches prepared the way for a true comedy of manners in *Turcaret* (1709) which ALAIN-RENÉ LESAGE (1668–1747) developed out of a few scenes of *L'Avare* and *Le Bourgeois gentilhomme*. Directed against the financiers as a growing danger to French society, this realistic play, without moral purpose, in which the central figure of Turcaret is surrounded by other strongly-drawn types of a corrupt age, makes a disagreeable impression at the first reading; but a better acquaintance reveals to us the merits of its close texture and, in spite of the absence of plot, its firm construction. The style is easy and vigorous, but Lesage has made the mistake of endowing all his characters alike, even Turcaret, with *esprit*.

As has been said above, all these three writers of comedy were influenced by La Bruyère. His portrait of Ménalque becomes, with little alteration, the hero of Regnard's *Le Distrait*; Turcaret is a development of Sosie in *Des biens de la fortune*, while many passages in the same chapter may be illustrated by Dancourt's comedies.

LOUIS DE SAINT-SIMON (1675–1755), *duc et pair*, the head of an old but not illustrious family of Picardy, did not begin to write out his memoirs till 1740, but from 1694 he was busy observing, collecting materials, and making notes. At least two-thirds of his work, greatly surpassing the rest in interest, is concerned with the last twenty years of the reign of Louis XIV, and his record of the Court during that period is of unsurpassed interest. We do not go to him for historical accuracy, for though he is honest, he is careless, uncritical, and above all prejudiced. But his ardent curiosity left no source of information untapped, and he had an incomparable genius for breathing life into his pictures. Like Fénelon he was an unsparing critic of absolute government; like Massillon he was a stern censor of a corrupt society; like Regnard and Dancourt and Lesage, though with far greater completeness and with infinitely deeper strokes, he portrayed the *comédie humaine* of his age. His account of the Dauphin's death is one of the marvels of literature. His portraits, whether rapid sketches or elaborate full-length paintings, stand out with arresting intensity. His style is the expression of quivering nervous energy, generated either by the keenness of his visualising power or by the heat of his passion. In fact the stronger his passion, the better he writes. It is a mistake, however, to suppose that he is always malignant and vindictive. He can love as well as hate; he can paint in soft colours as well as in black; the portraits of Beauvillier and Chevreuse, of Boufflers and Cardinal Jansen, are no less masterpieces than those of

Harlay and Vendôme and Cardinal Dubois. He is grossly unfair to Mme de Maintenon; he is less than fair to Louis XIV, but he does full justice to the courage and dignity with which the aged King, like the dying lion in La Fontaine, faced "the slings and arrows of outrageous fortune." When the end came on September 1, 1715, a great page in French history and literature was finally closed.

§ III. EIGHTEENTH CENTURY

The awakening of the critical spirit

The death of Louis XIV closed a page in history and literature; but the next chapter was already in preparation. La Bruyère might say *tout est dit*, but even as he wrote the words new things were being said, and he himself showed that they could be said in a new way. The 18th century may claim to have opened in 1687 with the "Quarrel between the Ancients and the Moderns," which was no storm in a tea-cup, as is sometimes held, but the first stage in a great new epoch. The poem which evoked it was as trivial as the occasion of the poem—the King's recovery from an operation for fistula—but Charles Perrault and his allies were the heralds of an era of capital importance, marked by all the qualities and defects of vigorous youth attacking a traditional fortress—hope and daring, impatience of authority, and boundless self-confidence.

Perrault was himself unconscious of the magnitude of the issue. He had a grand theme, if he had only known how to handle it. Boileau felt its importance, but rage blinded him. He was doubtless in a dilemma. To bless the Moderns was to betray his principles; to decry them was to stultify himself. He did not well know what to defend and what to attack. He knew *whom* to attack, and he did so blithely. But his replies to Perrault (except the last), whether in private conversation, flashing epigram, or set piece, are mere vituperation. In the end he was beaten, and he as good as allowed it. His *Letter to Perrault* (1700) surrenders nine-tenths of what he had fought for. The Moderns won all along the line, and their victory was more than personal. It gave to Frenchmen of the day a sense of their own dignity and of their right to criticise.

The new right, won in a battle of books, was openly applied

in the first instance to literature. The classical ideal was challenged. But criticism had already, though less noisily, been exercised in matters of religion by Fontenelle and Bayle.

BERNARD LE BOUYER, SIEUR DE FONTENELLE (1657–1757) belongs by every title to the 18th century—by his inquisitive spirit, his wit, his want of aesthetic sensibility. PIERRE BAYLE (1647–1706), on the other hand, is of the 16th century by his learning, of the early 17th by his style, of the 20th by his cast of mind. These two men, utterly different in character, circumstances, and ambition, between them sowed the dragon's teeth of "philosophy" so-called, and the good seed of religious toleration. They are the forerunners of Voltaire and the Encyclopaedists.

Fontenelle was born a man of letters. He began as a journalist in Paris under his uncle, Thomas Corneille, editor of the *Mercure Galant*; the example of his more famous uncle, Pierre, tempted him to try the stage, where he failed again and again. His dozen tragedies brought him the only disappointment of his hundred years of life. We may guess that chagrin and family jealousy of Racine, the great classicist, combined with his Cartesian trust in human perfectibility to draw him into the "Quarrel" on the side of the Moderns. His Norman caution, and the deliberate avoidance of all strong emotion, to which he largely owed his longevity, prevented him from pushing into the front rank of combatants, but the *Digression sur les anciens et les modernes*, appended to his insipid *Poésies pastorales* (1688), repeats a note already sounded in his brilliant *Dialogues des morts* (1683) and emphasises his total want of sympathy with the classical spirit. Aeschylus is a madman, Homer a modern cynic, Theocritus is too realistic, Virgil too ideal, etc. His own shepherds and shepherdesses are china figures. His criticism was no better than his poetry, and the *Réflexions sur la poétique* (1742) are only noteworthy for their definition, entirely characteristic of the age, which he gives of *esprit*. It is "la raison éclairée qui examine les objets, les compare, et fait des choix à son gré." But though no artist, he is a delightful writer, with an individual style and plenty of the *esprit* which he so greatly praised. A thorough sceptic, his thought is an acid whose solvent action he disguised under a pleasant irony. His manner is best seen in his capital work *L'Histoire des oracles*, of which the origin was as follows.

In 1683 a learned Dutchman published a stout Latin treatise, *De oraculis veterum ethnicorum*. The problem to be solved was twofold. (1) Were the oracles the work of demons? (2) Did they cease with the Advent of Christ? Van Dale solved both negatively, to his own satisfaction, but with no kind of grace. The theme attracted Fontenelle and he began a translation into French. He found the original too heavy, so he transformed it with infinite skill, and in so doing delivered a deliberate attack upon Christianity, which was far from the Dutch scholar's intention. Proving that the oracles were mere trickery, he hints that the early Christians were gullible fools; arguing that they did not cease in the presence of Christ, he seeks to depreciate the victory claimed for Him. Reason, which discredits heathen oracles, will presently overthrow many other superstitions. Fontenelle consistently protested that he had no ulterior motives, and he declined to enter into controversy.

Important as he is as a liberator of thought, Fontenelle's real claim to be remembered is as a populariser of science. He loved science for itself; he loved the Moderns because they cultivated it; he determined to bring it within the reach of the *beau monde*. His *Entretiens sur la pluralité des mondes* (1686) was written to teach a *marquise* the elements of astronomy. He set himself to educate the *salons* which he haunted for more than half a century, and he succeeded. Science became a fashionable game. Great ladies frequented laboratories and passed *pièces sèches* about in their drawing-rooms. But Fontenelle made his own contribution to the sum of knowledge. He proclaimed the stability of natural laws and the solidarity of the sciences, and as secretary of the *Académie des Sciences* from 1697 to 1739 he chronicled the achievements of that body and of its principal ornaments. His *Éloges des académiciens* are his best work.

Pierre Bayle was a man of different mould and belonged to another world. He was a recluse and a student, innocent of science, though a real searcher after truth. The quest brought him not certitude, but doubt, which he was nothing loth to spread. "Mon talent est de former des doutes; mais ce ne sont que des doutes." He knew too much to take a side, except against dogmatism and intolerance of any kind. Of these he was the sworn foe, and he had reason for his hostility. He was the son of a Protestant pastor in the county of Foix who died before the great persecution of 1685. But his brother fell a victim to it, and Pierre, a *relaps* (he had turned Roman Catholic for 17 months at the age of 17) and an exile in Holland, vented .his indignation in scathing pamphlets— *La France toute catholique sous Louis le Grand* (1685), the *Commentaire philosophique sur le "compelle intrare"* (1686), the *Avis aux réfugiés* (1690), this last being of uncertain authorship, but bearing undoubted traces of Bayle's hand. He found his co-religionaries as intolerant in their way as the King and the Church of France. It is immensely to his credit that the Rotterdam councillors, who deprived him on a charge of impiety of the chair of philosophy which they had founded in his behalf, should have drawn from him no explosion of resentment. "J'ai été heureusement délivré de plusieurs occupations qui ne m'étaient guère agréables," was his only public comment on the shameful treatment he suffered. But if his temper in this trial was Christian, this cannot be said of his writing whether controversial or erudite. The fact is that he took a humorous pleasure in shocking people, and his pages abound in irreverence and sheer indecency. But in spite of his mischievous flings and the unwearying war which he waged upon dogmatism and error, Catholic or Protestant, his moral life was blameless and his religious sentiment real. He remained in communion with his sect—he attended church and died, in his own phrase, as a Christian philosopher. It is a grave mistake to reckon him as a positivist or an anti-clerical before the time. He was from first to last a Protestant against bigotry and tyranny.

Fontenelle's main interest was scientific, and his object to convey instruction. Bayle is above all things a critic, bent on correcting opinion which his erudition told him was generally false. Thus his *Pensées diverses sur les comètes*, written ostensibly to remove the superstition which regarded Halley's comet of 1680 as a harbinger of evil, deals with a host of erroneous notions in history, ethics, theology, and politics. It has certain points of resemblance with Fontenelle's *Histoire des Oracles*, but it is far less subtle both in motive and manner.

His double appetite for knowledge and criticism found full gratification in two great literary undertakings, the *Nouvelles*

de la république des lettres and the *Dictionnaire critique et
historique*. The former was a monthly review conducted single-
handed by Bayle for three years (1684–7), which did for
Letters what the *Journal des Savants* was already doing for
Science. It brought all Europe to his feet. Theologians, historians, antiquaries, even poets, sought the approval of the
hermit of Rotterdam. It was the first, and by no means the
worst, of popular literary magazines.

The *Dictionnaire* was originally projected as a supplement to
the *Dictionnaire historique* of Louis Moréri (1674). The addition
of the word *critique* announces Bayle's purpose, viz. to correct
Moréri's many errors. But in Bayle's hands it quickly grew to
an original work, an independent monument of learning, and
became the vessel into which he skimmed his note-books. The
process began in 1694 (the first edition appeared in 1696) and
lasted until 1704. It cost him his chair on account of the
irreverence of his remarks, especially in the article on David;
but it solidly confirmed his reputation as *arbiter rerum scibilium*.
The Dictionary had effects deep and wide. Banned in France
and Holland, it spread light and learning in both. It was
translated into almost all the languages of Europe and it was
the arsenal from which the rationalists drew their weapons.

Fontenelle and Bayle, though they have points of contact,
are really worlds apart. Fontenelle is first and foremost a
littérateur. Bayle has no claim to that title. He paid attention to
style and he managed to make himself clear; but he has no sort
of art and his writings are a *causerie*. What gave him his power
was his vast accumulation of curious and exact knowledge, and
the remorselessness with which he made men face facts. He is
a sceptic of the school of Pascal, recognising the incompetence
of human Reason, but, unlike Pascal, refusing to take the leap
of Faith.

But it was not only literary ideals or articles of religion that
were being questioned at the close of Louis's reign. It was the
whole system of his government, which was rapidly bringing
ruin upon France. The first to see this and to protest was
the Norman economist, Pierre le Pesant, Sieur de Boisguilbert.
He diagnosed the disease and suggested the remedy in
two books, *Le détail de la France* (1695) and *Factum de la*

France (1705). He had neither the literary skill nor the force of character needed to win a hearing for his proposals, and it was only when he stood forth to champion Vauban for views closely like his own that he attracted attention and disapproval. His book was condemned and its author banished.

The signal services rendered by Sébastien le Prestre, Seigneur de Vauban (1633–1707) which won him a marshal's staff in 1703, did not save him from disgrace when, stirred like Boisguilbert by the wretched state of the country, he followed his lead and wrote his *Dîme royale*. This was twice submitted to the King in manuscript, but not published until 1707, to be at once censured and suppressed. Vauban's noble heart was broken by his failure and he died within a few days of the condemnation. Louis calmly remarked "I have lost a man greatly devoted to myself and to the state," and it was true. Saint-Simon describes him as "the most honest and most virtuous man of his age." He was a great patriot, and one of the very few who saw the moral and material disaster which the Revocation of the Edict of Nantes would cause.

But neither he nor Boisguilbert had ventured on open rebuke of the infatuated monarch. That was reserved for a churchman and a courtier, Fénelon, who in 1694 wrote, though he did not sign, a letter to the King in which he told him some home-truths. It is improbable that Louis saw it at the time, for next year he advanced Fénelon to the see of Cambrai, whence in 1699 there issued *Télémaque*. The avowed object of the romance was to hold up before the King's grandson and heir presumptive the ideal of the perfect monarch who exists for the sake of his subjects. Louis, though he could feel the satire, could not apply the lesson.

The writing on the wall, which Louis and his courtiers had no eyes to see, was plain to the rest of the world, and a sympathetic public was already formed when Montesquieu came forward as social reformer, first with his *Lettres persanes*, and then with his *Esprit des Lois*. This appears from the mildness with which the ABBÉ DE SAINT-PIERRE (1658–1743) was treated when he published his *Discours sur la polysynodie* (1718), condemning in unmeasured terms the despotic government of the late King. He was excluded from the *Académie* but the. Regent and his ministers let him be. "Ce sont," they said, "les rêves d'un homme de bien." The *Club de l'Entresol*, an anglophil society where he aired his views, was not closed till 1731, when its liberal tendencies became too alarming.

CHARLES DE SECONDAT, BARON DE LA BRÈDE ET DE MONTESQUIEU (1689–1755) was, like Montaigne, a Gascon and a magistrate, but there is little of southern exuberance in his style, and he hated the procedure of the law, though he loved its philosophy. True to the spirit of his age, he dabbled at first in science, but his real vocation lay elsewhere. In 1721 he awoke and found himself famous through his *Lettres persanes*, an oriental romance of feeble interest into which are woven pungent satire on contemporary follies, and serious thoughts, ironically expressed. Montesquieu fanned his sudden popularity by certain elegant *jeux d'esprit*, but his taste was for observation, and to gratify it he travelled far and wide—to Austria, Italy, and England. He came to our shores with a prejudice against us; he left them our sincere admirer, conquered by the order and freedom of our institutions.

When he returned to France in 1731, he sat down at his country seat, La Brède, and wrote *Considérations sur les causes de la grandeur des Romains et de leur décadence* (1733), a brief but penetrating study of the greatest political phenomenon the world has seen. The little book announces a new philosophy of history, which he was to develop magnificently. In mundane events, where Bossuet had seen the hand of Providence alone, Montesquieu watches the play of secondary causes. *L'Esprit des Lois*, to which the *Considérations* was the prelude, appeared in 1748 under the proud device, *Prolem sine matre creatam*; and it is a fact that all his friends counselled him to withhold it.

The work consists of six parts and three books: (1) laws in general and different forms of government, (2) military affairs and taxation, (3) climatic influences, (4) economics, (5) religion, (6) Roman, French, and feudal laws. A certain order of ideas is observed, but the thread is apt to disappear under the multitude of the subdivisions.

The mincing up of the matter—some chapters consist of a single sentence—the brilliant language, the lavish wit, the wealth of illustration, disclose the writer's anxiety to please and amuse an audience not averse to large ideas, provided they were tersely put, but *blasé* and easily bored. He succeeded so well that everyone applauded the saying of Mme Du Deffand, "Ce ne sont pas l'esprit des lois, mais de l'esprit sur les lois." Voltaire's judgment is sounder, "Le genre humain avait perdu ses titres; Montesquieu les a retrouvés et les lui a rendus." The book abounds in general notions and is ostensibly a work of theory, but Montesquieu's own character and personal preferences are not disguised. He abhorred despotism and intolerance. What he desired for France was a monarchy limited by privileged bodies—nobility, *parlement*, clergy—and he desired it not for the sake of his class but for his country's sake and the welfare of the race. It was no self-seeker who could write, "Si je savais quelque chose qui fût utile à ma famille et qui ne le fût pas à ma patrie, je chercherais à l'oublier." It was no ordinary patriot who could add, "Si je savais quelque chose utile à ma patrie et qui fût préjudiciable à l'Europe et au genre humain, je le regarderais comme un crime."

L'Esprit des Lois is a work of the most fertile and original power. The Declaration of the Rights of Man is there in germ. And although time has found flaws in his learning and in his theories, Montesquieu remains one of the greatest if not the first of the social philosophers (see below, ch. XIII).

The Philosophers

In style and spirit *L'Esprit des Lois* is entirely of the 18th century. The year before its publication there died a young writer in whom the moralists of the 17th century live again. This was LUC DE CLAPIERS, MARQUIS DE VAUVENARGUES (1715–1747). His life was tragic. He longed for glorious action; he was doomed to poverty and obscurity. Beginning as a soldier, ill-health compelled him to resign his commission and to renounce the career of diplomacy. He turned to letters, and died in misery within twelve months of the anonymous appearance of his solitary book, *Introduction à la connaissance de l'esprit humain*, with which are bound up *Réflexions* and *Maximes*.

The portraits and maxims which it contains depict the man and fix his position. Outwardly he is an imitator of La Bruyère and La Rochefoucauld, but he has a message and a manner of his own. He too watches the men of his time, and, though he lacks La Bruyère's gift of realism, he paints in one portrait at least closer to the life. For *Clazomène, ou la vertu malheureuse* is a picture of himself; "né pour les plus grands déplaisirs, il a eu de la hauteur et de l'ambition dans la pauvreté." His ambition and his hope were to reconcile in a synthesis the contradictions of previous moralists. All he could accomplish was the *Introduction*, but the titles of its divisions indicate his purpose, *De l'esprit en général, Des passions, Du bien et du mal moral*. It is a study of man, to which the maxims and characters which follow serve as illustration. Pascal and La Rochefoucauld had both studied man, but Vauvenargues goes the whole way with neither. He shrinks alike from the former's ruthless judgment of human effort and merit, and from the latter's cruel analysis of human motive. He holds man capable of good, and asks with equal wit and generosity; why "alors que le corps a ses grâces et l'esprit ses talents, le cœur n'aurait, lui, que des vices"? Of the two writers, the Christian attracts him more than the cynic; he was even tempted to the impossible task of a verbal imitation of Pascal. Like him he rates Intuition above Reason. But whereas Pascal uses it as a means of finding God, Vauvenargues applies it as a guide to action. Longer experience would doubtless have pointed out to him the danger to morality thereby involved. As it is, he remains a Stoic of the early 17th century, outside, but not far from, the Christian fold. The brightest spot in Vauvenargues's story is his friendship with Voltaire. They came together in an academic discussion on the respective merits of Corneille and Racine, and their correspondence settled the place which Racine has since held in French opinion.

FRANÇOIS-MARIE AROUET, "VOLTAIRE" (1694–1778), a sickly and precocious child, was the son of a Paris notary. He went to school at the Jesuit College of Louis le Grand, and he never lost a friendly feeling towards his masters, although he came to be the arch-foe of all they stood for. They taught him Latin and developed his dramatic sense. He was, so to speak, sealed for his future vocation, the pursuit of ease and pleasure, by the aged but by no means venerable Ninon de Lenclos, to whom he was presented by his godfather, her lover, at the age of eleven. She gave him literary advice and left him 2000 francs to buy books with. From Ninon's boudoir to the Temple was but one step, and it was to save him from the tastes which he formed in such undesirable circles that his father packed him off to the Hague as page to the French ambassador there. When after three months he was sent back in disgrace, M. Arouet tried to chain him to an office stool. But the youth had other ambitions. He rhymed and he wrote. He challenged Sophocles and Corneille with an *Œdipe*; he planned a great French epic which presently appeared under the title first of *La Ligue* (1727) and later of *La Henriade* (1728); he launched into the whirlpool of dissipation and fashion; he concealed his *bourgeois* name under the anagram which he rendered immortal—Voltaire = Arouet l(e) j(eune); he found his way to court; he saw the inside of the Bastille for a lampoon upon the Regent; he laid the foundations of a great fortune by happy speculation. But the course of the *parvenu* seldom runs smooth, and Voltaire had, together with great social success, his painful passages. He was twice publicly chastised, and, when he would challenge his noble assailant, he was rewarded for his insolence with a second dose of the Bastille, and, on leaving it, with a notice to quit France for England. Here he remained three years (1726–9), and here he fixed the character which he had been forming during thirty feverish years. What he brought back with him from London was the memory of the great men he had met, a vision of a new kind of drama, and, above all, a vast enthusiasm for English science, English toleration, English freedom, together with the will and the material to attack the thought and life of his own land at all its points of difference.

The attack, which was to last his lifetime, opened with the *Lettres philosophiques* or *Lettres sur les Anglais*, first published in a pirated English translation in 1733. Seven of them deal with English religion in its manifold forms, three with politics. Seven are devoted to Bacon, Locke, and Newton, seven to literature and its rewards in our happy island. Praising England, even while he praised with a gibe, he brought a railing accusation against France, and threw into consternation, and into coalition against him, court and *parlement* and Church. The book was condemned to be burnt and ran through ten editions in five years.

Paris became too hot for Voltaire and he spent the next sixteen years (1733–49) at Cirey, on the Lorraine border, with the Marquis and Marquise de Châtelet—a *ménage à trois*. She was a remarkable woman, linguist, physicist, mathematician, metaphysician. Voltaire, sharing her studies with passion, worked also at the subjects for which he was best fitted, poetry, drama, *contes*, and history—he had already produced his *Histoire de Charles XII* (1733) and had embarked upon his *Siècle de Louis XIV*. It was his most fruitful period of strictly literary production.

On the death of his mistress, who had recovered for him a footing at Versailles, Voltaire returned to the capital. But favour at court was precarious, and he was glad to accept in 1750 the invitation of Frederick the Great to go to Potsdam as his friend and literary adviser. The position, which dazzled him at first, soon became intolerable, and in 1753 he resigned his "bells and bauble." Despite his disappointments, his time in Prussia was not wasted. He saw the world; he learnt through servitude the value of freedom; he was master of his weapons, and now at the age of sixty he was ready to reap the full harvest of his wide and varied experience.

He settled at Geneva, first in a house he christened *Les Délices*, just outside the town, and then, when the Calvinists hampered his passion for staging plays, at Ferney, half an hour distant, on French soil. Here he lived his last eighteen years, a country gentleman, keeping open house, an ardent social reformer and champion of the down-trodden, the untiring enemy of tyranny and bigotry, waging a fierce and cunning campaign, openly or by anonymous pamphlets, against what he called the accursed thing, *L'Infâme*—superstition in all its forms, Jewish, Christian, heathen. At Ferney he was the cynosure of intellectual Europe, and he assiduously cultivated attention not only by public performance but by private correspondence. His letters, of which nearly 10,000 have come down to us, and of which he threw off thirty in one day, are his most enduring monument.

When at the age of 82, in February 1778, he paid a long-deferred visit to Paris, he was literally killed by kindness. He and his effigy were crowned with laurel in the *Théâtre français* during a performance of his twenty-seventh tragedy, *Irène*. Twc

months later, as he lay dying in the rue de Beaune, he signed
a confession of orthodox faith, and immediately withdrew it.
His real religious opinions are contained in a paper he wrote
a few weeks before, on the first threatenings of the end; " Je
meurs en adorant Dieu, en aimant mes amis, en ne haïssant pas
mes ennemis, et en détestant la persécution." The utterance was
no doubt sincere, but his life belied it. He was a convinced
theist, though a violent anti-Christian; but the God he worshipped
was but a kind of *gendarme* whose presence in the world was
needed to keep order. He was a good friend when it suited him.
But if his treatment of his opponents (Rousseau for example)
was not inspired by hate, it was by a contempt not less bitter
and implacable.

He had wished to be buried at Ferney. They took the body
to Scellières in Champagne, whence it was removed and laid
triumphantly in the Panthéon in the full flood of the great
Revolution which he had unwittingly done so much to prepare,
and which in most of its features he would have loathed.

Voltaire is the most universal figure that France has produced.
His eighty-two years of life were all too short for his astonishing
activity. *Nullum fere scribendi genus non tetigit.* And little of
it survives to-day, except one or two *contes* (*Zadig, Candide*),
the *Siècle de Louis XIV*, and his matchless correspondence.
Yet his effect has been prodigious, both on letters and on life.
The former will be seen in our account of the *genres*. Some
notion of the latter, which it is impossible to define precisely,
may be gathered from the bibliography of his works. M. Lanson
has pointed out that the curve of their sale corresponds
closely to that of the spread of liberal ideas, and that there
has been a special demand for them at all times when those
ideas are in peril. Thus the seven years of the Bourbon Restoration, from 1817 to 1824, saw an output of twelve complete
editions, numbering 1,598,000 copies. It is difficult to say
whether he led or followed popular opinion. He gave a marked
impulse to the study of science, but it was already in the air.
He finally dethroned Descartes in favour of Locke and Newton,
but Descartes's supremacy was already threatened. He developed the *esprit critique*, but Bayle had already aroused it.
He was in fact an incomparable journalist, grinding grist for the

masses. No cause could have had a better or a more effective exponent. He knew how to state in simplest terms a complicated problem, and how to cover the other side with ridicule. His style has been, and is, the model of all who value the essential qualities of French prose, grace, clearness, wit, irony. He did not invent the short, alert phrase. That was already so familiar to readers of Montesquieu and La Bruyère that they had almost forgotten the sonorous periods of Bossuet. But he used it with unerring skill. What he lacks is warmth and imagination, and when the Romantic movement added these elements, the perfect instrument was ready for the hand of a Flaubert or an Anatole France.

The Encyclopédie

The great movement of emancipation and criticism of which Voltaire was a central figure had also its group of adherents—les philosophes—and its organ—l'Encyclopédie. This was a dictionary of arts, sciences, and crafts, suggested by the English Cyclopedia of Ephraim Chambers, and edited by JEAN LE ROND D'ALEMBERT (1717–83), mathematician and man of science, and DENIS DIDEROT (1713–84), man of letters. Diderot drew up the prospectus (afterwards incorporated in a Discours préliminaire by D'Alembert) in 1750, and the undertaking was floated in 1751. It took twenty years of stormy voyage to reach port. In 1752 it was very nearly suppressed because one of the collaborators, the Abbé de Prades, had also written an unorthodox thesis for his doctor's degree. In 1757 an article on Geneva unchained the whirlwind. D'Alembert, prompted by Voltaire, praised the Genevan clergy for their liberal, not to say Socinian, theology, and their moral excellence, but reproached them for the narrow mind with which they regarded the theatre. This pleased nobody. The pastors refused the imputation of Socinianism, the Jesuits denied their moral excellence, Rousseau fulminated against the supporters of the stage in his Lettre sur les spectacles. D'Alembert resigned his post as editor and left Diderot to face the storm. At that moment there came out a frankly materialistic book, Helvétius's L'Esprit. Its author was known to be an ally of Diderot and both were involved in the same condemnation. The Encyclopédie was suspended in mid-

career. ·But Diderot, single-handed as he was, refused to give in.
He had the support of Malesherbes the press censor and of
Mme de Pompadour, and he managed to complete the publication. Ten volumes appeared *en bloc* in 1766 and the plates
followed in 1772. The *Encyclopédie* was a financial success, but
Diderot got no more than £1500 for a work to which he gave
twenty years of life and the best of his powers. He had come
to Paris from Langres as a boy and lived a difficult and obscure
life until 1749, when a scandalous book brought him notoriety,
and imprisonment in Vincennes. Then came his editorship of
the *Encyclopédie*. Such time and energy as this left him were
given to journalism, in which he excelled—he taught himself
art criticism and his *Salons* are justly admired—and to dramatic
theory and practice. He had many friends, but his best patron
was Catherine of Russia, who bought his books at a crisis, had
him to visit her in St Petersburg, and paid for the apartment
in Paris where he died.

His value as philosopher (ch. XIII), literary artist, and dramatist is indicated under other headings. Victor Hugo calls him
l'aigle de vol inégal and the description is exact. His reputation
has increased since his death, for the very good reason that his
best works were published posthumously. He was from first
to last an *homme du peuple*—not a great character, but a
splendid worker.

Diderot's chief helpers in the *Encyclopédie*, besides D'Alembert,
were the Chevalier de Jaucourt, man of science and mathematician, who spent three years at Cambridge; Marmontel for
literature; Daubenton for natural history; D'Holbach for
chemistry; the Abbé Morellet for theology; Quesnay, the good
physician, and Turgot, for economics. Behind these stood a
notable group of philosophers, encouraging, but not directly
co-operating—Condorcet, Condillac, Helvétius (for whom see
ch. XIII), not to mention Voltaire, who contributed a few
articles.

Between them they constructed a mighty engine for the
overthrow of the existing order in thought and government.
But their aims were not merely destructive. They fought for
liberty in the State and mercy in the courts, collecting, concentrating, and communicating the ideas which had been in

process of formation for the last half century. The *Encyclopédie* is not a work of art—it is often loosely written, and its literary judgments are puerile—but a political and social manifesto of far-reaching effect.

Among the *philosophes* may be reckoned JEAN-LOUIS LECLERC, COMTE DE BUFFON (1707-1788), in virtue of the part he assigned to natural forces in the economy of the universe. But in most respects he stands apart from them and indeed from his age. He was involved in none of its controversies. He respected much that the *encyclopédistes* derided, and he was not loved by them. But he was too big a man to care, and he passed a serene and laborious life in two gardens, his own at Montbard in Burgundy and the Jardin du Roi in Paris which he directed from 1739 till his death, never raising his purblind eyes from his task of observation, or laying down his pen. Detached as he was, he shared the prevalent enthusiasm for England, "ce peuple si sensé, si profondément pensant." Milton, Richardson, and Newton were his favourite authors, and a portrait of the latter faced him in his study when he began his day's work at 6 a.m. The rich fruit of his labours, the *Histoire naturelle*, appeared in thirty-six volumes between 1749 and 1789. Down to 1767 he conducted it single-handed. Afterwards he had a tribe of assistants. He retained in his own hands the sections on man and on minerals, which admit of the broad treatment in which he excelled. His method became more scientific as the work advanced. Abstractions, classifications, and the appeal to final causes were always abhorrent to him, "La nature...ne comprend que des individus." So he set man in the centre of his canvas, grouping round him the domestic animals which minister to his welfare. This kind of composition is artistic rather than scientific, but Buffon was always ready to learn and to correct. Thus in 1778 he explains the formation of the earth by the action of fire, whereas in 1748 he had ascribed it to water. The progress of his own thought was the reflexion of his Cartesian belief in human perfectibility, which he hoped to see achieved by gradual movement, not by the revolutionary methods advocated by Diderot and Rousseau. His original contributions to knowledge are not small. He was the first to assert that the present state of the earth is the result of a long series of changes which can be visibly traced, and to appreciate the effect of climate on the distribution of species. He saw the narrow line that separates animals from vegetables. On the other hand no one ever had a loftier idea of man's greatness. He is the King of Creation; the beasts are for his use and pleasure; nature is fairest when his hand has cultivated it. Man was created last (Buffon admits the six days of creation, regarding them as epochs), because the earth was not fit for him before.

But his real genius lay in his picturesque presentation of scientific matter. He has not Fontenelle or Voltaire's light hand, but he has a strong sense of the value of style. He urged it on his helpers, and he proclaimed it in the famous *Discours de réception à l'Académie* (1753). This is not a treatise, but merely "some notes on style," especially on the way in which natural history should be written. In this matter he was opposed to current tendencies. He does not seek to please a jaded palate by flashes of wit or by short, telling phrases. He is eloquent in the manner of the 17th century, of Bossuet. But he never loses the essentially French gifts of logic, clarity, and taste. In his *Discours* he shows how these gifts can best be exercised. Every writer, he says, must have a plan. But to have a plan is not enough. You must write well. In order to write well you must be master of your theme. You must also feel it, feel the pleasure born of matured thought, from the act of creation. Hence will arise warmth—an intellectual glow, not a mere emotion. This must not be quenched by strivings after brilliancy. Flashes blind and do not burn steadily. You must moreover be natural —here again speaks the 17th century. Avoid pomposity—he himself did not altogether escape the snare. Then comes the famous, often misquoted phrase, "Le style est de l'homme même." No writer can claim a monopoly of his subject. The discoveries of science are common property. But the way in which he treats it, his style, is his own inalienable possession. Only by it can he win immortality. "Les ouvrages bien écrits seront les seuls qui passeront à la postérité." Buffon faithfully practised his own precepts. He mastered his subject; he felt its greatness, and, musing upon it, the fire kindled and his imagination found expression in terms not unworthy of it. He is profoundly reverent. There is no room in his system for special miracles, but to him God's creation was a perpetual miracle. Yet he cannot be claimed as a Christian writer, for the Christian doctrine of sin and redemption lies outside his scope.

It may be said of him as of Montesquieu, that he added a new kingdom to literature.

If Buffon stood aloof from the Encyclopaedists, JEAN-JACQUES ROUSSEAU (1712–78) came into sharp conflict with them and that not only because his philosophy was so different (see ch. XIII) from theirs, but because he quarrelled with every one in turn. He was always unbalanced, and in the end he went mad. But no one man has had a greater influence in literature, or on society by means of literature. This is the more remarkable because he was in many ways opposed to tendencies of his time and lacking in the gifts that make for popularity. He hated tradition and authority with the best; he was an optimist, but while his contemporaries hoped for the improvement of man through civilisation and the spread of knowledge, Rousseau depreciated knowledge and held civilisation to be the main cause of man's corruption from primitive goodness. He had not a spark of *esprit*, which he regarded as a peculiarly French vice.

What then gave him his power? First, an extraordinary sensibility and an imagination which enabled him, the most individual and self-centred of men, to feel acutely with others. Secondly an irresistible eloquence which expressed, as had not been done for centuries, the needs and yearnings of the people. It was the voice of democracy, which swelled to thunder at the Revolution and whose echoes have never died away.

Add to this gift of imaginative sensibility a strong feeling for the concrete and an appreciation of phenomenal nature, and you have the essential elements of Romanticism, of which Rousseau was the forerunner, or, as he has been wittily called, "the grandfather."

His character is largely explained by his life, and neither is particularly beautiful. He was the son of a Geneva watchmaker and was brought up on Plutarch and 17th century romances. He ran away at the age of sixteen and was taken up by a Mme de Warens, who tried to convert him to Catholicism and succeeded in attaching him to herself as a lover. After many more or less shady adventures he came to Paris in 1741 with fifteen *louis*, a comedy in manuscript, and a new system of musical notation. Through the good offices of Mme Dupin (the grandmother of George Sand) he became secretary to the French ambassador at Venice. Quarrelling with him, he was back in Paris in 1745, as poor as he had left it. He formed a liaison with a working girl, Thérèse Lavasseur, whom he married long afterwards, and who bore him five children. Rousseau sent them all to the Foundling Hospital as soon as they were born.

He was in misery, but he made friends—all of whom he ended by renouncing. One of them, Diderot, then in prison, encouraged him to compete for a prize offered by the Academy of Dijon for an essay on the moral effects of science and the arts. Rousseau won it with his *Premier discours* (1750). A *Second discours* (1755), which missed the prize, pursues the theme of the first, viz. that man's age of innocence was his happiest and best, and that civilisation has been his ruin. Rousseau sent a copy to Voltaire, who put it aside with a jest, and sowed the seed of a life-long quarrel. The two men were indeed in natural antipathy. Voltaire, frivolous, irreverent, artificial, aristocratic, was the embodiment of that culture which Rousseau detested. The open feud began when Voltaire used the Lisbon earthquake as an excuse for attacking the ways of Providence. Rousseau defended them with spirit, throwing all the blame on civilisation, which crowded men together in lofty houses, and twitting Voltaire with complaining of human misery while he was himself lapped in luxury.

Matters came to a head over the article in the *Encyclopédie* on Geneva. Rousseau touched Voltaire in a weak spot, his passion for the stage. Voltaire sneeringly asked whether Jean-Jacques had turned *père de l'Église*, and from that time never lost a chance of inflicting a blow or a scratch.

All this while Rousseau was living at the charges, first of Mme D'Épinay, then of the Duc de Luxembourg at Montmorency. Thence in two years—1761, 1762—he published three capital works which contain the sum of his philosophy, *La Nouvelle Héloïse*, the *Contrat Social*, and *Émile* (see ch. XIII). The last was condemned as irreligious by the Paris *Parlement* and its author sentenced to arrest, but suffered to escape. He fled to Switzerland, but the ill-fame of the book accompanied him. To the Protestant *Lettre de la campagne*, justifying the burning of *Émile* at Geneva, Rousseau replied by *Lettres de la montagne*, in which he criticises severely the constitution of the little republic and the Reformation from which it was derived, and sets his face against Calvinist and Catholic alike. He was hounded out of his native land, and sought refuge with David Hume in England. But the terror and agitation of the last years had told upon him. He grew morbidly suspicious of everyone—sure sign of mania—"Hume, like Grimm, Diderot, D'Alembert and the rest, was conspiring against him." He fled again, wandered for three restless years, and then from 1770 to 1778 he found comparative peace in Paris, copying music, botanising in the outskirts, writing his *Confessions*, which he had begun in England, the *Dialogues* which are the wildest, and the *Rêveries d'un promeneur solitaire*, which are the most beautiful, of his works. He died at Ermenonville, near Senlis, in a cottage lent him by the Marquis de Girardin.

If he was writing down to the last, it was not that this was an easy task to him. Not a page of his manuscript but was recopied four or five times. But the effort was worth making. His style presents a marked contrast to the hard glitter of ordinary 18th century prose. It is alive and warm, not with the *chaleur* recommended by Buffon, but with the glow of emotion. It is infinitely varied and changes with his theme—logical in the *Discours* and the *Contrat*, rhetorical in *Julie*, musical in the *Rêveries*, and all combined in the *Confessions*. The worst of it is that these are not, like Montaigne's autobiography, *de bonne foi*, and they leave an impression of radical insincerity, or at least of the writer's radical incapacity to distinguish truth from falsehood.

Feminine influence: the Salons

When Jean-Jacques failed to conquer the musicians and the men of science with his scheme of notation, a friend said to him, "changez de corde et voyez les femmes." The advice was good and might have been given to anyone at any time during the century, for throughout the influence of women was great and growing. In literature their power was felt, not only directly, in letters, such as those of Mme de Maintenon—an impeccable writer—and of Mme Du Deffand, in memoirs such as those of Mlle Delaunay (whose knowledge of science is a sign of the times) and of Mme D'Épinay, or in the reflective pages of Mme de Lambert; but also indirectly and most potently through the sharpening of minds in the conversation of the *salons*.

There were in particular seven famous ladies who held *bureaux d'esprit* or *salons philosophiques*, each with a character of its own. First the DUCHESSE DU MAINE, tiny in body but great in rank and of keen intelligence, granddaughter of Condé, wife of a legitimised Prince. Wearying of Versailles, she formed at Sceaux soon after 1700 a court of her own, which lasted, with the interval of her imprisonment for the conspiracy of Cellamare, until her death in 1753. Here she entertained the wit and fashion of the day with a perpetual round of fêtes. It was here that Voltaire wrote *Zadig*, that Mlle Delaunay, her companion and servant, found her talent for portraiture and description, that Lekain the actor made his *début*.

But the true *salon* was inaugurated by MME DE LAMBERT, who from 1710 to 1733 threw open her house in the rue de Richelieu, where the *Bibliothèque nationale* now stands, to men of letters and men of the world. The former were chiefly bidden on Tuesdays, the latter on Wednesdays; but she encouraged her guests to meet on both days. Both in purpose (the refinement of society) and style, Mme de Lambert's assemblies recalled the Hôtel de Rambouillet, but they were more serious—here was no practical joking—and definitely literary. She herself was an accomplished writer, though shrinking from publicity and the title of blue stocking, and her *Avis d'une mère à son fils* (1726), *à sa fille* (1728) and her *Réflexions nouvelles sur les femmes* (1727) are of interest both as echoing the past and as heralding the future. Thus she defines religion very much as Rousseau defines it a generation later.

MME DE TENCIN, whose *salon* ran from 1726 to 1729, took over the guests of Mme de Lambert, and added to them birds of passage (e.g. Bolingbroke and Chesterfield) and specimens of the *bourgeoisie* and of the world of finance. The *salon* becomes variegated and cosmopolitan, in her own words, a veritable "*ménagerie*." She was a woman of unrivalled wit but of dubious character—D'Alembert was her natural son, whom she deserted.

When Sceaux closed, MME DU DEFFAND, one of its most faithful adherents, established her court in what was once the apartment of Mme de Montespan in the Convent of St Joseph. All went well till 1763, when MLLE JULIE DE L'ESPINASSE, whom she had taken to herself as reader on the failure of her eyesight, began to steal her guests. They used to assemble in the companion's room while the mistress slumbered upstairs. Julie was turned away, but she carried with her the pick of Mme Du Deffand's *salon* and kept them with her till her death in 1776. The depth of Mme Du Deffand's wound may be gathered from her comment, "Elle aurait bien dû mourir 15 ans plus tôt; je n'aurais pas perdu d'Alembert."

But the queen of the *salons* was MME GEOFFRIN, who reigned in the Rue Saint-Honoré from 1749 to 1776, winning a world-wide fame.

Il m'en souvient, j'ai vu l'Europe entière
D'un triple cercle entourer son fauteuil,

says the Abbé Delille. Her *salon* combined the qualities of all previous *salons*, together with a new element, the artists and musicians. But her great service to literature lies in her encouragement of the *Encyclopédie* towards which she advanced 300,000 fr. She was however herself no sceptic, and she kept her free-thinking friends within bounds while they were with her.

The same restraint was exercised by MME NECKER, wife of the great minister and mother of Mme de Staël, whose *salon* (1763–83) closes the series. Christian and protestant though she was, she befriended the philosophic clan, and when reproached with compromising acquaintance, she said, "Pourquoi non? ce sont des amis malheureux." She won their confidence; they repented before her with tears for their escapades. Buffon adored her, and she closed his eyes in death. It must be admitted that her literary taste was poor. Delille and poets worse than he were her favourites, while Bernardin de Saint-Pierre had no success when he read *Paul et Virginie* to her.

The *salons* play a very important part in the social and literary history of the century. Besides the impulse which they gave to feminine influence they greatly fostered *esprit*. But it is noteworthy that the two most independent and striking figures, Diderot and Rousseau, kept aloof from them, while Voltaire and

Buffon, who were assiduous in their attendance when in Paris, wrote their masterpieces far away in the quiet of the country.

The 18th century talked and thought more than it wrote, but the forms of art which had reached so high a perfection under Louis XIV did not stand still. If in some ways there was retrogression, in others there was marked development.

The Novel

Mme de La Fayette had shown the more excellent way, but it was not until 1731 that her call was answered. Between her and Marivaux came Lesage with his social satire *Le diable boiteux* (1707), in which an imp unroofs houses and shows what the inhabitants are about, and his picaresque epic *Gil Blas* (1715–35). This is a regular *comédie humaine*, depicting on a vast canvas the adventures not only of the hero, but of everyone he meets—doctors, bishops, poets, ministers. There is no single plot, but there is material in the work for as many tales as it took years to write. For this kind of performance realism is essential, and Lesage is a realist, though not of the class of 19th century naturalists, for he remembers Boileau's warning and exercises choice. His pictures are not ugly. But if his satire is on the whole good-tempered, his morality is not more than that. Virtue is as a rule rewarded and vice punished, but the character of Gil Blas, amiable rascal that he is, fails to move us either to admiration or wrath. In a word, the book is wanting in warmth and sentiment.

Very different are the novels of PIERRE CARLET DE CHAMBLAIN DE MARIVAUX (1688–1763). With him begins the reign of sentiment. He was a Parisian, a man of the world, a frequenter of *salons*, a close observer of men and especially of women. After one or two false starts—burlesque and heroic romance—he found himself in *Marianne* (1731–41), the autobiography of a young woman who successfully evades the traps laid for her and would probably have married happily if Marivaux, the laziest of men, had had the energy to finish his tale. He spends himself in analysing the moods and feelings of his tearful and coquettish heroine. This he does with consummate skill and charm. His other study, also unfinished, the *Paysan parvenu* (1735) has

more movement but less subtlety. It is however very valuable
as a mirror of *bourgeois* manners.

With these two works the psychological novel is fairly
launched. The style of Marivaux, artificial if not affected, has
given a new word to the language—*marivaudage*, the rather
spiteful invention of Voltaire. It is excellently defined by Sainte-
Beuve as *badinage à froid*. Marivaux defended himself stoutly,
maintaining that a man who thinks subtly must express himself
with subtlety. This is true, and Marivaux is not the only writer
whose characters talk too well to the accompaniment of "precious"
reflexions by their creators. But in any case the effect is somewhat cloying.

What is lacking in the novels both of Lesage and of Marivaux
is passion. The defect is made more than good by ANTOINE-
FRANÇOIS PRÉVOST D'EXILÉS, the Abbé Prévost (1697–1763).
For passion, deep feeling is needed, and for deep feeling, simplicity. And Prévost was a most simple-minded being. He had
likewise a great variety of experience. After three years' noviciate
with the Jesuits and another three years as a soldier, he returned
to religion as a Benedictine and showed himself not unworthy
of that laborious order by editing a volume of the *Gallia
Christiana* with his own hand.

But the world was calling him even in his cell, and after
writing there his *Mémoires d'un homme de qualité*, he escaped to
Holland and then to England (1727). Here he founded a journal
Le Pour ei le Contre, something in the nature of a modern
magazine, which had a successful career of seven years. Here he
also gathered material for several novels and read Richardson,
whom he introduced to France through translations of *Pamela*
(1742) and *Clarissa Harlowe* (1751). Returning home in 1733,
he became a secular priest and chaplain to the Prince de Conti,
but his chief means of livelihood was hack-work for the publishers.
Some 112 volumes are placed to his credit, among them a lengthy
Histoire générale des voyages. But the only one that lives is
Manon Lescaut, an episode detached from the *Mémoires d'un
homme de qualité*. It is the first of the novels of passion, either in
France or England, for Richardson, whom it recalls, had not
published his masterpieces when *Manon* appeared in 1732.
Prévost, like many other novelists, including Richardson,

protests that his object is to deter men from vice by painting its terrible results. We may believe him, and at the same time see in the adventures of the Chevalier des Grieux a reminiscence of personal experience.

The influence of Richardson is clearly seen in Rousseau's *La Nouvelle Héloïse* (1761). The situation is that of the *Princesse de Clèves*, a wife tempted and remaining faithful, but the form (a series of letters) and the principle (love yielding to duty) are those of *Clarissa*. Yet *La Nouvelle Héloïse* is no slavish imitation. Rousseau has written us a page of his own life, and Saint-Preux, the hero, is a true portrait of himself. His special gifts as preacher and teacher are given full play, and the long digressions on education, music, the French stage, etc. are most valuable to the student of history and morals.

Émile contains a thin strain of romance—a young woman, destined to be Émile's wife, appears in the last book—but it is in reality a treatise on education.

Rousseau's object in fiction as in all else is to move the reader. This he achieves not only by the torrent of his rhetoric and his sentiment but by the dramatic skill with which he draws his characters. They are not merely vehicles for his own opinions, but living beings. He notes their outward appearance, their gestures; he is careful with their setting and background. And no poet has more success than he in evoking sensation through the manipulation of sounds and words.

This gift belongs in a marked degree to his disciple, BERNARDIN DE SAINT-PIERRE (1737–1814). After a career of adventure and travel, he came under the personal influence of Rousseau during the last stage of the latter's life, and he took the torch from his hand. In 1784 he published his *Études de la Nature*, in which he opposed the materialism of the philosophers and betrayed the extreme poverty of his own scientific equipment. Sharing his master's belief in the goodness of man and Buffon's high idea of his place in the universe, Saint-Pierre makes all nature tend to serve him. His science is indeed sentiment run to seed. The cow has four teats, two for her calves and two for you and me. The flea is providentially black, that it may show up on a white ground, etc. Yet Louis XVI made him in 1792 director of the *Jardin des Plantes*, which he turned into a menagerie. The disciple of Jean-Jacques had little to fear from the Revolution. He was only taken from his garden, and put to lecture at the *École Normale*. He flourished under Napoleon and he died in easy circumstances.

This unscientific sentimentalist brings us one step nearer to Romanticism. He deepens and widens Rousseau's appeal to emotion and his love of nature. He manages to move you by mere description; he paints nature not only at home but in the tropics, and that with a minuteness of detail unknown hitherto. His art is best seen in his only work which survives, the incomparable *Paul et Virginie*. The bringing up of two children of nature in Mauritius, the death of the girl and the grief of the boy—that is all the story. But the eclogue had a profound effect. The characters are of the kind which Byron and Chateaubriand and Lamartine were to carry to perfection, and they are a sign of the growing revulsion against hedonism.

The Conte

Besides the great romances, with which on account of its influence *Paul et Virginie* must be reckoned, there were the *contes*. Of these there are two kinds: (*a*) mischievous and humorous stories with a philosophical or political intention. Such are the *contes* of Voltaire, *Zadig, Candide, Micromegas*, etc. which treat deep topics in highly indecent terms. Their wit is undeniable—their tone deplorable, especially when they speak of woman. (*b*) Accounts of actual occurrences—*faits divers*. Diderot excelled in these. His best tales are transcripts from life, e.g. *Ceci n'est pas un conte* and the brilliant *Neveu de Rameau*, which, being in all probability a fantasy woven out of actual conversations with a living person, may fairly be classed under this head. But neither kind had any influence on the development of the Novel, which in the next century was to be the most powerful of all instruments for touching men's hearts.

The Drama: Tragedy

There is only one tragic writer who counts, and that is Voltaire. While not averse to the terror of which the elder Crébillon (1674–1762), author of *Atrée et Thyeste*, etc. was the contemporary exponent, Voltaire was chiefly concerned with arousing pity. He abandoned himself to the wave of sentiment which was sweeping over France, and he measured the value of a tragedy by the volume of tears shed over it. The three of his plays which kept their vogue into the 19th century—*Alzire, Zaïre, Tancrède*—are especially praised by Mme de Staël for this hydraulic power.

But his real contribution to the theatre was his development of spectacular effect begun by *Athalie*, which he worshipped, and of the hurry of visible action as he had seen it practised by Shakespeare, "the inspired barbarian." To this end he used the space gained on the stage by the removal of intruding spectators for the manœuvring of crowds of actors; he elaborated scenery and costume; he forsook the classical rut and ranged in search of subjects from China to Peru (*Alzire, L'Orphelin de la Chine*) and up and down the national history (*Zaïre, Adélaïde du Guesclin, Tancrède*). Having found them he laid on "local colour" with a lavish hand. He would have done better to have boldly surrendered the "Unities," into which his ingenious complications fitted ill. His genius was rather that of a stage manager than of a dramatist, and he lacked, or forwent, the essential talent of letting his characters develop themselves. His hand is all too visible among the strings, his voice too audible in the words. He cannot ride free from his schemes and reforms, and many of his plays do more credit to his heart than to his head (*Les Guèbres ou la Tolérance, Mahomet*). But both his merits and his defects were fruitful of artistic result. The Romanticists learnt from him the use of history and local colour, and the *drame bourgeois* is founded on his contention that natural sentiment, maternal or filial affection, etc. can produce emotions as poignant and as dramatic as those evoked by Love.

The Drama: Comedy

Regnard, Dancourt, and Lesage really belong to the 17th century (see above, p. 460). They are the direct heirs, however little worthy, of Molière and they simply continue a tradition. There were also two comedies in the course of the century built on classical lines, Piron's *La Métromanie* (1738), an amusing piece, and Gresset's *Le Méchant* (1747), a terrible satire on his age, which contemporary opinion said fell short of the truth. A new note is struck by Marivaux. He hesitated, like Lesage, between the stage and the novel, and, though he does wonders with the latter,

his strongest originality is in his plays. He set out deliberately
to find a new comedy, in which love should be the mainspring
and not a mere accessory. "J'ai guetté dans le cœur humain
toutes les niches différentes où peut se cacher l'amour," and he
discovers many effective situations missed by his predecessors—
unconscious love, love which dares not show itself, love half
suspected and trembling into life. He always brings it to a
triumphant issue, for "Quand l'amour parle, il est le maître." He
is the first to bring out the comic side of the passion which, when
pushed to an extreme, often turns to tragedy. So whether in
Le jeu de l'amour et du hasard (1734), or *Le Legs* (1736), or *Les
fausses confidences* (1737), or *L'Épreuve* (1740), he is always
amusing, and generally true. By his delicacy of analysis he
recalls Racine; by the pretty play of his fancy he foreshadows
Musset. As for his style, there is less *marivaudage* in his plays
than in his novels, and it is really only the *valets* and the
soubrettes who talk in terms above their quality.

But the public, whose emotional appetite was well awakened,
was no longer content to be amused. It wanted to be serious,
even to weep. The former need was catered for by PHILIPPE
NÉRICAULT DESTOUCHES (1680–1754) with well written but unconvincing comedies, *Le Glorieux*, *L'Irrésolu*, etc., reminiscent
of La Bruyère; the latter by the *comédie larmoyante* of NIVELLE
DE LA CHAUSSÉE (1691–1754). Henceforward, men were no
longer to laugh at human weaknesses but to lament the sufferings of innocence. La Chaussée's plays, *Le préjugé à la mode*
and *Mélanide*, fail to touch us to-day both because of their
sentimental matter and of their form. Verse, as Diderot saw,
is unsuited to the purpose.

At this point in stepped that great *Encyclopédiste* with a
couple of plays (*Le père de famille*, 1757, *Le fils naturel*, 1758) and
a whole bundle of theories. The plays richly deserved their
failure. They are quite inferior to their English models (e.g.
Lillo's *Gamester*). But Diderot's dramatic theories are highly
interesting and have had a wide effect, although the *Paradoxe
sur le comédien* (advocating a self-control in the artist such as
Diderot himself entirely lacked) was not published till 1830, and
cannot have greatly influenced contemporary practice. He
admired the great masters of the classical age, but he challenged

the truth of their drama with its long tirades and its tiresome antitheses. What was needed was a moral drama, painting in strong colours, not the deep passions, but the domestic virtues and duties; and for their presentation, a large empty stage where natural characters, speaking prose, should group themselves in striking *tableaux*. The result would be a new form, the *drame sérieux*, midway between comedy and tragedy, dealing realistically with the relations of the modern man to the family or society, in a word, the 19th century problem play, which Diderot had the genius to forecast but lacked the dramatic touch to achieve.

The most successful play of the kind is Sedaine's *Le philosophe sans le savoir* (1765), which with its large morality, simple action, and correctness of staging, exactly answers Diderot's ideal.

PIERRE-AUGUSTIN CARON DE BEAUMARCHAIS (1732–99) tried his hand at the *drame sérieux* with *Eugénie* (1767). Failing signally, he turned back for inspiration to Regnard and Molière, profited by the critical spirit set in motion by the social reformers and philosophers, and produced two masterpieces, *Le Barbier de Seville* (accepted in 1772 and played in 1775) and *Le Mariage de Figaro* (accepted in 1778 and played in 1784). From that moment French comedy has not been suffered to be dull. The classical types reappear, but they are brought up to date—they are of their age; the *spectacle* aimed at by Voltaire in his tragedies; the treatment of social problems in their appropriate setting advocated by Diderot; the brilliant dialogue of Marivaux—all this is pressed into service and stamped with Beaumarchais's own genius. It is the beginning of modern comedy in which French histrionic power is displayed with such marvellous effect.

Beaumarchais's great creation *Figaro* is the reflexion of his own adventures if not of his character. He was a man of restless activity, always on the stage and in the limelight. He rose from nothing; he made and lost fortunes; he ran a fleet of privateers in the war with England; he printed an edition of Voltaire with Baskerville's type; he had endless lawsuits, one of which, *l'affaire Goëzman*, finally discredited the Maupeou *Parlement*. He ran a tilt against the abuses of the *ancien régime*, he was the mouthpiece of popular discontent. But the social effect of his plays has been exaggerated. He did not pull down the Bastille; he only threw some stones which hit their mark.

Poetry

The 18th century had no lack of men who wrote in verse, but only one poet. The truth is that the atmosphere of the age was fatal to those qualities which make a poet—imagination and self-surrender. At the outset we hear it proclaimed by La Motte and Fontenelle that the sole charm of poetry lies in the overcoming of difficulty, and Voltaire himself, who championed verse, had no notion of rhythm and harmony. Poetry became a trick of periphrasis, which is all very well in comic verse but is intolerable when great themes are handled. Now and again a true note is struck, as by Gilbert (1751–80) in his touching *Adieu à la vie*. But ANDRÉ CHÉNIER (1762–94) is the only writer who deserves to stand beside Ronsard and Racine on the French Parnassus. He had Ronsard's high conception of the poet's function. He felt that he had it in him to be great. He was half Greek by birth, and more than half Greek by genius. His natural bent was fostered by the revived interest in classical antiquities and art which marked the second half of the century. The systematic excavation of Pompeii was begun in 1755; general archaeology received a great impulse from the *Antiquités* of the Comte de Caylus (1752–7) and the *Voyage du jeune Anacharsis* of the Abbé de Saint-Barthélemy (1788); Brunck was publishing his *Analecta* from 1772 to 1776; and Winckelmann's *Ancient Art* was thrice translated into French between 1766 and 1793.

Before Chénier took seriously to writing he served as soldier and as diplomat. He was at the French embassy in London, which he cordially hated, when the Revolution broke out. He hastened home. An ardent advocate of the principles of '89, he protested vigorously against the excesses of '93 and he paid the penalty with his head in '94. Some of his best pieces are dated from the prison of Saint-Lazare.

His poems, which, with the exception of two revolutionary odes, remained unpublished till 1819, reveal the writer in four separate aspects, as philosopher, elegist, patriot, and Greek. These, taken together, form a very complete poet.

(1) The philosopher appears in *L'Invention* and *Hermès*. Full of the zeal for science which is a sign of the times, he projected a

great scientific epic, in the manner of Lucretius, inspired by Buffon and Newton. Loosely connected with *Hermès* is *L'Amérique*, the song of the new world, containing attacks on England and Christianity. (2) His elegies show the influence of the Latin amorous poets, especially Catullus, and the degenerate taste of the century. There is little real passion, but a strong vein of sensuality. (3) Two phases of patriotism are clearly marked. These are the appeals to the triumphant people to exercise moderation—*Le Jeu de Paume*—followed by fierce invective when those appeals failed. For this he invented a new and telling instrument, the *iambe*, a combination of 12-syllable and 8-syllable lines which he wove into a continuous strophe. (4) The poems in which the influence of Greece comes out are his best-- but it is not the Greece of the great age that appeals to him, but the Greece of the later vases. He is indeed Hellenistic rather than truly Hellenic, of Alexandria rather than of Athens, inspired by literature more than by life. Yet his claim and his ambition were magnificent, and the boldness of the title which he gives to the poem containing his theory of art declares this. *Invention*! It is not enough to recover ancient thought. The poet must create new things. The century which began with *Tout est dit* has travelled far from that cry of weariness and despair.

The Revolution

The great explosion of 1789, when all the criticism which had been gathering for a hundred years found expression in acts of extreme violence, gave birth to two new literary forms—political oratory and political journalism. In the former, while two men of genius, GABRIEL HONORÉ DE RIQUETTI, COMTE DE MIRABEAU (1749–91), the "Shakespeare of eloquence," as Barnave called him, and GEORGES-JACQUES DANTON (1759–94), the "Mirabeau of the crowd," spoke straight from the heart under the pressure of the extraordinary events in which they were principal actors, the majority wrote their speeches with an eye upon Demosthenes and Cicero, e.g. Vergniaud, the brilliant Girondin. French patriotism had, from the time of the Renaissance, an antique flavour, and the Revolutionaries were not the first Frenchmen to regard themselves as the direct heirs of republican Rome, Athens, and Sparta. But the classical revival, to which reference has already been made, fostered this tendency, and the soldier who silenced the professional orators by the 18 Brumaire addressed his troops with tags of Lucan and Livy. Pictures and statues tell the same story (see ch. x). David, who could, when he cared, paint portraits like John Sargent, is remembered as the artist of the pseudo-classical *Serment des Horaces, L'Enlèvement des Sabines, Le serment du jeu de paume*; and Chaudet the sculptor dressed the figure of a Roman general for the top of the Vendôme column.

The political journal, as distinguished from the literary or scientific review, dates from 1789, with the foundation of the *Journal des Débats*. This was originally meant to be a mere record of discussions, but it quickly grew to represent liberal and bourgeois sentiment in politics. Alongside of it during the revolutionary period appeared and disappeared a swarm of newspapers, which hardly count as literature, although great men of letters contributed to their columns. Thus André Chénier showed by his articles in the *Journal de Paris* that his prose was hardly inferior to his verse. But the journalist *par excellence* is CAMILLE DESMOULINS (1760–94), whose *Le Vieux Cordelier* poured irony upon the Terror. His last number, Feb. 3, 1794, ends with the words "*Les dieux ont soif.*" The writer was guillotined on the 5th of April following.

The Revolutionary drama calls for little remark. Patriotic and political tragedies had a great vogue. The classical influence is seen in the choice of subjects—*Marius, Lucrèce, Gracchus*. All, except the *Agamemnon* of Népomucene Lemercier (1771–1844) which was vastly admired for its Greek (?) feeling, bristle with allusions and ancient instances. The history of France supplied Marie-Joseph Chénier (1764–1811) with a fine declamatory topic in *Charles IX*, in which the hero denounces the wickedness of his royal race. Comedy is a negligible quantity. If mention is made of the *Philinte de Molière* by Fabre d'Eglantine, in which an attempt is made to furnish a sequel to the *Misanthrope*, it is only to pillory the decay of taste.

With the end of the Revolution there arises a new *genre* suited to the popular appetite for blood and thunder and common-place notions of justice, viz. the melodrama. Guilbert de Pixeré-court (1773–1844), its great exponent, "the Corneille of the boulevards," began producing melodramas as early as 1793, but it was not till August 1800 that he deliberately used the name. The subject therefore lies outside this present section—and in any case it is hardly literature!

§ IV. NINETEENTH CENTURY

Romanticism

The Romantic movement in French literature was a reaction from the literature of the 18th century—from its exclusive devotion to reason and intellect, from its subservience to the tyranny of rules and taste, from its indifference to form, from its dry and monotonous style—in a word, from a literature which through the gradual paralysis of creative impulse was no longer true classicism, but a slavish and unintelligent imitation of it.

This reaction was begun by Rousseau in *La Nouvelle Héloïse*, but it was arrested by the wave of neo-classicism which has been described in the preceding section, and the only writer of the last quarter of the 18th century who stands forth as a precursor of Romanticism is Rousseau's friend and disciple, Bernardin de Saint-Pierre. It was not till the first year of the 19th century that a more powerful disciple of Rousseau, RENÉ, VICOMTE DE CHATEAUBRIAND (1768–1848), brilliantly inaugurated the Romantic movement with *Atala*. This was a detached episode from a long work called *Les Natchez*, which, as the fruit of a nine months' sojourn in North America, he had written in England during his seven years' residence there as an *émigré*. It was followed in 1802 by *Le Génie du Christianisme*, with which was incorporated *Atala* and also another episode, destined to become even more famous, *René*.

The most conspicuous feature of Chateaubriand's great work from the point of view of its influence on literature was his insistence on Christianity, and particularly on medieval Christianity, with its chivalry, crusades, and Gothic architecture, as an unrivalled theme for the poet and the artist. But it had other novel features. It judged literature without any reference to the "rules" or to *le goût*. It described nature with the knowledge of a first-hand observer and with the imagination of a poet. It gave, in *Atala* and *René*, full play to the passionate demands of individualism. Finally, it was written in an enchanting style, which was warmed, like Rousseau's, by emotion, but which was heightened by imagination instead of rhetoric, and which moved with an easy freedom only attained by Rousseau in his *Confessions* after many years of patient toil.

Le *Génie* was followed by *Les Martyrs* (1809), a prose epic, the scene of which is laid during the persecution of Diocletian. Its hero, Eudore, whose autobiography fills eight of the twenty-four books, is René without his *ennui* and melancholy. He is Chateaubriand in action. The other characters, with the exception perhaps of the Druidess, Velléda, are purely conventional. But the merit of *Les Martyrs* is not in its characters, but in its grandiose conception of the contrast between the pagan and the Christian world, in what Mr Saintsbury aptly calls its panoramic action, in its brilliant episodes, such as that of Velléda, such as the battle between the Romans and the Franks, in its historical imagination, and in its descriptions of nature. The style suffers in places from the *clichés* of neoclassicism, but it has to the full the easy sweep of language and the plastic imagination which were Chateaubriand's birthright.

Neither *Le Génie du Christianisme* nor *Les Martyrs* had any immediate effect upon literature. This was partly because Napoleon discouraged all literature that did not conform to his own taste or to the supposed interests of the State, and partly because Chateaubriand, who posed as an amateur and a conservative in literature, was the last man to put himself at the head of a literary revolt.

It was therefore left for MME DE STAËL (1766–1817), a woman of warm heart and clear active brain, to formulate in *De l'Allemagne* (1813) the new literary ideas that were already in the air. In the chapters entitled "Poetry," "Classical poetry and Romantic poetry," "Taste," "Dramatic art," she criticises the whole 18th century conception of literature, and points to German and English literature as sources from which the artificial and worn-out channel of French poetry might be replenished and vivified. The book gave a strong impulse to the study of foreign literatures, especially of the northern literatures, and between 1813 and 1820 much work was done in the way of translation, particularly of Byron and Scott. During these years Romanticism meant chiefly the cult of English and German literature.

In March 1820 appeared a slim volume of twenty-four poems entitled *Méditations*. Its success was immediate and electrical; it was like a fountain of living water in the desert; it was the very essence of poetry as conceived by Mme de Staël. Its author was ALPHONSE DE LAMARTINE (1790–1869), the son of a country gentleman who had a small estate near Mâcon. He had written much verse after the 18th century pattern, when a brief love-affair, which terminated with the lady's death (1818), awakened in him "the rare gift of revealing in words what he felt in the depths of his heart." He was a great reader, chiefly of poetry and novels, and his range included Latin, English, and Italian authors. Like many Frenchmen of his day he was greatly drawn to Ossian, and he had read Mme de Staël's novel *Corinne* with enthusiasm. But the chief literary source of his poetry was *Le Génie du Christianisme*, particularly the episode of *René*. In *L'Isolement*, perhaps the most perfect poem that he ever wrote, there is hardly a stanza that cannot be traced to Chateaubriand[1]. Yet every line in its perfect phrasing, its pure harmony, its spiritualisation of the material universe, proclaims Lamartine as France's "most authentic poet." His subsequent volumes, *Nouvelles Méditations* (1823), *Harmonies poétiques et religieuses* (1830), *Jocelyn* (1836), a narrative poem inspired by Rousseau's *Émile* but of real originality, and *Recueillements poétiques* (1839), contain many beautiful poems and passages; but, in spite of the richer vocabulary and more elaborate harmony, there is nothing that can quite compare with the eight or nine masterpieces of the first *Méditations*, which, while they are romantic in their passion, their imagination, and their true lyrical cry, are classical in their generalising spirit.

In 1832 and 1833 Lamartine travelled in the East, and recorded his experiences in *Souvenirs d'Orient*. In his absence he was elected to the Chamber of Deputies, where he acquired a great reputation as an orator. But being disappointed in his political ambitions, he joined the opposition, wrote the emotional

[1] See F. Page in *The French Quarterly* for April and July, 1919.

but untrustworthy *Histoire des Girondins* and played a conspicuous part in the Revolution of 1848. Then on the election of Louis Napoleon as President of the Republic he retired into private life and lived in straitened circumstances, vainly trying to free himself from debt by literary toil.

Like Chateaubriand he posed as an amateur in letters, and this foible was not only prejudicial to his later poetry but it kept him aloof from the Romantic movement, which developed independently of him under other leaders. Its organ was *La Muse française* (July 1823–June 1824) of which the most active editor was Émile Deschamps, while among the chief contributors, besides Deschamps himself, were Victor Hugo and Alfred de Vigny, both of whom had published volumes of verse— Hugo, *Odes et poésies diverses*; Vigny, *Poésies*—in 1822. A new phase in the movement began in April 1824, when meetings of the contributors to *La Muse française* began to be held every Sunday at the official residence of Charles Nodier, recently appointed librarian of the Arsenal. The attitude of the reformers was at first timid and conciliatory, but under the attacks of their orthodox opponents they became more definitely romantic. In September a new journal, the *Globe*, was founded, with J.-J. Ampère, Charles de Rémusat, Thiers, Jouffroy, Dubois, and Sainte-Beuve for contributors. They were all liberals in literature as well as in politics, and they believed in individual taste as opposed to a universal standard. Their watchwords were Nature and Truth. In 1826 Hugo and Vigny each produced a novel and a new volume of poems. In 1827 Sainte-Beuve, who had formed a close friendship with Hugo, began a series of articles in the *Globe* on the literature of the 16th century. Reprinted with alterations and additions in 1828 they provided Romanticism with a distinguished ancestor in the Pleiad, and at the same time impressed upon its upholders the need of a thorough and systematic reform in language and metre. In the famous preface to *Cromwell*, which was printed with the play in December 1827, and which rallied to the Romantic standard a host of young and ardent combatants, Hugo enlarges on this point with insistence and effect. A year later he brilliantly illustrated his doctrines in a new volume of poetry, *Les Orientales*, which was highly successful and gave an additional stimulus to the movement. A new *Cénacle* was formed, which had its meetings at Hugo's house and included not only younger men of letters— Sainte-Beuve, Alexandre Dumas, Alfred de Musset, Gérard de Nerval—but distinguished artists, like the painter Delacroix, and the sculptor David d'Angers. They were far more uncompromising than the *Cénacle* of Nodier, and on February 25, 1830, they made the production of Hugo's *Hernani* at the *Théâtre français* the occasion for a pitched battle with the classicists. Their noisy demonstrations, rather than a genuine success, won them the victory, and the play ran for thirty-eight nights.

The Revolution of July broke up the *Cénacle* and scattered the writers for the *Globe*. This was not altogether a bad thing, for it impelled writers to follow their own genius instead of working on common lines. The next five years (1830–1835) were years of active production in poetry, drama, and romance, in which Hugo, Dumas, Vigny, Alfred de Musset, George Sand, Balzac, Sainte-Beuve, and Gautier all played a prominent part. Romanticism, though still regarded with disfavour by the Academy, became popular with the public, and in 1835 the sale of Hugo's works exceeded those of any living writer. But during these years Romanticism in one respect changed its character; from being conservative it became almost revolutionary. *Bourgeois* though most of the Romanticists were by origin, they hated the *bourgeoisie*, and the *bourgeois* government of Louis Philippe was fruitful in disappointment to young and generous hearts. In the plays of Hugo and Dumas, in the poetry of Musset, in the novels of George Sand, we hear the same cry of revolt. Didier and Antony, Rolla and Lélie are all true romantic types.

About 1835 the excesses and absurdities of the minor Romanticists led to a reaction. What may be called the realist wing—Sainte-Beuve, Mérimée, Gautier, Balzac—began to draw away, and up to a certain point they were followed by Vigny and George Sand, while Alfred de Musset rallied the whole movement in the witty and amusing *Lettres de Dupuis et Cotonet* (1836). Only Victor Hugo and Dumas still fought under the Romantic flag, and before long Hugo, in whose poems the echo of social and political questions became more and more audible, was, like Lamartine, drawn into the vortex of political life. In 1843 his play, *Les Burgraves*, proved a complete failure. From this time Romanticism began to lose its attraction for young aspirants to literary fame. The death of Chateaubriand in July 1848, four months after the Revolution of February, may be said to close the Romantic era in France, as that of Scott in 1832 may be said to close the Romantic era in England.

After this brief sketch of the movement as a whole it remains to say something about its individual productions, and it will be convenient to consider them under the four headings of Poetry, Drama, the Novel, History and Criticism.

Poetry. Romanticism being in its essence the revival of imagination and emotion, it was natural that its chief glory should be its poetry. Three names stand out: Hugo, Musset, Vigny.

In VICTOR HUGO (1802–1885) plastic imagination absorbed nearly every other faculty. He saw and he thought in images. Nothing was too complex, nothing too remote, nothing too impalpable for him to materialise in a concrete vision. His knowledge of the French language was complete; he had an immense vocabulary and a scholar's reverence for grammar and syntax. Though, like Coleridge, he lacked a musical ear, he had a strong feeling both for rhythm and for the character of sounds. Further, he had the faculty of constructing a long lyrical poem, or, so to speak, of orchestrating his verse. In his *Odes et Ballades* (1826) and *Orientales* (1829) he proved himself an incomparable virtuoso; but the later volume contains passages which reveal the vision of a true poet, and one poem, *Mazeppa*, which is a masterpiece. There are many masterpieces in his next volume, *Les Feuilles d'Automne* (1831).

His great periods of poetical production were the years 1835–1840 and 1852–1856. To the former belong *Les Chants du Crépuscule, Les Voix intérieures, Les Rayons et les Ombres*, and most of the poems in books I and II of *Les Contemplations* (1856); to the latter, books V and VI of *Les Contemplations, Les Châtiments* (1852), and the first series of *La Légende des Siècles*. The third book of *Les Contemplations* was written chiefly in 1843, and the fourth, *Pauca meae*, which commemorates his daughter's tragic death by drowning, in or after 1846. The second series of *La Légende des Siècles*, greatly inferior to the first, appeared in 1877, and during the last ten years of his life he published several volumes of apocalyptic poetry, in which amidst exaggerated technique and increasing obscurity of thought may still be found rifts of pure ore.

In his mature lyrical work Victor Hugo is inspired by genuine emotion. Much of it indeed is purely self-regardant, springing from a sense of his own greatness, his own wrongs, his own sorrows. But he has also altruistic emotions—the love of children, and sympathy for the poor and the oppressed and for humanity in general. Some of his finest poems are inspired by the sea, or by nature in her various forms and moods. Death, mystery, infinity, fascinate him strongly, but he contemplates them with a haunting dread.

Les Châtiments (1852), the first fruits of his exile, reveal him as a powerful satirist. As an indictment of the Second Empire the volume fails from its violence, its repetitions, and its bad taste, but many of the individual poems, whatever may be thought of them "in the order of charity," are magnificent as literature. Some of the finest are lyrical in form and the first two movements of the famous *L'Expiation* (Moscow and Waterloo) are an epical fragment. Seven years later what he calls "the fourth wind of the Spirit of Poetry" inspired him with a whole volume, *La Légende des Siècles* (1859), and in the opinion of many French critics revealed him as a master of epic. But granted that the portrayal of Humanity in its successive stages is a fitting subject for an epic poem, to which "the thread of Progress, sometimes invisible," suffices to give unity, it may be objected that the first *Légende des Siècles* is admittedly fragmentary and incomplete, and that its successors, however well they may fill up the gaps, are greatly inferior to it in execution. Thus the whole remains a patchwork. Not even in the original volume does Hugo achieve, except occasionally, the note of true epic narrative. He is too jerky, too unequal, too elaborate; he had not the large and simple nature requisite for the writing of a great epic poem. "He who would write a heroic poem must lead a heroic life." But if the "mosaic"— the simile is Hugo's—fails as a whole, it contains some splendid stories. *Booz endormi* is a model of classical simplicity; *Eviradnus* and *La confiance du Marquis Fabrice* are enthralling narratives; *La rose de l'Infante* is a charming idyll; and *Le Satyre* is a great symbolical poem.

ALFRED DE MUSSET (1810–1857) was as a man and a poet almost the complete antithesis of Victor Hugo. He was without vanity; he had *esprit* and a sense of the ridiculous; he was weak-willed and indolent, the creature of caprice and impulse, sometimes charming, sometimes odious. Thus he marred his own life, and scarred the lives of others. Nearly all his best poetry— the immortal *Nuits*, the *Lettre à Lamartine*, the *Stances à la Malibran*—was written between the ages of twenty-five and twenty-seven. The wonderful *Souvenir* however, the last of the poems inspired by his ill-starred passion for George Sand, belongs to 1841. His marvellous facility of expression enabled him to record his passions and emotions while they were still fresh, and thus his poems appeal to us with the force of absolute sincerity and spontaneity—as true cries of the heart. Except when he was moved by strong emotion he was at his best on the lower slopes of poetry, in exquisite lilting songs, or in *causeries en vers*.

ALFRED DE VIGNY (1797–1863) was a finer character and a better thinker than either Hugo or Musset. But he was inferior to them in poetical endowment. Musset's passion and natural ear for harmony, and Hugo's brilliant and learned workmanship, were wanting to him, nor had he their command of the long poetical phrase. His poems are the result of reflection rather than of inspiration; they are well constructed and carefully thought out, but the execution lacks spirit and *entrain*. His imagination is soon exhausted; beautiful similes are followed by flat passages which drop into prose. It was his just pride that he was a pioneer in the Romantic movement. His earliest volume of verse preceded Hugo's. *Cinq Mars* appeared five years before *Notre-Dame de Paris* and *Le More de Venise* a year before *Hernani*. Among his early poems the finest is *Moïse*, on the solitariness of genius, while *Éloa*, inspired largely by Chateaubriand and Milton, has some passages of great beauty and tenderness. After 1835 he was silent for four years, and then he began to publish at intervals in the *Revue des deux mondes* a series of poems, strongly impregnated with pessimism, which were collected after his death under the title of *Les Destinées*.

Vigny was a pessimist by temperament, an idealist who was

constantly being disillusioned by contact with a vulgar and
self-seeking world. The key-note of many of his poems is love
for humanity and pity for the unfortunate. This softened his
pessimism, which never had in it a touch of scepticism. He
seems to have believed in a God, but in a God who had no power
over evil. Hence the hopelessness of man and fate. Nature
brought Vigny no consolation—*la stupide nature nous insulte*.
Yet latterly he had one hope—in the future of science, a hope
which he expresses in the fine poem, *La bouteille à la mer* (1854).

Drama. The Romantic drama was the result of two influences working upon Voltairean tragedy, that is to say upon
classical tragedy as modified by Voltaire in the direction of
more visible action and more spectacular effect. These two
influences were the popular melodrama founded by Guilbert de
Pixerécourt and the tragedies of Shakespeare. From melodrama
the Romanticists learnt lessons of action and movement in a
more thorough and more democratic school than that of
Voltaire. Shakespeare, whose chief tragedies were given at
Paris in 1827 and 1828 by an English company which included
the three most eminent English actors, Kean, Macready, and
Charles Kemble, inspired them with a larger conception of
tragedy, and with a desire to portray the passions of men and
women of real flesh and blood. To this common aim HUGO and
ALEXANDRE DUMAS (1802–1870) brought very different gifts,
Hugo a strong plastic sense and a superb poetic style, Dumas
an inborn facility for dramatic movement and a style which,
however unliterary, has the power of bringing out the salient
features of actions and characters. Their productive period was
from 1829, when Dumas made the first attack on the classical
citadel with *Henri III et sa cour*, to 1836, when he produced
Kean. The same period covers six plays of Hugo's, three in
verse and three in prose. In the year of *Ruy Blas* (1838),
Rachel began her reign at the *Théâtre français* as an actress of
classical tragedy; two months after the disaster of *Les Burgraves*
(1843) Ponsard's dull and commonplace tragedy of *Lucrèce* was
acclaimed as a masterpiece.

Romantic drama had failed—partly by reason of its exaggera-
tions and absurdities, partly on account of its psychological
emptiness and its inability to create other than melodramatic

character. *Hernani* and *Ruy Blas*, however, still survive, preserved by the splendour of their verse. Dumas's stirring melodrama, *La tour de Nesle*, still attracts large audiences. *Henri III
et sa cour* may still be read as an example of dramatic construction, while *Antony*, as the realisation of that *tragédie bourgeoise*
which Diderot advocated but did not himself attempt, may be
regarded as the parent of modern French drama.

One Romantic play remains to be mentioned. VIGNY's
Chatterton was produced in 1835, and, partly owing to the acting
of Geffroy in the title-rôle and of Marie Dorval as Kitty Bell,
it was enthusiastically received. The plot is simplicity itself, and
the subject is treated with sincerity and sobriety, but the play
is deficient in dramatic movement and the characters are
without life.

Meanwhile ALFRED DE MUSSET was publishing in the *Revue
des deux mondes* comedies which have nothing to do with
Romanticism except that they are the work of a Romanticist
and that they are expressions of his own personality. Their
stage-history is a curious one. An actress, Mme Allan, saw one,
Un caprice, played in Russian at St Petersburg, was struck by
its merits, and brought it to Paris, where it was produced at
the *Théâtre français* (1847) with great success. Others followed,
though some not till after the author's death. These comedies,
so called because they are written in a more or less familiar
style and include a comic element, owe nothing to Voltaire or
melodrama, but something to Marivaux, more to Shakespeare,
and most of all to Musset's own genius. From Marivaux,
Musset learnt that outward incident is not necessary to a drama,
but that movement is, and that this movement may be purely
psychological. Thus through Marivaux, whom he also resembles
in the subtlety of his dialogue, he is descended from Racine.
From Shakespeare's comedies, to which he acknowledges his
debt by borrowing the names of some of the characters, he
gets the idea of the fantastic world which serves as his framework,
but his drama, like Shakespeare's, is true to life, because it
represents without convention the conflict of souls at high
pressure. He has only one theme, love; and only one hero,
himself, sometimes doubling the part as in Coelio and Octavio
(*Les Caprices de Marianne*). But, unlike Byron, he can look at

himself with detachment, and so his heroes are alive. His young girls—Camille, Elsbeth, Cécile—are all charming, but each has her own individuality. The other characters are mere types like Clavaroche and Jacqueline in *Le Chandelier*, or oddities like those which, in his masterpiece, *On ne badine pas avec l'amour*, contrast so effectively with its poignant tragedy. His dialogue is not only subtle and alert with *esprit*, but it is sometimes, as in *Fantasio*, deeply philosophical. *Lorenzaccio*, which was first staged in 1896, with Sarah Bernhardt in the title-rôle, stands apart. It is a historical tragedy treated as a modern drama. It is the work of a student of Shakespeare, but it has the concentration—the action only occupies a few days—of a French classical tragedy and there is no attempt to develop character. Lorenzaccio is the same at the end of the play as he is at the beginning, but he is drawn with great force and penetration, as are in a less degree some of the other characters. The picture of Florentine life, with touches added from the Paris of Louis-Philippe, provides an effective setting, all the more effective, because, as in Shakespeare, the atmosphere is spiritual as well as historical.

The Novel. Besides *Atala* and *René* only two novels of any note were produced in the pre-Romantic period, the *Corinne* (1802) of Mme de Staël and the *Adolphe* (1816) of BENJAMIN CONSTANT (1767–1830). *Corinne*, with its eloquent descriptions of Italian scenery and art, is akin to *René* in its melancholy and to *La Nouvelle Héloïse* in its passion and rhetorical style. *Adolphe*, a psychological study of great penetration, has stood the test of time better than *Corinne*, for it has the power which comes from truthful observation of facts. Corinne is an idealised Mme de Staël, but Adolphe is Constant himself.

In the year in which *Adolphe* was published a new impulse was given to the French novel by the translation of *Guy Mannering* and for the next twenty years the popularity of Scott in France was "prodigious." In a review of *Quentin Durward* (1823) Victor Hugo pointed out that Scott had substituted for the *narrative* novel of the first half of the eighteenth century and for the *epistolary* novel of the second half a *dramatic* form which combined epic narrative with dramatic dialogue. The first Romanticist to follow in Scott's footsteps was VIGNY with *Cinq Mars* (1826). HUGO'S own attempt, *Notre-Dame de Paris*, did not appear till 1831. Both novels contain fine scenes, characteristic of their authors. Vigny's are affecting and picturesque; Hugo's are brilliant and powerful; equally so is his description of 15th century Paris as seen from the tower of the great cathedral which he has made the central figure of his book. But neither novel is successful as a whole; for neither writer had Scott's power to create character, or his genius for portraying the society of a vanished age.

ALEXANDRE DUMAS was the last to enter the field of the historical novel, but he reigned over it as a king. In the power to reproduce the atmosphere of the past he is the rival of Scott; he has the same instinctive faculty of projecting himself into the age or society which he is describing. Whether it is the France of Henri III or of Louis XIV, or the Naples of Ferdinand I (*Il Corricolo*), whether his imagination is working upon contemporary memoirs or upon his own observations, he transports his readers into a new world. His best characters are at once thoroughly individual and intensely alive. There is no pretence at psychological analysis; they simply speak and act. He has wit, humour, incomparable verve, and the power of vivid presentment, and English readers, at any rate, do not discover his deficiency in the higher qualities of style. So prolific a writer was bound to be unequal, but his successes are numerous and they are by no means confined to the *Trois Mousquetaires* and its sequels *Vingt ans après* and *Le Vicomte de Bragelonne*, the equally great 16th century trilogy (*La Reine Margot*, etc.), the stories of Marie Antoinette and the Revolution, and the first part of the most famous of his non-historical novels, *Monte-Cristo*. The ten volumes of his *Mémoires* and the admirable little *Histoire de mes bêtes* are delightful expressions of his exuberant sense of life and his ever-present imagination.

Great though Scott is in novels of a distant past, such as *Ivanhoe* and *Kenilworth* and *Quentin Durward*, he is greater still in the Scottish and Border novels in which he is portraying a society known to him from uninterrupted tradition or from actual survivors. GEORGE SAND (1804–1876) recognises this when she records with pride that she has been called the Walter Scott of Berry. For it is not by the lyrical and passionate novels

of her youth, of which the strongest is *Mauprat*, nor by the
socialistic novels which she wrote between 1838 and 1848, but by
her rustic idylls (*La Mare au Diable, La petite Fadette, François
le Champi*) that she is likely to live. After *Les Maîtres sonneurs*
(1853) she returned to the novel of society, but in an idyllic
instead of a lyrical spirit (*Jean de la Roche, Le Marquis de
Villemer*). In the fifty-odd volumes which she was still to write she
retained her power of telling a story, her *lactea ubertas* of style,
and her rose-coloured view of life. They comprise an excellent
historical novel (*Les beaux Messieurs de Bois-Doré*), a romantic
tale of much charm, the scene of which is laid in Sweden
(*L'Homme de Neige*) and the admirable *Histoire de ma vie*, which
for truth of observation is superior to any of her novels.

Among Scott's warmest admirers was HONORÉ DE BALZAC
(1799–1850), and his first novel of any merit, *Les Chouans* (1829),
is generally called a historical novel. But the events described
in this fine picture of the struggle between Royalists and
Republicans in Brittany only preceded Balzac's birth by two
or three years, and he had made careful studies for it on the spot.
For the historical novel in its true sense he had little vocation,
and when he went to the days of Louis XI or Catherine de'
Medici for his subjects it was chiefly as a student of passion and
character. He applied Scott's art of portraying a social epoch to
the age in which he lived and in 1830 he published six short tales
under the title of *Scènes de la Vie privée*. *La Peau de Chagrin*
(1831) with its supernatural element made him famous, and it
was followed by other short stories of a romantic character. In
1834 appeared his first realistic novel of any length, *Eugénie
Grandet*, and it was a masterpiece. From 1834 to 1837 he collected his works under the title of *Études de mœurs au xix*e *siècle*,
with the sub-divisions *Scènes de la Vie privée*, etc. with which we
are familiar. They included *Le Père Goriot* (1835) and *La vieille
Fille* (1836). The title of *Comédie humaine*, which appears for the
first time in the sixteen-volume edition of 1842–1846, indicates
Balzac's ambition to portray a society which "should compete with
that of the state," and though his early death in 1850 prevented
him from filling up all the departments which he had mapped
out, he has left a work of imposing dimensions and tolerable
completeness. How far is the result a success? As a picture of

an imaginary society in which the various classes and the individual men and women act and react upon one another, it is astonishingly successful. But as a picture of French society of Balzac's day it has defects which arise from its creator's limitations. He does not portray all classes with equal truth. He succeeds with business-men, lawyers, doctors, authors, journalists, artists, bagmen, money-lenders, actresses, partly from observation and partly by intuition. But his dandies, his wits, his statesmen, above all his great ladies, are insufferable. He is unfair to provincial society, and, except in *Le Médecin de Campagne*, to the peasants. Lastly, though he protests that it has been his constant endeavour to present the good side of life as "a salutary counterpoise to the evil," it is evident that evil appeals to his imagination more powerfully than good. His good characters are simple and colourless and they are generally sacrificed to the bad characters. Balzac was a pessimist; if "he saw life steadily" he did not "see it whole."

This brings us to the much disputed question as to the relative parts played by observation and imagination in his work. It has been said that he toiled so assiduously that he had little time for observation. But, on the other hand, in his younger days he had a varied experience, spending eighteen months in a lawyer's office, another eighteen with a notary, and working for three years as a type-founder, printer, and publisher. He paid frequent visits to the provinces and was familiar with many provincial towns. Moreover he took in at a glance the physiognomy of persons and places and he had a prodigious memory. "Il ne regardait rien et se souvenait de tout." He says himself that observation was intuitive with him. "It penetrated the soul without neglecting the body...it gave me the faculty of living the life of the individual to whom it was directed[1]." As Gautier says in his admirable account of Balzac, he was a visionary as well as an observer. But if observation was the starting-point for the creation of the great majority of his characters, the greatest are rather creations of the imagination alone. Such are Grandet, Goriot, Philippe Bridau, Balthazar Claës, Baron Hulot d'Ervy, all victims of an absorbing passion. Such are Mme Marneffe, *la cousine* Bette, and *le cousin* Pons.

[1] *Facino Cane.*

But though Balzac idealised his chief characters so as to make
them types of humanity as well as living individuals, he equally
believed in the importance of details and especially of physical
and material details. So he gives us elaborate descriptions of
persons and things, and sometimes forgets, as his great admirer,
Taine, points out, that "a description is not a picture." It is
this defect as well as his pessimism and his preference for the
sinister aspect of life that has been most assiduously copied by
his followers. He has other defects, pretentiousness, want of
taste, and a bad style. But when all is said, he is a giant; he is
a prolific creator of character, he has an unrivalled insight into
the workings of human passion, and he has given to the novel
a scope and an importance which it never before possessed.

HENRI BEYLE (1783–1842), who adopted the pseudonym of
Stendhal, had nothing in common with the Romanticists but
his dislike of Classicism. His centre of interest was himself, but
he combined with an absorbing egoism a strong admiration for
Italy, Napoleon, and women. These, with an unrivalled faculty
for the analysis of character and motives, which he cultivated
by an assiduous study of Marivaux, were the mainsprings of his
two famous novels, *Le rouge et le noir* (1830) and *La Chartreuse
de Parme* (1839). Balzac hailed the second as a masterpiece,
but his later disciples preferred the first—and rightly from
their point of view. For its hero, Julien Sorel, is a superb
example of psychological analysis. He is the embodiment of
cool, calculating, ungenerous, unscrupulous ambition, a true
representation of a type common enough in Stendhal's day.
Fabrice del Dongo, the hero of *La Chartreuse de Parme*, is an
Italian Julien Sorel, but though he is in some ways more human,
he is less firmly drawn, and the best character in the book is his
aunt, the Duchess of Sanseverina. The picture of a petty Italian
Court provides the setting. It is skilfully drawn and it is none
the less true because it suggests the 16th century as well as the
19th. Stendhal had only a modest reputation in his lifetime, but
after an article on him by Taine in 1864 he began to be famous,
and by 1880 he became the object of a veritable cult. The
chapter of his influence is not yet closed, but, except in his
worship of energy, he represents all that is most antipathetic to
"the young men of to-day."

PROSPER MÉRIMÉE (1803–1870) was only a Romanticist by virtue of his interest in foreign civilizations and literatures and his love of the fantastic and the bizarre. In his regard for form and style and in the sobriety of his execution he was classical; in his careful observation of fact he was a realist. His contribution to the historical novel, *Chronique du règne de Charles IX* (1829), in which his aim was to give "a true picture" of the period, is only a partial success. Drawing chiefly from Brantôme he paints only the more frivolous side of the age; he gives us a series of clever sketches, but they have not been fused by the imagination into an organic whole. On the other hand, his short stories—*L'Enlèvement de la Redoute, Mattéo Falcone, L'Abbé Aubain*—are models of the art of pregnant concentration, while his longer ones—*Colomba* (1841), *Carmen* (1846), and *Arsène Guillot* (1846)—are powerful examples of accurate observation, straightforward narrative, and finished style. Similar qualities, with less art and more emotion, are shown in Vigny's three tales of military life, entitled *Servitude et grandeur militaires*, while in *Sylvie*, in which that lovable oddity, GÉRARD DE NERVAL (1808–1855) depicted the landscape and customs of his native Valois, the sobriety of tone and delicacy of observation are enhanced by a peculiar charm. "Le bon Gérard" also wrote delicate verse which foreshadows Verlaine, and translated *Faust* to the satisfaction of Goethe.

History and Criticism. The sympathetic interest in the past which produced the historical novel also led to the serious study of history. AUGUSTIN THIERRY (1795–1856) was inspired by Chateaubriand and Scott to write *Histoire de la Conquête de l'Angleterre par les Normands* (1825) and *Récits des temps mérovingiens* (1840), both remarkable for their imaginative sympathy and for the warmth and colour of their style. But he attained to a larger measure of historical truth in the *Essai sur l'Histoire du Tiers État* (1853), in which he gave definite expression to his idea that the true basis of history is the psychology of nations.

JULES MICHELET (1798–1874) widened the sources of history by consulting unpublished documents as well as printed ones. Like Thierry, he studied national psychology, giving however less weight to race and more to geographical position and climate.

Like Thierry too, he had strong imaginative sympathy with the past, but his imagination was that of a poet and a philosopher. His *Histoire de France* is full of errors and prejudices, but he has put into it ideas as well as life, and some of his ideas, such as his conception of France as a living organism, are illuminating. His earliest volumes (1833–1843), ending with the reign of Louis XI, are far the best. After these he wrote his moving account of the French Revolution (1847–1853), and then returned to the 16th century. But political partisanship had warped his judgment and narrowed his vision. Moreover, the glowing style of the earlier volumes with its musical cadences was ill replaced by the apocalyptic utterances and monotonous chant of the later ones.

From the psychology of peoples we pass to the psychology of individuals as represented by CHARLES-AUGUSTIN SAINTE-BEUVE (1804–1869). He began as an ardent disciple of Romanticism, to which he rendered great service by providing it with ancestors and critical ideas; but after the dispersion of the *Cénacle* of Victor Hugo in 1830 he drew away, and in 1840, after some abortive religious experiments and some unsuccessful attempts to achieve fame as a poet and a novelist, he definitely separated from the romantic school and settled down to scepticism and criticism. His work as a critic is sometimes divided into two periods, that of the *portrait* (1829–1849) and that of the *causerie*; but the *causerie* is only a condensed *portrait* written in a more familiar and personal style, and it is truer to say simply that Sainte-Beuve's powers reached their highest point in the *Causeries du Lundi* (1849–1861). His master-work, *Port-Royal* (1840–1859), and his malicious *Chateaubriand et son groupe littéraire sous l'Empire* (1861) also contain much first-rate criticism. His merits are exact scholarship, tolerant catholicity, and penetrative sympathy which rises to real creation. He has two limitations: he is too sceptical and unspiritual to appreciate the noblest and loftiest flights of literature, and his criticism of his contemporaries, though not so unappreciative as is sometimes made out, is, at least, ungenerous. His method is mainly psychological; his aim is not merely to appraise a writer, but to lay bare his soul. For the 17th and 18th centuries and the early years of the 19th no student can dispense with his guidance.

In the first of three "Mondays" which Sainte-Beuve wrote in 1850 on Chateaubriand's *Mémoires d'Outre-tombe*, then in course of publication, he says that the author had only produced one perfect work—*René*. The *Mémoires* are certainly not perfect, but they are to Chateaubriand what the *Confessions*, upon which they are modelled, are to Rousseau. They consist of three parts written at different times and after different methods; the first autobiographical, the second historical, and the third in the form of a diary. All alike are strongly coloured by imagination; in all alike there is the same charm of narrative, the same genius for description, the same outbursts of illuminating thought and lofty sentiment. Behind his posing and his colossal egotism Chateaubriand appears in them not only as a great man of letters, but as a great man.

They form a noble epilogue to the Romantic movement. They remind one that its true essence was not the cult of Gothic architecture or foreign literatures, but the revival of imagination and emotion. It is true that imagination became riotous and emotion hysterical, and the inevitable reaction followed. But imagination and emotion, tempered and purified, continue to inspire literature; the imaginative truth of Flaubert and Baudelaire, the exquisite sensibility of Verlaine and Anatole France are alike due to the liberating movement known as Romanticism. And to this movement Chateaubriand, after Rousseau, gave the first impulse. "Nous sommes tous partis de lui."

The Second Empire

Most of the chief writers of the Romantic movement continued their activity till the fall of the Second Empire, but the two who exercised the greatest influence on the literature of the new epoch were Sainte-Beuve and a writer who has not yet been discussed, Théophile Gautier. Sainte-Beuve's influence on thought generally was very great, but in the domain of pure literature it was overshadowed by that of Gautier, who as early as 1834, in the preface to *Mademoiselle de Maupin*, had enunciated in an exaggerated and aggressive form that theory of Art for Art which was to play so important a part in the literature of the Second Empire. It was a development of the Romanticist claim for freedom in art, but it was also a protest partly against

the "industrial" art of *La Presse* and the *feuilleton* novel, and
partly against the "social" art preached by Victor Hugo and
others. But the theory did not have much influence upon
literature till the days of the Second Empire, when Gautier
found adherents in Leconte de Lisle, Théodore de Banville,
Baudelaire, Flaubert, Jules and Edmond de Goncourt, and
Renan. They did not form a school, for their aims and ideals in
literature differed widely, but they agreed in the view that
art should be independent of religion and politics and
morals.

"Art for Art" is almost a truism, but the majority of its
advocates were not content with the simple meaning of the
phrase. They stretched it to mean "Art for the Artist"—Art,
not for the multitude nor even for the person of education and
culture, but Art for a select coterie of artists and critics.
Moreover, by way of reaction from the too personal art of
lyrical poets like Alfred de Musset, they added a new theory,
that of impassivity, and so alienated still further the sympathies
of ordinary men and women.

Along with this Art for Art movement, and often coalescing
with it, there developed another movement, that of Realism.
Its origin was quite distinct from that of Art for Art. It was a
painter, Gustave Courbet, who opened in 1848 the realistic
campaign, and it was he, or one of his friends, who invented the
word *Réalisme*. Then Champfleury applied the theory to literature and in the preface to *Les Aventures de Mlle Mariette* (1853)
defined it as "the choice of modern and popular subjects" and
elsewhere declared that the essential formula was "sincerity in
art." The chief god of the new school was Balzac, but they also
venerated Stendhal. They were helped by the growing reaction
against Romanticism, by the increase of observation among the
Romanticists themselves, and by the rising tide of scientific and
positive thought. Then *Madame Bovary* was published in the
Revue de Paris (October 1–December 15, 1856) and attracted
by its prosecution the attention of all literary Paris. Flaubert
felt nothing but contempt for the unimaginative Champfleury,
and though he greatly admired Balzac, he hated Stendhal. Yet
it is true that he "founded realism in France" (Faguet), and he
did so because, underlying all theories of art, he believed in art

itself. Before however considering his work, we must go back to his brother-craftsman, the author of *Émaux et Camées*.

THÉOPHILE GAUTIER (1811–1872), who began his career in a painter's studio, was a remarkably prolific writer and his work has been very variously judged. His account of himself as "a man for whom the external world exists" gives the key-note to his genius. Add to this, that he had a strong sense of form and style, a wide and intimate knowledge of the French language, an absorbing devotion to the aesthetic side of life, and a tendency to melancholy and pessimism which a sense of humour saved from becoming morbid. His romanticism took chiefly the form of a cult for Hoffmann and the *genre macabre*, and after a volume of verse entitled *La Comédie de la Mort* (1838) he definitely abandoned it. His later and more characteristic work includes four remarkable volumes of descriptive travel, of which the earliest, *Voyage en Espagne* (1843), is perhaps the best; *Émaux et Camées* (1852), in which the same descriptive qualities are displayed in elaborately chiselled verse; short stories, sometimes overweighted by description, but otherwise excellent in form; and much miscellaneous criticism of admirable quality, of which the most important is the volume *Les Grotesques* and the essay entitled *Rapport sur le Progrès de la Poésie*.

In the same year as *Émaux et Camées* appeared a volume of verse by CHARLES LECONTE DE LISLE (1818–1894) entitled *Poèmes antiques*, with a preface in which he inveighed against personal poetry and advocated the union of art and science. Like Gautier, whose influence he had strongly felt, he was a believer in form and style, and both in this volume and in *Poèmes barbares* (1862) he maintains an astonishingly high level. His style has the dignity of marble and the polish of metal, but it has also their hardness. He excites admiration, but he does not invite companionship—partly by reason of his monotonous perfection, chiefly because he shows little interest in human beings as individuals. He was born in the island of Bourbon, and his finest poems are descriptions of tropical scenery and animals (*La Fontaine aux lianes, Le Panthère noir*), for in these observation is quickened by imagination and feeling. On the other hand his more ambitious poems, in which he endeavours to reconstitute ancient civilisations, seem cold to the lover of poetry, and untrue to the scholar. Leconte de Lisle has not succeeded in wedding art to science, and his assumed impassivity is really a mask for strong and sincere personal sentiment. In the fine sonnet in which he protests against personal art (*Les Montreurs*) he is personal to the point of passion.

Under the aegis of Leconte de Lisle a new *Cénacle* was founded, and in 1866 appeared *Le Parnasse Contemporain*, to which thirty-seven poets, including Gautier, Leconte de Lisle, Théodore de Banville, and Baudelaire, contributed. It was followed by a second *Parnasse* in 1871 (postponed from 1869) and by a third in 1876. The earlier Parnassians practised with patient docility the aesthetic doctrines of their master. They were meticulous in their observance of metrical rules, and in their anxiety to be impersonal they chose trivial themes. But as invariably happens in poetical schools the more original—Mallarmé, Verlaine, Sully Prudhomme, François Coppée, Anatole France—left the school to strike out independent lines. The one true Parnassian who has achieved fame which promises to be permanent is JOSÉ-MARIA DE HEREDIA (1842–1905), born in Cuba, the descendant of a *Conquistador*. His only volume of verse, *Les Trophées*, was not published till 1893 but his poetry was known long before this and he is honourably mentioned by Gautier in his *Rapport* as one of the contributors to the first *Parnasse*. Like his master, Leconte de Lisle, his aim was to resuscitate vanished civilisations—Greece, Rome, the Renaissance, old Japan—but he realised that his peculiar art, which he happily compares to that of a worker in enamel, was best expressed in a short but stately poem like the sonnet. Consequently more than two-thirds of his work consists of sonnets, in which he combines the glowing colour of the worker in enamel with the firm outline of the medallist. But the finest of all are those which end on a note of imaginative vision.

In originality, in imagination, in the subtle adaptation of form to thought, both Leconte de Lisle and Heredia were inferior to CHARLES BAUDELAIRE (1821–1867). An idealist, a Catholic with a horror of vice, he sinned from sheer perversity, and he believed that perversity is natural to man. He preferred artificiality to nature and he held that modern civilisation is so artificial that it can only be represented by subtle thoughts and bizarre emotions. These ideas, which largely inspire his only volume of verse, *Les Fleurs du Mal* (1857), are the cause of a certain inequality in his work. But except when his perversity impels him to choose a repulsive and unpoetical theme he is a true poet. His imaginative symbolism heralded the reaction against the clear-cut precision of the Parnassians, while the delicate and varied music of his verse was a contrast to their too rigid harmony.

Les Fleurs du Mal and *Madame Bovary* (in book form) both appeared in the same year, and both were the subject of a prosecution by a government which thrived on corruption. To the production of his masterpiece GUSTAVE FLAUBERT (1821–1880) had given six years, working at it with frenzied industry at Croisset, near Rouen, where, except for a journey to the East in 1849, and occasional visits to Paris, he lived for thirty-four years. *Salammbô* was published in 1862, *L'Éducation sentimentale* in 1869, *La Tentation de Saint-Antoine*, an elaborate nightmare of the imagination which he had begun in 1846, in 1874, and *Trois Contes* in 1877. His last book, *Bouvard et Pécuchet*, in which his creative faculty failed him, was unfinished at his death. Faguet in his informing monograph on Flaubert has dwelt on his double nature, distinguishing between his Romantic and his realistic novels. But this leaves out of sight the important truth that Flaubert's method is the same in all his writings and that it rests on three processes: (1) the careful collection and observation of facts, (2) the fusing of these facts by the imagination into a concrete vision, and (3) the faithful presentation of this vision by means of language.

Much has been said of Flaubert's style and of the effort he expended on it. But his theory was at bottom a simple one—that the right idea produces the right word, and that "style is only a manner of thought." Fix your thought on your image, and then find the corresponding word or phrase; there is only one that will express it with adequacy.

The other doctrine which Flaubert held consistently throughout his career was that of impersonality. "Every work," he said, "in which you can divine the author is self-condemned." Like Leconte de Lisle he hated Lamartine and Alfred de Musset and other *montreurs*. Yet he had the greatest admiration for

Chateaubriand and Hugo, from whose work the *moi* is never absent. And if he supposed that his own novels were entirely impersonal, he greatly deceived himself. We learn from these that he had a poor opinion of human nature, judging most men to be fools; that though a *bourgeois* himself he hated the *bourgeoisie*; and that he thought nothing interesting which did not interest himself, and that anything which interested him must also be interesting to other people.

Partly for these temperamental reasons, and partly from the touch of pedantry—for pedantry it is—which his theory of Art for the Artist has introduced into much of his work, *Madame Bovary* is the only one of his novels, for all their power and craftsmanship, that will ever be widely read. It may or may not be true that it is the novel of the century, but beyond question its influence on the novel in France has been immense.

Of the chief novelists who worked on Flaubert's lines none came to maturity before 1870 except the brothers de Goncourt, who were very little read before 1880. But realism did not occupy the whole field, and the romantic tradition was carried on not only by George Sand, but by younger writers who followed in her footsteps. Such was OCTAVE FEUILLET (1821–1890), the novelist of aristocratic society, who made his name with *Le Roman d'un jeune homme pauvre* (1858), an admirable example of the romantic novel of sentiment, which still retains its enormous popularity. When he attempted stronger work, and dealt with passion instead of sentiment and crime instead of infirmity, his lack of psychology led him into melodrama, as in *Monsieur de Camors*; but his dramatic experience, if it sometimes betrayed him, sharpened his sense of construction, and *La Morte*, one of his latest novels, however unfair as an attack on materialism, is the work of a finished artist.

The psychological truth which is wanting in Feuillet is the making of *Dominique* (1863), the solitary novel of the painter, EUGÈNE FROMENTIN (1820–1876), who had already shown in *Un été dans le Sahara* and *Une année dans le Sahel* that he could paint with his pen as delicately and as truthfully as with his brush. His novel is habitually compared by French critics to *La Princesse de Clèves*, and the comparison is as just as it is honourable. He also wrote a volume of art-criticism, *Les Maîtres d'autrefois*, which in its combination of technical knowledge with power to interest the reader who is not an expert has never been surpassed.

The reaction from Romanticism was even more pronounced in the drama than in the novel. As early as 1849 ÉMILE AUGIER (1820–1889) produced a play of modern social life, *Gabrielle*, in which the romantic heroine is saved from the fate of Mme Bovary by the good sense of her *bourgeois* husband. It was in verse, but after some experiments in both verse and prose Augier realised that for a drama of modern life prose is the better medium. So from 1858 to 1870 he wrote in prose social comedies, *drames sérieux*, on the lines partly of *L'Avare* and partly of *Turcaret*. During his lifetime they were a great success, not only in the theatre, but with literary as well as dramatic critics. Now they have lost their savour and it is not difficult to see why. Augier had neither Molière's power of creating character nor Lesage's skill in selecting types. Moreover his style, though vigorous, is commonplace; his dialogue lacks taste and tact; he strains after *esprit* and he has no sense of humour. Thus in spite of his stage experience, his true conception of comedy, and his healthy, if commonplace, morality, even his strongest plays—*Les Effrontés, Le Fils de Giboyer, Maître Guérin*—just miss success, and *Le Gendre de Monsieur Poirier*, in which he had the assistance of Jules Sandeau, only achieves it in the last two acts.

ALEXANDRE DUMAS *fils* (1824–1895) was a more original thinker and a better writer than Augier; but he was a moralist first and a dramatist only second, and he ruined his plays by turning them into pamphlets. The best instance of this is *Les Idées de Madame Aubray* (1867), which opens admirably but ends as a mere problem-play. Further, his characters are either conventional or unreal, the only exception being the hero of *Un père prodigue* (1859), who is his own father. Yet in the social history of France as well as in the history of the French stage this experienced and skilful playwright, this sincere moralist, has a place. As M. Doumic says, "his work will remain considerable by reason of his influence."

The lighter forms of comedy, opera-bouffe and vaudeville, greatly flourished under the Second Empire. In the former

Henri Meilhac and Ludovic Halévy, with the collaboration of
the German musician Offenbach, reigned supreme, Meilhac
contributing the boisterous mirth and Halévy the delicate
irony. The master of vaudeville was EUGÈNE LABICHE (1815–
1888), who had an inexhaustible fund of mirth and gaiety and
an intimate knowledge of the machinery of stage construction.
But he was also a shrewd, if superficial, observer of life, and he
had in him the makings of a psychologist. Thus his published
plays include not only riotous and delightful farces, but also
true comedies, the best of which, such as *Le Voyage de
Monsieur Perrichon, Moi, La poudre aux yeux*, were produced
during the years 1860–1864. In many of his pieces the theme
is borrowed from Molière, though a farcical turn is given to it,
and like Molière's *Les Précieuses ridicules* they can be read now,
because underneath the farce they are founded on the eternities
of human nature. They also give us an excellent picture of
bourgeois life under Louis Philippe and the Second Empire.
The characters themselves may be caricatured, but the picture
of customs and manners is a true one.

Taine and Renan are too near to us for a just estimate of
their work to be possible. Historians, philosophers, critics, they
exercised a dominating influence well into the first decade
of this century, and, though they are now affected by the inevitable reaction, they have fertilised the whole field of French
literature. Profoundly though they differed in temperament,
they had certain characteristics in common—great industry and
courage, a child-like faith in science, and a pathetic belief that
their own work was strictly scientific.

HIPPOLYTE TAINE (1828–1893) was endowed with so many
mental gifts that they clashed with one another. His visualising
faculty hindered his power of abstract thought, his love of
simplification and types and formulae was injurious to his work
as a historian and a critic. No one now believes in his once
famous theories of the "predominant faculty" and "*la race, le
milieu, le moment*," but they have had a permanent influence
on literary criticism. His history of English literature is incomplete and full of mistakes, but its very mistakes are stimulating. His *Origines de la France contemporaine* is, says Acton,
"not history," but it stirred better-equipped historians to study

the French Revolution and the Empire in an impartial spirit. He was a great admirer of Balzac and at the age of twenty-six he had read Stendhal's novels more than sixty times, but he was far from pleased when the founder of Naturalism claimed to be his disciple. His positivism and his pessimism are out of date, but his intellectual probity and the courage and energy which he showed at the crisis of his country's fortunes are still beacons of encouragement. His style, though it lacks the spontaneity of Renan's, combines in a remarkable degree the visualising faculty with the power of concrete and imaginative expression.

ERNEST RENAN (1823–1892) was destined for the priesthood, but, ceasing to believe in Christianity except as providing a moral ideal, he devoted himself to learning and literature, became a great Oriental scholar[1], and contributed to the *Revue des deux mondes* original and suggestive essays on criticism, morals, and religious history. A mission to Palestine inspired him to write his monumental work, *Histoire des Origines du Christianisme* (1863–1881) followed by *Histoire du peuple d'Israel* (1887). The first volume, *Vie de Jésus*, made a great sensation, though his friends Berthelot and Taine told him that he had substituted romance for legend. The next two volumes were less successful, but *L'Antéchrist* charmed by its clever, if fanciful, portrait of Nero, and the last volume by its equally clever and equally unconvincing portrait of Marcus Aurelius. Renan was a positivist in philosophy and a firm believer in the future of science; but he was also an idealist and a man of imagination, and he left a gap in his philosophy which he filled with spiritual mysticism. After 1870, when all his props seemed to fail him—France, Germany, and even science—he became more sceptical, and he wrote philosophical dialogues and dramas (*L'Eau de Jouvence, Caliban*), in which he played with paradoxes in the manner of Montaigne, and developed an intellectual spirit which received the name of "dilettantism." At bottom, however, he remained an idealist, for to the mysticism of a Celt he united the obstinacy of a Breton. Everything that he wrote bears the stamp of great originality and intelligence, but much of his work is arbitrary, fantastic, and even puerile. He was an intellectual egoist in the fullest sense of the term, and

[1] See above, p. 395.

this absorption in himself may tend in the future to diminish his influence on others. But he has in his favour the perennial charm of style, of a style which owes nothing to books, but which is the natural expression of a singularly clear, subtle, and refined intelligence. There is no better example of it than the delightful *Souvenirs d'Enfance et de Jeunesse.* Like Rousseau, like Chateaubriand, Renan is at his very best when his theme is himself.

In his *discours de réception* at the French Academy he paid a remarkable and admirably phrased tribute to his predecessor Claude Bernard (1813–1878), the great physiologist, whose striking *Introduction à la médecine expérimentale* (1865) was widely read by men of letters and had a certain share in determining the direction of French literature.

§ V. AFTER 1870

The War of 1870 did not, properly speaking, make a break between the literature which preceded it and that which followed it. Nevertheless, so violent a disturbance could not take place without colouring its evolution, and finally giving it a certain bias. After the treaty of Frankfort literary life revived, and at first the existing schools continued to share the favour of the public. But they seemed to be in haste to finish their work and they aged visibly. New men appeared, and French mentality itself underwent a sort of crisis which continued till 1912, when there began a reaction against the past in the moral and intellectual as well as in the aesthetic order. Then came the Great War, which may perhaps alter the course of its development.

Of this literary movement of nearly two generations we propose to portray the chief features and to notice the principal figures.

The Novel

One form, born, or rather revived, late, and for long held, at least by the best minds, in low esteem, has made a great advance under the influence of romanticism and is on the high road to absorbing all other forms. This is the novel. After 1870, it continued to be represented for a time by Flaubert and the so-called naturalistic school. On the eve of the war, in

1867, FLAUBERT produced *L'Éducation sentimentale*, which is regarded as one of the types of naturalism. Of an impetuous temperament, he sometimes, fortunately for himself, soared above his usual style, and in *Madame Bovary*, in *Salammbô*, and perhaps above all in *La Tentation de Saint-Antoine*, there are lyrical outbursts, and picturesque visions, which relieve the somewhat colourless texture of these works. But in *Bouvard et Pécuchet* Flaubert reached the height of naturalism and depicted two fools with a detail that becomes repulsive.

The fact is that only mediocrities have ever been bound by formulas; writers of great personality have always escaped from them. For instance, the brothers de Goncourt, or to speak more correctly, EDMOND DE GONCOURT (1822–1896), while remaining faithful to the description of details, render what they see as they see it, and, having the eyes of artists, give artistic impressions. Their style has been called literary impressionism, and rightly so, if by this is understood that they devoted themselves to reproducing in full detail the impressions they received of persons and things. In this way they have succeeded in producing curious works, which are not lacking in life, although they remain somewhat superficial in psychology, and although such a book as *Madame Gervaisais* fails to do justice to a fine subject. They inaugurated a tradition which still continues. Every year the *Académie Goncourt*, which was founded by them, crowns the novel which seems to it the most significant, and brings together the writers who best continue the work of the masters. Their cult is thus assured. The *Journal* of Edmond de Goncourt contains most valuable and piquant information about his life and his surroundings.

But this school has its most distingui~hed representatives in ÉMILE ZOLA (1840–1903) and his group. Here again we must not deceive ourselves. In spite of his exaggerated manifestoes and his pseudo-scientific manner, Zola (*L'Assommoir*, *Travail*) is above all a poet and a visionary. In this lies his principal merit. His works are large frescoes, the lines of which appear distorted when examined too close, but which viewed from a suitable distance regain their striking perspective and relief.

It is, moreover, interesting to notice in connexion with this current of realism—which has always existed in French literature, but which since Balzac has specially pervaded the novel—that original writers have always freed themselves from it in some way or other, while the rest, by subjecting themselves too closely to its formulas, have ended by falling into insignificance.

The vibrating personality of GUY DE MAUPASSANT (1850–1893) soon freed itself from the rules of the school by which he was enslaved when he wrote *Boule de Suif*. He is an infallible painter of surroundings as well as a sure analyser of the human heart. In works such as *Bel Ami, Notre Cœur, Fort comme la Mort*, he paints man in the grasp of love and suffering, and by their structure no less than by their insight they attain the perfection of classical works.

ALPHONSE DAUDET (1840–1897) adds to the realism of the novel an element of picturesqueness and poetry. No one has represented so well the impressions of home, the aspects of town or of country, the freshness of morning, the melancholy of twilight. He is almost a pure poet, and adorably so in *Les Contes du Lundi* and *Les Lettres de mon Moulin*. In his novels, and especially in masterpieces such as *Le Nabab* or *Numa Roumestan*, he reveals himself as a historian and a psychologist, and as gifted with an instinct and insight into life which have not been surpassed.

Thus it was that Maupassant, by the delicacy and depth of his observation, and Daudet, by the exercise of an almost morbid sensibility, constructed novels of the first rank which only reveal the authors and the society which they wish to delineate, and thus it was that less original authors such as M. Henri Ghéon, Charles-Louis Philippe, or M. Charles-Henri Hirsch, imprisoned by the strict application of rules, have not been able to give life to books such as *Le Consolateur* or *Le Père Perdrix*.

Two contemporaries furnish us with a striking example of the difference between theory and practice. The brothers who write under the collective pseudonym of J.-H. ROSNY (b. 1856; b. 1859 respectively) have in *Le Termite* carried out step by step the work of accumulating notes and cutting up "slices of life." But they themselves have nothing of the "white ant" which they track out so thoroughly, and the subjects of *La Charpente*—the

society of the future—or of *Vamireh*—the prehistoric world—
are conducive rather to epic treatment than to that of an
auctioneer's inventory.

Moreover, naturalism freed itself from its chains, less by reaction than as the result of normal development, and it ended by
becoming so wide a system that any narrative could find a place
in it. J.-K. HUYSMANS (1848–1907) in *La Cathédrale* has applied
an ultra-realistic manner and language to an entirely new subject
—his own religious life; and if, in our own days, M. BARBUSSE
(b. 1874) (*Le Feu, Clarté*) has returned strictly to the methods
of the school of Zola, most of our novelists are content to be
themselves, and to tell a story with skill and feeling, like the
brothers PAUL and VICTOR MARGUERITTE (b. 1860; b. 1866) in
Le Désastre, while we see M. RENÉ BOYLESVE (b. 1867) in *La
Becquée, La Jeune Fille bien élevée, La Leçon d'Amour dans un
Parc,* crowning naturalism, as it were, by making one forget it.

Contemporaneously with naturalism had appeared a less
conspicuous, but equally popular, development. The romantic
novel, in the hands of Octave Feuillet and Victor Cherbuliez,
the former with more imagination, the latter with more
ingenuity, had continued its course until it relapsed into the
feuilleton novel of George Ohnet. MM. RENÉ BAZIN (b. 1853)
(*La Terre qui meurt, Le Blé qui lève*) and HENRI BORDEAUX
(b. 1870) (*Les Roquevillard*) at the present moment are carrying
on an analogous method. Gifted with much higher powers,
some women novelists, such as Mmes MARCELLE TINAYRE (*La
Maison du Péché, La Vie amoureuse de François Barbazanges*),
GÉRARD D'HOUVILLE (*L'Inconstante*), CAMILLE MARBO (*Le Sur-
vivant*) and COLETTE WILLY (*La Vagabonde* and *L'Entrave*) show
both observation and sensibility in their charming novels;
a master, HENRI DE RÉGNIER (b. 1864), produces from all sorts
of material a masterpiece like *Tito-Bassi*; and the novel of
adventure is revived by M. Pierre Benoît in a more discreet but
less frank form than in that of Ducray-Duminil.

If there was an intentional reaction against naturalism, it must
be placed about 1880 and be associated with the names of Paul
Bourget and Melchior de Voguë. The influence of foreign
literature undoubtedly contributed to it and made it a forward
rather than a backward movement. We hear of the Dickens

"side" of Daudet, and there is no doubt that acquaintance with the Russian novelists enlarged French observation, which was perhaps too minute and too worldly. PAUL BOURGET (b. 1852) in his somewhat artificial analyses (*Cruelle Énigme, Le Disciple*) knows how to preserve the gift of impassioned narrative, but in psychology he is greatly surpassed by ÉDOUARD ROD (1857–1910) (*La vie privée de Michel Tessier*). MELCHIOR DE VOGUË (1829–1910) reintroduced national spirit into the novel. But the idea of a school was thenceforward given up. Rustic manners are depicted with strength and simplicity by MM. FERDINAND FABRE (1830–1898) (*L'Abbé Tigrane, Le Chévrier*) and ÉMILE POUVILLON (1840–1896) (*Cesette, Les Antibel*). It is by the force of personal genius that M. PIERRE LOTI has given us under the name of novels (*Pêcheur d'Islande, Mon frère Yves*) books which are poems, and that MM. Barrès and France, of whom we shall speak again later, have enclosed the essence of their thought in a loose and ill-defined framework.

The Drama

The drama perhaps expresses the character of a period even better than the novel. We see it follow the general evolution, accentuating its phases instead of shading them off. The name of Alexandre Dumas *fils* (Émile Augier being already out of date) towers above his colleagues until his death in 1895. This realist, who was an observer as well as a moralist and a theorist, with the instinct for action and dialogue which he inherited from his father, represented and pilloried the whole of society on the stage. Nevertheless he kept his representations true to life, and showed, as was said by M. Larroumet, a philosophy which was within the comprehension of man. Always alive and sincere, he is a little exclusive in his moral prejudices, and, at this distance, one cannot help finding him rather narrow.

He seems so entirely to have absorbed theatrical activity in his time that originality in this line had to devote itself either to dramatic technique with Victorien Sardou whose sole merit, if he has any, is that he adapted feuilletons cleverly for the stage, or to operetta and vaudeville, which were charmingly exemplified by Meilhac, Halévy, and Labiche. But after Pailleron, who was ingenious, agreeable, and simple, after a few happy experiments in rhymed plays, and after the somewhat academic heroism of Henri de Bornier and the truculent and laboured affectation of Edmond Rostand, who discovered a few new subjects only to spoil them, we must turn to our contemporaries to find dramatic writing which equals, if it does not surpass, that of Alexandre Dumas.

MM. François de Curel, de Porto Riche, Bernstein, and H. Bataille are writers full of sober energy. It may be said, in a certain sense, that Henri Becque (*Les Corbeaux*) and the *Théâtre Libre* showed them the way by an active and sardonic spirit of observation, which delighted in the least agreeable aspects of life. But certainly they went further. The psychology of M. de Curel, which is social and perhaps a little elementary in his theses and his deductions, does not prevent him from dealing with subjects which concern the future of society. M. de Porto Riche, occasionally rather brutal, sets forth the deplorable excesses of almost exclusively sensual love. MM. Bernstein and Bataille, whose methods are superior to the somewhat easy-going ones of Hervieu, of Lavedan, or of Fabre, assert themselves as the masters of the contemporary stage, the former by his satire, vigorous sometimes to excess, the latter by a psychological intuition, which would remind us of Racine, were it not that he writes in a deplorable style. Both are conspicuous for sound technique, poetical feeling, and an acute sense of reality.

Poetry

The current of naturalism lost itself in poetry, where it barely found a place in that attempt at impersonality which was the boast of the Parnassian school. But we must not be misled by words. The poet is defined as a "naked soul," and he cannot hide himself without becoming insignificant. As a matter of fact, Leconte de Lisle is a powerful lyrical poet, as can be seen in *Les Montreurs*, and the work even of Heredia, antique and external in appearance, is full of feeling. What, however, characterises contemporary poetry is a kind of dissolution, followed by a reconstruction of forms and numberless experiments, which bear the mark of a multitude of schools and temperaments.

In the contempt for all form and for all rules it was enough that the imagination should conceive some new, or apparently new, mode of writing or not writing in verse, for a crowd of imitators at once to take the field. It was in this way that the fashion, soon to become a mania, of the *vers libre* was spread, and symbolists and decadents, vying with each other in boldness and too often in absurdity, brought what they called the poetry of unintelligibility, which was still melodious in the hands of Stéphane Mallarmé, down to the fantasies of Marinetti, whom no one, fortunately, takes seriously.

And yet, if poetry is sensibility, no period seems more fitted for it than our own, refined by centuries of civilisation, by the quest at any cost for new emotions, and by convulsions through which no social body has ever passed before. The Romanticists thought that they had sounded the whole gamut of human sensations, but they have been left behind, and the heart has been excited to such a pitch that no words have been sufficient to express it, and the whole vocabulary has been robbed of meaning in order to restore to it a purely musical value.

Three poets, foreign but French-speaking, have exercised a fruitful influence in this matter. Rodenbach, Maeterlinck, and Verhaeren, by the freedom of their forms and the almost sickly delicacy of their temperaments, have opened new paths to modern sensibility. They have been widely imitated. Possibly they prepared the public to accept, after an unpardonable hesitation, a genius great in spite of his blemishes—PAUL VERLAINE (1844–1896), who, following Baudelaire, has carried the expression of human sensibility to a point which cannot be surpassed. It may be said without hesitation that Verlaine is a great poet, perhaps pre-eminently *the* poet. The author of *Sagesse* and *Poèmes Saturniens* surpasses not only the symbolic school, but all other schools. In the course of an unhappy and sometimes degraded life he felt all that it is given to man to feel, and he knew how to concentrate in a poem or in a single verse all the experience which a human soul can acquire, all the suffering which can strike an unfortunate man, and this with an art which is full of imagination and variety and for the most part flawless.

Amidst the multitude of poets a twofold current is clearly

visible. Some, following Sully Prudhomme, Albert Mérat, Léon Dierx, and Emmanuel Des Essarts, keep, so to speak, to the high road, and make their art before all things a kind of eloquence. Amongst these should be mentioned as most representative, MM. Jean Richepin, Jean Aicard, Edmond Haraucourt. The others continue the tradition of our great emotional poets, and speak above all to the heart, the most secret chords of which they succeed in touching. Of these (after the vanished masters, Albert Samain and Charles Guérin), we may mention such men as MM. Maurice Magre, Henri Bataille, and Henri de Regnier. A double reaction, at first neo-classical with Jean Moréas and Raymond de la Tailhède, then neo-Catholic with Péguy and M. Claudel, has also left deep traces on French literary art. To these, in our own days, must be added the marvellous poetess, Mme la Comtesse Mathieu de Noailles, who rises above these diverse tendencies.

The literature of ideas

One merit of French literature, at least until recent and less favoured days, was to possess historians, philosophers, and men of science who were also men of letters. If, after 1870, Fustel de Coulanges and Taine carried on with less brilliancy the work of Michelet and Victor Cousin, they surpassed their former masters in knowledge, in severity, and in sobriety of style, which, while not devoid of picturesqueness, was much more impressionist. Taine, in particular, has stamped his influence on a whole generation of thinkers, the last of whom are dying out under our eyes. From him sprang Théodule Ribot and all the school of psycho-physiology, while, as to the historians, they have only surpassed him, at least in exactness, by perfecting his methods; and our writers of monographs, as well as our sociologists, even while sometimes pretending to repudiate him, do not fail to follow in his footsteps.

His influence has perhaps been most marked in criticism, the *genre* which has collected round it, since 1870, the most original thinkers. Nevertheless, the native genius of the writers has exceeded the limits fixed by the *Philosophie de l'Art,* and has only retained its spirit. Paul Bourget, who has best kept within these limits, has enlarged them by a psychology superior to that of his novels. The great work of Sainte-Beuve and of Scherer fell into not unworthy hands with Jules Lemaître, Ferdinand Brunetière, and Émile Faguet. By a charm which does not exclude depth, by a dogmatic strength which yet remains intelligent, by an incredible flexibility of mind, these writers have left inexhaustible treasures of ideas in the mass of their books and articles. In our day too, critics such as MM. Lanson and Doumic are not unworthy of their predecessors.

We have alluded to a certain tendency to literary heaviness, caused by the abuse of technical terms and erudition. The merit of form however has contributed to the success of M. Bergson, and in the most specialised works of science, as in entomology with J.-H. Fabre, we find too some charming authors.

But, by way of conclusion, let us give ourselves up to the great currents of thought which prevailed at the end of the last century and the beginning of this; in this way we shall be best able to appreciate their full artistic and intellectual development.

Conclusion

A considerable part of the literary period of which we have broadly sketched the outlines is dominated by the great names of Renan and, later, of Anatole France. We find in them the same art, the same spirit, the same supreme genius in plan and execution. The inheritors of centuries of civilisation, which they were so marvellously fitted to understand, these two men have looked on modern existence with a glance which pierced it through and through, and have explored the chain which links us with the invisible abyss of nothingness. Renan wove for Christianity the "purple shroud where sleep the dead gods" and placed it in the grave with pious impiety. Nevertheless, being systematically an idealist and an optimist, he could not resign himself to the renunciation of hope, and he chose to believe in the religion of progress, and in a kind of evolution, by which God, really absent, would fashion himself by degrees. He believed in science and in Germany, two errors which he paraded too complacently to be altogether deceived by them.

M. France, who knows everything, is not a historian by profession nor a systematic philosopher. He has simply drawn from the aspect of things and from the annals of men all the beauty to be found in them, and in books which escape all classification by their variety and all analysis by their perfection, he has written some of the most luminous and the most profound pages which ever came from the hands of man. Seeing that he has so fully possessed and reflected life, it is curious to see him treated as a nihilist, did not one know that, to those who have a faith, nihilism consists in the mere absence of that faith.

It is by these directions and under these influences that a state of mind has been formed, which has been much attacked, which presents some dangers, but which, all allowances being made, is eminently favourable to artistic development. Writers and philosophers, somewhat depressed by recent reverses, touched by scepticism, and robbed both of religious beliefs and political faith, turned away from direct action and a world which they found repulsive, to seek for their ideal in themselves, and to console themselves by the worship of the Muses for the failure of the old values. They are still accused of dilettantism, and it is true that they professed a great contempt for contingent realities and took refuge willingly enough in their "towers of ivory." But even so, their generous souls did not give up hope, and their industry struggled to define the ideal which they had conceived, and to invent new forms of expression. It is to these anxieties, to these cares, to this untiring work that we owe a form of literary art which is rather strained, rather diverse, and sometimes a little deceptive, but which has been able to make itself famous by masters who are the equals of the classical writers, and to give an original and definite note to the novel, poetry, and the drama.

Thought is in a perpetual state of oscillation throughout the ages, and a reaction was bound to come. Attempts have been made to date it from M. Barrès, without observing that in his search for sensation at any price and his cult of the *moi* this writer is closely allied to his predecessors. In reality this movement appeared about 1912, as is evident by the inquiry published by MM. Henri Massis and Alfred de Tarde under the title of *Les Jeunes Gens d'Aujourd'hui*[1], and it was, above all, a movement in the moral, social, and religious order.

[1] See G. Truc, *Une crise intellectuelle*, 1919.

Men wished to resume the taste for action, to interpret the word in its physical and even brutal sense, to regenerate politics, to establish the world on its old foundations, and to restore the old virtues to their former lustre. Sports have been cultivated, business carried on, colonisation encouraged. The literature which helped these new ideas affected strength and sobriety, and even a certain contempt for ideas.

Some men of genius appear at this stage of the literary history of France. CHARLES PÉGUY (1873–1914) started *Les Cahiers de la Quinzaine* and did the work of a historian, a polemical writer, and a poet. With powerful irony he attacked the methods of the Sorbonne, which were founded on German erudition; as a mystic, he wrote a long and grandiose poem, in a singular and difficult form, midway between prose and verse, in which in order to relate the history of the inner life of Joan of Arc he revealed a mind akin to the 16th century, even while belonging profoundly to his own age.

M. Paul Claudel, who followed a similar path, together with works of less merit, brought out an admirable trilogy: *L'Otage*, *Le Pain dur*, and *Le Père humilié*, wherein he contrasts the inflexible harshness of the law of justice with the beneficent "free gift" of Christian charity. On the other hand, Charles Maurras returned to the simpler beauty of the classical style, and, although his claim to be a political thinker may be denied, as a man of letters he is accepted by everyone.

Such was the evolution which was brutally arrested by the War. The blow was so heavy that we must not hope to see it resume its course all at once, and it is probable that it will not do so without its character being modified. The men who have lived through such terrible years will no longer weave theories about "action." On the other hand, literature like the arts is becoming the victim of a strange disaffection. In these difficult times more thought is given to business than to good education and good literature. Nevertheless, the soul does not die. If it seems hard to formulate even an approximate judgment on the French literature of to-morrow, we may hope all things from the French genius, which has survived such terrible trials, and which has already borne such splendid fruit.

BIBLIOGRAPHY

General

G. Lanson, *Manuel bibliographique de la Littérature française moderne*,
with a supplement, 1909–1914. *Histoire de la Langue et de la Littérature
française*, ed. L. Petit de Julleville, III.–VIII., 1897–1899. G. Lanson,
Histoire de la Littérature française, 14th ed. 1918. G. Saintsbury, *A short
history of French literature*, 7th ed. 1917. C. H. C. Wright, *A history of
French literature*, 1912. E. Lintilhac, *Histoire générale du théâtre en France*,
4 vols. published, 1904– . G. Saintsbury, *A history of the French novel*,
1917–1919.

Excellent monographs on most of the principal writers have appeared
in the series of *Les grands Écrivains français* edited by J.-J. Jusserand.
Sainte-Beuve's numerous volumes; E. Faguet, *Études littéraires*, 4 vols.
(one for each century from the 16th to the 19th), 1885–1893; F. Brunetière, *Études critiques sur l'Histoire de la Littérature française*, 8 vols.
1880–1907 will all be found of great service.

Admirable critical texts have been published by the *Société des Textes
français modernes* since 1905.

16th century

Revue du seizième siècle, 1913– ; a continuation of the *Rev. des
Études rabelaisiennes*. 10 vols. 1903–1912. A. Tilley, *The literature of the
French Renaissance*. 2 vols. Cambridge. 1904.

Marot, ed. Jannet. 4 vols. 1868–1872. Rabelais, ed. Marty-Laveaux.
6 vols. 1868–1903; edd. Lefranc, Boulenger, Clouzot, Dorveaux, Plattard
and Sainéan. 2 vols. published, 1912– . Marguerite d'Angoulême,
L'Heptaméron. 3 vols. 1879. Calvin, *Institution de la Religion Chrétienne* (text of 1560), ed. F. Baumgarten; (text of 1541), edd. A.
Lefranc and H. Chatelain. Des Periers, *Œuvres français*, ed. L. Lacour.
2 vols. 1856. Ronsard, ed. P. Laumonier. 8 vols. 1914–1919. Du Bellay,
Œuvres poétiques, ed. H. Chamard. 3 vols. published, 1908– . Desportes,
ed. A. Michiels. 1858. Garnier, ed. W. Foerster. 4 vols. Heilbronn.
1883.

Monluc, Brantôme, and D'Aubigné's *Histoire universelle* have all been
edited for the *Soc. de l'hist. de France*. A new edition of Monluc, by
P. Courteault, is in process of publication and one of D'Aubigné's works,
other than the *Histoire universelle*, is announced.

Montaigne, edd. E. Courbet and Ch. Royer. 5 vols. 1872–1900 (text of
1595); ed. F. Strowski (reprint of the Bordeaux text). 4 vols. 1906–1921.
La Satire Ménippée, ed. Ch. Read, 1876. Bertaut, ed. A. Chenevière,
1891. Regnier, ed. Courbet, 2nd ed. 1875. Henri IV, *Lettres intimes*,
ed. L. Dussieux, 1876. François de Sales. 12 vols. 1857–1859.

17th century

There are admirable editions of Malherbe, Corneille, Pascal, De Retz,
La Rochefoucauld, Mme de Sévigné, Molière, Racine, La Fontaine, La
Bruyère, and Fénelon's *Télémaque* in *Les Grands Écrivains de la France*.
Descartes, edd. C. Adam and P. Tannery. 12 vols. published, 1897–1910;
ed. V. Cousin. 11 vols. 1824–26. Boileau, ed. Berriat Saint-Prix. 4 vols.

1830. Bossuet. 43 vols. Versailles. 1815–19. Bourdaloue. 17 vols. 1822–26. Malebranche, ed. J. Simon. 2 vols. 1842. Fénelon. 34 vols. Versailles. 1820–30. Massillon, ed. Blampignon. 4 vols. 1865–84. Regnard. 6 vols. 1822. Dancourt. 12 vols. 1760. Saint-Simon, edd. A. Chéruel and Ad. Regnier *fils*. 22 vols. 1873–81; ed. A. de Boislisle in G.E.F. 1879– . (32 volumes published.)

18th century

Fontenelle. 8 vols. 1790–92; *Histoire des Oracles*, ed. L. Maigron, 1907. Bayle, *Dict. historique et critique*. 5th ed. 4 vols. 1740; *Œuvres diverses*. 4 vols. 1727–31; *Pensées sur la Comète*, ed. A. Prat. 2 vols. 1911–12. Montesquieu, ed. E. Laboulaye. 7 vols. 1875–79; *Lettres persanes*, ed. Barckhausen. 2 vols. 1915. Vauvenargues, ed. Gilbert. 2 vols. 1857. Voltaire, ed. Beuchot. 72 vols. 1828; ed. Moland (22 vols. 1880–85); *Lettres philosophiques*, ed. G. Lanson. 2 vols. 1908. G. Bengesco, *Bibliographie des Œuvres de V.* 4 vols. 1882–90. Rousseau, ed. Musset Pathay. 23 vols. 1823–26; *Political writings*, ed. C. E. Vaughan. 2 vols. 1915. Diderot, ed. Assézat and Tourneux. 20 vols. 1875–79. Buffon, ed. Lanessan. 12 vols. 1883. Lesage, 12 vols. 1821. Marivaux. 10 vols. 1825–30. Chénier, *Poésies*, ed. L. Becq de Fouquières; *Prose*, ed. L. Becq de Fouquières. 1872; *Œuvres*, ed. Dimoff. 2 vols. published, 1906– .

19th century

G. Pellissier, *Le Mouvement littéraire au xix* *siècle*, 1889; *Le Mouvement littéraire contemporain*, 1901. Jules Lemaître, *Les Contemporains*. 8 vols. 1885–89; *Impressions de Théâtre*. 10 vols. 1888–98. F. Brunetière, *Le Roman Naturaliste*, 1883. P. Bourget, *Essais de Psychologie contemporaine*, 1883; *Nouveaux Essais*, 1886. M. de Voguë, *Le Roman Russe*, 1886. A. Poizat, *Le Symbolisme de Baudelaire à Claudel* [1919].

There is an *édition définitive* of Victor Hugo in 62 vols. 1880–98 and one of Balzac in 24 vols. 1869–1876. Critical editions of Lamartine's *Premières Méditations* and Hugo's *La Légende des Siècles* have recently been published in the *Grands Écrivains de la France*.

CHAPTER IX

ARCHITECTURE

THE "Gothic art of France expired in a blaze of glory"[1], the glory of the Flamboyant style; and by its death French architecture was reborn in such wise as to meet the needs of an altered civilisation.

If the obvious and superficial character of this rebirth is the imitation of the monuments of Greece and Rome, this was not the result, as was once maintained, of a perverse craze introduced from Italy by pedantic nobles and *literati*. The phenomenon is too wide-spread and too persistent to be so explained. It prevailed because it expressed deep underlying movements.

Europe since the Middle Ages has built in a quasi-Classic manner because with the Renaissance her life and thought came nearer than at any time since the barbarian invasions to the life and thought of the ancients.

More than other lands Italy had maintained the Classical tradition in architecture as in other things. Gothic, the expression of all that was most foreign to it, had struck no deep roots there, but remained an exotic influence affecting little more than the decorative system. At the Renaissance Italian builders cast it aside to resume national methods and to reform their own national style in the light of their own ancient monuments.

France and England, when they experienced a similar evolution in civilisation and thought, made independent attempts to adapt their native Gothic to the new conditions. But in their case it was a sturdy growth not easily bent, so that eventually they too trod the path cleared by Italy towards the style from which Gothic itself drew its origins, a path peculiarly congenial to an age enamoured of humanistic studies.

The three great moulding influences of medieval society affecting architecture were the Church, feudalism, and corporate

[1] Sir T. G. Jackson in *Medieval France*, p. 386.

life. The Gothic style grew up from first to last under the inspiration of the ideals of the Church, the all-embracing medium in which human life moved; so much was this so that features evolved under stress of church needs were transferred to domestic and military architecture. Secular architecture was further conditioned by the prevalence of feudal warfare. Its most imposing works were fortresses. Domestic building had but little scope for development either in the confinement of walled cities or in the insecurity of the countryside, where it was all but limited to castles and monasteries. Building was largely carried out either by religious communities or by guilds of craftsmen.

Now the 15th and 16th centuries were marked by a great shrinkage in the influence of the Church and the destruction of its monopoly of education, by the rise of national monasteries and the suppression of private warfare, by new methods of warfare against which the old fortresses were useless, and by a decay of corporate life. With increased security and wider dissemination of knowledge a large class of peaceful, educated, and wealthy laymen emerged. Society came to be organised on an individualistic basis. Last but not least the rediscovery of Classical literature and art exercised a notable influence in modifying men's outlook.

Such were the conditions which were to remould the spirit as well as the forms of architecture by altering the character of its aims, its purposes, and its workers. Fewer churches, convents, and castles were to be built, more palaces, mansions, manor-houses, and public buildings. The latter, not the former, set the standard. The craft guilds were superseded by individual architects.

It is scarcely more fanciful to see in the hazardous equipoise of rib-vaulting and flying buttress, in the upward rush of pointed arch and spire, in the mysterious intricacies of plan and detail a reflection of the restless physical energy, the ardent spiritual aspirations, and imaginative mysticism of the Middle Ages, than of its turbulent unrest in the crenellated towers, loop-holed walls, and scant windows opening on to narrow courts.

As the generous fenestration and airy galleries of the Renaissance expanding towards the sun and the open country testify tó a sense of security allowing free indulgence in comforts and pleasures, so the calm reign of law and the habit of intellectual reflection find their expression in an architecture of order and repose, where schemes are clearly thought out from the first, where dead weight construction satisfies the eye of its stability, where breadth is sought rather than height, and the qualities most valued are spaciousness, symmetry, and proportion, where the dominant forms are the cornice and the lintel, the round arch and the dome.

Now these were precisely the characteristics of ancient architecture, and the example of Italy in studying ancient architecture merely hastened and coloured a process which must in any case have taken its course in England and France. But such was the charm and novelty of Italian detail and ornament, that it was this side of the movement which at first had most effect, and it was somewhat later that the basic principles, which Italy had rediscovered, or rather had never wholly abandoned, gained full influence on the architecture of her neighbours.

English builders began to enter upon this course in the 14th century, by the invention of the Perpendicular style and pursued it further in the later Tudor. They depressed the two-centred arch to the four-centred form and eventually to the lintel; they elaborated a system of vaulting akin to the Roman; they expanded their windows laterally into many lights; they delighted in long, low, parapeted roofs and a general horizontality of effect; and lastly they began to aim at symmetrical arrangements of plan. All this was without the aid of Italian example, which had no serious influence till the second half of the 16th century.

In France, where the curvilinear manner grew up later and was carried further than in England, the same tendencies, if less marked, are traceable from the middle of the 15th century onwards. The arch loses its point and begins to assume a flat semi-elliptical or five-centred form and is eventually replaced by a lintel, first with, afterwards without, curved haunches, but occasionally becomes semi-circular. A certain predisposition to horizontality and to spacious or even symmetrical setting-out appears here and there, and external galleries become frequent. But rib-vaulting and high-pitched roofs with tall dormers and chimney-stacks persist and the window of two lights remains the rule; it expands by adding lights above, not at the side. The cross formed by the single mullion and transom give it the name of *croisée*.

§ I. TRANSLATION AND EARLY RENAISSANCE (1494–1589)

Styles of Louis XII and Francis I—French Masons and Italian Decorators

A few minor works in the Renaissance manner were executed in French churches between 1460 and 1480 by Italian sculptors in the employ of the House of Anjou, such as the chapel of St Lazarus in the old cathedral of Marseilles.

But the first introduction of any large number of Frenchmen to Renaissance art was brought about by the expedition of Charles VIII to Naples (1494–5), after which kings, prelates, and nobles frequently imported Italian artists to assist in the decoration of their buildings. Charles VIII himself brought a group of such craftsmen and designers to work at Amboise. Others settled at Tours and other places in and about the Loire Valley, then the chief resort of the Court. Few of these were architects in the full sense of the word, or, if they were, had much opportunity of influencing the general design of edifices. But many buildings erected during the reign of Charles VIII and that of Louis XII (1498–1515) show features and ornament of Italian character, woven almost haphazard into the web of native Gothic design. For instance, the façade of St Pierre at Avignon is decorated with beribboned medallions, a cornice in Louis XII's wing at Blois (finished 1503) shows an egg and dart member, while Italian elements are introduced more liberally at Gaillon, the country seat of the Archbishops of Rouen (1497–1510), the stair towers at Châteaudun and St Ouen, the Archbishop's palace at Sens, the Hôtel d'Alluye at Blois, and the Hôtels de Ville at Dreux and Orleans. This mixed manner is generally known under the name of "Style Louis XII," and the first generation of Italian workers in France as the "School of Amboise."

These for the most part came from the north of Italy. The most eminent among them was FRA GIOVANNI GIOCONDO, the architect of the charming Palazzo del Consiglio at Verona. But no work in France can be certainly traced to him except the Pont Notre-Dame in Paris, though he is believed to have had some share in directing the works at Gaillon. They did not therefore represent the austere Tuscan school, in whose work a building told preeminently by its general proportions, and ornament was confined to a few crucial points, but the more luxuriant Lombardo-Venetian school, with whom ornament took a more important place and whose buildings were lavishly adorned in every part with delicate decoration small in scale and low in relief. Their ideal was not the Strozzi Palace at Florence but the Certosa at Pavia.

These superficial aspects were naturally the first to be imitated by the French, and indeed this was inevitable where the tasks assigned to Italians were mainly decorative.

By the opening years of Francis I's reign (1515–47) many French builders had learnt to work *à la mode d'Italie* in matters of ornament and detail, and even perhaps to conceive whole designs in the new manner. But a great influence was probably exercised at this time by BOCCADOR (Domenico Bernabei of Cortona, d. 1549), who carried out works in wood for the royal family, including models for castles, and in 1531 was summoned to Paris to act as architect to the new Hôtel de Ville.

In buildings sacred and secular, the aim of both Frenchman and foreigner had not advanced beyond the stage of clothing a French plan and conception in the new spirit and detail, enriching it with the new ornament, pilasters and arabesques, dolphins, *amorini*, and shells, and adding a few comforts while omitting no accustomed features, even, as in matters of fortification, long after they had outlived their use. Thus machicolations survived till late in the 16th century and moats in some cases till the 18th. In church building this conservatism was even more marked. There Gothic survived, almost unaffected, here and there, while many of the medieval crafts, such as that of stained glass, carried on their methods well into the 17th century.

Thus, however Italianate the builders and their employers might be in intention, their buildings remained French at the core though robed in Italian dress. Nothing could be more unlike than two such houses—both it may be observed rising out of the water—as the Palazzo Vendramin and the Château of Azay-le-Rideau, or than two such churches as S. Spirito of Florence and St Eustache of Paris.

The resultant style known by the name of Francis I has thus the picturesqueness of medieval work with the exquisiteness of Renaissance decoration. Its exuberant invention and youthful vitality, its spirit of adventure and romance, combined with the beauty and accomplishment of its craftsmanship, are full of fascination.

No completer example of the process of translation being carried out at this time could be found than St Eustache, in all respects of structure and arrangement a typical Gothic church, but detailed and decorated in the same manner as the châteaux of the Loire. It is one of the very few churches built as a whole in this style, though the works, begun in 1532, dragged on for over a century. But large portions of many others illustrate it with perhaps even greater charm, e.g. at St Étienne du Mont, Paris (1517–60); St Pierre, Caen; St Michel, Dijon; SS. Gervais and Protais, Gisors (1497–1558), St Pierre and Notre-Dame, Tonnerre (c. 1535–40); and several of the churches of Troyes. Charming examples of church fittings and tombs occur at Rouen, Beauvais, Evreux, and Sens cathedrals, St Bertrand de Comminges, St Florentin, La Ferté-Bernard, Beaumont le Roger and elsewhere.

The main work, however, is secular, particularly in great country houses, in which the castle plan survives. Such houses have retained the name of *château* ever since, though nothing castle-like may remain in them. Their buildings—with round towers jutting out on the external angles and other points of vantage—were grouped as convenience and the nature of the site might suggest and enclose one or more courts. Entrance to these was by a gate-house and from them spiral stairs in projecting towers or turrets led to the upper storeys. Communication on a level between the various blocks was still rare and only by means of external galleries, or of the sentry's walk carried on machicolations which still crowned the outer walls.

The town mansion or *hôtel* only differs from the *château* in not being free on all sides or surrounded by a moat. In both the front of the court was often closed by a mere curtain wall with or without a covered way running along its inner side and broken by the gate-house.

On this canvas the Renaissance builders embroidered, at first merely decorating in the new manner, but later reducing the whole to an ordered symmetrical scheme laid out on a rectangular plan, and gradually substituting square towers for round, stairs in straight flights for the spiral *vis*, and generally eliminating the fortress element.

Francis I, an ardent art-lover, was a liberal promoter of Renaissance architecture. Some of the best work of the day is to be found in his buildings, few of which he was able to complete. The N.W. wing at Blois (begun 1519 but not finished till 1570) is notable for the three tiers of galleries on the outer front, and for its court façade with windows grouped in vertical lines framed in pilasters—a feature characteristic of the period—a noble *cornicione*, and a richly sculptured open polygonal stair (Plate I). The building in its early stages was carried out by Jacques Sourdeau (d. 1530) and his son Denis (d. 1534).

The castle of Chambord (begun 1526) with a regular plan preserves the tradition of the donjon or keep and ponderous round towers, but has its walls adorned with delicate pilasters and cornices, and bursts forth at the roof level into a rich efflorescence of dormers, turrets, and chimney-stacks carved and panelled and inlaid with marble. Its donjon is divided at each storey into four self-contained suites by a hall planned as a Greek cross; in the centre of this rises a great spiral staircase in which two independent goings are intertwined (Plate II). The model was made by Boccador, and the building carried out by Denis Sourdeau, Pierre Nepveu (d. 1538), Jacques Coqueau (d. 1569) and others.

The château of Madrid in the Bois de Boulogne (begun 1528, destroyed at the Revolution) consisted of a rectangular block with external galleries running between square turrets, and was faced with enrichments in enamelled terra-cotta by Girolamo della Robbia (1480–1566), who was probably also the architect. The builders were Pierre Gadier (d. 1531) and Gatien François (d. after 1561). Colour decoration here gave the same joyous character which the delicately carved stone-work imparted to buildings in the Loire region, among which the châteaux of

PLATE I

FIG. I. CHATEAU OF BLOIS
Francis I's Stair (1515–19)

PLATE II

FIG. 3   NANTUA
Reredos in Church of St Michel (c. 1535)

FIG. 2.   CHATEAU OF CHAMBORD
(1526–44).   The Roofs

Azay-le-Rideau (1521), Chenonceaux (1520), Valençay (c. 1540), Villandry (c. 1540), the Hôtel de Ville at Beaugency (1526), and many lesser houses in Bourges, Orleans (Plate III), Tours, and Angers, deserve mention. Noteworthy buildings of a similar character in other parts of France are portions of the châteaux of Ecouen, La Rochefoucauld, Le Rocher-Mézanger and Fontaine-Henri, several hotels at Toulouse, Caen, and Troyes and the timber house of Diane de Poitiers (so-called) at Rouen.

Style of Henry II—The first architects

Till the middle of the reign of Francis I building was carried on largely under French master masons, who, if versatile, were men of lesser calibre than the great cathedral builders who had preceded them, and had little definite architectural training. Occasionally they had the assistance of Italian architects and generally of an army of accomplished decorators both Italian and French.

The newly imported ideas had hitherto affected rather the surface than the essence of architecture. The further development, which was inevitable as soon as the new spirit penetrated deeper, showed itself in the more virile qualities which the early Renaissance, with all its charm, still lacked—the qualities of breadth and repose obtained by greater sureness of proportions, a more monumental scale, fewer and larger parts and less ornament more judiciously distributed. These were the qualities which had come to be valued in the great architectural school fostered in the first quarter of the 16th century by the building activity of the Papal Court at St Peter's and in Rome at large. This school was much influenced by a closer study of ancient monuments and the works of architectural writers who, following in the steps of Vitruvius, sought to systematise the principles of design, and in particular the proportions and relations of the "Orders," i.e. the Roman column and its accompaniments, which, in earlier work, had been treated with great freedom. While these were applied with ease to Italian buildings with their lofty storeys, one of the initial difficulties with which French architects had to grapple was to adapt them to their own comparatively low storeys.

In the latter part of Francis I's reign the works at Fontaine-

bleau were largely in the hands of two painter architects—
"IL ROSSO" (1494–1541) and FRANCESCO PRIMATICCIO (1504–
70); and Francis gave a sinecure post there to the scholar architect SEBASTIANO SERLIO (1475–1554), to enable him to continue
his treatise on architecture and give architectural instruction.

At the same time, there was growing up a generation of
Frenchmen, no longer "master masons" but architects in something of the modern sense, who had made theoretic studies,
especially in Italy, where they would draw the ancient monuments and visit new buildings in course of erection. Among
these were the engraver architects, JACQUES ANDROUET DU
CERCEAU of Orleans (b. c. 1505–10—d. c. 1585), who after three
years in Rome spent his long life in producing architectural
designs and treatises and, though it is not certain that he
carried out any important building, was the founder of a family
of distinguished architects; and PHILIBERT DE L'ORME of Lyons
(b. c. 1505–10, d. 1570), who likewise studied in Rome and was
later employed to carry out many important works for the
French Court, and published several valuable treatises.

The earliest extant works to show the bolder manner of this
generation of workers are the Galerie de François I and its
decoration by Rosso (1530–3) and possibly the "Grotte des
Pins," all at Fontainebleau; and the Brézé tomb in Rouen
Cathedral (begun 1535) by JEAN GOUJON, mason, sculptor, and
architect (b. c. 1505–10, d. between 1564 and 1568).

The first important building in this manner is Primaticcio's
great château of Ancy-le-Franc, built for Catherine de' Medici
when Dauphiness (1538–46). The court is square and surrounded
by buildings of equal height like an Italian palazzo, but the
French tradition of steep roofs and towers, which are represented
by square angle pavilions, is followed. Its elevations are treated
with pilasters and show all the sobriety of the Roman School.

On similar lines was the rebuilding of the old castle of the
Louvre[1], begun in the last year of Francis and continued under
his son and grandsons[2] by PIERRE LESCOT (b. c. 1500–15, d.
1578)—a gentleman of scholarly tastes who had studied archi-

---

[1] The locality of a building when not mentioned is Paris.
[2] Only the western and half the southern sides were rebuilt at this time.
The old court was less than a quarter of the size of the present one.

PLATE III

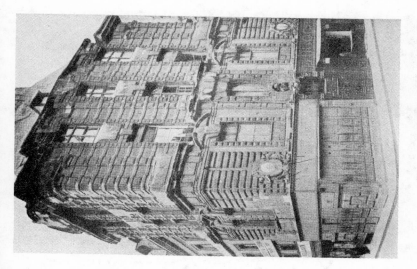

Fig. 5. ROUEN

House in Rue du Gros-Horloge (c. 1600)

Fig. 4. ORLEANS

So-called House of Agnès Sorel (R. c. 1530; L. c. 1500)

PLATE IV

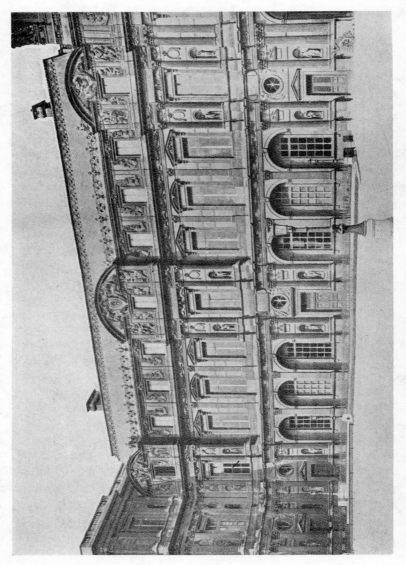

Fig. 6. THE LOUVRE COURT. By P. Lescot and J. Goujon (1546–78)

tecture and painting—assisted by Goujon. But, if the exterior
was even more austere than at Ancy, the façades of the court
were infinitely richer, the pilaster treatment being supplemented
by exquisite sculptural decoration concentrated on the most
telling points. The French character is maintained not only in
the high roofs and rich crestings but in the strongly marked
vertical divisions (Plate IV).

Other works of the same partnership are the Hôtel de Ligneris
(later Carnavalet, 1544–6) and the Fontaine des Nymphes
(1547–9).

Contemporary with the Louvre were some of De l'Orme's great
works. One of the earliest is the château of Anet (1548–54), built
for Henry II's mistress, Diane de Poitiers, which shows the now
standard type of plan for a great house—a central rectangular
Court of Honour with a screen-wall and gate-house in front,
flanked by subordinate courts and with a formal garden behind.
In other châteaux the main court is often approached through
one or more Fore Courts or Base Courts. One of his last works
was Catherine de' Medici's Palace of the Tuileries just outside
the walls of Paris, a magnificent scheme, only a fragment of
which was carried out (1564–70).

In both he displays a capacity for planning on a large scale,
hitherto rarely seen, and technical knowledge of mason craft
inherited from the old master masons, great beauty of detail
and occasionally of features, but also a tendency to restlessness
and over-elaboration foreign to the suaver manner of Lescot.
His other titles to fame are the invention of a system of wood-
vaulting and of the so-called "French Order" in which the
drums in the shaft of a column are variously enriched.

JEAN BULLANT (b. c. 1515–25, d. 1578), who had also made the
Italian tour, though not always happy in his handling of the
Orders, made great strides towards a monumental conception of
design, as may be judged from his additions to the castles of his
patron the Constable Montmorency at Chantilly and Écouen.
He succeeded De l'Orme at the Tuileries.

Other noteworthy examples of the style of Henry II, which at
its best was one of rare distinction, are the eastern half of the
"Grande Galerie" running along the river from the Tuileries
towards the Louvre and the "Petite Galerie," joining this with

the rebuilt Louvre and possibly a work of Lescot; the châteaux of Bournazel, Graves, Sully, Le Pailly, and Tanlay; the Hôtels de Lamoignon in Paris and d'Assézat at Toulouse. The vast châteaux of Charleval and Verneuil, perhaps by Jacques du Cerceau, but more probably by his son Baptiste, no longer exist.

Church-work of the period is not important, but interesting examples of attempts to graft the new manner on to Gothic design are to be seen in the fronts of the Cathedral of Evreux, the church at Villeneuve-sur-Yonne and St Pierre at Auxerre and the transept at Le Grand Andely. The two chapels at Anet are noteworthy as exhibiting early attempts at classic planning as well as classic detail. One is a domed chapel by De l'Orme, the other, possibly by Bullant, has a barrel vault. Primaticcio's Valois mausoleum at St Denis, a radiating domical edifice in pure classic forms, was never completed and has disappeared.

The tombs of Francis I and Henry II at St Denis and church fittings such as those in the chapels at Écouen and Chantilly are admirable of their kind.

§ II. MATURE CLASSIC (1589–1793)

Style of Henry IV and Louis XIII—Utilitarianism and Baroque

The period of the Wars of Religion, which for thirty years devastated France under the last three Valois and continued till the first Bourbon was accepted by all parties, was unfavourable to building, but it was resumed with vigour under the re-organising government of Henry IV and Sully.

This was an age of practical common sense, when utility and economy were much studied, but which suffered from the coarsening effect of prolonged disorder. All this can be read in its architecture, which is solid, substantial, comfortable, and which makes large use of the cheaper materials such as brick for walling and wood for window frames.

It indulges as a rule in but little ornament, but when it does it is of a somewhat over-massive type with a tendency to the grotesque, betraying the influence of Italian, and still more of the heavier Flemish Baroque.

But the lesson of breadth and bold scale had been learned; and if the proportions incline to the ponderous, they are of monumental effect, and the ornament, if coarse, betrays sound

decorative feeling in its design and application. It is characteristic of the style that great play is made with "rustication"—
or the bossing out of stones, especially on angles and basements
—not only in the bands and coigns of stone introduced into
brickwork, but also in buildings wholly of stone. Openings one
above another are often connected by vertical strips of rustication known as *chaînes*, and the intervening wall surfaces are
decorated with panels and niches.

Typical of this vernacular architecture are the Place Royale
(now Place des Vosges) and the Place Dauphine built for Henry IV
(1600–4) by Nicolas de Châtillon (1547–1616), with their brick
walls supported on massive arcades and surmounted by tall slated
roofs with metal finials (*épis*), and the stone Hôtel Sully by
Jean du Cerceau (b. before 1590, d. after 1649) with its clumsy
sculpture and fine grouping. Other examples of the manner
are the châteaux of Les Ifs (*c.* 1612), Beaumesnil (1634–40),
Balleroy (1626–36) (Plate VI), Cany Barville (1640–6), Courances,
and Cheverny, and the Hôtels de Montescot at Chartres and de
Vogüe at Dijon (1607–14) (Plate V), as well as the Galerie des
Cerfs, Horse-shoe Stair, and Baptistère de Louis XIII (*c.* 1600)
at Fontainebleau.

On a more monumental scale is the Palace of the Luxembourg
(Plate XI), built (1615–24) for Marie de' Medici, widow of
Henry IV, by the leading architect of the day, SALOMON DE
BROSSE (b. *c.* 1560, d. 1626), like Jean du Cerceau, a grandson
of Jacques Androuet du Cerceau. In plan and conception it is
a typical French château, with a one-storeyed screen and two-
storeyed wings leading up to the loftier main block at the rear
of the courts. From the fact that its decorations are rusticated
throughout from top to bottom it is supposed to be in imitation
of the Queen's early home, the Pitti Palace at Florence.

The work of JACQUES LE MERCIER (1585–1654), De Brosse's
successor as royal architect, is typical of the age of Louis XIII;
while making no advance in planning or refinement it maintains
its monumental character.

He continued the interrupted rebuilding of the Louvre on an
extended scale, doubling in length the western side of the court,
and adding as a centre-piece the somewhat heavy Pavillon de
Sully crowned with a square dome or hipped roof with curved
sides, a feature henceforward common in France. His most

important work, the Cardinal-Minister's vast château of Richelieu (1627–37), with its stately lay-out of courts gradually
increasing in dignity, no longer exists.

Style of Louis XIV—Baroque-Classic Compromise

The central years of the 17th century, the years of the Fronde,
of Corneille's *Cid* and of *Le Grand Cyrus*, were the heroic age of
the French nobility. A dying glow of chivalry then blended with
a new intellectual brilliance and the roughness of feudal manners
softened to a courtly urbanity. As is fitting, it was an age of
great houses in town and country, and these show considerable
advance in elegance and conveniences of planning. A society
refined in the *salons* of Madame de Rambouillet demanded it.

The stately but wind-swept grand staircase was moved from the
centre to one side, thus permitting of an uninterrupted range of
reception rooms *en suite*, facing the garden, and separated by
one or more courts from the filth and hubbub of the streets;
a new method of planning rooms back to back in each block,
where a single room had hitherto occupied the full depth,
ministered to cosiness.

The master mind in architecture was FRANÇOIS MANSART
(1598–1666), like Le Mercier probably a pupil of De Brosse, but
less successful in obtaining royal favour. It was largely his work
to wed an element of refined and classical taste and of sureness
of proportion to the Baroque monumentality of his day and thus
to prepare a style adapted to express the splendours of the
Grand Règne.

One of his earlier works, the Orleans Wing at Blois (1635–40),
a stately but somewhat grim pile, illustrates his feeling for
grandeur and noble scale, but as yet there is little of the refinement, which in his magnificent creation, the château of Maisons
(1642–51) (Plate XI), and his masterly additions to Madame de
Sévigné's town house[1] (Plate VII)—deftly incorporating Lescot
and Goujon's work—invests every line with an incomparable
distinction.

At Blois the quadrant sweeps of colonnade which lead up to
the main entrance may be noted as an example of a fashion
which long prevailed in French houses.

[1] Hôtel Carnavalet. See above, p. 541.

PLATE V

DIJON. HOTEL VOGUË (1614)

FIG. 7. ENTRANCE TO COURT   FIG. 8. CHIMNEY PIECE

PLATE VI

FIG. 9. CHATEAU OF BALLEROY (*c.* 1630)

FIG. 10. CHATEAU OF VAUX-LE-VICOMTE
By L. Le Vau (1656–60)

Mansart is credited with the type of roof bearing his name, in which the lower part of the slope is at a steeper angle than the upper, thus affording better attic rooms. This change was accompanied by the disappearance of the tall stone dormers (*lucarnes*), which were replaced by less conspicuous ones in wood covered with metal (*mansardes*). In the windows, about the same time, the *croisée* began to be omitted and simple "French windows" used, with wood glazing bars instead of leading. The sash-window had but a short vogue in France.

Several of the great houses of Louis XIV's minority were the work of LOUIS LE VAU (1612–70), an accomplished architect, more pliant to the behests of imperious clients than his older contemporary, but without Mansart's supreme sureness of touch.

In his Hôtel Lambert (1649), in the Ile St Louis, is a graceful example of the old central open staircase, while at Vaux-le-Vicomte (1656–60)—Plate VI—the splendid Fouquet's palatial seat, the centre is occupied by a great oval domed saloon, the stiras are relegated to the sides, and various internal *dégagements* are provided between the apartments.

The sumptuous interiors were confided to that great organiser of decoration, CHARLES LE BRUN (1619–90), and express the character of the age by the enhanced scale of their features and the elimination of the coarse and grotesque and the over-elaborate from their ornament.

The balustraded court of honour—still surrounded by a moat—is approached through a vast fore court flanked by stately kennel and stable courts, and closed in by an iron screen supported by gigantic hermae. The further setting of the mansion was entrusted to ANDRÉ LE NÔTRE (1613–1700), whose work as garden designer was to sweep away the old system of niggled pleasances and make the garden co-extensive with the park, and to subordinate individual features—*parterres, boulingrins, cabinets de verdure, treillages*, fountains, gazebos—to a broad axial lay-out, with vistas bounded by walls of greenery and refreshed with sheets of water.

Le Vau's next important work was the Collège des Quatre Nations (now Palais Mazarin or de l'Institut) designed as a *vis à vis* to the enlarged Louvre. The domed chapel containing Mazarin's tomb is effectively led up to by curved wings between massivesquarepavilions. In this fine composition Le Vau combines a "Giant Order" (i.e. one running through more than one storey) with small Orders more successfully than he had done at Vaux.

Interesting extant examples of town houses of this period are the Hôtels d'Aumont by Mansart and Le Vau, d'Avaux by Pierre Le Muet (1591–1669), and de Beauvais (1656) by Antoine Le Pautre (1621–91). The last illustrates the charm that may be created out of the chaos of a shapeless and confined site by skilful geometric planning. Another example of fine planning with a vista through arcades and courts is the Hôtel de Ville at Lyons (1646–54) by Simon Maupin, restored (1674) after a fire by the younger Mansart.

An age of hôtels and châteaux was now to be eclipsed by one of palaces. With the death of Mazarin (1661) Louis' personal reign began. The *Roi Soleil* could only allow princes and nobles to shine as his satellites. Autocratic centralised government had reached its zenith, and while with Molière and Racine the French genius was producing the masterpieces of classical literature, the "Grand Manner" in architecture, brought to maturity by Mansart, enriched and expanded by the creators of Vaux-le-Vicomte, expressed the pomp and majesty of the monarchy in a series of splendid public works.

Architecture, however, needed one more element if it was fully to represent the unifying, centralising character of its period. The element of unity which Le Nôtre had introduced into garden design was to be contributed by the example of BERNINI and the performance of Perrault in the completion of the Louvre (1665–74). Le Vau had all but finished the enlarged court which only lacked its eastern front. To obtain an elevation of the required impressiveness a competition was held. Mansart's design, at first accepted and then rejected on account of his reputation for extravagance, is unfortunately unknown. Those of Le Mercier, Le Vau, Marot and others fell short of the desired degree of grandeur. The matter was referred to Bernini, who came from Rome and produced a scheme—which he claimed to be divinely inspired—and which though eventually discarded as too subversive of national traditions supplied the key to the situation. Its rugged Baroque feeling could hardly please in France, but while all previous designs were composed as groups

PLATE VII

FIG. 11. PARIS. HOTEL CARNAVALET

Front by F. Mansart (1661); Doorway by Lescot and Goujon (1544)

PLATE VIII

FIG. 12. CHATEAU OF VERSAILLES
Garden Front by L. Le Vau (1668–74) and J. H. Mansart (1678–81)

FIG. 13. PETIT TRIANON, VERSAILLES
By J.-A. Gabriel (1762–8)

of several units Bernini showed the way to treat a front more than 550 feet long as a single unit.

While the highly paid, but disgusted, Cavaliere was travelling homeward, an official of the Royal works obtained the king's acceptance of a design by his brother CLAUDE PERRAULT (1613–88), a scholar and savant who had seriously studied architecture. Perrault had learned Bernini's lesson of unity. He treated the front as a single unit almost devoid of vertical divisions, with a continuous basement and an all but continuous balustrade, which by the abandonment of high separate roofs forms the crowning member of the design, and is broken only by a central pediment. But by the pure classicality of his detail he made the innovation palatable to French taste. He enhanced the dignity of its effect by the noble range of coupled Corinthian columns which run between the solid blocks at the ends.

The greatness of the Grand Monarque was proclaimed with less suavity but equal insistence in the Porte St Denis (1672) by François Blondel and Le Brun and in the Hospice des Invalides (1671–4) by Libéral Bruand (1635–97).

But the turbulence of Paris had disgusted Louis and his supreme work was to be elsewhere. On the disgrace of Fouquet he inherited the band of distinguished men which the luxurious financier had gathered to minister to his ostentation, and gave ever wider scope for their genius. Molière was to delight him with *Tartuffe* and the *Bourgeois Gentilhomme*. Le Vau, Le Brun, and Le Nôtre were to create Versailles.

The stages by which the dainty little brick hunting lodge of Louis XIII, the "card castle" built by an unknown architect (1624), grew in the great years of his son's reign (1660–90) into the complex of buildings, housing not only the premier Court of Christendom but also the offices of the Royal government, cannot be described in detail here.

The original courtyard coincided with the present "Cour de Marbre" (Plate VIII), which preserves some vestiges of its ordinance. Before his death (1670) Le Vau had more than quadrupled its size by encasing it on its three outer faces in a building of stone, and prefaced it by a double fore court. What is now the central block towards the garden was thus formed with its long balustrade supplanting the peaked slated roofs and gilded *épis* and *lucarnes* of the original building. With its pleasant proportions and the quiet dignity of its pilastered elevations enriched with good sculpture the effect must have been more excellent than can be guessed from the completed palace as we know it. For this has faults due to and inevitable in later additions.

Le Vau's extensions soon proved inadequate and JULES HARDOUIN, called MANSART (1646–1710), a great-nephew of François, who was soon to be in sole control of the Royal works, began (1678) to provide further accommodation by building the two long wings which reduce the palace proper to the proportions of a mere central block, while leaving its projection excessive for such a feature. This had the effect of making the scale of Le Vau's detail too small, and, though Mansart did what he could to correct this by arching the windows and filling up the long recess in its main front, he could not entirely rectify it.

This last alteration gave Le Brun the opportunity for his "Salon des Glaces," the culmination of the gorgeous works of decoration by means of which, with the aid of an army of artists of all kinds, he had enriched not only the long suites of royal apartments, but also the gardens and minor residences with which they are dotted.

Among Mansart's works at Versailles are the "Grand Commun," the twin stable blocks, the [Grand] Trianon, whose two blocks were united later by the "Péristyle" designed by his pupil and brother-in-law ROBERT DE COTTE (1656–1735) and—most impressive of all—the noble orangery. His too, a few miles away, was the so-called Hermitage of Marly, a square block round an octagonal top-lit hall approached between a double range of isolated pavilions flanking a water-garden, and, at Paris, the Places des Victoires and Louis le Grand (now Place Vendôme), in which the motive of the Louvre Colonnade is applied to the grouping of a number of separate houses in a single architectural scheme.

Styles of the Regency and Louis XV—Rococo

When the 18th century opened, French architecture had attained to a settled framework not to be seriously shaken till struck by the general disturbing influences of the early 19th. But during the intervening years the outward and inward decking of this framework varied widely from time to time under the action and reaction of movements in social and political life.

The glamour of the *Grand Règne* faded before its sun had set. From the splendid discomforts of Versailles, from the restraints imposed by its rigid etiquette and the solemn pietism of Louis' declining years, society swung round to the pursuit of ease, amusement, and licence. Denied outlet in action, the nobles found it in talk and dalliance, and they cultivated brilliant conversation and amorous intrigue as fine arts. An age of *salons* and *boudoirs* and *petites maisons* succeeded one of stately halls and majestic palaces. The Rococo ousted the Grand Manner in internal decoration and even invaded architecture proper.

From Francis I to Louis XIII decoration had steadily grown in scale and depth of relief. If, with Le Brun and his contemporary, Antoine Le Pautre (1621–91), it had been purged of coarseness and confusion, it was still formal. Already, however, the 17th century showed symptoms of a change of taste in the dainty and capricious arabesques of Jean Bérain (1638–1711). Under the Regency and Louis XV the schemes of Watteau, Audran, Gillot, the Huets, and Cuvilliès became more and more fantastic. The graceful and the humorous, the exotic and the wanton mingle in their piquant compositions. Colour, delicate rather than gorgeous, is enhanced by gilding of varied tint and brilliance, and a profusion of mirrors adds to the general sparkle. The *rocaille*, a form of shell ornament, the palm branch and scroll in cunningly contrasted curves lend their sinuous lines. The Rococo like the Flamboyant allies itself with naturalesque forms, emancipates itself from the straight line and right angle, and has a vertical trend. Sometimes even symmetry is replaced by subtle schemes of balance.

The glittering *Galerie Dorée* of the Hôtel de Toulouse (now the Bank of France, 1713–19) by De Cotte is typical of the transition stage known by the name of *Régence*. Here the dado, the pilasters, the cornice still hold their own, though they swell and surge and taper. In the Oval Saloon of the Hôtel de Soubise (1735) by GERMAIN BOFFRAND (1667–1745), another pupil of Mansart, they disappear altogether in a ripple of subtle curves, while in the designs of J.-A. MEISSONNIER (1693–1750) all solidity of consistency appears to have vanished.

Except in such matters as the rounding-off of corners, the flowing outlines of stair treads and balconies, of vases and panels, the sinuosities of iron-work and the gesticulation of statues, architecture proper is little affected by the fashion and maintains its monumental character. Here and there a garden pavilion or a minor town house would allow itself greater licence, but such a design as that of Meissonnier for the façade of St Sulpice (1726), in which the sway of curve and counter-curve is supreme both in plan and elevation, had little chance of being erected. Apart from such minutiae as those mentioned, the great buildings of this period might belong to the age of Louis XIV. Such are the stupendous stables of Chantilly (1719–35) and the aristocratic Hôtel de Biron (1728), both by Aubert, the Hôtel de Matignon (1721) by Courtonne, the stately buildings on the quay at Bordeaux (begun 1730) by the elder Gabriel (1667–1742), the Capitole at Toulouse (1750–3) by Cammas, and even the Hôtel de Ville at Nancy (1750–7) by Héré de Corny a pronounced Rococo designer. None of these overstep the limits indicated or depart from established standards of composition, the last three examples being in fact based on the system of Perrault's Louvre. The Place Royale at Bordeaux and the buildings of Duke Stanislas at Nancy forming a group of effectively linked *places* are examples of fine town planning.

Style of Louis XVI—Classical Reaction

Before 1740 in the height of the Rococo movement symptoms of an impending return swing of the pendulum began to show themselves in the chaste and restrained classicality of designs for theatrical scenery, and for the façade of St Sulpice (1733) by JEAN-NICOLAS SERVANDONY (1695–1766), who had studied under Panini in Rome, and in Bouchardon's Fontaine de Grenelle (1739). This reaction was hastened by the interest aroused by the discoveries at Pompeii and Herculaneum. Architectural students woke up to the fact that classical studies did not begin and end with the works of Bernini, but might be extended with profit to the remains of ancient Rome and even to those of Greece hitherto practically unknown. This was the course taken by JACQUES-GERMAIN SOUFFLOT (1709–80) who visited Paestum in 1748.

By 1750 JACQUES-ANGE GABRIEL (1699–1782), the Royal Architect and the descendant of a long line of architects, had gone over to the side of the purists. Every one was then reading Rousseau and a new-born enthusiasm for the simple life began to associate the Rococo of the gilded *salons* with the vice and artificiality of a corrupt society. Classicism with its severer lines was hailed as the outward sign of virtue and of a life in accordance with nature. The popularity of the movement was thus assured. Nobles, whose sons were being taught a trade, and ladies who were nursing their own babies banished the scroll and the *rocaille* from their drawing rooms to reinstate the rectangle and the classic column. On their walls and ceilings Chinamen and monkeys made way for Pompeian mythologies, and shepherdesses in sacques and rose garlands for farm labourers with ploughs and hay-rakes, while none but pure geometrical or definitely architectural forms were admitted in plan and elevation.

The general character of buildings of the style of Louis XVI, which thus began more than twenty years before that king's accession and lasted till the Revolution, came to be much what the style of Louis XIV had been at its best, but more refined and restful in effect, less pompous and overbearing. Its treatment of detail is based on a closer study of classical precedent, and its sculpture and ornament is of a quieter type. Yet freed though it is from the Baroque tradition it is still capable of vigour and originality.

The great exponent of the manner was J.-A. Gabriel. Admirable in the reposeful dignity of its long horizontal lines and reticent ornament is his Palace of Compiègne (rebuilt 1752–72), with its Doric colonnade in place of the customary screen to the court of honour, and its ingenious treatment of an awkward site and levels. The Place de la Concorde, which was laid out in 1753 from his designs, with the statue of Louis XV in the midst within an elongated octagon of terraces with lodges at the angles —later utilised as pedestals for statues of the great French cities—afforded him a rare opportunity for a monumental façade at the northern end. He used Perrault's Louvre motive, splitting it into two so as to make way for a central street, and substituting single for double columns above and an open arcade for a solid basement below.

The same period produced many other schemes—not in all cases carried out—of town improvements combined with monumental public buildings in provincial cities, e.g. Reims, Metz, Strasburg, Rouen, Tours, and Nantes.

At the École Militaire (before 1752) Gabriel used the now traditional square dome as a centre-piece for a stately building of court-yard plan. His example in this was followed by the architects of the Cour du Mai at the Palais de Justice completed (1776) by DENIS ANTOINE (1733–1801). Antoine also followed Gabriel's manner with much distinction at the Hôtel des Monnaies (1771–5).

The remodelling of the Palais Royal (originally Palais Cardinal) produced characteristic and varied types of Louis XVI design in the front (1763–70) by Moreau-Desproux and the garden court (1781–6) by VICTOR LOUIS (1731–c. 1810).

At this period much attention was given to theatre design. Gabriel's Opera House at Versailles and, on a miniature scale, R. Mique's theatre at Trianon are admirable in the arrangement and decoration of the interior, while the unobtrusive façade of the theatre of Amiens (1778–80)—Plate X—by Jacques Rousseau is a little *chef d'œuvre* of delicate and appropriate design. The greatest achievement in this department is the *Grand Théâtre* of Bordeaux (1777–80), planned in masterly fashion on axial lines by Victor Louis and imitated by M.-J. Peyre and Ch. de Wailly at the Odéon in Paris (1779–82).

The great châteaux of the second half of the 18th century are neither numerous nor remarkable, but among the smaller suburban houses many show a gem-like finish and reticence of expression which gives them marked distinction. Pre-eminent among these is Gabriel's Petit Trianon (1762–8)—Plate VIII— beloved of Marie Antoinette, but originally given by Louis XV to Madame du Barry. Bagatelle in the Bois de Boulogne, built for a wager in 64 days by the Comte d'Artois from the designs of Bélanger, is less completely successful.

Of hôtels and lesser town houses the period has left a large crop of examples. The Hôtels de Fleury, de Salm (Palais de la Légion d'Honneur), and Rogès in Paris, the Préfecture of Dijon,

PLATE IX

FIG. 14. LOUIS XV DOORWAY AT ABBEVILLE

PLATE **X**

FIG. 15. THEATRE AT AMIENS
By J. Rousseau (1780)

the Archbishop's Palace at Bordeaux may be instanced as examples of the former, while the streets of most cities, including those mentioned and also Amiens, abound in lesser town houses.

Classical Church Architecture

Under the early Bourbons a few attempts were made to carry on the system of St Eustache, i.e. that of clothing a Gothic structure in contemporary detail. Of these the Jesuit Chapels at Eu and St Omer and the façade and rood loft of St Étienne du Mont are pleasing instances.

But church architecture of the 17th and 18th centuries, as a whole, derives its inspiration from the adoption of the dome and the Roman vault, and its interest from the variety of attempts to adapt these singly or in combination to Catholic worship under the influence of St Peter's and the Gesù in Rome. In the exteriors, which are on the whole less successful than the interiors, interest centres in the gracious lines of the dome or on the façade, which is usually the Vignolan version of the Italian basilica front—a high pedimented nave front connected by scrolls with the lower aisle fronts. Variations on this theme may be seen at St Gervais (1616–21) by De Brosse, at the Sorbonne by Le Mercier, and at the Val de Grâce by F. Mansart, both about 1650; also at the Cathedral of Nancy (1703–40) by J.-H. Mansart and Boffrand. In the last instance it is combined with a pair of towers standing beyond the aisles.

Servandony at the outset of the classical reaction gave it its *coup de grâce* by substituting colonnaded galleries of a noble simplicity of design running between similarly placed towers.

At Ste Marie (Rue St Antoine, 1632–4), Mansart used, perhaps for the first time, another form of *portail*, which has remained popular to the present day in France—that in which the main cornice is carried up in the form of a great arch (cp. the Invalides and Petit Palais).

The interior is subject to greater variety of treatment according as a simple basilican, a radiate, or a mixed type of plan is adopted, as the dome space is the dominant feature or not, and as the Gesù type of nave section with vaulted clerestory carried on arcades is used or departed from.

Of domeless and transeptless basilicas good examples are the older church of the Invalides (1671–4) by L. Bruand and the chapel of Versailles (1696–1710) by J.-H. Mansart. Both are peculiar in section in that they have an important storey—or gallery—at triforium level. At Versailles indeed this is the principal storey, and, further, has a colonnade instead of an arcade. This chapel is a very beautiful building in its proportions and decoration. Some of its fittings and the almost contemporary stalls at Notre-Dame by De Cotte are examples of delicate *Régence* work.

St Roch by Le Mercier and St Sulpice by Le Vau, both begun soon after 1650, while of the Vignolan type in section, show traces in the planning of their transepts and apses of the tradition of Notre-Dame and St Eustache. They have low timber domes at the intersection concealed in the roofing.

The great examples of the mixed type are the churches of the Sorbonne by Le Mercier (1635–53)—Plate XII—and the Val de Grâce begun in 1645 by F. Mansart but completed by others. In both the dome is a nobly designed feature—an inner stone dome covered by an outer one in timber. In the former church, which is somewhat severe in treatment, the dome, in order to conform with the axis of the College buildings, rises in the centre of a basilican plan.· In the latter church, which is of richer and warmer effect and in which public and conventual purposes had to be combined, the dome space with radiating chapels forms the termination to a basilican nave.

F. Mansart's Ste Marie is the earliest 17th century church of the radiate type, and though on a small scale is internally very effective from the manner in which the dome dominates all else. This is somewhat less the case with the elliptical dome combined with a sort of Greek cross plan in the chapel of the Collège Mazarin by Le Vau (1660–8).

The two great radiate churches of France are J.-H. Mansart's Dôme des Invalides (1692–1704)—Plate XI—added at the end of the older church but back to back with it, and Soufflot's Ste Geneviève (now the Panthéon, 1757–c. 1820)—Plate XI. Both, like our St Paul's, have a triple dome; but the construction in each case

PLATE XI

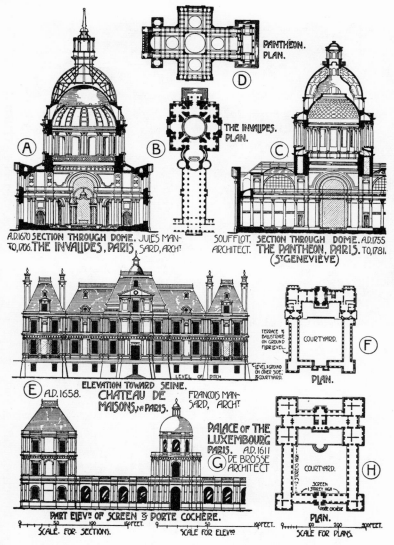

A.D.1670 SECTION THROUGH DOME. JULES MAN-
TO,1706. **THE INVALIDES, PARIS**. SARD, ARCH^T

PANTHÉON.
PLAN.

THE INVALIDES.
PLAN.

SOUFFLOT. SECTION THROUGH DOME. A.D.1755
ARCHITECT. **THE PANTHEON, PARIS**. TO,1781.
(S^{T}GENEVIÈVE)

ELEVATION TOWARD SEINE.
**CHATEAU DE
MAISONS,** N^R **PARIS.** FRANCOIS MAN-
SARD, ARCH^T

A.D. 1658.

LEVEL OF DITCH

TERRACE &
BALUSTRADE
ON GROUND
FLOOR LEVEL.

COURTYARD.

LEVEL: GROUND
ON OTHER SIDE.
& COURTYARD.

PLAN.

PALACE OF THE
**LUXEMBOURG
PARIS.** A.D. 1611
DE BROSSE
ARCHITECT

PART ELEV^N OF SCREEN & PORTE COCHÈRE.

2 STORIES HIGH

COURTYARD.

SCREEN
1 STOREY HIGH

PORTE COCHÈRE.

PLAN.

SCALE FOR SECTIONS.   SCALE FOR ELEV^NS.   SCALE FOR PLANS.

FIG. 16. A, B. DOME DES INVALIDES, by J.-H. Mansart.
C, D. PANTHÉON, by J.-G. Soufflot.
E, F. CHATEAU DE MAISONS, by F. Mansart.
G, H. LUXEMBOURG PALACE, by S. De Brosse.

PLATE XII

Fig. 18. THE PANTHÉON

By J.-G. Soufflot (begun 1757). The Interior

Fig. 17. CHURCH OF THE SORBONNE

By J. Le Mercier (1635–53). The Façade

is different. At the Invalides the two lower domes are in stone, the
first being widely pierced to give a view of the second, while the
third with its lantern is in timber. At the Panthéon all three are
in stone, the first having a small *oculus* and the second and third
carrying the stone lantern between them.

At the Invalides the dome rises from the centre of a Greek
cross contained in a square the angles of which are occupied by
domical chapels. It adequately dominates the interior, which,
with its varied vistas, its rich decoration and fine lighting is
extremely impressive, if not very devotional.

At the Panthéon (Plate XII) the dome covers the central square
of a large Greek cross, while over each arm is a saucer dome, but
the supports of the main dome contract the openings to the arms
by a third of their width. A colonnade running round each arm
divides them from a continuous aisle. The church is lighted
entirely from the dome and the clerestory windows, which are
concealed from outside by the windowless outer walls carried up
to the roof level somewhat as at St Paul's.

The dome space cannot in the nature of things be completely
dominant, and the arrangement of the supports with vistas
round them seem to isolate it from the halls which constitute
the arms. But the interior with its imposing scale and fine
lighting, its purity of detail and the beauty of its Corinthian
colonnade, is most impressive, if somewhat chilly and lacking in
Christian feeling.

Externally the dome is not quite happily managed. The
upper drum is too high and the colonnade round the lower drum
lacks the strength and repose which that of St Paul's derives
from the introduction of solid masses at intervals.

§ III. ECLECTICISM

Style of the Empire—Archaeological Classicism

The era of Revolution appears at first sight to have produced
upon architecture the paradoxical result of intensifying conservative—that is classical—tendencies. It did so only to a
superficial observer and in reality fostered disruptive forces.

Antiquity was still accepted as a guide in the "Age of Liberty,"
whose prophet was Plutarch as well as Jean-Jacques, while both

the Republic and the Empire set great store on classical precedent, regarding the ancients as models of civic and military virtues. But the copying of antiquity *in vacuo* without regard to national tradition was in fact a revolutionary process and opened the door for departure from tradition in other directions.

Since French architecture had readjusted itself to new conditions at the Renaissance with the help of classical forms and methods, there had been a continual grafting of these on to the native stock and a gradual laying aside of old elements as they became obsolete.

Various agencies had lent their aid to the formation and maintenance of a body of national classical traditions of composition and design. Among these were, first, an unbroken series of architectural writers, who sought to bring the Vitruvian system into relation with daily requirements, secondly, the handing on of acquired experience in families of architects such as those of Du Cerceau, Mansart, and Gabriel; thirdly the influence of the Academy of Architecture and its school founded by Colbert in 1671 concurrently with studentships in Rome.

Almost to the threshold of the Revolution the general authority of this tradition was hardly questioned even by those who least conformed to it. But the wider knowledge gained in the 18th century of ancient architecture proved the groundlessness of many of the Vitruvian assumptions as to the uses, proportions, and relations of the Orders; and while the archaeologisers copied classical prototypes more minutely, reproducing not merely details and proportions but entire features and edifices, and the rationalisers reduced classical features to their presumed structural origins, both broke away from traditional composition. The younger generation was thus left rudderless in a sea disturbed by the abolition of the Academy and the currents set in motion by the Romantic Movement, accompanied by royalist and Catholic reaction and by the invention of new materials and mechanical appliances.

Nevertheless from the great Revolution to that of July (1789–1830) the architecture of France is inspired in overwhelming proportion—often pedantically so—by classical examples. The actual Revolutionary Period was naturally infertile, but the reconstruction era of Napoleon, like that of

Henry IV, built largely and with the same aims of public utility.

The characteristic decorative side of the Empire Style was the result of the collaboration of CHARLES PERCIER (1764-1838) and PIERRE FONTAINE (1762-1853), who had both studied in Rome. It is a stiffer, more mechanical, version of the Louis XVI manner, influenced by Pompeian, and to a less extent by Egyptian, ideas. While, catering as it did for a society largely composed of military and *parvenu* elements and devoid of the minor social graces, it lacks the tender charm and rounded urbanity of its predecessor, it has an individuality and a severe refinement of its own. It can be studied in the Imperial apartments at Compiègne and Fontainebleau, Josephine's château of Malmaison, and many private houses. Externally decoration is used with an extremely sparing hand.

The monumental works of the period are largely in the nature of reproductions. The Colonne Vendôme (1805-10) by Gondoin and Lepère is based on that of Trajan, the Arc du Carrousel on those of Septimius Severus and Constantine, while the portico of the Palais Bourbon (1807) by Poyer, the Madeleine (1807-42) by Vignon and Huvé, and the Bourse (1808-27) by Brongniart and La Barre find their prototypes in Roman temples and basilicas.

More original is the Arc de Triomphe (1806-36), a noble work begun by Chalgrin and completed by Blouet. It is identical in purpose with Louis XIV's Porte St Denis—the glorification of the armies of France—but hardly more telling in effect in spite of its vastly greater scale, which is partly neutralised by the open nature of its site.

Napoleon gave a salutary lead to modern Parisian street architecture by the combined scheme of sober and dignified façades of the Rue de Rivoli, cut through crowded quarters—a lead followed in some measure to the present day and particularly—though with feebler architecture—by Baron Haussmann under the Second Empire.

The general character of Empire architecture may be summed up as one of austere dignity, sober in the matter of detail and ornament and sometimes carrying simplicity to the verge of baldness.

Modern Styles—Revivals and Classical Tradition

Till the close of the first quarter of the 19th century the authority of each style, when once established, had been acknowledged with practical unanimity throughout France, and had absorbed or eliminated conflicting tendencies.

Thenceforward this unanimity was to disappear in France, as in England and elsewhere. In France, however, the succeeding anarchy was less pronounced. The classical tradition was too deeply rooted to be altogether overthrown and has maintained a somewhat diminished authority to the present day.

Inherently congenial to the French temperament, it was supported by the centralised system of architectural training, which in spite of the abolition of the Academy of Architecture and its school in 1793 had not altogether lost its continuity. A private school opened soon after by Le Roy, one of its professors, was adopted by the *Institut* which replaced the old academies, and under the name of *École des Beaux Arts* has ever since been the focus of architectural education.

As stated above, an excessive tendency to archaeology was one cause of disruption, and archaeology was now to be pushed into domains other than classical antiquity—the Romanesque and Byzantine, the Gothic and Early Renaissance. That these revivals were not carried so far or cultivated with such success as in England was no doubt due to the greater strength of classical tradition. And French architecture in the last hundred years has on the whole been successful in proportion as it kept near to it, steering clear of ultra-Romanticism and ultra-Rationalism.

The Gothic revival—apart from such restorations, or rather reconstructions, as those of the learned enthusiast EUGÈNE VIOLLET-LE-DUC (1814–79) at Pierrefond and Carcassonne— was almost confined to churches, and much the same may be said of Romanesque and Byzantine, while the influence of the styles of Francis I, Henry II, and Louis XIII was not strong till the latter part of the century.

The dangers of anarchy presented by these revivals in themselves showed the necessity of avoiding undue archaeology and reknitting classical elements into the national tradition. But so rich is this national tradition that it may be followed along a diversity of lines.

The line which derives from the rationalistic idea received most brilliant expression in the Bibliothèque Ste Geneviève by HENRI LABROUSTE (1801–75), inaugurated in 1851. Dispensing with all the usual paraphernalia of columns and pediments and contenting himself with a reticent use of "Empire" ornament he makes his elevations tell in the most direct manner the tale of unlit stack rooms below and windowed reading-rooms above.

Another school making freer use of classical motives is exemplified in the work of JACQUES DUBAN (1797–1870) at the École des Beaux Arts (1835–58). Cognate to this is the so-called *néo-grec*, Greek rather in chastity of detail and line than in features or profiles. Under this label may be classed such work as the new buildings of the Palais de Justice (1857–68) by JEAN-LOUIS DUC (1802–79) (completed later by JEAN-LOUIS PASCAL), where in somewhat frigid forms he achieves the Grand Manner, the more harmonious École de Médecine (fin. 1900) by GINAIN and even the Faculté de Médecine by Pascal, though this leans decidedly to the Louis XVI manner.

A third school, inclining to greater pomp and richness, was more congenial to the "showy and flaunting" character of the Second Empire. Duban, who had made a scholarly restoration of the water-side façades of the Louvre (eastern half) and the Galerie d'Apollon, was not allowed to complete the long contemplated scheme of joining the Louvre with the Tuileries, for which he had prepared plans. The junction was carried out (1854–7) under the gaudier inspiration of Visconti and Lefuel in a manner, which, if skilful in the grouping of masses, exhibits a taste at once poor and aggressive. It was Lefuel, too, who after the destruction of the Tuileries rebuilt (1871–6) the Pavillons de Flore and de Marsan and the water-side gallery (western half) in a florid style similar but inferior to that of the supreme achievement of the Second Empire, the Paris Opera (1861–75) by CH. GARNIER (1825–98). This building, somewhat overcharged with coloured marbles and flamboyant sculpture, has monumental simplicity in its main lines, and its majestic, if tawdrily decorated, staircase is a conception full of imagination.

The influence of the early French Renaissance made itself widely felt in the last quarter of the century, particularly in the design of municipal buildings. The desire to reproduce the work of Boccador accounts for its adoption by Ballu and Desperthes in the rebuilding of the Hôtel de Ville, burnt down in 1871. But it has no obvious appropriateness at the Mairie of the 10th arrondissement by Eugène Rouyer or the Hôtels de Ville of Sens and Tours, while at Versailles among the works of the Grand Siècle its lack of repose is positively out of place.

In Ginain's exquisite Musée Galliéra, built in the eighties, suggestions from the style of Henry II and particularly from the Petite Galerie are utilised with excellent results.

More eclectic in their inspiration are the reconstructions of the Sorbonne (1897–1900) by Nénot of the Bibliothèque Nationale, recently completed by Pascal, and of the château de Chantilly (1876–82) by HONORÉ DAUMET (1826–1911). In all these, intricate problems of planning, complicated by the necessity of retaining historic buildings, are handled in a masterly manner, and both unity and monumental results are attained, if the elevations and decoration are not altogether convincing.

In the forty years preceding the war, considerable influence was exercised upon architectural design by the three International Exhibitions, in which the ruling ideas appear to have been the exotic in 1878, undisguised construction treated decoratively in 1889, and monumental architecture with concealed construction in 1900. Their several legacies are the Trocadéro, the Eiffel Tower, and the Pont Alexandre III with the two adjoining *Palais*. The first two can hardly be said to have seriously contributed to the beauty of Paris on the progress of architecture. The Trocadéro by Davioud and Bourdais, if grandly planned, is of ungainly outline, not redeemed by its pseudo-oriental style, while the Eiffel Tower, whatever its merits, is a work of engineering rather than of architecture.

But the products of the last exhibition are of greater artistic import and in the direct line of the national tradition on its more exuberant side. Both the *Palais* exhibit a consummate grasp of planning and of the resources of design. The *Grand Palais*, which may be reproached for a somewhat meretricious taste in ornament and the restlessness of its skyline and sculptural adjuncts, is the work of THOMAS, Louvet, and Déglane. The *Petit Palais* by GIRAULT has greater repose and a more refined taste in decoration. The *Pont Alexandre III* with its four splendid pylons, though perhaps unduly wide for its length, is a grand architectural composition.

Another architectural tendency brought into prominence by the 1900 Exhibition has fortunately proved ephemeral. The so-called *Art Nouveau* or *Style Moderne*—the vorticism of the day—sharing with the Flamboyant and the Rococo a horror of the straight line and a predilection for naturalism in its decorative forms, but without their sense of style, quickly died of its congenital inanity.

It cannot escape any trained English observer that the results of architectural education as practised in France are seldom satisfactory outside the province of the monumental and the grandiose. Studies are pursued under the most eminent architects of the day in the intense emulation and close collaboration of *ateliers* more or less connected with the Ecole des Beaux Arts and in its atmosphere of frequent competitions in subjects largely of an ideal order. The system has inestimable results in training men to grapple with problems, however complex, as a whole, to disengage the essential from the accessory, and then to relate the component parts in the most efficient juxta-position. It thus raises planning and the grouping of masses to the plane of serious art, and collaterally develops a high standard of draughtsmanship. It has also safely steered French design between the Scylla of pettiness or confusion to which the would-be monumental in England is too often a prey and the Charybdis of the forced and the *kolossal* in which it is engulfed in Germany.

But this concentration on the general to the overlooking of the particular, this absorption in vast problems and those mostly connected with city life, as well as the super-draughtsmanship fostered thereby, tend both to blunt the sense of refinement in matters of detail and to unfit the student for a tasteful and appropriate treatment of the lesser problems of ordinary practice.

To this system must, therefore, be attributed in great measure not only the deficiency in taste of many of the great monuments in the matter of ornament but also the failure of modern France to produce good domestic architecture other than in great town houses, which are often admirable, and particularly a good country-house architecture, which is the special forte of the English school. The modern "château," "villa," and so-called "cottage," too often fail to strike the domestic and intimate note. When attempts are made to reproduce types from foreign or old French sources, the spirit is lost and the proportions are ill understood. When originality is aimed at the result is even more deplorable. Occasionally a group of villa-residences, such as one finds at Paris Plage, produces in the mass an effect of coquettish gaiety, but examined individually they prove to be miracles of bad taste and misapplied ingenuity. The effect of such structures in the open country is altogether pitiable.

Modern Church Architecture

No great church building effort took place between the Revolution and the Restoration. The Madeleine was not built as a church but as a Temple of Glory, externally a Roman temple and internally a hall similar to those of Roman baths or law courts. It was adapted about 1842 for Catholic worship.

In modern times French architects seem never to have been quite at home in church design, and in whatever style they have worked they have not succeeded so well as their English contemporaries in recapturing the spirit with the forms, or in creating a devotional atmosphere. But it is a tribute to the strength of the classical tradition that their most successful experiments have been those which kept closest to it.

The idea of the primitive Christian basilica with its colonnade and triumphal arch was a popular one in the second quarter of the 19th century. The best examples are Notre-Dame de Lorette (1823–36) by Hippolyte Lebas and St Vincent de Paul (1824–44) by Lepère and Hittorf.

But the mediaeval trend of Catholic opinion favoured a return to Gothic, and a crop of archaeologically correct, but unsympathetically treated, Gothic churches sprang up. The best known of these is Ste Clothilde (1846–59) by Gau and Ballu.

Various compromises were also attempted in which the detail is Renaissance and the effect vaguely Gothic, though the construction is not so. Such are La Trinité (1861–7) by Ballu and St Augustin (1860–8) by Baltard, the latter with a visible iron roof. Again in certain churches, such as that of Merville and Notre-Dame at Armentières, destroyed in the late war, the system of St Eustache was followed.

But the most popular church style during the last half-century has been neo-Romanesque with Byzantine and other trimmings. Of this type the new cathedral of Marseilles by Vaudoyer and Espérandieu is considered the most successful. At the Sacré Cœur at Montmartre by PAUL ABADIE (1812–84) the crypt, the only portion he lived to see built, is a genuinely imaginative work, but the uncouth superstructure carried out by inferior hands has attained, at vast expenditure and with the aid of a unique site, a merely theatrical effectiveness, and is in every way inferior to Westminster Cathedral which is also more definitely Byzantine in its inspiration.

In Notre-Dame de la Consolation or Chapelle Expiatoire, erected on the site of the Bazar de la Charité, burnt in 1897, ALBERT GUILBERT (b. 1866) returns to the classical traditions of the later 18th century. This tasteful work has been described as an instance of "pure thought in architecture," "a new conception of old materials."

French architecture of to-day derives with no breach of continuity from that of the Middle Ages. If at the Renaissance it underwent a great transformation, this was by re-infusion of the elements from which Gothic architecture itself had sprung, and since then it has retained certain characteristics developed in the Gothic period. Among these may be reckoned a persistent fondness for vertical expression emphasised by tall roofs, a great technical proficiency, particularly in mason craft, a delight in exhibiting it for its own sake, and a recurrent rationalistic trend in design.

It is more obviously the direct descendant of the Renaissance, or re-absorption of classical elements through Italian channels, repeated at intervals under varying influences. But whatever it has absorbed it has assimilated, invested with a national character, and woven into the national tradition.

We have seen through what varied phases this tradition has

passed—each phase instinct with vitality and brimming with invention. In the 16th century its almost riotous exuberance in delicate and exquisite ornament is a pure delight, sobering later into a more chastened, more strictly architectonic distinction. In the 17th century a homely solidity tinged with the robustious Baroque spirit gradually draws an ample and richer majesty suited to the pomp and splendour of the *Grand Règne*, a manner which remains a national asset through passing fashions of taste, and which adapts itself to the dainty caprices of the Rococo, the chaste classical graces of the style of Louis XVI, and the chillier antiquarianism of the Empire.

If, in the last hundred years, French architecture has known hesitation and some degree of failure, it has kept a firm grasp on essential principles and shown vigour in the exploration of new fields. It has a wide range of achievement to its credit. A generation which has produced the École de Médecine, the Petit Palais, and the Pont Alexandre, the Musée Galliéra and Notre-Dame de la Consolation may look forward with confidence to a splendid future.

BIBLIOGRAPHY

For the period 1495–1830—W. H. Ward, *The Architecture of the Renaissance in France*, 1911.

For the period 1495–1661—Sir R. Blomfield, *A History of French Architecture from the reign of Charles VIII to the death of Mazarin*, 1911.

For the period 1495–1755—Baron H. von Geymüller, *Baukunst der Renaissance in Frankreich*, 2 vols. Stuttgart, 1898–1901.

For the modern period—H. H. Statham, " Architecture " in the *Encyclopaedia Britannica*, 11th ed., and *A Short Critical History of Architecture*, 1912.

CHAPTER X

PAINTING, SCULPTURE, AND DECORATIVE ART

RENAISSANCE is the name applied to the artistic period which corresponds to the return to antiquity at the end of the Gothic period. This term was at first used to describe a complete Renaissance of the arts, by men who thought that the Middle Ages were a period of barbarism. Since then the meaning of the word has become restricted to the sense of Renaissance of antique inspiration and plastic art. If this meaning is given to it, the term, in French history, designates a period which began approximately with the 16th century, that is to say, with the Italian Wars. At that time the French monarchy and its feudal system came into contact with Italian art, which carried on the traditions of ancient art. When the kings of France, Charles VIII, Louis XII, and Francis I, and the great feudal nobles who followed them, returned to France, they had learnt to appreciate the Italian palaces and gardens, the marble statues and painted galleries; they brought back precious pictures, antique casts, and sometimes even illustrious artists, whom they took into their pay. Leonardo da Vinci ended his days in France; Andrea del Sarto, Benvenuto Cellini, Primaticcio, Rosso, Niccolo dell' Abbate, and many others came to work at the court of Francis I.

Thus at the beginning of the 16th century the penetration of Italian fashions was general in France. We can trace their appearance in many parts of French territory, in provinces then only slightly attached to the kingdom as well as in the central regions of the monarchy. In the first thirty years of the 16th century classical forms appeared everywhere. Figures of Italian mythology replaced Gothic allegorical figures and religious statues. In all the arts, in decorative sculpture, in tapestries, in stained glass, in illumination, enamels, each province can quote some famous name as a type of this evolution: Bernard Palissy in Saintonge, Hugues Sambin at Dijon, Philibert de L'Orme at Lyons, Ligier Richier in Lorraine, Dominique Florentin in Champagne, Michel Colombe in Touraine, Jean

Goujon at Rouen, Jean Cousin at Sens, Nicolas Bachelier at Toulouse, Léonard Limousin at Limoges.

Henceforth we shall apply the name of "Classical Art" to this new form of French art. In architecture classical art replaced Gothic decorations by the use of antique orders, columns or pilasters, capitals, entablatures, and pediments. In religious architecture the ogee vault disappeared to make way for the Latin vault. In sculpture Gothic realism, statuary with long robes and voluminous folds, was replaced by heroic figures and flowing draperies. In painting, as antiquity had left no models, it was the Italian models of the 16th century, and especially the Florentine and Roman Schools, which transformed the decorative art of the Gothic masters, patient and truthful, but devoid of breadth and amplitude. Naturally the change from the Gothic to the classical style was not the work of a moment; the two styles were combined in some charming productions during the early years of the 16th century, before the severity of the classical style had entirely eliminated the fancies of the disappearing Gothic. This wavering between two tendencies is one of the charms of French art under Charles VIII and Louis XII. Under Henry II French art shows more logic, but greater coldness.

§ I.   PAINTING

It was in painting that Italian influence made the strongest impression, because it encountered no national tradition, as it did in architecture and sculpture. Decorative painting was unknown to the Middle Ages; its place was taken in religious architecture by stained glass, and in civil by tapestry. When the French kings returned from Italy, they brought back not only the finest works they had admired, but also artists capable of teaching their art and practising it. Francis I brought back Leonardo da Vinci; but he was very old and died soon after his arrival in France. Then came Andrea del Sarto, who only made a short stay. Finally Rosso, a Florentine, and Primaticcio, a pupil of Correggio, settled at Fontainebleau, where they supervised the decoration of the royal château and founded a school which survived until the end of the first third of the 17th century. These artists taught a new style of decoration, which is specially characterised by a love of physical beauty and a bold use of nude figures. Religious painting was forgotten and replaced by heathen mythology.

Along with this large ambitious style of decoration there existed the more modest tradition of portrait-painting. The illustrious figures of France of that period are well known to us from innumerable paintings or drawings. The most celebrated of these portrait-painters were the two Clouets—Jean and his son François, nicknamed Jannet—and Corneille, called of Lyons, because he lived for long in that town. Their painting is light and delicate, rather than robust; it gives a marvellous rendering of the delicate pallor of the court ladies, the elegant and crafty type of the men who waged the religious wars, and the degeneracy of the later Valois. Colour at times seems unnecessary to these portrait-painters, and pencil tinged with red-chalk is a sufficient medium to give a life-like presentment of their sitters. The Louvre, the Bibliothèque Nationale, and the Musée Condé at Chantilly, have preserved a great number of these paintings and crayon sketches.

Italian art also had a marked influence on JEAN DUVET (1481–after 1561), the best engraver on copper of the 16th century. The precise forms, learned modelling, and flowing draperies of Mantegna and Leonardo da Vinci, particularly attracted him. His compositions are over-burdened with details, which fatigue the eye and distract the attention; but we must admire the originality of his conception and execution. Among his works, the series of the *Apocalypse* and the *History of the Unicorn*, celebrated in his own day, have a strange charm, arising from the free play of a highly poetic imagination.

It was only during the course of the 17th century, and particularly during the reign of Louis XIII, that a really national school of French painting came into being; between the brilliant development of the Fontainebleau school in the time of Francis I and Henry II and the resumption of artistic activity in the time of Louis XIII and Richelieu there was a long period of minor activity of a character hard to define. Henceforward the fate of French art was too intimately connected with that of the central power not to suffer from the disasters of the monarchy. During the religious troubles at the end of the 16th century many of the grandiose schemes of the Renaissance were abandoned. It was not until Richelieu became minister that there was a revival of artistic life.

The new architecture welcomed the help of painting much more than had Gothic architecture. In the churches of the Jesuit style, constructed at the beginning of the 17th century, there was room on the altars for large religious pictures. At that time began the custom by which each year, in the month of May, the confraternity of goldsmiths and silversmiths presented a large religious picture to Notre-Dame de Paris. Most of our artists of that period are represented in this "May" series, now for the most part dispersed or vanished; a few examples are still in the galleries of the Louvre (Le Sueur, Le Brun).

At this time the French school of painting was invigorated by an influx of Flemish painters. As in the Middle Ages, the artists of these rich northern towns were in the habit of leaving their homes, either to study the Italian masterpieces, or simply to look for rich clients. In France, and particularly in Paris, they found work in the new churches and in the hôtels of the *bourgeoisie*. The traces of their passing can still be found in the churches of that period and in the hôtels of the Marais, which under Louis XIII was the fashionable quarter of Paris.

The most illustrious of these Flemings who came to work in France was the Antwerp painter, Peter Paul Rubens, who journeyed to Paris in order to hang in the Luxembourg Palace the twenty-five great compositions in which he had chronicled in the heroic style the life of the Queen-mother, Marie de' Medici. These fine pictures have since been moved to the Louvre, where they form a series unique in the world for breadth, rich colouring, and excellent preservation.

Another Fleming, PHILIPPE DE CHAMPAGNE (1602–1674), settled in Paris and mixed in the intellectual life of the time so thoroughly that he almost forgot his own country. He was court painter to Marie de' Medici; he has left a fine *Portrait of Cardinal Richelieu* (Louvre) and portraits of the most important personages at court; but, while painting according to the principles of Flemish realism, he allowed himself to be influenced by the moral attitude of French society, and particularly by the Jansenist circle in which he lived.

As to those artists who were really French, they did not possess, like their Flemish and Italian neighbours, a tradition which they had only to follow. At the beginning of the 17th century, at a time when all European art was under the influence of the Italian Renaissance, they too inevitably fell under the sway of Florentine or Roman masters.

After the decorators of the Fontainebleau school, the master who had most influence was SIMON VOUET (1590–1649), who owes all his importance to the fact that in his studio were collected the masters of the classical French school, Le Sueur, Le Brun, and Mignard. As for Vouet himself, he was a facile and prolific decorator, an imitator of the Venetian masters, especially of Veronese, the charm of whose colour he did not succeed in reproducing.

One of his best pupils was EUSTACHE LE SUEUR (1617–1655) who did not go to Italy, but who none the less was an admirer and imitator of the Renaissance masters, especially Raphael. We owe to him some charming mythological decorations which adorned the galleries of the Hôtel Lambert in Paris, and also a series of facile and emotional paintings, which recount the principal episodes of the life of St Bruno (formerly in the Carthusian church in Paris, now in the Louvre).

We must find a place beside these painters for the engravers, some of whom, such as ABRAHAM BOSSE (c. 1602–1676) and JACQUES CALLOT (1592–1635), displayed great originality. We specially admire the fine engravings of Bosse, which show us fashionable life in Paris under Louis XIII. Jacques Callot was an aquafortist, full of life and fancy, who travelled from Lorraine to Italy. The spirituel and grotesque silhouettes of Italian actors, the brutalities of soldiers, the operations of famous sieges such as La Rochelle and Breda, and some scenes of witchcraft and devilry, these are the principal subjects treated by his genius.

The three brothers LE NAIN (Mathieu, Antoine, and Louis), though painters, did not share any of the decorative ambitions of the artists of that day. They were content to remain faithful copyists of their contemporaries. Their great success to-day comes from the fact that they portrayed peasant life. *The Blacksmith* in the Louvre is in its simplicity one of the most touching works of the French school.

Many other masters, such as La Hire, Sebastien Bourdon, and Valentin, deserve mention. They have left numerous works, pictures of saints in relief on a black background, after the manner of the late Bolognese artists, who served as their models, and their pictures are still to be found in great numbers in our churches and picture galleries. But there are two, Poussin and Claude Lorrain, who hold a dominating position in their period.

NICOLAS POUSSIN (1594–1665) may be considered as the leader of the French classical school, because of the extraordinary influence he exercised on his contemporaries and on later art. His work is the best expression of all that French art at that time sought to borrow from the Italians and from antiquity— ideal forms and the poetry to be found in history. Furthermore, he expressed in his painting the qualities of logic and reason which French writers of that period held up to admiration in their tragedies and their moral treatises; his work has been rightly compared to that of Corneille or Racine. Like them, he presented old stories in perfect settings, and gave life to figures whose attitudes reveal their souls as clearly as the heroes of classical tragedies.

He was born at Andelys in 1594, and, after having received his early training as a painter from an obscure wandering artist, he determined to make the traditional journey to Italy to study on the spot the models which he knew only from copies or engravings. After many fruitless attempts, he succeeded in reaching the city of Rome, which he hardly ever again left. From that day onward, he steeped himself in Italian art and the memories of antiquity which still haunt the Roman ruins. His first paintings reveal him as a pupil of the late Bolognese school, then he appears as a great admirer of Titian, and finally of Raphael, who remained his favourite master. But his imagination specially inclined him to the ancient world, which he animated with a spirit of real poetry. He only left Rome to make a short journey to Paris in 1640–41, at the invitation of the King of France. His fame had spread from Rome to Paris, and his pictures were for the most part commissioned and bought by Parisian amateurs. He was summoned to decorate the great gallery of the Louvre, but he left before it was finished and never returned. He spent

the rest of his life in Rome in his house on the Pincian, painting
pictures which generally made their way to Paris.

Towards the end of his life, when his hand had become heavy
and tremulous, he gave less and less prominence to figures, and
his pictures were above all landscapes: landscapes which are
interpretations of the spirit of the Roman Campagna, and which,
even when not peopled by human or divine personages, always
seem appropriate settings for some mythological or historical
scene. Poussin is the great master of "historical landscape."

He has also proved a model to our classical painters by his ingenuity in composing perfectly clear scenes, in which each person
plays an easily recognisable part. In front of one of Poussin's
pictures there need be no fear of seeking for the psychological
meaning of the artist. Purely pictorial qualities, cleverness of
drawing, brilliancy or harmony of colour, are not the principal
features of his work. The artist speaks to the mind as much as
to the eye, and for this reason he was so greatly appreciated by
the French of the 17th century, who were interested in all moral
questions. When he died in Rome in 1665, he was regarded as
the leader of the French school.

The Louvre is richest in his paintings, which are to be found
chiefly in England and France. Among the most celebrated are
*Shepherds of Arcady, The Finding of Moses, The Conversion of
St Paul, Eliezer and Rebecca, The Triumph of Flora, The
Flood*, etc.

CLAUDE GELLÉE (1600–1682), called LORRAIN, also spent
most of his life in Italy. He early left his native Lorraine to cross
the Alps, in order to study and reproduce the most beautiful
scenes in Italy and the radiant light of the Mediterranean. But
his art differs greatly from that of Poussin, although his landscapes too are composed with careful balance. The effect which he
chiefly strives for is an effect of light, and, more particularly, he is
attracted by the softness and brilliancy of the light of sunsets.
He is not even afraid to introduce the sun itself into his compositions, and in his pictures he succeeds in giving us the effect
of dazzling light. Very often the chosen setting is a sea-port, and
the rays of the sinking sun play on lines of fine architecture, on
the masts of ships, on the clouds, and on the crests of little waves.
His compositions had so great a success that he saw his manner

imitated and copied even during his lifetime, and in order to protect himself against his copyists, he left his *Liber Veritatis*, a series of autograph drawings which reproduce his authentic compositions.

His principal works are in the Louvre and in English collections. In the Louvre are *Cleopatra at Tarsus, Chryseis restored to her Father, The Campo Vaccino, The Pass of Susa, A Sea-port, The Ford, The Setting Sun*, etc.

The personal rule of Louis XIV began in 1660. France was all powerful in Europe. The policy of Richelieu and of Mazarin had brought the kingdom to such a degree of power that Louis XIV had merely to reap the political results. He was born with an inordinate passion for glory, and he realised how the Arts could help to perpetuate the memory of men. Therefore all through his life he sought fame by achieving conquests and by erecting buildings. French art under Louis XIV was therefore, above all, French art in the service of Louis XIV.

In order to realise this plan, the Government undertook the administration of Art. Colbert, who was the chief minister, was "Superintendent of Buildings," and under this title he had control over the artistic activity of the kingdom. From his ministry date a number of institutions which had for their object the instruction of sculptors and painters. Most of these institutions survived him and have greatly influenced the evolution of art in France.

Some years earlier, in 1648, the sculptors and painters, to defend their artistic independence against the workmen's guilds, had founded an Academy and placed it under the patronage of the king. By means of this institution Co'bert had at his disposal all the artistic circles in France. The *Académie Royale* became a State Institution which undertook to teach. This teaching itself assumed an official character under the direction of an authoritative painter, Le Brun, who was technical adviser to Colbert and who supervised the decorations of the Louvre and Versailles.

Furthermore, the State, in undertaking the education of young painters and sculptors, founded in Rome an Academy to receive those students who were sent to Italy to complete their education, and as the artistic superiority of Italy was attributed to the great number of ancient monuments which she possessed, Colbert applied himself with all his might to obtain and convey to France statues and antiques unearthed in Italy. Failing originals, he ordered casts and copies to be made, and henceforth the *Académie de France à Rome* was bound to send to France copies after the antique or the Italian Renaissance. It was thus hoped that the French atmosphere might be rendered as favourable to the development of artistic vocations as was that of Italy.

From 1670 to 1683 it may be said that the artistic activity of France was entirely devoted to the work at Versailles. All the artists of France came to collaborate; the architects were Le Vau, Mansart, Robert de Cotte; the leader of the painters and sculptors was CHARLES LE BRUN (1619–1690), first painter to the king, who possessed the necessary qualities for so gigantic a work, facility of invention, prompt execution, and authority to organise the work amongst painters, sculptors, cabinet-makers, and upholsterers. It is thus the stamp of his prolific and facile genius which is found in the decorations of the palace of Versailles and in everything which can be called the style of Louis XIV. As a painter, he has left us a few good portraits, and, above all, several series of great decorative paintings, which are still in the palace of Versailles or in the galleries of the Louvre. In his *Battles of Alexander*, now in the Louvre, may be recognised his gift of composition, his real ingenuity in expressing feelings by gesture and by play of feature, but also his limitations as a painter. He had to make use of the brush of his pupils to execute landscapes, animals, and the thousand accessories which are a trifle to real painters.

Many of his pupils were of Flemish origin. One of them, ADAM FRANZ VAN DER MEULEN (1632–1690), deserves to emerge from the obscurity of the school. He has left a number of small pictures representing the campaigns of Louis XIV and the sieges of Flemish towns. He brings to the glorification of the king the qualities of accuracy and brightness which he owes to his Flemish origin. To blend mythology with reality is not his aim; the history of his own time has known no more faithful chronicler.

As a rival to Le Brun his contemporaries were accustomed to hold up PIERRE MIGNARD (1610–1695). When Le Brun died, it was Mignard who took over all his commissions, but in any case, the great period of expansion of the Louis XIV style was past. Mignard will live chiefly as a facile and fashionable portrait-painter, who knew how to give beauty to his female models while preserving a likeness, which is the most important quality for all painters of women. His friend Molière has sung the praises of his decoration of the Val de Grace cupola, which nowadays seems to us rather feeble.

Another portrait-painter, CLAUDE LEFEBVRE (1632–1675), has left some good pictures, which are preserved in the gallery at Versailles, but in reality these formal countenances are less pleasing to us than the admirable figures of the designer and engraver, ROBERT NANTEUIL (c. 1623–1678), which seem to be true and candid records. Another engraver, GÉRARD EDELINCK (1640–1707), translated into black and white the portraits painted by Rigaud, and, in spite of the simplicity of his medium, his engravings are as full of life and colour as paintings.

The period between the death of Louis XIV in 1715 and the personal government of Louis XV is called the Regency. In French history, periods of regency have always proved times of more or less violent reaction against royal authority. During the Regency of the 18th century, it was not against the monarchical power, too strongly established, that attempts to gain political independence were directed; but there was a change in habits that can only be explained by a reaction against the crushing authority of the absolute monarchy. Moreover, people had not waited for the death of Louis XIV to shake off the somewhat gloomy moral and intellectual discipline which surrounded the king. While Versailles was depressed by the long period of the old age of Louis XIV, the court mourning, and the reverses in the war of the Spanish Succession, Paris had already begun that independent, witty, and licentious existence which was characteristic of the whole 18th century. Therefore we must not date what is known as Regency Art from the death of Louis XIV, but from a much earlier period.

The artists domiciled in Paris now led a much more brilliant and independent life than those of previous centuries; they were no longer classed with mere workmen nor depended closely on the patrons for whom they worked. They belonged to fashionable society and took part in the social life of the cultured *bour-geoisie*. In the portraits which they have left us it is easy to see this social transformation; it had naturally an immense influence on the evolution of painting. Henceforth there existed what may be called the Parisian School, in which is resumed and concentrated the whole of French artistic activity.

It was above all in painting that the spirit of the Regency manifested itself. The artists took part in the decoration of rooms, and the pompous and somewhat ponderous style of Le Brun's time became clearer and lighter in the modern fashion. It was at this time that the custom began of leaving the white plaster of ceilings untouched; larger windows too, mirrors, and lighter panels forced the artists to lighten the shadows of their pictures. Then began the period of lighter colouring.

The most celebrated successors of Le Brun were first Charles de La Fosse, and then Le Moyne, who showed great ingenuity in his rendering of figures on ceilings and in peopling a celestial land-scape with flying figures. When the details of the drawing are examined, it is clear that the faces have lost the cold regularity which was derived from imitation of the antique. The noses are less straight, the eyes are more living, the draperies are arranged in broken folds, so as to give spirit to the attitudes and vivacity to the faces.

Jean Jouvenet and Restout, two Normans, one from Rouen, the other from Caen, still display a little of the majestic tradition of the great century. Their principal works are in the Louvre and in the Paris churches. But in the pictures of Antoine Coypel and François de Troy, although the subjects treated and the persons represented are borrowed from Poussin or Le Brun, the figures show the affectation which is learned in drawing-rooms or the theatre.

Santerre painted a *Susanna Bathing* (Louvre), which is not even an antique Venus, but a Parisian model. As to the artist Raoux, some of whose charming portraits are in the Louvre and a few provincial picture-galleries, he was content to paint pretty figures and beautiful silk dresses.

Once more the influence of Flemish masters, which has appeared at all periods of our history, is discernible in the French school of painting. One of these masters, Rubens, had, as we have seen, left in the Luxembourg galleries a series of marvellous paintings, which at first passed unobserved, but which soon excited the admiration of a few experts. Watteau was one of those who studied these works closely and who profited by it. The best painters of this period were therefore more or less admirers and almost copyists of the great master of Antwerp. FRANÇOIS DESPORTES (1661–1743) was an animal-painter, who was clever in rendering the fur and feather of game. He was granted the honour of painting the dogs of the royal kennels and he has also left us some good portraits. But the best portrait-painters of this period were Hyacinthe Rigaud and Nicolas Largillière.

HYACINTHE RIGAUD (1659–1743) was the official portrait-painter of the nobility and great personages at the end of the reign of Louis XIV and the beginning of Louis XV. He saw the men of his own time, kings, princes, marshals, and bishops, with the accessories of their position and the majestic frame which surrounded these figures in the social hierarchy. His colour and his brush were moreover admirable, and there had not yet been any portrait-painter of the French school capable of rendering with such success velvet hangings, brocaded stuffs, and metal cuirasses. Rigaud was also an observer of human physiognomy, and his figures of the aged Louis XIV and Bossuet are unforgettable.

NICOLAS LARGILLIÈRE (1656–1746) worked less for the court and more for the *bourgeoisie*. He was one of the official painters of the aldermen of Paris and also a very favourite master with ladies, to whose faces he knew how to give delicacy and brilliancy of complexion and grace of attitude. His *Family Portrait* in the Louvre is full of a perfectly sincere *bourgeois* inspiration; his palette is rich with striking and luscious tones, which owe much to his study of Rubens.

But of all these disciples of Flanders, the most artistic, the most poetical, and also the most representative of the lively society of the Regency was certainly ANTOINE WATTEAU (1684–1721). Watteau was one of the many Flemings who came to Paris in the course of the 17th century; but he holds a particularly important place in history, because to him it was given to express his time and to put into his refined painting the witty and pleasure-loving spirit of the Regency. Thus the public which honoured him during his life deserted him when the intellectual and political changes had effaced the memory of this period of fashionable licence, and it was not until the 19th century with its taste for all the artistic phases of the past that Watteau regained all his old popularity. Nowadays, lovers of art are inclined to regard Watteau as one of the greatest masters of the French school, if not the greatest.

Watteau is, in the first place, admirable for his qualities as a painter; he is truly Flemish in the refinement and brilliancy of his colour. When he came to Paris, he finished his education by drawing and painting in the Luxembourg galleries in front of the pictures of the life of Marie de' Medici by Rubens. He also studied the Venetian pictures in the collection of his friend Crozat; he thus derived from the greatest painters their best qualities, to concentrate them in his small pictures.

In order to understand the surroundings, real and imaginary, amongst which his figures move, it must be remembered that Watteau worked for the decoration of the opera and designed costumes for actors. His personages are clothed with an elegance and a fancy which recall both the world of fashionable circles and of the theatres. Watteau has also closely observed the beauties of French parks. He remembered them when he sought a background for his small figures, and in his landscapes are blended the unexpectedness of a fairy scene with the natural charm of a real horizon.

Watteau's characters too are borrowed from the stage, whence they derive their attractive pose. Their only occupation consists in conversing gallantly with each other in beautiful parks, irradiated by the golden light of evening, and their attitudes bring before our eyes the amusing mimicry of coquetry and refined love-making. His contemporaries called these little scenes *Fêtes Galantes*. The most celebrated is the *Embarkation for Cythera* (in the Louvre), a bevy of loving couples, who decide after more or less hesitation to embark in the ship of love, which will carry them to the Happy Isle, blue in the distance, enticing and unreal like a mirage.

Watteau had great influence on the taste and art of his time: he had even direct imitators, such as JEAN-BAPTISTE PATER (1695–1736), a Fleming like himself, who came from Valenciennes and was gifted with the picturesque qualities of his race, but who did not, like Watteau, succeed in catching the artistic spirit of the Regency. On the other hand, NICOLAS LANCRET (1690–1743) painted the society of Louis XV with much charm, but the brilliant palette of Watteau has become somewhat paler in his hands.

As the century advanced, the Parisian public interested itself increasingly in the work of painters and sculptors, and, after 1737, the Salons, which opened regularly every second year, attracted an ever greater number of people to see the pictures and statues. Thus the public became educated and it was no longer only the patrons who came into contact with the artists: they lived in a society which was interested in them, which applauded or criticised them; hence art began to express the feelings of this public to which it addressed itself.

The king, therefore, was no longer, as in the time of Louis XIV, the only patron; his influence is less noticeable. Nevertheless, the government of Louis XV was far from losing interest in the fine arts. The superintendents of building who succeeded Colbert continued to support the institutions founded by him. But intervention by the government could no longer influence the style of artists, as in the Versailles days. The artists now rather sought the approbation of Paris than that of the court. The king was only a richer customer than others; he did not demand from Boucher and Fragonard his glorification under some mythological form, but merely asked for witty or agreeable pictures to please the eye.

The historical painting dear to the *Académie Royale* of painting and sculpture never ceased to be the "grand style," from Le Brun to David. Every year, large compositions continued to be exhibited in the Salon, with subjects taken from mythology or Greco-Roman history. But nevertheless this grand style at length lost some of the ponderous majesty of the early classical artists, and the painters contrived to depict the gravest personages in a more pleasing fashion.

The painter who best represents the French school in the middle of the 18th century is FRANÇOIS BOUCHER (1703–1770). He treated mythology simply as an ordinary decorative subject.

Historical painting became with him decorative love-scenes. The figures usually treated in his pictures are Venus and her nymphs, or little naked Cupids. These pink and white bodies flit among clouds. When they are clothed, Boucher's figures are comic-opera peasants. Unfortunately, the landscape in which they move is entirely artificial with its blue vegetation and rockwork ruins. Boucher was extremely clever in composing a harmonious whole without a real subject and with insignificant details. They are always charming decorative panels, which we must look at without close examination, for fear of discovering many flaws and becoming wearied of their superficial character.

Round Boucher there were many painters with the same sort of inspiration: Natoire, van Loo, etc., all artists of extreme cleverness, but without depth. Not only painters must be mentioned, but also charming engravers, who brought to the illustration of books as much grace and lightness as the artists applied to the decoration of rooms; Cochin, Gravelot, Saint-Aubin, Moreau le Jeune, have left us witty pictures of 18th century Paris.

Amongst these artists special mention is due to those who represented the life of their period, and first of all to the painters of portraits; they were very numerous in fashionable salons. The man who nowadays seems to us to have best analysed the figures of his day is MAURICE-QUENTIN DE LA TOUR (1704–1788). He painted in pastels, which permits liveliness and lightness of execution; the touch remains visible; the dashes of the pencil give the details of the facial movements; the muscles are ready to relax themselves in smile or speech. The fire of the eye, the mobility of the mouth, betray awakened thought on the point of expressing itself in words. We are really transported into the literary and aristocratic salons of the 18th century. But the people are not shown to us surrounded and encumbered by the countless accessories of costume, as in the paintings of Rigaud. They stand out in their individuality and thus appear more lifelike and closer to us.

JEAN-BAPTISTE PERRONNEAU (1715–1783), another pastellist, rivalled La Tour in public favour.

In contrast to the truthful La Tour, JEAN-MARC NATTIER

(1685–1766) liked to give a flattering picture of his models. Instead of bringing out the personal peculiarities of his sitters, he modified their features so as to give them that fashionable elegance which the hairdresser and dressmaker supply to their customers. Nattier, painter of women, has stereotyped the Louis XV style of beauty: delicate colouring, rounded curves, a rosy face, under a powdered wig. He was the regular painter of the court-ladies, and has left us a charming series of the daughters of Louis XV in the Versailles picture-gallery.

The painters of the period of Louis XV did not work only for the aristocracy of birth and of finance. The Dutch masters, very fashionable in France, had taught that interest can be inspired by the representation of very simple scenes, taken from modest surroundings and enclosed in a small frame. They had shown us that it was possible, by picturesque qualities, to give charm to objects, fruit, vegetables, or game, which lie about on the kitchen table. JEAN-BAPTISTE-SIMÉON CHARDIN (1699–1779) surpassed the Dutch in the charm and sympathy with which he has represented little household things. He was a modest worker, without classical culture or historical pretensions. He first became known by exhibiting pictures of still life. His small pictures charm us by their simplicity of inspiration, and by a marvellously clever technique. Not that Chardin aspires to virtuosity, but his work is impeccably honest; he does more than give us the illusion of silver, fruit, or china: he has discovered and revealed the secret soul which lives in inanimate objects. Later he ventured to put figures into his small compositions, figures which hardly show any more movement than the accessories of his still life. They equally belong to the intimacy of home life; they are the mother of the house, the maid, the child. Chardin shows them, not agitated by some out-of-the-way or unforeseen occurrence, but in every-day attitudes. They do not know that they are being observed. It is impossible to render with greater sympathy or simplicity the ordinary life of the lower middle class; works such as the *Benedicite* (Louvre) are amongst the rarest jewels of French art. In the midst of so many mythological deities, pure products of the imagination, it is a surprise and a delight to come upon so much truth and poetry.

The second half of the 18th century beheld a gradual transformation in the general atmosphere of literature and art, a kind
of reaction against the abuse of intelligence and wit. It would
seem that the world, after having overworked its brain, felt the
need of returning to the life of the heart. In literature this return
of sensibility showed itself by the success of sentimental comedy
and romance. This general tendency of the cultured public also
affected painting; it explains the huge success obtained by
Greuze.

JEAN-BAPTISTE GREUZE (1725–1805) succeeded in harrow-
ing the feelings of his contemporaries by putting before them
scenes of melodrama. His pictures arouse emotion, pity, and
despair, while showing us virtue rewarded or vice punished.
The *Betrothed of the village*, in the Louvre, is a pretty scene of
comic opera; the *Paternal Curse* is a scene of pathetic melodrama. However, Greuze is not devoid of charming pictorial
qualities. They are specially to be admired in his portraits
of young girls, whose ingenuous expressions, tearful eyes, and
ruffled draperies he enjoyed painting. In this way Greuze, the
preacher and moralist, truly belongs to his century. When he
speaks to us of vice, he tries to convince us that he wishes to
reprove it; in reality he enjoys the pleasure of describing it.

HONORÉ FRAGONARD (1732–1806) sometimes, like Greuze,
fell into the emotional style, but he is a finely gifted painter,
with a fire and spirit which give life and vivacity to even
his simplest compositions. He only requires the most insignificant subject, the most modest colours and, if need be, a few
touches of ink, to give life to interesting figures and to compose
pretty decorations. He has left a large number of small works,
animated by extraordinary life and spirit.

The portrait-painters followed the fashion, and while Nattier,
under Louis XV, represented women of the world in their
drawing-rooms or amidst mythological clouds, Drouais, or
Mme Vigée-Lebrun appeal to our emotions by painting Queen
Marie-Antoinette in the midst of her children and the great
court-ladies.

The somewhat artificial life of the salons had also provoked a
reaction of public feeling towards the simplicity of country life,
or at least the love of nature. Just as Marie-Antoinette played

at being a shepherdess in the park of the Petit Trianon, so the Parisian public showed an increasing taste for the objects of the country and for natural surroundings. This new taste, which was manifested in literature by numerous descriptions of sunsets, was soon reflected in painting, renewing the success of landscape. No doubt this kind of painting had never entirely disappeared, but nature had never been presented except when blended with historical memories; the surroundings, always carefully arranged, were generally taken from Italy and for the most part from the neighbourhood of Rome. JOSEPH VERNET (1714–1789), the successful landscape-painter of the 18th century, owed his success to the fact that he discarded these historical pretensions, and was content to paint the scenes such as he saw them, or at least only changing them so far as the picturesque habits and the taste of his period obliged him. The Naval Gallery in the Louvre has preserved the series of *French Ports* which he executed by order of the king. The sincerity of these landscapes is beyond doubt, but the vision of the painter is not yet practised enough to enable him to note with precision the difficulty of differentiating between northern and southern, morning and evening light.

Another landscape-painter, HUBERT ROBERT (1733–1808), also obtained a great success in painting old ruins, on which he depicted the play of a fanciful light. He amused himself by grouping together capriciously, like the flowers of a bouquet, the most celebrated Roman monuments. These pictures of venerable ruins must not be taken too seriously. Hubert Robert only wished to make decorative pictures which should please the eye. He is moreover one of those artists who painted models of those so-called English parks which replaced the geometrical regularity of the French style by the fanciful and the unexpected, by the mingling of trees of various species and the varied combinations of trees and ruins. The closing 18th century thought this was the best way of imitating the irregularity of nature.

At the end of the 18th century, during the reign of Louis XVI, architecture and painting showed once more submission to classical rules, that is to say, they returned to the faithful imitation of ancient art. An extraordinary fact is that political events accentuated this return to a severe style of art; the courtly pictures after Boucher seemed to be the expression of the corrupt aristocracy, which had just been overthrown; the art of the Revolution had a moralising and archaeological tendency. Moreover, at this period, the discovery of the little town of Pompeii, unearthed from the ashes of Vesuvius, made known to modern man the life of antiquity, shown not only in works of art, but unveiled in its private life. The decorations and furniture of Pompeii supplied archaeological art with a quantity of information which had been lacking to archaeological artists, so numerous since the Renaissance. The Revolution had other reasons for admiring and copying ancient art; the Republicans of the Convention and the Directory, and, no less, the men of the Empire sincerely intended to re-establish the institutions and customs of the Roman Republic and Roman Empire, and just as they borrowed the vocabulary of the Roman orators and gave to their magistrates the names of consuls and tribunes, so they sought to revive the life of antiquity by their architecture, their furniture, and even their dress.

The name of LOUIS DAVID (1748–1825) dominates the revolutionary and imperial period as powerfully as Le Brun dominated the reign of Louis XIV. Even during the reign of Louis XVI he had become known by his paintings, *Horace*, *Brutus*, the *Death of Socrates*, in which already is felt the stoical breath of conventional authority. Moreover, David was a deputy during the Convention and a faithful partisan of Robespierre. Under the Empire he remained the leader of the French school and painted the two most expressive compositions of this passing fashion, *The Coronation* (Louvre) and *The Distribution of Standards* (Versailles). When he was not working for Napoleon, he returned to his beloved heroes of antiquity, painting *Leonidas at Thermopylae* and *The Rape of the Sabine Women*. David is one of those artists, of which there are several in the French school, who were richly gifted by nature, but who were spoilt by the spirit of the school. He had a profound respect for truth and opposed with happy effect the futile art of Boucher's last pupils. But this love of reality was thwarted in him by a fanatical admiration for the art of antiquity. Instead of merely painting humanity as he saw it, he strove to correct according to the Greco-Roman canon the proportions of the models who were posing for him, and he affected to despise the picturesque resources and rich colours of reality, because ancient art only showed him statues of marble against the grey walls of a gallery. With his qualities and his defects, his pomposity and his eagerness for a difficult form of art, David strongly represents revolutionary and imperial society.

Round David were collected his imitators and pupils. The most celebrated paintings of PIERRE-NARCISSE GUÉRIN (1774–1833), which are in the Louvre, were scenes of classical tragedy. We find in them theatrical attitudes and the costumes which had recently been introduced on the stage by Talma. FRANÇOIS-PASCAL GÉRARD (1770–1837) was an artist of less ambition: his easy and agreeable talent enabled him to compose scenes in the ideal and antique manner, and also to record the features of great ladies and high dignitaries of the Empire and the Restoration in formal and finely posed portraits.

ANNE-LOUIS GIRODET (1767–1824) was one of David's pupils in whom the restlessness of a new art is already discernible: romanticism, whose gorgeous dreams are magnificently expressed in Chateaubriand's works, found in him its first painter. Unfortunately, Girodet did not possess the pictorial means necessary to express the new sensibility. He was content to wrap the pale statues of David's school in grey mists. His *Atala*, his *Endymion*, and his *Flood* (Louvre), give us the impression of great attempts which have failed.

The two best painters of this period were Prud'hon and Gros. PIERRE PRUD'HON (1758–1823) had the greatest talent. He succeeded in imbuing his colour with the delicate sensuality of the 18th century and the soft melancholy of romanticism. He had studied, like all David's best pupils, the purity of Greek plastic art, but he took good care not to impoverish his painting by contenting himself with copying the smooth coldness of marble. In his painting of flesh there is a warmth and play of light imparting an appearance of life which immediately distinguishes them from all the other works of the school of David. Though as graceful and delicate as Praxiteles and Correggio, Prud'hon was nevertheless able to rise to the execution of noble mythological and allegorical compositions.

His *Psyche carried away by Love* and *Justice pursuing Crime*
are the finest pieces of painting of this period, and one of the best
portraits of the French school is that of *Josephine*, dreaming
sadly in the seclusion of her park at Malmaison.

ANTOINE-JEAN GROS (1771–1835) was the appointed battle-
painter of the Empire; he had seen war and taken part in the
Italian campaign; hence his battle-pictures are not, like those of
other military painters, the recollections of a man who has only
seen soldiers on the parade-ground or at reviews in the square
of the Carrousel. Moreover, he was a great admirer of Rubens,
the painter of spirited movement and brilliant colour, who was,
before Gros, the most capable of rendering the heat of battle
and the splendour of uniform. In his best works, his easy
and brilliant brush softened and warmed the somewhat rigid
coldness of his David-like drawing. Moreover Gros greatly
ennobled and amplified the art of military painting; before him,
a battle-picture was only a picturesque subject to please the eye,
as with Salvator Rosa, or, as with Van der Meulen, a formal
scene designed to show off the glory of the king. Gros put
thought into his battle-painting. In front of *The Plague-stricken
at Jaffa* and especially of the *Battle of Eylau*, the spectator
cannot escape the emotion caused by the human suffering
which the artist has had the courage to depict by the side of
military glory.

The period which extends from the end of the Empire to the
Revolution of July was filled by the development of what is
called Romanticism, and by the struggle of its literary and artistic
principles with the classical tradition. Literary romanticism is
well known; it was manifested in the works of Lamartine, Victor
Hugo, Vigny, and Musset. There was also a romantic movement
in art: it was clearly expressed, especially in painting, and the
other arts likewise interpreted, each in its own way, this new
form of French thought and sensibility.

Once again, at the close of David's school, we see artists who
outlived the influence of their work. David ended his days in
Brussels, where he lived in exile after the fall of the Empire.
And while he was painting his last pictures in Belgium, already
in Paris young artists were criticising his teaching and ex-

hibiting paintings in contradiction of his principles. Already
Girodet had disturbed his master by his effects of light and his
choice of subjects. However, his manner of painting still remained
in comparative agreement with the teaching of the school.
But now we see young painters, in front of the pictures exhibited
in the Louvre, which set before their eyes the finest examples
of the art of Flanders, Spain, and Bologna, learning to
model with delicacy and force, and to fashion bodies made
of solid matter. JEAN-LOUIS GÉRICAULT (1791–1824) admired
the expressive power of naturalism as shown by Caravaggio
or Rubens. His vigorous painting showed the followers of
David that their ideal and abstract art could no longer satisfy
a generation of men brought up in the fever of the Revolution
and the Empire. Géricault was one of the first naturalists of
the French school, and it is worthy of note that he learnt to
see and reproduce by the study of pictures in museums. In
the very height of David's sway, he distinguished himself by
violent paintings, representing horsemen fighting. But when the
Restoration sent the soldiers home to their firesides, Géricault
painted his famous *Medusa's Raft* (Louvre), a spirited composition, a mass of corpses and dying men, above whom a few
figures, supported by hope, make appealing gestures and
stretch their hands towards rescue. This vigorous painting, these
violent contrasts of light and shade, this storm and stress, all
had their effect on budding romanticism. We must also recall
the numerous pictures of horses and horsemen which Géricault
executed in England in the latter part of his short life. He died
too soon for it to be possible to fix with certainty the place
which his sturdy talent was destined to fill.

The friend of his youth, EUGÈNE DELACROIX (1798–1863),
was the leader of the Romantic school. It was in the Salon of
1822 that he made his name known by a picture of *Dante and
Virgil in Hell* (Louvre); a picture of tragic figures, writhing con-
vulsively in a sinister light. A little later, the *Massacre of Scio*
(Louvre) shocked the classicists and served as a rallying point
to the Romantic school. The choice of subject, the agitated
and unbalanced composition, the original colour, the nervous
touches, all shocked classical taste, and Delacroix was accused
of having painted with a "drunken brush." In truth, the

work which had just appeared was a revolutionary one, and we find in it all that constitutes the inner soul of romanticism.

It is not easy to explain exactly what is meant by romanticism; it shows itself under many varying aspects according to individuality, and it is one of its essential characteristics that it accentuates the originality and personality of the artist. In general terms it may be said that while the classical school believed in the existence of an ideal beauty, accessible to all and dominating all schools and individuals, and expected every artist to strive after this beauty as his aim, romanticism founds its aesthetics on individual sensibility, and regards a work as more beautiful in proportion to its sincerity and originality and as it represents more faithfully the personal genius of its creator. Several consequences result from this general principle: the classicist is an imitator; the romanticist rejects all slavish imitation of a model; the classicist bases his art on reason and mistrusts the caprices of feeling and imagination; the romanticist, on the contrary, allows himself to be carried away by his sensitive qualities and fears lest reasoning and reflection should destroy his emotions and the fire of his inspiration. Other differences separate the romanticist and the classicist; the classicist worships antiquity and despises the Middle Ages; the romanticist betrays his weariness of the long reign of ancient art and turns with relief to the dark and mysterious centuries of the Middle Ages. Finally—and this is perhaps where the opposition between the two schools is most violent—while the classicist, an admirer of the Greeks and of Raphael, shows himself a purist in the matter of drawing and seeks for balance of composition and for purity of line, the romanticist affects, sometimes sincerely, a certain inaccuracy of drawing, and, when he is not a great painter like Delacroix, clothes an extravagant composition with a medley of violent colours.

Delacroix represents all that is best in romanticism. He expresses in his feverish work the exaltation and passion of his nervous and ungovernable nature. He throws on the canvas his harmonious or discordant colours by violent strokes of the brush. The classicists accused him of inaccuracy, and it is true that his drawing lacks the purity and restraint to which the French public had become accustomed by the school of David. Delacroix so greatly prized the independence of his personal sensibility that he not only rejected the teaching of the school, but even refused to copy faithfully the model which he had under his eyes. He consulted nature, not in order to give a speaking likeness of it, but to supply himself with a subject which he could use according to his fancy. We do not find in any of his pictures that careful conscientiousness which implies an attentive study of the model. He has indeed left some portraits, but his genius was too ungovernable to submit to the necessity of a likeness. He said one day when speaking of his manner: " I begin by painting a woman and I end by painting a lion." This independence is also to be found in his historical paintings. Because he loved the Middle Ages, it is not to be supposed that he attempted to give an accurate reproduction of them. The Middle Ages were for him only a subject which enabled his imagination to indulge in all sorts of fancies. The Middle Ages pleased the Romantic school so much because, being little known, they gave to these visionary painters every scope for invention. Delacroix was as incapable of being bound by historical truth as by the truth of reality.

The universe in which he moved was entirely derived from his own imagination; the men and things, the animals and plants, all reflected his feverish melancholy. We see in them all the emotion of his time, the exaltation of a reader of romances, the dreams of Dante, the dramas of Shakespeare and of Goethe, the poems of Byron and of Walter Scott. His works also illustrated the actual life of his time, the episode of the war for Greek independence, the barricades of 1830; pages which call up memories of the Middle Ages, the *Battle of Nancy*, the *Battle of Taillebourg*, the *Taking of Constantinople by the Crusaders*; and also numerous oriental scenes, displays of Arab horsemen, sleepy harems, the hunting of big game, all recollections of a journey which he made to Morocco. Finally, Delacroix was one of the finest decorators of his day; he finished the roof of the Gallery of Apollo in the Louvre, which was begun by Lebrun. And in the church of Saint-Sulpice, his mural paintings in the chapel of the Holy Angels should also be seen.

Delacroix had not and could not have pupils, because art, as he conceived it, could not be a subject of instruction; nevertheless he was the originator of all the great pictorial innovations of the 19th century: firstly, because he taught that the artist has the right of his own opinion against everyone, when he is capable of imposing by his genius a new point of view; and secondly, because by new combinations of colour, harmonies, or contrasts, he proved that painting was still very far from having exhausted all the expressive resources of colour. Thus the modern Impressionists, though they copy real life and never paint except from Nature, have nevertheless found in Delacroix the first example of a painter who, in order to render it better, resolved a tone into its primary colours.

Round Delacroix collected many young painters, who profited both by his fame and by his unpopularity, but none shared his genius, and, after some youthful manifestations, most of them settled down and returned to the influence of the school. Most, like Deveria and Boulanger, were far from fulfilling their early promise. Another, Paul Delaroche, who by his choice of subjects and his love of historical scenes, might have passed for one of the Romantic school, gradually showed that he was a prudent follower of the classical masters. As for Ary Scheffer, if his sentimental prejudices sometimes attracted him to the inspiration of romance, the poverty of his artistic resources kept him wisely faithful to academical principles.

The true romanticists showed themselves in small works, engravings or lithographs. There exists a whole library of romantic books illustrated by drawings by Célestin Nanteuil, Tony Johannot, Deveria, and Delacroix himself. These illustrations, now a little out of fashion, are the product of feverish imaginations and visions of nightmare; people dressed in Gothic style, with angular gestures and picturesque costumes, have taken the place of the linear designs and correct anatomy of Girodet and Flaxman.

Among the painters who avoided the struggle between the romantic and classical schools, and who succeeded in rousing admiration in both camps, it is necessary to mention ALEXANDRE-GABRIEL DECAMPS (1803–1860), an artist of refined technique, a colourist who loved uncommon effects, and a fervent Orientalist. But he cannot be placed on an equality with Delacroix, because in his temperament there was no place for the fire of passion. When his small pictures, full of intense colours, are examined, it is evident that for him painting reduced itself to technical experiments.

But over against Delacroix and his group we must now place the artist who faced the leader of the romantic school, JEAN-AUGUSTE-DOMINIQUE INGRES (1780–1867). Never were two natures more opposed, and the antagonism between the two schools was rendered more bitter by the antipathy which separated the two men. Just as the work of Delacroix is full of passion and emotion, so that of Ingres is pure and serene. He was above all things an artist; he valued above all things the purity of an outline, the rounding of a curve. It must not however be imagined that he was a follower of the manner of David. David had a tendency to reduce everything to a type. Ingres, on the contrary, with his flexible and bold drawing, accentuated the differences which David was inclined to efface. Hence this pupil of David's, when he was in Italy, showed a preference for the Florentine Primitives of the 15th century, which surprised and alarmed the masters of the school. Perhaps the desire of representing classicism in opposition to Delacroix caused Ingres to defend theories which he would not naturally have applied.

The ruling passion with him is the love of fine drawing, the charm of sinuous lines executed by a sure hand. This is perceptible even in his first works, in which the desire for a beautiful outline plainly predominates over the love of modelling. He did not admire the developed muscles of the Greco-Roman statues as much as did the school of David. On the other hand, he appreciated better the nervous delicacy of Florentine drawing; perhaps he even admired those Greek vase paintings, on which the figures are expressed by outlines made with the point of the brush. We may sometimes raise objections to Ingres's paintings, but only admiration can be felt for his drawings. He knew the full value of a lead pencil, and often at the beginning of his career to make a living, and later to amuse himself, he drew pencil portraits which are little masterpieces.

When he allows himself to follow his personal preferences, he returns naturally to the soft curves of nude female figures. If it had not been necessary for him to accept the commissions of his admirers, and to paint portraits and large decorative pieces,

perhaps he would have been content to paint naiads and oda-
lisquès. In these the drawing of the nape of the neck, the supple
line of the shoulder and the arm, the turn of the torso on the hip,
the long curves of the legs in repose, become so many examples
of incomparable purity and perfection. Every time that a female
figure appears in his work, whether it be the Virgin, or allegorical maidens of the *Iliad* and the *Odyssey*, or the youthful
figure of the *Source*, always by force of perfection he avoids the
commonplace and attains to unforgettable beauty.

As the leader of a school, he was repeatedly compelled to force
his talent a little and to attempt ambitious compositions. His
Apotheosis of Homer, in the Louvre, with its beauties and its
flaws, marks an important date in the history of decorative
painting in France; by the symmetrical arrangement of the
figures, the rejection of all attempt at realism, the deliberately
pale colouring, the intangible atmosphere of the whole, this
painting opened the way to a style of decoration, which did not
come to perfection until in Puvis de Chavannes there appeared
a painter who was capable of placing these abstract figures
in an atmosphere where it is possible to breathe. Ingres
seized this opportunity to group together all the divinities of the
classical Pantheon and to expel from the picture, or to put in
the worst places, the writers and artists who were too greatly
admired by the Romantic school.

Numerous pupils continued the decorative work of Ingres,
Amaury Duval, Mottez, and above all, HIPPOLYTE FLANDRIN
(1809–1864). This group of painters found a vast field for their
activities in the Parisian churches constructed under the July
Monarchy and the Second Empire. The style inaugurated by
Ingres was continued and exaggerated by his disciples. Its
principal defect is that it tends to an abstract and cold form of
art. We see dawning little by little that affectation of simplicity
which eventually led to the imitation of the Primitives. The
best of these followers of Ingres is Flandrin, whose decoration
of Saint-Germain-des-Prés has been much admired. There we
find the pages of the Gospel interpreted by an art which is
somewhat devoid of distinction.

Subjects derived from the Middle Ages were not confined to
the Romantic school; the last of David's school, Ingres and his

pupils, treated them almost as often as they did antiquity. The middle of the 19th century witnessed the birth of an extraordinary movement of national history and the curiosity of the cultured public was directed to the origins of French civilisation. Moreover, the July Monarchy had just converted the palace of Versailles into a museum of the history of France; the best painters were commissioned to show in large compositions its most famous events, from the Baptism of Clovis to the conquest of Algeria. The chapters devoted to Louis XIV and Napoleon had already been supplied by the painters of the schools of Lebrun and David. For the earlier reigns the pictures seemed often to have been executed by artists with little feeling. It is however to this undertaking that we owe Delacroix's two fine pictures of the *Battle of Taillebourg* and the *Crusaders at Constantinople*.

HORACE VERNET (1789–1863) was one of the most gifted of all these painters, thanks to his facility and his unpretending good humour. He was the clever illustrator of the Algerian war. But PAUL DELAROCHE (1797–1856) was the most representative of these artists devoted to history. He succeeded in giving a dramatic personality to historical personages, Elizabeth of England, Charles I, Cromwell, Henry III, Richelieu, whose activities were recounted by eminent historians, such as Guizot and Barante. Delaroche was a clever stage-manager, who pleased the *bourgeoisie* of his time all the better because he did not shock their taste, like Delacroix, by lively sallies. Some other painter-historians deserve mention, such as Tony Robert, Fleury, and Isabey, who, in his small compositions, however, made little claim to great historical painting and was content to make light play on the fine costumes of his subjects.

Mention also is due, along with the great historical painters, to the less ambitious masters who were content to use lithography, a process of engraving which had just been invented and which was very fashionable in the Romantic period. NICOLAS CHARLET (1792–1845) and DENIS RAFFET (1804–1860) helped to preserve in Orleanist France the memory of the Revolution and the Empire, the volunteers of '93 shod in sabots, the old soldier of the Great Army, the conscript of 1814, and finally the Emperor, on his white horse, with his overcoat and small hat. Raffet by his lithographs gave form to the Napoleonic legend of which the romantic soul dreamed. His lithographs of the *Alarm* and the *Night Review* are admirable examples, which have felt the breath of the epic spirit.

Lithography played a polemical part. It could appear daily, like a newspaper article; and it took its share in the political battles of the July Monarchy. During the first years of his reign, the few years of liberty, Louis-Philippe continually recurred as a subject for the pencil of the caricaturists. HENRI MONNIER (1805–1877) created the type of Joseph Prud'homme, which showed the successful *bourgeois* bursting with importance and swollen with conceit. GAVARNI (1801–1866) wittily depicted the life of the grisette, of the student, and of the National Guard. But HONORÉ DAUMIER (1808–1879) surpassed all these little masters by the power and extraordinary raciness of his pencil. He treated the human body with surprising audacity; he has left unforgettable pictures, which are eloquent invectives against the *bourgeois* monarchy. He also executed a few paintings, which are much sought after by collectors.

One of the greatest achievements of romanticism was the cult of Nature. It had its reflection in painting, and the first half of the 19th century witnessed the rise in France of a school of landscape painters, who did not at first receive recognition from the general public, but whose fame has never ceased to grow. It is called the school of 1830, or the Fontainebleau school. Since the end of the 18th century, the Parisian public had become enamoured of the wild beauty of the forest of Fontainebleau. This forest, quite close to Paris, enabled the Parisians, when they left the city, to enjoy the charm of unexplored country. Already, under Louis XVI, some rather mediocre painters, such as Bruandet, had settled there, in order to paint the scenery. Under the Restoration this movement became accentuated; some modest painters, devoid of ambition, settled among the peasants on the outskirts of the forest and devoted their days to painting the old trees. Thus were formed little colonies of painters in villages whose names have since become famous in the history of art: Barbizon, Marlotte, etc. They led a simple life, shod in sabots, engrossed in the pleasure of admiring and painting nature, and did not always trouble to exhibit their pictures in the Paris Salons. Moreover, the most famous of them, Rousseau and Millet, were not always well received by the hanging committees; they shared the habitual fate of all innovators—they were for long slighted. But later, popularity came to them, and their works now fetch in public auctions prices which are constantly increasing.

Nevertheless, the landscape painters of this school were not absolutely a novelty in the history of art. They were connected with the Dutch school, that of Ruysdael and Hobbema, and derived their general principles from them—the proportion of sky to earth, and many technical details. One of the earliest landscape-painters in the 19th century, Gustave Michel, in painting scenes of the suburbs, imitated the tawny colour of the ground and the grey skies of Holland so well, that at first sight his pictures give the impression of being by Ruysdael, and the mills of Montmartre seem to be the mills of Haarlem.

But the Fontainebleau artists were not bound by these memories of the Dutch masters; they were directly inspired by nature in the effects which they reproduced. The earliest of them still show a little indecision, either because they wished to inspire their landscapes with romantic expression, like Paul Huet, or because, like Cabat, they still preserved some of the ambitions of historical landscape, or because, like De la Berge, they examined things too closely to see them well.

By 1830, JEAN-BAPTISTE COROT (1796–1875) was far enough advanced in the discovery of nature to be completely free from all the difficulties which beset his predecessors. Properly speaking, he did not belong to the Fontainebleau group, and his very long career enabled him to get beyond the point of view of the artists of his generation. In his first works he is still connected with the historical landscapes of Aligny and his master Bertin, and his last works show him as belonging to the painters of light of the Impressionist school. Corot was a much-travelled Parisian; he had journeyed in Italy, sketching the landscapes of Tuscany and Umbria, and also painting among the ruins of Rome and the Roman Campagna; he travelled in France; and finally settled in the suburbs of Paris, at Ville d'Avray, and in the north near Arras, fascinated by the transparent grey tints of the sky and the delicate haze of these damp regions. Corot was above all things a painter of light; his attention was not arrested by the objects themselves, but by the varied effects of light and shade. Never, in his pictures, is the light garish, or the shadow opaque. It is always between these extremes that he finds endless resources for producing varied effects. Moreover, he dreams as much as he beholds, and his memories of Rome easily blend with the landscapes of the Ile-de-France. A passing figure changes spontaneously into a mythological personage, and, without ceasing to be true, his landscape seems to be entirely poetical; the white forms which rise from the damp sward under the warmth of the morning rays become dancing nymphs. Furthermore, he always chooses the hours of twilight or dawn, when slanting rays cast long transparent shadows. In his last works, the substance of things has, so to speak, vanished; there remain only floating shadows, among which shine, here and there, like pearls, the sparks of his silvery light. Nature painted by Corot is at once poetry and reality.

THÉODORE ROUSSEAU (1812–1867) did not reduce the varied effects of nature to one favourite theme, like Corot; he allowed himself to be distracted by her variety, and he applied himself to reproducing her aspects with accuracy. He painted the plains of the Landes and the hills of Auvergne, but he spent the greater part of his career in the forest of Fontainebleau, at Barbizon; he portrayed its old trees with fervent application and indefatigable analysis. Sometimes, perhaps, he has given too much detail; but he has succeeded admirably in expressing the soul of the vegetable kingdom and particularly of the old oaks, which have developed through suffering, which have battled with the hurricane, and which find it hard to obtain from the sandy soil the means for supplying their sap. With minute touches, he has painted the detail of the leaves, of the brushwood and the mosses, of the rugged trunk and the gnarled branches. One of his comrades narrates that he remained so long motionless in attentive contemplation, with his pointed hat and his cloak, that the birds came fluttering round him, taking him for a hive. Rousseau remains the most characteristic landscape-painter of the forest, the master of the true Barbizon school.

JEAN-FRANÇOIS MILLET (1815–1875) lived near Rousseau at Barbizon. And yet their works are not at all alike. While Rousseau went into the forest to paint the vegetation, Millet left it to cross the fields and to observe the life of the peasant. The theme of his work is the struggle of the husbandman with the earth, which he forces to support him; the peasants are not the heroes of an eclogue, but rough labourers. The soil which he paints is that which is crushed by the foot of the sower, or which the peasant turns with his hoe; even when he shows the land without its inhabitants, some implement, the harrow or the plough left behind, recall the interrupted work which will be resumed on the morrow. Millet's peasants are shown in grand attitudes and are so expressive that their emphasis is sometimes criticised. Generally they stand out against the sky and their silhouettes thus shown to advantage possess singular majesty. Whatever their occupation, these peasants take on as it were a symbolical value, so much does their attitude express the effort and suffering of the peasant of all ages, that is to say, the essence of human labour. In this sense, Millet's peasants, although they are real husbandmen, with horny hands and coarse clothing, are the expression of thought, just as much as the figures of Poussin. Each of his compositions invites serious meditation. Like our classical painters, Millet addresses himself to the eyes, but it is in order to reach the thought. This thought is impregnated with romantic melancholy. With eloquent simplicity it interprets the monotony and sadness of the struggle, as old as Humanity, between man and the earth. We feel how much this pity corresponds to our modern feeling. The work of Millet has therefore had immense consequences on our contemporary art.

Near Rousseau we must place the painter NARCISSE DIAZ (1809–1876), who, like him, is the landscape-painter of foliage and underwoods. But Diaz is less truthful and more fanciful; he plays with the rays which pass through the leafy road to illumine some tree-trunk or pool in the mysterious underwood.

JULES DUPRÉ (1811–1889) composed strongly and modified forms by sacrificing details to the effect of the whole. Besides, he condensed intense colours in a compact glaze; he corrected in the studio the effects sketched from nature, amplified them and forced them, so that a very humble motive became a majestic scene. In short, he seems less preoccupied than Rousseau with representing what he sees.

Some younger landscape-painters may be mentioned in connexion with this group such as ANTOINE CHINTREUIL (1816–1873), a few of whose large paintings are in the Louvre. They are somewhat empty and bare, but possess great freshness. In the work of CHARLES-FRANÇOIS DAUBIGNY (1817–1878) there is facility, and we feel the artist's joy in painting. He was especially the painter of the Oise valley, where poplars and willows are reflected in a calm stream.

Finally, among these landscape-painters a place must be found for the painters of animals. While CHARLES JACQUES (1813–1894) was the special painter of sheep, which he represents as woolly and dirty, the animals of CONSTANT TROYON (1810–1865), generally cows and oxen, aim at a decorative effect.

During the second half of the 19th century it was painting which best displayed all the shades of contemporary feeling. And the first thing that strikes us in it are the naturalistic tendencies which dominate the whole of our intellectual life. The romanticists, whether painters or poets, only consulted nature in order to find subjects round which their fancy could play. Now, it was nature which guided inspiration. Painters and sculptors, like writers, thought that the great ambition in art should be absolute accuracy. This submission to the object painted is a virtue proper to scientists. And, in fact, scientists have taken the place of poets in the general direction of the intellect.

A new artistic revolution reflected this intellectual transformation. The work of GUSTAVE COURBET (1819–1877), which appeared at this moment, is as much opposed to the classicism of Ingres as to the romanticism of Delacroix. Courbet was a strong artist, who painted boldly and in its entirety the model which he had under his eyes. This method was new in France, for up to this time, though French painters doubtless drew from nature, yet when they painted, their mentality interposed between the sketch and the finished picture. Perhaps for the first time we have a painter who painted large figures in this way, as had been done by the great naturalists of the Neapolitan,

Flemish, Dutch, and Spanish schools, and this direct contact with reality gave to his work a fine strength and spirit in execution. No intellectual process intervened between the observing eye and the executing hand. This way of painting was a great surprise to his contemporaries, and Courbet came into collision with prevailing taste, which inclined to the small, careful, and delicate pictures of the followers of Ingres. But owing to his pride, which was stupendous, he had the courage to hold out against ridicule and to impose his style on the public. His pictures were rejected by the Salon, so he exhibited them to the public in defiance of the official decision, and his bold experiments encouraged new attempts and founded the school of naturalism in painting.

However, when we examine the work of Courbet nowadays, even while admiring the fine technique of this strong artist, we cannot fail to perceive the limits of his talent and the point beyond which this innovator was unable to advance. Indeed, naturalist though he was, Courbet had learned to paint from pictures in galleries. He had too much admired the Bolognese and Neapolitan works of Guercino and Caravaggio. From them he had learned his sombre style and the heavy shadows which serve to throw up his figures in such strong relief. But an out-and-out naturalism is bound to paint men and things in the surroundings where they most often present themselves to observation, not in the four walls of a studio, but in the open air. Now the open air dissipates shadows, and violent contrasts of light and shade no longer come into play. The robust method of Courbet was powerless when he had to represent figures walking in sunlight. He could only lighten the general tone of his painting, and he lost the best qualities of his style, without giving the equivalent of real light. We had to wait to resolve this difficulty until other artists had analysed light in itself. This was the task of the impressionists. Nevertheless, Courbet remains as one of the innovators who begin a movement which leads to new achievements.

But before following the history of naturalism up to its latest consequences, we must pass in review the principal forms taken by traditional painting. And first, as to historical painting. This kind of painting, created in the 17th century, and established by the work of Poussin, had followed French taste in its transformations. It had been psychological with Poussin and his followers, decorative and fashionable in the 17th century, ideal and moralising in the school of David. In the 19th century, historical painting was still pre-eminently the grand style of painting, and, in its own way, reflected contemporary ideas. Now, the 19th century was the century of historical study. Curiosity about the past was rife, and learned men wrote history which was much better supported by documents than in old days. Thence resulted a perfectly new historical colouring, which also supplied picturesque resources, of which painters took full advantage.

During the Second Empire, after Ingres had exhibited his small *Stratonice* (Chantilly) and Couture his very large *Roman Orgy* (Louvre), there was in painting a return to ancient history. Delacroix himself abandoned the Middle Ages for a time and painted his *Medea*. JEAN-LÉON GÉRÔME (1824–1904) continued the style established by Ingres in his *Stratonice* and depicted small figures in Pompeian surroundings. His compositions are always of great ingenuity; he is an interesting illustrator even when he sets before our eyes tragic or grandiose scenes. Gérôme also tried his hand successfully at sculpture, and left in this branch of art a few delicately chiselled bronze statuettes (*Bonaparte, Bellona, The Rubicon*) and some large marble figures, which he has inspired with a feeling of life (*Tanagra, The Player of Bowls,* etc.).

Boulanger also painted charmingly reconstructed Pompeian scenes. Cabanel too was a follower of Ingres, whom he imitated in the flowing lines of his drawing. Bouguereau was a draughtsman with a studied purity of line and monotonous cleverness. Jules Lefebvre and Luc-Olivier Merson deserve to be remembered for the honesty of their art. Moreover, Merson amplified his small historical compositions into large decorative panels which are really fascinating (Opéra Comique, and Chantilly). James Tissot, in his religious paintings, applied himself to reproducing with extreme accuracy the landscapes and costumes of the Gospel. JEAN-LOUIS MEISSONIER (1815–1891) was the painter of Napoleon. His small pictures were painted with great minuteness; he rendered faithfully the smallest details of the laced and iridescent costumes of the

Empire; he brought to them the same precision which the Dutch masters showed in their small pictures of interiors. But instead of painting what he saw, Meissonier went back to the past; he was the illustrator of one of the most brilliant periods of French history. He has shown us the Emperor and his Grand Army, the retreat from Russia, battle-scenes, quarrels, cavaliers in picturesque costumes, etc. Alphonse de Neuville and Édouard Detaille represented battles in large heroic pictures, in which the brilliant uniforms of Meissonier are often muddy and dirty; the battle is fought under a rainy sky, amidst ruins and the smoke of burning houses.

GUSTAVE MOREAU (1826–1898) was at once romantic by imagination and classical by the purity and finish of his painting. His brush depicted exquisite and fanciful figures, in strange landscapes, in costumes drawn from fairy-tales, overloaded with gold and precious stones. His Salome, his Peri, his Galatea and many others transport us to a mythological world, full of idle fancy, which bears no resemblance to reality.

JEAN-PAUL LAURENS (1838–1921) has admirably succeeded in rendering the Middle Ages, the dark fury of its fierce men, murderous kings, merciless inquisitors, cruel and deceitful princes. His painting is realistic and always touching, and his feeling is not crushed beneath the weight of research. The *Excommunication of Robert the Pious* (Luxembourg Gallery) is a fine canvas, which displays much poetry.

Historical painting, little by little, was abandoned. Most of the painters preferred portrait-painting to epic scenes. Aimé Morot, Machard, Ferrier, and Flameng cleverly reproduced the features of their contemporaries, successful *bourgeois*, or fashionable women of the world.

In the 19th century rose a style of painting—Orientalism— which was particularly successful, because it encouraged the romantic taste for exotic things and because it offered the painters very rich picturesque accessories. Already the 18th century, it is true, had known a rage for Chinese and Turkish ornaments, but as an amusement and partly by way of caricature. Here, as elsewhere, the 19th century brought a desire for accuracy. The conquest of Algeria, which interested the French public all through the reign of Louis-Philippe, also favoured

the development of African landscape. Decamps and Prosper
Marilhat were Orientalists. Delacroix in his turn made a voyage
to Morocco and brought back sketches and memories which very
often reappeared in his work. Ingres himself placed in harems
many of his nude figures, whom he represented as odalisques.
HORACE VERNET (1789–1863), the painter of the Algerian army,
painted with vivacity the beautiful Arab horses. These may also
be found in the work of EUGÈNE FROMENTIN (1820–1876), with
coats like satin, muscular legs, and long manes.

Orientalism was cultivated by many classical painters, who
permitted themselves in this exotic style a realism which they
would not have dared to indulge in representing the objects and
men of their own country and period, as though the remoteness
in distance conferred a kind of historical dignity on the subjects
painted. HENRI REGNAULT (b. 1843, killed in January 1871)
died before he could fulfil the promise of his precocious talent;
yet he left some brilliant canvases, inspired by a journey to
Morocco and a sojourn in Spain.

Benjamin Constant, a very clever artist, was especially
successful in rendering the richness of Arab trappings.
But the most sincere and faithful painters of Arab life were
Guillaumet and Dinet. With these masters the East is no longer
treated as a fancy subject which permits every caprice of colour.
Guillaumet painted the desert with absolute fidelity, and Dinet
applied to the painting of African light and Arab draperies the
division of tones to which our eyes have become accustomed in
impressionist painting. The landscape-painter Ziem was also an
Orientalist, who composed pictures with rare and dazzling tints
when depicting Venice or Constantinople.

The 19th century was also a century of eclecticism; the history
of art and the institution of picture-galleries caused the best
works of former schools to be known and admired. Therefore
artists were no longer content, like those who repaired to Rome
in the 16th and 17th centuries, to follow the reigning school. They
chose their favourite models in bygone ages and in various
schools. Hence it is not difficult to discover in the best painters
which model they have chosen and who has helped to form them.
We have seen how the landscape-painters received the stamp
of the Dutch masters and that Courbet was a pupil of the

Bolognese. We shall see that Manet never lost the impressions made on him by the Spanish masters and by Franz Hals.

But it is chiefly on the portrait-painters that the influence of older art is visible, for in a portrait, however little the artist may strive after style, it is almost inevitable that the great schools of former days should be recalled.

Ricard, who, under the Second Empire, excited admiration by his portraits of finished execution and profound expression, imitated the art of Venice or Antwerp sometimes so closely that we might believe that he had wished to produce a *pastiche* of Titian or Van Dyck. CAROLUS-DURAN (1837–1917) is, on the contrary, the painter of external appearances, with satin-like greys, complexions of dazzling freshness, and superficial facility of execution, which reveal him as a great admirer of Velasquez. As to LÉON BONNAT (*b.* 1833), he is also a disciple of Spanish art, and by the strength of his modelling he often reminds us of Ribera. A particular mention is due to him, because of his half official position in the art of the Third Republic. Bonnat was the authorised portrayer of illustrious persons, of great men in politics, literature, and art. The historian of the end of the 19th century who wishes to know the personality of those who filled the stage must perforce consult Bonnat's gallery of portraits.

The Italians and Spaniards must be counted among the masters of the French contemporary school. We must also recognise the profound influence exercised by the English portrait-painters of the 18th century; Reynolds and Gainsborough revealed the charm of beautiful patrician figures standing against the golden foliage of an autumnal park. The figure is thus imbued with the spirit of poetry which is breathed by the scene. The lesson was not wasted on clever portrait-painters, such as Benjamin Constant, and above all Ferdinand Humbert. The latter was not only a portrait-painter, but he has left some fine decorations in the Panthéon. Jacques Blanche, with his light touch and finished work, may also be counted amongst those who learnt their business from the best works of the English school.

Two portrait-painters stand out clearly from the rest of the school, by their intensity of feeling as much as by their originality

of treatment: IGNACE FANTIN-LATOUR (1836–1904) and EUGÈNE
CARRIÈRE (1849–1906). The flexible and delicate painting of
Fantin is as admirable as his models. They are careless about
elegance of costume or attitude and their painter arranges them
awkwardly enough, one beside the other. Neither the models
nor their painter seek to astonish or please us, but in the
painting there is such faithfulness that it compels admiration.
Besides, Fantin studied his sitters so profoundly that he
gives us the very rare impression of being face to face with
people of character. Carrière, in this search for the expression of
character, almost went so far as to suppress external appearances.
He softens colours, he effaces forms so as only to leave the
appearance of the general plan. It seems in this abstract
painting as though our gaze reaches the soul through the body.
Carrière has painted family groups, pictures of motherhood
(Luxembourg), on which the attitudes, the movements of the
arms, render visible the ties of blood and of affection. But this
colourless painting gives the impression of something unfinished,
which ends by wearying us.

In contrast to naturalistic painting, which was always advancing towards greater truth and accuracy, was the painting
which sought for decorative effects. The 19th century had need
of decorative painters, but it was not without difficulty that a
decorative art was created. The revolution of David had as its
first result the disappearance of the Boucher style, the charm
and spirit of which were so well suited to 18th century apartments. The severe figures of the new school, with their stiff
attitudes, the abstract bareness of their surroundings and
their moral pretensions, were not suitable for the adornment of
walls and ceilings. Then came romanticism, which considered all
these historical or mythological personages old-fashioned. As for
religious subjects, they could not be used outside churches.
Robbed of the resources of antiquity and Christianity, what
subjects then could our decorators treat?

However, Delacroix managed to get out of the difficulty by
reviving the richness of the Venetian masters, of brilliant colouring, of riotous compositions, in heavy gilt frames. In contrast
to this brilliant art, Ingres presented his compositions of
reposeful lines and quiet colouring. He thus recalled the fact

that the artist must simplify his modelling so as to adapt it to the surface of the wall, and that the balance of the attitudes should harmonise with the stability of the architectural lines.

It is from the manner of Ingres that is derived the large decorative painting by Delaroche in the semi-circular arena of the École des Beaux Arts. Recalling the *Apotheosis of Homer*, Delaroche has grouped together all the great men in the history of art, but he has not succeeded in giving expression to the common feeling which inspired this crowd and which gives the reason for bringing them together.

Although he has left no important works, the painter PAUL-JOSEPH CHENAVARD (1808–1895) must not be forgotten, on account of the influence which he exercised on the artists of his day. When the brush was in his hand, he was somewhat lacking in pictorial resources. His art is wanting in life, but he had the merit of showing that painting loses nothing by expressing noble ideas. Doubtless he tried to make it express too much; he had planned a decorative effect at the Panthéon, which would have been, under the form of pictures, a history of human thought. His attempt, which did not lead to anything, was not however useless, and, after his time, masters such as Puvis de Chavannes remembered that a large decorative panel is much more moving if, instead of showing only forms and colours, it suggests noble considerations.

THÉODORE CHASSÉRIAU (1819–1856) was also a painter who had not time to fulfil his destiny. He was one of the most gifted masters of our school, with a very impressionable nature; he followed Delacroix, whose violent colour and restless drawing he copied, after having practised the calmer style and peaceful harmony of the compositions of Ingres; but nevertheless his delicate personality was not destroyed by his contact with these dominating geniuses. His fine religious decorative works in the Paris churches of Saint-Merri and Saint-Roch deserve a visit; the remains of the paintings which he executed in the Cour des Comptes have been collected in the Louvre.

PAUL BAUDRY (1828–1886) will be remembered chiefly for his fine paintings in the foyer of the Opera. He had studied the masters of the Italian Renaissance. His very adaptable talent had successfully assimilated some of the best qualities of Raphael, Michael Angelo, and Veronese. In looking at his beautiful paintings, we are at every moment reminded of the pliant figures of the Florentine, the harmonious compositions of the Roman, and the delicate silvery light of the Venetian.

Another decorator of the Opera, ÉLIE DELAUNAY (1828–1891), was likewise a clever and intelligent painter, who knew how to gather from the past that which could be adapted to modern art. No reproach can be made against the painters of this school, except that they imitated too much and did not invent enough.

The greatest master of decorative art in the 19th century was PIERRE PUVIS DE CHAVANNES (1824–1898), a painter from Lyons like Flandrin and Chenavard, who before him had attempted to express great ideas in painting. A painting by Puvis de Chavannes is immediately recognisable by the tranquillity of line, the simplification of drawing, and the stability of composition, which always harmonises with the architectural design. The colours are attenuated, almost as if half effaced; the light and shades form a composition without accent and without violence. The general tone is, as it were, chalky; although he painted in oils, he apparently wished to give the effect of fresco, and on his palette the colours always seem to be mixed with white, as though they allowed the plaster of the wall to show through. Indeed, Puvis de Chavannes deeply considered the tones of the Italian frescoes, and even his drawing, which is of a somewhat studied simplicity and stiffness, carries us back beyond the Renaissance to the style of Giotto. Hence, his pictures have no need to be framed in gilded wood, like those of Delacroix and Baudry; they stand out against their background of grey stone and do not clash with the severe and light rooms of our modern palaces.

Puvis de Chavannes was not content to renew the means of expression of decorative painting: he showed also that in order to interest us this painting should express some clear and great idea. He did not return to mythological figures, but gave life to very simple and beautiful allegories, easy to understand and which avoid the commonplace, when they are treated by a painter who gives them noble attitudes and places them in a lovely landscape. In the picture-gallery at Amiens, to decorate the well of the staircase, Puvis de Chavannes painted vast symbolical compositions, Peace, War, and Work, in which are resumed the appearance of the country of Picardy and its manner of life. Several French towns also possess fine compositions by Puvis, which are generally appropriate to the district, whose geographical and historical features they symbolise. It is enough to enumerate them to understand the very simple method of his allegories. At Marseilles there is a picture to recall the foundation of the town, *Marseilles, a Greek colony*, and another to sum up the part played by it, *Marseilles the gate of the East*. At Poitiers there are compositions recalling the conflict between the civilisation of the Franks and the civilisation of the Arabs.

At Lyons, paintings in the gallery symbolise Christian inspiration and heathen inspiration meeting in a Sacred Wood, where they are reconciled. At Rouen the industries of the province are recalled, with the wide Seine landscape as a background. In Paris at the Panthéon, Puvis has gone back to the origin of the city and has revived the *Legend of St Geneviève*, patroness of the Parisians. In the Hôtel de Ville, he has summed up in powerful compositions the aspects of Summer and Winter. In the Sorbonne, in the temple of science, he has collected in a similar Sacred Wood the allegorical figures of sciences and letters, to whom he has given the appearance of life, by placing them in an atmosphere in which it is possible to breathe. Similarly inspired was his last work, the paintings which decorate the staircase of the library at Boston.

This art, which is dominated by thought, and which, in spite of the charm of its colour, lends itself above all to noble meditations, is truly according to the tradition of the French classical school. The work of Puvis de Chavannes is closely related to Poussin's, in spite of the difference between decorative and easel pictures. There is a certain carelessness of execution in both, and, in any case, a real disdain of virtuosity, which are characteristic of French art. It is to be noted, in fact, that in the artists most representative of the French spirit manual dexterity never takes the first place. It is as though, absorbed in higher considerations, they disdained the qualities of mere execution as being too mechanical.

The influence of Puvis de Chavannes has been very great

once the difficulty of accepting his manner, inherent in any really new work, was overcome. He has retaught French painters, too much taken up with the striving after naturalism, the necessity of the harmony and dignity of thought in art. We shall find his influence everywhere in contemporary art, even in the artists who least resemble him. If we had to name the two painters who have most revolutionised painting, not as regards technique, but from the point of view of sentiment, it would be Millet and Puvis de Chavannes.

As we approach contemporary art, it becomes increasingly difficult to appreciate works, because their proximity prevents us from seeing them at the necessary distance. Indeed, it is time alone that can judge of the durable value of art-forms, and there is much danger, in delivering a judgment on the works of our own day, of expressing an opinion which will be invalidated by the future. On the other hand, the extraordinary variety of contemporary art makes it very difficult to give a general picture of the schools of painting and sculpture. The individualism of the Romantics continued to develop in the course of the 19th century, and nowadays one of the conditions which we demand from an artist is that he should be original. How far this individualism may go, we may see by walking through an exhibition by our young painters. While in the Renaissance and up to the 18th century, the ambition of painters and sculptors was to continue the work of their masters, whence resulted a marked unity in each generation's way of painting and a continuity without violent interruption in its evolution; to-day, on the contrary, every painter or sculptor who has finished his apprenticeship or who thinks he has finished it, believes that his first duty is to differ from every one else. For all these reasons, it appears that the only way to describe the contemporary school is to enumerate the artists and to add appropriate epithets and criticisms. However, we may try to seek the general principles which are at the origin of so many divergent works. For this we must return to an earlier generation, which has already vanished, to discover the currents which feed contemporary art at their springs.

The great artistic revolution of the end of the 19th century, which opens the contemporary period, is the development of the so-called impressionist school. Impressionism is a name which was first employed to describe the landscapes of Claude Monet; the painter, exhibiting landscapes which were above all things effects of rapid light, caught in passing, called his work "Impression." If this term has made its fortune and serves to describe a whole school, it is because it was well chosen to define a fundamental principle. An impression, indeed, is not the same as a vision. A vision implies attention and an intervention of the mind; an impression is only a perfectly simple and instantaneous picture.

But before we say exactly in what consists the impressionist school, it is desirable to say in a few words how it was formed. In a word, it is a continuation of the naturalism of Courbet. Courbet placed himself in front of objects and painted them such as they were, without worrying about composition or psychological considerations. But we have seen that he carried the habits of the studio into open-air painting. The great originality of ÉDOUARD MANET (1832–1883) consisted in the fact that in the second part of his career he attempted to free painting from the deep shadows which darkened Courbet's work. Manet had an agitated career; each of his paintings appeared as a provocation to the general public and to traditional art. And yet he was a master of execution, who had studied the great Dutch and Spanish painters and retained some of their solid virtues. His brushwork, in particular, exhibited a vitality which more than once recalled Franz Hals, the master of Haarlem, and some of his pictures, after his return from Spain, showed that he had not misunderstood the fine lessons of Velasquez and Goya. He chose the subjects of his pictures in the actual world where he lived, the street or the suburbs. In his last pictures we see him trying to represent light and the open air; and it is owing to this fact that he is to be considered as one of the founders of the Impressionist school. These aims may also be found in painters who were less detached from the traditional school than Manet.

JULES BASTIEN-LEPAGE (1848–1884), on the whole, tried to suggest the open air by throwing an equal light on the landscape and the figure which it contains. But the delicate shades in his painting disappear at a distance, and are far from suggesting the light of the open air. Analogous attempts and similar results may be found in the work of Gervex and Duez, who lighted their large compositions with silvery tones. As to ALFRED ROLL (1847–1919), he was a vigorous painter of modern society, who succeeded in dissolving the shadows of studio painting in the light of full days, without, however, allowing the forms modelled by his strong colour to be effaced by the even light of the open air. The Versailles Gallery shows a large work of his, the *Centenary. of '89*. Since then, this strong naturalist has shown himself a brilliant decorator, with striking colours, who has replaced traditional allegories by modern symbolism. The Petit Palais and the Hôtel de Ville of Paris possess large decorative paintings by him. But the real painters of the Impressionist school are, above all, CLAUDE MONET (b. 1840), ALFRED SISLEY (1839–1899), CAMILLE PISSARO (1831–1893), ARMAND GUILLAUMIN and ALBERT LEBOURG (b. 1850). Without a doubt, the most brilliant is Claude Monet, who obtained from colour more than any one had yet done. It is in front of his art that we must pause to define the methods of the Impressionist school.

The impressionist painter is, in the first place, a painter of light, and he does not record this light in one of its general effects, such as sunrise or sunset. He observes it in its smallest shades, with an accuracy of analysis so complete, that the same subject, a stack of corn, the façade of a cathedral, a pond with water-lilies, painted fifteen or twenty times in the same morning, from dawn to mid-day, will furnish fifteen or twenty pictures differing absolutely from each other. Naturally, when the light assumes so much importance, the scene itself loses all interest; in Monet's painting objects only appear in order to serve as screens for the light of the sun.

In order to arrive at such accuracy and so much wealth of colouring, the impressionist artist, and particularly Claude Monet, was obliged to revolutionise the technical methods of painting and even the manner of seeing. His personal experience, like the law of optics, taught him that white light, when it passes through the prism, becomes decomposed into several simple colours, blue, yellow, and red, which blend to form the three composite colours, green, orange, and violet. Very often, when our sight is wearied by the dazzling effect of light, our retina still shows us objects, surrounded by the colours of the rainbow, which are only colours dissociated from the solar rays. Starting from this, the eye of the impressionist seeks methodically or instinctively to replace, as much as it can, the white colour of light, the black of shadows, the grey of half-tones, by the colours contained in this white, black, or grey.

The advantage the painter gains from this substitution is that he can, in the way of colour, equal or surpass nature herself, while his light is always inferior to that of the sun. He is thus compensated for the weakness of not being able to put the sun in his picture by putting in it the tones of the spectrum. In order that his colour may retain all its brilliancy, he uses it as pure as possible. The result of this is, that, at first sight, a picture of this sort may appear a somewhat confused medley of colours. The eye of the spectator has the task of blending the colours which have been dissociated by the impressionist brush. Pictures thus executed have a brilliancy which destroys everything round them.

But this exclusive preoccupation with light does not succeed without some sacrifices, and, though we are dazzled and charmed by the jewelled iridescence of Claude Monet, we must own that in front of his pictures we lose the habit of taking interest in objects themselves. By his method of painting, by his little touches thrown on as it were carelessly, the painter has to avoid modelling things. If these little flecks of colour seemed to be placed on the objects themselves, we might think that they were local tints, instead of suggesting the vibrations of light in space. Like Corot, the impressionist paints objects less than he paints the stratum of air which interposes between them and our eye. Only, while Corot reduces his light-effects to delicate differences of values, the impressionist seeks to accentuate the colour of the light and the shade. Impressionist painting has had so much influence on all our contemporary school that it has modified visual habits, even in the artists who seem most opposed to it. The impressionist method, with its brilliant use of many colours, seems especially appropriate to landscape. It does not give sufficient importance to form to be so well suited to the human figure.

ALBERT BESNARD (b. 1849) owes much to this impressionist vision, which profits by the use of light, by accentuating the liveliness of its reflections.

By extending the definition of impressionism, it is possible to include therein certain artists, such as EDGARD DEGAS (1834–1917), who were little interested in the experiments in light-effect. Indeed, if impressionism is a mental attitude towards objects, there may be an impressionism of drawing, of line, as there is one of colour. As impressionism of colour fixes the fugitive tints of light, so impressionism of line seizes or surprises the passing attitudes of movement. Modern painters, who owe much to contemporary sculpture, only record a figure in the attitudes taken by the model who is posing. A painter-draughtsman, such as Degas, on the contrary, delights in taking by surprise unexpected attitudes in men or animals. He is a trenchant artist who interested himself in showing unusual aspects of life, choosing, as his habitual types, jockeys on racehorses, dancers, and women bathing. Each of his pictures is a treasure-trove, which interests us by its unrehearsed attitudes and unexpected perspective. There is a certain irony in the work of Degas. It seems as though he delighted in showing his models under some condition which causes a smile. We find a somewhat analogous feeling in Toulouse-Lautrec, who pursued his research of character to the length of caricature.

There is another tendency in our contemporary painting, which it is necessary to mention, that of the so-called "advanced" painters, who insist on finding new points of view and a new way of rendering things. They are connected with the Impressionist group, although their intentions are different. Impressionism contented itself with noting light-effects but these artists demand more decorative and more expressive results from the treatment of colour. To speak generally, they give to objects a solidity which the impressionist painter dissolved in a luminous effect. Among the impressionists worked PAUL CÉZANNE (1839–1906), who, in his time, did not appear to have attained the effect he sought, but whose more or less successful works nowadays serve as models to some of the artists of this new school. Cézanne appears to have sought to obtain in painting an effect similar to that produced by a fine piece of tapestry. Even while painting from Nature with an apparent desire to copy faithfully, he put in juxtaposition strong flecks of colour encircled by vigorous lines.

In quite recent years, each exhibition of the Independents' or the Autumn Salon bring us the manifesto of some new school, and as one way of making people talk about us is to enter a house by breaking a window, these young painters do not mind clashing with our most inveterate prejudices and traditions. If up to the present every sort of fancy had seemed allowable in the domain of colour, at least a certain fidelity of drawing from the model had been respected. But these painters have not hesitated to play with figures with as much audacity as though they were mere reflections. This explains the drawing of this young school, which is amazingly impudent, if it is not excessively bold. Cézanne set the example. We have seen, since then, the so-called CUBIST painters, who wish to reduce the forms and appearances of objects to an incomprehensible confusion of polyhedra; others, the FUTURISTS, superimpose one incoherent picture on another under somewhat obscure pretexts. These attempts enrage some people, amuse others, and are perhaps taken seriously by a few amateurs, crazy for novelty. In following the very numerous exhibitions of these young revolutionaries, we must not be chary of sympathy, but we must avoid being duped.

§ II.   SCULPTURE

Italian art, when it reached France, encountered sculptors who executed tombs or carved figures of saints out of stone. Amongst the subjects which occurred most frequently were Our Lady of Pity, a sorrowing mother, weeping over the body of her son, who lies at her feet. This subject appeared very often at the end of the Middle Ages in all the churches of France. Another favourite subject was the so-called Sepulchre; there we see the usual figure of the Entombment, the body of Christ borne by Joseph of Arimathea and Nicodemus, by the side of the Virgin and the Holy Women. The two most celebrated Sepulchres are those of Ligier Richier at Saint-Mihiel, a work which betrays Italian influence, and an earlier one at Solesmes, which, on the contrary, is purely of French and Christian inspiration.

The name of the artist who dominated the French school at the beginning of the 16th century, before the triumph of the

Italian style, is MICHEL COLOMBE (c. 1435–1495), represented in
the Louvre by a *St George killing the dragon*, and whose chief
work is the tomb of Francis II, Duke of Brittany, in the
cathedral of Nantes. This work is characterised by the use of
the new style combined with great fidelity to the national style.
Nevertheless, the inspiration is no longer purely Christian, and
the duke in his tomb is no longer accompanied by gloomy
mourners, but is surrounded by four allegories, representing his
virtues, under the form of four beautiful and vigorous females.

It is in Saint-Denis that we can best follow this transformation
of sculpture, which not only shows an artistic evolution, but a
change in religious ideas. Louis XII, Francis I, and Henry II
are buried in magnificent monuments, animated by graceful
figures and decorated with bas-reliefs recording their exploits.
The first sculptors of the classical style came from Italy; the
tomb of Louis XII was executed by a family of artists from
beyond the Alps, but soon the French were able to compete with
the Italian artists. The monument of Francis I is by PIERRE
BONTEMPS and that of Henry II by GERMAIN PILON, who, with
JEAN GOUJON, was the most famous sculptor of the Renaissance.
Jean Goujon (born in 1515) succeeded in transferring to marble
bas-reliefs the long and elegant figures which the Italian
decorators of Fontainebleau executed in painting. The grace of
his style may still be seen in the *Fountain of the Innocents* in
Paris, decorated with bas-reliefs representing nymphs, whose
bodies and draperies are extremely graceful. In the château of
Anet, built for Diane de Poitiers, he executed a haughty figure
of *Diana* (Louvre).

The work of Germain Pilon (1515–1590) was more varied,
for it combines the violent realism of the Middle Ages with the
grace of the Italian Renaissance. We also find in it a great
variety in execution and technique, for he cast bronze and cut
marble with equal facility. In the Louvre, his funereal statue
of *René de Birague* is of great power, while his group called *The
Three Graces* or *Theological Virtues* is extremely attractive.

In Champagne we see the transformation of Gothic sculpture under the influence of Italo-antique art. About 1540,
DOMINIQUE FLORENTIN brought from Italy a new manner of
treating marble, and, in place of the heavy materials of medieval

costume, the sculptor's chisel applied itself to carving lissom bodies and light draperies.

In Lorraine, at Nancy, Charles IV caused a funereal chapel to be built, imitated from the Medici chapel in Florence. An artist of genius, LIGIER RICHIER (c. 1500–1567), succeeded in adapting Renaissance forms to Christian feeling. In the *Sepulchre of Saint-Mihiel* the elegance of attitude and form must be admired as much as the pathos and sincerity of the emotion. The church of St Stephen at Bar-le-Duc has preserved a "skeleton" by this artist, which is still inspired by the mediaeval spirit, but which, none the less, bears itself with the nobility of an ancient orator.

Normandy welcomed the new style; in Rouen cathedral, two famous tombs, that of the two Cardinals of Amboise and that of the Marquis de Brézé, mark two different periods of the Renaissance. That of the Cardinals is enriched by ornament after the Florentine manner of Michelozzo; the other by a portico of columns surmounted by caryatides, which reaches back through the Italian to ancient art.

During the difficulties which assailed France at the time of the wars of religion there was a cessation of artistic life. The artists who since the Renaissance had collected round the king suffered from the distresses of the monarchy. When at last, under Henry IV, peace was re-established, there was at once a renewal of artistic activity. Henry IV experienced much difficulty in entering Paris; when he had once settled himself there, he never again left it. It was then that Paris began to take a lead in the artistic life of France, and this has become accentuated in the course of the centuries.

It was at the beginning of the 17th century that modern Paris emerged from Gothic Paris. Quarters of the town were constructed in a style which still exists: very simple houses built of red brick, white stone, and blue slate, which give an impression of freshness and elegance without ostentation. A little later, this style appeared too modest and the façades became decorated with pilasters in the antique style. But for the moment, the *bourgeoisie*, the aristocracy, and even the French monarchy contented itself with this unpretentious architecture.

For these houses, hotels, and palaces, and for the Jesuit

churches, mythological or Christian ornamentation was perforce multiplied by the sculptors. The art of tombs was by no means interrupted; the churches found room for a large number, some of which, dispersed by the Revolution, have been collected and are now in the Louvre. As in the later Renaissance tombs, we generally find a portrait of the departed, in the attitude of prayer, accompanied by female figures which are allegorical of his virtues (tomb of Henri de Condé by Sarrazin at Chantilly; tomb of François de Montmorency at Moulins by François Anguier; tombs of the Duc de Longueville and Mazarin in the Louvre; tomb of Richelieu by Girardon in the church of the Sorbonne).

The kings were no longer content with funereal effigies on their tombs in Saint-Denis. After the manner of the Italian princes, they caused statues to be executed magnifying their persons and their royal authority. On the open space of the Pont-Neuf stood an equestrian statue of Henry IV. He was also to be seen in bas-relief on the spandrel of the door in the Hôtel de Ville. Pierre Biard erected a figure of Louis XIII in the middle of the Place Royale. Finally, opposite the Pont au Change stood a monument by Simon Guillain, which is now in the Louvre: Louis XIII in military costume, Anne of Austria, and, between them, the little Dauphin, the future Louis XIV.

Le Brun was not only the leader of the painters; his supervision also extended to the sculptors, whom he supplied with sketches and designs. FRANÇOIS GIRARDON (1628–1715) was the artist who best adapted himself to his wishes; his marble expressed in a natural manner the fluent and somewhat heavy figures dear to his chief. It was he who executed the statue of Louis XIV for the Place des Conquêtes (Place Vendôme). At Versailles, in the Grotte d'Apollon, he executed, in conjunction with Tuby and de Marsy, a threefold group of nymphs, horses, and tritons, in the midst of whom, the god of the sun, emblem of Louis XIV, descends from his chariot. He is represented in Paris by the very fine tomb of Richelieu, abovementioned.

ANTOINE COYSEVOX (1640–1720) had perhaps more originality; in any case, his work has more variety. He not only collaborated in the decoration of the park at Versailles by executing gods and nymphs of bronze for the fountains, but he has also left admirable portraits; his *Prince de Condé*, in the Louvre, leaves an indelible record in the memory. Coysevox was continued by the works of his pupils, NICOLAS and GUILLAUME COUSTOU, two vigorous sculptors, of whose works one at least is celebrated, the *Horses of Marly*, now in the Place de la Concorde.

The Versailles sculptors also executed works for tombs, some of which may still be seen in the churches of Paris. Besides Richelieu's tomb in the church of the Sorbonne, there is Colbert's in Saint-Eustache, Turenne's at the Invalides, and that of Le Brun's mother in Saint-Nicolas-du-Chardonnet.

Finally, we must give a special place to a very great artist, PIERRE PUGET (1622–1694), who lived outside the Versailles group. He was a Provençal from Toulon, where Colbert had made use of him for the decoration of the royal galleys. He was an artist of great spirit, less under the influence of Le Brun than under that of Bernini and the later followers of Michael Angelo. He enjoyed representing muscular effort and obtains pathetic effects from it. On the façade of the Hôtel de Ville at Toulon he placed two caryatides bearing a balcony, which crushes them under its weight. For the decoration of the château of Versailles, he sent an enormous high-relief, *Diogenes and Alexander*, of riotous composition, and a group of *Milo of Crotona*, whose body makes superhuman efforts to disengage itself from the tree which holds it fast, while a lion is about to devour him. This violent and restless work contrasts with the majestic and calm style of the divinities, with which Le Brun had thronged the galleries of Versailles and the avenues of its park.

Under LOUIS XV, sculpture followed the vagaries of fashion less closely than painting. It is more subject to technical considerations and has a greater respect for tradition. In spite of this slowness in evolution, it was none the less somewhat affected by the bad example of the sister art, and it copied the agitated draperies and figures made fashionable by the painters. Religious statuary art filled the Jesuit churches with figures whose long garments seem to be blown about by a storm. Adam and Slodtz had accepted the restless style of Bernini's art.

The greatest names of statuary art under Louis XV are those of JEAN-BAPTISTE LE MOYNE (1704–1778), who has left some very fine busts, Bouchardon, Pigalle, and Falconet.

EDME BOUCHARDON (1698–1762) opposed a somewhat studied simplicity to the affected style of his time; he followed the tradition of the Ancients and sometimes appears, in the very height of the 18th century, to belong to the style of Louis XIV or that of the Empire. His contemporaries admired his equestrian statue of Louis XV, now destroyed, which was in the Place de la Concorde. One important work by him remains and gives us a high idea of his decorative talent—the Fountain in the Rue de Grenelle.

JEAN-BAPTISTE PIGALLE (1714–1785) was also a sculptor of lofty inspiration, far surpassing the crowd of contemporary sculptors, who only possessed cleverness and wit. His most celebrated monument is the famous Tomb of Marshal Saxe at Strasburg. Here are seen allegorical figures of France and of Death attending the Marshal's descent to the grave. Nevertheless, in this tragedy in marble we feel the force of intelligence rather than the sincerity of emotion. Another tomb by the same sculptor is likewise worthy of our admiration, that of the Duc d'Harcourt in Notre-Dame de Paris.

As to ETIENNE-MAURICE FALCONET (1716–1791), he enjoyed high favour among the modern public because of the grace of his bathers and nymphs, which have been popularised by reproduction in porcelain. He was one of those who supplied models to the Sèvres factory. This delicate modeller of pleasing nymphs also erected the colossal statue of Peter the Great in Petrograd, and his contemporaries greatly admired the bold figure of the horse, rearing on a gigantic rock.

Among the sculptors of the time of LOUIS XVI, the statuary art of the 18th century showed itself increasingly instinct with life, mind, and feeling. They no longer sought to exhibit sublime works, they were content to execute nude figures full of grace, and faces full of thought.

AUGUSTIN PAJOU (1730–1809) and CLAUDE-MICHEL, called

CLODION (1738–1814), exhibited figures modelled in terra cotta or carved marble, in which we find as much life and voluptuousness as in the most brilliant sketches of Fragonard. JEAN-JACQUES CAFFIERI (1725–1792) left a series of busts, which all give an impression of life caught unawares. Many of them were executed for the Comédie Française, the foyer and vestibules of which they decorate. But the finest sculptor of this period and one of the greatest names in French art was JEAN-ANTOINE HOUDON (1741–1828), in whom are found all the qualities of the 18th century, with a depth of expression and a particular intensity of life when he represents the human countenance. The Louvre possesses a rich collection of his busts in terra cotta and in marble. The most illustrious men of the Revolution and the Empire are represented by his chisel, with as much vivacity and spirit as we admire in the pastels of Latour. The person who most often recurs in his work is Voltaire, who posed for him several times. The foyer of the Comédie Française contains the marble figure of the celebrated author, and neither in this nor any other school can be found a statue expressing with greater intensity the intellectual life and tension of a combative spirit. The whole critical and ironical 18th century breathes in this marble figure, executed a few years before the Revolution.

Romanticism did not affect sculpture in the same degree as painting. Sculpture is an art which is subject to certain material conditions and so limited in its resources as to be obliged always to follow tradition. Under the Empire the sculptors naturally consented to copy antique models, and it even occurred to sculptors of that period, such as Chaudet and Canova, to represent Napoleon in a Roman toga, or nude like an ancient hero. Even in representing the generals of the period, they did not hesitate to replace modern garments by an audacious lack of them. When romanticism had battered down the classical theories, the sculptors could not abandon their school habits as easily as the painters. It was thus often by Greek or Roman figures that romantic sentiment was perforce expressed.

The Restoration at once undertook to replace the statues of kings broken by the Revolution, Henry IV of the Pont-Neuf, Louis XIII of the Place des Vosges, and Louis XIV of the Place des Victoires. Louis-Philippe ordered a considerable number of statues, either to furnish his historical gallery at Versailles, or to decorate the Paris promenades, the Place de la Concorde, or the Luxembourg. But statuary art profited above all by the refreshing impulse of curiosity which carried France back to her past. It was at this period that historical heroes were honoured by statues raised in their native towns. The sculptor who did most work in this national glorification was DAVID D'ANGERS (1788–1856). He was by education and by technical habit a pure classicist, and he preferred representing breastplates rather than modern dress; but he was also affected by the passions of his time, and in the work of this idealist there is a spirit of energy to which we are not accustomed. Many statues of great men are the work of his chisel. In Paris, his most important work is the pediment of the Panthéon: "To great men, from a grateful country." We owe to him also a series of medallions representing the most celebrated personages of the literary, artistic, and political Paris of his day.

About the same time as the pediment of the Panthéon was finished the monument carved by FRANÇOIS RUDE (1784–1855) on the Arc de Triomphe de l'Étoile, the *Marseillaise*. Rude, like David d'Angers, speaks the classical language, that is to say, represents ancient heroes, but he inspires them with modern passions. The work which best expresses the patriotic exaltation of the Revolution attacked by Europe is the high-relief of the Étoile, showing the citizens departing for battle, while overhead the sculptor has rendered visible the mighty song which inspired them.

JAMES PRADIER (1792–1852) was, on the contrary, a graceful sculptor, who loved purity and elegance of form. He has left a very large number of monuments, fountains in public squares, and subjects for clocks for rooms of Louis-Philippe's period.

The sculptors who attempted to follow the romantic inspiration which animated painters at that time were not all successful in their undertaking. Jehan du Seigneur tried to express violent passions by exaggerating the play of muscles. Préault, in some curious works, sometimes succeeded in evoking a sort of passionate cry from marble or wood, but more often he failed, because his material is not flexible enough to express the fury of his inspiration.

ANTOINE-LOUIS BARYE (1796–1875) succeeded in creating a pathetic and decorative style, entirely free from classical tradition. He was a sculptor who studied wild beasts in museums and afterwards reconstructed their savage life in the desert. His animals are faithfully portrayed and not merely decorative images; he imitates their coats, he makes us feel the play of the muscles and the stretch of the tendons. The attitude which most often recurs is that of combat; he shows us the mortal struggle of animals who kill each other for food. Sometimes he is content with a tiny figure, but the animal is still faithfully rendered with its characteristic attitude. The work of Barye has enriched the realm of sculpture with a whole new province, for up to his day only horses had been admitted by sculptors. Since Barye there is an end of those stone lions, with one paw on a ball, who look at passers-by with a pleasant smile.

In the second half of the 19th century, although the same realistic tendency was visible in sculpture as in painting, nevertheless tradition showed a greater power of resistance; the statuary art developed slowly. While painters had already passed through several phases of realism, sculptors had always persevered in the endeavour to render their material more pliable to the changing aspects of life.

We may begin by referring to the sculptors who represent the traditional school. One prominent name is that of EUGÈNE GUILLAUME (1822–1893), whose work, full of pure and cold distinction, shows him to be a follower of the Ancients. He had a taste for typical figures and he corrected the faults or irregularities of real forms by correcting the model and reducing it to a kind of perfect geometry. He usually chose his subjects from antiquity, which gave him an additional reason for imitating Greco-Roman statues.

The influence of the antique was very happily united with that of the 15th century Florentine masters. While the Greek and Roman marbles inspired our sculptors with a noble but somewhat commonplace ideal, the highly artistic realism of Ghiberti, Donatello, and Verrocchio made them appreciate how much charm there is in slight outlines and the forceful slenderness of finely chiselled bronze figures. It is easy to recognise this Florentine

influence in the bronze works of Falguière, Frémiet, Paul
Dubois, Gerôme, Eugène Barrias, and Antonin Mercié. PAUL
DUBOIS placed on the tomb of General Lamoricière (Nantes
Cathedral) four meditative bronze figures, which remind
us of those by Michael Angelo in the Medici chapel. And more
than once, René de Saint-Marceaux transferred to his marble
the haughty elegance and the passion of the nude figures in the
Sistine chapel.

Again Florence appears in the revival of the medal. The artists
who attained most success were JULES-CLÉMENT CHAPLAIN
(1839–1909) and LOUIS-OSCAR ROTY (1846–1911). Chaplain
struck energetic effigies, which contain in their small dimensions
the power of great sculpture. It is impossible to give a stronger
impression of a definite subject. Roty's medals display delicate
allegories, executed with a charm and novelty, which have
completely revolutionised this art. He is the author of the
Sower, popularised by French coins.

In opposition to this sculpture which followed the antique or
the Renaissance, we must place that which took its inspiration
from reality. It was JEAN-BAPTISTE CARPEAUX (1827–1875), who
represented nature in sculpture with most vigour. He brought to
his art an extreme impetuosity of temperament and he imparted
the tremor of life to everything he modelled or chiselled. He was
the portrayer of the sensual society of the Second Empire, the
haughty princesses of the court, and the little dancers of the
Opera. He made his name by a restless group, *Ugolino*, in which
the pupil of Michael Angelo is again discernible. He was then in
Rome; but later he preferred less gloomy subjects and modelled
many female fauns and laughing nymphs, which recall the art of
Clodion. Carpeaux, in his statues, united the qualities of a
painter to the qualities proper to a sculptor. His figures do not
always conform to the plastic art of antiquity. This was because
in his manner of modelling there was real striving after the
qualities of a painter. Thus, when he represented eyes, he boldly
hollowed the eye-ball, so as to produce the shadow of the pupil.
This was one of the reasons why his works shocked his contemporaries. The public was not accustomed to find so carnal a
feature in the forms of classical divinities. His famous group,
The Dance at the Opera, is not composed of ancient divinities,

but of real living creatures, in whom the suppleness of the flesh may be felt. The *Four Quarters of the World*, on the fountain of the Observatoire, are also lively dancers.

Another realistic sculptor was JULES DALOU (1838–1902), whose abundant work sums up a great evolution in French sculpture. He too made the muscles of classical heroes supple in order to convey the elasticity of the human body. He too, in his busts, sacrificed less to style and sought rather the effect of life. He was one of those who have shown the plastic resources of the workman's or the peasant's dress. What Millet had achieved in painting to display the poetry of the attitudes of physical toil, he would have done in a monument which he had not time to finish, his monument to workmen. On the other hand, his *Triumph of the Republic* in the Place de la Nation, in Paris, is one of the most characteristic works of the 19th century, by its execution, importance, and moral significance. Dalou, who was a violent democrat, has therein symbolised the triumph of democratic rule. It depicts a Republic, on a car drawn by lions, and accompanied by workmen and by figures allegorical of fruitfulness.

Artists such as Falguière, Antonin Mercié and Injalbert cleverly reconciled the style of the traditional school and modern naturalism. Falguière left powerful female nudes, which possess the vitality and physical joy of beautiful living models and which assume the haughty attitudes of Juno or Diana. Antonin Mercié combined great qualities as a painter with his talent as a sculptor; in the work of Injalbert the figures are inspired with the joy of living. Excellent masters such as Denys Puech, Raoul Verlet, Marqueste, Aubé, and Coutan cannot be passed over in silence; their work often appears in parks and on the façades of public buildings. In all of them the frigidity of the classical style is fired with the expression of physical life.

Sculpture, in the second half of the 19th century, has continued to throng our public places with historical personages. Since it has ceased to be a decorative art in the service of architecture, as in the age of cathedrals, and since, together with religion, it has lost an important part of the place which it occupied in the life of former times, it has experienced some difficulty in playing a useful part in our modern world. Nothing would remain to it except to crowd our squares and museums with divinities or allegories, if the tradition of raising monuments to the memory of our great men had not been maintained. Unfortunately, this resource is not inexhaustible, and when sculptors are reduced to making statues of mediocrities, the sculptor suffers from the indifference which attaches to the false demi-god. Indeed, public opinion frequently expresses much ill-humour with regard to the multiplicity of these public monuments to the honour of people whom no one knows and who do not deserve to be known.

On the other hand, a few really national subjects have happily inspired our modern sculptors. The war of 1870 caused the erection of monuments which derive part of their beauty from the fact that they really express national feeling: for example, the *Quand Même* (Tuileries) and the *Gloria Victis* (Hôtel de Ville) of Mercié. In the court of the École des Beaux-Arts, the funereal monument to Henri Regnault, by HENRI-MICHEL-ANTOINE CHAPU (1833–1891), also expresses in a touching manner the gratitude of the country to its fallen heroes. Bartholdi has carved a roaring lion in the rock at Belfort to recall the heroic defence of that place; the lion in the Place Denfert-Rochereau in Paris is a replica.

Amongst the statues in glorification of historical figures, Joan of Arc often recurs. The best French sculptors have attempted to represent this heroine and some of these statues are among the finest of the modern school. Chapu's Joan (Musée Condé, Chantilly) is a peasant with a noble face, who dreams while in prayer. The Joan of Paul Dubois (opposite Saint-Augustin in Paris and opposite the Reims cathedral) is an inspired knight, who urges on her horse, her gaze fixed on some heavenly vision. Frémiet's Joan (Place des Pyramides, Paris) is a powerful woman-warrior, ready for the fray.

Finally, there are several monuments, which will continue to do credit to the generation of the close of the 19th century, the *Monument of the Republic* by Dalou, of which we have already spoken, and the *Monument to the Dead* by BARTHOLOMÉ, in Père-Lachaise. There we see humanity arrive trembling at the threshold of the grave; although the monument is religious in sentiment, the sculptor does not show himself to be a Christian and does not offer an image of the Resurrection as a consolation to mortals. But he has invested his figures with such beauty, and has put so much tenderness and love into the attitudes and faces, that this representation of the inevitable end brings a kind of alleviation by the spell of its loveliness.

In contemporary sculpture, one master towers above all the activity of our new schools. Here again, the artists have done everything to revolutionise the traditional conception of the figure. AUGUSTE RODIN (1840–1917) taught them the expressive resources of a form of sculpture which owes nothing to moulding. It is not that Rodin could not have executed figures of faultless modelling had he so desired—indeed, more than once, he has done so. But the result of his method is that he treated figures with successful audacity, so as to make them, above all, expressive. Already, sculptors, such as Michael Angelo, had demonstrated the moving eloquence of a body braced for an effort, or relaxed from weariness or despair. Rodin went further and did not shrink from portraying frenzied contortions showing passion in its paroxysm, as though the physical part of man could be as violently agitated as the moral part. Rodin also considered the material in which he worked. His bronze figures are rough and violent, while those chiselled in marble are treated caressingly. His *Thinker*, opposite the Panthéon, like his *Burghers of Calais*, are pathetic figures in their studied heaviness. The *Thinker* contracts his whole body from the nape of the neck to the toes, and this effort betrays the concentration of the first man in whom was kindled a glimmer of thought. The burghers of Calais walk with slow steps, their limbs heavy and their bodies crushed by sorrow and shame. On the other hand, the marble group *The Kiss*, as well as several others which represent bodies entwined, has been carved out of marble.

Rodin's manner brought into sculpture a poetical style such as Delacroix introduced into painting, which subjects reality to the exigencies of the artist's imagination and feeling; but this boldness seems even rasher in sculpture than in painting, because painting is, after all, only a convention, in which many fancies appear tolerable to us, while sculpture, which reproduces reality itself, seems always bound to respect appearances. It seems to us harder to accept a deliberately inexact figure than an inaccurate painting. And yet it was this new principle which the art of Rodin has made our modern school of sculpture accept. It can easily be understood what may be the advantages and the dangers of a method which rejects all considerations of literal truth as well as all respect for traditional style. In the current production of statuary, artists who are not gifted with great originality are yet able to execute figures sufficiently beautiful to keep their places in a decorative whole. The emancipation of sculpture, initiated by Rodin, deprives mediocre artists of the ordinary rules for their guidance. There is no sculpture whose influence has been so dangerous as that of Rodin.

Amongst the sculptors of our young school there are very few who have entirely escaped his influence. The best pupils of the traditional school sometimes follow, even against their will, the example given by his *Thinker* or his marble groups.

§ III. DECORATIVE ART

Renaissance. In the early years of the 16th century, classical forms revived alike in almost all kinds of art; mythological figures in the Italian manner became established in each of the traditional arts, in tapestry as in illumination, in glass as in enamels. The workshops of Limoges, which during the Middle Ages had produced cloisonné enamels, now produced painted enamels, which are real little masterpieces with mythological or allegorical subjects. The most celebrated of these enamellers were Léonard Limosin, the Pénicauds, Pierre Reymond, and Jean Courtois. The Louvre and the Cluny Museum possess fine collections of their cups, vases, caskets, and plaques.

Francis I wished to revive the superiority in tapestry, which the French had lost since the 14th century and which was now held by the Flemish and Italian ateliers; he therefore founded the royal factory of Fontainebleau about 1535. Here, under the direction of Ph. Babon de La Bourdaisière, superintendent of buildings, clever tapestry-weavers copied the cartoons of Primaticcio. It was probably from this atelier that the *History of Diana* and the arabesques in the style of Du Cerceau came.

During the reign of Henry II the direction of the atelier was entrusted to Philibert de L'Orme, but at the king's death it was broken up. On the other hand, a new atelier which he founded at Paris, in the Hospital of the Trinity, existed until about the middle of the 17th century. It was here that were woven the *Life of Christ* (Gobelins, Cluny Museum) by Dubout, and the *History of Artemisia*, in which the influence of Giulio Romano is discernible.

The influence of the Italian Renaissance made itself felt in stained glass later than in painting and sculpture. The Gothic forms persisted during part of the 16th century. Little by little, around figures which still preserved their religious severity there appeared little graceful angels fluttering amongst flowers and fruit. It is at Troyes in Champagne that the glass-painters have left the finest collection of stained glass: at Saint-Nizier, Saint-Jean, Saint-Pantaléon, and la Madeleine the inspiration of the artists resisted Italian influence for a long time. It was the same in Brittany and Normandy. Among the best decorators of stained glass, we must mention Engrand le Prince and his son Jean of Beauvais, the designers of the fine glass at Saint-Vincent at Rouen; and Jean Lécuyer, who decorated the windows at Bourges about the middle of the 16th century. At Paris, Pinaigrier left stained glass which can still be admired in Saint-Étienne-du-Mont and Saint-Eustache. These artists sought, above all things, to execute beautiful and faithful portraits of the donors, round the legends of the saints and the Virgin. The stained glass windows in the church of Montmorency and the church at Écouen are famous for the portraits of members of the Montmorency family. It was also for Écouen that the charming windows representing the legend of Eros and Psyche were executed (1542). Towards the end of the 16th century, the technique of stained glass became transformed by the use of enamels, which permitted a greater variety of tones; a regrettable innovation, which deprived glass of its brilliancy and its transparency. The leadwork was often arranged geometrically and lost the fanciful charm which may be seen in old stained glass. And in the 17th century the decadence arrived.

Classical decoration became adapted to each province. Local traditions have everywhere associated this widespread evolution with an illustrious name; HUGUES SAMBIN, at Dijon, carved

the heavy Burgundian furniture; in Saintonge, BERNARD
PALISSY (1510–1590), who was put on the track of a new
technique by Italian earthenware, was a learned man, a chemist,
and an artist, who passed his life in a struggle with poverty and
with the difficulties of execution of a new ceramic art. His finest
works are enamelled vases and dishes, on which are raised shells,
fishes, and serpents; the enamel renders in a marvellous way the
impression of dampness and of the sheen of aquatic animals and
plants. The factories of Oiron and Saint-Porchaire also produced
finely decorated vases and cups.

Louis XIV. During the age of Louis XIV Colbert had in his
hands the superintendence of buildings. It was Le Brun, chief
painter to the king, who received, among his other functions,
the direction of the manufacture of Gobelins tapestry, founded
by Colbert in 1662. This factory was enlarged in order to supply
the decorative necessities of Versailles. Le Brun, who lived
there, composed painted cartoons which were given as models
to the weavers of tapestry: the *Elements*, the *Seasons*, the
History of the King, etc. It was also in the Gobelins factory
that was constructed the furniture destined to fill the galleries
of Versailles. All kinds of artists, cabinet-makers, carvers, and
designers, brought together under the direction of Le Brun,
worked at the "furniture of the crown." Charles Boule constructed furniture of rare woods, inlaid with tortoiseshell, copper,
gold, and silver. Claude Ballin carved magnificent specimens of
the goldsmith's art. Bérain and Lepautre supplied models to
the sculptors in wood and metal.

Regency. Towards the end of his reign, Louis XIV himself
became weary of the pomp of Versailles, of its heavy and
ostentatious furnishing. Under the Regency, the change in
furniture showed the ingenuity with which public taste and the
requirements of comfort were satisfied. The tables and chairs
combined utility and grace; the backs and arms of arm-chairs
were curved so as better to receive the human body, and were
designed in so ingenious a manner that they seemed to retain the
attitudes of conversation. The decoration of interiors, hitherto
designed by architects, who reproduced the ornamentation of
façades, was now designed and executed by cabinet-makers. In
place of marble and heavy stucco we find panels of wood coloured

in light tints and framed by gilt mouldings, which were rounded at the corners and were sometimes expanded in a fantastic play of line. It was the age of rococo.

Louis XV. Under the reign of Louis XV admirable decorators adorned everything which they touched. Their lively figures and linear fancies spread through the work of goldsmiths and silversmiths, through carvings, china, tapestry, and engraving; rococo threw its elegant caprices on the pages of the most serious folios; the art of Louis XV was so greatly entertained by small and witty work because it was sure of the solid foundations of its principles. Meissonier, designer of the king's study, carved pieces of plate, very few of which have come down to us. Lamour, at Nancy, put the finishing touch to architecture with his wrought iron, the most *spirituel* of useless things, which conceals much logic in its caprice. Gonthières and Caffieri executed carved and gilded bronzes. The manufacture of Sèvres was started in 1748 by the financier Orry. Its productions in hard porcelain and his statuettes in biscuit china are remarkable for their delicacy and purity of paste, whiteness of glaze, and brilliancy of colour.

Louis XVI. During the second half of the century the tranquil geometry of the architects prevailed over the restless distortions of the cabinet-makers and the carvers. In the middle of Louis XV's reign there was formed a style known as Louis XVI, which combines elegance and simplicity; table-legs and chair-backs were straightened. The furniture of Rieserer had a sober elegance which recalled the antique. Ceramic factories were opened in the large towns; the most celebrated were those of Rouen, Nevers, Strasburg, and Moustiers, which produced fine earthenware, decorated with flowers, arabesques, and figures.

Empire. The empire style resulted partly from an effort of reconstruction in the antique style. We can distinguish vestiges of Pompeian, Greek, and even Egyptian influence; this style has a pompous and somewhat heavy gravity, which suited a serious society; it seems to protest against worldly frivolity. The shapes are massive and plain, with the corners clearly defined. It was archaeological architects, such as Percier and Fontaine, who were in part the creators of the antique style of Empire furniture. Even the fragility of porcelain was concealed; the Sèvres vases were covered with gold and displayed miniature reproductions of large historical pictures.

The July Monarchy continued the Empire furniture and made it *bourgeois*, at the same time that romanticism turned everything into pseudo-Gothic.

Contemporary decorative Art. At the end of the 19th century, as in the time of the Regency, the architects derived their decorative style from the furnisher. It was the cabinet-makers and designers who invented and made fashionable certain forms, which subsequently spread to the façades of houses. The term "modern style" has been applied to the work of numerous decorators, who for the last twenty years have been trying to revive among us the art of furniture-making. It has become wearisome to live among shapes borrowed from historical styles. It seems as though a modern generation like previous ones ought to create a style for its own needs. Unfortunately, a long period of imitation, during which people were content to revive artificially the Louis XV or Louis XVI style, had broken the continuity of our artistic industries. It was therefore necessary, not only to carry on a tradition, but to start anew, and nothing is so difficult in art as absolute creation. And indeed, in spite of their desire to be absolute innovators, our decorators have not succeeded in shaking off all influence. Only, instead of taking their models from the works under their eyes, they have sought them afar off, sometimes in the art of the Middle Ages, sometimes in Japanese art. However, after more or less successful experiments and furniture with contorted lines, furniture of elegant shape and subdued tone has made its appearance. In this style, the forms present fine continuous curves, which are linked one to the other by imperceptible gradations, like that of the branch which springs from the tree. There is no gilding, no paint, no tapestry; the wood is shown with its natural light colour. As to the proportions of chairs and tables, they recall by their simplified grace the outlines of Louis XVI furniture.

Still more recently, we have seen the birth of another style which differs essentially from that we have just described. It was shown in the last autumn Salons open before the war. In this new furniture the shapes have more solidity; they even affect a geometrical heaviness. And while the previous style was very sober in colouring, this new manner shows us furniture coloured sometimes with a certain crudeness. Its evolution however is not yet finished. But it is easy to note already a close relationship between this cubist furniture, painted in bright colours, and the most recent manifestations of our advanced painters. The war, by interrupting our artistic life, may perhaps have shortened the life of some of these young schools.

BIBLIOGRAPHY

Painting

E. Müntz, *La Renaissance en Italie et en France, à l'époque de Charles VIII*, 1888. A. de Champeaux, *Histoire de la peinture décorative*, 1890. E. Müntz, *L'École de Fontainebleau et le Primatice (Gaz. des Beaux Arts*, 1902, 11). H. Bouchot, *Le portrait en France au xvie siècle (G.B.A.*, 1887); *Les Clouet et Corneille de Lyon*, 1892. H. Lemonnier, *L'Art au temps de Richelieu et de Mazarin*, 1893. L. Vitet, *L'Académie royale de Peinture et de Sculpture*, 1884.

A. Felibien, *Entretiens sur la vie et sur les ouvrages des plus excellents peintres*, 1666–1688 (Vol. IV. contains an important biography of Poussin). R. de Piles, *Abrégé de la vie des peintres*, 1699. H. Bouchot, *J. Callot*, 1889. J. Guiffrey, *Antoine, Louis et Mathieu Le Nain, Nouveaux documents (Nouv. Arch. de l'art franç.*, 1876). A. Valabrègue, *Les frères Le Nain*, 1904. Gazier, *Philippe et Jean-Baptiste de Champaigne*, Paris, 1893. L. Vitet, *Eustache Le Sueur*, 1883. Nicolas Poussin, *Lettres publiées par Quatremère de Quincy*, 1824. M. Graham, *Mémoires sur la vie de Nicolas Poussin*. P. Desjardins, *Poussin*, 1903. Mrs Mark Pattison (Lady Dilke), *Claude Lorrain*, 1884. R. Bouyer, *Claude Lorrain*, 1904. A. Fontaine, *Les doctrines d'art en France, de Poussin à Diderot*, 1908. H. Jouin, *Charles Le Brun et les Arts sous Louis XIV*, 1889. L. Hourticq, *L'art académique (Revue de Paris*, 1904). P. Marcel, *Charles Le Brun*, 1909. Abbé de Mouville, *La vie de Pierre Mignard*, 1730. Ch. Thuillier, *Le peintre Claude Lefebvre (Réunion des Soc. des B.A. des Départements*, 1892).

J. Guiffrey, *Livrets des expositions de peinture depuis 1673 jusqu'à 1800*. P. Mantz, *Watteau*, 1892. E. et J. de Goncourt, *L'Art du xviiie siècle*, 1880. P. Mantz, *Largillière*. J. Foster, *French art from Watteau to Prud'hon*, 1906. P. Mantz, *Boucher, Lemoyne et Natoire*, 1880. G. Kahn, *Boucher*, 1904. G. Schéfer, *Siméon Chardin*, 1903. R. Portalis, *Fragonard*, 1899. Lady Dilke, *French engravers and draughtsmen*, 1902. Renouvier, *L'histoire de l'art pendant la Révolution*, 1863. M. Dreyfous, *Les Arts et les Artistes pendant la période révolutionnaire*.

Chesneau, *La peinture française au xixe siècle: les chefs d'école*, 1862. L. Rosenthal, *Louis David*. P. Gauthiez, *Prud'hon*, 1886. H.

Marcel, *La peinture française au xix* siècle*, 1908. E. Delacroix, *Journal*, 1893–98. M. Tourneux, *Delacroix*, 1903. P. Mantz, *Decamps* (*G.B.A.*, 1862). H. Delaborde, *Ingres*, 1870. H. Lapauze, *Portraits dessinés d'Ingres*, 1903. H. Marcel, *H. Daumier.* É. Michel, *Les maîtres du paysage*, 1906. Moreau-Nélaton, *Corot*, 1909. A. Thomson, *Millet and the Barbizon School*, 1903. H. Marcel, *J.-F. Millet.* G. Lafenestre, *La peinture française du xix* siècle*, 1893. C. Mauclair, *The Great French Painters, 1830 to the present day*, 1903. L. Gonse, E. *Fromentin*, 1881. Ary Renan, *Gustave Moreau* (*G.B.A.*, 1886, 1). Lorquet, *La peinture française contemporaine*, 1900. Th. Duret, *Manet et son œuvre*, 1902. C. Mauclair, *L'impressionnisme*, 1903.

Sculpture

Stanislas Lami, *Dictionnaire des Sculpteurs français.* Paul Denis, *Ligier Richier*, Nancy, 1906. P. Vitry, *Michel Colombe et la sculpture française de son temps*, 1907. R. Lister, *Jean Goujon, his life and work*, 1903. L. Palustre, *Germain Pilon* (*G.B.A.*, 1894). J. Gauthier, *Conrad Meyt et les sculpteurs de Brou* (*R.S.B.A.D.*, 1898).
L. Vitet, *L'Académie royale de Peinture et de Sculpture*, 1884. A. Samson, *Les frères Anguier*, 1889. Stanislas Lami, *Dictionnaire des Sculpteurs français sous le règne de Louis XIV*, 1906. P. Auquier, *Puget.* H. Jouin, *Ant. Coyzevox*, Paris, 1883. Lady Dilke, *Les Coustou* (*G.B.A.*, 1907, 1). A. Roserot, *Bouchardon*, 1894. S. Rocheblave, *Pigalle* (*Rev. d'art ancien et moderne*, 1897); *Jean-Baptiste Pigalle*, 1920. H. Cherion, *Les Adam et les Clodion*, 1889. J. Guiffrey, *Clodion* (*G.B.A.*, 1892, 11).
E. Guillaume, *La sculpture au xix* siècle* (*G.B.A.*, 1900). L. de Fourcaud, *Rude*, 1903. J. Cladel, *Auguste Rodin, l'œuvre et l'homme*, 1908.

Decorative Art

L. Bourdery et E. Lachenaud, *Léonard Limosin*, 1897. E. Dupuy, *Bernard Palissy*, Poitiers, 1902. A. Genevay, *Le style Louis XIV*, 1886. A. Bertrand, *La décoration de Versailles au xvii* siècle* (*G.B.A.*, 1899, 11). A. de Champeaux, *Le meuble*, 2 vols., 1889–1907. E. Molinier, *Le mobilier au xvii* et au xviii* siècles*, 1899. H. Havard, *Les Boulle*, 1893. J. Guiffrey, *Les Gobelins et Beauvais.* M. Fenaille, *État général des tapisseries de la Manufacture des Gobelins*, 1904–1909. É. Bourgeois, *Le biscuit de Sèvres au xviii* siècle*, 1908. G. Lechevallier Chevignard, *La manufacture de porcelaine de Sèvres*, 1909. Lady Dilke, *French furniture and decoration*, 1902. E. Molinier, *La collection Wallace, meubles et objets d'art français.* P. Lafond, *L'art décoratif et le mobilier sous la République et l'Empire*, 1900. V. Champier, *L'art décoratif* (*Musée d'art*, 1907).

CHAPTER XI

MUSIC

The Renaissance. There is a tendency among writers on music to assume that the art of music was not affected by the Renaissance until the end of the 16th century, more than a hundred years after the movement had made itself definitely felt in literature and the plastic arts. The ascription of the musical Renaissance to about 1600 is due to the fact that at that time an attempt was made in Italy to reproduce the musical declamation of ancient Greek drama, an attempt which was closely connected with a very important change in the technique of musical composition. There has also been a tendency to suppose that previous to this date serious musicians confined their activities almost exclusively to the composition of music for the rites of the Catholic Church. It is however abundantly evident that in the social life of the Renaissance, both in Italy and France, music, and especially secular music, played a very important part. Allusions to music are frequent in the literature of the period, and the enthusiasm with which certain composers are commended may be taken as showing that to their contemporaries at any rate they succeeded in expressing the spirit of their age.

During the 15th century the dominating musical influence was that of the French and the Netherlanders. It is impossible to separate them, and indeed there are cases in which a composer's precise nationality is uncertain. Flemish musicians were attached to the French royal chapel, to the court of Burgundy and to the Papal chapel during its residence at Avignon; they followed the Papal court back to Rome and were held in honour at most of the Italian courts. Some of them are best known to us under Italianised names. It is therefore convenient at this period to class together as French all those who set French words to music. The Renaissance in music may best be said to begin with Josquin des Prés, born about 1445, probably at

Condé in Hainault, where he died in 1521. He was a pupil of Okeghem, who from 1452 to 1495 was a member of the French royal chapel; he travelled extensively and appears to have held appointments at the Papal and Imperial courts as well as at those of Ferrara, Florence and France. Ambros describes him as "the first musician who impresses us as having genius." To the ingenious learning of the Netherlanders he added a new beauty, the first beginnings of the modern sense of harmonic relations, which enabled him to give expression to the words which he set in a way that no composer had ever done before. It was during his lifetime (1498) that music-printing with moveable types was first invented; and his works, both sacred and secular, are better represented than those of any other composer in the earliest collections of printed music.

Contemporary with Josquin were Anton Brumel, who went to Ferrara in 1505 and remained there for the rest of his life, Pierre de la Rue, from 1492 to 1510 a member of the Burgundian ducal chapel, and Loyset Compère, all distinguished composers of sacred music; to a rather younger generation belong Jean Mouton, a singer in the chapel of Louis XII (d. 1522), Éléazar Genet, called Carpentras from the place of his birth (1508–1518 a member of the Papal chapel), and Jacques Clément, known as Clemens non Papa (d. before 1558).

Still more characteristic of the Renaissance are the secular *Chansons* of the period, a large number of which were issued by the French and Italian printers. These are generally composed for four voices, sometimes plainly harmonised, more often treated with short points of imitation. Their composers were mostly pupils of Josquin and associated with the French court during the reigns of Francis I and Henry II. A collection was published by Attaignant in 1529 of *Chansons* by Claude de Sermisy, Consilium, Courtoys, Deslouges, Dulot, Gascogne, Hesdin, Jacotin, Jannequin, Lombart, Sohier, and Vermont, many of whom are mentioned in contemporary literature, notably by Rabelais and Ronsard. Clément Jannequin, about whose life nothing whatever is known, composed some remarkable descriptive works for four voices: *La Guerre* or *La Bataille de Marignan* (first printed about 1528, many times reprinted, and also arranged for the lute), *Le Chant des*

Oiseaux, La Chasse, Les Cris de Paris and others. Descriptive music was also composed by Nicolas Gombert and Guillaume Costeley. The *Chansons* in general represent all aspects of social life and are often broadly humorous. It was also the habitual practice at this time to use secular tunes as the themes of Masses which were openly called by the titles of the original songs. The mediaeval song *L'Homme Armé* was used in this way by many composers of sacred music including Palestrina himself.

The Huguenot Psalter. The French metrical version of the Psalms begun by Clément Marot and continued by Beza was provided with tunes between 1542 and 1562 by Louis Bourgeois. Some were of German origin, others were composed by Bourgeois himself or adapted from secular songs popular at the time. The melodies of the Genevan Psalter were popular amongst Catholics as well as Protestants. Claude Goudimel, a native of Besançon, then under Spanish rule, a well-known composer of *Chansons* and Masses, began harmonising them afresh in 1551 and completed the whole Psalter in 1564. He is said to have joined the Reformed Church; at any rate he was killed in the massacre at Lyons in 1572. The music of the Genevan Psalter was well known to English Protestants of the time and exercised a considerable influence on the music of the English Church. Some of its melodies are still sung, e.g. the "Old Hundredth."

The Music of the Pléiade. Ronsard and his circle were in the closest touch with the musicians of their time and were deeply interested in the musical setting of poetry. Ronsard himself, although gifted with a poor voice and afflicted with deafness, was passionately devoted to music. At his own request his poems were set by Jannequin, Pierre Certon, and Goudimel; Orlando Lassus, Claudin Le Jeune, Costeley and many others of less note followed their example. Good illustrations of their style are *Petite nymphe folastre* (Jannequin), the *Ode à Michel de l'Hospital*, and the sonnet *Quand j'apperçoy* (Goudimel). Among Ronsard's friends was Jacques Mauduit (1557–1627), who composed a Requiem for his death and collaborated with Baïf in his *Chansonettes mesurées*. If it seems strange to the modern reader that such delicate and intimately personal poems should have been set, not for a solo voice accompanied by an instrument, but for four voices moving for the most part in plain chords, or (as by Goudimel) embellished with contrapuntal devices, it must be remembered that the sense of modern harmony was still a comparatively new thing. The individual expression of a solo singer could not attain prominence until that sense of harmony had become firmly enough established in the minds of musicians for them to assume it instinctively. The study of stress and quantity both in France and in other countries is of great importance in the history of music. At this time the regular ictus of duple rhythm, on which the sense of tonality largely depends, was not assumed as a matter of course; but it was gradually gaining ground owing to popular and secular influences. In the 16th century, English, French, or Italian words are often set very carefully as regards quantity, but independently of regular periodic accents. The change which took place at the beginning of the 17th century was due to the acceptance of the general principle of a periodic strong accent, to which the declamation of words was made to conform. The invention of Recitative at this date draws attention sharply to the rhythmical differences of the three languages in question.

Instrumental Music. During the 16th century there was little distinction between vocal and instrumental music. In domestic chamber music viols might accompany or supply the place of voice parts; in performances on a large scale the instruments similarly played with the voices. The most popular of all instruments was the lute, which at that date held much the same position in social life as the pianoforte does now. It was the chief among what the middle ages called *bas instruments,* i.e. soft instruments for private music as opposed to the *hauts instruments* of louder character. We hear of lutenists at the French and neighbouring courts as early as 1396; Alberto de Ripa, an Italian lutenist under Francis I and Henry II, is mentioned by Pietro Aretino, as well as by Marot, Baïf, and Ronsard. The earliest lute-music printed in France was the collection issued by Attaignant in 1529. Certon's settings of the Psalms were published as solo songs with lute accompaniment in 1554. All sorts of music both instrumental and vocal was arranged for the lute, sometimes with variations, just as all modern music is transcribed for the pianoforte. A few severe moralists condemned the lute as worldly and effeminate, but to play the lute was a sure road to social success (cp. the *Cortegiano* of Castiglione). Even Richelieu took lessons in lute-playing to gain the favour of Anne of Austria. In the course of the 17th century lute music became so elaborate and difficult that no amateurs would take the trouble to learn it. They were content to vamp accompaniments according to popular labour-saving methods. Soon after the beginning of the 18th century the lute became obsolete; fashionable ladies had their lutes made into *vielles* (hurdy-gurdies) and for serious musicians its place had been taken by the harpsichord.

Mascarades and Ballets de Cour. As in Italy and England, so in France from the latter half of the 16th century onwards there were frequent semi-dramatic festivities connected with the court. Some took place out of doors and were of a quasi-impromptu character; others, for indoor performance, were prepared with great elaboration and expenditure. Ronsard and Mellin de Saint-Gelais were in many cases the authors of the words. Catherine de' Medici introduced Italian singers and players as well as Italian dancers; Brantôme gives an elaborate description of a ballet or masque which she had performed in honour of the Polish Ambassadors in 1573. The first example of what were called *Ballets de Cour*, a new form of art derived partly from the humanistic movement of Baïf's Academy and partly from the Italian entertainments, was the famous *Balet comique de la Royne*, organised in 1581 by an Italian known as Balthazar de Beaujoyeux. The word *comique* was intended to signify no more than that the ballet was dramatic and ended happily; its characters are all deities and heroes. The novelty of the form lay in the subjection of music, dancing, and scenery to a single dramatic idea. The story is that of Circe, whose enchantments are finally broken by Jupiter. Queen Louise and various noble ladies took part as naiads in the *grand ballet*, after Jupiter had led Circe captive to the King, seated as in the English masques at the opposite end of the hall. The words and music, neither of which are of the first order, were the work of various hands. There was a large band of instrumentalists, both strings and wind, and a chorus of singers in addition to

numerous dancers. The *Balet comique* is the original model for
the English Masques, containing their main characteristics—the
introductory allegory, the presentation to the King, the set
dance of the noble masquers, and the "revels" or general social
dances of performers and spectators. It lasted from 10 P.M. to
3.30 A.M. The most attractive musical episode is the *Son de
la clochette* accompanying the entrance of Circe; this has often
been reprinted and arranged in modern form under the title of
Air Louis XIII. It is probably an old French popular melody.

The *Ballet de Cour* continued in favour up to the death
of Louis XIII in 1643. One of the best is *La Délivrance de
Renaud* (1617), conducted by Mauduit, in which the King
himself danced; there was a chorus of ninety-two voices and
a band of more than forty-five instruments. The music was
mostly by Pierre Guédron (1565–1620) and his son-in-law
Antoine Boësset (d. 1643). Guédron, who frequently set words
of Malherbe to music, was much admired for his *Airs de Cour*,
somewhat after the fashion of the contemporary Italian mono-
dies. They are free in rhythm without bars and sometimes very
dramatic in expression. Boësset had less dramatic feeling and
his airs are more obviously melodious and clearly rhythmical.
The *Ballet de Cour*, like the English masque, eventually degenerated into the *Ballet à entrées*, in which all dramatic idea
was lost and the dances became more and more grotesque.

The beginnings of Opera in France.   The musical drama
initiated at Florence in 1597 soon became the favourite diver-
sion of princes in other cities of Northern Italy. At Rome it
was much patronised by the Barberini family; it was taken up
at Venice in 1637 as a commercial enterprise. During the early
years of Louis XIV's minority Mazarin, who was a keen lover
of music and had previously been in the service of Cardinal
Antonio Barberini, made persistent attempts to establish Italian
opera at the French court. Mme de Motteville describes somewhat unsympathetically the performance of Cavalli's *Egisto*
(Venice, 1643) at the Palais-Royal in February 1646. In 1647
Mazarin produced *Orfeo*, specially composed for him by Luigi
Rossi, with magnificent scenery by Giacomo Torelli, and in
1654 *Le Nozze di Peleo e Teti*, by Carlo Caproli, which combined the form of the Italian opera with that of the *Ballet de*

Cour. At the Théâtre du Marais, where *tragédies à machines*
(plays in alexandrines with songs, ballets, and elaborate scenery)
were given, Chapoton's *Orphée aux Enfers* of 1640 was revived
in 1648 with stage effects cleverly imitated from Torelli's. In
1647 Corneille was commissioned to write *Andromède*, a play
with music and machinery, in order to utilise again Torelli's
scenery for *Orfeo*. It was produced in 1650 with music by
Dassoucy. Corneille's preface is extremely interesting as giving
the French view of the relation of music to drama. "*Andromède*," says M. Prunières, "presents an eminently French solution of the operatic problem. The play calls in the assistance of
music only when the attention of the spectators is not occupied
by the development of the plot; the music diverts the ear, as
the scenery delights the eye, but poetry alone is allowed the
right of appealing to the emotions." In 1660 Mazarin produced
Cavalli's *Serse* with only moderate success. He died in 1661,
having already begun preparations for the same composer's
Ercole Amante, produced at vast expense in 1662. But there
had always been a strong anti-Italian party in Paris, and the
music seems to have made very little impression compared with
that of the decorations. Cavalli went back to Venice vowing
that he would never compose another opera.

The First French Operas. In 1650 Dassoucy produced a
comédie en musique entitled *Les Amours d'Apollon et de Dafné*.
The legend was treated in a comic spirit; the dialogue was
spoken and interspersed with songs, including one in Italian,
and a duet in dialogue. In January 1655 *Le Triomphe de l'Amour*,
a pastoral modelled on Tasso's *Aminta*, set to music by Michel
de la Guerre, was sung before the court in Mazarin's apartments
in the Louvre. It consisted merely of a series of duets in dialogue in a definite metrical form so that all could be sung to
the same music. It was not given with action on this occasion,
but appears to have been acted in an enlarged form in 1657.
The *Pastorale d'Issy*, written by Pierre Perrin and composed by
Robert Cambert (d. 1677), often described as the first French
opera, was performed privately in 1659 at Issy near Paris, and
later before the court at Vincennes. This too is merely a series
of *Chansons* in dialogue. In 1669 Perrin obtained a patent from
Louis XIV for the establishment of a French opera-house,

which opened on March 3, 1671, with *Pomone* by Perrin and Cambert. The opera-house was a financial failure, and Perrin was imprisoned for debt in May.

Lully. In April 1644 the Chevalier de Guise brought back from Florence an Italian boy, Giovanni Battista Lulli (b. 1632), to be *garçon de chambre* to Mlle de Montpensier, who was studying Italian. He showed musical ability, and had every chance of developing it at the court of the princess, who was devoted to music. In 1652 she left Paris and placed herself at the head of the Frondeurs; when the King entered the capital she took refuge at Saint-Fargeau. The young Italian, finding country life tedious, begged her to release him; she did so, and he entered the service of Louis XIV. There is no foundation for the story that he was a kitchen boy and was dismissed for misbehaviour. He was by that time an accomplished dancer and a brilliant violinist. He danced with the King in the *ballets de cour* and became his intimate companion. Besides these diversions he studied composition with three organists of the day, Gigault, Métru, and Roberday, the last a musician of some originality, much influenced by Frescobaldi. From 1653 onwards he collaborated in the music of the ballets; he composed almost all of *La Galanterie du Temps* (1656) and had by that time become the favourite composer of the court. *Alcidiane* (1658) is the first of his own ballets, but even these later ballets, which were known by his name, were not always entirely his own work. In 1661 he became naturalised as a Frenchman and married the daughter of Michel Lambert, a composer with whom he had collaborated in the ballets. Hitherto his dissipations had given some cause for scandal; Benserade the poet now congratulated him in the *Ballet des Arts* on his conversion to a more reputable life. In 1664 Lully (as his name was generally spelt in France) began the series of *comédies-ballets* in collaboration with Molière, the first of which was *Le Mariage forcé*. The most famous of these was *Le Bourgeois gentilhomme* (1670); it is difficult for the modern reader to realise that in those days the music of Lully counted for far more than Molière's play. *Le Bourgeois gentilhomme* was merely the pretext for a Turkish ballet, orientalism being for the moment in fashion. Louis XIV was delighted with it and even in 1712 loved to have its music played to him.

The Académie de Musique. After the failure of Perrin's operatic enterprise Lully seized the opportunity of buying up his privilege and in 1672 was granted letters patent for the exclusive establishment of an *Académie de Musique* for the performance of operas. He opened it (probably in November 1672) with *Les Fêtes de l'Amour et de Bacchus*, arranged by the poet Quinault from previous ballets; the first real opera which he produced (in collaboration with Quinault) was *Cadmus et Hermione* (1673). Molière had died in February of that year. *Cadmus*, in spite of some hostile criticism, was a great success; but *Alceste* (January 1674) was unexpectedly ill-received. Quinault's enemies did their best to persuade Lully to get rid of him. Lully accordingly attempted collaboration with Boileau and Racine in *La Chute de Phaëton*, but, according to Boileau, the King, at the instigation of Quinault, commanded him to return to his former librettist. It is probable that Lully did not work happily with Boileau and used this means of setting himself free. The breach caused Boileau to be permanently hostile towards the opera. Lully returned to Quinault for *Thésée* (1675), *Atys* (1676), and *Isis* (1677); *Psyché* (1678) was a re-arrangement by Thomas Corneille of the *Psyché* of 1671, a *comédie-ballet* originally written by Molière and Pierre Corneille. Thomas Corneille and Fontenelle supplied the libretto of *Bellérophon* (1679); in 1680 Quinault reappeared as librettist for *Proserpine*, followed by *Persée* (1682), *Phaëton* (1683), *Amadis* (1684), *Roland* (1685), and *Armide* (1686). Racine wrote the words of *L'Idylle de la Paix* for a fête at Sceaux in 1685. *Armide* was Quinault's masterpiece and his last tragedy; *Acis et Galathée*, a pastoral (1686), was written by Campistron, who also wrote *Achille et Polixène*. Of this Lully only lived to compose the first act. Conducting his *Te Deum* for the recovery of Louis XIV from illness in January 1687, he struck his toe with the stick with which he beat time on the ground. An abscess was formed which was followed by gangrene, and after the amputation first of the toe, then of the foot and finally of the whole leg, Lully died on March 22, 1687.

Lully is the creator of French opera, but his real genius was not so much for composition as for organisation. He was an extraordinarily successful man of affairs, too successful indeed

to be a sympathetic character. His operas, when we read them
in a library to-day, are dreary and monotonous in the extreme,
so that it is difficult to understand how they should have held
the stage in Paris almost up to the end of the 18th century.
They must not be judged on their purely musical merits. It
must be remembered that Lully was responsible not merely for
the composition of the music, but for the whole production.
He chose Quinault as his poet, directed him largely in the planning of the drama, trained the singers and the orchestra, besides
inventing the dances. It was no small achievement to have
created the dignified and ordered magnificence of the Lullian
opera out of the traditions of the *Ballet de Cour* and the hetero-
geneous absurdities of Italian baroque opera. Lully's musical
style was founded partly on Cavalli and Rossi, whose operas he
probably heard in Paris as a boy, and very largely on his father-
in-law Lambert. Before 1671 he was a violent opponent of
French opera; as soon as he took matters into his own hands
he got rid of the Italians and adopted an entirely French style.
The *Ballet de la Raillerie* (1659) contains a duet between *La
Musique Française* and *La Musique Italienne* which illustrates
the difference of style between the two very pointedly.

Italian opera concentrated attention on the beauty of pure
singing and the poignant vocal expression of emotion. Even as
early as Rossi and Cavalli the main interest lies always in the
airs, the recitatives being comparatively unimportant. Musical
scene-painting in the orchestra it almost entirely neglected.
Lully's operas, on the other hand, seldom contain anything
which an Italian would recognise as an air. For him and his
audience the recitative is always the first thing. It is strictly
syllabic and in the opinion of his contemporaries represented
accurately the standard style of theatrical declamation. It has
the formality of its century; the perpetual dactylic rhythms
which distinguish it so sharply from English or Italian recitative soon become wearisome even to French ears; compared
with the recitative of Debussy it is turgid and exaggerated. The
instrumental portions of the operas are of great historical importance. Lully is the creator of the "French overture" form,
first used in his additions to Cavalli's *Serse* (1660), and afterwards by Handel and Bach. His dance music is simple and

direct in style and always admirably suited to its purpose. His descriptive scenes are the direct ancestors, through Rameau and Gluck, of the descriptive orchestral music of Weber and Wagner. How far he was personally responsible for the music which bore his name cannot be exactly defined. We know that he had the habit of composing at the harpsichord and dictating the upper part and the bass to his assistants, of whom Colasse was the chief, who filled in the inner parts. His method seems to have been very similar to that of Rubens and other painters who worked on a large scale.

Sacred Music in the 17th Century. It is curious that the age of Pascal and Bossuet should have produced so little of importance in the domain of sacred music. Jean Titelouze of Rouen (b. 1563) was the founder of a school of French organists, among whom the most distinguished were Nicolas Boyvin (b. at Rouen, d. 1706), Baptiste-François Roberday (b. at Paris, d. before 1695), Jean-Henri d'Anglebert (*fl.* 1689), Louis-Nicolas Clérambault (1676–1749), and Jean-François Dandrieu (b. at Paris, 1684?–1740). A large number of organs were built in France during the 17th century, some with pedal-boards of thirty notes. The French style of organ-playing was much lighter than the German; great attention was paid to ingenious combinations and contrasts of stops. Loud and full chords were seldom used, partly on grounds of taste, partly on account of inadequate wind-supply.

Nicolas Formé (1567–1638) was much admired by Louis XIII for his church music, which is in a plain harmonic style somewhat resembling that of Gabrieli. Like the Italians of that period, the French church composers wrote much for a double choir. Lully's motets and his celebrated *Miserere* show great dignity; Mme de Sévigné said of the *Miserere*, "Je ne crois pas qu'il y ait autre musique dans les cieux." The most important composer of sacred music in the 17th century is Henri du Mont (1610–1684), whose motets, often accompanied by strings, closely resemble the English anthems of the Restoration. Michel de Lalande (1657–1725) and André Campra (1660–1744) were also distinguished composers for the church.

Harpsichord Music. The style of French harpsichord music in the 17th century shows clearly that it was derived primarily from the music of the lute. A school of clavecinists was founded by André Champion, Marquis de Chambonnières (d. 1670), whose father and grandfather had also been organists and clavecinists. Among his pupils were the brothers Louis (1630–1655) and François (1631–1698) Couperin; a third brother, Charles (1638–1669) was the father of François surnamed *le Grand* (1668–1733). The last-named, who is the most celebrated of the family, published his *Pièces de Clavecin* between 1713 and 1730. These suites, or as he calls them, *ordres*, include, besides the usual dance forms, a number of little pieces with curious and amusing titles, some of which are descriptive, while others were intended as portraits. Many of them suggest ballets performed at the opera. They form altogether an exquisite and fascinating expression of the frivolities and sentimentalities of their age. It is characteristic of François Couperin that in his *Art de toucher le Clavecin* he advises the student to place a mirror on the desk, so as to learn to avoid making grimaces. "Il faut avoir un air aisé à son clavecin: sans fixer trop la vue sur quelque objet, ny l'avoir trop vague: enfin regarder la compagnie, s'il s'en trouve, comme si on n'étoit point occupé d'ailleurs...."

A set of pieces bearing the name *Les fastes de la grande et ancienne Ménestrandise* refers to the struggles of the French composers, organists and clavecinists, with the *Ménestrandise*. About 1330 the itinerant musicians of Paris formed the *Confrérie de Saint-Julien des Ménestriers*, presided over by a "king," the *Roi des Ménestriers*. Charles VI in 1407 granted them a privilege by which they claimed authority over all instrumental musicians and insisted that they should be subject to the rules of the confraternity. These privileges were extended in 1658, but the clavecinists, lutenists, and composers protested in 1691 and obtained a legal decision in their favour. The dancing-masters and violinists, who formed the confraternity, renewed hostilities in 1706, but in 1707 the organists obtained new letters patent which "faisaient défense aux maîtres à danser de troubler les harmonistes dans l'exercice de leur profession." It is to this rout of the *Ménestrandise* that Couperin's satire refers. There were further difficulties in 1750, and finally in 1773 Louis XVI abolished the *Roi des Ménestriers* altogether.

The French Violin School. The violin had already sup-

planted the viol in popularity during the reign of Louis XIII.
Under the direction of Lully the *Vingt-quatre violons du Roi*
reached a high standard of performance; French players were
in demand in other countries. There were five at the court of
the Elector of Saxony in 1679. One of the most distinguished
of the *violons du Roi* was J.-B. Anet (1661–1755), a pupil of
Corelli; his playing was one of the attractions of the *Concerts
Spirituels* founded by Philidor in 1725. Here too were heard
J.-B. Somis, a Piedmontese (1676–1763), J.-M. Leclair (b. at
Lyons in 1697), composer of several sonatas, and later Pierre
Gaviniés (b. at Bordeaux in 1726), whom Viotti called "le Tar-
tini Français." Other composers for the violin were J.-F. Rebel
(b. 1664?), G.-B. Senaillé (1687–1730) and Aimé Francœur
(1698–1787). Jean-Louis Duport (1749–1818) was distinguished
as a violoncellist.

The Followers of Lully. Lully permitted no rivals at the
Opera as long as he lived. By the time of his death he had
established a style of construction from which hardly any departure was made for nearly a century. *Achille et Polixène* was
finished by Colasse (1649–1709), who wrote a few more operas
of little importance to libretti by Fontenelle, La Fontaine, and
others. Marc-Antoine Charpentier (1634–1704) composed music
for Molière's *Le Malade Imaginaire*, but could not appear as a
composer of operas until after Lully's death. His *Médée* (1693)
is more Italian in style and at times more dramatic than the
operas of Lully. Campra, who produced his first operas under
the name of his brother Joseph, gave up church music definitely
in 1700 and devoted himself entirely to the stage.

Jean-Philippe Rameau (1683–1760), the most distinguished
French musician of the 18th century, also took to the stage late
in life, after he had made his name as an organist, as a composer
for the harpsichord, and above all as the author of a theory of
harmony. Rameau's *Traité d'Harmonie* (1722) is the foundation of the classical harmonic system. He was the first theorist
to formulate the principle of the inversion of chords and of the
basse fondamentale or system of roots, as well as the first to propose a theory of harmony based on acoustic phenomena. His
first opera, *Hippolyte et Aricie* (1733), was considered very ab-
struse and complicated. *Castor et Pollux* (1737) was received

with enthusiasm, and a week before the production of *Dardanus* (1739) all the boxes of the theatre were taken for a fortnight. His usual librettist was Gentil-Bernard; the words of *Le Temple de la Gloire* (1745) were written by Voltaire. As a musician, Rameau is one of the greatest that France ever produced; he is the incarnation in music of French intellectualism. Considered dramatically, his operas are monuments of formal and frigid pomposity. The conditions of performance were absurd. The chorus came on in two rows, men on one side, women on the other; the men stood with arms folded, the women all carried fans. The dancers wore masks and their dresses bore no relation to the subject of the drama. The singing and orchestral playing was described by many contemporaries as atrocious; the poet Gray in 1739 writes of the "cracked voices" accompanied by "an orchestra of hum-strums" and elsewhere sums up French music as "des miaulemens et des heurlemens effroyables, mêlés avec un tintamarre du diable."

The Guerre des Bouffons. A troup of Italian comedians (*les bouffons italiens*) came to Paris in 1752 and took the city by storm with Pergolesi's *La Serva Padrona*. Rousseau, whose little opera *Le Devin du Village* had been given at Fontainebleau a few months later, published in 1753 his notorious *Lettre sur la Musique Française* in which he maintained that such a thing as French music could not possibly exist. Rousseau had had very little musical training and was probably actuated by personal animosity against Rameau, who had criticised his compositions. The success of the Italian company was due to the natural vivacity of their performance as contrasted with the stiff traditionalism of the French opera; but it was hardly just to make comparisons between French tragedy and Italian farce. One result of the *Guerre des Bouffons*, as the controversy was called, was that Egidio Romualdo Duni (1709–1775), a Neapolitan composer of comic operas, established himself at Paris and founded a school of *opéra-comique* of which the favourite composers were Monsigny (1729–1817) and Dalayrac (1753–1809).

Gluckists and Piccinnists. The *Encyclopédistes*, D'Alembert, Diderot, Rousseau, and Grimm, were all enemies of the essentially aristocratic and reactionary art represented by Rameau's operas, though they were not without respect for his individual genius. There is good reason to suppose that Gluck in Vienna was already acquainted with their ideas and influenced by them in the composition of *Orfeo* (Vienna, 1762). His French comic operas (1758–1764) were composed not for Paris but for the Viennese court. In 1774 his *Iphigénie en Aulide* was produced in Paris. Gluck had the support of Marie Antoinette, to whom he had taught singing in Vienna, and he had taken considerable trouble to cultivate the favour of the men of letters, but there was a strong party against him. Mme du Barry was persuaded to invite the Neapolitan Niccolò Piccinni (1728–1800) to Paris to represent the Italianising party. Piccinni was the most modest and retiring of men and had himself a great admiration for Gluck. The war of the Gluckists and Piccinnists was a war of journalists rather than a quarrel of musicians. *Iphigénie en Tauride* (1779) finally decided the battle in Gluck's favour, but it is worth noting that Piccinni's *Didon* held the stage in Paris till 1826. Gluck's reform of the opera was dramatic rather than musical. On the general style of music outside France he had very little influence; Romain Rolland has well said that his reforms were primarily moral. In this way he prepared French music for the Revolution.

The Music of the Revolution. The history of the Revolution may be traced in its popular songs such as *Ça ira*, the *Carmagnole*, the *Reveil du Peuple*, and the *Marseillaise*. It also had its official music, and actually brought about a definite change in the artistic outlook of French musicians. Those who composed for its ceremonies had to abandon the complexities and the elegances of the century that was ending. The Revolution required music that was simple and direct, suitable for a large body of people in the open air, played by brass bands rather than by violins and harpsichords. The chief composers of music for the Revolution were Grétry (b. at Liège, 1741–1813), a charming composer of *opéras-comiques*, who modelled himself on Pergolesi and Rousseau; Gossec (1734–1829), composer of a *Hymne à l'Être Suprême* and the music for Mirabeau's funeral; Méhul (1763–1817), whose *Chant du Départ* (1794) is the most famous song of the period after the *Marseillaise* of Rouget de Lisle (1760–1836); Catel (1773–1830), Lesueur (1760–1837), the teacher of Berlioz, and Cherubini (1760–1842). The Revolution affected music beyond the frontiers of France, for it gave all composers the ideal of writing, as Beethoven did, not for a small circle of patrons but for humanity. Lesueur, one of the first composers to show the Romantic influence of Ossian, provided music on a gigantic scale for the coronation of Napoleon in 1804. Méhul, another early Romantic, won Napoleon's prize for the best opera in 1807 with *Joseph*. Italian composers were very popular in France at this period. Cherubini, a Florentine by birth, settled at Paris in 1788. Although he composed several French operas, he cannot be regarded as a French composer; but as Director of the Conservatoire (1822), which had been founded in 1795, he exercised a considerable influence on the training of the composers of the 19th century.

The Romantic Period. After the death of Beethoven in 1827 Paris took the place of Vienna as the musical centre of Europe. Mendelssohn and Wagner admitted that the classical symphonies were nowhere so magnificently played as at the concerts of the Conservatoire. French opera was best represented by the comic operas of Boieldieu (1775–1834), Auber (1782–1871), Adam (1803–1856), and Hérold (1791–1833), many of which are still popular both in France and in Germany. Auber's *La Muette de Portici* (1828), known in England as *Masaniello*, was the precursor of Rossini's *Guillaume Tell* (1829) and the operas of Meyerbeer. Halévy's *La Juive* (1835) is the chief French opera in the grandiose style of the period which was dominated mainly by the influence of Meyerbeer and Rossini. Parisian music was extremely cosmopolitan; besides these two, Chopin, Liszt, Paer, and Cherubini were all living there, while Paganini was a frequent visitor.

Berlioz. Hector Berlioz (1803–1869), the chief representative of the Romantic movement in French music, though never fully understood or appreciated by his contemporaries, was born near Grenoble, the son of a country doctor. He was sent to Paris in 1822 to study medicine, but gave it up in disgust and much against the will of his parents devoted himself to music. He became a pupil of Lesueur and entered the Conservatoire in 1823. After constant rebellion against his teachers (except Lesueur, for whom he always cherished an affection) and many struggles with poverty he won the Prix de Rome in 1830; in

1832 he returned to Paris and married in 1833 the Irish actress
Henrietta Smithson, from whom he separated in 1840. His first
important works were *Eight Scenes from Faust* set to Gérard de
Nerval's translation (1828–1829), some songs translated from
Thomas Moore (1829), and the *Symphonie Fantastique* (1830–
1831). *Harold en Italie*, a symphony with viola obbligato, was
written for Paganini in 1834; it was followed by the *Symphonie Funèbre et Triomphale* and *Roméo et Juliette* (1838). The
Requiem was composed in 1837, the *Te Deum* in 1849–1854. In
1846 he completed *La Damnation de Faust*, the work by which
he is best known; the oratorio *L'Enfance du Christ* belongs to
1850–54. Of his operas *Benvenuto Cellini* was first performed in
1837; *Béatrice et Bénédict* was written in 1860–1862, and his
last work, *Les Troyens*, which he regarded as his masterpiece,
was produced in 1863.

"Berlioz," says M. Combarieu, "a été plus qu'un musicien
romantique: il fut le Romantisme personnifié." His influence on
the music of the 19th century may be compared to that of Victor
Hugo in literature. In considering the dates of his compositions
it should be noted that Wagner did not write *Der Fliegende
Holländer* till 1843, and the first of Liszt's symphonic poems
dates from 1849. Berlioz unfortunately did not possess the
technical ability to correspond with his extraordinary powers
of emotion and imagination. His passion for expressing in
music all that was gigantic and terrible suggests the influence
of the Revolution. He loved to write for an enormous orchestra,
and the modern conception of orchestral colouring as a means of
poetic expression is entirely due to his genius. It was a genius
in some respects more literary than musical, and his memoirs,
letters, and critical essays are as important an expression of his
personality as his music. He was an uncompromising advocate
of descriptive music, and the story of the *Symphonie Fantastique* well illustrates both his aesthetic principles and his
peculiar personal temperament.

This *Épisode de la vie d'un artiste*, as he calls it, represents a
young musician of sensitive temperament who attempts to
poison himself after a disappointment in love. The poison is
not sufficient to kill him, but produces a series of dreams, in
which the idea of the woman he loves takes the form of a melody

designated as *l'idée fixe*. In the first movement he recalls his *malaise de l'âme* before he met her; the fury of passion which she inspired, his jealousy, tenderness, and religious consolations. In the second movement he meets her at a ball; the third shows him wandering in the country, soothed by its pastoral sounds, until the *idée fixe* reappears in his mind. A storm rises and dies away into silence. In the fourth movement he dreams that he has murdered the woman and is being taken to the guillotine. The knife falls, and in the fifth movement he finds himself in the midst of an orgy of witches and evil spirits. The woman again appears, horribly transformed, to join in the parody of the *Dies Irae* and the witches' sabbath. We see here the perpetual preoccupation of Berlioz with the grotesque, the horrible, and the *macabre*, as well as the passion for self-torture which made his life a continuous martyrdom. But he possessed an unfailing nobility and tenderness of character, which found expression in almost all his works, notably in *Roméo et Juliette*, *L'Enfance du Christ*, and *Les Troyens*. "No composer," says Saint-Saëns, "has done so much in the way of opening up new paths of art and preaching throughout his life the love of beauty and the veneration for great works."

The Second Empire. The period covered by the life of Berlioz was an age of great *virtuosi*, both vocal and instrumental, but it did not in France produce much music of importance outside opera. A composer who sets out to make a name in opera is obliged to write what will please the public, and the operas of this period are all very obviously designed to be successful operas rather than studies in dramatic idealism. The influence of Rossini and Meyerbeer was predominant throughout the Second Empire and even for some time afterwards. Ambroise Thomas (1811–1896), a clever and accomplished composer, is still remembered by *Mignon* (1866), the delicate sentimental charm of which has secured its popularity. The Shakespearean subjects which he attempted later were beyond his powers. Charles Gounod (1818–1893) was a man of deeper musical temperament, influenced even in his operas by his profound religious convictions. It is this blend of idealism and sensuousness which has made him one of the world's most popular composers both of opera and of sacred music. In his early days he was accused

by contemporary critics of following the dangerous path of
German music. He was in fact, as his operas show, a devoted
student of Mozart. Of his operas *Faust* (1859), *Mireille* (1864),
and *Roméo et Juliette* (1867) are the only ones which have survived; in sacred music he is best represented by the *Messe de
Sainte-Cécile* (1855), and the beautiful commemoration of the
war of 1870–1871, *Gallia*. His oratorios *Rédemption* (1867–1882)
and *Mors et Vita* (1884) have been more popular in England
than in France.

Ernest Reyer (1823–1909) is little known outside France, but
his operas *La Statue* (1861), *Sigurd* (1884), and *Salammbô* (1890)
are still performed.

By far the most original composer of this period is Georges
Bizet (1838–1875), composer of *Les Pêcheurs de Perles* (1863), of
incidental music to Daudet's play *L'Arlésienne* (1872), and of
Carmen (1875). He was a pupil of Halévy, but was influenced
further by Meyerbeer and Gounod. In *Carmen* he also made use
of Spanish themes, although Spaniards do not regard the opera
as at all typical of Spanish music. Bizet's style is eclectic and
facile, but even in his simplest movements he employs unexpected
turns of melody or harmony which, without the least trace of
affectation, give his music a singularly individual novelty and
piquancy. *Carmen* took some time to establish its popularity,
but it is now an opera which the most ordinary listener enjoys
at a first hearing, while the most cultivated musician never
wearies of it. Other composers of this period were Léo Delibes
(1836–1891), a charming writer of ballets, and Jules Massenet
(1872–1912), who continued the tradition of Gounod with several
operas and oratorios, in all of which the charm of femininity
finds a peculiarly emphasised expression. The brilliantly amusing
operettas of Jacques Offenbach (1819–1880), a German Jew who
came to Paris as a youth and opened the *Bouffes-Parisiens* in
1855, were entertainments eminently characteristic of the
pleasure-loving days of the Second Empire.

Symphonies, Chamber Music, etc. The catastrophe of 1871
seems to have turned the thoughts of French musicians into
more serious directions than before. The only contemporary of
Berlioz who made a name as a composer of symphonic music
was Félicien David (1810–1876), remembered now only by his

Ode-Symphonie, Le Désert, a remarkable study of Arab local colour. After 1871 the influence of German music begins to be more apparent, both in the actual technique of composition and in the tendency towards a revival of chamber and concert music. At the same time there was naturally a very strong national feeling among musicians, and, whatever contemporary listeners may have thought, it is evident now that the French composers always put their own impress upon every idea that they adopted from outside. The most conspicuous representative of the new movement was Camille Saint-Saëns (1835–1921). In opera he was at first unsuccessful; *Samson et Dalila,* now his most popular work, was originally produced by Liszt at Weimar in 1877. A brilliant pianist and organist, he has composed music in all styles; but his most important works are his symphonies, his symphonic poems (*Le Rouet d'Omphale, Phaëton, Danse Macabre* and *La Jeunesse d'Hercule*), and his concertos for pianoforte and for violin. Few musicians have even shown such skill and ingenuity in the technical handling of all problems of composition, but his creative power has never been sufficient to place him on the highest level. At the same time his versatility and accomplishment have had a noteworthy influence on French music in drawing attention towards other fields than opera and in setting the example of a high standard of workmanship.

A much deeper creative nature, though in his life-time less esteemed, was César Franck (1822–1890), a native of Liège. He was organist of Sainte-Clotilde at Paris from 1858 until his death, and devoted his entire life to his organ, to teaching, and to composition, hardly even conscious of the indifference with which the outer world regarded his music.

The influence of German composers, especially of Wagner, may be traced in the extremely chromatic harmony which is his most conspicuous characteristic, but his creative mind was that of a religious dreamer and mystic. Many of his works give the impression of having been originally extemporised at the organ. His most important work is the oratorio *Les Béatitudes* (1870), which in its more devotional portions maintains a very rarefied atmosphere of spirituality. Its weakest parts are the episodes dealing with illustrations of wickedness; Franck, like Fra Angelico, was quite unable to depict evil. He left one symphony and three symphonic poems; his chamber-music (violin sonata, pianoforte quintet, and string quartet) suffers from excessive length, but is otherwise on an extremely high level.

Édouard Lalo (1823–1892) is known by his popular *Symphonie Espagnole* (1875) as well as by concertos for violin and violoncello. Emmanuel Chabrier (1841–1894) wrote two operas, *Gwendoline* (1886) and *Le Roi malgré Lui* (1887), but is better known by his brilliant rhapsody *España* (1883) and several clever and vivacious songs. Gabriel Fauré (b. 1845), a pupil of Saint-Saëns, was till recently the head of the Conservatoire and the teacher of several distinguished modern composers. His best works are his chamber-music and his songs. He set many poems of the "Parnasse" and his music, delicate, restrained, and exquisitely finished, well reflects the Parnassian spirit at its best. César Franck's chief pupils were Alexis de Castillon (1838–1873), one of the leaders of the revival of chamber-music; Ernest Chausson (1855–1899), best remembered for his chamber-music and his songs, notably the *Serres Chaudes* of Maeterlinck; Henri Duparc (b. 1848), also a composer of songs, whose career has been unfortunately cut short by ill-health; and Vincent d'Indy (b. 1851) who with Charles Bordes and Alexandre Guilmant the organist founded the *Schola Cantorum* at Paris in 1894, originally designed for the study of sacred music but now a complete musical training school. D'Indy has composed two operas, *Fervaal* (1897) and *L'Étranger* (1903), a symphonic poem, *Wallenstein* (1880), two symphonies and much chamber-music.

Modern Tendencies. Alfred Bruneau (b. 1857), a pupil of Massenet, struck out a new line in his operas *Le Rêve* (1891), *L'Attaque du Moulin* (1893), and *Messidor* (1897), all based on prose libretti after Émile Zola, who was his intimate friend, and all dealing with modern life. Bruneau's music was considered extremely daring and original at that time. He has also set several poems of Catulle Mendès to music. Gustave Charpentier (b. 1860), another pupil of Massenet, pursued a similar idea of opera in modern dress with *Louise* (1900); it has obtained more popular success but is on a lower artistic level. Claude Debussy (1862–1916) was the leader of the modern school, which has broken completely with the traditions of the 19th century. Various factors have contributed to the change which Debussy more than any other originated. The influence of painting and poetry has been more apparent than real. The titles of many of Debussy's works suggest that he has aimed merely at the reproduction of atmosphere, and more especially of a poet's or painter's synthetic vision of external objects; but in almost every case the work can be understood on a purely musical basis and is constructed with a logical sense of form. The first new factor is the desire to create a new type of melody, new both as regards intervals and as regards rhythm. This new type of melody was derived partly from mediaeval plainsong, which had for other reasons been very assiduously revived in ecclesiastical circles, and partly from the music of non-European peoples which had been heard at various exhibitions in Paris. There was further the deliberate creation of new scales on a mathematical basis. To these influences Debussy owed the five-note scale (black keys of the pianoforte), common to the music of Scotland, China, and various other countries, and the six-note scale of whole tones derived from the artificial twelve-note scale of equal temperament. Debussy's system of harmony is the natural outcome of his new experiments in melody and rhythm; its principles are only a further development of the older system and may be seen foreshadowed in the music of Grieg, by whom Debussy was strongly influenced. Another strong influence upon him was Moussorgsky, whose curious originality was not recognised until long after his death. As a song-writer Debussy has been associated chiefly with the poems of Verlaine, Mallarmé, and Pierre Louys. His opera *Pelléas et Mélisande* (1902) applies to the stage the same principles of delicate and natural diction supported by an orchestral background which aims more definitely at "atmosphere" than the independent orchestral works. The subdued colouring of the whole easily produces a certain sense of monotony, but when properly performed it gathers to a powerful climax by the gradual cumulative effect of quickening rhythm in the vocal declamation. In any case *Pelléas et Mélisande* is a landmark in the history of opera.

Paul Dukas (*b.* 1865) is best known as the composer of a symphonic poem *L'Apprenti Sorcier* and the opera *Ariane et Barbe-Bleue* (1907), which show the influence of Debussy. Maurice

Ravel (b. 1875), like Paul Dukas, represents a modern return to the intellectualism of Rameau. He has composed much original and interesting music for the pianoforte, a string quartet dedicated to his teacher Fauré, and a very witty and amusing comic opera, *L'Heure Espagnole*.

From the time of Lully almost to the end of the 19th century, French music appears to have been largely dominated by foreigners; yet whatever new impulses they brought into the music of France, they were all of them subjected to influences of French literature and French taste which gave their music a very definitely French character. This is as true of Meyerbeer and Offenbach as it is of Lully and Gluck. To define the French musical style in words is hardly possible. The rhythms of the French language have naturally affected the shape of vocal melody, and have thus set the general style of instrumental melody also. As in literature, so in music, the French have always aimed at the highest standard of lucidity, economy of means, and fineness of workmanship. They have regarded music on the whole in a different way from their neighbours. French music has never had the spontaneous passion of the Italians nor the philosophical meditation of the Germans. Berlioz and Franck are perhaps exceptions, but Franck was a Belgian by birth, and Berlioz is not to be defined by any generalisations. One might say that the French have regarded music always as a consciously practised art, and one practised with the principal aim of giving pleasure. At its worst, French music has been frivolous and trivial, at its best intellectual rather than emotional. To the French mind music is a thing apart from reason, and therefore incapable of transcending reason; the only possible relation into which the two can enter is that reason should dominate music.

BIBLIOGRAPHY

J. Combarieu, *Histoire de la Musique*. 3 vols. 1913–1919. M. Brenet, *Musique et Musiciens de la vieille France*. 1911. R. Rolland, *Musiciens d'Autrefois*. 1908; *Musiciens d'Aujourd'hui*. 1908. H. Prunières, *Le Ballet de Cour en France*. 1914; *L'Opéra Italien en France avant Lulli*. 1913; *Lully*. 1910. E. Newman, *Gluck and the Opera*. 1895. C. Pierre, *Les Hymnes et Chansons de la Révolution*. 1904; *Musique des Fêtes et Cérémonies de la Révolution Française*. 1899. J. Tiersot, *Rouget de Lisle, son œuvre, sa vie*. 1894; *Hector Berlioz et la Société de son temps*. 1903. C. Saint-Saëns, *Portraits et Souvenirs*. C. Gounod, *Mémoires d'un Artiste*.

Modern Reprints of Old French Music

J. Tiersot, *Mélodies populaires des Provinces de France*; *Noëls français du XVe au XVIIIe siècle*; *Chants de la vieille France du XIIIe au XVIIIe siècle*. H. Expert, *Les Maîtres Musiciens de la Renaissance française*, 23 vols.; *Airs français des XVIe et XVIIe siècles*; *Répertoire classique de musique religieuse et spirituelle*: Série A. *Musique d'église des XVIIe et XVIIIe siècles*. Ch. Bordes, *Chansonnerie du XVIe siècle*; Cl. Jannequin, *Trois fantaisies vocales*; *Chœurs extraits des plus célèbres opéras de nos maîtres français des XVIIe et XVIIIe siècles*; *Les chefs-d'œuvre de l'opéra français*.

F. Couperin, *Pièces de clavecin*, 4 livres, ed. L. Diémer. J.-P. Rameau, *Œuvres complètes de clavecin*, 4 vols., ed. L. Diémer.

CHAPTER XII

THE STAGE

THE theatre is made up of three elements: the intellectual element, the human element, and the material element; the first being the literary work, the second the actors, and the third the house, stage, scenery, and costumes. We propose here to deal with the history of the last two only: the human element and the material element.

The actors and the costumes, the stage setting and the arrangement of the house, are, so to speak, the external means and conditions of the theatre, the literary work being its mind, its soul, and its internal spirit. And just as the literary work always more or less reflects the ideas, sentiments, and manners of the moment at which it appears, in the same way the stage setting, the arrangement of the house and the style of acting (subject of course to the limitations of the mechanical and scientific knowledge of the day) show the tendency of the artistic and social aspirations of each period. By simply following the evolution of theatrical production we could build up an historical picture of society. From a mystery play of the 13th century to the last play of M. François de Curel, *L'Ame en Folie*, passing through the *Tartuffe* of Molière, the *Turcaret* of Le Sage, *Le Mariage de Figaro* of Beaumarchais, the *Antony* of Dumas, the *Hernani* of Hugo, *Le Gendre de M. Poirier* of Augier, *Le Demi-Monde* of Dumas *fils*, *La Course du Flambeau* of Hervieu, *Les Affaires sont les Affaires* of Mirbeau, *Les Corbeaux* of Becque, the *Blanchette* of M. Brieux, the *Amoureuse* of M. de Porto-Riche, and *Les Ventres dorés* and *La Vie publique* of M. Émile Fabre, it is possible to follow the changes of feeling and the political and moral evolution of French society from the Middle Ages down to our own day.

The result would not be different if we restricted ourselves to the study of the external conditions of the theatre. In both cases it would be evident that the development of the drama

follows a continuous if fluctuating tendency to return slowly
but surely to the populace from which it originated, but from
which it became more and more remote as the populace
declined in political importance. From this point of view the
recent experiments of M. Gémier at the Cirque d'Hiver are particularly interesting; they illustrate and, as we shall see later
on, make clearer the truth of what has just been said.

§ I. THE MIDDLE AGES

The Theatres and the public

The sacred drama was the first play, the church the first
theatre. What a play and what a theatre! The Mass—I speak
with all the respect the ceremony commands—by its mystic
meaning and the participation of the faithful in its celebration,
is the highest and most complete form of spectacle.

This has been said long ago. The Mass stirs the heart and the
mind, the soul and the senses, of all the *actors*. What theatre
can be compared to a cathedral? No modern building is so
appropriate to its purpose, so perfectly adequate to the drama
performed there. In the Middle Ages, religion being the basis
of philosophy and of society, it was only natural that the Church
should initiate spectacles for the people apart from the religious
ceremonies. The mystery plays originated within, and under the
fostering care of, the Church. They were merely objective commentaries on the Scriptures and the life of Jesus, a supplement
to the ceremonies of Palm Sunday and the Way of the Cross.

Given at first in the choir, they soon overflowed into the
cloister and then into the parvis under the very porch of the
cathedral. Finally they were performed in the public square
and as they developed from the sacred to the profane the crowds
before whom they were played became more and more mixed
and noisy. When these performances were given in the open
air the spectators were just massed together anyhow, the lucky
ones on tiers of steps facing the stage, the rest on benches, chairs,
and ladders, or even on bundles of hay. The boldest sat astride
the gargoyles of the neighbouring houses, the windows of which,
richly bedecked with flags, garlands, and flowers, were occupied
by the best people. But indeed there was at this time little

class distinction, especially in the 12th and 13th centuries. In spite of all that has been said to the contrary, the nobles were nearer to the people then than the wealthy middle class is to the working class to-day.

The earliest fixed theatre which existed in France was that which the *Confrères de la Passion* opened at the Hôpital de la Trinité in Paris in 1402; it measured 43 yards long and 12 wide. In 1516 the town of Autun constructed a theatre which, according to one chronicler, could hold 4000 people, everybody being "sheltered under canvas." In addition to the tiers of steps this theatre contained "240 rooms (or boxes), each entirely separate, so that the occupants of one had no access to another and the occupants of the upper boxes could not disturb the occupants of the lower[1]."

Stage and Scenery

The mysteries were eminently popular spectacles, as well in their spirit and their purpose as in their execution. The authors, ecclesiastics for the most part, aimed at the edification and religious instruction of the masses; by language and scenery they did their utmost to strike the imagination of the populace. Moreover the public always took an active part in the performance, either by helping to build the platform, by making the costumes and properties, or by actually appearing on the stage. The mysteries demanded a numerous cast. *Les Actes des Apôtres* by the *frères* Gréban needed no less than 494 persons.

The stage was divided into three parts, corresponding to the three regions in which the action took place—Heaven, Earth, Hell. When the theatre was within a building these three parts were placed one above the other, as there was not sufficient space to arrange them on the same plane. But for open air performances in the public square the stage was as much as 50 metres long by 25 metres deep.

One of the characteristics of the medieval theatre was simultaneous action. Unless the public could see everything, they could not understand. For example in the *Mystère de la Passion* the tortures of Herod's soul in Hell were shown at the very same moment as his burial upon Earth.

[1] L. Petit de Julleville, *Les Mystères*.

The sculptures of the cathedrals give an idea of the crude symbolism of the time. Passions and the most abstract sentiments took material form in the medieval drama. The stage was crowded with mechanical monsters and animals, angels and saints; nor must we forget to mention the dummies carefully rigged out to take the place of the actors when the time of torment arrived.

Hell was represented by the monstrous mouth of an animal recalling the leviathan of the Book of Job, out of which issued with a deafening clamour devils dressed up in skins and heads of beasts, clanging cymbals and bells, and brandishing torches. In the centre of the stage, where most of the action took place, were several structures called *mansions*—houses, palaces or monuments: the Tower of Limbo, the House of Pilate, the Temple of Jerusalem, Golgotha, the cave in which Christ was buried. Explanatory placards were hung up to make things clear to the audience amid all the maze of historical and symbolical constructions. Very complicated machinery was brought into play for the angels who flew across the stage, or the temples which fell into ruins; galleys manœuvred in miniature seas; Jesus Christ ascended to heaven to a height of 40 feet; the sun darted huge rays, which were turned by a handle and rotated like a lottery wheel at the fair.

For profane plays, such as the *soties* and *moralités*, which were numerous during the 15th century, the scenery was rudimentary; a symbolic attribute was sufficient to designate the characters: scales for Justice, a looking-glass for Truth.

Actors and Costumes

The Mysteries were at first acted by clerks in orders and members of religious bodies. They were soon joined by amateurs, and, as we have seen, the common populace provided the supers' parts. The *jongleurs* were professional actors, but the celebrated *Confrères de la Passion* were citizens and artisans. Later the *Fous* made their appearance, then the *Sots*, who must not be confounded with the mountebanks and players of farce. Amongst the *Sots* special mention must be made of the *Enfants sans Souci*, the *Basochiens*, and the University students. The *Sots* wore a yellow and green hood with donkey's ears (*chaperon*

de fol), and a vest likewise of yellow and green. They were
acrobats as well as actors. Jean de l'Espine, surnamed Pont-
Alletz because his booth was near the Pont des Halles, was
trebly famous above all the *Sots* as actor, author, and acrobat.
At Paris the *Sots* were chiefly represented by the *Enfants sans
Souci*; the *Prince des Sots* and the *Mère Sotte* presided at all
their meetings. Pierre Gringore, or Gringoire, whose device
"Tout par raison, raison partout, partout raison" is sufficient
proof of his independent spirit, was an *Enfant sans Souci*; so
was Clément Marot.

The *Basoche* drew its members from the "Parlement": they
were all men of law. The *petite Basoche* was restricted to the
personnel of the Châtelet.

The style of acting, like the stage setting and the written
text, was very realistic. On the other hand historical costume
was as fantastic as it could be. Whatever the character represented, the actor wore the fashionable dress of his time: God the
Father appeared in the costume of the Emperor or the Pope;
Nero in the *Actes des Apôtres*, as given at Bourges in 1536, was
arrayed in a robe of blue velvet embroidered with gold, lined
with crimson satin and slashed at the waist; in his hand he
carried a magnificent battle-axe.

Not for centuries was any attention paid to historical accuracy
on the stage, and moreover the medieval attitude towards the
art of costume was not as ridiculous as it seems at first. It was
justified in view of the conceptions of the very public for which
authors and actors worked. Herod in the dress of a king of
France was at once fraught with meaning. The poets, writers,
and actors of the Middle Ages made these transpositions for
the benefit of their contemporaries; moreover, the historical
deeds and characters were often but a pretext for the portrayal
of sentiments and manners peculiar to the moment. Racine
did much the same sort of thing.

§ II. SIXTEENTH AND SEVENTEENTH CENTURIES

The Evolution of Ideas and their Influence on the Theatre

The Renaissance marks an epoch in the evolution of ideas; it left a profound impression on Politics, the Church, and Society. The theatre, as always, felt the effect of the events of the times. By bringing about the free discussion of ideas the Reformation enlarged the intellectual horizon of the stage. But above all, the essential fact, so far as we are concerned, was the importance of the Court in the Society of the 16th century, and the formation of an ever-growing cultivated circle. The poets were thus brought to write for a select public and the theatre consequently became more and more detached from the populace. The stage-setting, the arrangement of the house, even the style of acting, reflected these developments.

Note that the Parlement of Paris, by a decree dated the 17th November 1548, gave a theatrical monopoly to the *Confrères de la Passion* and prohibited the performance of Sacred Mysteries; but this did not prevent the *Confrères* from performing them from time to time. Note also that the Renaissance was almost exclusively inspired by Antiquity.

Addressing a smaller and more refined public, the authors gave all their attention to the literary part of their work, neglecting the external part. For the Mysteries the traditional stage-setting was maintained; for any other kind of play the scenery was reduced to a minimum. On the appearance of the first tragedies and comedies of character, the saints of Heaven, the monsters of Hell, and all the machinery necessary for the representation of miracles, disappeared. The public square was abandoned. Plays were performed in colleges and at court in halls of moderate size.

We must not generalise too much however. For a play by Hardy, now lost, the stage-setting called for a palace in the centre, on one side the sea with a ship from which a woman jumps into the water, on the other side a room with a bed. The staging of the tragi-comedies, therefore, had not given up the simultaneous setting of the Middle Ages. For the performance of *Cléopâtre* by Jodelle in 1552 the stage was erected at one end of a courtyard against a wall, and the windows looking on the courtyard served as boxes just as in the 13th century.

We must remember also that at this period companies of strolling players began to wander up and down the country. It is obvious that they would not care to encumber themselves with a heap of scenery and stage properties, and this helped to make for the simplification of stage-setting. In every age the playwright must reckon with the material possibilities of his stage; in our day there are many dramatists who write for touring companies plays which call for very few actors and no special scenery.

The Theatres and the Actors

Theatres were rare. In the reign of Henry III (1551–89) there were only two in Paris, one occupied by the Italian comedians in a building which formed part of the Hôtel du Petit-Bourbon, the other in the Hôtel de Bourgogne of which the *Confrères de la Passion* became the proprietors in 1548. Owing to this lack of theatres the strolling companies were forced to utilise tennis-courts. They were of very fair size and somewhat similar in shape to the Petit-Bourbon and the Hôtel de Bourgogne. Galleries were constructed for the audience, and the stage was erected at one end.

The stage, about the middle of the 16th century, consisted of a platform without wings, enclosed at the back and on both sides by tapestries or draperies. As tapestries were very costly they were replaced by painted canvas. Scenery as we understand it, made of canvas stretched on a frame, did not come into use until after the League. Scenery of this type was a substitute for tapestry and intended only to enclose and limit the stage; it had absolutely nothing to do with the subject of the play. The medieval realism was forgotten; true psychology was sought after rather than picturesque symbol. When they decided to paint on their canvases something more than mere decorative themes, they invented the three scenes which are still to-day the basis of all stage scenery; a rather rich interior, a public square, and a garden.

With regard to the theatre of the Petit-Bourbon, which Molière occupied for a short time, we find a certain amount of

information about it in the description of a ballet given there in
1615:

> This hall is 36 yards long by 16 yards wide at the end of which there
> is in addition a semicircle 14 yards deep and 17 yards wide, the whole
> covered by a coved ceiling strewn with fleur de lys. All around it is
> adorned with columns having their pedestals, capitals, architraves,
> friezes, and cornices of the Doric order, and between the said cornices
> arcades and niches....At one end of the hall, directly opposite the daïs
> of Their Majesties, was erected a large stage 6 feet in height, 16 yards
> wide and as many yards deep.

We know also that two staircases led to two rows of balconies
one above the other, running along the wall and arranged in
the form of boxes. The stage communicated with the pit by a
flight of steps, and above the stage was a loggia with a balcony.
The prompters were stationed on one side of the stage.

The theatre of the Hôtel de Bourgogne built in 1548 was of
smaller proportions and more modestly decorated. In 1588 it
was in such a bad state that it was described by one chronicler
as a "sewer."

At the beginning of the 17th century the number of theatres
increased; they were indeed for the most part little more than
tennis-courts converted and more or less adapted to theatrical
purposes. From this time on, however, speaking generally, the
external theatrical conditions improved. Italy was the chief
source of inspiration. The celebrated engraving by Abraham
Bosse shows that in 1634 the "interior" scene of the Hôtel de
Bourgogne was in the Italian style with cornices, pilasters,
volutes, mouldings, and other architectonic ornaments. This
famous "interior," in the antique style of "plantation[1]," had
three doors, one at the back and one at each side. Instead of
footlights, which had not yet been invented, ran a balustrade
intended to separate the stage from the pit.

Another engraving shows us the public square, one of the
three essential scenes. The back scene represents a street seen
in perspective; at each side are flats with houses painted on
them; these flats, set obliquely, allowed the actors to make their
entrances and exits. Nothing better or more simple has ever
been thought of.

---

[1] Plantation is the method of setting the scenery on the stage.

The *Confrères de la Passion* had been the most active workers for the theatre in France, but curiously enough their activity slackened from the moment they entered into possession of the Hôtel de Bourgogne. This was due to the fact that the same decree of the Parlement which granted to them a theatrical monopoly robbed them of the greatest part of their repertory by prohibiting the performance of sacred mysteries. They then decided to let their theatre to a troupe of actors under the leadership of Valleran Lecomte, which in the reign of Louis XIII took the title of "Troupe Royale." In order to get full profit from a monopoly which they did not themselves exploit they authorised another troupe, for a consideration, to open a theatre at the Hôtel d'Argent. Under the leadership of Mondory this company, known as the "Troupe du Marais," became the rival of the company at the Hôtel de Bourgogne, the most illustrious members of which were Montfleury (1600–1667), La Champmeslé (1642–1698), the interpreter and inspirer of Racine, and Baron (1653–1729), the pupil of Molière himself.

Jean-Baptiste Poquelin, who was to render for ever glorious the pseudonym of Molière, began by touring the provinces. Tradition has it that he had lessons from Scaramouche, the celebrated Italian buffoon. It was in 1658 that he made his début in Paris before the King. At first the company was under the patronage of Monsieur, the King's brother, and shared the Théâtre du Petit-Bourbon with the Italians. When, in 1660, this hotel was demolished, Louis XIV placed at the disposal of Molière the Théâtre du Palais-Royal built for Richelieu, and in 1665 authorised his company to take the title of "Troupe du Roi." At the death of Molière his company under the leadership of La Grange was successively installed in the rue Mazarine, and then in the rue Guénégaud, near the Institut.

The year 1673 saw the death of the author of *Tartuffe* and the breaking up of the company of the Marais. Some of the actors joined the Hôtel de Bourgogne, others the Troupe du Roi. On the other hand the Hôtel de Bourgogne lost La Champmeslé, who in 1679 brought over with her to the troupe of Molière the repertory of Racine. It was at this time that by order of Louis XIV the two remaining companies were united into one. Thus came into being the *Comédie-Française* in the year 1680.

To complete this rapid survey it is necessary to add that, concurrently with these companies, troupes of *farceurs*, of whom Tabarin was the most famous, gave to the populace grotesque shows on the Pont-Neuf, or at the fairs of Saint-Germain or Saint-Laurent.

The performance of the Mysteries called only for realistic acting in keeping with the spirit of the text and the mentality of the audience. The evolution of the literary forms of the drama brought with it the evolution of the actor's art. The comic plays had brought into being a type of comedian who was at once acrobat, conjuror, and actor, and whose traditions were continued in the Italian Comedy and the farces of Molière. But as the dramatic repertory became more refined, more literary, and thus more remote from the populace, the comedians gained in dignity what they lost perhaps in imaginative vigour. The introduction of tragedy gave birth to a new kind of interpreter. To Montfleury is due the honour of having created the dramatic school from which our modern tragedians have descended.

At the time of Richelieu the development of the theatre was more rapid. The cardinal's influence was considerable. The literary value and the high moral tone of the dramatic works made it henceforth possible for women to take part in the performances both as actresses and as spectators. Women had appeared on the stage in the Middle Ages during a short period, but licentiousness of subject and dialogue drove them away, and a woman of quality could not even witness the performance. During the 17th century actresses did not play all the female parts, but they did at least play the noble ladies and princesses. The soubrettes and the old women and nurses continued to be impersonated by men.

To prevent disturbance of the performance by riots, as happened only too often, the lieutenant of police prohibited any armed person from entering the theatre. Noisy persons were thrown out by force. In short the theatre became a place fit for good company.

Eager to add to the glory of French literature and of the reign of his master, Richelieu took an interest in all that appertained to the theatre—men and things. Not content with writing plays and competing with Corneille, he wanted a theatre worthy of himself, and the one he had built in his palace in 1640 was long considered a model. For the first time we find a rectangular hall with a rounded end giving it thus the shape of the letter U. Another feature was that "the architect had constructed a long series of wooden benches, which covering only two-thirds of each tier of steps left a space for the feet[1]."

The comfort of the public was beginning to be considered. In this I see a proof of what I have advanced with regard to the evolution of dramatic forms and of the externals of the theatre. So long as plays were given before the populace there was no thought of comfort; the spectators remained standing or were crowded on the stone steps. It is by no means impossible that the custom of placing seats upon the stage originated in the rudimentary equipment of the theatre. Deference was shown to persons of importance by allowing them to be comfortably seated, and by sparing them promiscuous contact with the common herd[2]. When the theatres became more comfortable, the nobles and the *bourgeois* refused to mix with the common people; the seats on the stage disappeared; the galleries, balconies, boxes, and amphitheatre made it possible to keep the classes apart.

It was on the 30th April 1759 that the stage was cleared of the benches, which encumbered it to such an extent that in 1739 Racine's *Athalie* could not be given in entirety. With regard to the removal of these benches Collé the song-writer wrote a few years later:

Stage illusion is now perfect [he exaggerated]; we no longer see Caesar forced to turn a coxcomb out of his seat, Mithridates expiring amidst men of our acquaintance, the ghost of Ninus bumping against a farmer of taxes, and Camilla [in the *Horace* of Corneille] dying in the arms of well-known authors of comedies, who lend a hand in the assassination of this Roman lady by her brother.

The "Salle des Machines" constructed at the Tuileries by order of Louis XIV and intended for the performance of huge ballets could hold, it appears, from 7000 to 8000 spectators. Luxurious in the extreme it was considered the finest theatre

[1] Sauval, *Antiquités de la Ville de Paris*.
[2] This is my personal opinion. It is generally supposed that the seats placed upon the stage were reserved for poor authors and pages; that, when it became the fashion to parade oneself on the stage, the great nobles took possession of these seats; and that when the fashion changed again the lackeys took the place of their masters.

in Europe. Louis XIV, indeed, was passionately fond of shows of all kinds, and he was not too proud to take part in them. At his various palaces of Saint-Germain, Fontainebleau, and Versailles he was always organising fêtes. *La Princesse d'Elide* by Molière was first given at a fête at Versailles upon a stage erected in the open air. For a background it had the central avenue of the park with the Palace in the distance. Versailles for that matter could not boast of a fixed stage before the year 1700.

Stage, Scenery, and Costumes

The opening of the theatre of the Palais Richelieu (which later became the Palais-Royal) took place with the performance of *Mirame* by Richelieu and Desmarets. A great effort after stage effect had been made. The scene represented a garden surrounded by a colonnade adorned with statues and surmounted by urns, and thick bushes with a balustrade behind them, and the sea on the horizon.

The machinery, which stirred everybody's wonder, consisted of apparatus by means of which people popped up through the stage floor or disappeared through the flies. As there was no ceiling as yet, it was quite easy to do so, either by lifting them up with steel wire or by some other equally simple means.

Till the middle of the 17th century performances were given in the day-time; the police regulations ordered them to be over by half-past four at latest in winter. The theatre was probably darkened, as we know that in 1581 at the performance of *Circe* oil lamps a hundred candles and innumerable luminous stars shed a brilliant light. *Circe* was only a ballet, but it is regarded as the first opera given in France; it contains the three elements—dancing, singing, and orchestral music—which distinguish opera from comedy, drama, or tragedy. It was played at the Petit-Bourbon, not on the stage, but in the middle of the auditorium cleared for the purpose.

The scenery was composed of artificial beds of flowers and fruit, bordered with lavender, rosemary, and sage; the balustrades were of silver gilt; the trees and their fruit were imitated in gold, silver, silk, feathers, and colours. A large golden sun spread its rays over the whole.

This kind of show was often characterised by the most ridiculous costumes. In the ballet of *Les Femmes Renversées*

(1626) all the performers, by means of masks, had two faces. In another, where the idea was to represent humanity upside down, the actors apparently walked with their feet in the air. Ballets enjoyed a great vogue for a long time. Molière composed them, Louis XIV danced in them.

The staging of *Mirame* created such a sensation that all the theatres of the time were influenced by it, and began competing with each other for the finest scenery. It was however impossible as yet to change the scenery during the performance; so that they had to be content with one scene unless they followed the medieval method of a simultaneous setting. But the stage was barely 7 metres wide, while for the medieval mysteries the stage was 30, 40, and even 50 metres wide. To make up for the lack of space they contented themselves with painting various scenes on the side flats and on the back scene. Changes of scenery were all the more difficult because there was no entr'acte. They knew the use of a curtain however, the first being installed at the Hôtel de Bourgogne in 1630, but it was only dropped at the end of the play. Not until the performance of Rossini's *Guillaume Tell* in 1828 was the curtain dropped after each act.

Notwithstanding the great luxury displayed, the stage-setting of the 17th century shows no remarkable improvements, at least so far as works of literary value are concerned. However the spectacular shows, which correspond practically to the pantomime of to-day, already called for complicated machinery. The principle of the three unities simplified the stage-setting, since one single scene sufficed for all the acts, and it was probably for the sake of this simplification that the principle was accepted. At any rate the result remains the same. Historical accuracy, as is indeed obvious, was not encouraged. Racine demanded a Turkish palace for *Bajazet*, but elsewhere costumes and scenery followed the fashion of the day. In the time of Louis XIII the same accoutrement (cuirass and corselet, buskins and plumed helmet) served for an Asiatic monarch, Caesar, or Charles V. When they made an effort after local colour the actors impersonating Turks wore turbans on their heads. Imitating the actors of Antiquity, the comedians of the 16th and 17th centuries wore masks, or else covered their faces with flour. The celebrated Gauthier Garguille, who played the parts of old men at the

Hôtel de Bourgogne, always wore a bearded mask and a black skull-cap on his head. This tradition was brought into France by the Italians, and indeed Molière borrowed Sganarelle, Scapin, and Mascarille from the Italian Comedy. The costume of Molière himself as Sosie in *Amphitryon* was composed of

a *tonnelet* or short tunic of green taffeta with fine silver lace, a vest of the same taffeta, two cuisses of red satin, a pair of shoes laced with silver braid, willow-green silk stockings, belt, tunic, and a cap embroidered with scallops of fine gold and silver[1].

Here is a description of an antique costume, a costume for a mythological character, worn by Armande Béjart, the wife of Molière, in the rôle of Psyché.

A gown of cloth of gold garnished with silver lace and an embroidered bodice with a jacket and sleeves of fine gold and silver; another gown of silver cloth, the front of which was adorned with three rows of lace of fine silver, with a mantle of crêpe likewise trimmed with lace; another gown of green and silver moiré trimmed with imitation lace, with an embroidered bodice, the jacket and sleeves trimmed with fine gold and silver; and a fourth gown of blue English taffeta trimmed with four rows of lace of fine silver.

Happy age! in which they were so lavish with their gold and silver—and fine gold and silver to boot.

The opera costumes differed only from those of comedy by more embroidery, gold, and jewellery. The dancers still wore the long ballet skirt.

§ III. EIGHTEENTH CENTURY

With the 18th century profound social changes took place. From the Middle Ages to the reign of Louis XIV the political and social development may be said to have ended in the establishment of authority and aristocratic rule. For a moment Versailles is a symbol of royal power; the whole intellectual life of the country converges at the court and centres around it. The theatre took the tone and attitude which the age of the "Roi Soleil" demanded. When the reign of the *bourgeoisie* began the aspect of the theatre was once more modified. It was precisely during the 18th century that the *bourgeoisie*, or third estate, increased in influence, because it began to organise itself and because it was rich. In real life the *bourgeois* got the better

[1] E. Soulié, *Recherches sur Molière et sa famille*.

of the aristocrat more and more, and the same took place on the stage. Thus a new source was opened to the dramatist and at the same time considerable changes followed in the external conditions of the theatre.

The Society Theatres

But there was also a reaction. The nobility, feeling itself menaced, withdrew into itself, bent on having its life apart and on protecting itself from the current which was hurrying all the middle classes to an attack on their privileges. Whenever the highest circles try to isolate themselves and lose contact with the masses whom they despise, society suffers from arrested development and is subjected to profound changes. When we come to study our own contemporary history we cannot help being struck by its resemblance to the latter part of the 18th century.

The result of the attitude of the aristocracy towards the rising middle class was that a large number of small theatres were opened. The great nobles, whose example was soon followed by the men of letters and the financiers, competed with the professional theatres. Mme de Maintenon at Saint-Cyr, the Duchesse du Maine at Sceaux, Condé at Chantilly and the Duke of Orleans at Villers-Cotterets produced plays in theatres built for them. The prettiest and most luxurious perhaps of these little theatres was the one which the Mlles de Verrières had installed at their hotel in the Chaussée d'Antin. The theatre contained seven screened boxes like the *baignoires* of modern French theatres. Mlle Guimard, a famous actress, also had her theatre, decorated by Fragonard. Voltaire followed the fashion. According to Bachaumont every lawyer had his theatre and company in his little country house. Adrienne Lecouvreur, the greatest actress of the 18th century, made her début at the age of fifteen in the theatre of the hotel of the Présidente Du Gué.

At Versailles Madame de Pompadour opened the Théâtre des Petits Cabinets. This was the most celebrated of the "society" theatres. In order to have it built the favourite caused one of the rooms in the Palace to be altered. Madame de Pompadour herself acted comedy before the King, and the greatest nobles of the realm played with her. The Duc de Luynes relates in his

Mémoires that in 1748 the Théâtre des Petits Cabinets was replaced by a larger one built in the well of the great staircase of the Ambassadors. This was a theatre which could be taken down, and caused no architectural alterations in the Palace. It was Madame de Pompadour again, ever anxious to please Louis XV, who had a stage erected in the Château de Bellevue, which she had had built for her royal lover. The theatre was in the Chinese style just introduced into France, and Boucher the painter was entrusted with the decorations.

Later Marie-Antoinette organised performances in the "Orangerie," and even had a theatre built in the park at Versailles. It still exists.

It was thus described by Edmond de Goncourt, one of the writers who has done most to make people of taste take an interest in the 18th century:

> The theatre is white and gold; the seats in the orchestra and the fronts of the boxes are covered in blue velvet; the supports of the first balcony are pilasters, of the second trophies of lions' heads with skins and oak branches. Above, on the front of the *œil-de-bœuf* boxes, Cupids carry hanging garlands. On the ceiling Lagrenée has painted clouds and Olympus. On each side of the stage are two gilded nymphs with limbs intertwined and carrying torches; two more nymphs above the curtain bear the arms of Marie-Antoinette.

The Queen appeared on this stage in the *Devin du Village* by J.-J. Rousseau.

The society theatres disappeared at the Revolution; they revived for a time under the Directory. The aristocracy, if one may use the term, of the Revolution had a craving for festivities. With the Restoration, which brought back the nobility, the private theatres enjoyed a new vogue, but we must wait for the 20th century before we shall see, in another form, the appearance of numerous little theatres.

The Large Theatres

The 18th century gave to France a theatre of a new type—the national theatre. It was different from the Italian type, of which the Scala at Milan is the perfect example and which at first was imitated both in Paris and the provinces. The auditorium of the Italian type is an oval and shows as it were an immense wall from top to bottom pierced with boxes. The effect is very monotonous, though there are acoustic advantages. The French type is less uniform; instead of having five or six storeys of boxes it combines boxes with balconies. In the final arrangement (as for example in the auditorium of the Comédie-Française and of the Odéon to-day) the boxes are so open and are carried so far back that we see only immense hanging balconies.

At the beginning of the 18th century Paris boasted only two theatres, the Comédie-Française and the Opera. In 1754 there were five, and twenty years later there were ten. In 1791 there were fifty-one.

As often happens, the provinces were ahead of the capital in the organisation of theatres. Thus it is at Lyons that we find the first big modern theatre. Built by Soufflot, the architect of the Panthéon, although influenced by the Italian conception, it already heralds the French type with balconies. At Bordeaux in 1780 was inaugurated the theatre designed by Victor Louis, a veritable monument which still remains to-day one of the finest of its kind. It is famous for its grand staircase (which was to serve as a model for the Paris Opera House by Garnier), for the majestic architecture of exterior and interior, and for its cupola. For the first time in France a theatre was built on a vast open space and entirely isolated from any other buildings. For the first time too the French type was completely developed. The auditorium is in the shape of a horse-shoe decorated with twelve columns engaged in the encircling-wall; in the intervals between the columns there are projecting balconies. The theatre of the Comédie-Française which was burnt in 1900 was built in 1787 by the architect of the theatre of Bordeaux.

Gabriel, to whom we owe the plans for the Place de la Concorde, was entrusted with the design of the theatre in the Palace of Versailles, inaugurated in 1770 on the occasion of the marriage of Marie-Antoinette. Its chief feature was the large stage, which was so large that it was itself fitted up as a ball-room with its own boxes and balconies. It boasted of a considerable amount of mechanical appliances. I cannot say what state the stage and machinery are in to-day, but the auditorium is still charming, although the imitation of *verde antico* marble has been ill-advisedly taken down and the hangings of blue velvet have been replaced by red velvet and paint of the same colour.

Scenery, Costumes, and Actors

In the 18th century, the art of stage setting made no less progress than architecture. Indeed the greatest painters of the time did not disdain to paint scenery. But the man who transformed stage scenery was an Italian, Cavaliere Girolamo Servandoni (1695–1766), who came to France in 1724. In his hands Nature took possession of the stage; he presents to the eye a variety of points of view; he daringly carries his trees and monuments high up into the flies out of sight of the audience. Before his time a tree had to be represented in its entirety, which meant that it had to be reduced to the scale of the stage. The same thing applies to buildings, which were visible from top to bottom. He broke away from the symmetrical setting, and showed oblique perspectives and buildings on the slant.

This was indeed a revolution. The stage was given up to realism, and the costumes soon showed the effect of the same influence. Historical accuracy was not yet insisted on, but at least they ceased to follow solely the fashion of the day. In Voltaire's *Zaïre* (1732) there was an effort after originality; the actors wore Polish and hussar costumes for a play dealing with the period of the Crusades! In 1747 was introduced a great novelty: *L'Amour Castillan* was played with Spanish costumes. For Voltaire's *Orphelin de la Chine*, played at the Comédie-Française in 1755, Mlle Clairon wore an extraordinary get-up, which both she and the audience thought pure Chinese. The great tragedian Lekain supported his comrade and the pair are regarded as the real reformers of stage costume.

The *tutu* or short ballet skirt of gauze was first worn by Mlle Sallé, a celebrity of the Académie Royale de Musique. Mlle Saint-Huberty, a famous opera singer, who had to play the part of a Greek, appeared on the stage dressed in a white tunic fastened below the breast, her legs bare and her hair down. The scandal was so great that she was ordered to refrain from appearing again in such guise. Another singer, Mme Favart, was even more remarkable for her search after picturesqueness and truth. It was she who introduced real peasant costumes. For the performance of *Les Trois Sultanes*, composed by her husband, she had a costume brought from Turkey. Favart insisted on a great deal of accuracy in the staging of his operas as regards costume, furniture, and other properties.

At the Comédie-Française Talma (1763–1826), whom Napoleon honoured with his friendship, showed the same attention to the staging of tragedy. Whilst on a visit to England he had the opportunity of appreciating the innovations of Mrs Bellamy, Macklin, and Kemble in the same direction. Encouraged by the painter David, whose studio he frequented and whom he asked to design his costumes, he had the courage, although he was the youngest member of the Maison de Molière, to play the small part of the Tribune Proculus in Voltaire's *Brutus* dressed in a real Roman toga with short hair and Roman sandals. The day was won for reform.

The Theatre during the Revolution and the Empire

During the Revolution the theatre was naturally affected by the agitated state of the period. An actor cannot help being a man, and though he may wear the costume now of a great noble, now of a poor beggar, he none the less has his own convictions, his own political ideals. It often happens that his political and artistic ideals are in harmony. Talma the actor was a man of progress, so was Talma the citizen; and he persuaded some of his comrades of the Comédie-Française, then established in what is now the Odéon, to follow him to the theatre built by Victor Louis in the Palais-Royal, where they were free to realise their dramatic conceptions and welcome daring works born of the times.

Moreover it often happened that the real drama took place in the auditorium. Passions ran high; the public was excited by the actors' speeches, and real battles ensued between the spectators. On one occasion at the Comédie-Française the orchestra dared even to play the incendiary *Ça ira*. The bust of Voltaire was crowned and the crowd demanded that his ashes should be transported to the Parthenon. On another occasion one of the men who had helped to take the Bastille, who was present as a spectator, was recognised; he was torn from his seat and carried on to the stage where an actress crowned him with flowers amid the acclamations of the audience. At a performance of *Dumouriez à Bruxelles*, a play as famous then as it is forgotten now, by Olympe de Gouges (a fierce revolutionary who was beheaded in 1793 because she had the courage to become reasonable again) the public in the pit rushed on the stage and danced the *Carmagnole* around the Tree of Liberty. During the Terror these outbursts ceased, to begin again after the 9th Thermidor but in a totally different spirit.

The stage-setting and the accommodation in the house also showed the influence of external events. The subscribers had always for the most part belonged to the wealthy classes, and when these more or less disappeared the boxes they had occupied were suppressed. The whole house was democratised. In place of the stage-boxes statues of Liberty and the Republic were set up. The walls and ceiling were covered with tricolour paper. The upper galleries were adorned with busts of the chief heroes of the Revolution. On the curtain, covered with tricolour like the rest, were seen the symbolic features of the goddess Reason.

The Consulate and the Empire put an end to these crazes, to which art was too often a stranger. Political plays were no longer given. The Emperor allowed only eight theatres in Paris. There appears to have been no real scenic innovation except perhaps at the Opéra. Some great artists added glory to the Comédie-Française; Talma above all, then Mlle Georges (1787–1867), both in tragedy; Mlle Mars (1779–1847), Mlle Contat (1760–1813) in comedy. In 1821 Talma, playing the part of Sylla, made up as Napoleon with his famous lock of hair.

§ IV. NINETEENTH CENTURY

The Lighting and the Auditorium

No really interesting innovations took place until the time of the Romantic Movement. Up till the 17th century, it will be remembered, the performances were given during the day; it was only in the middle of the reign of Louis XIV that evening performances, and consequently theatres lit by artificial light, came into fashion. In 1719 the lighting of the Comédie-Française took 268 candles; in 1764 the footlights alone needed 128 wax candles. The first oil lamps appeared twenty years later at the Odéon. It was only in 1821 that gas, already in use for some time in London, took the place of oil at the Opéra. It was the Opéra again which first made use of electricity in 1887.

During the 19th century a great number of theatres were built in France, especially in Paris. The most important were the Châtelet erected in 1860, the Opéra, the Opéra-Comique and the new Comédie-Française. The efforts of the architects chiefly centred on subsidiary things like the staircases, the passages, the public foyer, and the actors' dressing-rooms. Some attention was also devoted to hygiene. That is why the subsidiary portions of the building were considered so important.

The Opéra, built between 1862 and 1874 by Charles Garnier, was inaugurated on January 5, 1875, its principal features being its vast proportions and the beauty of its architecture. The grand staircase suggested by that of the theatre of Bordeaux is celebrated. The house holds 2200 spectators. The general arrangement is according to the French type with balconies, but on three storeys the balconies are entirely divided up into boxes. However, and this is a happy peculiarity, instead of an ordinary balcony in front of the first tier of boxes is a vast amphitheatre, a sort of second pit overhanging the orchestra stalls. The stage is 60 metres high, 17 metres wide, and 22 metres deep; this depth can be increased to 50 metres, if necessary, by including the dancing-room behind the stage.

The Opéra-Comique having been burnt in 1887 a new theatre was built according to the plans of M. Bernier and opened in December 1898. Unfortunately the confined site prevented the architect from giving the theatre its proper proportions; the public foyer, the passages, and the staircases take up too much room by comparison with the stage, which is too small. The house, rather sober in decoration, can hold 1500 people.

It was after a fire also that the present Comédie-Française was constructed. The work was carried out quickly: destroyed on March 8th, 1900, the new theatre was inaugurated on December 29th of the same year. The architect, M. Guadet, limited himself to a recast of the plans of the old theatre by Louis, the architect of the theatre of Bordeaux. On either side of the stage are two caryatides; there are no columns; only balconies entirely split up into boxes in the second and third tier. There are 1500 seats. The stage measures 11·50 metres in height, 15·40 metres in width, and 13 metres in depth. Under the stage there is a depth of 7 metres and the flies also are 7 metres high. The subordinate parts of the building are very fine. On the other hand the stage can boast of none of the improvements installed at Bayreuth (built upon the plans of Richard Wagner himself) and at Wiesbaden, where powerful electric machinery takes the place of the stage hands to great advantage.

In reality, nothing essentially new has appeared since the 18th century but, thanks to scientific discoveries, improvements have been made in certain parts of theatrical equipment.

Scenery, Costumes, Actors

On the other hand the scenery, influenced by the aesthetics of the Romantic period, and later by the realistic formulae of which M. Antoine was the chief exponent, developed in an extremely interesting way. With Alexandre Dumas, Alfred de Vigny, and Victor Hugo the theatre began to aim at historical accuracy. The literary work, the costumes, and the scenery formed one homogeneous whole. Each part one might say helped to achieve a common result.

February 11th, 1829, was an important day for the Romantic theatre: on that day *Henri III et sa Cour* by Alexandre Dumas was performed at the Comédie-Française with a very unusual display of scenery and costume. Both were entirely in keeping with the play; it was an attempt to reconstitute history. Henceforth all the theatres and all the dramatists showed the same attention to historical accuracy. Victor Hugo, whose extraordinary talent as a draughtsman is well known, himself made the sketches for the scenery of his plays. Nothing is left to chance or the imagination. All the places represented and all the properties are copied from the real thing. The Opera imitated so perfectly the marvellous cloisters of Saint-Trophime at Arles for Meyerbeer's *Robert the Devil* that *L'Artiste*, a journal keenly interested in innovations, declared the day after the performance "that it was cold beneath those deserted vaults, that the cemetery smelt of moisture and that the sight of these spots, consecrated to silence and to death, stirred the emotions profoundly."

The art of costume progressed side by side with the art of decoration. In both cases accuracy was sought after. In the *Don Juan* of Casimir Delavigne, the sword of Francis I, which Charles V bestows upon his son, was copied from the real sword in the Musée de l'Armée.

Under the influence of the realistic writers this desire for accuracy soon became excessive. M. André Antoine at first at the Théâtre Libre (1887), later at the Théâtre Antoine, and finally at the Odéon, pushed this system to an extreme. Even for a *comédie bourgeoise* the scenery and the interpretation were governed by a constant desire to reproduce nature and reality. The actors no longer declaimed, they spoke naturally, so naturally that one did not always hear what they said. Breaking every tradition, every rule, every convention, they did not hesitate to turn their backs to the audience. It is impossible to put on the stage real walls, real houses and real trees, but at any rate the properties had to be authentic. The furniture was of the correct style, the paintings were signed by masters. The mirrors, the ironwork, the locks, were real, and the coal was so real that the dust reached the audience.

The great actors of the romantic theatre were Mélingue, Marie Dorval, and Frédérick Lemaître. Rachel (1821–1858), without doubt the most admirable tragic actress of France, was somewhat apart from the movement of which Victor Hugo was the high-priest; he himself called her *un drapeau ennemi*. After her came Agar (1832–1891), and at length Mme Sarah Bernhardt, who gave her beauty, her genius, and her passionate imagination to the service of tragic and dramatic poetry. Mention must also be made of "the divine" Bartet, whose pure rhythmic diction made her an ideal interpreter of Racine, and of Mounet-Sully (1841–1916), the most illustrious tragedian since Talma and certainly the most impassioned. The verve of Constant Coquelin in classic and modern comedies was incomparable. The greatest actor of contemporary France and the one whose style has most profoundly influenced other actors of to-day is Lucien Guitry; beside him may be placed M. Le Bargy and M. Maurice de Féraudy. The greatest *comédienne* of our day, Réjane, has just died; she was born in 1856.

Conclusion

This, in bare outline, is the history of what I call the externals of the theatre. A great deal has been left unsaid. I think however that this concise summary is sufficient to show what has been the development of the stage, scenery, and costume, and even of the style of acting from the Middle Ages to our own day. As I pointed out at the beginning, this development has taken place along lines parallel to those of the ideas and manners of the time; the theatre has been moulded by society.

The 19th century and the first twenty years of this century saw social politics taking every day a more democratic turn, and the populace holding a more and more important place, though the *bourgeoisie* did not, for all that, cease to be supreme. The romantic and realist movements were expressions of *bourgeois* ideals in literature.

Speaking of the private theatres which flourished towards the end of the 18th century I went so far as to say that whenever the élite attempts to isolate itself society is on the eve of some brutal transformation.

No one will deny that society is undergoing a crisis to-day. Well then, just as in the time of Louis XV and Louis XVI, we have seen in Paris, during the last fifteen years, the opening of numerous pretty, but often uncomfortable, little theatres. It is true that anyone who wanted could not have gone to the private theatres of the Duchesse du Maine, the great Condé, and Mme de Pompadour, while the tiny theatres of to-day are open to the public; but, as in the old days, only the élite goes to them. The men wear evening dress, the women *decolleté* gowns and all their jewels; they are very much at home there, and far from the populace.

In an opposite direction, but under the same spirit of social influence, M. Gémier, a good actor and above all a master of stage-craft, has for a long time tried to establish a theatre for the people. Inheriting the realistic methods of M. Antoine, he applies them on a grand scale. A wonderful inspirer of crowds, he aims at colossal effects. Finding the stage too narrow at the Théâtre-Antoine of which he is the Director, he has produced plays in a circus. At the performance of the *Œdipe* of M. Saint-

Georges de Bouhélier, runners, athletes, dancing girls, and a whole tribe of supers moved about the stage mingling with the principal action of the play. It recalled the simultaneous methods of the Middle Ages; moreover the tragedy was conceived in the form and spirit of the ancient mysteries.

Finally—and this is the last innovation I shall record—M. Jacques Copeau, an able writer who is also an actor of merit, is bringing about a revolution in spite of his modest materials. In a very small theatre he applies a symbolic and synthetic system of stage-setting in opposition to the realist formula. At the Théâtre du Vieux Colombier the scenery is reduced to a minimum. The scene is suggested rather than represented. The system of M. Antoine ended in burying the text beneath the stage-setting; M. Copeau tries on the contrary to give to the text its full meaning and importance, making the stage-setting subordinate to it and serve to set it off. All the same M. Copeau continues to seek after scenic accuracy. The footlights which light the actors from below seem to him an anomaly —so he suppresses them. He insists on his players acting simply and truly, so simply and truly that they give the impression of real life. Again he holds that the acting must vary according to the work interpreted. After being realistic he is not afraid to be poetic. For him the same setting does for plays that are utterly different; a few properties cleverly arranged give the necessary atmosphere.

Let us not be deceived: in spite of appearances M. Jacques Copeau is working in the same direction as M. Gémier. In different ways they are both breaking away from the aesthetic aims of the *bourgeois* stage. They bring the stage once more into line with social development. And just as French society tends to become organised on very much the same plan as medieval society—the Trades Unions are a modern edition of the guilds, and the political decentralisation clamoured for on all sides will bring about a return to provincialism—so the theatre tends more and more to return to the symbolism and realism of the centuries which preceded the Renaissance. Thus the wheel comes full circle—only to go on turning.

BIBLIOGRAPHY

G. Bapst, *Essai sur l'histoire du Théâtre*, 1893. Gustave Cohen, *Histoire de la mise en scène dans le théâtre religieux*. L. Petit de Julleville, *Les Mystères*, 2 vols. 1880; *La Comédie et les Mœurs en France au Moyen-Age*, 1886; *Les Comédiens en France au Moyen-Age*, 1886. Émile Morice, *Essai sur la mise en scène des Mystères*. Les Frères Parfait, *Histoire du Théâtre-Français, 1745–1749*. E. Rigal, *Les décors, les costumes et la mise en scène au xviie siècle*, 1869. Nuitter et Thoinan, *Les Origines de l'Opéra français*, 1886. J. Moynet, *L'Envers du théâtre (La machinerie théâtrale)*, 1893. A. Pougin, *Dictionnaire historique et pittoresque du théâtre*, 1885. L. Becq de Fouquières, *L'Art de la mise en scène*, 1884. Joseph de Filippi, *Parallèle des principaux théâtres de l'Europe et des machines théâtrales françaises, allemandes et anglaises*, 1860. Adolphe Thalasso, *Le Théâtre Libre*, 1906. Jacques Rouché, *L'Art théâtral moderne*.

CHAPTER XIII

PHILOSOPHY

§ I. SEVENTEENTH CENTURY

THE history of Modern Philosophy it is universally agreed, opens with Descartes, and the history of French philosophy in the 17th century is, in a word, the history of Cartesianism in France. The most famous names, after that of Descartes himself, are those of Malebranche, who followed Descartes pretty closely, and of Pascal, whose all too brief contributions to philosophy disclose some essential differences from Cartesianism.

RENÉ DESCARTES was born at La Haye[1] in the province of Touraine on March 31, 1596. His mother, Jeanne Brochard, died of consumption a few days after his birth. His father, Joachim Descartes, was a Councillor of the *Parlement* of Brittany. René was sent in his eighth year to the Jesuit College of La Flèche. His educational experiences there are described in his *Discours de la Méthode*: "I found myself embarrassed with so many doubts and errors, that it seemed to me that the effort to instruct myself had no other effect than the increasing discovery of my own ignorance." Thus early was doubt present in a mind destined to adopt it as a philosophical method. At La Flèche Descartes began his lifelong friendship with Mersenne. In 1613 he went to Paris, where he spent two years in amusement and two in study. In 1617 he enlisted as a volunteer in the Army of the Netherlands under Prince Maurice of Nassau; in 1619 he went to Bavaria, and served under Maximilian and afterwards under Ferdinand II. His military career ended with the battle of Neuhäusel in 1621. For five years he had no settled abode, after which he lived for three years in seclusion in Paris. In 1629 he went to Holland, where he spent twenty years. Finally, in 1649, at the invitation of Queen Christina of Sweden, he went to Stockholm, where he died in 1650.

Descartes approached philosophy with a firm conviction of the pre-eminence of mathematical demonstration. He held that the subject-matter of Mathematics is peculiarly suited to methodical treatment, but that the soundness of its methods is

---

[1] Now called La Haye-Descartes.

not dependent on its subject-matter Philosophy, then, must proceed from what is clear and certain to the explanation of what is complex and doubtful. First principles are obtained by intuition, which is "the undoubting conception of an unclouded and attentive mind, and springs from the light of reason alone" (*Rules for the Direction of the Mind*, Rule iii). We know by intuition, for example, that a triangle is bounded by three lines, and (a vital principle for Descartes) that the effect cannot contain more than the cause. In intuition two conditions are necessary: the proposition which is to be known must be clear and distinct, and it must be apprehended completely at one and the same time, not successively (*Ib.* Rule xi). In intuition, therefore, according to Descartes, we become aware of a necessary connection between two or more distinguishable elements. Deduction is a chain of intuitions along which thought moves, each transition being seen to be necessary, and the movement of thought guided by the *lumen naturale*, which discloses self-evident propositions or axioms. In the enumeration of his axioms Descartes falls short of his mathematical ideal.

The philosophy of Descartes found its starting-point in doubt —not the doubt which despairs of reason, but that which believes itself a stage on the way to truth and is based on faith in the power of reason to attain truth. Descartes thought that the search for truth could only begin by doubting everything that can be doubted. He found that we are deceived by our senses, that we fall into error even in mathematics—in short that the mist of uncertainty wraps almost the whole field of knowledge. The ideas are in the mind, no doubt, but the moment we assert any relation between our thoughts and the things to which they seem to be related, the possibility of error slips in. So most of what we think we know must be discarded, but not all. There is in the mind one thing that cannot be denied or doubted, its own existence in thinking. This is the famous first principle of Cartesianism—*je pense, donc je suis*. In spite of its form this must not be taken as embodying an inference. Descartes was not so naïve as to make his starting-point depend on something else: it is attained by intuition, not by deduction. It is simply impossible to believe that what thinks does not, at the time of thinking, exist. If the proposition, I think, therefore I am, be accepted, what follows? First, we know the essential quality of mind: it is simply a thinking thing, and nothing more. No bodily qualities or actions can belong to it at all, still less be essential to it. Next, there follows the universal criterion of certainty—whatever is clearly and distinctly conceived is true. So far Descartes is imprisoned in his own mind, for all the objects he is aware of through the senses in any way may be merely modifications of his own mind. The *cogito* establishes the existence of the mind, but what establishes the existence of anything more and other than the thinking mind? The things of which our senses inform us have merely possible or contingent existence, but it is necessary existence that is needed. Descartes found his solution in the necessary existence of God, which he established by the help of the principle of causation, for he held that we know intuitively that the effect cannot contain more than the cause. Consequently if I, a finite being, have the idea of an infinite and perfect being, it is equally impossible that I should have manufactured it myself, or that a finite external cause should have produced it in me. Unless the notion of cause is to go, God, a perfect and infinite being, must be the author of the idea. The existence of a perfect and therefore veracious Deity enabled Descartes to pass the circle of his own consciousness. It would be repugnant to the nature of an infinite Creator to deceive his creatures. Therefore he knew that the external world which seemed to exist was not a mode of his own mind, but did actually exist. Thus an objective science became possible. There still remained a difficulty. God is absolutely free, and cannot therefore be subject even to a logical necessity. In the language of Descartes He establishes the laws of nature as a king the laws of his realm. God wills freely and indifferently. He could have made it untrue that the three angles of a triangle are equal to two right angles. Yet, thought Descartes, there is still a guarantee for science, for though the laws of nature are not absolutely necessary, since God could have ordained them other than they are, yet still they are eternal, because the will of God does not change.

There next emerges the Dualism of Descartes, which has had such a far-reaching effect both in metaphysic and psychology, even to this very hour. Matter and mind were taken to be two substances, each with a single attribute, the attribute of matter

being extension, of mind, thought. In the strict sense of the
term Descartes held there is one and only one substance, that
is, God. For substance is defined as "an existent thing which
requires nothing but itself in order to exist" (*Principles of
Philosophy*, I. 5). It is only in a relative or secondary sense,
therefore, that matter and mind are called substances, on the
ground that "they are things which need only the concurrence
of God (*Concursus Dei*) in order to exist" (*Principles*, I. 52).
Mind and matter are therefore substances in the sense
that each can exist without the other. Matter, however,
is taken to be something quite other than the common notion
of it. The nature of matter for Descartes did not consist in its
being hard, or heavy, or coloured. These are secondary qualities
dependent on external factors and on the sensibility of the percipient, and do not belong to the material object *per se*. Matter
has only one essential attribute, namely extension. A material
body is therefore simply the space which it occupies. There is
no vacuum, no atoms: every extended thing may be divided
ad infinitum. Movement is defined as "the transference of one
part of matter or one body from the vicinity of those bodies
that are in immediate contact with it, and which we regard
as in repose, into the vicinity of others" (*Principles*, II. 25).
Matter is thus reduced to its geometrical qualities, for extension, divisibility, and mobility are at once the simplest and
clearest of our ideas of matter, and we cannot get rid of them
even in imagination. With these elements Descartes framed a
mechanical theory of nature—*terram totumque hunc mundum
instar machinae descripsi*. The first and original movement came
from God, and as He is unchangeable, the quantity of movement
in the universe is constant. The particles of matter once set going
move in *vortices*—circular movements in a *plenum*, the change
in one part being simultaneous with the compensating change
in the other parts. In this was found an explanation of
gravitation and the planetary system. The whole Universe,
according to Descartes, is a machine which can be understood
simply by a consideration of the shapes and movements of its
parts. Final causes are rejected on the ground that it is impossible for us to discover the purposes of an infinite being. The
machine which Descartes described was destined to be conceived

by later thinkers as capable of going without the Maker and Mover to whom he ascribed it. The theory of vortices failed to account for the elliptical orbits of the planets and for the fact that falling bodies are attracted to the centre of the mass, and not to the axis of rotation. Descartes made his greatest contribution to science by the application of Algebra to Geometry, thus founding Analytical Geometry. He showed that any equation may be represented by a special figure whose every characteristic corresponds to a characteristic of the equation. According to Descartes, just as the essence of matter consists in one attribute, extension, so does the essence of mind consist in one attribute, namely thought. It follows that as matter is always extended, so mind always thinks or is conscious; that we cannot always remember our thoughts is due to the bodily conditions of memory. Sense-perception is due to stimuli (such as undulations of light or air) which affect our organs, but sensations are not like the object perceived, nor are they qualities of it, but modifications of the percipient. Quite naturally this philosophy is strained to the breaking-point at the problem of the relation of mind and body. Since mind and body are substances and so mutually exclusive, there could strictly be no connection of any sort between them. But Descartes was constrained to admit that in man mind and matter were *somehow* united. The ineradicable contradiction was thinly disguised by the theory of animal spirits (adopted with modifications from the current physiology) and the action of the pineal gland, with the further qualification that the relation of mind and body is, after all, supernatural. The more subtle parts of the blood, when filtered and warmed in the heart, rise as animal spirits to the brain and enter the pineal gland, which Descartes regarded as the special seat of the soul, and to which ordinary blood was too gross to be admitted. "The small gland which is the main seat of the soul is so suspended between the cavities which contain the spirits that it can be moved by them in as many different ways as there are sensible diversities in the object, but that it may also be moved in diverse ways by the soul" (*Passions of the Soul*, I. 34).

Thus sensation, perception, and the emotions are due to the animal spirits and their action on the pineal gland. Mental control is nevertheless indirect or through ideas: for we can replace the thought which is by nature joined to each movement of the gland by another thought (*Passions of the Soul*, I. 50). When the animal spirits revive their former traces, we remember. Unfortunately scarcely any part of the brain has less to do with thought than the pineal gland. Quaint as the theory is, it is important because subsequent thought tried to improve this lame solution of the psycho-physical problem with considerable consequences to the development of philosophy.

It is interesting to note that Descartes differed from the modern theory of psycho-physical parallelism. He held that there are acts of mind which do not involve any corresponding physiological change. Of this sort are understanding, and *émotions internes*, such as the love of God.

In the opinion of Descartes animals are automata. In a letter to Henry More in 1649 he said: "But the greatest of all the prejudices we have retained from infancy is that of believing that brutes think." Again (in a letter to the Marquis of Newcastle): "Doubtless, when swallows come in the spring, they act like clocks." Descartes held to his opinion in spite of numerous arguments—and anecdotes—brought forward by his opponents. But he explains in the letter to More quoted above that he did not deny that animals possess life and sensibility: "I do not refuse to them feeling even, in so far as it depends only on the bodily organs. Thus my opinion is not so cruel to animals as it is favourable to men." Whether or not the theory deserves the epithets "barbarous and cruel" applied to it by More, the experiments on the living machinery made by Descartes and his followers unfortunately do. Descartes gave to philosophy a new method and a new direction, but his system was loosely knit in many important respects, and in fact the development of Cartesianism is largely governed by attempts to bridge the gaps left therein by its founder.

BLAISE PASCAL (1623–1662) conceived the Universe to be infinite in two directions, infinite in greatness, infinite also in smallness. Between these infinities man is placed, a mean between nothing and the All. The Universe, as such, is therefore incomprehensible. Our knowledge can only lay hold of what lies midway between the infinitely great and the infinitely small, and before it and behind it lies an abyss of ignorance. If we compare the two orders, that of matter and that of mind, the material shrinks into comparative nothingness before the mental. Man, the feeblest reed in nature, is a reed which thinks, and therein lies his dignity. But even reason is not supreme. Pascal differs from Descartes as to the test of truth; an inner feeling is not a final proof. When we think we are awake, our apparent waking might be another sleep. Strictly speaking we cannot know even that God exists—a fundamental truth according to Descartes. Nature at once reveals and conceals the Deity, thought Pascal. We see too much for doubt, too little for belief. Still we cannot find an abiding place in scepticism; that is impossible, since we are obliged to act, though theoretically possible if we had nothing to do save to know. But Pascal did not find himself without a refuge. Above the order of matter and the order of mind, there is a third—the order of charity. Just as all matter in the Universe could not give birth to a single thought, so all the bodies and all the minds could not originate a movement of charity—that, says Pascal, is impossible and belongs to another order. Charity is imparted to us by the Grace of God, and it is imparted by the attraction of pleasure which is the only object to which the will is ever directed. The love of God and of man is a supernatural gift. Left to ourselves we could only fear God, not love Him.

Thus Pascal did not share the confidence of Descartes in the power of reason to comprehend the Universe. Though geometry be the perfect science, there are regions beyond it where its inadequacy is glaringly revealed—the world of concrete and living things, where *l'esprit· de géometrie* must give place to *l'esprit de finesse*. Thus, in the greatest things of all, reason fails and faith steps in, while the crowning glory and joy of human life must be received from the hands of God, a gift at His good pleasure.

NICOLAS MALEBRANCHE (1638–1715) received his philosophical awakening from the study of Descartes' *Traité de l'homme*, and from that day philosophy became his dominating interest. He is broadly classed as a Cartesian, but he diverged from his master on several points, and in addition his general tendency was towards the theological side of philosophy, whereas the main current in the mind of Descartes seems to have set in the direction of the establishment of an unimpeachable basis for science. All the same the philosophy of Malebranche is based on the Cartesian principles, (1) that the mind is a thinking substance, (2) that matter is an extended substance, (3) that the existence of the idea of God in us is absolute proof of His real existence. We have seen that Descartes had left a serious difficulty at the very centre of his system, namely, the inconsistency of holding that God is the absolute or primary substance, and that matter and mind are relatively substances to the extent that, though God can of course act on both, neither can act on the other. The pressure of the difficulties involved in this position led Malebranche to form two of his most characteristic and famous doctrines—the vision of all things in God, and the theory of "occasionalism." Malebranche argued that as matter cannot act upon mind and cannot be present to it, we can only know ideas. These exist in the mind of God which contains the intelligible world, and it is through them as a medium that we are able to know the external world, the existence of which cannot be demonstrated but must be believed on the authority of Scripture, which, Malebranche says, tells him positively that there are thousands and thousands of creatures and things (*Entretiens sur la Métaphysique*, VI. 8).

We have an immediate and direct knowledge of God *alone*, for He is not known by means of an idea; the Infinite (i.e. God) is its own idea and has no archetype (*Ib.* II. 5). Every spirit is not merely dependent on God, but is immediately united to Him— God is *the place of Spirits*, as space is of bodies.

Natural causes, thought Malebranche, are not real causes. The movement of one material thing is not the real cause of the movement of another material thing. The creature is impotent, all power belongs to God. If God wills the existence of a thing, He must at the same time will the *place* of its existence, for it must exist *somewhere*, and how can it be moved except by the will of God? So it is absurd to say that all the angels and devils together could stir a piece of straw (*Entretiens*, VII. 10). In the idea of extension (and it is extension which constitutes matter) it is vain to look for the idea of movement. The moving body *A* strikes the body *B*, and *B* moves. The collision between the two is the *occasion* on which God according to His universal laws moves *B*. Through all nature the same thing holds. Plants grow and animals live by the sole activity of God. Without the power of God, the mind could neither know nor feel nor will. This line of reasoning applies still more strongly to the relation of mind and body, for they are substances which cannot interact. There can be no necessary relation between a change in the mind and a change in the brain; we must therefore have recourse to a power not found in either, namely, the efficacy of the divine decrees. Man would be dead and without movement, were it not that God has decreed to join His will, which is always efficacious, to the desires of man, which are in themselves always impotent. God alone can move the "animal spirits," which are, after all, minute bodies (*petits corps*). "He has willed that I should have certain feelings, certain emotions, when there exist in my brain certain traces, certain disturbances of the spirits. He has willed in a word, and wills unceasingly, that the modes of the mind and of the body should be reciprocal. This is the union and the natural dependence of the two parts of which we are composed" (*Entretiens*, VII. 13)[1].

Malebranche held that while we know the existence of our minds more distinctly than that of our own bodies or of other bodies, we do not know the nature of the soul as perfectly as the nature of the body. The parts of what is extended may be clearly known, because we can see the ratios between them, but we cannot discover the ratios between mental events. So Psychology is hampered because it can make no use of Mathematics, and must be an experimental science based on reflection. Malebranche studied the illusions of the senses, the nature of colour differences, and the visual perception of depth. But, in spite of a true psychological gift, his results suffered from his theological and metaphysical conceptions. Yet, according to M. Duhem (*Rev. de Métaphysique*, January 1916), it is to Malebranche that we really owe the vibration theory of colours.

---

[1] Probably Malebranche was not indebted to those who had developed an occasionalist theory before him. Traces of such a theory are found in La Forge, a French physician, and in Cordemoy, a lawyer and tutor to the Dauphin (Höffding, *Hist. of Modern Philosophy*, I. 244). Geulincx (1625–1669) at any rate had published such a theory in the first part of his *Ethica* in 1665. Malebranche's *Recherche de la Vérité* appeared in 1674.

§ II. EIGHTEENTH CENTURY

It is not necessary to debate the question whether VOLTAIRE (1694–1778) was really a "philosopher," though with Kant's authority in support one might maintain the affirmative with a good courage. It is quite beyond doubt that Voltaire was at any rate a philosophic influence. In his *Lettres sur les Anglais* (1732) he made Locke and Newton known to France. He expresses the deepest admiration for Locke, who had written a history of the mind, whereas others had written its romance. In 1738 Voltaire published an excellent exposition of Newton (*Éléments de la philosophie de Newton, mis à la portée de tout le monde*). In this he also gives an account of Berkeley's theory of vision and Cheselden's operation on one born blind. Although Locke's essay had been translated and published by Pierre Coste in 1700, there is no doubt that Voltaire's exposition of the English philosophy stirred widely and deeply the speculative spirit of France. Voltaire followed Condillac's development of Locke's sensationalism, but on the problems of metaphysics his verdict was, in his own words, *non liquet* (*Dictionnaire philosophique*—Bien (Tout est)).

The Materialists

JULIEN OFFRAY DE LA METTRIE (1709–1751) may fairly be regarded as the pioneer of Materialism in France. His best known work is *L'homme machine* (1748), in which he maintains that there is no difference in kind, but only a difference in degree of organisation, between man and animal. It is the physiological mechanism which thinks and feels and wills. When the body is out of order the soul is out of order too; the soul is entirely dependent on the body, they appear, change, and disappear together. Why introduce a special substance to explain man's nature, when his nature is so obviously continuous with that of the animals, and differs only in complexity? Perhaps the most interesting and important thing in the theories of La Mettrie is that here is (possibly for the first time) more than a hint of a genuinely biological view of man, whom La Mettrie did not conceive as a machine in the same sense as Descartes conceived of animals as automata. It is more than probable that the development of La Mettrie's thought found its origin in the physiological discoveries which the microscope had rendered possible. Boerhaave was his teacher. Certainly his materialism is not an extract from Cartesianism. Plant, animal, man, form a line of development, the impulse to which is the growing needs of the organism. La Mettrie assumed an agnostic position on the questions of immortality and the existence of God. His ethical outlook was hedonistic. His influence seems to have been considerable, extending to the general thought of his time.

DENIS DIDEROT (1713–1784) spent twenty laborious years on the Encyclopaedia. Had he spent this time on philosophy proper, it is impossible to imagine what might have been the achievements of a mind so fertile and so unfettered. In philosophy he started in general from Locke, and from Locke's remark on the possibility of thinking matter he seems to have gradually passed to materialism—with qualifications. In the Article on Locke in the Encyclopaedia, after quoting Locke's statement that it is not impossible that matter might have the capacity of thought, Diderot maintains that it makes no difference to justice, immortality, politics, or religion. "Supposing sensibility were the primitive germ of thought, and a common property of all matter, scattered through all the products of nature in various proportions, manifesting itself in weaker or stronger degrees according to the varying complexity of different organisms, what evil consequences could any one possibly infer from all this? None. Man would still remain what he is and would continue to be judged solely by the good or evil uses to which he may devote his activities."

In the Rêve de d'Alembert, however, Diderot seems to hint that he found a crucial difficulty in conceiving a self conscious of its own unity to be merely a material aggregation. Still Diderot seems to have become more materialistic in his later years; he aided Holbach and applauded the Système de la Nature.

Diderot's Pensées sur l'interprétation de la nature (1754) abounds, as might be expected, in suggestive statements, and shows that Diderot was not merely a philosopher by flashes, but also possessed the philosophic appetite for the continuous and systematic. "Nature has perhaps in reality never produced

more than one single act. It seems even that, if nature had been
under the necessity of producing several acts, the different
results of such acts would be isolated; that there would be
collections of phenomena independent of one another, and that
the general chain, of which philosophy assumes the continuity,
would break in many places. The absolute independence of a
single fact is incompatible with the idea of a Whole, and without
the idea of a Whole, there can be no philosophy" (*Pensées*, XI.).

The prophecy of Rousseau that after ages would look upon
Diderot as that age looked upon Plato and Aristotle has not
been fulfilled, perhaps ought not to be; still there is in Diderot
a rich harvest of suggestion not yet reaped.

PAUL-HENRI THIRY, BARON D'HOLBACH (1723–1789) reduced
materialism to systematic expression in his work *Le Système de
la Nature*, published under an assumed name in 1770. Diderot
and Lagrange certainly assisted in the work, to what extent is
doubtful. The effect of the book was extraordinary. "No book
has ever produced a more widespread shock. Everybody insisted on reading it, and almost everybody was terrified"
(Morley). Goethe described it as gray, Cimmerian, and corpse-
like, too unattractive to be dangerous. Voltaire hastened
to refute it. Holbach reduced all philosophy and all science
to physics. The only ground for believing in God and the
soul is the false supposition that matter is dead and inert.
Such a supposition is seen to be otiose when it is realized
that motion is an essential property of matter. The notion of
the soul and the notion of God are merely used to fill up gaps
in our knowledge: they are survivals from the efforts at explanation made by savages. Consciousness is a molecular motion: its
mysteries are not explained by the theory of a spiritual substance. With Holbach natural and revealed religion are in the
like ill-repute. In a well-known paragraph he says: "If we go
back to the beginning we shall always find that ignorance and
fear have created Gods; fancy, enthusiasm, or deceit has adorned
or disfigured them; weakness worships them; credulity preserves
them in life; custom regards them, and tyranny supports them
in order to make the blindness of men serve its own end"
(*Le Système de la Nature*, II. 200).

Holbach's ethics were utilitarian: men are united by self-interest; free-will, of course, is rejected. His influence was very considerable, a result to which his personal popularity contributed.

Condillac. The Ideologists

ÉTIENNE BONNOT, ABBÉ DE CONDILLAC (1715–1780), started from the philosophy of Locke, but essayed an achievement which Locke had not touched, namely an account of the genesis of the mental faculties. Locke had distinguished two sources of our ideas—sensation and reflection; Condillac set out to prove that there is only one, that is, sensation, and that perception, comparison, judgment may all be genetically derived from it alone; they are transformed sensations. Many of Condillac's points were included in his first work (*Essai sur l'Origine des Connaissances Humaines*, 1746) but were developed further in his best known work, *Traité des Sensations*, 1754. It is in this that Condillac introduces the fiction of a statue potentially conscious, whose senses are opened one at a time, beginning with smell, and uses this method in order to show the process by which a mind may be built up from sensation only. There has been considerable controversy as to the source of this illustration. We may accept Condillac's statement that it was suggested to him by his friend Mlle Ferrand. No doubt the device tended to popularise his theory; as a demonstration it cannot be considered successful. A few examples will show how Condillac's method works. If a number of sensations of the same degree of vividness existed at the same time, man would only possess the sensibility of an animal, and would display no mental activity. But suppose there is either only one sensation, or one peculiarly vivid sensation along with others less vivid, then that sensation becomes attention. Attention, therefore, is nothing but a single sensation, or one sensation more vivid than the rest. The more vivid a sensation the greater its tendency to be preserved. Hence arises memory. Condillac's single-sense statue remembers when it dimly feels what it has been, and feels strongly what it is at the moment. Thus man becomes capable of two directions of attention, one by way of the memory, the other by way of the senses, the former active, the latter passive. Comparison is merely attending to two ideas at the same time. But we cannot compare two ideas without perceiving resemblance or difference between them, and this is judgment. So attention, memory, comparison and judgment are nothing but *sensations transformées*.

There are no absolutely indifferent sensations; each has its affective tone of pleasure or pain; in the former case we tend to preserve it, in the latter to escape from it. By the help of memory we become capable of desire, which is composed of an idea of a better (i.e. more pleasurable) state along with the experience of pain. Will is an absolute desire, the object of the desire being in our power.

Condillac's theory does not deserve the somewhat extravagant admiration of his contemporaries, but on the other hand it has been considerably underestimated by later critics. He clearly saw the necessity of conceiving the mind as a unity, and he made a very considerable, if defective, attempt to derive mental processes from a single principle. Hegel saw both his merit and defects. "In Condillac's method there is an unmistakable intention to show how the several modes of mental activity could be made intelligible without losing sight of mental unity, and to exhibit their necessary inter-connexion. But the categories employed in doing so are of a wretched sort" (Hegel, *Philosophy of Mind*).

Condillac held that the self is the totality of sensations, the consciousness of what one is together with the recollection of what one has been. But under this empirical mass and supporting it there is, in his view, a spiritual substance whose nature we cannot know. The suggestion of Locke that the faculty of thinking *might* be annexed to matter did not commend itself to Condillac, as it did to many of his contemporaries. That which thinks must be one, and matter is a multitude, and behind it is another substance. Consequently a bodily event cannot be the real cause of a mental event, only its "occasional" cause. The existence of God is proved by the argument from design.

The method on which Condillac relied he called analysis, which he regarded as the great secret of discovery. He illustrates the process by comparing it to taking a watch to pieces and putting it together again. Hence it is obvious he included in his method what is ordinarily meant by synthesis. The synthesis which he condemns is dogmatic and abstract deduction starting from general principles. In a word his method is empiricism.

The direction taken by Condillac was followed by the Ideologists, of whom we have only space for Destutt de Tracy and Cabanis. ANTOINE-LOUIS-CLAUDE DESTUTT, COMTE DE TRACY (1754–1836), understood by Ideology the analysis of sensations, the metaphysical systems of the past he contemned. He was a genuine and independent thinker. He threw overboard Condillac's account of mind as being transformed sensations, and recognised four faculties or primary modes of sensation, sensibility, memory, judgment, and volition. Condillac had attributed our knowledge of external objects to our active sense of touch; by passive touch he thought we could never know that anything existed which was not a modification of ourselves. Tracy developed this point and forms a link between Condillac and Maine de Biran. According to Tracy, the knowledge of the external world is given us in our consciousness of resistance to an action we feel and will. Mobility is the only link between the self and the sensible universe. Further, without it we could not distinguish a sensation from a memory, and could not form a judgment. It is curious that Tracy resolved will into two passive factors, a sensation of movement and a feeling of desire, and held that it is only by an illusion that man believes himself to be peculiarly active in volition.

Tracy also rejected the logic of identity which Condillac had elaborated, and maintained that the ideas related in a judgment are equivalent but not identical, and that this is true even of equations.

PIERRE-JEAN-GEORGES CABANIS (1757–1808) is often hastily described as a materialist, in fact he was neither materialist nor immaterialist, but disclaimed metaphysics altogether. He knew nothing, he says, of *causes* and *effects* except in so far as they express order of succession, and so are just antecedents and consequents. Science is concerned with facts and their order of succession. Experience teaches us that there are relations between mind and body. If we leave out all metaphysical notions of substance and causation, there are relations of antecedence and consequence between physiological facts and mental facts. Here lies the true meaning of the oft-quoted saying of

Cabanis, "The brain in some sort digests impressions, it produces an organic secretion of thought." It is a functional not a material or substantial relation that is meant. Cabanis has the merit of having observed the existence and importance of organic sensations, of mental dissociation and the unconscious, and his thought marks a distinct stage between the psychology of Descartes and modern psychology, in that it is positive, and pays due regard to other than intellectual factors in mental life, and to the evolution of that life itself.

The Social Philosophers

CLAUDE HELVÉTIUS (1715–1771) has at any rate the merit of having perceived the dependence of the individual on the society to which he belongs. His treatise *De l'Esprit*, which appeared in 1758, was condemned by judges so diverse as the Pope, the *Parlement* of Paris, and Rousseau, and was burnt along with Voltaire's poem on Natural Religion. The views of Helvétius were based on sensationalism—*dans l'homme tout se réduit à sentir*. In man there is one and only one spring of action, and that is interest: we always act either to procure pleasure or avoid pain. Hence our moral judgments on others are derived; what we call probity is simply the habitual performance of actions which are advantageous to us. Of intentions we cannot judge. Thus the laws of interest are as absolute in morals as the laws of motion in physics. According to Helvétius differences in character are due to differences in environment and education. He protests (and with evident truth) that he was not actuated by love of paradox, but by a desire for the happiness of his fellows. Naturally he was led to emphasise the importance of legislation and education. Education he considered all-powerful, but it should be public and include physical and moral training. The latter he urges is generally neglected, and more time is spent on Latin verse than on the study of morals.

CHARLES-LOUIS DE SECONDAT, BARON DE MONTESQUIEU (1689–1755), set himself the task of investigating the nature of laws; his chief work, *L'Esprit des Lois*, representing more than twenty years of laborious research, was published in 1748. Laws are taken to be the necessary relations which spring from the nature of things. An intelligible order must have its source in an original reason, therefore laws are either the relations which hold between the *raison primitive* and different beings, or the relations which hold between these different beings themselves. Laws in this sense are prior to their positive enactment. Human reason is the true law of Humanity; positive law arises from its application to particular cases. Laws, however, do not spring forth ready made and absolute from the depths of a pure reason, they are relative to exterior conditions, to the nature of the government, country, climate, mode of life, etc. There are, according to Montesquieu, three types of states, despotism, limited monarchy, republic. In despotism a monarch rules without laws save his own will, and his rule is based on fear. On the part of the governed it is an effort to obtain security. But a genuine civil order implies a union of the citizens which is impossible under a despotism, inasmuch as security is incompatible with fear, and this inner discrepancy is invariably fatal to a despotic government. "When the savages of Louisiana," says Montesquieu, "wish to have fruit, they cut down the tree, and gather the fruit. There you have despotic government" (*L'Esprit des Lois*, v. 2). In a monarchy the power of the ruler is limited by rules, not by laws in the proper sense of the term, for laws must emanate from the whole nation, and not from a part. The power of the ruler rests on privilege, it is limited by the privileges of others. Honour is the cement which binds the structure together, creating a spirit of loyalty to place and privilege. In a republic or democracy the people is at once monarch and subject, being the subject of laws which it has itself made, and of magistrates whom it has itself appointed. The virtue essential to a republic is, according to Montesquieu, the love of one's country, that is, the love of equality. This he calls a political virtue, not a moral, nor a christian virtue; and as honour is the spring which moves a monarchy, so is the love of equality the spring which moves a republic. As everybody knows, it was in the English limited monarchy that Montesquieu found a practical compromise of the theoretical types of state, deeming the English constitution best adapted to preserve liberty and initiate reform. He attached the highest importance to the principle of limiting the power of one person or body by the power of another person or body, and the separation of the legislative, executive, and judicial powers.

Montesquieu has the honour of being the first philosopher in France to protest against slavery, which had been approved by the theologians, including Bossuet. He protested also against severity in punishment, which defeats its own end, and leads to the worst sort of corruption in a state, for it is a corruption engendered by the laws themselves—the disease is in the remedy.

JEAN-JACQUES ROUSSEAU (1712–1778), born at Geneva of a family of French origin, brings us forthwith into an atmosphere quite distinct from that of the Materialists, Encyclopaedists, or the School of Condillac, and in him we find the most far-reaching philosophic influence of the eighteenth century in France. There is in his thought little formal metaphysic or psychology. He takes his stand on an element in human nature which had been neglected; the foundation is not to be reason and culture, but nature and immediate feeling. Science and art alone cannot benefit man. Civilisation, largely through the division of labour, had made men slaves. What is needed, thought Rousseau, is a culture and a state which do not crush, dull, and deform humanity, but which give it an environment in which it can grow and develop in accordance with its own nature; it needs scope and sustenance, not bonds.

Rousseau's philosophy is largely an *exposition du sentiment*, and this is obviously to be expected when we remember his point of view. As such it is easy for unsympathetic criticism to find contradictions enough and to spare, but on the other hand any one who cares can find, in broad outline, a view of nature and man so warm and penetrating, that it becomes easy to understand Rousseau's enormous influence on modern thought and action.

Man, in a state of nature, he conceived as not devoid of sympathy, but mainly guided by instincts, in particular by that of self-preservation. Wants are few and easily met. But as men begin to form societies, the new complexity of relations produces troubles, rivalries, and dissatisfactions. Self-preservation develops into selfishness. But no steps backward are possible. Social life and civilisation there must be. The inevitable question is, what sort of civilisation and what sort of society. Rousseau's answer is found in *Émile* and the *Contrat Social*, both published in 1762.

In *Émile*, Rousseau set forth his theory of education, in which the scholar plays the leading part, and the teacher mainly sees that he has every chance to do it. His system is, as he himself says, negative and not positive. Man is by nature good; it is a false civilisation which has corrupted him, and the aim of education is to remove obstacles which block the self-development of human nature. A positive education prematurely forms the mind, and seeks to teach a child the duties of a man. Rousseau realised the truth that, rightly regarded, each stage of a child's life is not merely a preparation for something yet to come, but is itself a life worth living as an end and not merely as a means. At the age of twelve positive instruction (though somewhat limited) begins, and the mind is to be occupied as a safeguard against awakening passions. Books are to be avoided as much as possible; they only teach people to talk about what they do not understand. Let the pupil learn from things. Quite naturally we find Rousseau teaching that religion is a matter which must develop from within, and not be imposed from without. His views are expressed by means of the Savoyard Vicar, whose confession of faith is introduced in the fourth book of *Émile*. Philosophers merely multiply doubts; in the inner light therefore we must seek for guidance.

The first principle or dogma is that a will moves and animates the world, for matter being in itself inert, and an infinite chain of causes incredible, we must find the first cause in a will.

The second article of faith follows on the first. As the movement of matter displays a will, its movement according to laws proves an intelligence. We can know the order of the World, and yet be unable to know why it exists. We know that God is, that He is intelligence, will, goodness, but His substance we cannot know. In that direction it is wise to look with fear, for it is a greater impiety to think ill of the Deity than never to think of Him at all. What then is man, wherein lies his dignity? He is above all other animals in that he alone is able to contemplate them all, and in his rule over them. But while the animals are happy, their king is miserable. Providence rules all, yet there is evil on the earth. Its source is a duality or discord in

man's nature; he is at once slave and free; he sees and loves the
good, and does the evil.

The third article of faith is that man is free in his actions
(otherwise he would not be a will) and animated by an immaterial
substance. It follows that evil is not a part of the providential
order, but arises from man's abuse of his liberty, which was
given him not to do evil, but to do good, from choice. Should
man be shut off from being wicked at the price of restricting him
to instinct and making him a brute? The triumph of wickedness
and oppression in this world forces us to believe in the immortality of the soul. The virtuous who suffer in this world must be
recompensed in another, but the strongest foundation for this
belief is not to be found in human merit, but in Divine Goodness.

It is irreverent to say our souls are spirits as God is a spirit,
His substance is inconceivable by us, *and is to our souls what our
souls are to our bodies*. The Divine intelligence has no need of
reasoning; there are for it no premisses, no conclusions, no propositions even, for it is absolutely intuitive. While human power
acts by means, the Divine power acts by itself.

How then shall man's conduct be guided? By conscience
which never deceives us; it is the instinct of the soul. The
morality of our actions lies in the judgment we pass on them
ourselves. We have not only self-regarding feelings, but also
altruistic, and one sort is as innate and natural as the other, for
man is by nature sociable, or at any rate made to become so.
"Whenever there is sentiment and intelligence there is a moral
order. The difference is that the good man orders his life in
accordance with the whole, and the evil man orders the whole in
accordance with himself. The latter makes himself the centre of
all things; the other measures the radius and holds himself at
the circumference. So he is placed by relation to the centre,
which is God, and by relation to all the concentric circles which
are the creatures."

For contemplation, meditation, adoration, there is every place,
for thanksgiving also, but not for prayer. For what should we
ask of God? To distrust His own wise order? Such a prayer
should be punished rather than granted. To change our will?
That is to ask of Him what He asks of us.

Rousseau's theory of the state was expounded in the *Contrat*

Social. It follows Hobbes and Locke in basing the state on a contract, but Rousseau mainly uses the notion as a vehicle for conveying the conditions expressed or implied on which society rests. In sum these come to this, that the individual gives up unrestricted and individual liberty for a greater good to be found in social life: if social life cannot realise this greater good, it is irrational and unjustifiable. This greater good must be won for the common people; they are the human race. To the people sovereignty belongs—Rousseau is the prophet of democracy.

There is a distinction between the general will (*volonté générale*) and the will of all (*volonté de tous*). The latter aims at the individual's own interest (*l'intérêt privé*) and is merely the sum of individual wills. The former aims at a common good, and at the same time tends to realise more adequately the true good of the individual than the latter would do. Rousseau felt, though perhaps not clearly, that a man's true self is not mutilated, but expressed in social life. In practice, however, it is mere majority rule which prevails. Rousseau summarises in the *Social Contract* (Bk I. ch. VIII.) the effects of the passage from a state of nature to the civil state. "Let us draw up the whole account in terms easily commensurable. What man loses by the social contract is his natural liberty and an unlimited right to everything he tries to get and succeeds in getting; what he gains is civil liberty and the proprietorship of all he possesses. If we are to avoid mistake in weighing one against the other, we must clearly distinguish natural liberty, which is bounded only by strength of the individual, from civil liberty, which is limited by the general will; and possession, which is merely the effect of force or the right of the first occupier, from property which can be founded only on a positive title. We might, over and above all this, add to what man acquires in the civil state moral liberty, which alone makes him truly master of himself; for the mere impulse of appetite is slavery, while obedience to a law which we prescribe to ourselves is liberty."

It is a difficult task to reconcile man's natural freedom and the autonomy of the state, and there must remain a sense in which man is less free after the "social contract" than before it. But freedom, as Rousseau conceived it, is not merely absence of restraint; the will is not an abstract and unqualified potency of which anything may be the issue, nor is a being ruled by appetite free, but rather a slave. The social union is based on will, and that will is *rational*; therefore freedom is not lost but realised by reasonable action. But there can clearly be no contest between *rational* wills. That is to say, the apparent conflict between the interest of the sovereign and the interest of the individual is only apparent because the conflicting interests can never both be real interests. So it is only the "freedom" of the individual to do what is bad for himself and others which Rousseau sacrifices to the autonomy of the state. Representative government is rejected because no man can alienate his will, while sovereignty is inalienable as being the exercise of the general will. It should be remembered in this connexion that the actual representative governments of Rousseau's time did not present an impressive spectacle. This rejection inevitably involved a serious limitation in the application of his scheme to actual politics, so that a city-state, or at all events a small state, was all that it could cover.

The idea of freedom as the essence of man the world owes to Rousseau, and this idea has penetrated and swayed all succeeding ethical and political thought. Kant was deeply influenced by Rousseau. We are told that the perusal of *Émile* upset the clock-like regularity of his daily walks. In a striking passage Kant says (*Werke*, ed. Rosenkrantz, p. 240): "I am myself a student of inclination. I feel the whole thirst for knowledge, and the covetous restlessness that demands to advance in it, and again the satisfaction of every step of progress. There was a time when I believed that all this might constitute the honour of humanity, and I despised the crowd that knows nothing. It was Rousseau who set me right. That dazzling privilege disappeared; and I should think myself far less useful than common artisans, if I did not believe that my line of study might impart value to all others in the way of establishing the rights of humanity[1]." In Kant's development of Rousseau's conception, however, the moving force becomes purely rational, whereas Rousseau, faithful to his fundamental view, held it to be feeling.

---

[1] See also Bosanquet, *Philosophical Theory of the State*, ch. IX.

§ III. NINETEENTH CENTURY

(a) 1800–1850

The century opens with a reaction against Sensationalism. This reaction, psychological in its basis, begins with Maine de Biran, and afterwards with Cousin develops into Eclecticism—long the official philosophy in France. From Eclecticism, Ravaisson marks a divergence. The attempt to reduce philosophy to science is seen in Comte, and the attempt to base it on probability in Cournot.

FRANÇOIS-PIERRE-GONTIER MAINE DE BIRAN (1766–1824) was to begin with largely a follower of the School of Condillac. But in his *Mémoire sur l'habitude* (1803) he gradually broke away in quite another direction. Perception, memory, will, are not transformed sensations. The term sensation should be restricted to passive impressions; perception comes by way of the mobility of our organs, although in most of our experiences the sensible and the active elements are combined. Biran instances as "pure sensations" those which are now called organic; in these there is no effort, no distinctness, no recollection, because there is no active movement. It is in virtue of our activity and not of a mere sensation that we come to know the external world. The *fait primitif* is voluntary effort in which is given the awareness of the self and the not-self; both of these are given at the same time and with the same certainty. The general law of habit is that it weakens sensation—the passive element—and strengthens perception—the active element. But although habit dulls sense it may awaken passion and desire.

Maine de Biran further developed his ideas in the *Essai sur les fondements de la psychologie*, which was not published until 1859. His basis is the consciousness of personality given in the *fait primitif*. In the experience of voluntary activity we obtain the idea of a cause, which is neither innate, nor a habit, nor *a priori*, but a datum of our immediate inner experience. Causation and the other categories are thus views rooted in personal experience, and spring from the analysis of it. The true philosophic method is not to look outwards but inwards; by an act of *reflexion* the thinking subject can lay hold of itself in its living action. Previous philosophers, thought Biran, had gone astray through turning their regard to objects apart from the subject. Even

Descartes, who began rightly, went beyond the facts in maintaining the existence of a thinking *substance*.

In this work also there is a forecast of the modern psychology of the unconscious. The affective element, it is suggested, which is closely allied with the functions of organic life, may maintain an existence dissociated from personality and consciousness.

In his *Anthropologie*, an unfinished work published in 1859, he passed to a mystical view, where he no longer regarded personality as the highest stage of human life, but as a stage intermediate and transitional to an existence where persons are absorbed in God. In man there are three lives. There is the animal life, bound up with the organic life. This life man lives in his passions and in his dreams. There is also the peculiar life of man as a conscious subject, liable to animal passions, but capable of free action, and so a moral person, a self. The third is the spiritual life, to which man tends because in the personal life he is unable to attain the perfection and the happiness which hover before him. Love is the mark of the last stage, as spontaneity is of the first, and consciousness (i.e. self-consciousness) of the second. In love, at once the supreme perfection and the supreme joy, the duality of the human life with its attendant conflict is enfolded and lost.

The Scottish philosophy was made known in France by PIERRE-PAUL ROYER-COLLARD (1763–1845) and on this basis he opposed the tradition of Condillac. Royer-Collard formed an interesting theory of duration, which he considered to be a presupposition of succession and derived ultimately from the continuity of our action. The reaction against sensationalism was continued by VICTOR COUSIN (1792–1867), the founder of Eclecticism, a school which obtained and held a prominence quite out of proportion to its actual merits. Cousin followed the principle of Leibniz that philosophies are true in what they affirm, false in what they deny. Philosophies he divided into four classes, Idealism, Sensationalism, Scepticism, and Mysticism. The gold, at first, was to be separated from the dross, by the agency of the "common sense"; afterwards he sought refuge in an impersonal and universal reason. His later views were inspired by Hegel, whose thought he introduced to France. When Hegel read Cousin's lectures in the course for 1828 he remarked,

"I provided him with the fish, and he has served it with his own sauce."

Cousin's greatest services were rendered to the history of philosophy. He edited the works of Descartes, and discovered the original text of Pascal's *Pensées*. He translated Plato and Proclus and inspired his followers with a like zeal for historic research.

THÉODORE-SIMON JOUFFROY (1796–1842), Cousin's most distinguished disciple, expressed the hope that French thought might bring about the reconciliation of systems and a treaty of peace to be concluded in Paris. He remained faithful to the point of view of psychology and the introspective method, and was far superior to Cousin in precise expression.

FÉLIX RAVAISSON (1813–1900) was influenced largely by Maine de Biran, Leibniz, and Schelling among the moderns, and Aristotle of the ancients. His *thèse de doctorat* at the Sorbonne (1838) entitled *De l'habitude* has become classical. Therein he started from the point where Maine de Biran had left off, and sought an explanation of the fact that habit weakens passivity and increases activity. This he found in the development of an unconscious spontaneity outside will, personality, and consciousness. Under the influence of habit sensation becomes feebler, but the effect is stored, forms part of our life, and may reappear as a want. Similarly habit makes action more facile by the realisation in us of a new power, able to act of itself. In habit thus conceived is found the middle term between nature and spirit. Accordingly the activity of spirit comes first and passes into matter through the unconscious spontaneity which is habit. The mechanical view of the world is totally reversed, life is the explanation of matter, and thought the explanation of life. This is "the lofty doctrine which teaches that matter is only the last degree and as it were the shadow of existence; that the true existence of which all other is only an imperfect sketch, is that of the soul; that, in reality, to be, is to live, and to live, is to think and will" (*Rapport sur la philosophie en France*, p. 282). Memory and association are derived from the activity of mind; we forget only because our senses are partly under the dominion of matter. The true system of metaphysic must be based on an intuition to which the absolute stands revealed without a veil, and whereby we are, as it were, placed within it and identified with it. Empiricism fails, not so much by what it affirms, as by what it leaves out, while the philosophies of the understanding make mind active, but hem it in by limits beyond which it cannot pass, so that the absolutely real is left for ever beyond its reach.

Ravaisson distrusted the analytic method; once break the real in pieces, he thought, and there is no device cunning enough to re-make the shattered universe. His philosophy was an absolute idealism, based on intuition and with a tendency to the oracular. One of his many great services to philosophy was that he aided in the dethronement of Eclecticism; another, and by no means lesser one, was the preservation of metaphysical enquiry against the positivist spirit.

ANTOINE-AUGUSTIN COURNOT (1801–1877) based his philosophy on his conception of philosophical probability, for certainty in metaphysic he held to be unattainable. Chance is not merely a name for our ignorance, it is also an objective fact in nature. Events are said to happen by chance when they are brought about by the meeting of causal series otherwise independent. The probability of such conjunctions can be calculated mathematically, but mathematical must be distinguished from philosophical probability. The foundation of philosophical probability according to Cournot is the idea of order and of "the reason of things." The essential difference between mathematical and philosophical probability is that the latter cannot be expressed numerically; for number can only be arbitrarily applied to the simplicity of laws, the perfection of forms, and their relative values, all of which demand appreciation and not merely bare logic. Philosophical probability is thus, so far, subjective and its force varies downwards from its highest point, where it is capable of excluding doubt and producing a certitude *sui generis*.

Cournot conceived order as objective; order exists in nature, thus does the world become knowable to us. It is not the mind which puts order into things, so the understanding does not make nature. On the contrary, it is because there is an order in things that there is the notion of it in our minds, so that our faculty of reason is, so to say, constituted by something objective and independent.

The critical method as followed by Cournot consists in a careful analysis of concrete science, not of forms of knowledge. Philosophy has not a particular and peculiar subject-matter of its own, except in so far as it is a search for "the reason of things"; therein lies its difference from scientific knowledge, which is occupied with the observation of facts and the deduction of consequences. In the "reason of things" more is implied than the mere relation of cause and effect. It is a kind of coherence, lateral as well as linear, and applies in regions where the relations are other than causal, and its watchwords are simplicity, unity, and harmony.

All our faculties are not on the same level, but form a hierarchy over which reason is supreme, and gives the final verdict after the various faculties have been checked one against another. There is a distinction between appearances and phenomena in that the former do not exist independently of the observer, while the latter do. Sight, and to a certain extent touch and hearing, Cournot considered to be "representative," that is, they give us knowledge of something which exists independently of us, and which we know therefore as it really is. The characteristic of the representative sensations is that to suppress them involves the overturning of the whole system of knowledge. The human understanding is compelled to use signs, words, and symbols which are discontinuous to deal with a reality which is continuous. This is a native defect in logic, and limits its field of application.

Cournot's views met for long with quite undeserved neglect. He was a vigorous, careful, and concrete thinker, and is now meeting with some degree of the attention which his works undoubtedly merit.

CLAUDE-HENRI DE ROUVROY, COMTE DE SAINT-SIMON (1760–1825) essayed the reorganisation of society. What the eighteenth century had destroyed must be replaced in a new form, and the business of the nineteenth century was precisely, he thought, to construct a scientific and social system, so inaugurating the true golden age whose dwelling was in the future and not in the mists of the past. He maintained a positive tendency in philosophy which must throw overboard metaphysical speculations. Society, like nature, is subject to inevitable laws, including a law of progress. The reorganisation of society was to be carried out by the aid of science, industry, and finally a new religion able to make each one love his neighbour. The temporal and the spiritual powers are to be separated, the former to be wielded by the workers and producers, the latter by a new priesthood of scientists and artists. Women were to receive full civil and political rights and share in the labours and rewards of the renovated order.

AUGUSTE COMTE (1798–1857), who derived some of his inspiration from Saint-Simon and Condorcet, set before himself the foundation of a new philosophy and a new religion. Opinions differ as to his success in these attempts, but it is certain that he succeeded in founding a new science, namely Sociology. Comte called his philosophy *positive*, as he explains, because that term is universally understood to imply reality, usefulness, certainty, precision, and a tendency to organise. The latter characteristic is held to be conspicuously absent from the metaphysical spirit, which only availed for criticism.

Positivism begins by a general clearance of most of the problems with which traditional philosophy had been chiefly concerned. By our senses we know reality, and there is no other reality to know. The search for causes is necessarily futile. All we can know about a change is not its cause, nor the force that produces it, but simply its time-order. Forces are merely movements or tendencies to movement. Phenomena are simply perceptible facts; we can know them and their laws, but by laws we must rigidly understand nothing but invariable relations of succession and resemblance. The ordinary subject-matter of psychology is also excluded, for the mind can only observe what is external to it. All absolute knowledge is beyond the pale save the one absolute principle— that there is nothing absolute.

Comte's classification of the sciences is one of the most prominent features of his system. Science has for its subject-matter perceptible objects and their relations of antecedence, simultaneity and succession—that is, the whole of possible knowledge. It is therefore possible to arrange the sciences in order of complexity. Mathematics is at one end as the simplest, sociology (later ethics) at the other as the most complex, having the most concrete object. The simpler phenomena are necessarily also the most general and appear in the more complex. The laws of mathematics have the widest range, for everything can be measured. After mathematics come astronomy, physics, chemistry, biology, sociology, in order of increasing complexity and decreasing range of applicability. Also the simpler a science is, so much the more must it lean on induction. All the same, no science is purely deductive, but in mathematics the simple inductions on which it rests tend to be overlooked, partly because the facts may be understood as well in imaginary instances as in real. Though each science after mathematics leans on and uses the simpler science or sciences beneath it, yet no science is reducible to a lower one, so that each higher science involves a principle which cannot be deduced from any or all of the lower sciences. Such an attempt Comte entirely condemns, and asserts that between plant and animal there is an absolute discontinuity without possibility of transition. Such a view is, one may remark in passing, just as little likely to find favour with scientists as with philosophers, for the progress of a science is bound up with the effort to extend its field, and to find one science of nature.

According to Comte, the human mind necessarily passes through three stages, the theological, the metaphysical, and the positive. In the first two stages men seek vainly for causes, in the last stage they restrict themselves to order in time and space, and prevision is alike their aim and criterion. In the theological stage, events are explained by the will of personal agents; it is the stage of the supernatural and the miraculous, in which the uniform is less regarded than the strange and unforeseen. In the metaphysical stage the supernatural is ousted more or less by abstractions, occult causes, scholastic entities, and the *a priori* is its sovereign method. In the positive stage man realises that he really only needs facts and their relations of co-existence and succession; more than this is unknowable and useless if it could be known. What man needs is to foresee and to control. The individual, if left to a spontaneous education, goes through the same stages as the race. In childhood we are naturally theologians, in youth metaphysicians, in manhood physicists. The third stage is permanent, the second transitional, the result of metaphysic is to do away with theology. But until

the great consummation the three stages may co-exist in different
individuals at the same time, or even in different compartments
of the same mind. The law of the three stages has been traced
back to Saint-Simon and Turgot.

The aim of the Positivist Ethics is universal love; consequently
the transformation or over-ruling of the self-regarding impulses
is a capital point. By what process can social feeling be made
stronger than selfish feeling, which naturally holds sway?
Comte's remedy is in the effect of the social state, which naturally
enlarges and strengthens social sympathies, while it just as
naturally restricts and atrophies the selfish impulses. But there
is also an art of morals the object of which is an active intervention in the interests of the sympathies and against self-love.
The goal is the expansion of the benevolent emotions in which
lies the basis of individual and social well-being, for they are at
once the sweetest and the only non-exclusive or common good.
Comte held that the Ethics of the metaphysical systems and of
Christianity were essentially selfish, for he located, strangely
enough, the essence of Christian morality in the effort of each
individual to save his own soul. There are three stages of moral
progress as there are three stages of human life—the personal,
the domestic, and the social. The practical problem of morality
largely depends on the second, for the family leads man from
love of self to love of humanity. It is a grave error to neglect
this intermediate stage.

In his later years, Comte, to the consternation of some of his
disciples, endeavoured to found a new religion. It contained no
theology and no god. The object of worship was to be the
supreme being—Humanity. Comte proposed a solemn commemoration of great men, and an equally solemn reprobation
of bad men. Under the former, Caesar, St Paul and Charlemagne
were selected for special reverence. On the bad eminence stood
the Emperor Julian and Bonaparte—the latter being adjudged
the greater criminal and the former the greater fool. This
religious proposal has had little influence. Comte's greatest
achievement, and a great one it is, remains the foundation of a
new science, sociology—no unnatural offspring from a philosophy which was in fact and by profession, science, and whose
central conception was the *esprit d'ensemble*.

(b) 1850–1870

Broadly this period displays both a Hegelian tendency united with a faith in positive science, as in Taine and Renan, and a development from Kantianism in Renouvier's Neo-criticism.

HIPPOLYTE-ADOLPHE TAINE (1828–1893) published in 1857 an attack on the Eclectic school—under the title *Les philosophes classiques du xix*ᵉ *siècle*. "The little spiritual entities hidden under phenomena as under garments" are the objects of a brilliant and piquant criticism, but it is difficult to see why Maine de Biran should be classed with Cousin and Jouffroy. Taine's own philosophic masters were Condillac, Spinoza, and Hegel. The ruling idea of his view was necessity, inferential and causal. Thought can proceed from experience beyond the relative and accidental to the absolute and necessary. It was from Condillac that Taine's method started. Analysis, he thought, is the master-method, the method moreover best adapted to the French genius, and applicable not only to ideas, to which the Ideologists had restricted it, but also to things. But the mind of Taine was winged for higher flights than his predecessors. Holding with Spinoza that the causal relation is reducible to the logical relation of ground and consequent, he conceived nature as "a hierarchy of necessities." The world is pictured as "a living geometry," man as "a walking theorem." These results are reached by *abstraction*, "the interpreter of nature, the mother of religions and philosophies." The first step is taken by analysis, which shows that the causes of events are the inborn laws of things, and so the source of things is a system of laws; then metaphysic can reduce these particular laws to a universal formula and nature to an indivisible whole. It is impossible to avoid remembering Taine's own remark in his *Notes sur l'Angleterre* that the remains of the great German systems mark at once the goal at which philosophy ought to aim and the way it ought not to go.

Taine's psychology was chiefly expounded in his book *De l'intelligence*. There is, he maintained, neither mind nor body, but merely groups of movements present or possible, and groups of thoughts present or possible; there is no substance, only a system of facts. Mind and matter are two aspects or modes of being, as in Spinoza. In man, mentally a theorem, and physically a machine, virtue and vice are products "like vitriol and sugar." But they are not chemical but moral products, and the business of Ethics is simply to ascertain in what circumstances and under what conditions vice and virtue happen. Taine had intended to write also a treatise on the will, but—fortunately or unfortunately is hard to say—historical interests prevented the completion of his psychology.

To the Hegelian School belonged also ERNEST RENAN (1823–1892). Like Taine he believed in the rule of necessity. This view of course left no room for miracles and involved a breach with religious orthodoxy. So for Renan religion became the sense of the unity of things and the conception of the ideal which is their end. God is "the category of the ideal." The ideal is not however merely a possibility at the realisation of which we aim, it is also the idea in the Hegelian sense, the infinite mind whose evolution is the Universe. The true support of faith in God is a moral one; to a man merely intelligent atheism is inevitable.

CHARLES RENOUVIER (1818–1903) ultimately preferred for his system the name of "Personalism," in place of that of Neo-criticism by which it has become generally known. Each name has its peculiar applicability. Neo-criticism points to its relation to the Kantian criticism, with which Renouvier agreed in adopting the method of concepts and the notion of belief instead of evidence in regard to the super-sensible world, that is, in effect, to metaphysic and "transcendental" psychology. But on the other hand Renouvier's finitism and relativism differed *toto coelo* from the views of Kant, and found no place for the unconditioned and for things-in-themselves which were regarded as sheer intellectual fictions. The name Personalism emphasises the claim that consciousness is the foundation of existence, and the person the first causal principle of the world. Renouvier was a vigorous and audacious thinker, and exercised a very considerable influence in France, though outside his own country his philosophy has not had the attention which it indubitably merits.

Renouvier saw in every philosophical system not so much a rigidly logical construction as a purely personal belief. In Descartes, Leibniz, Berkeley, Malebranche, Hume, he thought he saw this exemplified, and concluded that belief must intervene where observation fails.

The doctrine of Personalism may conveniently be summed under its leading concepts: (1) the law of number, (2) the principle of relativity, (3) the absolute beginning, (4) free-will, (5) the unity of God, (6) creation.

(1) Renouvier, holding that number is applicable to everything, found himself at the commencement faced with a choice between a theory of knowledge which accepted the concept of infinity (as he understood it) and one which rejected it. To his mind there could be no actual infinite, for an infinite must consist of units and therefore its actuality would imply that it was complete and could not be added to, whereas on his view the fact that addition was always possible was essential to the notion of an infinite. Hence he thought infinity involved a contradiction so radical, that if he adopted it, there would scarcely be ground for refusing to accept any other contradiction which arose in the course of his subsequent speculations. The actual world must therefore be finite.

(2) "No object of thought can be known and defined, save in the idea which we have of it, and this idea asserts always a relation to the idea of some other thing whether subject or object of thought matters not" (*Le Personnalisme*, p. 21). The idea of God, for instance, is neither definable, nor even thinkable, save by relation to the idea of a world of which he is the author or governor or essence or substance. In virtue of this principle Renouvier reached a sort of phenomenalism, for which reality consisted of phenomena and their general laws or relations, and which dispensed with noumena and substance whether material or spiritual. The principle of relativity, like the principle of contradiction, is a postulate and cannot be demonstrated.

(3) The Infinite being regarded as unthinkable, the world must have had a beginning—and so must God, neither nature nor God can be eternal. Renouvier, largely influenced by Hume, held that it is not necessary that everything which has a commencement should have a cause of its existence. Similarly there may arise in nature new beginnings which are not themselves effects. God cannot be eternal because by the law of number His existence resolves itself into a series of thoughts, and an infinite series

cannot be real, which it would have to be if God's existence was eternal.

(4) In the beginnings of his speculation, Renouvier was opposed to the doctrine of free-will, but modified his position after he had adopted the theory of an absolute commencement. This once admitted, the way was open to the admission of relative and partial commencements as acts of free-will. Here, he says, as in the question of infinity, he follows logic; for with a universal necessity morality and the distinction of truth and error are incompatible.

(5) Renouvier at first thought that some form of pluralism or polytheism followed from his conception of relativity, but later he came to believe that the unity of God follows from the unity of Nature as seen in its laws, for law to him implied representation in a mind. He conceives of God as non-eternal and limited, so remaining faithful to his initial rejection of the infinite. Once admit, he thought, the eternal and the infinite, and the distinction of good and evil, vital for ethics, must disappear.

(6) God is not eternal, and can only be called *causa sui* in the sense that He has no cause and no antecedent, and so simply *began*. But it was necessarily involved in His beginning to be, that He should at once be the cause of other existences, and this is Creation. God could not exist without at once and necessarily creating the world. An act of will originating the world is a more intelligible and logical supposition than an infinite series of phenomena without origin.

(c) 1870–1900

During this period psychology and sociology become independent sciences. Philosophy, largely idealistic, ·centres round the problems of Contingency and Evolution.

French philosophy has been to a large extent psychological and sociological, but in the development of thought, psychology and sociology have come to occupy definite positions as autonomous sciences. THÉODULE RIBOT (1839–1916), in the introduction to *La Psychologie Anglaise contemporaine* (1870), traced the outline of a scientific psychology, which was to replace the abstractions and metaphysical discussions in vogue. "The psychology in

question here will then be purely experimental; it will have no
other object than phenomena, their laws, and their immediate
causes; it will concern itself neither with the soul nor its essence,
for this question, being above experience and beyond verifica-
tion, belongs to metaphysics." The method will be neither
entirely subjective as in Jouffroy, nor entirely objective as in
Broussais, but a combination of both. Ribot's demarcation of
the objective sphere in psychology is important. "The natural
expression of the passions, the variety of languages, and the
events of history are so many facts which permit us to trace the
mental causes that have produced them: the morbid derange-
ment of the organism which produces intellectual disorders;
anomalies, monsters in the psychological order, are to us as
experiments prepared by nature, and all the more precious
as the experimentation is more rare. Study of the instincts,
passions, and habits of the different animals supplies us with
facts whose interpretation (often difficult) enables us by induction, deduction, or analogy, to reconstruct a mode of
psychological existence." The study of pathological processes
of mind has been brilliantly pursued in France, especially by
Charcot and Pierre Janet. Ribot published a crowd of distinguished works on heredity, the diseases of memory, attention,
etc., in which his method was consistently applied to the great
advantage of psychology. To Ribot also we owe the foundation
of the *Revue philosophique* in 1876.

Sociology started as we have seen from Saint-Simon and Comte
—the latter indeed may fairly be considered its true founder.
But the science did not at once develop, and only attained its
greatest activity towards the end of the century. Amid a
crowd of able workers, especially noteworthy contributions have
been made by Espinas, Tarde, and Durkheim. ALFRED-VICTOR
ESPINAS (in *Les Sociétés animales*, 1877) regarded sociology as a
branch of biology. Societies are conscious organisms, systems
of representations. The consciousness of a society and the
consciousness of an individual are alike produced by a fusion of
more elementary consciousnesses; so society is really a self.

GABRIEL TARDE (1843–1904) initiated a reaction against the
positivist element in sociology, resting his views on a psychological basis. The central fact of society, he thought, is invention

followed by imitation, not indeed an imitation operating mechanically but by a specific mental contagion. The effect of this principle was to install in society a certain element of chance or spontaneity.

ÉMILE DURKHEIM (1858–1917) aimed at freeing sociology not only from philosophy but from psychology as well, making it an autonomous science. In every society there are phenomena clearly outside the purview of the other sciences. These are the social facts, which possess a specific nature, and cannot be simply resolved into the sum of individual consciousnesses. The collective life is as distinguishable from the individual as the mental life from that of the body. The method of sociology is analytical and historical. Durkheim and his collaborators have published many careful researches on the sociological side of religion, economics, law, and morals.

JULES LACHELIER (1832–1918) was above all a teacher of philosophy—*son œuvre, ce sont ses élèves*. His object was not to impart dogma, but to inspire in those whom he taught at once the desire and the capacity to think for themselves, and so his influence survived their changes of opinion. He is one of the few philosophers who have written too little—a thesis *Du fondement de l'induction*, an article *Psychologie et Métaphysique*, and a small volume entitled *Études sur le syllogisme*. The philosophy of Lachelier was largely inspired by Kant and Leibniz. But he differed essentially from Kant as to the nature of knowledge, though they agreed in the principle that knowledge would be impossible unless the laws of thought are also constitutive laws of nature. Knowledge according to Lachelier is not merely relative, but under the form of reflexion attains the absolute, and thus for him the unintelligible residuum of things-in-themselves falls away. In his enquiry into the nature of induction Lachelier rejected the empiricism of Mill, whose theory left the inductive principle in the strange situation of being applicable only to the past, and certain only where no further induction need be made. Cousin and his school had failed to give a precise idea of the order they held to exist in nature. What then is the basis of induction? Thought and its relation to phenomena. Induction implies (*a*) the serial sequence of phenomena and (*b*) their union in a system or systems.

Lachelier's argument is directed to prove that without both these conditions thought is impossible. The former gives efficient, the latter final causes. The distinction between abstract and concrete, mechanism and finality, is relative to the distinction of our faculties. It is finality—the hidden spring of mechanism —which gives the only complete explanation of thought and of nature alike. Reality is thus at once mechanical, final, and free; and similarly the order of thought and the order of existence being absolutely identical, every act of thought implies the knowledge of a material mechanism, the feeling of an organic unity, and freedom.

ÉMILE BOUTROUX (1845–1921) is akin in spirit to Ravaisson, to whom he dedicated his brilliant little book, *De la contingence des lois de la nature*, his thesis for the doctorate in 1874. Its plea is for liberty and against necessity. The aim of science is held to be to reduce the complex to the simple, the contingent to the necessary—an aim which only partially succeeds. For the different sciences stand at different levels, and a higher or more concrete science is not completely reducible to or deducible from a lower or more abstract. Here Boutroux agrees with Comte. The supreme form of necessity is the law of causation, but this is abstract and analytic and does not exhaust the whole nature of reality. At every step we find that no concrete whole is simply equivalent to the elements of which it is composed—a man for instance is not simply equal to his physiological constituents. Nature provides us with something new in the course of its development, and wherever there is novelty there is contingency, for the new cannot be necessary since it is not attainable by analysis. The fact that we must appeal to experience testifies to the contingency of nature. Permanence is a result of change. The laws of nature are the habits of an agent which itself is spontaneous and free. Necessity is therefore not of the essence of being, but merely marks a stage of its development, and that development free. Of course science and experience cannot *prove* freedom, for they only present things actually realised. But freedom is a creative power anterior to the act. As we ascend the scale of being from the abstract to the concrete we find developing at every step the principle of finality, the good and the beautiful attracting not necessitating.

Should these triumph, the laws of nature in the exact sense would disappear, replaced by a free effort of will towards perfection, by "the free hierarchy of souls."

These views maintain, as against materialism and scientific determinism, a conception of the world in which mind is free and values rule. The notion of contingency finds further development in Bergson.

The philosophy of ALFRED FOUILLÉE (1838–1912) combines an extraordinary comprehensiveness with an equally notable unity of principle. The centre of his system is found in the conception of *idées-forces*. First suggested in *La philosophie de Platon* (1869), it runs through all his theories, and is developed fully in *La psychologie des idées-forces* (1893). The problem which presented itself to Fouillée can scarcely be expressed better than in the words of M. Augustin Guyau: "To show by what evolution Reality results in man in the conception of ideals which go beyond it, then how these ideals, once conceived and desired, become forces in Reality and so make it go beyond itself" (*La philosophie et la sociologie d'Alfred Fouillée*, p. 3). Philosophy, according to Fouillée, must rest on experience, not on a transcendental dogmatism; with Plato and Aristotle as examples it must study being both universal and individual, and also *thought*, taken in its widest sense of the whole of consciousness including sensation, feeling, tendencies, and appetitions, as well as judgment, reasoning, and the idea in its usual application. Thus the "classical separation of faculties" is rejected; every mental act involves three aspects or moments, thought, feeling, and appetition. Psychology is essentially philosophic; philosophy in a sense a universal psychology. Above all, there is no reason to suppose that Reality can be expressed in the most elementary forms into which we can analyse it, or the most abstract views that we can take of it.

The essential characteristic of consciousness is not that it is "representative" or "formal," but its union of sensation and appetition. Under the term *ideas* Fouillée includes all mental states more or less conscious of themselves or their objects. The force or activity inseparable from ideas implies: (*a*) an appetitive element by which every state of consciousness tends to realise its object and every idea of an end to realise itself;

(b) a movement in the organism (though not a merely mechanical movement) which tends, unless inhibited, to realise its idea; (c) the efficiency of the mental side as an actual factor in evolution, so that consciousness cannot be regarded as an epiphenomenon or inactive accompaniment of physical events, a sort of uncalled-for illumination of certain regions of mechanical changes. It results that mind is the actual spring of things, mechanism an abstract and symbolic view of them.

Can the determinism of science be reconciled with the conception of liberty which seems necessary for Ethics? This is a pressing problem which Fouillée endeavoured to solve from the time of his thesis *La Liberté et le Déterminisme* (1872) until his last days, and we find it discussed in his *Esquisse d'une interprétation du Monde* published after his death. In his view Renouvier's solution of absolute beginnings was impossible. Fouillée accepted throughout his speculations the principles of contradiction and of causality, and did not like Renouvier elect to discard the latter and make what shift he could with the former. Nor could he accept contingency as found in Boutroux and Bergson. Faithful to his conception of a *synthèse concilia-trice* whereby philosophy may garner what truth is in each opposing claim, he sought a higher synthesis in which the contradictions of determinism and indeterminism might be reconciled after the actual claims of each had been duly assessed. The doctrine of *idées-forces* is Fouillée's means of solution and is used as a mean term between the conflicting theories. We all have the idea of liberty which enfolds the love of liberty—that is "the idea of the maximum independence possible for an intelligent and loving self" (*Histoire de la philosophie*, p. 531). This idea being an *idée-force* tends to realise itself and wins in practice a relative liberty capable of indefinite increase. It is true, thought Fouillée, that the determinations of mechanism and of mathematics do not exhaust reality. That is the truth in the doctrine of contingency; but its error lies in supposing that the conclusion to be drawn is that therefore there is room for indetermination, whereas the true conclusion is that there are other determinations than the mechanical and quantitative, and these determinations are psychic. So is reached the notion of a psychic auto-determinism, and man is like "a star which

conceived the possibility of departing from its orbit by the idea
and the desire of an orbit larger and more beautiful" (*Esquisse*,
p. 359). One person can only become conscious of himself along
with other selves; there is no self which is not also a social self.
Hence Fouillée's saying, *cogito, ergo sumus*. This is specially
important for Ethics, for egoism is already condemned where
there is solidarity between selves, and this is why the immoral
is also the irrational. Fouillée's activity touched most of the
problems of philosophy—metaphysical, psychological, ethical or
social, and all to good purpose. He was a philosopher *de tout
son âme*.

In JEAN-MARIE GUYAU (1854–1888) we find the poet and
philosopher so inextricably united, that his philosophy often
finds its choicest expression in his poetry, his poetry in his
philosophy. The concept of life for him is fundamental. Life is
the concrete thing in which we distinguish such "extracts and
abstracts" as force, movement, existence. Inanimate things,
said Guyau, are much more living than the abstractions of
science. Deep in the nature of life lies a tension from which
springs the development of the capacities of the individual, and
an expansion in virtue of which they overflow the individual's
limits. So morality becomes for him not a limitation and
cramping of life, but its outpouring and abundance. Thus the
"supreme virtue is greatness of soul"—*la générosité*—and this
is also the fullest and truest expression of the life which is
nature. The old notion that the impulses of the individual are
all egoistic and have to become or to be made altruistic is wrong.
The original impulse embraces both the self and others; it is
strengthened by reflection—not weakened or suppressed as it
might be if it were merely a social or herd instinct.

Art, according to Guyau, is an enlargement of life, which being
cramped by its ordinary and every-day setting frees itself by the
help of imagination, imitation, and play. Unreality, however, is
not a condition of Art, but rather a limit against which it
unavoidably finds itself. It remains, however, inevitable that
nature should surpass Art.

The foundation of religion is the conception of a social bond
between man and the universe. Just as the object of Guyau's
work *Esquisse d'une morale sans obligation ni sanction* (1885)

was not to subvert morality, but to show that it implies more
and better than a mere imperative, so in *L'irréligion de l'avenir*
it is not so much religion as a certain conception of it which
disappears; for religion is taken to imply mythology, dogma,
and the cult of the supernatural. The human spirit, thought
Guyau, will win a freer and higher flight without such weights;
and those who can essay the fair adventure of the ideal will draw
all men after them. His aspirations are best expressed in the
enthralling charm of his own words, engraved on his tomb:
" Je suis bien sûr que ce que j'ai de meilleur en moi me survivra.
Non, pas un de mes rêves peut-être ne sera perdu; d'autres les
reprendront, les rêveront après moi, jusqu'à ce qu'ils s'achèvent
un jour. C'est à force de vagues mourantes que la mer réussit à
façonner sa grève, à dessiner le lit immense où elle se
meut."

To HENRI BERGSON (born 1859) philosophy owes a debt which
as yet can scarcely be realised or assessed. His works display a
width of outlook, a subtlety of insight, and a felicity of expression
as obvious and admirable to the critic as to the disciple. In
Bergson's view philosophy is not an extension and completion
of the ordinary process of thought, nor is its instrument intelligence as ordinarily understood. For intelligence proceeds by
analysis and so has to express one thing in terms of another;
and—equally important—intelligence has been evolved as an
instrument of action. It spatialises, and is consequently
limited in its proper action to spatial objects, and if applied
to the non-spatial, for instance, the activities of the mind,
its effect is to misrepresent, turning a reality which is a
continuous and undivided movement into a set of frames and
symbols in space. Philosophy rests on intuition, but the vision
is not vouchsafed to the first look. When we gaze into our minds,
it would be a mistake to suppose that reality becomes at once
apparent and transparent to us; our minds are full of the
products of intellect, and these must be cleared away before
intuition can seize and possess the reality which is essentially
mobility, not things made but in the making, not states, but
processes. Intellectualism fails, not because it maintains that
concepts can be extracted from reality, which is true, but
because it maintains that reality can be reconstructed from

concepts, which is false. We may pass from intuition to analysis, but from the analysed to intuition there is no road.

Contrary to the tradition of Plato and the Platonists, Bergson holds that change is real and original and not apparent and derived. In short there is nothing but change, there are no things which change. In a pure intuition we cannot see *things*; though we may think we see them, they are not true ultimate elements of reality, but surviving relics of the practical activities of the intelligence, and must be got rid of if the intuition is to become pure.

Clearly on the principles which have been briefly sketched many of the problems current in philosophy would turn out to be artificial, that is to say, actually engendered by the method in which the study of reality had been approached.

Three such problems Bergson has examined in detail. His first important work was *Essai sur les données immédiates de la conscience,* his doctoral thesis, published in 1889, which deals with the notion of freedom—a rock strewn with the wrecks of ages, and a stern coast for a first adventure.

If, as seems probable, the states of mind as we think we perceive them are really seen through forms borrowed from the external world, these forms must be cleared away. When we look at psychic states as isolated units they seem to possess degrees of intensity; as they unfold in time they constitute duration; in their mutual relations they seem to determine one another. Intensity resolves itself on inspection into pure quality, its cause in space is quantity, and so the intensity of a psychic state is not a quantity, but the qualitative sign of a quantity. There is a wide distinction between a multiplicity of discrete or discernible units, which involves space, and the multiplicity of conscious states, which is entirely qualitative. In the notion of the duration within us we come across one of the vital points of Bergson's philosophy. "What is duration within us? A qualitative multiplicity, with no likeness to number; an organic evolution which is yet not an increasing quantity; a pure heterogeneity within which there are no distinct qualities. In a word, the moments of inner duration are not external to one another" (*Les données immédiates*, p. 174). In the external world there is no such duration but only simultaneity. Now the common conception of time is a blend—"the mixed idea of a measurable time which is space in so far as it is homogeneity, and duration in so far as it is succession" (*Ib.* p. 176). The problem of freedom thus approached takes on a new complexion. Both determinists and libertarians have failed to eliminate space from the inner world. The former made the error of denying freedom, the latter of defining it in terms covertly spatial. Freedom can only be denied if time is identified with space; it can only be defined if space adequately represents time. In *Matière et Mémoire* (1896) Bergson attacked his second problem—the relation of mind and body. The brain does not store memories, neither does it create ideas. A perception is an action in outline, virtual not actual, and the function of the brain is the carrying out of action. Perception depends on memory, not memory on perception. There are two forms of memory, motor habits and recollection or pure memory; the former is exemplified in a poem learnt by heart, the latter in the recollection of a particular occasion in the learning of it: the former can be repeated; the latter is unique and cannot be repeated; it has a date. Perception and memory differ in that the one gives us matter, the other spirit. Their point of contact is in action which they direct and in which alone they are united, and the instrument of this action is the body. The third problem— evolution—forms the subject of *L'Évolution créatrice* (1907). Here the mechanical and finalist theories of evolution are discussed and rejected. They are both infected by the same vice; they both assume that life works by bringing part to part, by association. But this is exactly untrue. "Life does not proceed by the association and addition of elements, but by dissociation and division" (*L'Évolution créatrice*, p. 97). For a mechanical aggregation or a pre-conceived plan Bergson substitutes an original vital impulse—*élan vital*—which splits as it proceeds and takes divergent directions, towards instinct for instance and towards intelligence. "From our point of view, life appears in its entirety as an immense wave which, starting from a centre, spreads outwards, and which on almost the whole of its circumference is stopped and converted into oscillation: at one single point the obstacle has been forced, the impulsion has passed freely. It is this freedom that the human form registers.

Everywhere but in man, consciousness has had to come to a stand; in man alone it has kept on its way. Man, then, continues the vital movement indefinitely, though he does not draw along with him all that life carries in itself. On other lines of evolution there have travelled other tendencies which life implied, and of which, since everything interpenetrates, man has doubtless kept something, but of which he has kept only very little. It is as if a vague and formless being, whom we may call, as we will, man or superman, had sought to realise himself, and had succeeded only by abandoning a part of himself on the way. The losses are represented by the rest of the animal world, and even by the vegetable world, at least in what these have that is positive and above the accidents of evolution" (*L'Évolution créatrice*, pp. 288–9.)

Conclusion

From France there have set out four currents which have deeply influenced European thought—the philosophy of Descartes in the seventeenth century, that of Rousseau in the eighteenth, the Positivism of Comte, and Bergson's philosophy of change in the nineteenth. These, nevertheless, by no means represent the whole philosophy of France, for it is exceedingly hard to say where its philosophy begins and ends. The reason is simple; the French mind is by a gift of nature inclined to "the thinking consideration of things" and to looking at them in a larger setting. Hence the abundance of writers of whom it is easier—and truer—to say that they are more or less philosophic than that they are, or are not, philosophers. Hence also the risk run by a breathless survey like this of being somewhat arbitrary or capricious in its inclusions and exclusions.

Bergson, with his own clearness of vision, has set down as the salient characteristics of French philosophy its simplicity of form, and its close union with science (*La Science française*, I. 30–1). One result of the former is the notable absence of any abuse of technical phraseology in French philosophic writers, and—as a consequence of this—the fact that they may be and are understood outside professional circles. There is no thorny hedge to keep out the layman. Meanwhile philosophy, in touch with actual science which is ever progressive, tends to preserve the suppleness necessary to follow the subtle movements of increasing knowledge, and as errors are cast off in its career, draws visibly nearer and nearer to the supreme goal—the holding in translucent synthesis logic and life.

BIBLIOGRAPHY

For Descartes, Pascal, Malebranche, Voltaire, Diderot, Montesquieu, Rousseau, see the bibliography to chapter VIII.

La Mettrie. *Œuvres Philosophiques.* 2 vols. London and Berlin. 1751.

D'Holbach. *Système de la Nature.* 2 vols. 1770.

Condillac. *Œuvres Complètes.* 32 vols. 1803.

Destutt de Tracy. *Œuvres Complètes.* 4 vols. 1824.

Cabanis. *Œuvres Complètes.* Éd. Thurot. 1825.

Helvétius. *Œuvres Complètes.* 10 vols. 1796.

Maine de Biran. *Œuvres Posthumes.* Éd. Cousin. 3 vols. 1841; *Pensées.* Éd. Naville. 1857; *Œuvres Inédites.* Éd. Naville. 3 vols. 1859.

Royer-Collard. *Fragments philosophiques.* Éd. Schimberg. 1913.

Cousin. *Œuvres Complètes.* 22 vols. 1846–7.

Jouffroy. *Mélanges philosophiques.* 1833; *Nouveaux Mélanges philosophiques.* 1842; *Cours d'Esthétique.* Éd. Damiron. 1843.

Ravaisson. *De l'habitude.* 1838 (reprinted, *Revue de Métaphysique,* Janv. 1894); *La philosophie en France au xixe siècle.* 1868; 5th ed. 1904.

Saint-Simon. *Œuvres Choisies.* Éd. Lemonnier. 3 vols. 1859–61.

Comte. *Cours de Philosophie positive.* 6 vols. 1894; *Système de Politique positive.* 4 vols. 1851–4.

Cournot. *Essai sur les fondements de nos connaissances et sur les caractères de la critique philosophique.* 2 vols. 1851; *Traité de l'enchaînement des idées fondamentales dans les sciences et dans l'histoire.* 2 vols. 1861. (These two works have recently been reprinted.)

Taine. *De l'intelligence.* 2 vols. 1870; *Les philosophes classiques du xixe siècle.* 1875.

Renan. *Dialogues et fragments philosophiques.* 1895.

Renouvier. *Essais de critique générale.* 4 vols. 1854–64; *Le Personnalisme.* 1903.

Lachelier. *Du fondement de l'induction.* 1896.

Boutroux. *De la contingence des lois de la nature.* 1875; *De l'idée de la loi naturelle dans la science et dans la philosophie contemporaine.* 1895.

Ribot. *Les Maladies de la mémoire.* 1881; *Les Maladies de la volonté.* 1883; *Les Maladies de la personnalité.* 1885; *La psychologie de l'attention.* 1889; *L'hérédité psychologique.* 1882; *La psychologie des sentiments.* 1896; *L'évolution des idées générales.* 1897.

Pierre Janet. *L'automatisme psychologique.* 1889.

Espinas. *Les Sociétés animales.* 1877.

Tarde. *Les lois de l'imitation.* 1890; *La logique sociale.* 1894.

Durkheim. *De la division du travail social.* 1893; *Les règles de la méthode sociologique.* 1895.

Fouillée. *La liberté et le déterminisme.* 1873; *L'évolutionnisme des idées-forces.* 1890; *La psychologie des idées-forces.* 1893; *Esquisse d'une interprétation du monde.* 1913.

Guyau. *Les problèmes de l'esthétique contemporaine.* 1884; *Esquisse d'une morale sans obligation ni sanction.* 1885; *L'irréligion de l'avenir.* 1887.

Bergson. *Essai sur les données immédiates de la conscience.* 1889; *Matière et Mémoire.* 1896; *L'Évolution créatrice.* 1907.

CHAPTER XIV

MATHEMATICS

§ I. SEVENTEENTH CENTURY

THE transition between two periods in the history of a science can hardly be defined by a date. The achievements of Galileo, Descartes, Newton, and Leibniz really divide modern from mediaeval mathematics, their names marking epochs in the mathematical studies of Italy, France, England, and Germany.

In France Descartes had several contemporaries of the first rank, Fermat, Pascal, and Desargues. But none of them succeeded in turning the thoughts of the generation which followed into new channels; indeed their work bore little immediate fruit; as we shall see, much of it was buried for many years and, when at length exhumed, excited the kind of wonder aroused by works of art of an almost forgotten civilisation when re-exhibited to public view. The work of Viète, though earlier than that of Descartes, owes much of its importance to the fact that it was adopted and adapted by Descartes. The secret of Descartes's influence lies in the philosophical trend of his mind; he was distinguished by his attitude towards mathematical studies as much as by direct contribution to their advancement. He was the first perhaps who looked beyond the actual problem to the general conditions underlying its solution and indeed its existence. Even though he was unable to answer the question proposed, he had the gift of looking for the solution in the right direction. It is his passion for the general that makes his work so modern, and it is this quality which justifies us in placing him at the head of the roll of modern French mathematicians.

For the life of RENÉ DESCARTES (1596–1650) the reader is referred to the preceding chapter, in which his philosophy is treated. We know that at the age of twenty-two he was engaged in physical speculations, for it was in 1618 that he met Isaac Beekman, who kept a diary recording the subjects of their daily discourses. It is from this document that we learn that problems of mechanics and hydrostatics largely occupied the attention of the two students. After leaving Holland in 1619, Descartes travelled, and in the winter of that year on the eve of St Martin he tells us that, filled with enthusiasm, he discovered the foundations of a marvellous science. In the *Discours de la méthode* his words are: "Je demeurois tout le jour enfermé seul dans un grand pöesle, où j'avois tout le loisir de m'entretenir de mes pensées." We may reasonably entertain the conjecture that it was at the age of twenty-two that the foundations of Cartesian geometry were laid in the mind of its author. From 1620 to 1629 Descartes travelled much, studying, as he said, "le grand livre du monde." From these years we date his friendship with his life-long correspondent, Marin Mersenne, and with Claude Mydorge, a fellow-student in optics. At this time too he met the founder of the congregation of the Oratory, Cardinal Bérulle, who perhaps decided the most important step in his life; it was by his advice that Descartes decided to devote his life to philosophy. To this end, in 1629, he selected Holland as his place of residence. The States offered many advantages to the scholar and the artist at that time, but chief amongst its privileges Descartes prized the liberty which a wise and stable government assured to those who lived within its boundaries. Here he worked for twenty years in friendship and in controversy with Dutch scholars, and in correspondence, amiable and otherwise, with his French contemporaries. No one who reads the ample correspondence of this period, which by good fortune we possess, can doubt that Descartes found in the country of his adoption not only the external calm and peace which were so essential for his work but also the friendship and appreciation upon which he showed himself sometimes a little too dependent.

His first publications were designed to arouse interest in his new scheme of philosophy; and with this object he compiled three small treatises, the first upon a subject of mixed mathematical and physical interest, the *Dioptrique*, the second upon pure physics, the *Météore*, and the third upon mathematics, the *Géométrie*. For these *Essais philosophiques* he prepared a preface, the *Discours de la méthode*. In the *Dioptrique*, Descartes enunciated the laws of the refraction of light and applied them to the theory of lenses; part of the treatise is concerned with the grinding of lenses, a problem which occupied his attention and his correspondence for many years. In the *Météore* he discussed such problems as rainbows and parhelia. The importance of these tracts for us, though perhaps not for his contemporaries, is inferior to that of the *Géométrie*, which was written while the previous tracts were passing through the press. Whatever may have been the actual hurry in writing the last tract, the ideas unfolded in it must have been long in its author's mind. The obscurity of certain passages and its infelicitous arrangement are explained sufficiently by the circumstances of its composition; it is characteristic of the author and of the age that he ascribes his obscurity to design, stating that the treasures of the book were reserved for those who had the skill and patience to extract them. The *Géométrie* is divided into three books. In the first the value of the use of algebraical symbols is demonstrated by the solution of a famous problem proposed by Pappus. The introduction of algebraical symbols into geometry marks a new era in mathematical investigation; and algebra owes perhaps as much to Descartes's improvements in its notation as arithmetic does to the unknown inventor of the symbol 0. In the second book curves are introduced by their equations and a general definition of the tangent of a curve is given. The third book is a treatise on the theory of equations, the earliest tract on this subject. The mathematical and physical theories of Descartes aroused much criticism in detail, and at first their importance was hardly recognised. Fermat was their acutest critic and Florimond de Beaune their warmest defender.

The *Discours de la méthode* contains a statement of the functions of mathematics in the search for truth which Descartes regarded as the goal of philosophy. He insists upon the unity of mathematical studies and the value of coordination. Two and a half centuries have passed since this short essay was written; but its appeal to-day is as strong as when it was first penned, perhaps stronger, for it excited little contemporary comment.

In studying physical phenomena, Descartes introduced principles as far reaching and as bold as his new ideas in pure mathematics. He enunciated with precision the law of the conservation of momentum, and foreshadowed modern views of physical phenomena. "C'est le mouvement seul qui selon les différens effets qu'il produit s'appelle tantost chaleur tantost lumière." It is unnecessary to discuss how much Descartes owed to the initiative of other men; it was perhaps more than he would have conceded, but it was small when weighed in the balance against his own achievement. We know that he had few books and that he was not addicted to reading; he relied upon himself, for, as he says with self-conscious power, "Je voy que la plupart des hommes jugent si mal, que je ne dois point arrester à leurs opinions." But Descartes, if he relied little upon his contemporaries, was ever willing to be taught by nature. It was by experiment that he investigated the problem of the refraction of light and the pressure of the atmosphere. If he failed to appreciate the value of Galileo's results, it was because he regarded the resistance of the atmosphere as a necessary condition in the fall of heavy bodies. Incorrect as his dynamical theories sometimes are, Descartes's theories always have in them something that surprises us by its originality and penetration.

In his relation to his fellow-workers Descartes has so often been judged by one set of utterances that it is perhaps fair to balance the verdict passed by him upon his contemporaries, which has been given above, by a second quotation in which the truer voice of the philosopher may be heard. In a letter to an unknown correspondent he writes:

La recherche de la verité est si necessaire & si simple, que le travail de plusieurs milliers d'hommes y devroit concourir; et il y a si peu de personnes au monde qui l'entreprennent à bon escient, que ceux qui le font se doivent d'autant plus cherir les uns les autres & tâcher à s'entr'aider en se communiquant leurs observations & leurs pensées, ce que je vous offre de ma part avec toute sorte d'affection.

The work in which Descartes published his theory of the universe was published in 1644 by Louis Elzevir and was entitled *Principia philosophiae*; it was intended to contain six parts, but the last two were never written. Knowledge and the phenomena of the heavens and the earth are the subjects treated; the plan of the book contemplated further sections upon plants, animals, and men. The emancipation of natural philosophy from its position as a section of metaphysics was a result of this treatise.

It is from his letters, of which a large number remain, that we judge the fertility of Descartes's mathematical genius; many of these letters were replies to Père Mersenne, the Minim friar, who corresponded with the mathematicians of France, Italy, and Holland, acting as a kind of clearing-house for problems and new ideas. The problems were often used as challenges, and Descartes, as the writer of *La Géométrie*, found himself called upon to answer not only questions which arose in connexion with his own work but any problem which engaged at the moment the attention of any mathematician. The worthy Minim sent to Holland problems which do not seem to have been intended for Descartes; but these mathematical conundrums were solved with the ease and dexterity which reveal the true master. The area of the cycloid, the tangent to the roulette are solved as a reply to Roberval's challenge, and solutions of problems on numbers are provided for Fermat at Toulouse. The philosopher who left France for quiet found himself pursued by problems and controversies in his Dutch retreat, and these often arrived at a time when his mind was considering larger questions. Can we wonder that Descartes showed impatience, and that at times he renounced all mathematical problems and their solutions? In 1646 he wrote to Mersenne after a tiresome struggle with Roberval:

> Quoy qu'il en soit, je vous suplie, encore un coup, de ne m'envoyer jamais de sa part, ny aussy de la part d'aucun autre de ses semblables, je veux dire de ceux qui ne cherchent pas ingenuement la verité, mais taschent d'acquerir de la reputation en contredisant. Enfin je declare, des a present, que je ne sçay plus lire aucuns escrits, excepté les letres de mes amis, qui m'apprendront de leur nouvelles et en quoy j'auray moyen de les servir; comme aussy je n'escriray jamais plus rien, que des letres a mes amis, dont le suiet sera, *si vales, bene est*, &c. Je ne me mesle plus d'aucune science que pour mon instruction particuliere.

The philosopher who renounces mathematical disputations in this vigorous fashion is engaged in correspondence with Princess Elizabeth of Bohemia. The letters were written for the purpose of instructing the Princess in mathematics and ethics, and we have the letters of the pupil as well as those of the teacher. The letters of Descartes do not possess the charm of other parts of his correspondence, but persons of understanding will always be interested in the elegance of mind and the sweetness of character of the granddaughter of James, the first of England and the sixth of Scotland.

Princess Elizabeth was not the only lady of high birth who sought instruction from the philosopher; but his intercourse with Queen Christina of Sweden had tragic consequences. Induced by his friend Chanut, ambassador of France at Stockholm, Descartes left Holland on Sept. 11, 1649, to take up his residence near the young queen. The experiment was unsuccessful; life at Stockholm did not fulfil the philosopher's expectations. From letters we know that he intended to leave Sweden in the spring; but that was not to be; the northern winter proved fatal to him, and he died on Feb. 11, 1650. Mersenne had predeceased Descartes, and the series of letters from which we learn so much had terminated in 1648. An attempt was made by Carcavi to renew the correspondence, and Descartes welcomed the opportunity of hearing from his friends in Paris; but when Carcavi showed that his intention was to reopen the old controversy with Roberval which had been closed before Mersenne died, Descartes refused to write again.

Three mathematicians of commanding power and singular originality lived in France while Descartes was writing in Holland—Desargues, Fermat, Pascal. Descartes, though he corresponded with both Desargues and Fermat, never met either of these great contemporaries, nor did he realise the importance of their work. Pascal on the other hand was known personally to him, and a visit of Descartes to Pascal is described in a family letter from Jacqueline Pascal to her sister.

GIRARD DESARGUES (1593–1662) was born at Lyons. He came to Paris as an architect, and was well known to the circle of scholars who lived there and were interested in mathematical studies. Little is known of his life, but he returned to Lyons in 1650. He published in 1636 a work on Perspective in which a treatise by his disciple Bosse is included, and in 1638 a treatise on Conic Sections entitled *Brouillon Project d'une atteinte aux événements des rencontres d'un cône avec un plan*. Of the first of them a single copy exists; the latter was known only by an abridgement made in 1679 by La Hire and preserved in the

Bibliothèque de l'Institut until in 1845 a copy was discovered by Michel Chasles; this copy contained also an *Atteinte aux événemens des contrarietez d'entre les actions des puissances ou forces* under the title *Leçons de ténèbres*. Desargues's third work, which again is known by a single copy, is on a professional subject, *Brouillon Project d'exemple d'une manière universelle du S.G.D.L. touchant la practique du trait à preuves pour la coupe des pierres en l'Architecture; et de l'éclaircissement d'une manière de réduire au petit pied en perspective comme en géométral et de tracer tous quadrans plats d'heures égales en Soleil.*

Desargues engaged in violent dispute with two authors, Tavernier and Langlois, who pirated and mangled his work on Perspective; he placarded Paris with notices *Erreur incroyable*, etc. and *Fautes et faussetés énormes*, etc. There were retaliatory pamphlets, *Avis charitables sur les divers œuvres et feuilles volantes* du Sieur Girard Desargues, Lyonnais. The only relics of this typical controversy are the pamphlets of Desargues's unworthy opponents.

The great importance of Desargues's work was unrecognised until long after his death; its very originality stood in the way of ready acceptance, and it was further obscured by the introduction of a cloud of new terms. In order to emphasise the distinction between his own work and the ancient geometry, the author decided to discard the old notation as much as possible. Descartes in a letter pointed out the folly of this policy; if, wrote the philosopher, you are writing for scholars, there is no need to use terms other than those to which they are accustomed, but if you are writing for the curious, you will have to explain your meaning at very great length to "ces messieurs qui n'estudient qu'en baillant." Of all the cargo of new words one only remains in the science of pure geometry, and that holds the field because it was attached to a new and fertile idea, involution. Desargues's work was continued, rediscovered in part, by Poncelet in the beginning of the 19th century. Amongst his contemporaries Desargues found a disciple in Blaise Pascal. The real importance of the work of both master and pupil can be judged by the high place occupied to-day by projective geometry among mathematical sciences.

PIERRE DE FERMAT was born at Beaumont-en-Lomagne in 1601 and died at Castres in 1665. He was educated at Toulouse, where he passed his life, attaining the dignity of *conseiller au parlement*. He was well known to his contemporaries and esteemed as the finest geometer of his time; but this reputation did not rest upon printed works, as he published only one dissertation during his life and did not attach his name to it. He gained his fame by issuing his mathematical discoveries in the form of enunciations to his Paris friends. It is probable that Carcavi, who was transferred from the magistracy at Toulouse to Paris, introduced Fermat's work to Beaugrand, Frénicle, Roberval, and Mersenne, the latter of whom brought it to the notice of Descartes. Fermat also corresponded with Sir Kenelm Digby, and problems sent by him from Toulouse form the groundwork of the *Commercium Epistolicum* (Oxford, 1658) in which John Wallis exhibits a vivid and not always pleasing picture of the methods of some of our learned forefathers.

Fermat was distinguished by simplicity, candour, and generosity in all his relations with his correspondents. At the time of his death he was engaged upon the collection of his numerous papers, some on loose sheets and others written upon the margins of books. We owe the preservation of most of what remains of Fermat's work to the piety of his son, Samuel Fermat, who in 1670 published an edition of Bachet's *Diophantus*, in which were incorporated the observations of P. de Fermat, and *Doctrinae Analyticae inventum novum collectum Ex varijs eiusdem D. de Fermat epistolis*. This was followed by the publication in 1679 of *Varia opera mathematica D. Petri de Fermat, Senatoris Tolosani, accesserunt selectae quaedam ejusdem epistolae, vel ad ipsum à plerisque doctissimis viris Gallicè, Latinè vel Italicè, de rebus ad Mathematicas disciplinas, aut Physicam pertinentibus scriptae*. Unfortunately the letters are very incomplete; some of Fermat's correspondents perhaps did not reply to his son's invitation to contribute letters written to them, while one of them, Roberval, selected those which redounded to his own credit and recast even these. These two books are the main source of our knowledge of Fermat. His fame rests principally upon his discoveries in Arithmetic or the theory of numbers; the various problems are usually enunciated without proof, and the most remarkable of them were attached to the propositions of Diophantus or the commentary of Bachet, and written in the margin of the book. The so-called last theorem of Fermat is the second commentary upon Diophantus given in this way and has attained the widest fame; it has never been solved in its general form, though the greatest mathematicians have attacked it with varying success. The enunciation of the theorem and the author's comment are still worth citation:

cubum autem in duos cubos, aut quadrato-quadratum in duos quadrato-quadratos et generaliter nullam in infinitum ultra quadratum potestatem in duos ejusdem nominis, fas est dividere; cujus rei demonstrationem mirabilem sane detexi. Hanc marginis exiguitas non caperet.

Euler showed that there was no solution of $x^n + y^n = z^n$ when $n = 3$; Lagrange extended the proof to the case of $n = 4$; Legendre to $n = 5$; and others have gone farther, but no one has yet found the proof which the margin could not hold, nor has anyone disproved the theorem. In geometry Fermat arrived independently at the principles of Cartesian geometry, indeed his conception of a curve is in closer agreement with modern practice than that of his great contemporary. In the discussion of *maxima* and *minima* he anticipated the methods of Leibniz. In the tract *De Aequationum localium transmutatione* he writes upon problems of the integral calculus and arrives at results which are particular cases of integration by parts and change of the independent variable. In another sphere of mathematics Fermat showed his power by laying the foundations of the theory of probabilities. The subject arose from a problem submitted to him by Pascal regarding the proportions in which the stakes of an unfinished game of skill should be divided when the scores were taken into account. At the end of an amicable exchange of letters Pascal writes, "Je vois bien que la vérité est la même à Toulouse et à Paris."

The correspondence between Descartes and Fermat was not always amicable. Truth at Toulouse and in Holland were not always identical, and the differences were perhaps accentuated by temperament. "M. de Fermat est Gascon; moi, non," Descartes is reported to have said. But in the end Descartes frankly recognised the greatness of his rival; "Je n'ai jamais connu personne, qui m'ait fait paroistre qu'il scust tant que vous en Geometrie." The two men were profoundly different: Fermat was a pure mathematician whose imagination in the realms of space and number provided subjects of his analysis; Descartes studied pure mathematics because he needed them in his physical speculations. Fermat adhered to the old notation of symbols; Descartes adopted the newer methods. Descartes wrote in French, reserving Latin for metaphysics, while Fermat used Latin. A passage of a letter of Pascal to Fermat is of interest in this connexion; in the middle of a letter he breaks off with " Je vous le dirai en latin, car le français n'y vaut rien." The difference in language was not an essential distinction, but it was one of those straws which prove that Descartes discerned modern tendencies which neither Pascal nor Fermat saw.

The name of BLAISE PASCAL (1623–1662) is associated with the *Provinciales* and the *Pensées* more than with mathematical and physical discoveries. But it is impossible to study either Pascal or Descartes from one side only; in their aesthetic development both owed much to their mathematical studies. One difference between them is fundamental. In Descartes's life the streams of philosophy and mathematics flowed fairly evenly side by side; in Pascal's there were periods in which mathematics were completely banished; the first conversion separated two periods of mathematical study, while the second was divided or interrupted by an interval in which important mathematical discoveries were published.

Born at Clermont on June 19, 1623, the young Pascal was taken to Paris at the age of seven. Here he showed such aptitude and interest that he was admitted as a boy to the meetings at which Étienne Pascal (his father), Mersenne, Mydorge, Roberval, Desargues and others discussed the new mathematical and physical speculations. At the age of sixteen Pascal wrote a treatise on conic sections; this was abstracted in 1639–40 under the title of *Essai pour les coniques*, and Mersenne sent the abstract to Descartes. The philosopher was not in sufficient sympathy with Desargues's work to understand the importance of the young author's discoveries. The full treatise was never published, but we know its contents from a letter of Leibniz, who, in 1676, saw the manuscript in Paris and suggested its publication. There is no doubt of the fertility and originality of Pascal's early geometrical work; Desargues and Pascal advanced the study of geometry into regions where no writer followed for more than a century and a half. Geometry was not the only subject at which Pascal, as a boy, worked; at an early age he devoted himself to the construction of a calculating machine. Study was frequently interrupted by serious illness; but even on his sick bed in 1646 Pascal was occupied with theorems of the vacuum, and in 1647 he published a book, *Nouvelles expériences touchant le vide*, which aroused general interest. On November 16, 1647, he wrote to his brother-in-law and detailed experiments which he desired to be made upon the Puy-de-Dôme. It was not however until September 19, 1648, that these experiments were carried out, and the difference ot the lengths of the column of mercury at two heights proved to be proportional to the difference of the altitudes of the two places of observation. The problem was discussed by Descartes with Pascal at visits paid by the former in Paris on September 23 and 24, 1647. It is unnecessary to apportion how much is due to one and to the other in this matter; great men share discoveries more easily than lesser men choose to allow. In 1651 Pascal wrote the *Traité de l'équilibre des liqueurs* and the *Traité de la pesanteur de l'air*; in these he lays down the theory of the equilibrium of gases and liquids. In 1653–4 he wrote the *Traité du triangle arithmétique* and the *Traité des ordres numériques*. About this time he corresponded with Fermat on the theory of probability, and, to the satisfaction of both, their conclusions were found to be in accord. At Port-Royal in 1658 Pascal again turned to mathematics, and in sleepless nights meditated upon problems which are now recognised as part of the infinitesimal calculus. The geometrical properties of the cycloid had occupied the attention of mathematicians for many years, and Pascal applied the method of indivisibles of Cavalieri to the discovery of very remarkable properties of the curve. He published his work by issuing through Carcavi a challenge with a prize to any who before a certain date sent a solution. His own solution was published under the name of Amos Dettonville, an anagram of Loüis de Montalte, the name of the author of the *Provinciales*. The skill of Pascal as shown in these problems places him high among those mathematicians whose work was crowned by the discoveries of Newton and Leibniz.

In 1660 he had renounced mathematical study for the last time; and when Fermat, also broken in health, wrote suggesting a meeting, Pascal is unable to make the exertion necessary to meet his old correspondent, though he esteems him the greatest man in the world. He writes:

mais il y a maintenant ceci de plus en moi que je suis dans les études si éloignées de cet esprit-là [geometry] qu'à peine me souviens-je qu'il y en ait. Je m'y étais mis, il y a un an ou deux, pour une raison tout à fait singulière, à la quelle ayant satisfaite, je suis au hasard de ne jamais plus penser.

These words were written by one whose natural aptitude for geometry may have been equalled but has rarely been surpassed.

Of the less important contemporaries of Descartes, mention may be made of GILLES PERSONNE DE ROBERVAL (1602–1675). He held the chair of mathematics in Paris at the Royal College for more than forty years and, while displaying fertility and ingenuity in mathematical speculation, proved that these virtues are sometimes divorced from amiability. During a period in which honourable traditions of courtesy and cooperation were established Roberval adhered to the older methods. His name is associated with the Roberval balance and the theory of roulettes; if he had not wilfully held back what he called his method of *indivisibles*, he would have had more credit both in his own and in our day for the discovery of processes which heralded the birth of the infinitesimal calculus.

The vicissitudes which the work of Fermat and Desargues suffered demonstrate the value of a central institution which encourages scientific cooperation and records contemporary work. Such institutions were created in Italy at an early date, the *Accademia dei Lincei* having been founded in 1603; their importance must have been recognised by the group of French mathematicians who met regularly in Paris in the middle of the 17th century, their guiding spirit being Père Mersenne. He died in 1648, eighteen years before the foundation of the *Académie des Sciences*, but his labours had accustomed his fellow-workers to the advantages of keeping in touch with the world outside Paris, and rendered them familiar with the methods of establishing and effecting cooperation. The *Académie des Sciences* was founded in 1666 and supported by royal bounty; it conferred pensions upon the academicians and enjoyed a grant of 12,000 livres for experiments and the purchase of instruments. The first list of academicians contains the names of Carcavi, Huygens, Roberval, Frénicle, Auzout, Picard, and Buot. The Proceedings of the Academy were published in 1699 as *Histoire de l'Académie...avec des mémoires de mathématique et de physique*, but the *Journal des Savants* appeared in 1665; it was founded to promulgate the discoveries of the group whose names are given above, and was endowed by Colbert. The new journal was followed in Italy by the *Giornale dei Literati* and in Germany by the *Acta eruditorum*.

The institution of the *Académie royale des Sciences* in Paris and of the sister Royal Society in London was followed by the establishment in London and Paris of astronomical observatories. These observatories played a notable part in the advancement of science in the 18th century, and French mathematicians recognised their importance. The Observatory at Paris was placed under the charge of the *Académie des Sciences*; its first chief was GIOVANNI DOMENICO CASSINI (1625–1712). This distinguished astronomer was Italian by birth, and at the age of twenty-five was chosen to occupy the chair of astronomy at Bologna. Here he conducted a notable series of observations, by which the value of the obliquity of the ecliptic was determined and the alteration of the position of stars due to refraction was established; at Rome in the presence of the Queen of Sweden, Descartes's pupil, he observed a new comet and amongst other discoveries in the period 1665–8 he ascertained the periods of revolution of Jupiter, Venus, and Mercury and published ephemerides of the satellites of Jupiter. At Bologna and at Rome his reputation as an engineer was high. But Colbert induced him to visit France and the visit was prolonged until France became his home; in 1673 he was naturalised on the occasion of his marriage. At Paris in the new Observatory he determined the period of rotation of the Sun, discovered several satellites of Saturn and made measurements of the

length of an arc of the meridian. He was the first of a distinguished family whose names are associated with the Paris
Observatory.

He was succeeded in direct line by Jacques Cassini (1677–
1756), César-François Cassini (1714–1784), Jacques-Dominique
Cassini (1748–1845). The Observatory became independent of
the Academy in 1771. The long connexion between the Academy, the Observatory, and the family of Cassini is remarkable
not only for astronomical progress but also for the great geodetical work carried out. In this period the map of France was
correctly determined as well as the position of a series of places
outside France, and the first correct measurement of an arc of
meridian was effected. The calculations made in the great survey
by Picard allowed Newton to revise his earlier calculations on
the motion of the moon, and justified him in continuing his
speculations on gravitation. Officials organised the work, but
their success was due to their association through the Academy
with men trained in theory; some of the French mathematicians
who were engaged upon geodetical work are Maupertuis,
Clairaut, Legendre, Deleambre, and Arago.

In another branch of studies closely related to mathematics
France has led the way, and it is convenient to mention this
sphere of work before turning to the mathematicians of the
18th century. The first history of mathematics was attempted
by Claude-François Dechales (1611–1678) who wrote a *Cursus
seu mundus mathematicus* (1670); appended to the second edition
of this work appeared a *Tractatus procemialis de progressu mathe-
seos et illustribus mathematicis* (1690). This humble beginning was
followed by the more ambitious work of Jean-Étienne Montucla
(1728–1799), who in 1758 published in two volumes his *Histoire
des mathématiques*. This work was edited and extended in 1799
and is still of great interest. The memoirs of the *Académie des
Sciences* furnish a contemporary commentary upon the history
of science in the form of memoirs of the lives of the academicians.

§ II. EIGHTEENTH CENTURY

In the first half of the 18th century the great studies founded
by Descartes, Newton, and Leibniz were developed, but it
was not France that took the lead in this work. It is Holland

and Switzerland that we associate with the achievement of Huygens, Euler, and the Bernoullis. But though the greatest work was not performed by Frenchmen, France has a long roll of names which occupy an honourable place; Abraham de Moivre (1667–1754), Jacques Ozanam (1640–1717), Philippe de La Hire (1640–1718), Guillaume-François de l'Hôpital (1661–1704), Antoine Parent (1666–1716), Joseph Saurin (1659–1737), Pierre Varignon (1654–1722), all did work of permanent value.

The career of VARIGNON illustrates the changed conditions under which work was carried on at this period. Varignon was born at Caen and educated at the Jesuit college; a copy of Euclid found in a bookseller's shop turned his attention to mathematics. A generous fellow-student, the Abbé de Saint-Pierre, provided a modest allowance for his impecunious companion; with this support Varignon is able to go to Paris where he studies mechanics and anatomy and meets members of the Academy. In 1687 he publishes a *Projet d'une nouvelle mécanique*, which is dedicated to the Academy. This work procures for its author admission to the Academy and a professorship at the Mazarin college. In 1690 Varignon writes *Nouvelles conjectures sur la Pesanteur*. Fully launched on his career, he now engages in those seemingly interminable controversies which surrounded the early stages of the infinitesimal calculus. He enters into correspondence with the great mathematicians, contributes regularly to the proceedings of the Academy and becomes a corresponding member of the Academies of England and Prussia. In spite of teaching duties and correspondence he prepares a large and valuable treatise upon mechanics. This was not however published until after his death; it is a monument of his scholarship, and contains the theorem of moments which will always be associated with his name.

In the first half of the 18th century the *Académie des Sciences* was established after many vicissitudes upon a firm basis; in the revival of mathematical studies in the second half of the century it played an important part by encouraging youthful talent. The system of adjoint and associate members gave direct support to the younger men; we find these junior members taking part in the weekly meetings of the Academy and reporting upon papers. In the second half of the 18th century the work of Descartes and Newton was carried forward by brilliant and original thinkers into new fields; two names are associated with the new epoch: ALEXIS-CLAUDE CLAIRAUT (1713–1765) and JEAN LE ROND D'ALEMBERT (1717–1783). Their careers, while proving the impossibility of prescribing the way in which genius works, unite in demonstrating the value of the help which an academy may render to youthful ability. Clairaut was taught at home, the second of a family of twenty-one, the father being a teacher of mathematics and a fellow of the Royal Prussian Academy of Sciences. Precocious even amongst those most remarkable for the exhibition of early powers, the young Clairaut was wisely restrained and then skilfully directed. His first mathematical paper was written at the age of thirteen; a paper on curves in space obtained his admission to the *Académie des Sciences* at the age of eighteen *en qualité d'adjoint mécanicien*; the qualifying age of twenty was reduced in his case by special resolution. On the other hand d'Alembert was abandoned as an infant on the steps of the little church of Saint-Jean-le-Rond (now demolished) from which he takes his name, and was brought up in the family of a glazier in humble circumstances. The child was not however permanently left to himself, as his father provided for his education at the *Collège des Quatre-Nations*. Jean le Rond graduated bachelor of arts at eighteen and was admitted *licencié-en-droit* in 1738; he took up the study of medicine, but, finding geometry absorbed his attention, he decided to devote his life to science and to live on the annual allowance of 1200 livres which his father assigned. He turned to mathematics, and it is interesting to note that his second communication to the Academy was reported upon by Clairaut in 1740. At the age of twenty-four, in 1741, he was elected *adjoint astronome*, and in 1746 became *associé géomètre*; but it was not until 1765 that he became *pensionnaire titulaire* with the full rank of member.

Clairaut after his early success was appointed with Maupertuis to measure an arc of the meridian; he visited Lapland, and published his *Théorie de la figure de la terre*, 1743. This work was followed by a study of lunar inequalities and the problem of three bodies. He published the *Théorie de la lune* in 1752 and 1765, and the *Prédiction du retour de la comète de 1682* in 1760. In pure mathematics his name is associated with the theory of the singular solutions of differential equations.

The first notable contribution to mathematics of d'Alembert is the *Traité de dynamique* (1743); it contains the enunciation of the celebrated principle which did so much to advance dynamical science. This book was followed by the *Traité de l'équilibre et du mouvement des fluides* (1744) and the *Réflexions sur la cause générale des vents* (1744). In these treatises d'Alembert investigated partial differential equations, then an unexplored field; the dedication of the second edition of the latter book in 1747 introduced him to the notice of Frederick of Prussia, who caused him to be elected a member of the Prussian Academy. The presidency of this academy was offered to him in 1752, and in 1754 Frederick made him an annual grant of 1200 livres. In 1747 d'Alembert obtained the solution of the differential equation to which he had reduced the vibrations of a stretched string; this is the starting-point of much of the work on mathematical functions which was done in the 19th century. He also continued his work on the problems of astronomy, investigating the precession of the equinoxes and the obliquity of the ecliptic; these papers were collected in the *Système du monde* (1754–1756).

Clairaut and d'Alembert died before the Revolution, but their successors took part in the great political upheaval of the end of the century, some on scientific commissions, others on active service and most of them in the great schemes by which Napoleon recast the French educational system. In the new model there was one feature which gave a remarkable impulse to mathematical studies, the establishment of schools of higher studies in intimate relation with the state service. The *École Normale* and the *École Polytechnique* have since their foundation provided regular courses in higher instruction; how important this work proved will be seen by the part which these schools played in the lives of the mathematicians of the 19th century. But before dealing with this period two great mathematicians have to be considered, Laplace, who in a certain sense continued and completed Clairaut's work, and Lagrange, who may be regarded as d'Alembert's successor.

JOSEPH-LOUIS LAGRANGE (1736–1813) was born at Turin, his grandfather having settled in Italy. It is his close association with the educational system of France as well as his parentage that justify us in calling Lagrange a French mathematician. A tract by Halley first fired his imagination, and two years of close application enabled him to master the theory of mathematics; at the age of nineteen he communicated to Euler a general method of dealing with isoperimetric problems which became the basis of the calculus of variations. Euler wrote generous encouragement to his young correspondent, but even before the arrival of his letter Lagrange was appointed professor of geometry in the military school of Turin. Here he took a prominent part in the establishment of the learned society which in 1784 became the Academy of Turin; in its proceedings, *Miscellanea Taurinensia*, a paper entitled *Recherches sur la nature et le propagation du son* appeared, in which he solved a problem which had engaged the attention of Newton, d'Alembert, and Euler. In subsequent papers he foreshadowed the reduction of mechanical problems to differential equations. From Turin he gained on five occasions the prizes offered by the *Académie des Sciences* of Paris for essays on subjects connected with astronomy. The years from 1766 to 1787 were spent in Berlin, where he succeeded Euler as director of the mathematical department of the Academy; in these years he wrote the *Mécanique analytique,* the sequel to Newton's *Principia*. At this period his mind was so active that every branch of mathematics was enriched by his work, and yet in all there was unity of conception. His task was the reduction of mechanics to analytical processes; the development of the differential and integral calculus with the investigation of differential equations formed one side of his work, while in problems of mathematical astronomy he found the great field of application for his theory. In the study of planetary disturbances and the stability of the solar system, Lagrange touched problems which were beyond the reach of his predecessors. The death of the King of Prussia released Lagrange from residence in Berlin, and in 1787 he came to Paris and received the honour due to his great achievement. But Paris at first gave no inspiration; melancholia succeeded enthusiasm, and it is related that for two years the pages of the *Mécanique analytique,* the printing of which had been supervised by Legendre, lay unopened on their author's study table. The Revolution came and seems to have aroused him to the exercise of his powers. Exempted by name from the proclamation which banished all foreigners, he gave his powerful help in the introduction of the metric system of weights and measures; in 1795 he was appointed professor at the *École Normale* and in 1797 at the *École Polytechnique,* where he exercised a far-reaching influence upon his students. In 1810 Lagrange began a revision of the *Mécanique analytique* which was however never completed; he died on April 8, 1813, and was buried in the Panthéon.

PIERRE-SIMON LAPLACE (1749–1827) was born at Beaumont-en-Auge. The son of a small farmer, he owed his education to the interest which his early promise aroused in a wealthy neighbour. At a later stage, d'Alembert, always a generous friend to merit, came to his assistance and obtained for him a professorship at the *École militaire* at Paris; admitted in his twenty-fourth year to the Academy as *adjoint mécanicien,* he entered upon a career in which he earned the title of the Newton of France. In his great work, the *Mécanique céleste* (1799–1825), Laplace gave the first complete mathematical account of the solar system, bringing theory and observation into agreement. The nebular hypothesis was first stated in the *Exposition du système du monde* (1796); it was the basis of much interesting and fruitful speculation. Laplace was an applied mathematician; he looked to the physical world for the problems to which he applied his mathematical skill. But he also possessed the skill of the pure mathematician; it was in the discussion of the problem of a rotating mass of fluid under its own attraction that he introduced Laplace's coefficients and the potential function. Two other notable works are *Théorie des probabilités* (1812) and *Essai philosophique sur les probabilités* (1814). Laplace's career was one of uninterrupted prosperity; he was an associate of the Academy at the age of twenty-four, a full member at thirty-six; he held an official position at the *Bureau des longitudes* and at the *École Normale;* he sat on the commission which introduced the decimal system. His political fortune was distinguished by all the outward signs of success; in the republic, the empire, and the monarchy he reaped the fruit of his great scientific reputation and became Count and Marquis. There is however reason to doubt whether his administrative capacity equalled the profound scientific insight which he brought to bear upon mathematical and astronomical investigations.

In ADRIEN-MARIE LEGENDRE (1752–1833) we have another type. The genius which blazes forth in so many French mathematicians when young men was not shown by him; it was not until he was thirty that he gained the prize of the Berlin Academy by a paper on ballistics, and a year later he entered the *Académie des Sciences* at d'Alembert's death. His early work was geodetical and astronomical, and he was a member of the commission which determined the relative positions of Paris and Greenwich. His work on the theory of numbers is of first-rate importance; his discovery of quadratic reciprocity linked up French studies in this subject with Fermat's work. Legendre published the *Essai sur la théorie des nombres* in 1798, three years before Gauss wrote the *Disquisitiones arithmeticae*; thus the closing years of the 18th century and the opening years of the 19th saw the rebirth of a most fertile branch of modern pure mathematics. Another subject with which Legendre's name will always be associated is elliptic functions. For forty years, 1786–1827, he laboured patiently at elliptic integrals, calculating tables and meditating profoundly upon the theory, and then at the age of seventy-five he found the subject suddenly transformed by the independent discoveries of Abel and Jacobi. It is pleasing to record that the veteran welcomed the new work and incorporated it in a supplement of his own book. Legendre's power as a calculator was utilised in the great French tables of logarithms called the *Table du cadastre*; in the theory of the attraction of ellipsoids he introduced the coefficients known now by his name. He is famous also as the author of the *Éléments de la géométrie* (1794); the book displaced the text-book of Euclid in France and aroused interest in the parallel-postulate. Ingenious as Legendre's work is, it received additional importance from the discovery of non-Euclidean geometry in Eastern Europe. Legendre's great achievements become fascinatingly interesting when we notice how he just passed turnings which led others to greater discoveries; perhaps the new ways were invisible except to the eyes of youth.

GASPARD MONGE (1746–1818) is a geometrician whose name is associated with descriptive geometry, differential equations, and the theory of surfaces. His work in geometry stands side by side with that of Lazare Carnot, Brianchon, and Poncelet. These writers are responsible for the modern interest in a subject which had slept since the days of Desargues and Pascal. JEAN-VICTOR PONCELET (1788–1867) served in the Russian campaign, and was captured and imprisoned at Saratov in 1813. Here, cut off from books and other help, he set himself to follow out the consequences of certain theorems which he had already obtained. The results of his work are embodied in the *Traité des propriétés projectives*, published in 1822, and reported upon to the Academy by Poisson, Arago, and Cauchy.

§ III. NINETEENTH CENTURY

Lagrange and Laplace completed the cycle of thought which commenced with Descartes and Newton. A new era was opened in the first quarter of the 19th century by the study of the general forms of mathematical functions. In France the names particularly associated with this study are Fourier and Cauchy.

JEAN-BAPTISTE-JOSEPH FOURIER (1768–1830) was born at Auxerre of humble parentage. His admission to the military school of his native town, then under clerical direction, was due to the interest aroused in a patroness by his talents. Debarred by his social position from entering the army, he became a professor, but no drawback could hinder his scientific advance. In Paris he occupied a chair first at the *École Normale*, and later (1795–8) at the *Ecole Polytechnique*; then, called to Egypt by Napoleon, he commenced a political career distinguished by high success.

In 1789 he presented to the *Académie des Sciences* a paper written two years earlier *Sur la résolution des équations numériques de degré quelconque*. In 1807 he communicated an unpublished paper upon the conduction of heat: this paper has been recently discovered. In 1812 he obtained the prize of the Academy with a memoir, *Théorie des mouvements de la chaleur dans les corps solides*. The first part of this memoir was incorporated in 1822 in the *Théorie de la chaleur*, one of the great classics of mathematical physics. Fourier published papers in the *Annales de chimie et de physique* and wrote upon the theory of equations and statics. Like Laplace, Fourier was a mathematical physicist deriving the inspiration of his work from the phenomena of nature. The mathematical problem to which he applied himself had been discussed by d'Alembert, Euler, and Bernoulli, but Fourier's name will always be attached to the series of sines of multiples of a variable, for he was the first to perceive the nature of the functions represented by such a series. Fourier saw in them a means of attacking the physical problems which engaged his attention; he did not, he could not, know that his work would prove the basis of much modern analysis. His attitude to his own and to other studies is sufficiently indicated by an extract from the preliminary discourse of his great work.

L'étude approfondie de la nature est la source la plus féconde des découvertes mathématiques. Non seulement cet étude, en offrant aux recherches un but déterminé, a l'avantage d'exclure des questions vagues et les calculs sans issue; elle est encore un moyen assuré de former l'analyse elle-même, et d'en découvrir les éléments qu'il nous importe le plus de connaître, et que cette science doit toujours conserver; les éléments fondamentaux sont ceux qui se reproduisent dans tous les effets naturels.

AUGUSTIN-LOUIS CAUCHY (1789–1857) was born at Paris and received his early education from his father, a friend of Lagrange and Laplace, and subsequently attended the *École centrale du Panthéon.* Turning to mathematics, he gained after ten months' preparation the second place in the admission to the *École Polytechnique* and proceeded to the *École des ponts et chaussées.* But his success in pure science decided him to abandon engineering and adopt mathematics as a profession. In 1815 he gained the prize of the Academy for an essay on the propagation of waves. After the restoration the names of Monge and Carnot were struck from the list of the Institute and those of Briquet and Cauchy substituted. From 1816–30 Cauchy taught mechanics at the *École Polytechnique,* higher algebra at the *Faculté des sciences,* and physics at the *Collège de France.* In three years he played an important part in introducing the more exact logical methods which distinguish mathematics in the 19th century. At the revolution of 1830 he relinquished his posts, being unable to take the oaths, and left France. At Turin, 1831, he occupied a chair of *Physique sublime*, and undertook the tutelage of the grandson of the deposed Charles X. In 1848 he returned to France and resumed his post at the *École Polytechnique*; after the *coup d'état* he was exempted from the obligation of taking the oath.

As a mathematician Cauchy is remarkable for the range and number of his papers; he was a regular contributor at the weekly meetings of the Academy. He wrote upon geometry, theory of numbers, phys¹c₃ and astronomy, but his principal contributions were devot₃d to the establishment of the principles of the differential and integral calculus and to the construction of the theory of functions of a complex variable.

Louis Poinsot (1777–1859), André-Marie Ampère (1775–1836), Jean-Baptiste Biot (1774–1862), Siméon-Denis Poisson (1781–1840), François-Jean-Dominique Arago (1786–1853), Augustin-Jean Fresnel (1788–1827), Joseph-Louis Gay-Lussac (1788–1850), Gabriel Lamé (1795–1870), Urbain-Jean-Joseph Leverrier (1811–1877), Jean-Bernard-Léon Foucault (1819–1868) form a group of mathematicians and physicists trained in the *École Polytechnique*, where some of them were pupils of Lagrange. The modern theories of optics, heat, electricity, magnetism, elasticity, attractions, and dynamics rest largely upon their labours. Their scientific papers were published mainly in the *Annales de chimie et de physique*, founded by Arago and Gay-Lussac in 1816, and in the *Comptes rendus*, the great scientific journal issued in 1830 to supplement the *Mémoires de l'Académie des Sciences*. The dominating personality in this group is ARAGO; it was his eloquence combined with political sagacity which did much to establish the national faith in science which is so peculiar to France. It was under Arago's advice that a national system of canals and railways was designed and artesian wells made; it was also on his initiative that the chamber voted honour to Fermat, Daguerre, and Laplace. All democratic people believe that the highest honours are those that the nation's representatives sitting in council confer by their direct vote; France was the first country to confer such honour upon men of science.

Leverrier's name is widely known by the startling discovery of the planet Neptune. It was as a chemist in the laboratories of Gay-Lussac that he did his first scientific work, but he soon abandoned chemistry in favour of mathematical astronomy. It was by the advice of Arago that he undertook the great task of revising the tables giving the positions of the planets. In 1846, as a consequence of profound study of the irregularities in the movement of Uranus, he was able to announce to the *Académie des Sciences* the position of a new planet. This discovery, the result of patient scientific work of the highest order, brought Leverrier before the notice of every civilised country; he was the recipient of countless honours and distinctions. The achievement was so great that it was not diminished by the fact that the Cambridge student, John Couch Adams, arrived almost at the same time at the same result; the scientific world followed the lead of the Royal Society in awarding the Copley medal and divided the honour of the discovery of Neptune between the two astronomers. France elected Leverrier a member of the Legislative Assembly, but his genius was not political, nor did he succeed as an administrator when he followed Arago as Director of the Observatory. The great task of his life was the revision of the planetary tables, and this he just lived to complete, the last proofs being placed in his hands a few weeks before he died.

Even in a country so generous as France great men have lived whose work has remained unrecognised. Fermat and Desargues were acknowledged by those who lived and worked with them, but Sadi Carnot and Évariste Galois had no recognition in their lives, and were hardly saved from oblivion by the labours of the succeeding generation.

SADI-NICOLAS-LÉONHARD CARNOT (1796–1832) was the eldest son of Lazare Carnot, the great geometer who organised victory for the young republic. He was admitted to the *École Polytechnique* in 1812, but the services of the father stood in the way of the son's advancement in the period which followed the restoration. Carnot resigned his commission in the army in 1827; but already in 1824 he had published his only book, *Réflexions sur la puissance motrice du feu et sur les machines propres à développer cette puissance*. Though the importance of this book was not recognised for twenty-five years, its author is now known as one of the founders of the science of thermodynamics. An ardent student over the widest range of knowledge, Carnot weakened his health by excessive study, and died at the age of thirty-six.

ÉVARISTE GALOIS (1811-1832) is another of the many instances which prove that in France, at any rate, genius for mathematics may be exhibited at an early age. Galois was educated at the *Collège Louis-le-Grand*; being dissatisfied with the ordinary text-books, he turned at the age of fifteen to the works of Lagrange. At the age of seventeen he had made discoveries of the highest importance. Two memoirs presented to the *Académie des Sciences* have been lost, but in the *Bulletin de Férussac* of 1830 a two-page abstract of a memoir upon the algebraic resolution of equations shows that he had then obtained the results which under the name of the Galoisian resolvent now play a fundamental part in the theory. The papers published during his lifetime are all slight and bear the date of 1830. Galois's life was short and full of trouble. Rejected at the entrance examination of the *École Polytechnique*, he entered the *École Normale* in 1829, but was obliged to leave in 1830. In the last years of his short life he was involved in political agitation and passed several months in gaol; he was killed in a duel at the age of twenty-one. What is known of his work is derived principally from a letter written to his friend Auguste Chevalier on the night preceding the fatal duel. This letter was published in the *Revue encyclopédique* in 1832, but the editors did not carry out their intention of publishing the manuscript left by Galois. In 1846 Liouville published two of his papers, namely, *Mémoire sur la condition de résolubilité des équations par des radicaux* and *Des équations primitives qui sont solubles par des radicaux*.

It is impossible to write of Galois without being reminded of his comrade in genius who wrote

> When I have fears that I may cease to be
> Before my pen has gleaned my teeming brain.

John Keats and Évariste Galois are alike in genius and in promise. But while Keats received some measure of recognition in his lifetime, it was years before Galois's work was noticed. Indeed though Cauchy and others had studied the theory of groups no one realised their importance in the theory of equations. Of Galois's other writings nothing remains but his own parting references in the letter to Chevalier, but from these it has been conjectured that he was in possession of important theorems which now form the basis of the theory of algebraic functions. The editor of the thin volume of his collected works writes

L'influence de Galois, s'il eût vécu, aurait grandement modifié l'orientation des recherches mathématiques de ce siècle dans notre pays—aucun des grands mathématiciens de ce siècle ne le surpasse par l'originalité et le profondeur de ses conceptions.

Mathematics of yesterday and to-day are largely the outcome of the work of Fourier, Cauchy, and Galois, and their writings illustrate the double aspect of the subject. Fourier, as we have seen, was no believer in pure mathematics, a branch in which Galois's work entirely lay. By a sly stroke of fortune, it is from the work of Fourier that the most abstract of modern speculations of pure mathematics has grown. Mathematical analysis will always be one of the chief weapons by which knowledge of the universe is obtained, but greater than analysis, because containing it, are the conceptions of form and number, which constitute the problem of pure mathematics. It is the secret of French genius that an instinct for pure mathematics has always inspired its greatest mathematicians even when they seemed least conscious of the influence.

In the reconstruction of studies after 1870 the names of three great mathematicians may be recorded: CHARLES HERMITE (1822–1901), who proved a wise guide in the reorganisation which followed the crisis and whose work in the theory of functions and of numbers is of permanent value; JEAN-GASTON DARBOUX (1842–1917), who indicated the path of advance in geometry and differential equations; and JULES-HENRI POINCARÉ (1854–1912), one of those geniuses who find a field of activity in every branch of the subject which they enter.

To-day a large and increasing band of devoted mathematicians is engaged in advancing the great work of their predecessors. The *Encyclopédie des sciences mathématiques*, even in its unfinished bulk, is one of the monuments which attests their wide scholarship and varied activity.

BIBLIOGRAPHY

J.-E. Montucla, *Histoire des Mathématiques*, 2 vols. 1758. M. Marie, *Histoire des sciences mathématiques et physiques*, 12 vols. 1883–1888. M. Cantor, *Vorlesungen über die Geschichte der Mathematik*, 4 vols. 2nd ed. Leipsic, 1894–1908. M. Chasles, *Aperçu historique sur l'origine et le développement des méthodes de géométrie*, 2nd ed. 1875. W. W. Rouse Ball, *A short account of the history of Mathematics*, 1888. R. Grant, *History of physical astronomy*, 2nd ed. 1852. R. Wolf, *Geschichte der Astronomie*, Munich, 1877.

Descartes, *Œuvres*, edd. C. Adam and P. Tannery, 11 vols. 1897–Fermat, *Œuvres*, edd. P. Tannery and C. Henry, 4 vols. 1912. Desargues, *Œuvres*, ed. Poudra, 2 vols. 1864. Pascal, *Œuvres*, edd. L. Brunschvicq and P. Boutroux, 3 vols. 1908. Lagrange, *Œuvres*, ed. M.-J.-A. Serret, 14 vols. 1867–1892. Arago, *Œuvres*, ed. J.-A. Barral, 17 vols. 1854–1862.

CHAPTER XV

SCIENCE

§ I. THE BIOLOGICAL SCIENCES

In biological science useful work in France, or indeed elsewhere, hardly begins before the middle of the 18th century. At that period René-Antoine Ferchault de Réaumur (1683–1757) was at work in various branches and was leaving durable traces in each. It may be said that he was the first naturalist in the complete sense of the word. He did not confine himself to the collection and description of animals, but observed their manner of life and noted down their habits. Six thick octavo volumes which appeared between 1734 and 1742 (*Mémoires pour servir à l'histoire des Insectes*) contain the results of his researches, and inaugurate the science of behaviour (*comportement*), long neglected in the past but rapidly developing in our own day. Réaumur describes and makes no attempt to explain; but he describes with precision, and, remote though he is in point of time, it is impossible to undertake researches of the same order without taking his descriptions into serious consideration. Moreover, Réaumur was not without influence in his own day; and it is sufficient to recall that, in Sweden, De Geer both followed and rivalled him.

A few years his junior, Jean-Louis Leclerc, Comte de Buffon (1707–88), exercised a great and enduring influence upon natural history studies. His work bears upon various branches of zoology. If in the main morphological, it also touches on the habits of animals. It comprises, further, personal discoveries and views of a general character. It must not be forgotten that, if the discovery of fossil animals, due to Bernard Palissy, goes back to so early a date as 1580, Buffon investigated the dispersion of fossil shells, distinguished pelagic from littoral forms, recognised the extinction of some, and the first appearance of others, and had an inkling of the immensity of the geological periods.

The 18th century, too, marks an important stage in the process of classification. In 1789 appeared Antoine-Laurent de Jussieu's (1748–1836) *Genera Plantarum* conceived on an entirely new plan. He replaced Linnaeus's artificial system by the natural method, on the value of which time has set its seal.

About the same period the problem of what constitutes life and with it the experimental study of biology came to the fore. In 1777 Antoine-Laurent Lavoisier (1743–94) published his experiments on the respiration of animals and the changes which the air undergoes in passing through the lungs. He established that that portion of the air which is utilised in respiration is the oxygen, while the nitrogen remains unutilised. This discovery dealt a decisive blow at the phlogiston theory which then reigned supreme. In his later works, two of which were written in collaboration with Armand Séguin, Lavoisier further developed his discovery. By means of accurate measurements and a remarkable instrumental apparatus he laid down the quantitative variations of air breathed under various conditions; he noted the relations between respiration and the heat emitted by animals and concluded that respiration corresponds with a process of combustion. By thus laying the foundations of a physio-chemical explanation of the phenomena of life, he opened the way for all the studies of physiology and energy.

A few years later Xavier Bichat (1771–1802) contributed under a different form to the regeneration of physiology. While Lavoisier was destroying Stahl's sterile doctrine of phlogiston, Bichat aimed the first blow at vitalism, by depriving it of its metaphysical atmosphere and turning it into a scientific conception. Instead of conceiving an intangible principle which gave the illusion of an explanation rendering all research superfluous, Bichat faced the problem of the material properties of the tissues of the organs. It is true that without defining precisely the nature of these *vital properties* he opposes them to non-vital properties, and consequently appears to say that organised beings differ essentially from inorganic objects; he even declares definitely that these vital properties are distinct from physical properties and sees an antagonism between them— the latter tending constantly to destroy bodies animated by the former. Vital properties thus acquire the character of metaphysical entities, and this is wherein Bichat's error consists. But freed from this error, which is not an essential part of them, Bichat's views form the solid foundation of all modern physiology. Inasmuch as Bichat saw life incarnated in the tissues and connected its manifestations with the properties of the same tissues, he made life accessible to scientific analysis. Henceforward physiologists and physicians sought the explanation of vital phenomena in the condition of the tissues and traced disturbances in the working of the organs to deteriorations in their constituent elements. Moreover the radical opposition which Bichat supposed to exist between vital and physical properties grew progressively less under the influence of the continuous progress of physical and chemical science.

François Magendie (1783–1855) was one of the first to devote himself to estimating the true value of vital properties and to show that in a certain number of cases they can be reduced to physical properties having play under determined conditions. He thus inaugurated modern experimental physiology. He was himself a judicious experimenter who approached very varied subjects, among which must be noted his researches into the distinction between motor and sensory nerves. The English physiologist, Charles Bell, had established this distinction in 1811 on the basis of anatomico-physiological considerations which rendered it extremely probable. Magendie demonstrated it by experimental proof (1822).

About the same period Marie-Jean-Pierre Flourens (1794–1867) published his researches on the nervous system, attempting to determine the special functions of the various portions of the brain. These researches undoubtedly threw a certain light on the subject. He demonstrated the relative importance of the brain and of the medulla; drew attention to the part played by the cerebellum in equilibrium, and was the first to give the notion of *nervous centres* by his experiments on the vital nodes. But above all he had a clear view of the relations which exist between the mental manifestations of man and those of animals.

These researches constitute to an appreciable degree the starting-point of our present knowledge of the physiology of the nervous system. And that appears to be the extent of Flourens's influence. That of Magendie on the other hand was longer lived and dominates the entire evolution of physiology. Not that Magendie personally played a preponderant part in it; but his teaching determined the vocation of Claude Bernard (1813–1878), and it may be said that the advance of physiology dates from Claude Bernard's work. Moreover this remark refers not merely to the discoveries he made in various domains, important as these are, but in a special degree to the faultless method initiated by him and the directing principle in all research. Claude Bernard introduced *determinism* into the domain of physiology and merely gave the same certainty to the results achieved in the study of living beings as to those achieved in the study of inert matter. He overthrew the barriers set up between two orders of sciences; and in consequence—whether intentionally or not—deprived the sterilising ideas on vitalism of all their importance. His *Introduction à l'étude de la médecine expérimentale* (1865) is a monument containing the immutable rules of experimental method reduced to precise formulae, coordinated in a masterly manner, illustrated by the best examples, set forth with an elevation of view and a depth of thought which it seems hardly possible to surpass. Claude Bernard's own personal researches show to what results the application of his precepts leads. *Le diabète et la glycogenèse animale, La chaleur animale, Le curare, Les nerfs vaso-moteurs* represent so many first-rate discoveries, the result of a penetrating analysis, of rigorous and sagacious deduction allied with a prudent spirit of generalisation.

Thus, under the inspiration, or at any rate under the influence, of Claude Bernard's thought, the French physiological school has produced, and is producing, a number of men of science, the authors of important works. It is out of the question to mention them all and still more so to enumerate their works. We must confine ourselves to pointing out their essential characteristics.

The discovery of the glycogenic function of the liver brought to light an important general fact, that of a secretion entering the blood directly, without passing through the excretory canal. This fact did not escape the notice of Claude Bernard, who perceived the general character of these internal secretions (1867). He enumerates some of them and believed that they contribute to maintaining the composition of the blood constant. At the same period Charles-Édouard Brown-Séquard (1817–94) was experimenting on the supra-renal capsules and proving that their extirpation causes death. Various workers in all countries (Gratiolet, Vulpian, Philippeaux in France) were studying the effects of the extirpation of the thyroid gland. But this subject made no progress till the day when Brown-Séquard suggested the idea that internal glands evacuate into the blood products which act in an elective manner on other organs. All contemporary work flows from this fundamental conception of a *specific functional excitement*. In France the following works deserve mention: those of E. Gley on the thyroid and of Abelous and Langlois on the supra-renal capsules.

Brown-Séquard, however, by no means confined himself to the glands producing internal secretions. In fact this study was merely the occupation of the last phase of his career. He had previously devoted himself to the study of the nervous system, and it is right to attribute to him the discovery of two important facts: the variations in the reflex power of the medulla after section of the brain and the transmission by the grey matter of sensitive impressions into the medulla. Generally speaking Brown-Séquard made a contribution of first-rate importance to the physiology of the nervous system.

Étienne-Jules Marey (1830–1904), who was more directly under the influence of Claude Bernard, left a profound mark in the domain of physiology. It was he who discovered and brought into current use the graphic method in physiology. Invented in France in 1734[1], utilised in Germany by Ludwig and by Vierordt, it was taken up again by Marey, who by means of it achieved important results in respect of our knowledge of the circulation, of human locomotion and of the flight of birds. He brought to perfection—nay, he created—the instrumental apparatus necessary for the drawing of curves and for the photographing of movements. In this last matter he is one of the precursors of the cinematograph.

Marey's name should be coupled with that of his collaborator Jean-Baptiste-Auguste Chauveau (1827–1917) who had a share in the perfecting of the application of graphic processes. Chauveau

[1] The anemometrograph of the Marquis d'Ons-en-Bray.

further devoted himself to the study of other problems, notably those of energetics.

Other names, both of the past and of the present, would likewise deserve mention. Claude Bernard was the centre of a galaxy of men of science, each of whom contributed his quota of new results of varying importance: Paul Bert (1833-86), Louis Gréhant (1840–1910), Albert Dastre (1844–1917), and many others who continued the master's work with insight. Many physiologists of note still living might also be mentioned who can easily bear comparison with their colleagues in neighbouring lands. Among these a prominent place should be assigned to M. and Mme. Lapicque, whose researches on chronaxy (1903–5) cannot be passed over in silence. G. Weiss had previously established a relation between the duration of the passage of an electric current in a nerve and the intensity necessary to produce a contraction; the intensity is in an inverse ratio to the duration of the current. Lapicque demonstrated that the duration of the passage is an important element in its efficacity for excitation; but duration is not sufficient and there is a minimum intensity below which, whatever its duration, a current has no effect; and it is to this duration that the minimum intensity corresponds. It is for lesser durations that the necessary intensity varies and it increases in proportion as the duration decreases. There exists therefore a relation between duration and intensity to which Lapicque gives the name of chronaxy. Chronaxy varies from one nerve to another and all the consequences of this fact from the point of view of the general functioning of the nervous system are obvious. In fact the idea of chronaxy renders it intelligible that excitation should take one form or another as a simple result of the duration of the excitation or of its intensity without reference to the structure of the nervous system.

In another but equally important department, André Mayer and G. Schaeffer have devoted themselves to the quantitative analysis of living substance and have obtained highly important results from their researches (1913–14). After establishing the existence of a relative and constant proportion between the constituents of the substance of various kinds of cells, they show that this constancy maintains itself in spite of continual oscillations. Then, upon examining the distribution of these constituents they were led to admit that certain among them, such as the lipsoids, are distributed throughout the mass of the cell and not localised upon its surface, as Overton had presumed. This distribution of the lipsoids is regarded as playing an essential part in the penetration of water and of dissolved substances. This would no longer be a question of osmosis, but of imbibition, the passage to and fro of the water depending on the quantitative oscillations of the constituents about a constant mean. The importance and fecundity of this doctrine in relation to vital phenomena in general is obvious.

Finally, the physiology of vegetables, nearly allied in certain respects to biological chemistry, has been the subject of remarkable researches. Above all those of Félix-Victor Raulin must be mentioned, who in 1870 drew attention to the importance of zinc in very small quantities in the mutations of plants. Other subsequent investigators in France, under the influence of Gaston Bonnier, have extended this idea to other substances, and it tends to pass from vegetables to animals (Delezenne, 1918). The study of the function of chlorophyll has likewise produced various works, among which those of Molliard deserve special notice bringing, as they do, into prominence an antagonism between the chlorophyllic function and the absorption of juices by the radicular apparatus. Various other studies by Gaston Bonnier, Molliard, and other physiologists have made a very serious contribution to our knowledge of the physiology of plants, the conditions of parasitism, etc.

While French physiology was taking a leading place at the head of the scientific movement, France gave birth to a new science at the suggestion of Casimir-Joseph Davaine (1812–1882) and under the impulse of Louis Pasteur (1822–1895)—the science of bacteriology. As early as 1850 Davaine and Pierre-François-Olive Rayer (1793–1867) saw the anthrax bacterium in the blood of animals which had died of anthrax and maintained that this organism was the cause of the disease. From that moment bacteriology was in being. But its true development dates from the repeated discoveries and the rigorous demonstrations of Pasteur. It was not enough to show the constant existence of the microbes in diseased subjects; it was necessary to establish the relation of cause and effect between these microbes and the disease. The whole of Pasteur's work was the achievement of this result. It revolved round the fundamental idea of the specificity of microbes which perpetuate themselves in similar microbes and consequently determine the same effects on analogous organisms.

To those who maintained that the germs were born of fermentations, that diseased tissues generated the microbes, Pasteur replied by demonstrating the impossibility of spontaneous generation under present conditions. Resuming with faultless rigour the experiments of Spallanzani, he established, and this time with irresistible authority, that the air contains numberless germs which insinuate themselves everywhere and develop whenever they meet with favourable conditions.

It is unnecessary to-day to insist on the consequences of these demonstrations or on those which preceded and followed them. Modern pathology and hygiene are founded upon them: biology has been revolutionised by them with fertilising results. A whole generation of scientific men has grown up under the influence of Pasteur: Chauveau, Duclaux, Charrin, Chamberland, Roux, Yersin. To these must be added Charles Laveran, who by his discovery of the hematozoon of malaria has inaugurated the study of pathogenic protozoa. At the present day bacteriologists without number claim to be working on the lines of Pasteur or of his immediate pupils in utilising or perfecting methods calculated to track down microbes and discover their general and special characteristics.

But it should not be forgotten that the directing ideas and the discovery of the fundamental facts are almost all due to Pasteur or his *entourage*: the attenuation or weakening of virulence, the existence of the part played by toxins, the applications of inoculation. All subsequent discoveries, both in France and abroad, especially that of serum treatment (Richet and Héricourt) descend in a direct line from these original discoveries. The theory of immunity is likewise a consequence of them; but it belongs rather, at any rate as regards its point of departure, to Chauveau than to Pasteur. The latter believed that immunity was the result of the impoverishment of the blood in certain substances; the former showed that it resulted from a modification, which might be the addition of a substance due to the reaction of the organism which has been invaded by a colony of microbes. More recently still the theory of immunity seems to have been complicated by the discovery of anaphylaxis by Richet and Portier (1902). Without being the opposite of immunity, anaphylaxis corresponds with a state of extreme sensitiveness in the organism brought about by the penetration of toxins and other substances. Whether enduring or not, this hyper-sensitiveness exists, and while contributing to the understanding of a series of facts previously misconceived necessitates certain practical precautions.

In a word, Pasteur, his French precursors, and his school, not only founded bacteriology, but sowed the seeds of all subsequent discoveries. Without them neither the labours of Koch himself, nor those of Behring and Metchnikoff, would probably have seen the light.

In a very different region of the domain of biology, France has made contributions of equal importance, namely in that of zoology proper, of embryology, and comparative anatomy.

The initial impulse came incontestably from Buffon, who, with various collaborators and especially Louis-Jean-Marie Daubenton (1716–1799), devoted himself particularly to the description of external forms and internal dispositions. The considerable body of his work brought followers into the field and aroused an interest in zoological research and publications—witness the numerous sequels to Buffon which appeared at the beginning of the 19th century, and which are for the most part important works. That period produced a whole brood of naturalists, many of whom left works of durable value: Bernard-Germain-Étienne de la Ville, Comte de Lacépède (1756–1825); Pierre-André Latreille (1762–1833) who laid a solid foundation for the study of the arthropoda; Jean-Baptiste de Monet de Lamarck (1744–1829) who was an eminent descriptive botanist and zoologist, the French Linnaeus, before he became the illustrious author of *La philosophie zoologique*. A pause must be made at Étienne Geoffroy Saint-Hilaire (1772–1844), who was able to pass from pure description to the comparison of forms and to deduce general ideas from his researches. Comparative anatomy inspired him with a personal conception of organisms. He regarded them as all being upon a common plan, "essentially the same in principle," but infinitely diversified. From the unity of composition flows the principle of connexions ("an organism can be destroyed sooner than transposed") and that of the balance between organs ("the underdevelopment of one organ corresponds to an overdevelopment of another"). Many naturalists have admitted and still admit these conceptions; they dominate the study of comparative anatomy and provide it with a clue and a method of coordination.

They would perhaps not have been sufficient for this purpose had not Georges Cuvier (1769–1832)—at first in friendly and later in hostile rivalry with Geoffroy Saint-Hilaire—conceived independently the law of the subordination and correlation of characters. But discussions and disputes between these two men belong to another domain. In so far as they remained within the limits of comparative anatomy their efforts converged. Cuvier, it is true, wished to force his laws to yield excessive consequences, since in virtue of correlations he claimed to be able to deduce the entire constitution of an animal from the knowledge of a very limited portion of it. This claim, as it soon came to be recognised, was excessive; nevertheless, at the moment at which it was formulated it helped to give an impetus to comparative anatomy.

The influence of Geoffroy Saint-Hilaire was felt in another direction, that of normal and teratological embryology. Kaspar Friedrich Wolff had shown that the egg is in the first instance a formless mass within which the individual becomes progressively defined; but this discovery had not completely overthrown the hypothesis of the continuity of germs. It persisted obstinately and naturalists deduced from it the idea of original monstrosity. Geoffroy Saint-Hilaire while admitting that development took place in accordance with the unity of organic composition, also admitted that the formation of the parts depends to a certain degree on external circumstances: epigenesis thus came into conflict with preformation. In his view development may be effected, according to circumstances, either completely, or incompletely, or prolonged beyond its natural term. In the two latter cases monstrous births would be the result. Geoffroy

Saint-Hilaire strove to demonstrate his views by experiments in hatching birds' eggs by artificial incubation[1].

The same line of investigations gave Geoffroy Saint-Hilaire a clue to the study of monstrosities. Each of them represented a phase in the development. And since the various groups of animals seemed to differ from one another merely in the degree in which the scheme of their composition was realised, there would be a parallelism between the less developed adult forms and the embryos of the more developed forms. It thus followed that if a monster represented an arrested embryonic form the parallelism would extend to monsters themselves; and they would be the result of an arrest or an excess in the development, both arrest and excess originating in various traumatic actions.

Geoffroy Saint-Hilaire's teratological work was taken up again and developed by his son Isidore (1809–61), who studied in detail and classified animal monstrosities. Teratogenesis on the other hand owes its expansion to Camille Dareste (1822–1899), who by means of experiments in artificial incubation in normal and abnormal conditions proved finally the influence of external actions. Dareste also believed himself to have proved that the amnios played a part in the determination of monstrosities, and he was followed in this conviction by the majority of naturalists and physicians. But this view has now to be abandoned; I have been able to demonstrate that traumatic actions do not produce the regular and symmetrical forms which characterise monstrosities. It is nevertheless a fact that teratology in its various aspects is a science of French origin and it should be mentioned that the first experiments in the excision of the germ-cells, which, as is well known, had so important an influence on our conception of the organism, were carried out in France by Laurent-Marie Chabry (1855–93), while W. Roux was carrying out comparable ones in Germany.

Many naturalists followed up and continued the zoological work of Geoffroy Saint-Hilaire and Cuvier. Foremost among these H. and A. Milne-Edwards, Lacaze-Duthiers, and Quatrefages, deserve mention, and many others might be added to

---

[1] It would however appear that the first scientific attempts at incubation go back to Réaumur.

the list. Their merits are of diverse order; but all left works which extended the range of our knowledge, and some exercised a direct influence on the evolution of zoology. Henri Milne-Edwards (1800–85), regarding the organism from a general point of view, conceived the idea of the physiological division of labour. This idea has perhaps served its time; but the fact remains and it is right to give it its value. The career of Henri de Lacaze-Duthiers (1821–1901) left profound traces. By the creation of two fully equipped maritime laboratories, one on the Atlantic at Roscoff, the other on the Mediterranean at Banyuls, he gave an immense impulse to the study of marine zoology in France. He drew round him a large number of the young naturalists of his period, and some of them became masters in their turn.

Alfred Giard (1846–1908), a biologist in the widest sense of the word, clearly perceived that zoology was not bounded by the limits of systematics and anatomy; and had the wisdom to encourage the most diverse tendencies among the younger men. He showed, for example, that oecology, the study of organisms in their natural environment, the reactions produced by individuals one upon another, are all deserving of special attention by reason of their general consequences. His work on castration by means of parasites has become classical, as well as his researches on the parasitic isopoda; his published work on general questions of the most diverse nature has provided food for several generations of naturalists.

Marie-Yves Delage (1854–1920) deployed his activity specially in experimental work. His researches on the otoliths of crustacea and on parthenogenesis are important contributions to the study of difficult questions. He was certainly not inferior to Loeb, his fellow-worker in the same field. Before entering upon these researches he had devoted several years to the solution by simple observation of the questions of the development of sponges and of the relations between the Sacculine and its host.

Among the naturalists of the school of Lacaze-Duthiers, and the direct pupils of Giard, many names might be quoted as holding a very honourable place in French science and in science generally. Some cannot be passed over in silence, such as Paul Marchal (b. 1862), the author of *Polyembryonie, Biologie des*

Chermès, and many other works of first-rate importance; Lucien Cuénot, known by his researches on various questions both general and special, notably on heredity, which he was one of the first to take up after the exhumation of the works of Mendel; Charles Pérez and his researches on metamorphoses.

Mention should also be made, among investigators independent of all schools, of Charles Naudin (1815–99), who discovered the essential phenomena of heredity at the same time as Mendel and independently of him. Like Mendel he understood the necessity of experimenting on pure races, but, being more of a physiologist than his contemporary, he arrived at a conception fundamentally somewhat different, but equally lacking in precision; in his system "specific essences" take the place of "characters."

Next comes the names of Léon Dufour (1782–1865), Jean Pérez (1833–1914), Jean-Henri Fabre (1823–1915), François-Émile Maupas (1812–1916), Charles Ferton (1856–1921). Dufour devoted himself to the study of the anatomy of the habits of insects and left very useful contributions; Pérez left solid and penetrating works on the morphology and habits of insects and especially of hymenoptera; J.-H. Fabre, who gave himself up to the same studies, drew attention to a certain number of facts without analysing them very closely; in particular he attracted to this class of research the attention of young persons who might not otherwise have suspected their interest. Ferton, whose activity, exercised outside all official ties, is inexhaustible, likewise observes patiently and analyses rigorously the habits of hymenoptera, achieving precise results and contributions of the highest importance to a scientific theory of instinct. Finally Maupas will live as the initiator of precise researches by experiment and observation into the life of protozoa.

In two other directions slightly different from, but connected with, the former, those of histology and of anthropology, French science has made a fundamental contribution.

Histology under the name of general anatomy originated in France, for an accurate conception of tissues is due to Bichat (1800). Before him Aristotle and Galen had spoken of similar and dissimilar parts without any systematisation. Fallopius had had none but extremely vague ideas about tissues, and Théophile de Bordeus' (1767) knowledge hardly extended beyond the loose connective tissue. Bichat realised that tissues are the elementary portions of organs and possess properties which characterise them: his analysis did not get beyond this; he did not use the microscope; and the idea and the fact of the *cell* are not his. The fact was perceived by the botanist Mirbel (1820) and its importance was recognised in Germany by Schleider (1838) for plants and by Schwann (1839) for animals.

After Bichat histology seems to fall into oblivion, at any rate in France, till the day when Charles Robin (1821–85) realised its scope and advocated its study. He himself discovered a number of anatomical elements—the myeloplax of the marrow of the bones, the perineurium of the nerves, the lymphatic sheath of the cerebral vessels. But the final impetus with a new orientation, which passed the frontiers of France, is due to Louis-Antoine Ranvier (b. 1838) and to the group of scientists gathered around him.

By introducing the earliest improvements into technique without forgetting the physiological aspect, he founded the great school of histo-physiology, which counts Joseph-Louis Renaut (1844–1918), Louis-Charles Malassez (1842–1909), Vignal (1852–93), Georges Pouchet (1833–94), Mathias-Duval (1844–1907) and so many others, such as Henneguy, Prenant, Bouin, Nageotte, etc. whose work has left its mark. It is notably by the employment of the accurate technical methods advocated by Ranvier that Mathias-Duval was able to bring to a satisfactory issue his classical researches into the true origin of the cranial nerves, the extreme importance of which from the point of view of the general physiology of the nervous system it is needless to emphasise.

The study of anthropology had received its first impetus in France from the two volumes of Buffon on the "Human varieties" (1749) and the researches of Daubenton (1764). Its real development did not however begin till the discovery made at Abbeville of the first prehistoric axes by Jacques Boucher de Perthes (1788–1868). This discovery forced upon the world the idea of the antiquity of man, which the researches of Buckland in England (1820), and of Tournel, E. Dumas, Marcel de Serres (1830) in the south of France, had given reason to suspect. Analogous discoveries have since followed. In France the following must be mentioned: the pliopithecus found by Edouard Lartet (1801–1871), a prelude to that of the fossil man, whose antiquity he already foresaw (1860); the skeletons of Cro-Magnon (Dordogne) exhumed by Louis Lartet (1868); the Mentone man by Rivière (1872); the Chancelade (Dordogne) man studied by Testut (1888); the man of La Chapelle-aux-Saints (Corrèze), the subject of Marcellin Boule's remarkable studies (1908); the skeleton of La Ferrassie (Dordogne) brought to light by Peyrony (1909); that of La Quina (Charente-inférieure) by Henri Martin (1911). The study of the civilisations corresponding to these types of early man has in its turn given rise to French works of first-rate importance, among which those of Gabriel de Mortillet, and Émile Cartailhac must be cited.

The study of fossil man cannot be dissociated from that of the various human races. The utility of the discoveries could only make itself felt because anthropology existed as a distinct science gathering individual efforts into one. Investigators remained isolated in spite of certain attempts at association in Paris and London during the first half of the 19th century. But it was not till the foundation of the *Société d'Anthropologie* of Paris (1859) by Paul Broca (1824–1880) that the study of man began to acquire importance or to develop. The impulse once given, similar societies sprang up everywhere in Europe and America. By Broca's agency men of science such as I. Geoffroy Saint-Hilaire, Louis Pierre Gratiolet, Camille Dareste, Émile Godard, Charles Robin, Béclard and others, were drawn into a group which encouraged investigators and supported them by their advice and their works. Broca's own works on the comparative morphology of men and monkeys (1869), those of Armand de Quatrefages and Hamy on the principal cranial types (1873–1882), have remained classics. The impetus given has never lost its power, as is proved by the works published in the *Mémoires de la Société d'Anthropologie*, and in *L'Anthropologie* touching on the most diverse questions in palaeontology, anatomy, ethnography, etc.; and as is also proved by the accurate studies of Cartailhac and Breuil on the drawings with which the various caves are decorated.

While all these scientists were exerting themselves in such various domains, enriching our knowledge with a large number of particular facts, a few of them and others also attempted and are still attempting to solve more general problems connected with the origin of living beings.

From time immemorial thinkers have tried to penetrate the mystery of origins, and traces of this preoccupation are found in the most ancient writers. But it only began to take a scientific form towards the beginning of the 18th century with Buffon, Lamarck, and Geoffroy Saint-Hilaire. Buffon maintained successively two opposite opinions. At first he defended the absolute invariability of living beings, but later admitted the possibility of extensive transformations, and finally concluded upon a mixed conception consisting in the admission of the invariability of species in its essentials combined with a relative variability within certain limits and as regards secondary characteristics; he thus combines the idea of species with the idea of race. In his view external conditions were the determining causes of modifications.

These different phases of Buffon's thought may not, perhaps, have been devoid of influence on the ideas of his immediate successors. A great distance, however, separates Buffon from Geoffroy Saint-Hilaire, and a greater from Lamarck. Both the latter admit variability, not within the limits of species but of such a nature as to allow species to be transformed one into another; and, if these two thinkers diverge on certain points, in reality they complete one another. Lamarck makes a frontal attack on the question of species and endeavours to show that species has no real existence. Living forms are not constant but subject to transformation, all originating from a living substance born of inert matter under the action of the physio-chemical forces. Organisms remain subject in a constant fashion to these forces, and they become modified in the course of ages; acquired modifications pass from one generation to another; they are hereditary. Lamarck, however, places a restriction on the period of individual existence during which modifications are possible;

the young only and not adults are capable of experiencing durable modifications. In any case the organism does not submit passively to external influence; the organism has needs and has to form habits as a function of its environment; it is therefore active. Thus Lamarck does not separate the organism from its environment, and regards their connexion as necessary. In a more general point of view Lamarck understood that biological phenomena obey a fixed determinism and in so far he placed the question of the origin of life in the domain of science.

A few years later and perhaps more directly under Buffon's influence, Geoffroy Saint-Hilaire came to similar conclusions. Defining in detail what must be understood by environment, developing that idea which had already been clearly pointed out by Lamarck, Geoffroy Saint-Hilaire repudiates the view that the organism plays any active part in its transformations and thinks that it submits passively to external influences. On the other hand, he corrects Lamarck on an important point, when he expresses the view that effective transformations do not take place either in the adult or in the immature form but in the embryo in the course of its development.

At bottom, however, Geoffroy Saint-Hilaire's views are extremely close to those of Lamarck. His great merit is to have maintained the variability of species as against Cuvier. It was in 1830 that a widely celebrated discussion took place, in the course of which Cuvier made use of every scientific and theological argument to secure the triumph of his doctrine. He succeeded for a time and the idea of evolution ceased to dominate the thoughts of men of science both in France and outside France.

A few men, however, did not feel debarred from facing these fundamental problems, and it is only just to recall that Henri Ducrotay de Blainville (1777–1850) never ceased to proclaim the influence of environment or the transformations of organisms. Naudin, likewise, remained a convinced "transformist." In his view the likenesses observed between living beings imply community of origin; he presupposes a certain *plasticity* in living beings and admits that they are transformed under the influence of environment; he considers that transformations once effected become the object of a process of selection; from this idea he deduces processes of artificial selection. In the main

Naudin regarded the mechanism of evolution with great breadth of view, borrowing ideas from Lamarck but adding others peculiar to himself.

But it must be admitted that Naudin's published work exercised no marked influence. Cuvier's doctrine reigned supreme and its reign lasted till the day on which Darwin's *Origin of Species* appeared.

The French scientific world received this work very favourably. Controversy revived on the Continent, as it had done in England. In spite of a certain timid but courteous resistance on the part of Quatrefages and of the work of Jordan, which claimed to prove by experiment the fixity of species, the idea of evolution took its place once more in scientific speculation; it inspired numerous works by naturalists, and especially by palaeontologists, the latter perceiving more clearly than the former the succession of forms under the influence of the succession of environments.

From the outset of his scientific career Alfred Giard endeavoured to confront the theory with the facts and quickly understood that so far from contradicting the views of Lamarck those of Darwin completed them. According to Giard organisms are subject to two classes of influence, the primary or Lamarckian and the secondary or Darwinian, the former determining, the latter selecting the modifications. Giard defended to the end of his life this point of view, which corresponds in the main with that of Naudin, and succeeded in exercising a considerable influence both in his own entourage and further afield.

At the same period Gaston Bonnier was approaching the problem through experiments; by cultivating plants under differing conditions he obtained well-characterised correlative modifications.

For his part Félix Le Dantec (1869–1917) undertook to show that variations and selection are traceable to a strict physio-chemical determinism. After first establishing that the properties of living matter are reducible to the properties of matter in general, he then proceeds by a logically reasoned argument to draw from this a complete series of deductions relative to the interpretation of fundamental facts, while constantly eliminating metaphysical and verbal explanations. His numerous and widely circulated publications have had a large share in accustoming the French public to the idea that evolution is effected in accordance with a determinism accessible to research.

Such, briefly indicated, are the phases traversed by biological studies in modern France; and such is the state in which they stand at present. I have no doubt been obliged to pass over in silence the names of many sound workers who have made appreciable and useful contributions to the common stock; in the impossibility of naming all, for they are too numerous, I could not do more than take cognisance of general results and personify them under the most representative names.

§ II. CHEMISTRY

Whoever undertakes to write the history of chemistry in France must begin by calling up the great figure of Antoine-Laurent Lavoisier (1743-1794). The period when he lived was one well suited for the unfolding of his genius. It was the century of philosophers; its whole tendency was favourable to the growth of scientific studies, and chemistry, which was taught at the Jardin du Roi by the famous Rouelle, found ardent devotees, among whom were Diderot and later Lavoisier. Abroad too, and especially in England, chemistry attracted great minds. Black, Cavendish, and Priestley may be regarded as the pioneers of the chemistry of gases. Black, following up the work of Hales, had discovered the " fixed air " of limestone (carbonic acid) in 1755. In 1765 Cavendish discovered "inflammable air" (hydrogen), and in 1774, almost simultaneously with Scheele and Lavoisier, Priestley was discovering the "air eminently proper to combustion" (oxygen). While Lavoisier was not thus an isolated researcher, it may be said that he was a great innovator, for by instituting the gravometric method he brought into chemistry a new thing—order.

Chemists had undoubtedly made use of the balance before him, but merely for the preparation of substances, and not for the interpretation of the transformations which were occurring under their eyes. Let us consider for instance the phenomenon of combustion. Jean Rey, a physician of Tours, had pointed out as early as 1630 the increase in weight which metals undergo during calcination. Boyle and Mayow had observed it in their turn. But chemists regarded this variation of mass as a secondary detail. The only thing which had importance in their eyes was the heat given off, and they explained it by Stahl's "phlogiston." This was a subtle principle, a sort of fire demon, which quitted the metal during combustion, leaving it reduced to the state of a "calx," but it was possible to borrow it from coal and restore it to the "calx," thereby producing the metal again. Lavoisier proved conclusively by a judicious use of the balance that the combustion of a metal is attended by *addition of matter*. The matter added is oxygen, and the increase in weight observed is exactly equal to the weight of the oxygen which disappears from the atmosphere surrounding the metal. Thus chemical reaction is accompanied by a displacement of matter, and every displacement of matter is betrayed by a displacement of weight. Such is the fundamental law which it is Lavoisier's merit to have established in all its rigour and all its universality. He thus placed the idea of elements upon an experimental basis, and founded analytical chemistry.

In a career all too short he found time to demonstrate by his work the fruitfulness of his method. He determined the composition of water and that of carbonic acid gas; he established the constitution of the chief oxy-acids (the acids of sulphur, phosphorus, and nitrogen); he pointed out the part played by bases in the formation of salts. Finally he carried his studies into physiological phenomena, and explained the respiration and perspiration of animals[1]. The complete exposition of his teaching is found in his *Traité élémentaire de chimie*, the first edition of which appeared in 1789.

The new theory gave birth to a new language, both more expressive and more accurate. Thus arose a rational nomenclature, the principle of which has persisted to the present day. First suggested to Lavoisier by Guyton de Morveau, it was built up in collaboration with Fourcroy and Berthollet and contributed greatly to the spread of the new ideas.

The Elements

After Lavoisier chemistry guided by analysis was destined to make rapid progress. The conception of a simple substance

[1] See above, p. 756.

became definite. Chemists now taxed their ingenuity to isolate them, and in particular those metals which according to this theory must be united to oxygen in alkalis. Just at that period (1800) they received powerful assistance from Volta, the inventor of the electric battery. Nicholson and Carlisle demonstrated the decomposition of water by electric currents. The Swedish chemists Berzelius and Hisinger subjected solutions of acids, bases, and salts to the same process. Immediately afterwards —in 1807—Sir Humphry Davy succeeded in a celebrated experiment in isolating potassium by electrolysing caustic potash with a cathode of mercury. This discovery at once became known in France, and without delay Joseph-Louis Gay Lussac (1778–1850) and Louis-Jacques Thénard (1777–1857) set to work to prepare potassium on their own account.

A constant and noble emulation is thus seen to have reigned between English and French *savants* to the great advantage of science. But Gay Lussac and Thénard, not yet having at their disposal a battery so powerful as Davy's, attacked the problem by another route, and it was entirely by the means of chemical actions (the treatment of iron with caustic alkali at a high temperature) that they succeeded in isolating the alkaline metals. This was an important discovery, for Davy could isolate potassium and sodium only in minute globules, while Gay Lussac and Thénard were in a position to prepare them in considerable masses. It is a further fact that alkaline metals are themselves first-rate reducing agents, capable of bringing other elements to light by liberating them from their oxides or chlorides. The most important acquisition of this kind is undoubtedly aluminium. In 1827 Wöhler reduced for the first time the chloride of aluminium by means of potassium. And Sainte-Claire Deville, repeating his method in 1854 with sodium, rendered it practicable, prepared the first ingot of aluminium, and created the aluminium industry at the factories of Salindres (Gard). Calcium and magnesium and, speaking generally, all metals with stable oxides were prepared for the first time in the same manner. But it is curious to observe that at the close of the 19th century, thanks to the progress of the electric industry, the electro-chemical progresses founded on Davy's experiments came back into favour to such a degree that at the present day aluminium, magnesium, and even sodium are once more prepared by electrolysis. This evolution has taken place almost entirely in France, where the electrical preparation of aluminium was perfected by the engineer Héroult. One other element must be added to the list, namely fluorine, which hitherto electrolysis alone has been able to liberate. Its discovery is due to the patient researches of Moissan (1886).

Analysis made it possible not only to prepare known elements from their compounds, but also to reveal new elements in unknown compounds. Among the most important brought to light by analysis may be mentioned bromine and iodine. Bromine was discovered in 1826 by Balard in the brine of salt marshes. Iodine was discovered at Paris in 1811 by the salt-petre-maker Courtois in the ashes of kelp. It was studied first by Clément-Désormes, then by Gay Lussac, who devoted a masterly study to it (1813-14). Thus the halogen group of elements was completed in a striking manner.

This was the origin of the rational classification of metalloids by Dumas (about 1835), a classification which was to fall into its place in a wider system with the periodic law of Mendeléeff. But it should be remembered that even before Mendeléeff the periodic law was recognised in France by Béguyer de Chancourtois. He wound a spiral round a vertical cylinder, disposed the symbols of the elements upon it at heights proportionate to their atomic weights, and recognised that the analogous elements of each group fall together periodically on the same generating line of the cylinder.

Meanwhile the progress in physics furnished more and more delicate means of identifying substances, and thanks to Bunsen's spectroscope Lecoq de Boisbaudran discovered gallium (1875) and Crookes thallium (1862), each of which fitted into a place left blank in the classification. Similarly in the complex and closely united group of rare earths the spectroscope made it possible to detect the twin elements. Lecoq de Boisbaudran, Demarçay, and Urbain distinguished themselves in these researches. We owe to them the description of samarium (Lecoq de Boisbaudran), of the constituents of didymium (Demarçay), and of those of ytterbium (Urbain). But the most remarkable discovery and the most decisive for the future of science is unquestionably that of radium.

At the end of the year 1895 Röntgen made known the penetrating rays issuing from Crookes's tubes and the method of making them visible by means of fluorescent screens. Immediately physicists everywhere began to study these curious phenomena. Poincaré suggested that fluorescent substances might themselves give birth to radiations analogous to the X-rays, and Henri Becquerel subjected this hypothesis to the test of experiment. In this he was unsuccessful, for all his fluorescent screens failed except the one made from a double sulphate of uranium and potassium. This salt revealed itself as the source of a radiation which, if very feeble, was as penetrating as the X-rays, and the radiation seemed to continue indefinitely *without any external exciting agency.* Becquerel soon found that this was a property common to all the compounds of uranium and to uranium itself. He further found the electroscope an instrument convenient for measuring radio-activity. These data formed the starting-point of the labours of Pierre Curie (1859–1906) and his wife. The electrometric measurements taken by Mme Curie first revealed the radio-activity of thorium; then a comparison between the different salts of uranium shewed that radio-activity was a property of the atom which varied with the mass of the atom and was independent of the compound chosen. But Mme Curie extended her study to the minerals themselves which contained uranium, and a surprising fact appeared; pitchblende, an ore of uranium, is three times as radio-active as pure uranium. The learned investigators at once suspected that pitchblende must contain an element more radio-active than uranium. A methodical separation was undertaken and a ton of pitchblende yielded eight kilogrammes of barium chloride, evidently accompanied by an unknown element, and sixty times as radio-active as uranium. As it was impossible to separate this unknown element from the barium chloride by chemical means, physical means were employed, i.e. successive crystallisations were undertaken with the electrometer as a guide, till the moment when the electroscope revealed a new ray. At the same time the determination of the atomic weight made it possible to follow the progress of purification. After several thousands of such recrystallisations M. and Mme Curie were able to obtain pure radium chloride. Starting with a ton of the pitchblende residues, they isolated twelve centigrams of radium chloride. But the radio-activity of their specimen proved to be several million times that of uranium. The consequences of this discovery for the future of chemistry and of physics are incalculable [1]. Thus from Lavoisier's time onwards the number and order of the elements formed a regular system.

The Compounds

We must now consider how the system of compounds was established. In mineral chemistry co-ordination is easy. They are almost all built up from the elements by a gradual process and by combining together those of an opposite electro-chemical character. Thus oxides of metals form the group of bases; oxides of non-metals form the group of acids; and bases combined with acids form salts. By this simple scheme almost the whole of mineral chemistry can be represented. It is Lavoisier's conception, developed subsequently by Berzelius, whose dualistic theory long remained in favour. It is also found in another form in modern electro-chemical theories.

But in organic chemistry the problem was much more complicated. There one had to deal with an infinite variety of natural compounds, which it seemed impossible to synthesise from elements. They were, therefore, characterised and classified by analysis alone. And this was a work of patience and sagacity which reflected great credit on those who accomplished it. In this connexion the names of such Frenchmen as Rouelle, Vauquelin, and especially Chevreul, must be mentioned. To Michel-Eugène Chevreul (1786–1889) belongs the credit of having established the true nature of fats. He it was who first demonstrated the breaking up of fats into fatty acids and glycerine by the addition of the elements of water. This fundamental discovery dates from the years 1813–15, and its consequences were propounded in a paper which has remained a classic (*Recherches chimiques sur les corps gras d'origine animale*, 1823). At the same time Chevreul was providing chemists with whole groups of methods for the analysis of organic compounds. It is at this period too that numerous discoveries were being made

---

[1] Besides radium two other radio-active elements were discovered, polonium by Mme Curie and actinium by Debierne.

of definite substances—they were then termed "active principles"—in natural products. The discoveries of Pelletier and Caventou (strychnine 1818, brucine 1819, quinine 1820) deserve special mention. Chevreul in his long career carried out other important works, notably on dyes. But the breaking up of fats by hydrolysis was the one instance of a general method of work which was to prove singularly fertile. A similar decomposition was brought about later in the case of glucosides. Similarly, too, it was in hydrolysing gelatine that Braconnot of Nancy discovered glycocoll, the first type of aminoacids.

Finally, a little later Paul Schützenberger (1829–1897) studied in a celebrated work the decomposition products of albuminoid matters, described the characteristics of aminoacids derived from them, and prepared the way for the modern researches on polypeptides.

By analysis not merely were compounds discovered, but they were also broken up into simpler substances, and the more the process was continued the greater was the need for classification. In this work of co-ordination the French school of chemistry played an important part. The names of Jean-Baptiste Dumas (1800–1884), Auguste Laurent (1807–1853), Charles-Frédéric Gerhardt (1816–1856), and Charles-Adolphe Würtz (1817–1884) will always be famous in the history of chemistry.

The fundamental conception which first emerges from their work is that of classes of organic compounds. Four groups of organic substances were described, all possessing the same properties. Thus from the comparison of spirits of wood with spirits of wine, and of the latter with potato-oil, arose the conception of an alcohol or the group of alcohols. It is clearly established by Dumas and Péligot in their classic papers on spirits of wood (1835), and its consequences are very important, for alcohols produce acids by oxidisation (e.g. formic, acetic, valerianic). Now such acids fall immediately into a much larger series of analogous acids (butyric, caproic, œnanthic, capric, etc.), in which one passes from one acid to the next by the addition of one carbon atom and two hydrogen atoms. If this series be imagined complete, a parallel and complete series of corresponding alcohols must also be imagined, and likewise a series of aldehydes, carbons, hydro-carbons, etc. And thus a whole region of organic chemistry is subjected to regular co-ordination, a co-ordination by two factors in which each substance is characterised by the name of the series (alcohol, acid, carbide, etc.) and by the position which it occupies in this series. And this co-ordination represents so well the nature of the known phenomena that it at once calls up new relationships. The man who had the clearest vision of this great general system was Charles Gerhardt, a young Montpellier professor of twenty-eight, who expounded it for the first time in *Précis de Chimie organique* (1844). Yet it was not enough to create systems for grouping the multiplicity of species; the conditions of their genesis and the laws of their relationship must be understood. These found their perfect expression in the atomic theory, the development of which must now be traced.

Atoms and Structure

Here the great name of John Dalton should first be recalled. His genius outran, so to speak, experience. About the years 1802–4 he had realised that the whole edifice of chemical combinations could be erected upon the idea of molecules and atoms. But in 1808 Gay Lussac enunciated the law of simple relations in gaseous combinations. In 1811 Avogadro and Ampère gave to this law its physical interpretation and the experimental bases of the atomic theory were laid down once for all. Elementary atoms may themselves form groups, which are preserved from one molecule to another and which are termed "radicals." Gay Lussac discovered a striking example, the radical cyanogen, formed of carbon and nitrogen, which resembles chlorine in its combinations. With atoms and radicals it seemed that it would be possible to build up molecules by the process of addition. But the dualistic theory of Berzelius, valid as regards mineral chemistry, shewed itself unfruitful here. In order to understand the relationship of organic species another concept is required, that of substitution. Just at this time Dumas discovered chloracetic acid in which, as was clearly proved, chlorine substitutes itself for hydrogen. This substitution was demonstrated even in hydro-carbons by Laurent, Regnault, and Malaguti, and the importance of the new conception, brought into prominence by Dumas, impressed itself on the minds of chemists. From that moment Laurent, and especially Gerhardt, began to give the theory of substitution its full value by associating it with a new and fertile idea, that of chemical types. Thanks to them the real relationship of species now appeared with perfect clearness. It is operated by the substitution of atoms or radicals in the types. In 1849 Würtz provided a timely and remarkable illustration of the *chemical* type by his great discovery of amines[1]. The ammonide type was created and it became clear that the amines are derived from it by substitution of the alcoholic radicals for hydrogen. Finally in 1851 Williamson discovered mixed ethers and brought into prominence the water type, and in 1852 Gerhardt connected it with the anhydrides of acids.

Meanwhile the theory of chemical types was undergoing a further evolution under the influence of the discovery of polyhydric alcohols. This was in 1854, when Marcellin Berthelot (1827–1907) was making known the synthesis of neutral fatty bodies. Chevreul had demonstrated the hydrolysis of fats into glycerine and acids. Berthelot succeeded in reconstituting the fatty body from glycerine and the acid. For instance a prolonged heating of glycerine and stearic acid at 200° Cent. gave him stearine. But the result was quite unexpected. The new stearine with the same quantity of glycerine contained only a third as much stearic acid as natural stearine. Berthelot heated it in its turn with stearic acid, and obtained a new fat, in which the proportion of acid was doubled. Finally, treating this second stearine by the same process, he obtained a third variety containing three times as much acid as the first and in every respect identical with natural stearine. Shortly before this discovery Graham had introduced into science the conception of polybasic acids. A comparison of glycerine with these acids was inevitable. Berthelot had realised this, but Würtz went further in the investigation of the structure. He recognised glycerine to be an alcohol, predicted by analogy the possibility of the existence of glycol, and immediately produced it (1856). But if common alcohol is regarded as constructed on the type of water, $O \begin{cases} C_2H_5 \\ H \end{cases}$, on what type is glycerine to be constructed?

[1] Completed by Hofmann.

Würtz conceived it as being derived from the radical C_3H_5,
OH
which was attached to three residues of water (C_3H_5) OH. The
OH
whole interest now centred on these radicals, the capacity of
which for saturation determines the number of hydroxyl groups
in the alcohols. It was necessary to analyse them in turn to
determine their constitution. Kekulé in Germany made this
analysis (1858) and deduced from it with perfect clearness
the idea of tetravalent carbon. Thenceforth carbon with its
four valencies became the single and fundamental type and the
modern atomic theory was fixed.

There remained but one final advance to make to reach the
clear understanding of all the groupings of atoms, and this advance was due to the genius of Louis Pasteur (1822–1895)[1]. This
great scientist, whose discoveries have, it may be said, renewed
biology, had won his spurs in science by the crystallographic study
of isomeric tartrates. The isomerism of the tartrates appeared
to him to be in some way connected with a dissymmetry of their
molecules in three-dimensional space. This is the fundamental idea of stereochemistry. It gained precision later on
(1874) in the mind of Le Bel, a French chemist, who at the same
time as Van 't Hoff and independently of him settled the geometric figure of the tetrahedron of carbon and defined asym-
metry. As is well known their conceptions gave rise eventually
to researches of the highest interest into molecular structure, and
they may be regarded as the crowning feature of the atomic theory.

It has been necessary to insist on the development of the
atomic theory because it is one of the most remarkable examples
to be found in the history of sciences. Nowhere else has the
influence of tabular representation and of language on the discovery of the actual facts affirmed itself so clearly. The atomic
representation of chemical species is such a perfect language that
it not merely figures known realities but suggests possible ones
and indicates the means of creating them. The list of important works to which the atomic theory gave rise in France is a
long one. Dumas and Würtz were really the heads of the school
and inspirers of genius. One dare not quote, for fear of omitting

[1] See above, pp. 761–762.

some great name, the men of science who collaborated in or continued their work, and space fails to give even a brief indication of their labours[1]. Whether they demonstrate the constitution of natural compounds, or multiply new compounds by powerful methods of synthesis, their discoveries may be said to have enriched chemistry, and done honour to French science. Grignard's method was particularly helpful; he invented in organo-magnesium compounds a chemical agent of the first order, many reactions of which give rise to innumerable syntheses.

Chemical Energy

While chemistry was thus developing within the framework of the atomic theory, there appeared another trend of ideas which was full of interest in its principle, but which unfortunately kept apart from the other branch of chemistry—namely, the study of chemical energy. Berthelot, its protagonist, was both an experimenter and a thinker of genius. But the principle of his work is quite different from that of the school of Würtz. While the supporters of the atomic theory consider structure as a guide in their researches and establish the relationship of species by their forms, Berthelot fixes his whole attention on a study of the energy which brings about chemical changes. From the very outset of his career, when he was endeavouring to synthesise organic compounds from their elements, his main interest lay in the study of the stability of the compounds. He was attempting to synthesise from mineral carbon, the elements of water, and nitrogen, certain of the more important simple compounds from which the rest could be derived. It is remarkable that he obtained them by the process of addition according to the laws of mineral chemistry. Hydrogen and carbon in the electric arc produced acetylene, the condensation of which by heat furnished benzene. Acetylene with hydrogen gives ethylene, and the latter fixing the elements of water through the medium of sulphuric acid furnishes alcohol. Later on Sabatier, one of Berthelot's best pupils, was to develop in collaboration with Senderens yet another part of his work by improving by catalysis the processes of fixing hydrogen. Researches of this kind are an

[1] Malaguti, Regnault, Cahours, Chancel; and later, Friedel, Grimaux, Jungfleisch, A. Gautier, Haller, Béhal, Bouveault, Grignard, Moureu, Blaise, etc.

admirable school. The number of products obtained is of little moment, but the means set in operation, the light which they throw on the mechanisms of the most delicate reactions, are of the highest instructive value for the future of chemistry.

In Berthelot's brilliant career two things are to be deplored. First that, having grasped the importance of the idea of energy in the study of chemical changes, he did not take into consideration the question of structure. If the genius of Würtz had been able to combine with that of Berthelot to found a common school, it might have meant the gain of half a century in the progress of chemistry. Another cause for regret is that after his first experimental discoveries, that is after 1860 (when he summed them up in his *Leçons de chimie organique fondée sur la synthèse*), he directed his attention almost solely to the measurement of the heats of reaction. Undoubtedly his labours and those of his pupils in this domain constitute as a whole an admirable achievement, and the body of teaching contained in them remains—with some weak points—a very important acquisition to science; but though his main success, the fixing of the conception of chemical stability, was a decisive result for the orientation of ideas, it is permissible to think that time would have been gained had he given more attention to reversible reactions[1].

The importance of reversibility had been grasped before him by Claude-Louis Berthollet (1748–1822), a contemporary of Lavoisier. As early as 1803 in his *Statique chimique* he considers the chemical system as the resultant of an equilibrium between opposing reactions such as the mutual reactions of salts in solution, and forestalling Guldberg and Waage he conceived the idea of "active mass." Unfortunately, starting from these sound ideas and pushing them to extremes, he went so far as to deny the law of "definite proportions." Hence arose the discredit into which his work fell. It was not till the work of Sainte-Claire Deville and the discovery of the phenomena of dissociation are reached (1867) that the importance of reversibility became undoubted.

Henry Sainte-Claire Deville (1818–1881)[2], already famous for

---

[1] His work on etherification, in collaboration with Péan de Saint-Gilles, was a masterly beginning, but he does not seem to have gone on with it.

[2] See above, p. 775.

his work on aluminium, sodium, and the synthesis of crystallised minerals, was led by the nature of his researches to explore the chemistry of high temperatures. In studying the oxyhydrogen flame, which he used for melting and refining platinum, he made the fundamental discovery of the dissociation of water. Admirable for the experimental sagacity with which he succeeded in demonstrating the traces of free elements (hydrogen and oxygen) in the vapour of water, he was even more admirable for the clear-sighted genius with which he was able to generalise the new fact and found the doctrine of chemical equilibria. Professor at the Sorbonne and Director of the chemical laboratory of the *École Normale,* he was able to surround himself with a galaxy of pupils who developed brilliantly the experimental consequences of his theory. Mention must be made of Debray, Troost, and Hautefeuille; also of Lemoine, who worked on the same lines and whose paper on hydriodic acid (1877) remains a model of precision. The study of reversibility begun in this manner was now to find support in thermodynamics and acquire the full development which characterises modern physical chemistry. Van 't Hoff and Arrhenius are the remote disciples of Sainte-Claire Deville, but in France the man who may be regarded as his worthiest successor is Henry-Louis Le Châtelier (b. 1850).

The law of the displacement of equilibria which bears his name really sets forth the clear and fruitful idea which was to be the guide of investigation along the new road. The modern work on the syntheses of nitric acid and of ammonia is, so to speak, a consequence of his theoretical views. He has also other titles to fame. In particular, he has created in the domain of metallurgy methods of investigation which are universally applied and have assisted the progress of that science.

Apart from the great theoretical laws, the exploration of high temperatures has yielded other results for science. The researches of Frémy and his pupils have led to the synthesis of rock minerals, e.g. the preparation of artificial rubies by Frémy and Verneuil, from which Verneuil discovered an ingenious process for the industrial manufacture of these stones. Later —about 1890—Moissan, a pupil of Frémy, in the course of researches which remained purely experimental, carried his investigation on to the temperature of the electric arc, and this resulted in the carbide industry.

A feature still lacking in our picture is the study of mineral compounds at low temperatures. Here complication is by no means rare, and the problem of constitution has a renewed interest. The work of Frémy on cobaltammines is extremely noteworthy in this respect. So also is that of the school of Sainte-Claire Deville and Debray on the chemistry of the platinum metals, and that of Recoura on the complex compounds of chromium. They form the experimental foundation of Werner's later theory.

The need for brevity has confined this account to the general lines of the subject, and much important work in theoretic chemistry has been passed over in silence. Much also might be said on the subject of applied chemistry. In this domain France has had no lack of great inventors. In mineral chemistry Berthollet created the industry of bleaching by chlorine, and Le Blanc the soda industry (1798). Schloesing and Rolland prepared soda in bulk by the ammoniac process before Solvay. Marguerite and Sourdeval gave a practical demonstration of the synthesis of ammonia by the use of cyanides. Sainte-Claire Deville, as above mentioned, created the industry of aluminium, and Moissan that of calcium carbide. Osmond presented metallurgists with that remarkable instrument of progress, metallography. In organic chemistry the industry of fatty acids owes its birth to Chevreul, and that of colouring matters to Verguin, Rosenstiehl, Roussin, Lauth, etc. Finally in bio-chemistry occur the most striking examples of the reciprocal influences of practical application and scientific theory. Thus the study of the soil and manures set the problem of the nitrogen cycle. Boussingault, Berthelot and Schloesing are the principal men of science who have thrown light upon it. They recognised and measured the fixation of free nitrogen in the soil, and pointed out the part played by living matter in this fixation. For Pasteur, too, the desire for practical application acted as a constant guide in his memorable labours. Starting with the biological separation of isomeric tartrates, he was led on to the study first of fermentations, then of the diseases of wines

and beers, and lastly of viruses and vaccines. It would be difficult to enumerate the benefits which humanity owes to his
labours, and to those of his pupils (Duclaux, Metchnikoff, Roux,
etc.). But be it noted that by a fortunate reciprocity they
helped to impart a new impetus to theoretical chemistry itself.
For the consideration of "organised ferments" leads back inevitably to that of "soluble ferments," and once more raises
the question of the mechanism of reactions by catalysis and
the rôle of the "infinitely small in chemistry." Bourquelot's
work on reversible hydrolysis of glucosides and sugars, that
of Gabriel Bertrand on oxydases and on the biological rôle
of manganese, arsenic, zinc, etc., are among the most notable,
on account of the new outlook they give to the chemistry of
living matter.

To sum up, when the history of chemistry in France is looked
at as a whole, when we see a succession of such names as
Lavoisier, Dumas, Würtz, Berthelot, Sainte-Claire Deville, and
Pasteur, we may have confidence in the future and feel assured
that the flame will not die out. This confidence is increased
when we think of the restricted number of workers and the
scanty material resources from which so many splendid discoveries have issued successfully. They are the sign of a strong
vitality. This vitality has again revealed itself in the recent war,
when we had suddenly to face the colossal effort of German
industry in the chemistry of gases. In future years, when France
has renewed her vigour and has risen from her ruins, we may
be sure that, advancing resolutely towards scientific progress,
she will continue to hold her place side by side with England
among the *élite* of the nations.

§ III. PHYSICS

The prodigious development of Physical Sciences will always
be a distinguishing mark of the 19th century. By the public at
large this will be remembered as the period in which man learnt
to make use of steam and electric currents. Such applications
were rendered possible by the repeated discoveries made during
that century, and above all in the heroic period which followed
the fall of the First Empire. It is a remarkable thing that in a

few years Davy, Young, Fresnel, Oersted, Ampère, Arago, Carnot, and Faraday were able completely to renew the aspects of science. It is a remarkable thing, too, that these discoveries were made by young men, as if the atmosphere of revolution had emboldened them to overthrow ideas then regarded as classic, and to explore hitherto untrodden fields of research.

It is not possible to determine with exactitude the share of France in the development of Physics in the 19th century, for that was precisely the period during which science tended to become more and more a collective work. It will nevertheless be the aim of this rapid sketch to indicate the part played in France by a few leaders of science under the headings of Heat, Optics, Electricity and Magnetism, and the Physics of Electrons and Radio-activity.

Heat

The first name that calls for mention is that of Jean-Baptiste Fourier (1768–1830)[1], for it is one which constantly recurs; wherever in fact periodic functions are met with, Fourier's method of developing a function in a trigonometrical series is used. His work on the Theory of Heat is one of the most remarkable examples of the influence which Physics can exert on the development of mathematical analysis. Fourier, like Laplace and Poisson and all the men who formed the brilliant school of mathematical physics of the beginning of the last century, believed that questions of natural philosophy should be the chief object with mathematicians. Without going as far as that, and without in the least regarding mathematical analysis as a mere instrument, one may regret that mathematicians have deviated too much from that view.

One of the greatest conquests of Physics in the 19th century is the discovery of the two principles of thermodynamics which govern the transformation of energy. It was in 1824 that Sadi Carnot (1796–1832)[2], the son of the "organiser of victory," published his *Réflexions sur la puissance motrice du feu*, in which one of these two principles was enunciated for the first time. His book remained almost unknown for a quarter of a century; Clapeyron was alone in making an interesting application of its

---

[1] See above, pp. 748–749.   [2] See above, p. 751.

principle (1834), and of rendering the exposition of Carnot's ideas more clear by the introduction of graphic methods. Lord Kelvin relates that when he went to Paris he had infinite trouble in obtaining a copy of the book. To him is due the credit of having brought into prominence the importance of the principle enunciated by Carnot in connexion with heat-engines, and of having demonstrated that this principle indicates in a general manner the direction of the evolution of energy. But though Lord Kelvin—and also Clausius in Germany—undoubtedly perfected the work of Carnot by bringing out clearly the ideas of absolute temperature and entropy, the latter's glory remains undiminished.

The other principle of thermodynamics, that of the conservation of energy, was not enunciated till after Carnot's time. It was long supposed that he had not even an inkling of it, but though in his book he does, indeed, use the language of his day in speaking of heat as matter, he certainly did not regard it as indestructible matter. Here again his ideas were those of a precursor. There is even to be found in his book—a book more often cited than attentively read—a calculation of the value of the relation between the work which is done by an engine and the heat which disappears. Unpublished notes found recently by M. Raveau (*Comptes rendus*, 1919) among Carnot's papers leave no doubt upon this point, and indicate the calculation by which he arrived at the figure given in his book.

The principles of thermodynamics are not capable of practical application and cannot even be verified in the absence of the numerical data necessary for utilising them. France may claim to have carried out an important body of experimental work on heat to supply this need. This may be grouped round the work of Henri-Victor Regnault (1810–1878), which he was called upon to undertake at the moment when the first railway company was formed in France (1841). The problem comprised two parts. The first was to determine the motive power an engine could produce. This demanded the determination of the vapour pressures and also of the density of the fluids used. The vapour pressures of steam vary greatly with temperature. For the first part of the work it was therefore necessary to make accurate measurements of temperature. This led Regnault to take up again studies begun by Gay-Lussac and Dulong and to make a methodical study of the dilatation of gases, liquids, and solids, to compare the indications of different thermometers, and to fix his choice on the gas-thermometer. The process of determining the curve of vapour pressures of the steam of water and of some thirty other substances which he believed utilisable in heat-engines provided him with the occasion for improving the measurement of pressures and volumes. It was his methods, boldly applied to pressures of thousands of atmospheres, which were used by Cailletet and Amagat in their researches on the characteristic equations of the fluid state. His great work on the density of vapours and gases, in which he corrected the measurements of Dumas and of Boussingault, fixed definitively the value of constants such as the mass of the litre of air or the density of mercury, which crop up at every turn in physical measurements.

The second part of Regnault's work was to ascertain the quantity of heat communicated to a liquid during its vaporisation and during its evaporation. Regnault's work on the measurement of atomic heats was an improvement upon the hitherto known processes by means of which Dulong and Petit had succeeded in establishing the celebrated law of specific atomic heats. In this domain Regnault's results are still regarded as classic. But what is more important still, the care for simplicity and accuracy with which he carried out his measurements has inspired the bulk of subsequent work.

This work of Regnault's was carried out between 1840 and 1856. He completed it later by introducing the recently accepted idea of the mechanical equivalent of heat. In order to calculate this equivalent from the measurements of gases, it was necessary to ascertain the ratio of the specific heat when the gas is kept at constant pressure to that when it is kept at constant volume. This ratio may be deduced from the value of the velocity of sound in the gases, and so Regnault was led to carry out important work on the velocity of sound, whether moving freely through the air or travelling along pipes. The methods that he instituted for this study mark the beginnings of those registering apparatuses which were destined to render such good service to biologists as well as to physicists.

Optics

In the domain of Physical Optics France, thanks in particular to Fresnel, made important contributions in the early 19th century. The theory of emission then reigned uncontested, and yet in 1802 the Englishman Thomas Young had by his celebrated experiments brought into evidence for the first time the phenomena of interference. In France in 1808 the Academy of Sciences had had the idea of offering a prize for a new study of the phenomenon of double refraction, and Etienne-Louis Malus (1775–1812) had made the capital discovery of the polarisation of light. These were new facts which the theory of emission did not explain. The honour of having connected them both with the undulatory theory belongs to Augustin-Jean Fresnel (1788–1827). It was he who showed the importance of Young's experiment by pointing out the part played by interference in a number of phenomena which seemed independent of them. His success in this is due to the fact that he was one of those very rare minds which combine the genius for discovering ruling principles with the experimental skill required for controlling them.

This double character is already observable in his first memoir on diffraction. Fresnel, treating of the elementary waves of Huygens, admitted that they may interfere with one another. He was thus able to calculate in their smallest details the phenomena to be observed at any distance from the screen. He tested this theory by a careful comparison with experience, ingeniously inventing the needed apparatus in the solitary village where he was working, improvising a micrometer with the aid of the local locksmith, and utilising as the luminous point the image of the sun produced by rays passing through a drop of honey. Such were the rudimentary means by which he was able to show that the undulatory theory makes it possible to foretell the phenomena with all their details, even those which at first sight seem most paradoxical, "with as great precision as Newton's theory foretells the movements of the heavenly bodies." In this connexion he observed for the first time the simplest case of interference, that in which two waves only are involved, and when diffraction does not occur, as it did in Young's experiment. His celebrated experiment of two mirrors was carried out in the first instance with similar improvised means. The apparatus consisted of two pieces of plate glass, the angle of which was regulated by soft wax; yet it proved adequate for the taking of measurements.

Further, Fresnel's entirely new conception of transverse vibrations had an unsuspected and far-reaching effect on Physics. This hypothesis gives so simple an explanation of the phenomena discovered by Malus that one may well be surprised at Fresnel's difficulty in convincing others of its truth. But the conception ran so much counter to current ideas that physicists spoke of "the mechanical absurdity of transverse vibrations."

Even François Arago (1786–1853)[1], who was a man of open mind and who besides had collaborated with Fresnel in the famous experiments by which they had settled the condition of interference of polarised rays, refused to admit Fresnel's hypothesis, which explained everything so simply. Yet its importance is greater than the interest of the mechanical theory itself. Its essential feature is the introduction of a periodic transverse vector, and this part of Fresnel's work survived integrally when the electro-magnetic theory in its turn was coming gradually to be accepted. Periodically variable fields now replace mechanical vibrations, which were then regarded as existing in the ether, but apart from the names of the vectors there is nothing to be altered on the geometrical side of Fresnel's work.

In his further study of these transverse vibrations under varying conditions and of the results of their interferences, Fresnel explains a whole series of new results. For instance, Arago had just discovered the colorations of crystalline plates placed between two nicols; these Fresnel explains by the interference of two principal vibrations which may spread through the crystalline plates. Again, in England, Brewster had just discovered the double refraction of compressed glass; Fresnel explains this property by the propagation in the strained medium of two transversal vibrations at right angles, and he directly points out the difference of the principal indices. Arago had just discovered the rotatory power of quartz perpendicularly to its axis; Fresnel connects this new phenomenon with the interferences of polarised rays. But in this case the two interfering rays are polarised

1 See above, p. 750.

circularly, one to the right, and one to the left, and Fresnel demonstrates by direct experiments the double circular refraction of quartz along the axis.

One of the discoveries of Fresnel which struck his contemporaries most was that of the laws of refraction in biaxial crystals, which are by far the most numerous. He showed that in such crystals there is not, as was previously thought, an ordinary ray, but that nevertheless all the optical properties might be foreseen by the consideration of a single ellipsoid. To these purely geometrical considerations he added a mechanical theory. This theory, in which he propounded clearly for the first time a problem of elasticity, has since been the object of justifiable criticisms, as was also his mechanical theory of the reflection of light upon transparent substances. But the laws and formulae discovered by Fresnel have stood unshaken. In the matter of crystals the consideration of a single ellipsoid with three unequal axes representing optical properties was to prove very fruitful; even at the present day a similar ellipsoid is sufficient to represent in crystallised matter the variation with the direction of almost all physical properties.

When these discoveries are considered as a whole, and when it is realised from Fresnel's writings that he had a clear conception of the ground which optics still had to cover, increased regret is felt at his early death, and that the last years of his life should have been absorbed by work in connexion with lighthouses. These works are undoubtedly of great value in seafaring life, but they might have been carried out by others.

Next after Fresnel we owe to Amand-Hippolyte-Louis Fizeau (1819–1896) and to Jean-Léon Foucault (1819–1868) the most important progress achieved in optics. These two great physicists began by working together, and their names remain associated with the study of the phenomena of interference by means of fluted spectra. Both were skilful and bold experimenters, and it is interesting to see them both tackling the problem of the measurement of the speed of light on the surface of the earth, and both arriving at a satisfactory solution.

Foucault's activity bore on several branches of physics, and he left on each a personal mark. He possessed a keen sense for mechanics, which enabled him to guess at solutions which mathematicians discovered later by calculation. It is enough to recall his celebrated experiment of the pendulum (1851) and the invention of the gyroscope, the vivid impression made by which upon Lord Kelvin led to the latter evolving his gyrostatic theory of light. Without leaving this domain of pure optics it is necessary to make particular mention of the methods of study and of the accurate figuring of optical surfaces which have proved so useful and which have contributed largely to the progress of celestial physics.

Fizeau's activity was more concentrated, though touching upon many delicate questions of optics. He was the first to recognise that a ray of light with regular waves might be used as a perfect micrometer. His measurements of the infinitesimal layers of silver and of the dilatation of crystals, carried out by means of the measurement of interference, were the origin of all recent applications of optics to metrology in the work of Benoît, of Michelson, of Fabry and Perot, of Macé de Lépinay and Buisson, etc. For instance, one of his experiments on the striations on the surface of polished metals is the origin of Gouy's work on distant diffraction. It was he, too, who suggested the method now brilliantly applied by Michelson and used at Mount Wilson for measuring the apparent diameter of celestial bodies. To him too we owe the first positive experiment on the influence of the movements of matter on luminous phenomena.

The body of research on the rotatory power of organic liquids is one in which France may reasonably take pride. The discovery was due to Jean-Baptiste Biot (1774–1862), who had clearly perceived the importance which these researches might have for the progress of chemistry. In his great article in the *Annales de Chimie et de Physique* of 1860, "his last farewell to the sciences he had so greatly loved," in which he sums up the patient researches of forty years, he insists once again on the interest of this method of study which gives information about molecules without the necessity of touching them, and furnishes results which ordinary chemical analysis is incapable of producing. Nor does he conceal his delight that he had at last found a follower on that new path.

For Louis Pasteur (1822–1895)[1] had made the important

[1] See above, pp. 761–762; 782.

discovery of the two active isomers of tartaric acid, from which the whole of stereo-chemistry was to emerge, and for the first time, thanks to polarimetric researches, the distinction was clearly established between the molecules endowed with certain elements of symmetry which cannot act upon polarised light, and those which are devoid of them.

Drawn on, as is well known, to other discoveries, Pasteur was, to his great regret, unable to pursue his researches in pure physics. But he lived to see with pleasure his work continued in that laboratory of the *École Normale* which he had rendered illustrious. There Gernez discovered the rotatory power of vapours and Verdet the laws of rotatory magnetic polarisation, that beautiful phenomenon discovered by Faraday, and the first for which the mechanical theory of light could find no explanation.

In all the optical work which after Fresnel's time long engaged French physicists, attention was almost exclusively directed to the propagation of luminous rays, without studying the manner of their production and disappearance, though research also bore upon the visible spectrum. The progress in optics noticeable in the last part of the 19th century is due precisely to the fact that not only the propagation but the *absorption and emission* of light were studied. In addition the systematic study of invisible spectra was commenced during that period and the conception of radiation has been gradually evolved. The names associated with this work in France are those of Desains and La Provostaye, Mascart, Cornu, Gouy, Deslandres, Lecoq de Boisbaudran, etc.

In many of these researches in spectroscopy, as indeed in all departments of physics, photography has supplied particularly valuable methods; and it should not be forgotten that this is a French invention due to Niepce and Daguerre, that colour photography by the indirect method is due to Cros and Ducos du Hauron, and that it was Lippmann who discovered the interferential method. Entire industries such as those of photogravure and collotype have their origin in the work of Poitevin. Finally, Lumière's cinematograph is an application of the purely scientific researches of Marey and Demeny.

Electricity and Magnetism

Electricity also has its heroic age in the early 19th century. It was in 1820 that Arago announced to the Académie des

Sciences Oersted's discovery of the action of the current on the magnetic needle. This unexpected discovery produced an immense impression upon all minds and everyone set to work upon it according to his own bent. Biot and Savart, physicists of the classical school, strove to subject Oersted's experiment to quantitative measurements; by observing the oscillations of a magnetic needle they measured what we should now call the field of a long rectilinear current. Laplace deduced from it the field of an element of current, so that one is brought back to a definite mathematical problem if it is desired to know the action of a current on a magnetic pole.

On the other hand André-Marie Ampère (1775–1836) at a single bound advanced much further. Oersted's experiment suggested to him a clue which guided him throughout. He had an inspiration of genius that in the end magnets must be electric currents. This was enough to suggest to him that a magnet must act on a mobile portion of current, that the earth itself must act on similar elements, and that two currents must act upon one another. So this celebrated mathematician became at the age of forty-four an experimenter and invented ingenious devices to render currents mobile and to establish the results which he foresaw. Solenoids supplied him with an image of the constitution of magnets. Eventually he discovered a formula which expresses the action of one element of current on another, which in his view comes into play in every experiment whether of electro-magnetism or electro-dynamics.

Arago having just observed that a wire plunged into iron filings becomes coated with them as soon as it is attached to the poles of a powerful battery, it occurred to Ampère to insert an iron wire into a solenoid, and thus he discovered the first electric magnet.

This group of discoveries shows how fertile a single guiding idea may prove, and justifies Clerk-Maxwell's remark that Ampère was the Newton of electricity.

One of the inventions which resulted from these discoveries was that of the telegraph. Ampère had himself had an idea of it, but strange to say it had not occurred to him that it was not necessary to use as many wires as there are letters in the alphabet.

Electro-magnetic motors and generators were for a long time hardly seen outside the laboratory, and the earliest forms of apparatus required a delicate commutator to produce and utilise continuous currents. It was not till 1869 that a Belgian workman, Gramme, who constructed at Paris the magnetos then used in the lighting of the lighthouses, had the idea of his armature. This original arrangement appeared to the scientific men of the period to be too symmetrical; in fact they maintained that it could only work thanks to some defect of construction. As a matter of fact it was the first really practical solution, and the era of important industrial applications of electric energy dates from that moment.

Continuous currents were for a long time the only ones which it was known how to utilise. It was not till later that alternating currents entered into practical use in industry, for they could not be harnessed till it was possible to ascertain their exact form and distinguish the terms of Fourier's series, which represents them by means of stroboscopy (Joubert) and oscillography (Blondel). In all the problems which were successively presented by alternating currents, turning fields, etc., French engineers discovered neat solutions, which have their origin in Fresnel's work on alternating vectors.

Electrons and Radio-activity

The close of the 19th century is marked by a notable revival of activity among French physicists, recalling in some respects the singular energy of its opening period. This activity is to a certain extent explained by the emergence of new and unforeseen facts giving a similar impulse to that caused by Oersted's discovery. But a contributory factor was certainly the presence of important guiding ideas; for in this period kinetic theories assumed great importance, and the Dutch physicist Hendrik Lorentz introduced into science the study of electrons.

The kinetic theory of fluids led to the now reigning views on the discontinuity of electric charges. And in this connexion the brilliant confirmation recently received by this kinetic theory must not be passed over. The researches of Jean Perrin on the Brownian movement (1910) showed that this movement is really to be explained, as Gouy had hinted, by the incessant shocks of the molecules of the liquid on the particles in suspension visible by the microscope, and Perrin was able to determine by measurement Avogadro's constant. On the other hand, in an entirely different domain, Fabry and Buisson (1914) discovered another important confirmation of the kinetic theory by their study of the breadth of the spectral rays and of its variation with the temperature

Elementary electric charges were first revealed by the study of cathode rays, in which these "particles of electricity" are isolated and move in a vacuum with great velocity. Perrin's first work (1895) had been devoted entirely to these rays. At this time the views of Crookes, who had discovered them in England and who held them to be "radiant matter," were being discussed. The German Lenard had shown that it was possible to make these rays issue through a sheet of metal from the tube in which they were produced and to observe their propagation in the air. He regarded them as a form of radiation. Perrin's experiments showed beyond doubt that a negative charge was carried by these rays and everyone has since admitted that they are composed of charged projectiles. By measuring the deflection of| their paths in magnetic and electric fields J. J. Thomson estimated their velocity and also their mass, which proved to be less than the thousandth part of the lightest chemical atom. These particles are in fact electrons observed in a condition of separation from all ordinary matter. But Lorentz and Larmor have the credit of showing that these same elementary charges are to be found everywhere, even in the interior of atoms and molecules, and that their function must be an important one.

This function first came to light through the discovery due to another Dutchman, Zeeman, of the change produced in the lines of the spectrum by a magnetic field. French physicists made an important contribution to the study of this new phenomenon. Cornu, Deslandres, and Henri Becquerel brought to notice important cases of the decomposition of the rays; Jean Becquerel and Dufour discovered the changes of which the rays of absorption of rare earths and the banded spectra of gaseous compounds are susceptible. It was in France that the first precise measurements of Zeeman's phenomenon were published.

Kinetic consideration of the theory of electrons then came to light in the course of researches on magnetism. All recent experimental researches on the magnetic properties of matter and on its relations with chemical constitution are bound up with the work of Pierre Curie (1859–1906)[1]. His name is one of the purest glories of France. He is best known to the public at large by the discovery of radium, but his work is much vaster than is generally supposed. He had long worked alone with very restricted means in a wretched laboratory. When fame came to him, quite unsought, he was already exercising upon the younger generation in an ever-widening circle a profound influence, due as much to the qualities of the man as to those of the scientist. The stir made by the discovery of radium was irksome to him, and he would have liked to return to his favourite studies which related to symmetry and to crystals.

His first discovery had been that of "piezo-electricity," made in collaboration with Jacques Curie. As a matter of fact considerations connected with symmetry had preceded this discovery, and the two young physicists knew beforehand what were the crystals that could be electrified under compression. In his important work on magnetism Pierre Curie clearly established, by his calculation of the coefficients of magnetisation at varying temperatures, the different laws to which diamagnetic, para-magnetic, and ferromagnetic substances are subject. His name remains attached to the law whereby the coefficient of magneti-sation of paramagnetic substances varies in inverse ratio to the absolute temperature, and the "Curie point" is the name given to the temperature at which a ferromagnetic body becomes paramagnetic.

These experimental laws enabled Langevin to build up his theory of magnetic phenomena. According to him diamag-netism is a general phenomenon resulting from the action of the magnetic field on the electrons present in the molecule. Para-magnetism makes its appearance when the molecule has a resultant magnetic moment other than zero, and behaves like a small magnet. Taking then into consideration all the little elementary magnets which the magnetic field constantly tends

[1] See above, pp. 777–778.

to orientate and thermal agitation to disturb, he rediscovered by calculation Curie's law.

In a very important body of measurements made by himself or his pupils, Pierre Weiss has extended our knowledge of the magnetic properties of various substances. We owe to him in particular the discovery of the very curious properties of the crystals of magnetite and pyrrhotine, in which once more Pierre Curie's observations on symmetry are verified. His theory of the phenomena presented by ferromagnetic substances is a generalisation of Langevin's theory into which he introduced the mutual action of molecules. They led him to the conception of the magneton, a magnetic unit of invariable moment which he recognised in all paramagnetic and ferromagnetic atoms.

These theories of magnetism are kinetic theories, and electrons only come in to explain directive actions. These kinetic theories also play an important part in the explanation of new phenomena discovered in magneto-optics. Particularly deserving of mention is the discovery made in the physical laboratory of the *École Normale* of the electric magnetic double refraction of pure liquids. Like the electric double refraction discovered by Kerr, it is explained by molecular orientation.

The function of electrons, or more generally of electric particles, is being constantly identified in radio-activity. It was in France that Henri Becquerel (1852–1908) discovered in uranium the two characteristics which distinguish radio-active bodies, that of making gases conductors, and that of emitting radiations which act upon photographic plates. To Mme Curie is due the honour of having discovered by means of precise quantitative measurements that side by side with uranium there must exist other more active elements. She then carried out with Pierre Curie those prolonged labours by which they succeeded in extracting from several tons of raw material a few decigrams of salts of radium. As they returned in the evening to the shed which formed their laboratory at the *École de Physique et de Chimie*, they would notice with rapture that the glimmer emitted in the darkness by the products resulting from their laborious subdivisions gradually became brighter. At the same time as the measurements of the piezo-electric quartz were showing a progressive increase in radio-activity these singular properties were clearly manifesting themselves. Curie and Laborde found out the unexpected fact that radium constantly emits heat; Mme Curie measured its atomic weight; Demarçay discovered its characteristic spectral rays. The same methods enabled Mme Curie to discover polonium and Debierne actinium.

It was in France too that the various forms of radiation of radio-active bodies were distinguished. Mme Curie and Henri Becquerel recognised the existence of the α and β rays and Villard discovered the γ rays analogous to the X-rays. From the outset of their researches Pierre Curie and his wife had clearly enunciated the hypothesis which attributed radio-activity to an atomic transformation. The discovery of these phenomena of induced radio-activity, which decrease somewhat rapidly with time, and the researches of Rutherford and Debierne were to justify this hypothesis. Investigation founded on it eventually led to the general theory of Rutherford and Soddy on the relationship of radio-active elements, and an entire new chemistry thus had its birth in work which belonged to pure physics.

This necessarily very incomplete account of the part played by France in physics in modern times must here be brought to a close. The work of the men of science mentioned in it is sufficient to show that the part was an important one. But there are other forms of the contribution of French thought to natural philosophy which it may be useful to mention.

It is generally agreed that the writings of French authors possess qualities of order and clarity which explain their success. It would therefore be unjust not to recall that the works published in France during this period, whether periodicals such as the *Comptes rendus*, didactic works such as those of Verdet, Mascart, Joubert, etc., or high-class popular works, such as those of Henri Poincaré, have largely contributed to the progress of physics.

Then again France may claim a particularly important share in international congresses, in which men of science of all civilised nations have collaborated. It was in Paris that most of the meetings took place in which by common consent the names and values of electric units now in universal use were settled. Those who, like Dumas or Mascart, supported by his friend Lord Kelvin, assured the success of these congresses were inspired by the same generous idea which guided the founders of the metric system, and their efforts should not be forgotten. These gatherings have been extremely useful. In the first place solid work has been done at them, and secondly they have proved the starting-point for new and important researches. At one of the International Conferences (1882) Lord Kelvin insisted on this point, and he quoted Falstaff's saying, "I am not only witty in myself but the cause that wit is in other men." At the same time these gatherings have multiplied those direct relations between workers of different countries which are so highly profitable and which contribute so powerfully to the progress of civilisation.

BIBLIOGRAPHY

The Biological Sciences

I. Geoffroy Saint-Hilaire, *Vie, travaux, et doctrine scientifique d'Étienne Geoffroy Saint-Hilaire,* 1847.

M. Landrieu, *Lamarck, le fondateur de transformisme, sa vie, son œuvre,* 1909.

M. Boule, *Les Hommes fossiles,* 1921.

J.-B. Lamarck, *Philosophie zoologique,* 1809, 2nd ed., 1873; *Discours d'ouverture,* 1907.

A. de Quatrefages, *Charles Darwin et ses précurseurs français,* 1873.

X. Bichat, *Recherches physiologiques sur la vie et la mort,* 1809; *Anatomie générale appliquée à la physiologie et à la médecine,* 4 vols., 1812.

E. Gley, *Essais de philosophie et d'histoire de la Biologie,* 1900.

F. Le Dantec, *La Matière vivante,* 1899; *Théorie nouvelle de la vie,* 1896.

C. Dareste, *Recherches sur la production artificielle des monstruosités,* 2nd ed., 1891.

L. Ranvier, *Traité technique d'histologie,* 2nd ed., 1889.

Alf. Giard, *Controverses transformistes,* 1904; *Œuvres diverses,* 2 vols., 1911; *Facteurs primaires de l'évolution,* 1901.

Claude Bernard, *Introduction à l'étude de la médecine expérimentale,* 1865.

L. Lavoisier, *Mémoires sur la respiration et la transpiration des animaux,* 1920.

Ét. Rabaud, *La Tératogenèse,* 1914; *Eléments de Biologie générale,* 1921.

Y. Delage and Goldsmith, *Les théories de l'évolution,* 1909; *Le Parthénogenèse expérimentale,* 1913.

Chemistry

A.-L. Lavoisier, *Œuvres,* 6 vols., 1862–1893.

C.-L. Berthollet, *Recherches sur les lois de l'affinité,* 1801; *Essai de Statique chimique,* 2 vols., 1803.

N. Leblanc, *Mémoires sur la fabrication du sel ammoniac et de la soude,* 1798.

J.-L. Gay-Lussac and L.-J. Thénard, *Recherches physico-chimiques,* 2 vols., 1811.

M.-E. Chevreul, *Considérations générales sur l'analyse organique et ses applications,* 1824; *Recherches chimiques sur les corps gras d'origine animale* (1823), 1889.

J.-B. Dumas, *Leçons sur la Philosophie chimique, professées au Collège de France,* 1837.

Ch. Gerhardt, *Traité de Chimie organique,* 4 vols., 1853–1856; *Recherches sur les acides organiques anhydres, Ann.,* 3rd series, XXXVII.

Sainte-Claire Deville, *Sur les phénomènes de dissociation, Bibl. univ. de Genève,* Archives VI (1859); *De l'aluminium,* 1879.

H.-L. Le Châtelier, *Recherches expérimentales et théoriques sur les équilibres chimiques,* 1880.

Ad. Würtz, *Mémoire sur les glycols ou alcools diatomiques,* 1859; *Mémoires sur les ammoniaques composées,* 1850; *Leçons de Philosophie chimique,* 1864.

M. Berthelot, *Chimie organique fondée sur la synthèse,* 1860; *Essai de Mécanique chimique fondée sur la Thermochimie,* 2 vols., 1879; *Sur la force des matières explosives d'après la Thermochimie,* 3rd ed., 1883.

C. Friedel and Crafts, *Méthode de synthèse des carbures aromatiques, Ann.,* 6th series, I.

L. Pasteur, *Recherches sur la dissymétrie moléculaire des produits organiques naturels, Ann.,* 3rd series, XXIV ff.; *Recherches sur les propriétés spécifiques des deux acides qui composent l'acide racémique, Ann.,* 3rd series, XXVIII, 1850.

E. Duclaux, *Pasteur, histoire d'un esprit,* 1896.

V. Grignard, *Sur les combinaisons organomagnésiennes mixtes et leurs applications,* Lyons, 1901.

P. Sabatier, *La catalyse en Chimie organique,* 1913.

H. Moissan, *Le Fluor et ses composés,* 1900; *Le four électrique,* 1897.

P. Curie and Mme Curie, *Œuvres de Pierre Curie,* 1908; *Traité de radio-activité,* 2 vols., 1910.

Physics

Sadi Carnot, *Réflexions sur la puissance motrice du feu,* 1824.

V. Regnault, *Travaux publiés pour déterminer les lois et données physiques nécessaires au calcul des machines à feu,* 1847–1868.

A.-J. Fresnel, *Œuvres Complètes,* 1866.

J.-L. Foucault, *Recueil des Travaux scientifiques,* 1878.

E. Becquerel, *La lumière, ses causes et ses effets,* 1867.

A.-M. Ampère, *Théorie mathématique des phénomènes électrodynamiques, uniquement déduite de l'expérience,* 1826, 1883; *Mémoires relatifs à la physique,* 1885.

J. Perrin, *Les Atomes,* 1913.

Société française de Physique, Rapports présentés au Congrès international de Physique, 1900.

F. Billet, *Traité d'optique physique,* 1859.

É. Verdet, *Œuvres publiées par ses élèves,* 1872.

P. Janet, *Leçons d'Électrotechnique générale,* 3rd ed., 1921.

H. Poincaré, *Électricité et Optique,* 2nd ed., 1901.

INDEX

The letters ff. after an entry implies that there are references to the same subject on at least two immediately succeeding pages. Princes are indexed under their Christian names, persons of noble birth and those usually known by their surname under their surnames.